THE EUROPEAN COURT AND NATIONAL COURTS
—DOCTRINE AND JURISPRUDENCE

The European Court and National Courts—Doctrine and Jurisprudence

Legal Change in Its Social Context

Edited by
ANNE-MARIE SLAUGHTER, ALEC STONE SWEET
and J. H. H. WEILER

·HART·
PUBLISHING
OXFORD
1998

Hart Publishing
Oxford
UK

Distributed in the United States by
Northwestern University Press
625 Colfax, Evanston
Illinois 60208–4210 USA

Distributed in Australia and New Zealand by
Federation Press
PO Box 45, Annandale
NSW 203 Australia

Distributed in the Netherlands, Belgium and Luxembourg by
Intersentia, Churchillaan 108
B2900 Schoten, Antwerp
Belgium

Hart Publishing is a specialist legal publisher based in Oxford, England.
To order further copies of this book or to request a list of other
publications please write to:

Hart Publishing, 19 Whitehouse Road, Oxford, OX1 4PA
Telephone: +44 (0)1865 434459 or Fax: (0)1865 794882
e-mail: hartpub@janep.demon.co.uk

Payment may be made by cheque payable to 'Hart Publishing' or by
credit card.

British Library Cataloguing in Publication Data
Data Available
ISBN 1–901362–26–4 (cloth)

Typeset in 10pt Sabon
by Hope Services (Abingdon) Ltd.
Printed in Great Britain on acid-free paper
by Redwood Books, Trowbridge, Wilts.

Prologue – The European Courts of Justice

J.H.H. Weiler, Anne-Marie Slaughter, Alec Stone Sweet

This volume revisits a well know terrain: the relationship between the European Court and Member State Courts in the so-called constitutionalization of the Community legal order. Its contours have been clearly etched by the cartographers of the European Community legal system. The contributions to this volume come, however, to this landscape from a different shore, examine it through a different lens and ultimately, we hope, map it in a different way.

The title of this Preface—*The European Courts of Justice*—may seem to contain a typological error. After all there is, surely, only one European Court of Justice? The premise and defining approach of the entire volume is that the construction of the Community legal order is a tale in which national Courts (as well as other national and transnational actors) have played as important a role as the European Court of Justice itself; that constitutionalization is above all a "conversation" with a uniquely interesting grammar and syntax; that this conversation has taken place over time at differing levels of intensity and outcome; that this on-going conversation occurs in a context broader than a narrow discourse of legal rules and, finally, that this relational and process-oriented perspective has both doctrinal and extra-doctrinal manifestations.

The volume contains the results of a research project involving political scientists and lawyers from Europe and the United States who were asked to follow, loosely, this premise and approach in retelling and re-evaluating the story of constitutionalization. It follows the classical scheme of such projects. There are several "National Reports" or Studies from a variety of Member States—not all fifteen, to be sure—together with a selection of "cross-country", horizontal interpretative essays. It displays, we hope and acknowledge, both the virtues and vices that are typical of such collective scholarly enterprises. Inevitably, an edited volume of essays does not have the coherence of a singly authored volume. It suffers from lacunae and overlaps. But, as if to compensate for such vices, it is clear that in this field at least no single scholar can match the same range of erudition, insight and creative imagination of a group as diverse as the one represented here. And although the basic guidelines were the same for all contributors, the resulting reports reflect the rich diversity of the different legal cultures examined as well as the different intellectual sensibilities of the authors. Likewise, though the "cross-country" interpretative essays also aim in some way to make sense of, and give coherence to, the same factual matrix, the reader will find, here too, as much contrast and conflict as one finds in the affairs of courts and states. Scholarly sovereignty, every bit as artificial as national sovereignty, is no less jealously guarded and fought over.

Is there an overarching result to this research project, some short summary that encapsulates the essence of its findings? There is, but do not rush to the back of the book in search of conclusions, for the essence of this project was in the questions asked and the approaches adopted by its multiple authors rather than in the conclusions reached.

DOCTRINAL PERSPECTIVES

The key doctrinal dimensions of the so called constitutionalization of the Community legal order are so well known as to require only the briefest of allusions: Direct Effect, Supremacy, Pre-emption, Implied Powers and all the rest. In their classical presentation these doctrines are about norms—typically developing Community norms based on, and in relation to, Member State norms within the overall Community legal order. But one can flip this coin and examine these very same doctrines from a relational perspective: the ECJ set of obligations or rules of conduct "imposed" on, and within, national jurisdictions as they take part in the discourse of European law. There is nothing new to this: Direct effect situates a Community measure as part of "the law of the land." It is also a rule of conduct for national courts in dealing with parties in certain cases. But this side of the coin highlights the conversational aspects of constitutional doctrine. All the Member State studies follow the constitutionalization doctrine from this relational perspective. They treat it as a process that has happened over time and, most importantly, they tell the story from the vantage point of the Member States. In this volume it is as if the story of the Binding of Isaac was told not from the normal perspective of Abraham but from the far less usual perspective of Isaac.

WHAT MAY YOU EXPECT IN THE MEMBER STATE CHAPTERS?

Some aspects are "pure" doctrine. We asked our contributors to provide a relatively brief description of the reaction to and reception of the Direct Effect/Supremacy doctrine by national courts, in particular higher courts. This part is historical-doctrinal in nature. In most Member States the reception (or otherwise) of the Direct Effect/Supremacy cluster was not achieved by one national judicial move. It is thus important to trace over time the principal landmarks in this evolution bringing us to the present.

Note that the focus is both doctrinal and empirical. At one level it is important to establish the authoritative formal position as stated by national courts of the status of Community law within the national legal order. In a critical, but distinct, second question the Member State chapters deal with actual practice by the national judiciary. Here too, the explication of doctrine in these studies is typically done from a *national constitutional law perspective*, not from an EEC law perspective which sometimes differs from one part of the judiciary to another. The acceptance or rejection of, say, Supremacy is a tale that has different legal rationales in different national jurisdictions.

One doctrinal question, however has been examined only marginally from a European Community law perspective, and hardly at all (except for Germany as far as we know) from a national constitutional perspective and never before in a comparative context. This is the issue of *Judicial Kompetenz-Kompetenz*.

The ECJ and most national courts would now agree that EC law is supreme—understood in different ways—in the fields for which the Community has been given competences by the Treaty. Conversely, however, if the Community acts outside its designated sphere of competence, its acts should have no effect, much less take precedence over conflicting national law. Community measures that are *ultra vires* do not enjoy supremacy. On this there is unanimity. Likewise, there is unanimity that the Community is a system of Attributed Powers, meaning that the Community does not have plenary legislative or executive authority. Powers are, thus, limited though the definition of these limits is very difficult, given the open-textured nature of the controlling provisions in the Treaties and the past practice of the various interpretative communities that bear on this issue (Court of Justice, Council of Ministers, etc.).

That is why the institutional question of *who gets to decide this question* as the final legal arbiter is as important as or even more important than the material legal question of *what* are the actual substantive limits. Several different positions on this question are possible and already emergent in the case law of some countries. On the one hand, the ECJ maintains (in a case such as, say, *Foto-Frost*) that the question of the limits of Community competence is *itself* a question of Community law and consequently is a matter for the ECJ. The ECJ thus sees itself as possessing the *exclusive* competence or at least the *ultimate* competence to adjudicate the issue of limits to competence in the Community.

National courts, on the other hand, can take a different view. It is quite possible, for instance, for a national constitutional court to accept the supremacy of EC law, but to take the position that defining the material limits within which such supremacy operates—the limits of Community competence—is a matter of national constitutional law to be decided by itself. Thus in the Maastricht decision the German Constitutional Court essentially decided that Community competences could not pass limits set by the *German* constitution, limits within its own competence to decide with some unspecified cooperation with the European Court. This issue can be part of an even broader version of this conflict—namely the extent to which national courts accept that the European Court of Justice has exclusive competence *generally* over interpretation of the Treaty, not only on issues of material competences and jurisdictional lines. Narrow or broad, in most jurisdictions the doctrinal position on this issue is murky. Elucidating this issue, as far as possible, is an important part of some of the national studies.

One great advantage of shifting the perspective from European to national constitutional sensibilities is that the landscape becomes more varied and interesting, even if more difficult to traverse. The very notion of a *constitutional* legal order comes into question. For, on this view, the reference of the European Court in a case such as *Les Verts* to the Treaty as the Constitutional Charter of the Community (and we use this as a metaphor for all its constitutional doctrines) is but an offer, a gambit that requires a response. That response has not been an unambiguous acceptance. Doctrine thus easily slips to issues of legal theory—a second important dimension of the volume.

From Doctrine to Legal Theory

Consider, first, the following manifestations of these ambiguities in the broader political arena. Prompted by an almost continuous process of Treaty revision, the last ten years of Community evolution have witnessed a surprisingly intensive debate about the architecture of the Community and Union. It has not been a "one sided" debate nor have revisions gone in one direction. The imperative of "deepening" found expression in, for example, the monumental shift to majority voting introduced by the Single European Act, the plan for Economic and Monetary Union introduced by Maastricht and an appreciable increase in the powers of the European Parliament culminating in Amsterdam. But there have been counter-forces too, reflecting altogether more sceptical public and elite opinions as demonstrated in the pre- and post-Maastricht debates. These found expression in, for example, the "derogation clause" of Article 100a in the Single European Act, in a determined effort in Maastricht to reign-in the legislative profligacy of the Community as well as the explicit, and largely successful, attempts to exclude the Court of Justice from the Second and Third Pillars of the Union. Amsterdam, too, is marked by these countervailing forces: the lateral expansion in the powers of the European Parliament contrasts with the palpable failure to increase majority voting.

And yet, with all this give and take there seemed throughout this process of Treaty revision to be one "centrist" line-in-the-sand shared by all principal actors: the sanctity of the *acquis communautaire*. And within the *acquis communautaire* the "Holy of Holies" was the constitutional *acquis*. Various suggestions emerging from time to time from British, German, French and other quarters to, for example, clip the wings of the Court or modify key constitutional relations failed to gain wide support within the revision process. The only successes of this sentiment in some notorious protocols to the Treaties have been sporadic and specific rather than systemic.

Thus, the very process of Treaty revision, negotiated among its High Contracting Parties (rather than Member States) and requiring ratification in accordance with the constitutional provisions of the various Member States, is a sharp reminder, to some, of the *"international law"* dimension of the Community and its constituent Treaties. But in that same process, in the affirmation of the sanctity of the *acquis* these same High Contracting Parties seemed to acquiesce and express a commitment to its *constitutional* foundations.

Constitutional or international? We are not quite sure whether it is possible to give a decisive answer to this question nor, even, how interesting it is to give such an answer. Be that as it may, it highlights the critical relevance of epistemology. Perspective becomes all important.

If, as Carl Schmit insisted, the exceptional provides the ultimate definition of a system's essence, then the Community's constitutional claim may well be difficult to sustain from the perspective of Member State jurisdictions. Most Member States root their obedience to the Community rules of conduct in their own constitutions. A certain, impeccable, legal logic supports such a negation.

If, on the other hand, Holmes celebrated dictum holds, logic must cede to experience. And constitutionalism, real or virtual, has been a remarkable experience. Whatever its theoretical foundation, empirically, the constitutional myth (if that is what it is) seems to have taken hold of most forms of legal discourse, notably court decisions and doctrinal writing, so as to become a practical reality in all but, indeed, the exceptional case. Was there not something astonishing in the altogether no-fuss manner in which the House of Lords made the Reference and received the Ruling in *Factortame*? And whatever the exact contours, who can deny that a major shift in the direction of the Community and its Court took place by the French *Conseil d'Etat* in *Nicolo*? And is it not of more than transient significance that despite many a warning bell and tough doctrinal talk and posturing from some jurisdictions, open constitutional conflict between European and German legal orders always seems to be looming but never to materialize?

So which perspective is more valid—the theoretical or the pragmatic? The pathological or the physiognomic? Can both be correct? Politically (including the politics of academia) that actually seems to be the case. Once the international lawyer has proven the point that in the final analysis the Community legal order is no more than a Treaty, he or she is usually happy to return to the comfortable arena of custom and treaty and soft law and leave Community lawyers to their devices. And Community lawyers? Since a professional lifetime can pass without requiring that "final analysis", they can happily proceed on the constitutional and domesticated assumptions that characterize the humdrum of the system in its day to day operation. And so it is, or has at least been to date, with courts. The doctrinal position of the European Court of Justice and, say, the German Constitutional Court on the ultimate authority to interpret the jurisdictional limits of the Community legislator may be as conflicted as the old West and East during the Cold War. Both sides have gone to the brink, but studiously avoided open warfare. Whether and why this Cold-War logic may persist remains an open question reflected, openly or obliquely, in several of the essays in this volume.

Still, the lawyer's lawyer may object and argue that this very dichotomy between the pathological and the physiognomic is outside authentic legal discourse, that it is a yardstick from sociology or politics that is alien to law. Courts have to *decide* and lawyers have to give reliable and responsible advice to clients. But here, too, even through the "lawyer's" purest doctrinal prism, perspective becomes all important. Who is more of a "lawyer"? He or she who believes in scientific jurisprudence, in the pure theory of law, in the ability to move through accepted procedures from the system's *grundnorm* to its most specific application? Or the legal realist—neither an American invention nor an exclusive American trademark — who applies his or her finest professional skill to predict how the controlling court would decide the issue. Assume that the "purist" and the "realist" come out with different doctrinal positions. Whose statement of doctrine will be more "true"? The purist who will have to concede—"you may be right that the court will decide in this way, but both you and the court are wrong. The law is as I state it"; or the realist who will have to concede—"your analysis and reasoning may be more persuasive, but unless and until the court is persuaded it is not 'law.'

All sides of this timeless debate are reflected, explicitly or implicitly, in the various essays in this volume rendering them all the richer.

BEYOND DOCTRINE

Going beyond doctrine poses an overarching generic research assumption for obvious reasons; judicial acceptance of the constitutional doctrines and especially the Supremacy/Direct effect cluster, could not be expected in all Member States as a banal occurrence. Recall, simply, the political opposition in some of the submissions of intervening Member States in the leading cases or even some Opinions of Advocates General. Indeed, in many jurisdictions the history of constitutionalism has had its ups and downs until "final"—full or qualified—acceptance. Recent years have even seen a retreat in several jurisdictions.

It is thus foundational to this project that the attitude and behavior of national courts vis-à-vis this question cannot be explained simply by reference to the doctrinal theory on which their decisions were based. It is necessary to look *Beyond Doctrine* adequately to understand the evolving European and national judicial practice.

In taking this leap, legal sociology, political theory, judicial politics and personalities, economic interests, legal realism—all come into play. Any methodology or approach that sheds light on the doctrinal evolution was deemed Kosher in this project.

This extra-doctrinal approach to judicial doctrine is a dimension of the story that has surely not been fully exhausted over the years and to which this projects hopes to make an important contribution. Of course each Member State has its own constitutional and political specificity in this regard; no one template can fit all cases. As already noted, in some Member States there had been and continues to be a certain divergence among various judicial branches as well as among other constitutional actors.

Still, despite this inevitable diversity we developed an inventory of possible hypotheses to explain national judicial reaction to European constitutionalization. To conclude this Preface we wish to record here those hypotheses that received some confirmation in one or more of the national studies. These hypotheses conditioned the orientation and the general direction of the project and defined the scope of the part of the research protocol that we called *Beyond Doctrine*. We present in lieu of any general theory—we do not agree on any such theory among ourselves; moreover, some of the crosscutting essays attempt to do just that!

Here, then, is a selection of the most important hypotheses to explain in non-doctrinal terms the reaction of national jurisdictions to the constitutionalization process.

a. Judicial self-understanding: "National Identity" and National Political Culture

One analytical axis explores the extent to which national courts have taken on the coloration of a "national identity" and/or given expression to a particular political culture. More specifically, it examines the extent that a nation's attitude toward European integration operates as an integral element of its "national identity" or political culture. Examples of this phenomenon, contestable to be sure, include Germany's vision of itself for some time as the motor of integration and its Post-War search for re-legitimation via the Community, Great Britain's historically more sceptical stance (its alleged island mentality...) and the traditional internationalist outlook of the Netherlands. Could these self-understandings have had an influence on national judicial positions? Courts may emphasize the "national" in their identity when confronted with a transnational situation. Can changes in judicial positions on these issues signal a change in political culture towards Europe? Surely the political culture of Post-War Germany of the 50s and 60s is quite different from that of Post-Unification Germany of the 90s. Can it be that this shift has no impact on judicial attitudes? Can the judicial identity shift with time? Could it be that the more Europe ceases to be considered in the national political culture as "international" and more as an extension of the "domestic" the more willing judges will be to shed that "national" mantle?

There are issues of identity within each national judiciary as well. The usual focus is on the self-conception of *constitutional courts* as guardians and promoters of the constitution, and on the way in which constitutional courts may advance both this mission and their own power by opposing or supporting the ECJ and EC law. Yet to the extent that this line of analysis emphasizes judicial *politics*, in the sense of a struggle for power among different courts, it is also an important factor in considerations of judicial identity.

The previous point hypothesized the "national" as a principal variant in the self-conceptualization of courts. But beyond *national* identity, the impact of a specific *judicial* identity may also be related to a particular position in the national judicial system. Courts may, for instance, feel a particular obligation toward a particular segment of the population. The ordinary French courts, for instance, conceive of themselves as representing French business interests, a consideration that appears to have influenced their attitude toward EC law. The French *Conseil d'Etat*, on the other hand, has an image of itself as charged with the protection of the public interest.

b. Judicial Empowerment

The empowerment thesis rests on the proposition that accepting the Supremacy/Direct effect cluster of doctrine enormously empowers courts in systems that hitherto had no power of judicial review over, say, acts of the legislature. It may empower lower courts vis-à-vis higher (or constitutional) courts in systems in which power of judicial review is reserved to the highest courts. The permutations can vary. Some constitutional courts for example may display a greater reluctance to accept the discipline of EC law—in power terms they gain the least and maybe even lose. The notion of judicial empowerment should be handled with some delicacy. It is not meant, in and of itself, to be pejorative. It need not, perhaps should not, be understood as a crass grasp for power for its own sake. The allure of this type of judicial empowerment may be strongest to a court entrusted to "uphold the law" and unable to do so because of structural limitations.

c. Judicial Dialogue and "Cross Fertilization"

The phenomenon of judicial dialogue is potentially an important factor in the reception of European Community law by national courts. Much of this dialogue is "vertical"—carried out between national courts and the ECJ. Most previous scholarship has focused on a one-way conversation in which the ECJ seeks to communicate its ideas to the national courts; some of the most interesting findings in this volume of papers stress the extent to which national courts also shape the ECJ's deliberations.

Judicial dialogue can also be horizontal—among national courts of different countries. Such dialogue has multiple forms and uses. Sometimes it is not dialogue at all, but a simple usage of the jurisprudence of one court in the jurisprudence of another. It is quite revealing to see how much use was made of the decisions of courts of one jurisdiction in those of another even in some of the classical early decisions of the highest courts in Europe on the "Supremacy" issue.

d. National and European Political Context

We may distinguish judicial identity from the particular and more fleeting political, social and economic context of a particular decision or line of decisions. The EU has been constructed in relatively identifiable stages, typically accompanied by relatively wide swings in national and European public opinion. Do such sentiments appear to filter through to national judges? What was, if any, the possible effect of the post-Maastricht malaise on the German Maastricht decision? To what extent do judicial decisions themselves or extralegal sources suggest that national judges take "judicial notice" of these larger trends? And if they do, how precisely do these factors enter into their legal analysis. Do they, for instance, refer to a particular stage of the integration process as a justification for adopting a stricter or looser construction of a particular position? Or do their language and rhetoric seem to echo prevailing political debates about the importance of preserving democratic accountability?

e. The Deployment of Individual Litigants and National Courts

A number of both the legal and the political science analyses of the effectiveness of the ECJ have emphasized its ability to co-opt or "deploy" individual litigants and national courts in the construction of the EC legal system and, of course, in challenges to it. It is an interesting hypothesis to explore the extent to which national courts consciously try to manipulate individual incentives at the level of both litigants and lower courts.

f. The Role of Different Branches of Government and the Relative Power Balance between Them

Supremacy is often characterized as compromising the "sovereignty" of a Member State. But if we "disaggregate" the notion of the Member State as a monolithic concept, supremacy can also mean the strengthening of the Executive over the legislature, leaving the Executive free to make laws in conjunction with fellow Executives at the Community level that can no longer be overridden by national parliaments. This move has contributed to the so-called Democracy Deficit. How does this phenomenon impact on the doctrinal evolution and acceptance of it in the Member States?. Does the Executive understand the implications of this evolution? Is there evidence of an active Executive role in trying to convince the national courts to accord primacy to EC law even over subsequent national legislation? This paradigm is one of the most interesting in the national chapters.

g. The Impact of Legal Culture

Many different "legal culture" explanations are raised in the various chapters as explanations for different attitudes of national judiciaries at different times. Some of the dichotomies featured here are formalism *v.* pragmatism; internationalism *v.* parochialism; parliamentarism *v.* judicial activism (judicial review); and monism *v.* dualism. The traditional role and importance of doctrinal commentary (*La Doctrine*) also stamps a particular legal culture, as opposed to a greater openness to legal realism.

h. Judicial Composition and the Role of Individuals

Judicial biography is one of the most fascinating (and delicate) categories of explanation. Who the judges are as a category as well as the role of individual judges in doctrinal evolution cannot but be a major explanatory factor. It is remarkable to see the role that specific judicial personalities have played in different national jurisdictions as well as the background of judges as a class. The findings are never systematic but always revealing.

*   *   *

Doctrine, legal theory and "beyond doctrine"—these are the elements which combine together to give this volume its special identity. It is very much a collective product and an eclectic one. Its conclusions are more suggestive than systematic, more provocative than proven. Nevertheless the familiar terrain has some unfamilier obstacles and some surprising new vistas. We hope that even seasoned travellers will arrive at unexpected destinations.

Contents

Contributors

KAREN ALTER is an Associate Professor in the Department of Politics at Smith College.

HERVE BRISBOSIA is a Researcher at the European University Institute, Florence, and the Institut d'Etudes Européennes de L'Université Catholique de Louvain. He was formerly a Research Fellow of the European University Institute Florence.

MARTA CARTABIA is a Researcher in Constitutional Law at the University of Milan.

MONICA CLAES is Lecturer in Law, University of Maastricht.

P. P. CRAIG is Professor of Law in the University of Oxford and a Fellow of Worcester College.

JULIANNE KOKOTT is Professor in the Department of Foreign, International and European Law at the Heinrich-Heine-Universität in Düsseldorf.

FRANCESCO P. RUGGERI LADERCHI is a former assistant, Law Department, College of Europe, Bruges; Dottorando di Ricerca, University of Macerata.

WALTER MATTLI is Professor at the Institute for War and Peace Studies at Columbia University in New York.

JENS PLÖTNER is a civil servant in the German Foreign Office and was formerly a student of political science at the Institut d'Etudes Politiques in Paris.

ANNE-MARIE SLAUGHTER is the J Sinclair Armstrong Professor of International, Foreign and Comparative Law at Harvard Law School.

ALEC STONE SWEET is Associate Professor in the Department of Politics and Society, at the University of California, Irvine.

J. H. H. WEILER is the Manley Hudson Professor of Law and Jean Monnet Chair, Harvard Law School and Co-Director, Academy of European Law, EUI, Florence.

BRUNO DE WITTE is Professor of Law at the University of Maastricht.

ULRICH R. HALTERN, Dr. iur., LL.M. (Yale), was formerly a Visiting Researcher at the European Law Research Center at Harvard University.

Table of Cases

A. EUROPEAN COURT OF JUSTICE

NOTE:, where possible, the only reference given in this list is that to the *European Court Reports* (ECR), although alternative or further references may be given in footnotes in the text.

B. OTHER SUPRANATIONAL BODIES

International Court of Justice

C. NATIONAL COURTS

Table of Legislation

A. EUROPEAN COMMUNITIES

EC Directives

EC Regulations

B. OTHER SUPRANATIONAL LEGISLATION

World Trade Organisation Agreement

United States -Israel Free Trade Area Agreement 1985

C. NATIONAL LEGISLATION

Belgium
Constitution (old)
Constitution (revised)
Special Cour d'Arbitrage Act 1989

Denmark
Constitution

PART I: NATIONAL REPORTS

1

Report on Belgium

HERVÉ BRIBOSIA

GENERAL INTRODUCTION[1]

This chapter is divided into two parts. The first part describes the *doctrinal* (legal) evolution of the notions of direct applicability and the primacy of EC law in the Belgian legal order. However, it appears necessary to enlarge the scope of investigation in two directions; first, a full comprehension of the Belgian legal order's stance *vis-à-vis* the EC legal order requires an examination of its relations with international law in general; secondly, the direct applicability and the primacy of international/EC law are facets of more comprehensive concepts relating to relations between the international/EC legal order and states' legal orders, namely the conditions for the domestic applicability of international treaties and EC law, their domestic effects, and their domestic authority. In that respect, it will be sought to determine, in addition to the *content* of the rules governing the relations between the legal orders at issue, the legal *foundation*—municipal, international or EC—of those rules. This second enlargement of the study seeks to analyse the approach of Belgian law to the distinction between monism and dualism, and hence, to the *Kompetenz-Kompetenz* issue.

The second part makes some observations on the social and political *context* in which the Belgian doctrinal stance towards European integration has evolved. For this purpose, it endeavours to depict relationships and influences between the three highest Belgian courts, namely, the Cour de cassation (Cass.), the Conseil d'État (CE), and the new constitutional court, the

[1] I wish to thank M. Melchior, President of the Cour d'arbitrage, and P. Tapie, First President of the Conseil d'État for the interviews that they kindly granted to me in April 1994. I am also grateful to Luis Diez-Picazo and Renaud Dehousse (EUI) for the constructive critical responses to my report at the workshop held on 28 and 29 June 1994 at the EUI; to Jean-Louis Van Boxstael (Université Catholique de Louvain) for his helpful comments and to Michael Upton (Advocate, Edinburgh) for the improvement of the English writing. Of course, all views expressed in this report and any errors remain the author's own. This chapter is based on a report completed in May 1995 for the workshop held at the Harvard's Center for European Studies. A more comprehensive and updated legal study in relation to direct applicability and primacy of EC law in Belgium can be found in: Bribosia, H., "Applicabilité directe et primauté des traités internationaux et du droit communautaire—Réflexions générales sur le point de vue de l'ordre juridique belge", *Revue Belge de Droit International*, 1996/1.

Cour d'arbitrage (CA). Furthermore, it comments on the relationships between the various legal actors—"*la doctrine*" and "*jurisprudence*"[2]— between the politico-constitutional actors—the executive, the Parliament and the Constituent Assembly—and between the legal and politico-constitutional actors. Accordingly, the first part prepares the way for the second by narrating the parallel and chronological evolution of those actors.

DOCTRINAL REVIEW

The direct applicability of international treaties is a concept with two different meanings which are very often confused in both doctrine and jurisprudence. The first meaning refers to the *conditions of applicability* in the municipal system. Apart from rules requiring public notice, these pertain chiefly to constitutional requirements concerning *reception* in the domestic legal order. The applicability of an international provision is "direct"—it is better to say "immediate"[3]—if its domestic applicability is not subject to any requirements of this kind: it is sufficient that it has come into force in international law. The other—more common—meaning of direct applicability deals with the *domestic effects* of international provisions applicable in the state legal order. In its broadest definition, an international convention is "directly" applicable—or produces direct effect—if it can be applied in the domestic legal order without previous domestic normative *implementation*. As far as primacy is concerned, it is envisaged here firstly as a *rule of conflict* between municipal law and treaties/EC law. Then, the notion will be related to the *source* of domestic validity of international and EC law in general, and more specifically to the question of the competence to determine the competence of the European Communities (*Kompetenz-Kompetenz*).

Conditions of domestic applicability

International treaties: nature of the Parliamentary assent

Unlike international custom, treaties are not "immediately" applicable. Article 167 (previously 68)[4] of the Belgian Constitution provides indeed that treaties[5]

---

[2] For the purpose of this chapter, the French expressions "*la doctrine*" and "*jurisprudence*" refer to the world of academia and scholars, and case law respectively.

[3] Verhoeven, 1984, 14.

[4] On 5 May 1993, Belgium revised its Constitution in order to complete federal reforms that were started in the 1970s (*M.B.*, 8 May 1993). The numeration of the Constitution has been entirely revised as well, with effect from 17 February 1994 (*M.B.*, 17 February 1994).

[5] Concluded by the King (federal executive) or by the governments of the three Regions or of the three Communities, since 1993's reforms laid down the principle of sharing the international competences in parallel to the internal division of legislative powers between the federation and the two kinds of federate entities.

shall have no effect as long as they have not obtained (Parliamentary) *approval*.[6] The legal nature of such Parliamentary assent has been discussed in the Belgian doctrine in terms which may at times appear confusing. Various analyses have been advanced, from the most monist to the most dualist.[7] Yet, the prevalent conception lies somewhere in between: the Parliamentary assent amounts to a formal statute which introduces the treaty into the state legal order, and hence renders it applicable as such therein.

However, the statutory definition of the Cour d'arbitrage's jurisdiction may seem to challenge the legal nature of the Parliamentary assent, in a dualist manner. The Cour d'arbitrage is a constitutional court of limited jurisdiction which was created in 1983 in order to enforce the federal division of exclusive legislative competences between the federation and its federated entities, namely the Communities and the Regions. To this end, the court has been given powers—through annulment proceedings and through references for preliminary rulings—to review the conformity of federal statutes, decrees and ordinances[8] with the constitutional and legal provisions allocating powers. Since 1989, its jurisdiction has been extended to review the compliance of all legislative rules with the constitutional principles of equality and non-discrimination, and with the constitutional provisions regarding education (former articles 6, 6bis and 17 of the Constitution, currently articles 10, 11 and 24).[9] What is relevant for present purposes lies in the fact that, within the scope of its jurisdiction, the Cour d'arbitrage is also entitled to review the validity of federal statutes, decrees and ordinances functioning as Parliamentary assents.[10] How then can the Cour d'arbitrage's power to review the substantive validity of Parliamentary assents be explained other than by regarding them as substantive statutes? How may the fact that the unconstitutional character of a treaty rebounds on the Parliamentary assent thereto be explained other than by implying that the assent incorporates the content of the treaty? An answer—consistent with the prevalent more monist doctrine— has been inferred from the first decision of the Cour d'arbitrage that reviewed the constitutionality of a Parliamentary assent:[11] namely, that Parliamentary assents correspond to an "individual decision" consenting to the introduction

---

[6] By the Houses of Parliament or by the Councils of Regions or Communities, according to their respective competences.

[7] The most monist doctrine views the Parliamentary assent as a formal authorisation that is required prior to the international ratification of treaties: these become applicable as such in the domestic system upon their entering into force in international law. The most dualist view considers the Parliamentary assent as a substantive statute incorporating the content of a treaty, so that the treaty is applicable as a Belgian statute.

[8] Decrees and ordinances (Region of Brussels) are the legislative rules that the Regions and the Communities are entitled to enact within the scope of their competences.

[9] Articles 1 and 26 of the Special Cour d'arbitrage Act of 6 January 1989, adopted in pursuance of article 142 (formerly 107*ter*) of the Constitution.

[10] Article 3, § 2, of the Special Act cited above.

[11] CA, 16 October 1991, 26/91. More recently see CA, 3 February 1994, 12/94.

of the treaty. The validity of such consent accordingly depends on the constitutionality of the treaty.[12]

European Community law

The Community treaties do not exhibit any peculiarity as far as the conditions for their domestic applicability are concerned: as with any other treaty, they must be granted Parliamentary assent. Conversely, Belgian courts have never questioned the jurisprudence of the Court of Justice (ECJ) proclaiming the principle of the immediate applicability of secondary EC legislation, although the doctrine remains divided as to whether unilateral acts of international organisations in general must be granted Parliamentary assent.

With respect to directives, it may be wondered whether the states' powers over the "means and methods" are only a matter for implementation, or whether they also require an act of reception.[13] In any event, the Conseil d'État has implicitly admitted the immediate applicability of directives—at least after the deadline for transposition has passed—in a case in which it applied a directive which had not then been transposed, by annulling a conflicting ministerial decree of deportation.[14]

Direct applicability

Belgian courts have for a long time accepted their jurisdiction to apply and interpret international treaties, as well as to decide that they confer on individuals rights and obligations.[15] They did not wait either for the PICJ opinion of 3 March 1928 apropos the free city of Danzig's civil servants, or for the progressive jurisprudence of the ECJ or the European Court of Human Rights, though it is true that Belgian jurisprudence subsequently exhibited particular development in these two areas. The question of treaties' domestic effects has been dealt with abundantly by the doctrine and is one that arises before the Belgian courts with increasing frequency. Nevertheless, controversies remain over the definition and the basis of such effects. Not surprisingly

---

[12] Lejeune and Brouwers, *J.T.*, 1992, 673.

[13] Thus, K. Lenaerts believes that directives are not applicable in the state's legal order until their transformation into national law. The recognition by the ECJ of direct effects of untransposed directives is described as an "*accident de parcours*" that must be dealt along the lines of the estoppel doctrine or the continental principle *Nemo auditur suam propriam turpitudinem allegans* (Lenaerts (1986), 261, 263–5). It is true that the views of the ECJ itself on this point may have appeared somewhat ambiguous when it held against Belgium that: "A Member state has not discharged the obligation imposed upon it . . . if for the purpose of fulfilling the requirements under the directives in question, it simply relies on existing practices or even just the tolerance which is exercised by the administration", *Commission* v. *Belgium*, Case 102/79 [1980] ECR 1473, ECJ).

[14] CE, 7 October 1969, *Corvelyn*, *J.T.*, 1969, 694.

[15] See for instance Cass., 8 January 1925, *Osram*, *J.T.*, 1925, 52.

the answer to these two questions affects the extent to which treaties in general, and EC law in particular, are domestically applicable.

International treaties

The direct effect of a treaty provision is usually defined *senso stricto*, as the creation of rights in favour of individuals which they can invoke before their national courts, without need for domestic measures of implementation.[16] This conception is characterised by the combination of two criteria: individual applicability, and applicability without previous implementation. It presumes that treaties which do not confer rights on individuals before previous implementation in national law create obligations only in the international legal order, which are therefore enforceable only in that system. It implies that treaties' domestic effects amount to their direct effects *senso stricto*.[17] Such a conception was first propounded in 1963 by the Procureur général of the Cour de cassation, R. Hayoit de Termicourt.[18] It was espoused a year later by both the Cour de cassation[19] and the Conseil d'État.[20] The Cour de cassation proclaimed it in its landmark decision in the *Le Ski* case,[21] and has subsequently confirmed it [22] though often only implicitly. Lastly, the Cour d'arbitrage too—which includes international treaties in its reference standards, indirectly through the constitutional principle of equality of rights and liberties accorded to the individuals[23]—has confined itself to that strict conception of direct effect, and hence of domestic effect.[24]

Today this conception of direct effect is being undermined by the doctrine.[25] The definition of direct effect *senso lato* does not retain the criterion of individual applicability: a treaty provision is directly applicable if its domestic applicability does not require previous domestic normative

---

[16] In a more generalized version of the *senso stricto* definition, direct effect of an international provision can be characterised by its ability to confer, upon legal subjects of the domestic order, rights and obligations that can be enforced—without previous domestic normative implementation—before national courts, or even administrative authorities where they take individual decisions (Verhoeven (1980), 243–6).

[17] It will be shown hereafter that the assimilation of direct effects *senso stricto* with domestic effects has often been done while dealing with the issue of primacy, see pp. 13, 16.

[18] Hayoit de Termicourt (1963), 483.

[19] Cass.,13 April 1964, *Ananou, Pas.*, 1964, I, 849.

[20] CE, 13 March 1964,*Lippens*, no 10.501. More recently, see also CE, 12 April 1989, *Group. unions prof. belges médecins spec.*, no 32.346, *A.P.M.*, 1989, 58.

[21] See p. 14 below.

[22] See for example Cass., 10 May 1985, *Pas.*, 1985, I, 1122; Cass., 6 March 1986, *Pas.*, 1986, I, 853; and Cass., 20 December 1990, *Pas.*, 1991, I, 392. In the same way, also see Lejeune (1994), 320.

[23] See p. 20 below.

[24] CA, 23 May 1990, case no 18/90, B.11.3; CA, 5 June 1990, case no 25/90; CA, 14 June 1990, case no 26/90, 6.B.2.; CA, 4 June 1991, case no 22/91; CA, 14 November 1991, case no 33/91, 6.B.15.

[25] Coppens (1990), 611; Ergec (1986), 104; Leroy (1990), 197 and 198; Salmon (1971); 535. Verhoeven (1969,) 697–9; Verhoeven (1991), 904; Verhoeven (1980), 264; Waelbroek (1965/2), 356 *et seq*; Waelbroek (1972), 574 *et seq*; Waelbroek (1985), 33 and 34.

implementation.[26] In that perspective, treaties that simply require states to enact national rules[27] become part of "the law of the land" (*légalité objective*) as soon as the treaties have been introduced by Parliamentary assent, even though they do not necessarily confer subjective rights and obligations on individuals. The individual can invoke such a treaty, by means of the appropriate judicial remedies, in order to disapply or annul any national rule conflicting with it. He also could bring an action for damages because of the violation by a public authority of the treaty considered as a measure having validity in the national legal order.[28]

It is not surprising that it is has been the Conseil d'État,[29] and more recently the Cour d'arbitrage[30]—in cases referring to article 13 (2) of the International Covenant on Economic, Social and Cultural Rights—which have concurred with the doctrine and have accordingly reconsidered their jurisprudence. Their jurisdiction is indeed largely concerned with annulment proceedings or, in the case of the Cour d'arbitrage, with preliminary rulings on constitutional validity (*contentieux objectif*); and the *locus standi* to bring an action before those two courts consist of a mere interest, without need for the existence of a "subjective" right. Yet, such an evolution is remarkable in the case of the Cour d'arbitrage because—as mentioned above—its jurisdiction with reference to international law is only indirect.[31] As for the ordinary courts and the Cour de cassation—whose jurisidiction is mainly determined by the existence of subjective rights—they too have potential jurisdiction to recognise direct effects *senso lato* by setting aside a national rule, or by awarding damages for a breach of legality. However, in a recent case relating to the same article 13 (2), the Cour de cassation appears to have adhered to the strict definition of direct effect.[32]

---

[26] Verhoeven (1980), 244.

[27] By one means or another; for instance by means of incorporation of treaty provision into domestic law, by means of executive implementation of such provisions, by means of domestic legislation according to common principles provided by the treaty, etc.

[28] Ergec (1986), 104.

[29] " . . . *que la question ainsi posée n'est pas de savoir si le pacte . . . a conféré aux particuliers des droits subjectifs dont ils pourraient se prévaloir devant les tribunaux, mais de vérifier si la législation belge est compatible avec l'objectif inscrit dans la règle claire et précise de l'article 13, 2, a) du pacte (gratuité de l'enseignement primaire)*" CE, 6 September 1989, no 32.989 and 32.990, *R.A C.E.*, 1989, 66 and 71.

[30] "*L'article 13, 2, b) et c) du pacte . . . (relatif à l'enseignement secondaire et supérieur) n'a pas d'effets directs dans l'ordre juridique interne, et, en soi, ne fait pas naître un droit à l'accès gratuit à l'enseignement autre que primaire. Ces dispositions s'opposent toutefois, tout comme le littera a) du même article, à ce que la Belgique, après l'entrée du pacte à son égard, prenne des mesures qui iraient à l'encontre de l'objectif de gratuité qui doit être immédiatement atteint en ce qui concerne l'enseignement primaire et progressivement instauré en ce qui concerne les enseignements secondaire et supérieur*" CA, 19 May 1994, no 40/94, *A.P.M.*, June 1994, 109; in the same way, see also 7 May 1992, no 33/92, B.4.1.

[31] See also p. 23 below.

[32] Cass., 20 December 1990, *Najimi, Pas.*,1991, I, 392. Conversly, see the atypical case of 16 February 1970, in which the Cour de cassation seems to admit direct effects *senso lato* of a Convention on the status of refugees (*Pas.*, 1970, I, 533, cited by Ergec (1986), 104, and by Waelbroek (1985), 36).

As far as the *source* of direct effect is concerned, the traditional Belgian conception conforms with the 1928 PICJ opinion cited above: the intention of the contracting parties is a necessary and sufficient condition of the direct applicability of treaties. In contradiction to this, the new trend both in doctrine[33] and jurisprudence[34] tends to recognise direct effects of treaties lawfully introduced whenever their provisions are self-sufficient, i.e. they are sufficiently clear, precise and complete to be applied without prior implementation.

This trend of resorting to objective criteria—disregarding or even contradicting the will of treaties' authors[35]—stems from several factors.[36] Such a method simplifies the task of national judges who are confronted with more and more treaties, contracted by a larger and larger number of parties. It also allows the judges to interpret national law in conformity with the treaties as far as possible in order to prevent the state from failing to meet its international obligations. Above all, it is worth noticing that, apart from the Cour de cassation, the thesis of an objective source for direct effect has evolved alongside the extension of its definition: they both promote the extensive domestic application of treaties. This tendency of Belgian judges can be explained in part by their internationalist outlook, or by the fact that judges favour the application of rules irrespective of their source as long as they are relevant to the case at issue. Lastly, Belgian judges have undoubtedly been influenced by the ECJ's jurisprudence on this matter.

European Community law

The only measures for which EC treaties expressly provide direct application are regulations. Nevertheless, it is well known that the ECJ is inclined to acknowledge a general presumption in favour of direct applicability for both the EC treaties and secondary legislation. The Court's assumption of jurisdiction to rule on direct effect presupposes that the foundation for direct effect lies in the EC legal order. And by refering to the "nature",[37] the "essence",[38] or "the spirit, the general scheme, and the wording of the Treaty",[39] as well as by refering to the clear and unconditional expression of certain provisions,[40] the Court, by means of teleological interpretation, seems to have rendered objective the intention of the contracting parties. However, there is still support for the opinion that the Court did not create a specific concept of direct applicability based on objective criteria. This argument holds that those

---

[33] Verhoeven (1991), 897; Ergec (1986), 104; Waelbroek (1972), 574 *se seq*.
[34] CE, no 32.989 and 32.990 cited above, observations by Leroy (1990), 196 to 198; CE, 4 July 1989, no 32.945, *A.P.M.*, 1989, 103. Cass., 10 May 1985 and 6 March 1986 cited in n. 22 above.
[35] Leroy (1990), 196.
[36] Waelbroek (1985), 38; Verhoeven (1991), 897 and 898.
[37] ECJ, 19 December 1968, *Salgoil*, Case no 13/68.
[38] ECJ, 21 June 1974, *Reynders*, Case no 2/74.
[39] ECJ, 5 February 1963, *Van Gend and Loos*, Case no 26/62.
[40] *Ibid.*

criteria are meant simply to detect the intention of the contracting parties, and to allow the extension of the technique of direct effect.[41]

The point of view of the Belgian legal order is in accordance with that of the EC: national courts admit the supreme jurisdiction of the ECJ—by virtue of article 177—to rule on the direct effect of EC law in the domestic legal order, although they themselves often directly apply EC law independently, without reference to the ECJ.[42] The decision of the Conseil d'État in the case of *Corveleyn* in 1968[43] deserves to be mentioned as it precedes by a few years the ECJ's decision in the *Van Duyn* case (1974)[44] asserting the principle of the direct applicability of directives, or even the 1977 case of *Verband van Nederlandse Ondernemingen*[45] defining their direct effects *senso lato*.[46] Indeed, the Conseil d'État annulled a ministerial order of deportation that violated the 1964 directive, which, at the time, had not been transposed.[47] Commentators considered that the Conseil d'État had applied directly the directive,[48] or even that it had supported the definition of direct effect *senso lato*.[49] Since then, the Belgian courts have, with a few exceptions,[50] supported the direct application of directives,[51] at least in their vertical dimension,[52] in accordance with the ECJ's decision in *Marshall*.[53]

Supremacy over conflicting domestic law

The milestone decision of the Cour de cassation in the *Le Ski* case on 27 May 1971 was a watershed in Belgian jurisprudence as far as conflicts between

---

[41] Verhoeven (1980), 262.

[42] For recent case law, see Wytinck (1993), 986.

[43] Cited above; also published in *C.D.E.*, 1969, 343 and comments of Gigon.

[44] ECJ, 4 June 1974, Case 41/74, submissions Mayras.

[45] ECJ, 1 February 1977, Case 51/76.

[46] On direct effect *senso lato* of directives, see Waelbroek (1972), 580 and 581.

[47] Articles 2 and 3 of Directive of 25 February 1964 provided, respectively, that *"les mesures d'ordre public ou de sécurité publique doivent être fondées exclusivement sur le comportement personnel de l'individu qui en fait l'objet"*, and that *"la seule existence de condamnations pénales ne peut automatiquement motiver ces mesures"*. Thus, the ministerial order of deportation was annulled because it was based merely on a previous sentence.

[48] Ganshof van der Meersch (1970/2), 425; Waelbroek (1972), 573.

[49] Verhoeven (1969), 699.

[50] See for instance the judgment of Tribunal correctionnel de Bruxelles, 24 February 1976, *Pas.*, 1976, III, 24.

[51] See for example 7 January 1977, *Pas.*, I, 492, and the judgment of Tribunal correctionnel de Malines of 28 September 1987, *J.T.*, 1988, 48.

[52] On the absence of horizontal direct effect of directives, see the Belgian decisions cited by Wytinck (1993), footnotes 32, 33 and 35, 986 and 987.

[53] *Marshall* v. *Southampton and South West Hampshire Area Health Authority*, C-271/91, [1994] QB 126, ECJ. See also, in accordance with ECJ's *Marleasing SA* v. *La Comercial Internacional de Alimentacion SA*, C-106/89, [1992] CMLR 305, the decision of Cour d'appel de Bruxelles of 20 May 1992: it reversed a lower judgment for not interpreting national law by taking into account a not-yet transposed directive, disregarding the fact that it was invoked in a horizontal relation; similarly, see *Prés. Comm. Namur*, 23 December 1992 (*R.D.C.*, 1993, p. 254), cited by Wytinck (1993), 988.

treaties/EC law and domestic law are concerned. Before expounding on it, the situation before that decision will be examined; and following that, the reactions to which *Le Ski* gave rise are set out. In each section, it is sought to draw the developments of the doctrine together with the developments of the jurisprudence, as well as the politico-constitutional context in which those developments occurred. Moreover, each section endeavours to compare the special treatment of EC law with that of international treaties in general (this special nature of EC law is referred to in French by the expression "*spécificité communautaire*"; hereafter in this chapter, "specificity" is used accordingly).

Before 1971 (Le Ski): Lex posterior derogat legi priori

International treaties   In forty years, the Constituent Assembly has sought eight times to insert in the Constitution a provision providing for the primacy of treaties over conflicting statutes. Yet such a project has never been achieved. The first attempt in 1953 failed because it was objected that the judiciary would interfere in the executive's or the legislature's powers.[54] In 1959, the Parliamentary Commitee for the revision of the Constitution believed that it was premature to enact such a constitutional provision, and that the issue should be left to the evolution of international law and *jurisprudence*.[55] The 1965–68 and 1968–71 Constituent Assemblies considered the insertion of an article 107*bis*, but without success because of the early dissolution of Parliament. The provision—inspired by a University seminar held in 1965[56]— read: "Courts shall apply statutes and regulations only so long as they are in conformity with international law, and notably with treaties duly published".

The 1959 invitation has in fact been taken up by the judiciary, with the support of part of the doctrine which had qualified as "exceptionally retrograde"[57] the older jurisprudence dealing with relations beween international law and domestic law. Even so, the evolution will be gradual.

The solution provided by the Cour de cassation to the conflict between treaties and laws *formerly* enacted long remained immutable: subsequent treaties "suspend (*arrête*) the effects of statutes".[58] That wording was applauded for two reasons. First, since the conflicting statutes were not repealed, they became applicable again as soon as the treaties ceased to be effective. Secondly, such wording implied a difference in nature between treaties approved by a law and domestic laws.[59] Therefore, the adage *lex posterior derogat legi priori* should have seemed inappropriate to explain the

---

[54] *Doc. Parl.*, Chambre, 1952–1953, no 693, 54 and 55.

[55] *Doc. Parl.*, Chambre, 1959–1960, no 374–1, 14 and 15 (author's emphasis).

[56] Salmon and Suy (1966), p. 69 (author's translation).

[57] Rolin (1953), p. 561 (author's translation).

[58] Cass., 8 January 1925, *Osram, Pas.*, I, 101 (author's translation). Also see case law cited by Muûls (1934), 31 and 32; and by Hayoit de Termicourt (1963), footnotes 27 and 33, 482 and 483; by Salmon (1971), 516, footnote 60; and by Waelbroek (1965), 352.

[59] Hayoit de Termicourt (1963), 482; Ganshof van der Meersch (1966), 803, and (1968), 488.

ruling. As Hayoit de Termicourt conceded, the Cour de cassation never offered a very consistent justification.[60]

In the case of conflicts between treaties and *subsequent* statutes, the jurisprudence held that the latter would prevail. Such an outcome appeared to refer to the aforementioned *lex posterior* principle, and therefore implied that treaties approved by Parliamentary assent could be assimilated to laws, at least so far as concerned their authority. That is in any event how a decision of the Cour de cassation of 1925 has been interpreted for about forty years:[61] "Considering that it is for the legislature to assess the conformity of statutes with the treaties' obligations binding upon Belgium; that the courts are not entitled to disapply a statute for the reason that it supposedly does not conform with such obligations".[62] Such an interpretation is supported by an earlier case in 1916 which asserted that treaties approved by Parliament have "the authority of a law *(force de loi)*",[63] or by a later case in 1950 holding that treaties are "equivalent to a law *(équipollent à une loi)*".[64]

Accordingly, conflicts between treaties and regulations or other administrative acts inferior to laws were solved in favour of international treaties; hence, approved treaties have always been a source of Belgian administrative law.[65]

Prompted by the Procureurs généraux[66] of the Cour de cassation Hayoit de Termicourt and Ganshof van der Meersch, the resolution of the conflict between treaties and subsequent laws took a new approach. From being a conflict of law in time, it turned into a conflict of norms of differing authority. Besides, both the Procureurs généraux mentioned two cases decided in 1961 which implicitly admitted the precedence of treaties over domestic laws without regard to chronological order of enactment of the treaties and domestic provisions[67]. Surprisingly, those cases passed unnoticed.

---

[60] Hayoit de Termicourt (1963), 483.

[61] Cass., 26 November 1925, *Schieble, Pas.*, 1926, I, 76. Hayoit de Termicourt (1963), 483.

[62] (Author's translation). In the same way, see Cour d'appel de Bruxelles of 3 July 1953, published in *J.T.*, 1953, 518, commented on and strongly criticised by Rolin (1953), 561. Another interpretation was to consider the holding as an application of the traditional principle of separation of power according to which judges may not review the constitutionality of laws. Such a justification has been criticised by Hayoit de Termicourt (1963), 488. One can add that such a justification implied that treaties, like the Constitution, were formally superior to laws, but that judges had no jurisdiction to enforce the hierarchy in both cases. It was thus inconsistent with traditional case law that accepted the setting aside of laws contrary to subsequent treaties.

[63] Cass., 20 May 1916, *Pas.*, 1915–1916, I, 416.

[64] Cass., 27 November 1950, *Pas.*, 1951, I, 185.

[65] Waelbroek (1965/2), 358; Salmon (1987), 147 to 153.

[66] The Procureur général is the head of the prosecutor's office *(parquet)* both at the Cour de cassation, and for all the lower courts. Albeit under the authority of the minister of justice, he is quite independent. The *parquet* is a party to criminal prosecutions, and also to civil actions to defend public interests.

[67] Cass., 7 November 1961, *Pas.*, 1962, I, 261 and 291, exposed by Ganshof van der Meersch (1966), 807; and cited Hayoit de Termicourt (1963), p. 484, in footnote 53.

Moreover, in a *mercuriale*[68] that he delivered in 1963, Hayoit de Termicourt endeavoured to reconstruct the 1925 case cited above as providing no final answer to conflicts between *self-executing* treaties (i.e., having direct effect *senso stricto*) and subsequent statutes.[69] In his conclusions, he advocated that self-executing treaties should prevail over domestic law, unless there was express contrary provision in a legislative or constitutional measure.[70] In other words, it was assumed that such conflicts were in general the result of the legislature's negligence which therefore had to be adjusted by the judges. The courts seem to have shown implicitly some signs of acceptance of the new doctrine,[71] and the doctrine applauded the shift, except for one albeit important point which still remains controversial today: why should the primacy of treaties be confined to provisions conferring rights and imposing obligations upon individuals? In fact, that issue coincides with that of the definition of domestic effects and direct effects.[72]

In his 1968 *mercuriale*, the Procureur général Ganshof van der Meersch revealed his monist conception of law involving the supremacy of international law over states' legal orders. Indeed, he asserted that:[73] "The international legal order and the state's legal order are not separated, and must be considered as spheres of the general legal order . . . law can only be single (*unique*), under pain of not being". In addition, he justified the primacy of international law by virtue of its "very nature", "for reasons of social morality", and because "if international law would not prevail, it would be doomed". He then concludes that the subjection of state law "finds its basis in the international legal order", so that an express provision in the Constitution proclaiming such primacy is not indispensable and would have a purely declaratory effect.

European Community law   Belgian case law related to EC law was rather scarce during the first dozen years. The first ECJ preliminary ruling initiated

---

[68] A *mercuriale* is a speech delivered annually—usually by the Procureur général—at the ceremonial reopening session at the Cour de cassation which comprises a thorough doctrinal study adressing a topical issue.

[69] Indeed, he maintains that the statute supposedly inconsistent with the treaty, which the Court refused to set aside, was simply implementing an international obligation, which was binding on Belgium only in the international legal order. Since the Convention did not confer rights and obligations on individuals, it could not conflict with a domestic law (1963), 483.

[70] Hayoit de Termicourt (1963), 486. According to Joliet, the principle then asserted by Hayoit de Termicourt was not so much the one of primacy, but rather the technique of "interpretation in conformity" (1983), 357.

[71] See cases cited by Ganshof van der Meersch (1966), 805 and 806, and by Salmon (1971) 518 and 519. Also see the judgment of Tribunal civil de Bruxelles of 8 November 1966 in which the Convention on Human Rights takes precedence over national linguistic legislation (exposed by De Visscher (1968), 611); equally, see the judgment of Juge de paix d'Anvers of 24 December 1968, C.D.E., 1969, 603, commented on by Verhoeven, 702.

[72] See p. 6 above.

[73] Ganshof van der Meersch (1968), 494 and 495 (author's translation).

by a Belgian court dates from 1967.[74] The two Procureurs généraux were amongst the first to examine the specific features of the EC legal order.

Hayoit de Termicourt's *mercuriale* of 1963 appears to be somewhat paradoxical.[75] On one hand, he stressed the features specific to the EC, citing in a footnote the 1963 ECJ *Van Gend en Loos* case (see n. 95 below): an autonomous legal order with some federal aspects, the competences of EC institutions to enact self-executing legislation, the exclusive jurisdiction of the ECJ to assess the validity of EC secondary legislation, etc. Accordingly, he argued that the very existence of EC law depended on the recognition of its primacy over subsequent laws. On the other hand, he drew no specific legal consequences distinct from those that normally attend traditional self-executing treaties: a constitutional or even legal provision could expressly oblige national judges to apply a subsequent law conflicting with either self-executing treaties or EC law, either in particular case or in general. Therefore, it can be inferred that the Procureur général grounded the primacy of EC law in the domestic legal order.

In his 1968 *mercuriale*, Ganshof van der Meersch merely indicated that his argument for the primacy of international law in general applies *a fortiori* to EC law.[76] However, in an article published two years earlier,[77] he not only affirmed that the division of respective competences between the two legal orders made the concept of primacy unnecessary to settle conflicts between EC secondary legislation and national law; he also maintained that the very concept as well as the specific nature of the Community implies that EC law must also prevail over the national Constitutions.

1971: Le Ski *proclaims supremacy*

In 1970, the Constituent Assembly enacted the former article 25*bis* (now 34) of the Constitution. By stating that "the exercise of definite powers may be allocated by a treaty or by a statute to institutions set up under public international law", it intended to provide for a legal basis for the limitations of power that Belgium had consented to in 1950 (European Convention on Human Rights), in 1951 (ECSC Treaty), and above all in 1957 (EEC and Euratom Treaties). A part of the doctrine was inclined to find the justification for the supremacy of EC law in that provision.[78]

However, that view was not universal. Indeed, before the dissolution of Parliament in September 1971, a Parliamentary Committee for the Revision of the Constitution recommended the insertion of a specific provision (article 107*bis*) which held that: "Courts shall apply statutes and regulations only so long as they are in conformity with self-executing provisions of international

[74] Lenaerts (1986), 279.
[75] Hayoit de Termicourt (1963), 484–6.
[76] Ganshof van der Meersch (1968), 492 (footnote no 127) and 495.
[77] Ganshof van der Meersch (1966), 809 and 810 (author's emphasis).
[78] Louis (1979), 237, and see references cited.

treaties in force and duly published". This wording was undoubtedly determined by the decision in *Fromagerie Franco-Suisse Le Ski* v. *État belge*—examined below—which was delivered on 27 May 1971 by the Cour de cassation.[79]

International treaties   As the reader may have observed, *Le Ski* has completed a trend that both doctrine and jurisprudence had initiated ten years earlier. Nonetheless, the case is famous,[80] both in Belgium and abroad, for having settled the question of the stance of the Belgian legal order to the international and EC legal orders. In fact, the case is more remarkable for the fact that the Cour de cassation was swayed neither by the large sum at stake, nor by the legislature's pressure which tried to determine the outcome.

It is unnecessary here to go into the facts of the case.[81] Essentially, the Court had to rule on a conflict between article 12 of the EEC treaty—which prohibits the introduction of new customs duties on import or taxes having equivalent effect—and a subsequent Belgian law of 1968, which retroactively ratified taxes that a Royal decree had imposed on various imported milk products from EEC countries. The Cour de cassation held that:

> "in the event of a conflict between a norm of domestic law and a norm of international law which produces direct effects in the domestic legal system, the rule established by a treaty shall prevail. The primacy of the treaty results from the very nature of international law;
>
>   article 12 of the [EEC Treaty] is immediately effective and confers on individual persons rights which national courts are bound to uphold; it follows . . . that it was the duty of the judge to set aside the application of provisions of domestic law that are contrary to this Treaty provision".[82]

Procureur général Ganshof van der Meersch's submissions greatly affected the Court's decision, notably in so far as it based the supremacy of international law in its very nature. It has been rightly noted that such a doctrinal position has never been the object of thorough theoretical analyses.[83] In his submissions,[84] the Procureur général added little to what he had expressed in his 1968 *mercuriale*. The basic idea resided in the fact that the very existence of the international legal order implied its superiority: given that a legal order is superior to its legal subjects, it follows that the international legal order is superior to the states, and hence, to their legal orders. From the international point of view, these assertions are banal. But, in order to explain that the primacy of international law has implications inside the domestic system, one

---

[79] *Pas.*, 1971, I, 896 *et seq*, submissions of Procureur général Ganshof van der Meersch. Also published in *J.T.*, 1971, 471, and in English, in *International Law Reports* (1993), p. 203.

[80] The number of articles commenting on the case is impressive; see references cited by Naômé (1994), 37.

[81] For a detailed description of the case, see Salmon (1971), 529 *et seq*.

[82] Compare with ECJ's decision in *Simmenthal Spa* v. *Amministrazione delle Finanze dello Stato*, Case 70/77, [1978] ECR 1453.

[83] Naômé (1994), 39.

[84] Submissions, *Pas.*, 1971, 896–900.

must have in mind Ganshof van der Meersch's postulate: the international and domestic legal orders comprise a single legal order in which "a norm cannot be both valid and invalid at the same time, nor obligatory and non-obligatory".[85]

Furthermore, Ganshof van der Meersch stressed two consequences flowing from that monist postulate. Firstly, there is no necessity for the enactment in the Constitution of the principle of primacy; such provision would have only a "declaratory" effect.[86] Secondly, and more importantly, he strongly rejected the proposition that the courts should abide by any express legislative provision requiring that treaties conflicting with a subsequent statute be set aside.[87] Conversely, his monist doctrine was weakened by conceding supremacy only to international treaties, and then only if they were self-executing (*senso stricto*); and by expressing reservations about their supremacy over the Constitution.[88]

In *Le Ski*, the Belgian state argued in the Cour de cassation that courts do not have jurisdiction to set aside a statute conflicting with an earlier treaty because the legislature is sovereign, and and has an exclusive prerogative to assess the conformity of statutes both with the Constitution and with treaties binding upon the Kingdom of Belgium. Like its Procureur général,[89] the Court abstained from responding to that argument referring to the unanimously admitted principle that judges do not review the constitutionality of laws.[90] However, since primacy has been based on the nature of international law, as opposed to the constitutional legal order, setting aside a statute contrary to a treaty does not, formally, imply an exercise of constitutional review. Nevertheless, reviewing the compatibility of a law with a treaty is, in fact, as much a challenge to Parliament's sovereignty as is constitutional review. The following section (After 1971: reactions to *Le Ski*) describes the political reactions provoked by this alteration in the separation of powers. As for the doctrine, the predominant view was one of approval for the readjustment of powers, arguing that the legislature can always refuse to give its assent to treaties concluded by the executive, or can prompt the latter to reject or modify the treaties at issue [91].

European Community law   While all of the Court's reasoning in *Le Ski* is concerned with international law, and more particularly with its nature, one should not lose sight of the fact that the case was actually dealing with a provision of the EEC treaties. After asserting the principle of the supremacy of

---

[85] Submissions, *Pas.*, 1971, 896 and 897, citing Masquelin (author's translation).
[86] Submissions, *Pas.*, 1971, 889 and 899.
[87] Submissions, *Pas.*, 1971, 904.
[88] See p. 22 below.
[89] The Procureur général's submissions are rather ambigous on that point, *Pas.*, 1971, 893–6.
[90] Joliet (1983), 369.
[91] Salmon (1971), 535 and Waelbroek (1973), 521 go along with the Procureur général 's submissions, 905.

directly applicable provisions of treaties in general over conflicting domestic laws, the Cour de cassation continued:

> "this is a fortiori the case when a conflict exists, as in the present case, between a norm of municipal law and a norm of Community law;
>   the reason is that the treaties which have created Community law have instituted a new legal system in whose favour the member-states have restricted the exercise of their sovereign powers in the areas determined by those treaties".

So, by recognising the re-adjustment of sovereignties, the Cour de cassation proclaimed the supremacy *a fortiori* of both the primary EC treaties and secondary EC legislation. The terms of the judgment are borrowed from the leading ECJ case of *Costa* v. *E.N.E.L.* (1964), apart from the reference to the limitation of the *exercise of sovereign powers*, whereas *Costa* v. *E.N.E.L.* invoked *a definitive limitation of sovereign rights.*

To the extent that the Cour de cassation adopted the language used by the ECJ, the decision may have represented a retreat inspired by the Procureur général;[92] nevertheless, it was debated within the Belgian doctrine whether the Cour de cassation had acknowledged a "specificity" of the EC legal order. Various opinions were supported,[93] even one maintaining that the Court had not taken a stand on the matter.[94]

In his submissions preceding the *Le Ski* case, Ganshof van der Meersch expounded at length on the "specificity" of the EC legal order and on leading ECJ cases relating to the matter (*Van Gend en Loos, Costa, Walt Wilhelm,* etc.).[95] He appeared to differentiate EC law from other treaties on the ground that:[96]

> "Community law is a specific and autonomous law which is binding on the courts of member-states and makes it impossible to set against it any domestic law whatsoever. The very nature of the legal system instituted by the Treaty of Rome endows the primacy with its own foundation, independently of the constitutional provisions in states. This special character of Community law flows from the objectives of the Treaty, which are the establishment of a new legal system to which are subject not only states but also the nationals of those states. It also stems from the fact that the Treaty has set up institutions having their own powers and in particular the power to create new sources of law".

This passage seems thus to imply the primacy of EC law over the Constitution, and so to confirm what Ganshof van der Meersch had already affirmed in 1966.[97] Monism between member states' legal orders and that of

---

[92] Conclusions, *Pas.*, 1971, 902.

[93] Salmon sees a difference of degree (1971), 534, whereas Pescatore considers it to be a difference of nature (1971), 580.

[94] Waelbroek (1973), 520.

[95] Submissions, *Pas.*, 1971, 900–5. *Van Gend en Loos* v. *Nederlandse Belastingadministratie*, Case 26/62, [1963] CMLR 105; *Costa* v. *E.N.E.L.*, Case 6/64, [1964] CMLR 425; *Wilhelm* v. *Bundeskartellamt*, Case 14/68, [1969] CMLR 100.

[96] Submissions, *Pas.*, 1971, 903 (author's translation).

[97] Ganshof van der Meersch (1966), 809.

the EC appears to be deeper, and seems to imply the location of the *Kompetenz-Kompetenz* in the hands of the latter.[98] For the rest, it must be admitted that the doctrine does not draw any substantial legal consequences from any possible "specificity" of the EC legal order.

Whatever the special status of EC law may be, and whether or not it affects the meaning or the extent of its supremacy, Belgian doctrine praised the ruling in *Le Ski* for not having treated international law any less favourably than EC law.[99] Indeed, the Cour de cassation could have based EC law supremacy on the former article 25*bis* (now 34) of the Constitution (set out above).[100] By not doing so, the Court avoided several flaws. Basing EC supremacy on the constitutional provision could have entailed an *a contrario* interpretation when the authority of other international treaties in the domestic system was considered. Moreover, the effects of EC supremacy would have amounted to a constitutional review of laws that the ordinary courts in Belgium, including the Cour de cassation, may not carry out. Finally, it is logically difficult to conceive how the Constitution could provide for the supremacy of a rule over itself.

After 1971: reactions to Le Ski

It is not surprising that, on the whole, *Le Ski* was well received by both the politico-constitutional arena—which had suggested such a judicial shift as early as 1959—and by the doctrine, which had begun to encourage it even earlier. Yet, immediately after *Le Ski*, the doctrine was divided as to whether primacy should be embodied in a constitutional provision, or whether the jurisprudence should be allowed to evolve pragmatically, adapting to new realities in international and European relations. It was also argued that former articles 68 and 25*bis* (now 167 and 34) constituted sufficient grounds for the primacy of treaties and EC law respectively.[101]

As has been indictated above, there is today still no express constitutional provision regarding the authority of either international or EC law in the Belgian legal order. Moves were, again, made in 1978 and 1981 to insert an article 107*bis* but merely for the limited purpose of confirming the decision in *Le Ski*.[102] A 1987 project referred for the first time to the notion of "supranational law". As for the current Constitutional Assembly (1991–May 1995), it has not yet reached a consensus on this question and probably will not.[103]

However, it is worth mentioning, beside the projected article 107*bis*, other proposals, the genesis or abandonment of which have always been attributable to the implications of *Le Ski*. In 1972, a private member's bill, strongly

---

[98] On *Kompetenz-Kompetenz*, see p. 21 below.
[99] Salmon (1971), 533; Pescatore (1971), 581; Louis (1979), 237.
[100] See p. 14 above.
[101] Salmon (1971), 535; Wigny (1972), 364. See p. 14 above.
[102] Velu, Bruylant (1992), 72.
[103] *Doc. Parl.*, Chambre, s.e., 1991, no 626.

opposed to *Le Ski*, submitted that issues involving the conformity of domestic law with international and EC law should be referred to Parliament for a preliminary ruling. However, such a proposition tended in effect to challenge the very principle of the primacy of international and EC law by subjecting it to the will of the representatives of the state.[104] In 1975, a senator proposed to introduce the procedure suggested earlier in 1968 by Ganshof van der Meersch himself, namely that such an application for a preliminary ruling should be referred to the Cour de cassation. In 1980, during the preparatory work for the creation of the Cour d'arbitrage, a draft Government bill submitted that the new Court should have jurisdiction to rule on such preliminary references.[105] The Government's proposal was eventually abandoned largely for two reasons. First, it would have undermined the decision in *Le Ski* inasmuch as it would have deprived the ordinary courts of jurisdiction to rule directly on conflicts beween international law or EC law and domestic law. For the same reason, the bill was found to be incompatible with the ECJ's decision in *Simmenthal*,[106] which requires that any national court disapply municipal law to the extent that it is not in accordance with EC law, "of its own motion . . . and it is not necessary for the court to request or to await the prior setting aside of such provision by legislative or other constitutional means".

Thus, apart from a few reactions, the decision in *Le Ski* was relatively well accepted in Parliament. The same cannot be said of the Government, which took four years to accept the judgment and repay the unlawful duties to *Fromagerie Franco-Suisse Le Ski*. As for the doctrine, the principle itself was generally accepted, but not always its foundation in the international/EC legal order.[107]

Except for a few decisions, ordinary courts adhered to the principle laid down by the Cour de cassation.[108] Long before *Le Ski*, the Conseil d'État had construed its jurisdiction to entitle it to treat directly applicable treaties as a source of administrative law, in order to review the validity of regulations or administrative decisions. Unlike its French counterpart, it had no problem with conforming to the line drawn by *Le Ski*, through either the annulment[109] or the validation[110] of administrative acts (or municipal elections), by setting aside statutes inconsistent with directly applicable treaties, even where the statutes had been enacted subsequently.

---

[104] *Doc. parl.*, 1971–1972, Chambre, 200/1, 27 April 1972. The proposal was strongly criticised by Louis (1972), 437.

[105] *Doc. parl.* Sénat, s.e., 1979, no 100/14 and *Doc. parl.*, Sénat, s.e., 1979–1980, no 435/1.

[106] ECJ, 9 March 1978, *Simmenthal*, Case no 106/77.

[107] Joliet (1983), 367 and 368.

[108] See case law refered to by Louis (1979), 236; and by Velu, Bruylant (1992), 60–8 and 129.

[109] CE, 10 November 1989, *J.T.*, 1990, 608, observations by Coppens (1990), 608.

[110] In a case of 17 February 1989, the Conseil d'État refused to annul municipal elections that had infringed a 1985 statute on opinion polls, for the reason that the statute was not compatible with article 10 of the Convention on Human Rights proclaiming freedom of expression (*J.T.*, 1989, 254, commented on by Leroy).

What of the Cour d'arbitrage? Contrary to the Conseil d'État with respect to administrative regulations, the constitutional Court has no jurisdiction to invalidate legislative rules because of "direct violation of international law".[111] However, the Cour d'arbitrage does refer to international treaties and EC law, but only indirectly: [112] either where the rules dividing powers between the various legislators refer to such international or EC[113] provisions; or where the constitutional principle of equality of rights and freedoms accorded to individuals includes rights and freedoms provided for by international conventions[114] or EC law.[115] Such an indirect jurisdiction—construed by a constitutional Court eager to extend its jurisdiction—tends to promote *de facto* the primacy of both international and EC law over legislative rules. But such an indirect jurisdiction regarding EC law may also account for the fact that the Cour d'arbitrage had never until recently[116] requested from the ECJ a preliminary ruling in relation to a legislative rule submitted to the review of the constitutional Court.[117]

Could the Cour d'arbitrage, like the Conseil d'État, set aside one of its legal, or even constitutional[118] reference standards for the reason that its enforcement would be incompatible with a treaty or with EC law? The doctrine denies that possibility, arguing that such review does not fall within the Cour d'arbitrage's jurisdiction as determined by the Constitution and the Special Cour d'arbitrage Act.[119] The Cour d'arbitrage seems to be of the same view. [120] However, it could be argued that the Cour d'arbitrage, just like the

---

[111] CA, 14 July 1990, Case no 26/90, 6.B.2. It is however worth mentioning two Parliamentary draft bills concerning the status of the Cour d'arbitrage; the first one in 1983, and the second one in 1989. The idea was no longer to vest the Constitutional court with exclusive jurisdiction—through preliminary rulings—to rule on the compatibility of national law with international/EC law (see p. 19 above), but with a non-exclusive jurisdiction to rule on such conflicts through annulment proceedings, alongside ordinary courts' jurisdiction in accordance with *Le Ski*, and the ECJ's ultimate jurisdiction to rule on the matter (EC treaty, Art. 177), (see Velu, *J.T.*, 1992). The project to entrust the Cour d'arbitrage with such a jurisdiction may come up again in the future to ensure the effectiveness of EC law in the federal structure of Belgium.

[112] On that matter, see Bribosia and Van Boxstael (1994), 32–4, and 168–9.

[113] See for example CA, 25 February 1988, Case no 47; CA, 26 May 1988, Case no 55; CA, 14 November 1991, Case 32/91.

[114] Mainly the European Convention for the Protection of Human Rights and Fundamental Freedoms, and the two 1966 New York International Covenants.

[115] See the following cases in which the Cour d'arbitrage refers to a provision of the TEC or of a directive: CA, 15 July 1993, Case no 63/93; CA, 7 October 1993, Case no 72/93; CA, 29 September 1993, Case no 68/93; CA, 10 May 1994, Case no 37/94; CA, 2 February 1995, Case no 7/95 and 8/95; CA, 25 April 1995, Case no 37/95; CA, 14 December 1995, Case no 81/95.

[116] See CA, 19 February 1997, Case no 6/97, where the Cour d'arbitrage requests from the ECJ a preliminary ruling concerning the interpretation of the Directive 93/16 CEE in order to be able to construe a Flemish decree accordingly in conformity therewith, and hence, its conformity with the constitutional rules dividing the legislative powers.

[117] Compare with Ergec (1995), 220–5.

[118] If one accepts that *Le Ski* implies supremacy over the Constitution as well, *infra*, see p. 000 below.

[119] Ergec (1991), 648; Velu, Bruylant (1992), 114.

[120] CA, 23 May 1990, no 18, B.14.2. It is however uncertain whether the Cour d'arbitrage denied that it had jurisdiction to set aside a Constitutional provision contrary to conventions on

administrative and ordinary courts, could set aside a national reference standard which is incompatible with a treaty or EC law without referring to its constitutional jurisdiction. Indeed, such a power would derive from the logic of *Le Ski* which is supposed to apply to all the courts without exception, and arguably even from the "nature of international law". In any case, the ECJ's *Simmenthal* decision applies to all national courts, constitutional courts included, disregarding notably the domestic definition of their jurisdiction. That said, it is true that today the issue remains rather theoretical since the reference standards of the *Cour d'arbitrage* that might be inconsistent with international/EC law are not very numerous. This fact may also explain why to date the Cour d'arbitrage has never requested from the ECJ a preliminary ruling in relation to one of its reference standards. Nevertheless, the issue will become sensitive if and when the Cour d'arbitage's jurisdiction is extended to refer to the whole Constitution.[121]

Kompetenz-Kompetenz

In its broadest version, the *Kompetenz-Kompetenz* issue presupposes a monist doctrine of legal (sub)orders, and raises the question of which legal (sub)order—international/EC or constitutional—governs the domestic validity of treaties and EC law. In that respect, it has been indicated above that only EC secondary legislation is "immediately" applicable in the Belgian system, whereas all the treaties—including those of the EC—have to be introduced according to the constitutional requirements (i.e. Parliamentary assent). As for direct effect, despite the Belgian courts' general tendency to neglect the contracting parties' intentions—and thus the international basis—in favour of objective criteria, the ECJ's exclusive jurisdiction to determine the direct effect of EC law has not been questioned by the national courts. As for supremacy, some derive it from the international/EC legal order, others from the constitutional one; none of the views have sought to establish a consistent theoretical argument. Yet, as with direct effect, the Belgian courts have not challenged the ECJ's jurisdiction to interpret the extent of the primacy of EC law in the domestic legal order.

Similarly, as far as the author is aware, neither the national courts, nor the debates upon the ratification of the Maastricht Treaty, have ever challenged the ECJ's exclusive jurisdiction to rule on the question of whether a Community institution has acted *ultra vires*—the question which ultimately governs the issue of direct effect and primacy of EC law. More generally, it is accepted that the ECJ has exclusive jurisdiction to decide upon the formal

human rights, or denied the hiearchal superiority of international treaties over the Constitution (cited by Ergec (1991), pp. 647 and 648).

[121] The jurisdiction of the Cour d'arbitrage can be expanded without a Constitutional revision; a Special Act suffices (article 142 of the Constitution).

and substantive validity of secondary EC legislation, and to interpret the scope of the obligations imposed on the Member States by the Treaties.

However the position may have changed completely following a decision of the Cour d'arbitrage in 1991 in which it held that it has jurisdiction to review the constitutionality of treaties that have already come into force in the Belgian legal order (*ex post* review). If the Court had to follow the same kind of reasoning with respect to EC law, it would necessarily grant itself the *Kompetenz-Kompetenz*. Thus, in the Belgian legal order, the *Kompetenz-Kompetenz* issue is a question of the hierarchical relationship bewreen the Constitution and EC law. However, the issue must also be raised, once again, for international treaties in general.

Hierarchy between the Constitution and treaties

Le Ski did not rule explicitly on the relation between treaties and the Constitution. The doctrine inferred from the decision arguments both *a contrario* and *a fortiori*. Ganshof van der Meersch's submissions are somewhat contradictory in that respect. On one hand, since he pointed out that the supremacy of treaties is not incompatible with the Constitution,[122] he seemed to reaffirm what he had already maintained in his 1968 *mercuriale*, namely that the Constitution still prevails over treaties.[123] On the other hand, the arguments put forward by him to justify supremacy logically imply that the Constitution is also subjected to the international order. Equally, in his 1992 *mercuriale*, Procureur général J. Velu adopts the monist foundation of *Le Ski* by referring to the arguments of Ganshof van der Meersch's 1968 *mercuriale* in order to justify treaties' primacy over the Constitution as well: "law can only be but single under pain of not being (all law must comprise one single order, or be nothing at all) . . . The international and constitutional legal orders must be considered as spheres of a larger legal order, and not as being separated". J. Velu concludes that if *Le Ski* did not create a distinction between domestic law and the Constitution, that was because such a distinction was unjustified.[124]

Recently, a discussion has taken place in the Parliamentary Committee for the revision of the Constitution about the legal relationship between international treaties and the Constitution. The Parliamentary Committee's principal conclusion was that it was not the right time to take such a political

---

[122] Submissions, *Pas.*, 1971, 899.

[123] Commenting in his 1968 *mercuriale* on the project to insert a article 107*bis* in the Constitution, he held: "*on a entendu exclure le refus d'application de la Constitution elle-même. Et c'est sage, bien que ce soit une atténuation au principe de la primauté . . . Le gouvernement a eu égard aux principes fondamentaux inscrits dans les articles 130 et 131 (aujourd'hui 187 et 195), sur lesquels la Constitution elle-même repose et subsiste; l'article 130 interdit de suspendre la Constitution; l'article 131 ne permet pas de la modifier ou d'y déroger autrement que par la voie de révision . . . La Constitution continue à s'imposer au juge, qui tient d'elle ses pouvoirs, et à régir ses devoirs vis-à-vis de l'État*", (1968), 496.

[124] *J.T.*, 1992, 758 (author's translation)

decision, notably because divergences of opinion on the matter remained [125]. On the contrary, the judiciary will not wait for a "political decision" to take a stand, but rather for concrete—and rare—cases of application.

In fact, before the creation of the Cour d'arbitrage, the issue remained purely theoretical for the Belgian courts, including the Cour de cassation and the Conseil d'État. Indeed, when treaties were assigned the same authority as statutes, conflicts between treaties and the Constitution were logically settled in the same way as those between laws and the Constitution: the Constitution was considered to be formally superior, while the courts had no jurisdiction to review the constitutionality of either laws or treaties. As soon as primacy of treaties was recognised (in *Le Ski*), two positions could be defended. Either the Constitution was similarly viewed as subordinated to treaties; and therefore, it had to be set aside to the extent that there was a conflict with an international provision.[126] Alternatively the Constitution was viewed as superior to treaties, but such constitutional primacy remained merely formal since judges consistently declined to review the constitutionality of treaties.[127] Thus, in any case, treaties were applied, even though they might be considered to be unconstitutional.

The creation of the Cour d'arbitrage in 1983 will have revived the issue of the conflict between treaties and the Constitution. The constitutional Court's jurisdiction displays two correlative aspects that impinge upon the relationship beween the Constitution and international or EC law, and hence that affects the issue of *Kompetenz-Kompetenz*. First, it has been said that the *Le Ski* ruling does not seem to apply to the Cour d'arbitrage's reference standards; this could be seen as a limit to the primacy of international and EC law, as much over the Constitution as over laws.[128] Secondly and most importantly, treaties are indirectly—through the Parliamentary assents—subject to constitutional review. Indeed, articles 1 and 3, § 2 of the Special Cour d'arbitrage Act provide that the Court has jurisdiction to *annul* Parliamentary assents[129] inconsistent with its usual reference standards,[130] namely the constitutional and legal rules regarding the federal division of powers,[131] and the constitutional principles asserting equality of rights and freedoms and guaranteeing freedom of education.

---

[125] *Doc. parl.*, Chambre, s. o. 1993–1994, no 626/4–92/93.

[126] See Cass., 25 February 1974, *J.T*, 444, and judgment of Tribunal civil de Bruxelles of 9 February 1990, *J.L.M.B.*, 1990, 796, commented on by Naômé; discussed by Velu, Bruylant, 1992, 130 et 131.

[127] For a presentation of the doctrine supporting that position, see J. Velu, Bruylant (1992), pp. 141 and 142.

[128] See p. 21 above.

[129] Enacted by the Houses of Parliament or the Councils of Regions and Communities.

[130] See p. 5 above.

[131] In this way, Parliamentary assents could be annuled if the treaty at issue has been concluded in a field of competence belonging to another entity, or even concluded irregularly. Ergec (1986), 271; Brouwers and Lejeune (1992), 674.

This aspect of the Cour d'arbitrage's jurisidiction has recently given rise to a controversy between the constitutional Court and the present Procureur général of the Cour de cassation, J. Velu, whose 1992 *mercuriale* concentrates on the issue. Both[132] agree that the constitutional review of Parliamentary assents implies the confrontation of the approved treaties themselves with the constitutional—and even with the legal—reference standards. In other words, there is no doubt that the Special Act itself has provided for a substantive constitutional—and legal—review of treaties, and that such review presupposes the "primacy" of several legal and constitutional provisions over conflicting treaties. But the Cour d'arbitrage and J. Velu strongly disagree over the nature, and more precisely over the *appropriate stage* of such a constitutional review.

According to the Procureur général,[133] the constitutional review of treaties through their Parliamentary assents may only be carried out *prior to* the treaties coming into force in international—and thus in domestic—law. He points out that the Cour d'arbitrage's jurisdiction to make preliminary rulings on the matter has been implicitly excluded, and that the deadline to commence annulment proceedings has been shortened from six to two months. Accordingly, he argues that the spirit of the Special Act requires that the King—or the federated executives—should not ratify and commit Belgium in the international sphere before the deadline to commence annulment proceedings against Parliamentary assents has elapsed, or before the Court has ruled on such proceedings. In other words, such a constitutional review would amount to a kind of preventive review, similar to that exercised by the Conseil d'État but with three differences: the Conseil d'État merely delivers *advisory opinions* examining the compatibility of *draft Government bills* for Parliamentary assents, and does so with reference to the *whole* Constitution. He concludes his *mercuriale* thus: "once the directly applicable treaty has come into force, neither courts nor other public bodies could, under the pretext of intrinsic unconstitutionality, hinder its execution or ignore its effects".[134]

By so concluding, J. Velu directly addresses himself to the Cour d'arbitrage, which had considered itself to be entitled to carry out *ex post* constitutional review of international commitments. Indeed, one year earlier, the Court had accepted its jurisdiction to rule on a *preliminary reference*[135] concerning the

---

[132] As for the Cour d'arbitrage, CA, 16 October 1991, *Commune de Lanaken*, Case no 26/91, B.4.; CA, 3 February 1994, *École européenne*, Case no 12/94, B.6.; and CA, 26 April 1994, Case no 33/94. As for the Procureur général Velu, *J.T.*, 1992, 741. In the same way, Brouwers and Lejeune (1992), 673.

[133] Velu, *J.T.*, 1992, 737 to 741, and 760.

[134] Velu, *J.T.*, 1992, 761 (author's translation).

[135] The Court d'arbitrage held that, although article 3, § 2 of the Special Act only refered to annulment proceedings, its jurisdiction to rule on preliminary references was to be found in article 26 of the Special Act since it did not distinguish, amongst the laws, decrees and ordinances submitted to its review, between those assenting to treaties and the others.

compatibility of a Parliamentary assent to an international convention[136]—which was already in force—with the constitutional principle of equality. Though the Court did not invalidate the treaty at issue, attention must be paid to the consequences of such a ruling. While the Court tended to downplay the effects of preliminary rulings, authors have raised the possibility that such effects may lead to disapplication of treaties.[137] In a report submitted at the IXth Conference of European Constitutional Courts,[138] the Cour d'arbitrage itself admitted that ordinary courts[139] are bound, in similar cases, by previous preliminary rulings. It recognised that, although both Parliamentary assents and treaties thereby approved still belong to the Belgian legal order, they are in fact deprived of legal effect. Therefore, the Court concluded that, in such cases, the treaties at issue must either be amended or rejected.

In a 1994 case,[140] the Cour d'arbitrage, far from adopting the Procureur général's views, once again accepted its jurisdiction for a prelimary ruling on whether the Parliamentary assent to the international status of a "European school" in Belgium was in accordance with former article 17 (today 24) of the Constitution which provides for free education. Instead of trying to relativise the domestic effects of such a preliminary ruling, the Court held that:

"Incidentally, the Constituent Assembly, which has forbidden the legislature to pass rules contrary to those referred to by article 107ter (today 142) of the Constitution, may not be supposed to have authorised the same legislature to do so indirectly through the assent given to an international treaty".

The following dictum is somewhat enigmatic, but seems to entail a dualist connotation, or even an approach that combines monism with primacy of national legal orders:

"Besides, no rule of international law—which is a creation of the states—not even article 27 of the 1969 Vienna Convention on the law of treaties, allows states to conclude treaties which are contrary to their Constitution."

It is perhaps too early to apprehend the full significance of these statements. Nevertheless, contrary to the opinion of J. Velu, the Cour d'arbitrage has thus assumed that the Constitution is superior to international treaties. The court does not believe it to be necessary to challenge the *Le Ski* case, because it interprets that decision to proclaim the primacy of treaties over laws only, and not

---

[136] Case no 26/91, *Commune de Lanaken*, cited in n. 132 above. The Convention intended to suppress double taxation between Belgium and the Netherlands.

[137] Brouwers and Lejeune (1992), 672.

[138] Report presented at the Conference of European Constitutional Courts, 10 to 13 May 1993, by M. Melchior and L. De Greve, *Protection Constitutionnelle et protection internationale des droits de l'homme: concurrence ou complémentarité*, Bruxelles, Roneo, December 1992, 36 to 42, particularly 41 and 42.

[139] The Cour de cassation and the Conseil d'État must re-apply for a preliminary ruling.

[140] CA, 3 February 1994, Case no 12/94, *École européenne*, cited in n. 132 above, B.4. Also see CA, 26 April 1994, Case no 33/94, ruling that article 6, § 1er of the European Convention of Human Rights "and hence, the Parliamentary assent . . . do not infringe articles 10 and 11 of the Constitution" (author's translation).

the Constitution, and therefore to apply only so far as the treaties at issue are consistent with the Constitution.[141] In any case, the Court intends to enforce the primacy of the Constitution over treaties, at least to the extent of its reference standards. In that respect, it is remarkable that the Court has indicated, in its aforementioned report, that the two-month deadline for the commencement of annulment proceedings did not imply that the treaties at issue were not yet in force.[142] In other words, it is not only through preliminary rulings that the Court would be able to review the constitutionality of treaties, but also through annulment proceedings.

The Cour d'arbitrage is not the only court in Belgium to acknowledge, at least implicitly, the supremacy of the Constitution. Indeed, in order to respond to preliminary references, other courts must address references to the Cour d'arbitrage; by doing so, they seem to admit the Court's jurisdiction to review the constitutionality of treaties already in force. In his 1992 *mercuriale*, J. Velu expresses his concern about the influence that the Cour d'arbitrage could have on ordinary courts and the Conseil d'État in the realm of conflicts between treaties and the Constitution. Therefore, in his conclusion, the Procureur général recommends that "whatever the preliminary ruling by the Cour d'arbitrage be, it will be up . . . to the courts to detect conflicts between the Constitution and the treaty, and accordingly, to set aside the former to the extent of its incompatibility with the latter".[143]

We may be witnessing the basis for a potential struggle between the national courts, a struggle which is already being fuelled by the doctrine.[144]

Hierarchy between the Constitution and European Community law

Before setting forth the implications of the Cour d'arbitrage's jurisprudence on the issue of *Kompetenz-Kompetenz* in EC law, it seems appropriate, as a contrast, to show how little attention was paid to the Constitution at the time of Parliament's assent to the European treaties. Reference has already been made to the fact that the EEC, ECSC, and Euratom Treaties were approved by Parliament without waiting for a revision of the Constitution allowing transfers of powers to supra-national organisations: former article 25*bis* (now 34) was enacted only in 1970. Strict legality was departed from because of obvious political and economical necessities,[145] at a time when there was in any event no constitutional review of laws. Likewise, the Maastricht treaty

[141] Report of the Cour d'arbitrage, 1992, 43.
[142] Report of the Cour d'arbitrage, 1992, 32 and 35.
[143] Velu, *J.T.*, 1992, 761 (author's translation).
[144] Thus Brouwers and Simonart comment on Velu's thesis: "*Cette analyse appelle de sérieuses réserves. C'est à une véritable rébellion que les juridictions judiciaires et administratives sont conviées . . . Il convient d'insister sur le devoir de loyauté qui s'impose à tous les pouvoirs de l'État vis-à-vis de la Cour d'arbitrage*" (1995), 18. The same authors propose, however, to modify the constitutional jurisdiction of the Cour d'arbitrage regarding parliamentary assents, 22. Compare with Louis who supports Velu's thesis (1995), in particular p. 26.
[145] de Stexhe (1972), 232.

was approved by Parliament and ratified by the executive despite an opinion of the Conseil d'État advocating the prior revision of the Constitution. The need for such revision arose from the fact that European citizenship (article 8 B, § 1 of the Treaty on European Union) was incompatible with the Constitution's exclusive reservation of electoral rights to Belgian nationals.[146] In order to justify its depature from the Conseil d'État's opinion, the Government argued that article 8 B, § 1er was not directly applicable, and that it was preferable to wait for the EC to develop Union citizenship before revising the Constitution accordingly. The Prime Minister added that the Maastricht Treaty, once coming into force, would in any event prevail over the Constitution![147] This illustration of the Government's attitude was as remarkable as it may appear improper.[148]

That said, support for the view that EC law has primacy over the Constitution had previously been voiced by the Government,[149] by Procureur général Ganshof van der Meersch,[150] and today, according to an *a fortiori* argument, by Velu.[151]

How is the Cour d'arbitrage going to define the relations beween the Constitution and EC law? If it decides to remain consistent with its jurisprudence, it is likely to challenge the constitutionality of EC treaties or secondary legislation by invalidating the corresponding Parliamentary assents. Such an issue could have been raised if the Court had not dismissed, for lack of *locus standi*, an action seeking the annulment of the Parliamentary assent approving the Maastricht Treaty, the constitutionality of which is—as indicated above—at least questionable.[152]

In its report for the Conference of European Constitutional Courts, the Cour d'arbitrage has declared that constitutional review of the European treaties would have to take into account article 25*bis* (today 34) of the Constitution which relates to the granting of powers to international organisations such as the European Communities.[153] In the case of secondary EC legislation, it is true that its primacy can be explained as a corollary of a valid transfer of powers under article 25*bis*. However, it is doubtful whether that provision provides a justification for the primacy of the EC Treaties

---

[146] Former article 4, today 8, of the Constitution. CE, *section législation*, opinion of 6 May 1992 on the draft Government bill concerning the approval of the Maastricht Treaty, *Doc. parl.*, Chambre, s.e., 1991–1992, 482/1, 69–72: according to the opinion, former article 25*bis* (today 34) of the Constitution did not provide a legitimate ground to justify electoral aspects of European citizenship.

[147] Velu, *J.T.*, 1992, 737.

[148] Delpérée (1992), 649.

[149] Velu, *J.T.*, 1992, p. 736.

[150] See p. 17 above.

[151] Velu, *J.T.*, p. 760.

[152] CA, 18 October 1994, Case no 76/94. The statute of 26 November 1992 assenting to the Treaty of the European Union was the object of annulment proceedings invoking the breach of articles 6 and 6bis (today 10 and 11) of the Constitution combined with former article 4 al. 2 (today 8), (rôle no 620, M.B. 15/01 1994).

[153] Report of the Cour d'arbitrage, 1992, 44.

themselves.[154] In any case, the difficulties that result from deriving the supremacy of EC law from the Constitution have already been explained: namely, the logical inconsistency in inferring primacy over the Constitution itself, and the lack of any jurisidiction permitting the Cour d'arbitrage to refer to article 34 of the Constitution.[155]

It is worth noting a decision of the Court in a 1990 ruling on annulment proceedings in which several provisions of the statute of 23 March 1990 concerning elections to the European Parliament were challenged. The Cour d'arbitrage held that the "Act concerning the election of the representatives of the European Parliament by universal suffrage"[156]

> "cannot be interpreted in a way that would allow the legislature, when it organises the election procedures, to ignore constitutional provisions. The general principle of law, according to which an Act of the Council of ministers takes precedence over domestic law and even over constitutional rules, is not relevant in the matter".[157]

Nevertheless, the doctrine doubts that the Cour d'arbitrage intended to proclaim the supremacy of EC law over the Constitution.[158]

CONTEXTUAL OBSERVATIONS

As indicated in the general introduction, the first part of this chapter has been structured so as to prepare for the second one, which is devoted to some contextual observations. It sought to do so by narrating in parallel the chronological evolution of the various judicial actors, the doctrine and the politico-constitutional environment. Accordingly, this contextual part will largely—though not exclusively—confine itself to emphasising causal relations which are implicit in what has been described so far. To begin with, the "specificity" of EC law in relation to international law in general will be commented on. Then, the evolution of the Belgian legal order's position will be examined in its *politico-constitutional context*. As far as the *evolution of jurisprudence* is concerned, struggles for power between the highest courts will be expounded on (*"judicial empowerment"*), as well as influences from decisions of foreign courts and the ECJ. Lastly, the *doctrine* will be briefly analysed, in particular by highlighting different "schools".

"Specificity" of European Community law

For a study dealing with the application of EC law in a state legal order, the attention devoted to international treaties in general may strike the reader as

---

[154] Naômé (1994), p. 54.
[155] See p. 18 above.
[156] Annexed to the Council Decision of 20 September 1976, OJ L 278. 8 October 1976.
[157] CA, 14 July 1990, Case no 26/90, 3.B.3 (author's translation).
[158] Velu, Bruylant (1992),135; Ergec (1991), 647.

disproportionate. The three Procureurs généraux at the Cour de cassation—Hayoit de Termicourt, Ganshof van der Meersch and Velu—have been the principal advocates for recognising the existence of EC law "specificity". Yet, few legal consequences have been deduced from that peculiar status, apart from the superiority of EC law over the Constitution, advocated by Ganshof van der Meersch as early as 1966 (two years after *Costa* v. *E.N.E.L.*), and reaffirmed in his 1971 submissions.

It is tempting to conclude that it is the opening up of Belgian law towards international law—and more particularly treaties regarding the protection of human rights—that has rebounded *a fortiori* on the reception of EC law. J. V. Louis argues that what has in fact happened is the opposite: "The international order benefits from . . . the favourable treatment accorded to EC law. It is indeed without doubt the E.C. legal order's growth, and in particular the activity of the ECJ, that has orientated and accelerated the recognition of primacy for both international and E.C. law. The phenomenon is not restricted to Belgium".[159]

In support of that thesis, one could add the following example: the Belgian courts' generous tendency to attribute direct effect to international provisions, according to objective criteria of clarity and precision, is a direct influence of the ECJ 's case law on the matter.

In the future it may be the Cour d'arbitrage that will work out the legal consequences of the unique status for EC law when, through challenges to Parliamentary assents, it is called upon to review the constitutionality of international treaties and EC law. But it may also conclude that no distinction should be drawn between EC and international law.

Political and Constitutional context

What is striking about the evolution of the Belgian position towards international treaties and European integration lies in the rather passive attitude of the Constituent Assembly. On one hand, it is true that the ratifications of the EC treaties, and more recently of the Maastricht Treaty, have always been preceded by a debate in Parliament concerning a necessary prior revision of the Constitution. Similarly, the *Le Ski* case had been preceded by some proposals upon the matter, and above all has given rise to many reactions in Parliament and further proposals. Nevertheless, those debates and proposals have only rarely been enacted in a constitutional provision.

Indeed, the Constituent Assembly has pondered on and off for forty years, and continues to do so without result, about the insertion into the Constitution of an article 107*bis* designed to resolve conflicts between international or EC law and domestic law. Similarly, it took about twenty years

---

[159] Louis (1979), 237 (author's translation).

to straighten out limitations of sovereignty conceded as early as 1950 with the adoption of the former article 25*bis* (today 34) of the Constitution; article 8 (formerly 4) of the Constitution has still not been revised in accordance with the Maastricht Treaty. Another example is article 167 (formerly 68) which had not been revised for more than 140 years before its revision in 1992, although it was universally agreed that its wording was completely outdated. How is such inactivity on the part of the Constituent Assembly to be explained? A few reasons can be advanced, all related to the Belgian political context.

The first reason for such an inactivity stems from differences of opinion about proposals to revise the Constitution. Those divergences may have been doctrinal. While some maintained that transfers of powers to the Communities did not require prior revision of the Constitution, others argued that the basis for the primacy of treaties and EC law was to be found in (former) articles 68 and 25*bis* of the Constitution respectively.[160] Political differences also account for the repeated failure of attempts to add to the Constitution an article 107*bis* proclaiming the supremacy of international and/or EC law. They led to a *compromise* under which it was left to the courts to adjust the Belgian legal order progressively in accordance with the evolution of the international order. It is true that *Le Ski* has given rise to several critical reactions.[161] But those reactions were of minor significance in comparison with those that were caused by the decision in *Lecompte* three years later.[162] In that case, the Cour de cassation—once again largely inspired by its Procureur général Ganshof van der Meersch—timorously attempted to review the constitutionality of a statute, and hence to reverse the traditionaly-accepted principle that the assessment of the constitutionality of laws was a matter reserved exclusively to Parliament. The attempt was severely denounced by the Belgian Senate, which in June 1975 unanimously adopted a bill that read simply "courts are not to be judges of the constitutionality of laws and decrees". Although the House of Representatives never proceeded with the bill, the message was clear enough, and the Cour de cassation ventured no further.

The second reason for the Constituent Assembly's inactivity in the matter stems, at least indirectly, from the co-existence in Belgium of two main linguistic and cultural communities—Flemish- and French-speaking. In order to quell the ever-growing tensions between the two communities, over the last twenty-five years, the Constituent Assembly has been extensively engaged in reforming the national institutions to establish a federal state. There has been little time left to do much else, apart from, for instance, modifying for the first time the former article 68 (today 167), precisely in order to extend the federal division of legislative powers to external relations.

---

[160] For a survey of the debate, Velu, *J.T.*, 1992, 734 and 735.
[161] See p. 18 above.
[162] Cass., 3 May, 1974, *J.T.*, 1974, 564.

In the same way, it has already been explained that the Belgian Government decided to ratify the Maastricht Treaty in spite of the Conseil d'État's opinion advocating the prior revision of article 8 (formerly 4) of the Constitution so as to allow non-Belgian Union citizens to take part in municipal elections.[163] In fact, this was because the Government deliberately wished to postpone the modification of the Constitution on that matter. The Flemish community feared that European citizens living in the vicinity of the linguistic border would favour French-speaking canditates, and so alter electoral majorities that the Flemish have sought to consolidate for almost 30 years, particularly in the periphery of Brussels where the number of Europeans working in European and international organisations is relatively high.[164]

A third example is that after the European Court of Human Rights had agreed to rule upon a petition challenging the compatibility with the Rome Convention of Belgian laws concerning the use of langage, the Flemish Parliamentarians were reluctant to enact in the Constitution the principle of the international law's primacy over domestic law.[165]

The relative inactivity of the Constituent Assemby is not the only relevant aspect of the politico-constitutional context of the Belgian legal order that calls for comment. There is another variable which may account for political acceptance of integration, and hence of primacy. Belgium, like many other countries, is faced with deficiency in the Parliamentary system which is expressed notably in a shift of power from the legislature in favour of the executive. In other words, there is a tendency for Parliament to lose power in the decision-making process, be it in favour of the executive, or the inter- or supra-national level. Conversely, international relations involve a gain in power for the executive. Indeed, in Belgium, it is for the executive to conclude and reject treaties. The legislature can only refuse to assent to their domestic application. It is also the executive that takes part in the making of EC secondary legislation in the Council of Ministers, while national Parliamentarians tend to have little awareness of proposals coming before the Council, nor of decisions adopted therein. Hence, there is a convergence of interest between the executive and the doctrine of supremacy.

In the new federal structure of Belgium, the federalisation of Europe also seems to strengthen the power of the federal executive at the expense of the federated authorities, though the latter will henceforth take part in the decision-making process for EC secondary legislation. More generally speaking, European integration, and therefore the primacy of EC law, seems to favour federal unity, which is not without significance in a country periodically threatened by separatism.

---

[163] See p. 27 above.

[164] Delpérée (1992), 648. It is accordingly not surprising that Belgium asked for, and obtained, a derogation for elections concerning mainly municipalities in the Brussels area, the capital of Europe.

[165] De Visscher (1968), 607 and 608.

Lastly, a few words may be said about the general approval of Belgium and Belgians for European integration. Belgium is a small country. Community interests often coincide with its own interest.[166] The Belgian economy is highly dependent upon exports, and therefore takes full advantage of the internal market. Similarly, Belgium's influence on international relations is greater under the auspices of a common foreign and security policy than on its own. Today, it is willing to play host to the European capital in its own, Brussels.

The ratification process of the Maastricht Treaty illustrates that in Belgium, European integration is a *fait accompli*, as much as for the politicians as for public opinion. During the Parliamentary debates about ratification, there was a high level of absenteeism.[167] That indifference can be explained by two facts. First, all six traditional parties, the French and Flemish Socialists, Christian Democrats and Liberals, basically share the same favorable opinion towards the European Union. Secondly, both the House and the Senate have fairly active advisory Parliamentary Committees on European Affairs which enjoy close relations with the European Parliament, and wherein the main issues concerning European integration are discussed. Furthermore, the Maastricht Treaty, and in particular the convergence criteria for joining the monetary union, are a good pretext for the Goverment to adopt unpopular economic policies, especially to reduce the public debt which now totals more than 120 per cent of GDP.[168] In sum, apart from some criticisms directed at lack of democracy, lack of progress in fiscal harmonisation and social policy, and lack of transparency of the Treaty's structure, and a few attempts to submit the ratification to a referendum,[169] no heated debate occurred in comparison with those in France or Germany.[170]

As far as public opinion is concerned, the general acceptance of supranationality may be connected with the fact that regional or linguistic identities are stronger than national identity.[171] Some may even secretly hope for the disintegration of the Belgian state in the European Union. Besides, the public has a degree of indifference towards politics in general, and even their own federal institutions in particular.

---

[166] Vanhoonacker (1994), 52.
[167] Vanhoonacker (1994), 51.
[168] Vanhoonacker (1994), 53.
[169] Vanhoonacker (1994), 49.
[170] Colla (1994), 14.
[171] Vanhoonacker (1994), 53.

Evolution of jurisprudence

Gradual and prudent evolution

It is questionable whether the *Cour de cassation* would have adopted the *Le Ski* ruling as it did without the invitation implied by the politicians in 1959.[172] It is worth noting that, in two cases cited above adopted in 1961, thus only two years later, the Court enforced the primacy of directly applicable treaties over statutes, regardless of whether the legislation was enacted before or after the treaties. Yet, those two cases went unnoticed. In 1966, Ganshof van der Meersch applauded them as illustrating the gradual, discrete, implicit but firm new direction adopted by the Cour de cassation.[173] It appears, however, that the two cases themselves did not intend to establish the principle of supremacy, nor suddenly to reverse the traditional conceptions.

More generally, it can be observed that abrupt reversals of jurisprudence are avoided as much as possible thanks to a technique that one could identify as *reconstruction*. For instance, Hayoit de Termicourt and Ganshof van der Meersch endeavoured to re-interpret the expression of "act equivalent to the law"—referring to a treaty approved by a Parliamentary assent—so that it did not necessarily imply for the treaty an authority equivalent to a statute.[174] Similarly, Hayoit de Termicourt did not intend to reverse the 1925 decision of the Cour de cassation that had established the Belgian doctrine for many years: he re-interpreted it as not concerning self-executing treaties.[175] Likewise, the Cour d'arbitrage does not intend to challenge *Le Ski* jurisprudence since, according to the constitutional court, the decision does not concern conflicts between treaties and the Constitution.[176]

"Judicial empowerment"

The notion of judicial empowerment refers hereafter to the more or less conscious struggle for power, influence or prestige between courts and other institutions, or amongst the courts themselves. It has been said that neither the ordinary courts nor the Conseil d'État ever granted themselves the jurisdiction to review the constitutionality of laws, and that the attempt to reverse the traditional doctrine by the Cour de cassation in 1974 ended in failure. In such a context, the power to test the compatibility of statutes with international

[172] See p. 11 above.
[173] Ganshof van der Meersch asserts that: *"Le ministère public d'abord et la Cour ensuite s'engagèrent dans la voie nouvelle fermement et clairement sans doute, mais avec une discrétion caractéristique de l'attitude adoptée généralement par la Cour suprême de Belgique qui, n'aimant pas les éclats, choisit de préférence la voie de l'évolution jurisprudentielle implicite et 'par paliers'. Les arrêts, dans leur rédaction discrète et sobre, sont très remarquables".*(1966), p. 808. See also Submissions, 1971, p. 899.
[174] Ganshof van der Meersh (1968), 487 *in fine* and 495; Hayoit de Termicourt (1963), 483.
[175] See p. 13 above.
[176] Rapport de la Cour d'arbitrage, 1992, 42 to 44.

treaties can be viewed as an appreciable compensation. Therefore, it is not surprising that both the ordinary courts and the Conseil d'État accepted the Cour de cassation's decision in *Le Ski* without reservation.

Struggles for influence could be observed between the three Belgian highest courts. For instance, the Cour de cassation was quite unhappy at the creation of the Conseil d'État after the Second World War, and conflicts of jurisprudence were likely to occur. Indeed, either the two courts would deal with concurrent fields such as expropriation or the civil liability of public authorities, or they would have to interpret the same rules, notably constitutional provisions, in different fields. Similarly, the Cour de cassation has never been reconciled to the fact that the constitutional review of laws—albeit limited to the federal division of powers—was for about ten years allocated to the Conseil d'État, and, since 1983, to the Cour d'arbitrage, whose jurisdiction is now enlarged, and which is tending to become a fully-fledged constitutional court. Likewise, the Cour de cassation certainly did not appreciate a draft Government bill in 1980 that would have reserved to the Cour d'arbitrage all preliminary references made by the courts concerning the conformity of domestic law with international or EC law.[177]

As indicated above, the current controversy between the Procureur général at the Cour de cassation, J. Velu, and the Cour d'arbitrage concerns the hierarchical relation between treaties and the Constitution. Once again, that controversy can be explained in terms of power struggles. On one side, Velu supports the monist doctrine of one of his predecessors, Ganshof van der Meersch, so that ordinary courts, and eventually the Cour de cassation, have the jurisdiction to set aside constitutional provisions that are not compatible with treaties and EC law. On the other side, the Cour d'arbitrage maintains that the Constitution is supreme, not only because it has no jurisdiction to refer directly to international or EC law, but also because it has the exclusive jurisdiction to review—through Parliamentary assents—the constitutionality of treaties in the Belgian legal order.

Judicial dialogue and "cross fertilization"

There is clear evidence that the Belgian legal order is influenced by jurisprudence emanating from foreign courts and from the ECJ. For example, in his 1963 *mercuriale*, Hayoit de Termicourt surveyed the constitutional attitude of different countries towards the authority of treaties in their domestic legal order; and as he described the "specificity" of the EC legal order, he discretely referred to *Van Gend en Loos*.[178] Ganshof van der Meersch—in both his 1969 *mercuriale* and his 1971 submissions—also expounded on and approved leading ECJ decisions such as *Van Gend en Loos*, *Costa* v. *E.N.E.L.*, *Lütticke* (Case 48/65), *Mölkerei-Zentrale* (Case 28/67), *Fink-Frucht* (Case 27/67),

---

[177] See p. 19 above.
[178] Hayoit de Termicourt (1963), footnote 68, 484.

Salgoil (Case 13/68), and *Walt Wilhelm* (Case 14/68).[179] Likewise, in his 1992 *mercuriale*, J. Velu devoted himself to an extensive comparative study of relations between Constitutions and treaties.[180]

As far as foreign jurisprudence is concerned, the 1954 case of the Luxembourg Cour supérieure de justice is probably the one that has exerted most influence on Belgian doctrine, notably because the little neighbour, like Belgium, had no constitutional provisions regarding the domesic authority of international treaties. The Luxembourg court held that a treaty is a law of superior nature, stemming from higher origins than domestic organs; consequently, international laws prevails over national laws".[181]

While the Belgian legal order is affected by external influences, the opposite is also true. For instance, Procureur général Ganshof van der Meersch's submissions have been relied upon by the avocat général Cabannes in the landmark decision *Cafés Jacques Vabre* delivered by the Cour de Paris on 7 July 1973, and by Procureur général Touffait before the French Cour de cassation on 27 May 1975.[182]

Similarly, as has already been mentioned, decisions of the Cour de cassation in *Le Ski* (1971) and of the Conseil d'État in *Corveleyn* (1968)[183] can be seen respectively as precursors of, on the one hand, the ECJ's decision in *Simmenthal* (1978) and, on the other, the decisions in *Van Duyn* (1974) and *Verbond van Nederlandse Ondernemingen*.[184] It also seems that ECJ cases in *Zückerfabrik süderditmarschen* (Case C-143/88) and *Francovich* (Joined Cases C-6 and C-9/90) were adumbrated by decisions given earlier by Belgian judges.[185]

La doctrine

It has been shown at length that the main doctrinal contributions to the relations between the Belgian and the international/EC legal orders arose from

[179] Ganshof van der Meersch (1970), 423 to 432; Submissions, 1971, 900 to 910. *Van Gend en Loos* v. *Nederlandse Belastingadministratie*, Case 26/62, [1963[CMLR 105; *Costa* v. *E.N.E.L.*, Case 6/64, [1964] CMLR 425; *Lütticke Gmbh* v. *Commission*, Case 48/65, [1966] CMLR 378; *Molkerei-Zentrale* v. *Hauptzollamt Paderborm*, Case 28/67, [1968] CMLR 187; *Fink-Frucht Gmbh* v. *Hauptzollamt München-Landsbergerstrasse*, Case 27/67, [1968] CMLR 187; *Salgoil Spa* v. *Foreign Trade Ministry*, Case 13/68, [1969] CMLR 181; *Wilhelm* v. *Bundeskartellamt*, Case 14/68, [1969] CMLR 100.

[180] Velu (1992), *J.T.*, 1992, 750 to 758.

[181] Cour supérieure de justice, 14 July 1954, *Chambre des métiers c. Pagani*, *Pas. lux.*, XVI, 150; cited notably by Ganshof van der Meersch (1968), 495, and in his submissions, 1971, 897 and 898; by De Visscher (1968), 608 and 609 (author's translation).

[182] Louis (1994), 270.

[183] See pp. 6, 10 above.

[184] In the same way, Lenaerts (1986), 264. *Simmenthal* v. *Amministrazione delle Finanze dello Stato*, Case 70/77, [1978] ECR 1453; *Van Duyn* v. *Home Office*, Case 41/74, [1974] ECR 1337; *Verbond Van Nederlandse Ondernemingen* v. *Inspecteur der Invoerrechten en Accijnzen*, Case 51/76, [1977] ECR 133.

[185] Wytinck (1993), 989 to 994. *Zuckerfabrik Suderdithmarschen AG* v. *Hauptzollamt Itzehoe*, Case C-143/88, *The Times*, 27 March 1991; *Francovich* v. *Italy*, Joined Cases C-6/90 and C-9/90, [1992] ILRL 84.

the Procureurs généraux at the Cour de cassation in their submissions before rulings, and most importantly, in their *mercuriales*, i.e. speeches delivered each year at the ceremonial re-opening session which comprise thorough doctrinal studies addressing a topical issue: first Hayoit de Termicourt (1963 *mercuriale*), then Ganshof van der Meersch (1968 and 1969 *mercuriales*, and his 1971 submissions in *Le Ski*), and nowadays Velu, whose 1992 *mercuriale* runs to more than 200 pages. There is undoubtedly a common intellectual tradition and an intellectual continuity among the three Procureur généraux. The first one, Hayoit de Termicourt, opened the way for the primacy of treaties over domestic laws, including those enacted subsequently, but with several limits. The second one, Ganshof van der Meersch, set out his monist conception of law, involving the superiority of international law and EC law, and, for the latter, superiority even over the Constitution. And the third one, Velu, made his predecessor's monist doctrine his own in order to justify the primacy of both treaties and EC law over the Constitution.

A few words should be said about W. J. Ganshof van der Meersch. The Procureur général was also a law Professor at the Free University of Brussels, where he founded the active Institute of European Studies. In 1973, he became a judge at the European Court of Human Rights, and its Vice-President in 1985. His leading role in the legal doctrine went beyond Belgium's borders. The course on the Community legal order, which he taught at the Academy of International Law at La Haye, has been described as "the largest synthesis dedicated to EC law in the courses of the Academy".[186] It was also he who initiated the *Novelles* relating to EC law.

For the rest, Belgian doctrine is chiefly the work of university law professors. In the 1970s, three schools of thought could be distinguished by reference to their views on the constitutional review of laws, and consistently therewith, by their approaches to the relations between domestic laws and treaties or E.C law.[187]

The Brussels school (Free University: Ganshof van der Meersch, Velu; others are Louis, Waelbroek, Leroy, and Ergec) considered the constitutional review of laws to be a judicial function. Accordingly, it favoured a decentralised review exercised by all the courts, and ultimately supervised and harmonised by the Cour de cassation. As observed above, the Brussels school's theses prevailed apropos the review of the conformity of laws with treaties, but were not followed in the case of constitutional review.

Conversely, the Ghent school (State University: Mast) was opposed to any constitutional review of laws, arguing that such a review was a political concern falling within the domain of Parliament. The very reason why this school could accept the judicial review of the compatibility of laws with treaties was founded in the fact that the treaty-making power is a Royal (executive) pre-

---

[186] Louis (1994), 270.
[187] Dumont (1983), 75 *et seq*, and 101 to 105.

rogative, while the enactment of the Constitution is a prerogative of the legislature, albeit subject to special procedures.

For the Louvain school (Catholic University: De Visscher, Delpérée; others are Verhoeven, Lejeune), the power to review the validity of statutes was a judicial function. However, the political aspects of such function were held to require that the constitutional review of laws, or the review of their compatibility with treaties, be centralised to a special authority with a membership that reflected a certain political balance. The Cour d'arbitrage has been created accordingly, albeit that constitutional review is limited. However, proposals to vest the Court with jurisdiction to refer to international standards have never succeded.

Lastly, the existence of a Liège school (State University) may be pointed out, represented by its Professor of International Law, M. Melchior, who was formerly a member of the European Commission of Human Rights, and is now President of the Cour d'arbitrage; and by its Professor of EC Law, R. Joliet, who is also judge at the ECJ. Both seem to favour grounding EC supremacy in the Constitution.[188]

REFERENCES

BRIBOSIA, H., and VAN BOXSTAEL, J. L. (1994), *Le partage des compétences dans la Belgique fédérale* (la charte, Bruges, 1994).

BROUWERS, PH., and LEJEUNE, Y. (1992), "La Cour d'arbitrage face au contrôle de la constitutionnalité des traités", *J.T.*, 1992, p. 670.

——and SIMONART, H. (1995), "Le conflit entre la Constitution et le droit international conventionnel dans la jurisprudence de la Cour d'arbitrage", *C.D.E.*, 1995, p. 7.

COLLA, E. (1994), " La ratification du traité sur l'Union Européenne par la Belgique", *A.P.T.*, 1/1994, p.1.

COPPENS (1991), "Observations sous Conseil d'État du 10 novembre 1989", *J.T.*, 1990, p. 608.

COUR D'ARBITRAGE DE BELGIQUE (1992), Report to the ninth conference of Constitutional Courts on 10 to 13 May 1993 presented by M. Melchior and L. De Greve, *Protection constitutionnelle et protection itnternationale des droits de l'homme: concurrence ou complémentarité* (Bruxelles, December 1992).

DELPÉRÉE, F. (1992), "La Belgique et l'Europe", *J.P.*, 12 June 1992, p.14.

DE STEXHE, P. (1972), *La révision de la Constitution belge 1968–1971* (Bruxelles, Larcier, 1972).

DE VISSCHER, P. (1968), "Les positions actuelles de la doctrine et de la jurisprudence belges à l'égard du conflit entre le traité et la loi", *Recueil d'études de droit international en hommage à Paul Guggenheim* (Genève 1968), p. 605.

DUMONT, H. (1983), "Le contrôle de constitutionnalité des lois et des décrets en Belgique: fonction juridictionnelle ou politique?", in *Fonction de juger et pouvoir judiciaire* (Publications des F.U.S.L., Bruxelles, 1983), p. 71.

---

[188] See p. 19 above.

ERGEC, R. (1986), "Le contrôle juridictionnel de l'administration dans les matières qui se rattachent aux rapports internationaux: actes de gouvernement ou réserve du pouvoir discrétionnaire", *R.D.I.D.C.*, 1986, p. 267.

——(1991), "Note. Le droit international et le droit à l'égalité des étrangers dans la jurisprudence de la Cour d'arbitrage", *R.C.J.B.*, 1991, p.622.

——(1995), "La Cour d'arbitrage et le juge international et européen—La censure du législateur: le justiciable entre la Cour d'arbitrage, la Cour de Strasbourg et la Cour de Luxembourg", in *Regards croisés sur la Cour d'arbitrage*, F. Delpérée, A. Rasson-Roland and M. Verdussen, Bruxelles (eds.) (Bruylant, 1995), p. 191.

GANSHOF VAN DER MEERSCH, W. J. (1966), "Vues comparatives sur l'ordre juridique communautaire et l'ordre juridique national dans les droits belges, néerlandais et luxembourgeois", *R.I.D.C.*, 1966, p.797.

——(1968), "Réflexions sur le droit international et la révision de la constitution", address given to the official reassembly of the Cour de Cassation on 2 September 1968, *J.T.*, 1968.

——(1970), "Le juge belge à l'heure du droit international et du droit communautaire", address given to the official reassembly of the Cour de Cassation on 1 September 1969, *J.T.*, 1969, p. 537; also published as "Le juge belge et le droit international", *R.B.D.I.*, 1970/2, p. 409.

——(1971), submissions before the Cour de Cassation, 27 May 1971, *Pasicrise*, 1971, I, 886.

HAYOIT DE TERMICOURT, R. (1963), "Le conflit traité—loi interne", address given to the official reassembly of the Cour de Cassation on 2 September 1963, *J.T.*, 1963, p. 481.

JOLIET, R. (1983), *Le droit institutionnel des Communautés européennes* (Faculté de Droit, d'économie et de Sciences sociales, 1983).

LEJEUNE, Y. (1994), "§2.—La conduite des relations internationales", in *La Belgique fédérale* (Bruylant, Bruxelles, 1994), p. 313

LEROY (1990), "Le pouvoir, l'argent, l'enseignement et les juges", Observations on the Conseil d'État, 6 September 1989, M'Feddal, no 32.989, *R.T.D.H.*, 1990, p. 190.

LENAERTS, K. (1986), "The Application of Communiy Law", (1986) *C.M.L.R.*, p. 253.

LOUIS, J. V. (1979), "La primauté du droit international et du droit communautaire après l'arrêt 'Le ski' ", in *Mélanges Fernand Dehousse* (Bruxelles, 1979), p. 235.

——(1994), "Walter Ganshof van der Meersch et le droit européen", *J.T.*, 1994, p. 270.

——(1995), "La primauté, une valeur relative", *C.D.E.*, 1995, p. 23.

MASQUELIN (1980), *Le droit des traités dans l'ordre juridique et dans la pratique diplomatique belges* (Bruxelles, Bruylant, 1980).

MUULS, F. (1934), "Le traité international et la Constitution belge", *R.D.I.L.C.*, 1934, p. 451.

NAOMÉ, C. (1994), "Les relations entre le droit international et le droit interne belge après l'arrêt de la Cour d'arbitrage du 16 octobre 1991", *R.D.I.D.C.*, 1994, p. 24.

PESCATORE, P. (1971), note of submissions before the judgment in *Le Ski*, *C.D.E.*, 1971, p. 564.

ROLIN, H. (1953), "La force obligatoire des traités dans la jurisprudence belge", *J.T.*, 1953, p. 561.

SALMON, J. and SUY, E. (1966), "La primauté du droit international sur le droit interne", in *L'adaptation de la Constitution belge aux réalités internationales* (Bruxelles, l'Institut de Sociologie, 1966), p. 69.

SALMON, J. (1971), "Le conflit entre le traité international et la loi interne en Belgique à la suite de l'arrêt rendu le 27 mai 1971 par la Cour de Cassation", *J.T.*, 1971, pp. 509, 529.

VANHOONACKER, S. (1994), "Belgium and the ratification of the Maastricht Treaty", in *The Ratification of the Maastricht Treaty: Issues, Debates and Future Implications* (I.E.A.P., Martinus Nijhof Publishers, 1994), p. 47.

VELU, J. (1992), "Contrôle de constitutionnalité et contrôle de compatibilité avec les traités", address given by M. J. Velu, premier avocat général to the official reassembly of the Cour de cassation on 1 September 1992 (Bruxelles, Bruylant, 1992); also published in an abridged version in *J.T.*, 1992, p. 729 and p. 749 *et seq.*

VERHOEVEN, J. (1969), "Observations" on the Conseil d'État, 7 October 1968, *Corveleyn*, *J.T.*, 1969, p. 694.

—— (1980), "La notion d' 'applicabilité directe' du droit international", in *L'effet direct en droit belge des traités internationaux en général et des instuments internationaux relatifs aux droits de l'homme en particulier* (S.B.D.I., International Law series, 1980).

—— (1984), "Sources et principes du droit des gens et ordre juridique belge: certitudes et vraisemblance", in *Hommage à Paul De Visscher* (Paris, Pédone, 1984).

—— (1991), "Applicabilité directe des traités et 'intention des parties contractantes', *Liber amicorum E. Krings* (Bruxelles, Story-Scientia, 1991), p. 895.

WAELBROEK, M. (1965), "Le juge belge devant le droit communautaire", *R.B.D.I.*, 1965/2, p. 348.

—— (1972), "Effets internes des obligations imposées à l'État", *Miscellanea W. J. Ganshof van der Meersch* (Bruxelles, 1972), p. 575.

—— (1973), "Considérations sur le rôle du juge belge face au droit international", *Rivista di diritto internazionale*, LVI, 1973, p. 499.

—— (1985), Note following the judgment of the Cour de cassation on 21 April 1983, "Portée et critères de l'applicabilité directe des traités internationaux", *R.C.J.B.*, 1985.

WIGNY, P. (1972), *La troisième révision de la Constitution* (Bruxelles, Bruylant, 1972).

WYTINCK, P. (1993), "The Application of Community Law in Belgium (1986–1992)" (1993), *C.M.L.R.*, p. 981.

2

Report on France

JENS PLÖTNER

France is one of the Member States in which Community law has had the greatest difficulties to be fully integrated and recognised as supreme to national law. This observation fits into a line of events in which France has proven to be an essential, but sometimes difficult, member of the Community. The student of European integration has, however, learned that often the essential impetus for further integrative steps finds its origin in Paris; one must only think of the Schumann-Plan or the decisive French role in the draft-comity for the legal aspects of the EC Treaty. Especially this last example shows the thoroughly ambiguous, often contradictory, character of France's involvement: a leading role in the theoretic, intellectual construction of Europe finds its counterpart in an often "national" interpretation of Community rules. A recent example of this puzzling attitude is to be found in the French position concerning the GATT negotiations. The same applies to the discussion now starting to take place concerning the Maastricht Treaty review conference in 1996.[1] Although President Chirac has been keen to disperse tenacious voices blaming him of a lesser Euro-enthusiasm than his socialist predecessor, his campaign and his first weeks in office seem to confirm a more inter-governmental—Gaullist—approach towards the European Union.

As I hope to demonstrate in the following, the pure doctrinal approach doesn't allow us to fully understand French resistance towards legal integration. Here, the use of extra-legal tools has proven to be of great help. As will be argued, one of the main reasons for the non-endorsement of the "direct effect" and "supremacy" doctrine lies in the statics of the French legal and administrative system.

THE RECEPTION OF THE DIRECT EFFECT AND SUPREMACY DOCTRINE BY THE FRENCH SUPREME COURTS

The student of French and European law has, for the past twenty-five years, especially focused on the question of how Community law could be given full effectiveness within the French legal order.

---

[1] E. Baladur, "Pour un nouveaux Traité d'Elysée", *Le Monde*, 30 November 1994.

In order to understand the particularities of the French case, a few general remarks concerning the three supreme courts might be of use: the existence of a three-fold judicial system is rooted in history; being the successor of the ancient Kings Council, the Conseil d'Etat (CE) traditionally stood independent from the ordinary courts. The Conseil Constitutionel (CC) is the youngest of the three, it was established by de Gaulle as an innovation included in the Constitution of 1958. It is important to note that each of the three institutions stands alone and that there is no formal interaction between them, the only exception being the Tribunal de Conflits (TC), in which the Conseil d'Etat and the Cour de Cassation sit together in order to co-ordinate their respective spheres of competence.

Before retracing the history of the French reception of the "direct effect" and "supremacy" doctrine, it seems useful to describe the stage the development of this problem has reached today. All of the three French supreme courts (Conseil d'Etat, Cour de Cassation and, somewhat separated, the Conseil Constitutionnel[2]) have *de facto* accepted the supremacy of European Union law over national law as well as the integration of the former into the latter. The fact that the result achieved by each of the three courts seems comparable should not, however, conceal large differences regarding methods and pace. This first section will retrace the doctrinal development followed by each of the three courts by spotlighting the major events which led to the enforcement of the two founding doctrines of EU law. In a second section, we will turn our attention to a second doctrinal question which merits just as much attention, the *Kompetenz-Kompetenz* problem.

Doctrinal development of the three supreme courts

In contrast to Italy or Germany, France has a monist judicial tradition which finds its confirmation in article 55 of the fifth republic' constitution which states: "Treaties or agreements duly ratified or approved possess, from the moment of their publication, a superior authority to those of laws under the condition, for each treaty and agreement, of its application by the other party". Although one might feel that such an approach to the relationship between national and international law would provide for a swift reception of EC law, there are a few hints in French legal history for the problems to come. First of all, there is the tradition of separation of powers inherent in France since the Revolution which makes it quite unthinkable that a judge could censor the work of Parliament.[3] Even if parliament could be controlled, there remains the strong position of the Executive with the President at the top. Taking into consideration that de Gaulle had more or less tailor-made

---

[2] Supreme courts for administrative law, civil law and finally constitutional law.

[3] B. de Witte, "Retour à 'Costa'. La primauté du droit communautaire à la lumière du droit international" *R.T.D.E.* (1984), pp. 425, 444.

the Constitution of 1958 for his proper ideas of how a state should be led, it seems quite unlikely that "*La France*" would accept any uncontrolled influence from whoever it may be.

Bearing this in mind, we will now turn to the analysis of the three courts' jurisprudence.

The Conseil Constitutionnel, guardian of the French "*bloque constitutionnel*" (which includes the Constitution of 1958, the preamble of the Constitution of 1946, the Declaration of Human Rights of 1789 and some general legal principles) took the first opportunity to delegate the difficult task of enforcing the direct effect and supremacy of EU law. For the effectiveness of its move it matters little that the specific case had nothing to do with the European Community directly.

The question was to know whether Art. 55 of the French Constitution from 1958[4] had been violated by an abortion-liberating law because the latter was presumed to be in violation of the European Convention of Human Rights. For two reasons, the CC refused to control the conformity of the pending bill with the Treaty: according to the Constitution, the decisions the CC handed down were of absolute and definitive character whereas the superiority of a Treaty to a law could merely be of a relative and contingent nature. Relative, because the supremacy would be limited to the sphere of the Treaty (a law contrary to the Treaty could remain applicable if its sphere was larger than that of the Treaty) and contingent, because article 55 of the Constitution submits supremacy to the condition of reciprocity (and therefore a law contrary to the Treaty could nevertheless be applicable at certain moments towards certain nationals). In an enigmatic diction, the CC considered that "a law incompatible with a treaty is not, by the same means, incompatible with the constitution"; and since article 61 of the Constitution charged the CC with the task of controlling the constitutionality of laws, it did not intend to do more than that.[5] In two decisions handed down on 20 July and 18 January 1977, the CC reiterated this jurisprudence.

The reception of this decision by the legal community was generally positive. The commentators and convinced Gaullists Faverau and Philip praised the 1975 decision as a solution which gives "an interpretation to art. 55 and 61 which is in accordance with the spirit and letter of the text".[6] Underpinning this analysis was a distrust towards the integrative character of Community law which was considered as being in contradiction to the very principles of Gaullism: "It is clearly admitted that during the drafting of the constitution the framers thought to avoid European integration from advancing too

---

[4] If not specified otherwise, "Constitution" is always the French Constitution of 1958.

[5] C.C. 15 January 1975, IVG.

[6] L. Favereau, L. Philip, *Grands decisions du Conseil Constitutionel* (Paris: Sirey, 1979), pp. 301, 309.

quickly and from endangering national sovereignty."[7] For the Gaullist school of thought any other decision "would have lead to the path proceeding towards a government of judges."[8]

In the same time, this decision was partially understood as an open invitation to the other two supreme courts to take on this task themselves.[9] As we will see, the two of them did not accept the invitation with the same degree of eagerness.

Apart from its function as guardian of the Constitution, the CC may also be called upon as judge in electoral litigation. It was on such a matter that the CC then finally did have to at least state its attitude concerning the supremacy doctrine. Without even making a point of the potential problem, the CC examined the compatibility of a later national law with an additional protocol of the European Convention of Human Rights, thereby implicitly acknowledging its superiority[10]. This decision was, however, not yet in existence when the other supreme French courts started to develop their positions.

The first of them to respond substantially to the ECJ's fundamental jurisprudence was the Cour de Cassation, which has proven to be the most pro-European supreme court of France, and this despite the fact that in the early 1970s its starting position was identical with that of the Conseil d'Etat.

Having subscribed to the monist theory since her constitution of 1946, France should at first view not have had any problems concerning the supremacy doctrine. However, the traditionally very Parliament-centred philosophy of French law[11] led to a distinction between laws previous to an international treaty and those latter to it. Concerning the first case, the solution never caused any problems: by the simple force of the international treaty, mostly ratified by parliament, the previous law was automatically abrogated. The case of laws subsequent to a treaty was more complicated: if a court enforced such a treaty against a later law, it would thereby abrogate an Act of Parliament, quite unthinkable since Montesquieu wrote that judges were supposed to be the simple mouth of the law.

To reach a solution in this case, both Courts followed the famous "Matter" doctrine, named after an Attorney-General of the Cour de Cassation in the 1930s:

(i)   In a first stage, the judge should try to solve the apparent conflict between the two dispositions by conforming interpretation;

---

[7] L. Favereau, L. Philip, *Grands decisions du Conseil Constitutionel* (Paris: Sirey, 1979), pp. 301, 309.

[8] L. Favereau, *R.D.A.* (1977), p. 131.

[9] See L. Faverau, L. Philip, "Chronique Constitutionelle et Parlementaire Francaise", *R.D.A.* (1975), p. 193: "*On peut même dire (que) le juge constitutionel a implicitement confirmé le rôle exclusif du juge ordinaire, quand à la mise-en-oeuvre du principe de superiorité du Traité sur la loi*".

[10] C.C. 21 October 1988, *Election du député de la 5ème circonscription du Val d'Oise*.

[11] Two still valid laws dating from the French Revolution (16 and 24 August 1790) state: "The jurisdictions can not take any part whatsoever in the exercise of the legislative power, neither can it render impossible or suspend the execution of laws regularly promulgated without committing abuse of its power". At that time, judges still designated by the King were simply ignoring his orders since they were given under the pressure of the revolutionary National Assembly.

(ii)   if this should not be possible, he had to enact the national law since he "cannot know other will than that of the law".[12]

The landmark decision for the Cour de Cassation's final compliance with the supremacy doctrine, implying the abandon of the Matter doctrine, was the *Jacques Vabre* case, decided 24 May 1975.[13] The case which had been referred to the Court opposed article 95 of the EC Treaty to a more recent (1966) French fiscal law. The lower courts had already enforced the disposition of the Community treaty against the later law. This in itself was already remarkable, although, from an EU point of view, not quite flawless. The lower courts had indeed based their enforcement on article 55 of the French Constitution of 1958 translating the monist theory, and not on the famous "specific character" of Community law as set forth by the European Court of Justice in its *Costa* v. *E.N.E.L.* decision.[14]

Confirming the abandonment of the Matter doctrine in cases concerning the European Community, the Attorney-General Touffait invited his colleagues to modify the grounds for their decision; instead of choosing their own constitution he proposed to follow the ECJ in its *Costa*-logic.[15]

The Court finally chose to proceed by compromise concerning the reasons for its decision: it bases its enforcement of the EC Treaty on article 55 of the Constitution as well as on the specificity of the Community law. Although this combined argumentation has not found unanimous appreciation,[16] the Cour de Cassation has until today continued to use the same formula.

If we add to this development the fact that the Cour de Cassation has never had any problems with the doctrine of direct effect, its degree of compliance with the ECJ and EU law is almost perfect.

This can hardly be said about the Conseil d'Etat, as mentioned above a very traditional French institution. Confronted with the doctrines of supremacy and direct effect, the CE took a long time to develop a very differentiated position towards both.

After the Cour de Cassation's *Jacques Vabre* decision, it was quite obvious that the next step would be up to the CE. It had however as early as 1968 clearly pointed out that supremacy of EU law over later national laws was quite unacceptable: in the *Semoules* case,[17] the government commissioner Mme Questiaux affirmed that "the administrative judge can not make the effort demanded from him without modifying, by his own will, his place within the institutions". Three main reasons were given for this refusal: first of all, the CE believed that overruling a law in favour of an earlier treaty

---

[12] Conclusions of Attorney-General Matter, Cass. civ. 22 December 1931, *Dalloz* (1932) 1, p. 131.

[13] Chambre mixte, *Dalloz* (1975), p. 497; *A.J.D.J.* (1975), p. 567.

[14] *Costa* v. *E.N.E.L*, Case 6.64, [1964] CMLR 425.

[15] Conclusions of Attorney-General Tuffait, *Dalloz* 1975, p. 504.

[16] F. C. Jeantet, "La Cour de Cassation et l'ordre juridique communautaire", *J.C.P.* 2743, (1975).

[17] C.E., 1 March 1968, *Syndicat général des fabricants de semoule, A.J.D.A.* (1968), p. 235.

would be no less than a violation of the principle of separation of powers and that secondly, such a control of laws would be the work of the Conseil Constitutionnel. The third and final reason was of a quite pragmatic nature, but allows us to better understand the way the CE feels about its role: by accepting to take over the control of laws, the CE would sooner or later enter into conflict with Parliament; this in turn would then endanger its efficiency in exercising a control on administrative action.

The roots of this attitude were thus too deep for a change to occur soon and swiftly and this couldn't be changed by the harsh reminder quite obviously addressed to the CE by the ECJ in its *Simmenthal* decision: "The national judge has the obligation to assure the entire effect of community norms by leaving, if necessary, inapplicated, by his own authority, any contrary national legislation, *even subsequent*".[18]

Some first signs of a prudent reversal of this conservative attitude can only be found as late as 1986 in the CE's decision *Smanor*,[19] which admitted that the administrative judge could examine the conformity of regulations (based on a later law) with an international treaty.

This first step was made possible by a working distinction between laws which content themselves with attributing competence to the administration, and laws which fix detailed rules of execution. In the first case, the administrative judges were from now on free to examine the conformity of the (later) law with a Treaty; in the latter, this procedure remained impossible.

This first shift in jurisprudence was however still a long way from an effective enforcement of Community law by the administrative judge. The real breakthrough only came three years later with the famous *Nicolo*[20] decision, which the Conseil d'Etat—sign for an important case—took as an Assembly. In his conclusions,[21] the Government Commissioner Frydmann followed a double strategy: on the one hand it was important that the CE did not give the impression of yielding ground to the doctrine but, on the other hand, a path had to be found allowing the Assembly to adopt a decision which would end its no longer "splendid" isolation. The starting point was to confirm that the *Semoules* jurisprudence was by no manner erroneous today but that there existed another solution, legally just as valid but more appropriate and practicable. The key to this solution was found in a reinterpretation of article 55 of the Constitution: in the new reading, this article contained an implicit authorisation for judges to make treaties prevail over national law in order to render their supremacy ensuing from article 55 entirely effective. At this point, we already become aware of one of the major doctrinal deficiencies of the

---

[18] *Simmenthal*, Case 70/77, [1978] ECR 1453, ECJ, our italics.

[19] C.E., 19 November 1986, *Rec.*, p. 260.

[20] C.E. Ass., 20 October 1989, *Dalloz* (1990), p. 136. For a complete bibliography: D. Simon, "La C.E., la directive, la loi, le droit, *ad agusta per angusta*" *Revue Europe*, 4, chron (1992).

[21] Conclusions of Government Commissioner Frydman, *La semaine juridique* 48, (1989), p. 21371.

Nicolo decision: in contrast to the Cour de Cassation, the CE did not only base its decision on the French Constitution but it exclusively used the national text. In his conclusions, Frydmann even went further when he expressly pointed out that this new interpretation of article 55 should be applied to all international treaties and not only to the EC Treaty, since such a distinction would be without any legal basis. According to him, the E.C.J.'s *Costa* v. *E.N.E.L.* decision, solemnly declaring the specific character of EU law, led to a supra-national logic which in turn was in contradiction with the French Constitution.[22]

Although the legal foundation of the supremacy doctrine has so far proven to be of no practical consequence, it is worthwhile to keep in mind this quite anti-integrationist conclusion as well as the nuance between the Cour de Cassation's and the Conseil d'Etat's position in this question. As one author put it, the CE neither capitulated nor reviewed but installed its own "French garden".[23]

Apart from these—very important—doctrinal aspects of the case, the *Nicolo* decision left two important practical questions open:

(i) The first one concerns the reciprocity clause contained in article 55 of the French Constitution. Once again based on the specificity of EU law, the ECJ does not accept that national courts examine the faithful and loyal application of the EU treaties by the other contracting states; this is, however, exactly what article 55 asks French judges to do. In the *Nicolo* case, the CE did not say a single word concerning this problem,[24] but in a case involving the European Convention on Human Rights, the CE continued to practise the reciprocity examination.[25]

(ii) The second more important question left open by the Conseil d'Etat concerned the extension of the supremacy doctrine to derived EU law. In *Nicolo*, the French administrative judges were asked to apply article 227-1 of the EC Treaty—would they also extend the new approach to EU regulations, directives and decisions? The case of the regulations was the least complicated since article 189 of the EU Treaty stipulates their obligatory character in all elements; the CE therefore endorsed this first extension of the *Nicolo* jurisprudence in its *Boisdet*[26] decision. There remained the directives . . .

This final step to full *de facto* supremacy of EU law seemed almost as difficult as the step made by *Nicolo*. Not only does the directive[27] suffer from a very complicated and to a certain point still evolving legal nature even within

---

[22] Conclusions of Government Commissioner Frydman, *La semaine juridique* 48, (1989), p. 21371.

[23] P. Sabourin, "Le Conseil d'Etat face au droit communautaire", *Revue de Droit Public et de la Science Politique en France et à l'etrangère* 2 (1993), pp. 397, 399.

[24] Kovar, "Le Conseil d'Etat et la Cour de Justice des Communautes Européennes: De l'état de guerre à la paix armée", *Dalloz* (1990), p. 57.

[25] C.E., 21 December 1990, Conclusions of Government Commissioner Stirn quoted by P. Sabourin in *Dalloz* (1991), p. 283.

[26] C.E., 24 September 1990.

[27] Dir. No. 72/464, adopted December 19th, 1972.

the EU legal system itself, but also the French administrative law has, as we will soon see, considerable problems with their direct effect.

Although there had been some positive signs of movement in a pro-Communitarian sense,[28] it remained a surprise when the Conseil d'Etat implicitly closed this last gap as early as 1992 in two decisions, *Rothmans* and *Phillipp Morris*.[29] Not only does the CE in these cases assimilate the directive to an international convention with the effect that it gains supremacy over all national law, but it also accepts the interpretation of the directive as given by the ECJ ruling condemning the French Republic in an article 171 EC Treaty procedure. In its decision *Arizona Tobacco* taken the same day as the two aforementioned, the CE even complies with the ECJ *Francovich* and *Bonifacius* jurisprudence.[30] Under these circumstances, the only remaining problem once again is the legal basis; as the Government Commissioner Mme Laroque put it: the Conseil d'Etat intends to enforce EU law supremacy "without going as far as to conform itself to the conception of absolute supremacy of community law, maybe even supra-constitutionality as the ECJ understands it".[31]

Nevertheless, the attitude the CE has since adopted when confronted with the supremacy doctrine must be recognised as a full-blown success for European integration through law. The achieved progress would, however, in practice remain without effect in absence of any consequent enforcement of the direct effect doctrine.

Although here, too, the CE has *de facto* adapted its jurisdiction to the demands of the ECJ, the overall situation from the EU point of view still remains largely unsatisfactory.[32]

Concerning the supremacy doctrine, the line of events which essentially begins in 1978 with the famous *Cohn-Bendit* decision[33] actually runs parallel to the development just described. In this quite picturesque case, Mr. Cohn-Bendit claimed that an administrative measure taken against him was in violation of a Community directive. The CE's answer was clear: they result from 189 of the EC Treaty, Community directives are addressed to Member

---

[28] In C.E., 22 December 1989: *Cercle militaire mixte de la caserne mortier*, the C.E. accepted to interpret provisions of a domestic statutory law in the light of objectives determined by a EC directive.

[29] C.E. Ass. 28 February 1992: *S. A. Rothmans International France* and *S. A. Philip Morris France* (joint decisions No. 56776 and 56777); AJDJ (1992), 210 and CMLR (1993) 30, 137–198.

[30] C.E 28 February 1992: *Societé Arizona Tobacco*.

[31] See n. 29 above.

[32] For a general panorama of the situation cf. Bonichot, "Convergences et divergences entre le Conseil d'Etat et la C.J.C.E.", R.F.D.A. (1989), p. 579.

[33] C.E. Ass., 22 December 1978: *Ministre de l'Intérieur c/ M. Cohn-Bendit*. Cohn-Bendit, of German nationality, was one of the student leaders in the May 1968 revolts in Paris. For his active participation in these events he was expelled. On petition of Cohn-Bendit, the Paris administrative court suspended the expulsion order and addressed a preliminary reference to the ECJ concerning the conformity of the above-mentioned ordnance with Community law. The Minister of the Interior on his turn called upon the CE to invalidate the suspension in order to allow the immediate expulsion of Cohn-Bendit, which finally took place. Cohn-Bendit became a member of the Frankfurt city government and today is a Member of the European Parliament

States and bind these only regarding the results to achieve; directives cannot be referred to by a national of one of these states against an individual administrative act. This position was of course in complete contradiction with the ECJ *van Duyn* jurisprudence.[34] For this radical solution, the CE used two superposed lines of argument: the first was offered by a strictly textual interpretation of article 189–3 of the EC Treaty which specifies that directives bind the addressed states as to the results to be achieved. It would have required a certain amount of goodwill from the CE to follow the purely teleological interpretation of this article by the ECJ, and this certain amount was missing through a matter of principle: in its motives, the CE sharply points out that "no stipulation [of article 56 of the EC Treaty concerning public order] empowers organs of the Community to make regulations concerning public order . . . directly applicable in the member states . . . ".[35] What the CE actually feared—and what it tried to prevent by this decision—was a significant shift in the balance of power between Community and national state.[36] If in a field as sensitive as that of public order, Community directives could be directly referred to by an individual, a significant shift in competences would be the consequence. In the doctrinal reaction to the *Cohn-Bendit* case, very few became aware of an escape route left open by the CE which was to even the way to a more "citizen rights friendly" interpretation six years later.

In a case brought before the CE in 1984,[37] an association attacked a French administrative decree transposing a Community directive with the argument that the former was in violation of the objectives of the directive: quashing the decree, the CE decided in favour of the litigant. The method was quite simple: in its *Cohn-Bendit* decision, the CE had expressly pointed out that an individual could not validly attack an *individual* administrative act on the basis that it is in violation of a Community directive. If, however, the individual takes the detour to attack the general national regulation (transposing the directive), the administrative court can examine whether this national regulation is in conformity with Community law.

One year later, the CE took a further step by deciding that the French administration could not invoke a national regulation which is in violation of a directive, even if the directive has not yet been transposed.[38] Finally, the *Alitalia*[39] decision not only invalids a national regulation contrary to objectives contained in a directive—which now is quite common—but recognises furthermore that individuals have a right to ask their administration to take the measures necessary for the transformation of a directive and to invalidate former ones henceforth contrary to the community text.

[34] *Van Duyn* v. *Home Office*, Case 41/74, [1974] ECR 1337, ECJ.

[35] C.E. Ass., 22 December 1978, n. 33 above.

[36] See Paul Sabourin, n. 24 above, p. 424.

[37] C.E., 28 September 1984, *Confédération nationale des Sociétés de protection des animaux de France et des pays d'expression francaises.*

[38] C.E., 7 December 1984, *Féderation francaise des societés de protection de la nature et autres.*

[39] C.E., 3 February 1989, *Companie Alitalia.*

After these three decisions, the Community directive gained some of the force of which it seemed deprived since the *Cohn-Bendit* case. Nevertheless, two lacunae remain: the first consists in the CE refusal to examine a breach of Community law despite the appellants not invoking the breach of it. More important is however the possibility to invoke directly a directive before a French administrative court. This possibility becomes vital when no application measure whatsoever has been taken; the potential litigant then has no national text by the detour of which he can make use of the directive.[40] In this case, one can of course argue that the litigant has the possibility, as described by the CE in *Alitalia*, to ask the concerned administration to transpose national law. He must however be prepared to wait for three month after which silence can be interpreted as a tacit refusal. These three months can be a long time to wait, especially if the execution of the original administrative measure against which he wants to invoke Community law is not suspended. Taking into consideration the quite theoretical nature of the described possibility, one must admit that the problem of the direct effect of EU directives is more of doctrinal than factual relevance.

"Kompetenz-Kompetenz"

Apart from this first complex of problems which gained the centre of attention quite some time ago, the recent decision of the German Constitutional Court concerning the Maastricht Treaty has shown a second theme which is likely to become an equally important issue: the problem of the *Kompetenz-Kompetenz*. The question is simple: who decides who decides? In France, this question has never been widely discussed in a legal context, and the jurisprudence of the supreme courts, except perhaps that of the Conseil Constitutionnel, has so far not addressed the problem. Before trying to develop some hypotheses on the reasons for the silence of the two regular supreme courts, our attention will first of all turn to the position of the CC and its development.

Endowed with the task of examining wether the international treaties and certain agreements signed by France are compatible with the French Constitution(s), the CC had an early opportunity to take a position. The opportunity was seized by the Prime Minister in 1970, when the CC was asked to examine if the decision of the European Council from 21 April 1970 concerning the fusion of the EEC and the ECCS, and the new budgetary rules, were in contradiction with the French Constitution. The court answered in the negative; one of its arguments was that the above-mentioned decision only contained "dispositions concerning the inner functioning of the Community"

---

[40] Note, however, that in C.E., 8 July 1991, *Palazzi* the C.E. admitted the direct invocation of a directive by way of putting forward an *"exception d'illégalité"*.

and did "not affect the balance between the European Communities on the one hand and the member states on the other".[41]

The interpretation of this *a contrario* argument could have meant that if the above-mentioned balance had been affected, the international treaty would have to be considered as contrary to the Constitution. Further hints were soon added by a second decision handed down in a case concerning the election of the European Parliament: even if the preamble of the French Constitution of 1946, confirmed by the new Constitution,[42] allowed the *"limitations"* of sovereignty necessary to the organisation of the defence of peace, "no disposition of constitutional value whatsoever allows the *transfer* of all or part of national sovereignty to whatever international organisation it may be".[43] This sophisticated textual approach obviously had the major inconvenience that the difference between "transfer" and "limitation" would not always be an easy one to make.[44]

In a decision taken in 1985, the CC added that an international agreement would have to "preserve the essential conditions of exercise of national sovereignty", those being the state's duty to assure the respect of the Republican institutions, the continuity of life of the nation and the guarantee of civil rights and liberties.[45]

A first shift towards a new doctrine, more practical and pro-European, can be seen in the CC decision on the constitutionality of the Schengen Agreements,[46] where the CC for the first time does not recall its precedent jurisprudence and quite openly defies the distinction between transfer and limitation put forward by the plaintiffs without, however, explicitly mentioning it.[47]

The new doctrine was then finally established in 1992 with the *Maastricht I* decision when the CC stated that according to the preamble of the 1949 Constitution, France "can enter—under the condition of reciprocity—international agreements in order to participate in the creation or development of permanent international organisations, possessing a judicial personality and power of decision and that in consequence France, as other states, accepts the transfer of competences".[48] According to this new doctrine, the CC considers the existence of two potential cases of unconstitutionality: an international agreement may contain clauses in contradiction to the Constitution or violating the essential conditions of exercise of national sovereignty. The CC's *Maastricht I* decision has shown how it operates this distinction. Among the

---

[41] C.C., 19 June 1970, *Rec.* p. 15.

[42] Article 15 of the preamble of the Constitution of 1946 and implicitly article 53 of the Constitution of 1958.

[43] C.C., 30 December 1976, *Rec.* p. 15.

[44] D. Rousseau, *Droit du contentieux constitutionel*, Monchrestien 1990, p. 259 and following.

[45] C.C., 22 May 1985, *Rec.* p. 15

[46] C.C., 25 August 1991.

[47] See D. Rousseau, "Chronique de jurisprudence constitutionelle", *R.D.A.* (1992), I, pp. 92–4.

[48] C.C., 9 April 1992, *Maastricht I*.

considerable number of arguments brought forward by the opponents to the Treaty establishing the European Union, the CC recognised three Treaty dispositions as being unconstitutional.

The right to vote and the eligibility in municipal elections for non-French EU-citizens was considered to be in contradiction of articles 3, 24 and 72 of the Constitution, whereas the clauses concerning the monetary union and the common visa policy where regarded as violating the essential conditions of the exercise of national sovereignty. Following this decision, the government proposed a bill amending and changing the Constitution which was substantially amended especially in Senate before then passing the Congress in Versailles where both houses sit together. The ratification of the Treaty on the European Union as such was submitted to the people by referendum.

This jurisprudence gives us a first idea of how the CC intends to treat the *Kompetenz-Kompetenz* problem: it has clearly stated its intention to protect French sovereignty, as defined in the constitutional block, against silent enlargement of Community competence. If the Government nevertheless wishes to transfer sovereignty, it has to go through the complicated and politically delicate task of modifying the Constitution; and even this possibility might not always be assured: in its *Maastricht II* decision, the CC points to article 89 of the French Constitution which stipulates "the republican form of government may not be issue to revision".[49]

This very interpretable stipulation makes it difficult to say to what extent the CC will develop its doctrine of *Kompetenz-Kompetenz*. If in the future it should decide to make use of a historical interpretation of article 89 of the Constitution, every step toward supra-national integration short of founding a European Kingdom seems possible. On the other hand, a more extensive interpretation would be capable of freezing the integration progress at its current stage. Whatever the direction chosen, an important influence on the outcome will be given by French political developments since the members of the CC are nominated in equal numbers by the President of the Republic and by the Presidents of the two Houses.

Notwithstanding this aspect of the *Kompetenz-Kompetenz* problem, the CC has already taken its precautions for not being left out of the control mechanism: article 54 of the Constitution declares the CC competent for the examination of "international engagements". As those who have closely studied the CC's jurisprudence have demonstrated,[50] its interpretation of this definition is very extensive; the CC has thus declared itself competent for examining the legal commitments taken in application of the constituent international treaties.

It may be added that since the constitutional reforms of 1980 and 1992, any group of sixty members of Parliament and Senators are entitled to refer an

---

[49] C.C., 02 September 1992, no 19, *Rec.* p. 791.
[50] E. Zoller, *Droit des relations Extérieure* (Paris: PUF, 1992) p. 270.

international engagement to the court. Given the fact that, as mentioned above, the Assemblé Nationale amended the constitutional law enacting the Maastricht Treaty in order to oblige government to consult the Parliament before consenting to a European legal text,[51] one can presume that MPs will use their power to defer these texts to the CC as a political weapon.

The above suggests that the CC has not only pointed out the outer limits of European integration contained in the French Constitution, but also has opened the way for a potentially very extensive control of all European legal measures; and, as its first Community-related decision has shown,[52] this control will include the question of competence. It therefore seems, that as far as the CC is concerned, the *Kompetenz-Kompetenz* problem is solved: this competence finally remains with each Member State.

As discussed above, the Conseil d'Etat as well as the Cour de Cassation have neither directly nor indirectly addressed the problem of who was to decide over how far EU competence extends. Any hypotheses proposed below have even more the character of speculation than hypotheses always tend to have, since no thorough analysis of this aspect of European integration has been undertaken in the French legal literature.

A first approach leads us to believe that the absence of discussion might be the result of a certain legal tradition. This proposition becomes especially clear when we compare the French legal culture with the German: being of federal structure, Germany is well acquainted with the problem of attribution of competence between different levels of power and the problems which can arise from borderline conflicts. In France, the situation is and always has been totally different. United for centuries, Paris always represented the central power and had the last word in all matters. A first, quite simple explanation must therefore be that the *Kompetenz-Kompetenz* problem has historically never been a question to be solved or even discussed.

Moreover, the French legal system today still carries the imprint of the Revolution, which clearly subordinated the legal branch to political power;[53] this also became clear in the difficult enforcement of the supremacy and direct effect doctrine. It is therefore in the purest French legal tradition to turn to the political power for arbitration and not to count on the courts.

These reasons might, to a different extent, be true for each of the two courts. More intimately related to the political power in what concerns its history and scope of activity, the silence of the Conseil d'Etat as an institution

---

[51] The new article 88-3 of the Constitution reads: "The government submits to the National Assembly and to the Senate, by way of their transmission to the Council of the Communities, proposals of Community acts incorporating provisions of legislative nature. During session or outside of them, resolutions can be voted in the framework of the present article, according to the terms determined by the rules of each assembly". For the extension of the assemblies and the CC's competencies subsequent to the modification of the Constitution see F. Luchaire "L'Union Européenne et la Constitution", *R.D.A.* (1992) II, pp. 933, 965–71.

[52] See n. 41 above.

[53] See n. 12 above.

and of its members as individuals[54] should quite accurately be explained with the above. As a Conseiller d'Etat and former judge at the ECJ told us, he only became acquainted with the *Kompetenz-Kompetenz* problem while serving in Luxembourg, it was quite simply not a matter he had been taught at the ENA. The members of the judicial legal branch might not count on the political branch as much as their administrative law colleagues, but ignorance about typical federal problems was widespread there too.

As to what concerns the probable reaction of the two courts when confronted with the issue, our hypotheses can only be based on their past attitude towards the Communities' legal order. As a basic rule, one can presume that the Cour de Cassation's approach will be more pragmatic and therefore pro-integrationist than that of the CE. As we will see later, the members of the CCass have in the past proven to be quite frankly pro-European which may also result from the less doctrinal character civil jurisprudence tends to have.

Even though this is so, it would be pure speculation to say that the supreme civil court would accept finally subordinating itself to the ECJ, for the *Kompetenz-Kompetenz* problem ultimately deals with the question who is the supreme umpire. As we will see below, one of our explanations why the CCass enforced the two founding doctrines of EU law much more swiftly than the CE is that the CCass therein saw a chance to strengthen its position within the French legal system as a whole. Such an advantage can however not be expected from an enactment of the ECJ *Foto-Forst* jurisprudence.

The acceptance of the CE should be even weaker. Given the sophisticated doctrinal construction which finally allowed the CE to accept supremacy and direct effect, one can only imagine the difficulties connected to the *Kompetenz-Kompetenz*.

THE SOCIAL CONTEXT OF LEGAL CHANGE CONCERNING EUROPEAN UNION LAW IN FRANCE

For the analysis of the deeper, extra-doctrinal reasons for the legal evolution, or revolution (depending on the court) which took place in France during the last twenty-five years, this section will reconsider the chronology of events which led to today's situation, and hope to show to what extent the three supreme courts of France influenced each other. A second emphasis will be placed on the importance of the position each of the courts take within the French legal system as a whole, explaining that this position and the way the legal actors felt about it was a determining factor for their instinctive approach to supremacy and direct effect.

---

[54] The members of the Conseil d'Etat are almost entirely recruited from the best ENA (Ecole Nationale d'Administration) graduates, one of the Grandes Ecoles which prepares for the senior civil service as well as for political careers.

In a second section, our analysis will turn to a more specific issue which, however, also tries to explain the developments which led to a *de facto* enforcement of the two European Union law doctrines: the relationship between *doctrine* and *judicial decisions*, showing to what extent the influence of doctrine varied from one supreme court to another and how doctrine itself developed.

Chronology of the social context

Before entering into a chronological analysis of the social context leading to legal change or inertia, a few general remarks concerning social differences between the three courts might be of use.

As explained above, the first problem encountered on the way to full enactment of the two founding doctrines of Community law in France was the existence of the "Matter" doctrine.[55] More than a simple operational doctrine, this obstacle represented the very core of the French approach to statehood and the separation of powers. Differently from in the USA or Germany, France today still feels very strongly about this separation, which it has not attenuated by the system of checks and balances. By the end of the 1960s, it however became more and more clear that this doctrine, dating back to 1931, was difficult to maintain. In the more than thirty years which had passed, the number of international treaties had significantly increased and parallel to this the number of plaintiffs founding their action in court on such international texts. This development was of course of different concern for the judicial and administrative branch of justice. For the former, the steady growth of transnational economic exchanges brought along an internationalisation of civil and especially commercial law. This was only later the case for their administrative colleagues.

Subsequently, the differing litigation patterns with which the respective courts were confronted led to differences in their adaptation to growing interdependence. Therefore, it must be said that the 1968 *Semoules*[56] decision of the Conseil d'Etat was not a total surprise.

A second distinction with high social relevance is the total difference of a career in the judicial and in the administrative branch, especially the CE. Magistrates of the judicial branch have generally studied law at university and then taken quite a difficult exam to enter the Ecole de la Magistrature. Once they pass their final exams, they are posted all over France and work their way up through the courts of appeal to, eventually, the Cour de Cassation. Those judges who compose the CCass can therefore look back to a long career which often started in the *province*. The normal career of a member of the Conseil d'Etat follows a totally different logic. The CE almost exclusively

[55] See n. 13 above.
[56] See n. 18 above.

recruits its members from the very first ranks of each ENA graduation class. This very reputed Grande Ecole was founded with the aim of providing national administration with the most qualified recruits. The rank obtained in the final exams is the essential criterion for a future career; the first five to ten graduates enter the Conseil d'Etat, the next five the Cour des Comptes, then comes the Quai d'Orsay etc. It is important to understand that the new Maître de requettes, the lowest rank within the CE, are aware of being the most excellent servants of French Grandeur. In their future career, they will spend many years in leading positions of the administration, the ministries or in nationalised companies. In this, their work will often bring them very close to political power. This tendency is confirmed by the French political tradition of establishing a restricted circle of personal advisers around every minister; these then are frequently composed of members of the CE. Furthermore, the normal CE-member will spend the most of his working life in Paris; a recent project to transfer the ENA to Strasbourg had to be partially cancelled.

The contrast between these two groups of civil servants therefore already finds its roots in their education: while the members of the Conseil d'Etat have had the benefit of the finest studying conditions France can offer, their judicial colleagues had to take the long way through the less well-known universities. This discrepancy will then continue in the working conditions which, for the magistrates, are subject to growing complaint. All of this adds up to create a public opinion which has less and less esteem for magistrates and, in spite of some criticism concerning the CE members' detachment from the people, still rates a career in the CE very highly.

These fundamental differences provide a first explanation for the divergent jurisprudence of the CE and the CCass and must be kept in mind when analysing the reasons for the path each of the two supreme courts chose.

On the basis of these existing divergences in general, it seems worthwhile to have a closer look at how Community law has been integrated into the training of future judges. Here too, we can note a difference in the approach: even if the role Community law plays within the curriculum of both branches of justice could be improved, the basic attitude of the two formations towards the EEC/EU have differed in the past. Less centralised, the future magistrates simply didn't learn anything about Community law whereas the ENA students were taught in an atmosphere of distrust towards European integration for a long time.

A further important reason for the resistance the CE developed against the full implementation of EU law in France, resides in its somewhat delicate position within France's legal and institutional framework.[57] Concerning the problem of the control of laws, the CE finds itself in a quite different position to that of the CCass. The main task of the latter is to arbitrate between individuals and only quite seldom the action of the public administration is at

---

[57] For an in depth analysis of this problem by a member of the CE see B. Genevois, note on CE, 22 October 1979 in *Actualité Juridique* (1980), p. 43.

stake. Even when this is the case, the decision handed down by the CCass only concerns the individual case at stake. The CE, however, usually issues daily judgments on the legality of public administrative actions which, in quite a few cases, can have great political importance. The collective memory of the CE has still not forgotten the strong governmental reaction caused by its *Canal* decision in 1962.[58] In this decision, the CE had invalidated an order given by General de Gaulle which was to establish a special military court for crimes committed during the "events" in Algeria. Very upset about this decision, President de Gaulle is said to have considered the pure and simple dissolution of the Conseil d'Etat. In this affair, the CE learned two lessons. First, it should never forget that its existence has no constitutional guarantee whatsoever. Although—or because—it is the oldest French court, it is not mentioned anywhere in any of the Constitutions. The direct consequence of this deficiency is that, if he had decided so, the General could have dissolved the CE entirely legitimately.

The second lesson concerned its place within the institutional framework. Given the fact that the CE could not avoid handing down decisions now and then which did not please the Government, it was important to be on good terms with Parliament. In the eyes of the CE, however, declaring itself competent to control an Act of Parliament even though it was subsequent to the Treaty in question, would have meant leading the administrative jurisdiction into a conflict on two fronts. As a Conseiller d'Etat later put it, the CE already often had against it a "heterogeneous troop uniting the upholders of public power, annoyed by the very strict control of their measures, the supporters of deregulated liberalism '*à l'américaine*', contesting the distinction between private and public law and, of a more mediocre type, those practitioners of law who wished to be dispensed of studying a supplementary discipline".[59]

These considerations were, as the *Canal* case had shown, in no way purely hypothetical and it must be presumed that they played an important role in determining the CE's position in the early 1960s and the 1970s.[60]

A last and very important cluster of reasons for the conservative approach the CE adopted towards Community law might reside in its powerful position within the French establishment in its broadest sense. Up to 1958 the CE had the monopoly of interpreting public and constitutional law in France. Furthermore it participated in the elaboration of all legal norms. This had placed the CE in the very core of the French political system. From 1958 onwards, this predominance was under attack: the first assault consisted in the creation of the Conseil Constitutionel, whose judges—political nomi-

---

[58] CE, 19 October 1962, *Rec. Lebon*, p. 552.

[59] Yves Galmot, "Le Conseil d'Etat et le contrôle de la conformité des lois aux Traites", *Revista de Institucionas Europeas*, (January/February 1990).

[60] That this kind of reasoning was still current at the end of the 1980s can be read in a note under a CE decision confirming the *Semoules* jurisdiction. The note was written by Bruno Genevois, a younger member of the CE: B. Genevois, "Note sur l'arret du Conseil d'Etat du 22. 10. 1979, Union démocratique du travail", *Actualité Juridique* (1980), p. 43.

nates—were considered as "parvenus" in the public law establishment. Belonging to an institution which had been there for more than two hundred years, the members of the CE could not help asking "who are they to tell us what public law is?". The CE's position was further threatened when it finally became obvious in Paris that there was a court in Luxembourg which actually had the competence to intervene in what seemed to be French domestic affairs. If one adds to this France's accession to the amendment granting citizens direct access to the European Court of Human Rights in 1973, the predominance of the Conseil d'Etat's role had been seriously restricted within as little as twenty years. Notwithstanding the "*Canal*-syndrome", the CE as a corps had and still has a very strong hold on administrative power in the national bureaucracy.

This might have led its members to consider supremacy and direct effect as another threat to the status quo which for them was still, after all, quite favourable. Even if full enforcement of Community law was unlikely to substantially endanger their position, the awareness of a certain precariousness of their situation led the corps as such to defend their "*acquis*" in a static manner.

A first occasion for an elegant shift in its jurisprudence was offered to the CE in 1975, when the Conseil Constitutionnel decided not to examine the conformity of international treaties with national laws.[61] Before we try to understand why the CE did not make use of this occasion, let us have a look at the motives which drove the CC to its step.

As explained above, the doctrinal explication turned around the fact that the character and form of the control operated by the CC were inappropriate to the distinct characteristics of international treaties. To us, this reasoning seems quite convincing, although it might not be the only reason for a decision of such strategic character.

Among the three supreme courts, the Conseil Constitutionnel is the youngest, it was founded in 1958 by General de Gaulle. It therefore seems possible that such a relatively recent institution felt the explosive power contained in the issue and thought it wiser to leave such a difficult task to the century-old regular supreme courts.

A second hypothesis would be that the CC felt that the supremacy and direct effect problem demanded a different answer depending on the judicial or administrative character of the case. In this case, it would not have wanted to "force" a single solution on both of the two other courts.

The last aspect "spotlighted" here in our non-exhaustive list of possible motives is the two-fold political character of the CC which potentially weakens the court. This first of all stems from the nomination procedure of its members who are nominated by the President of the Republic and the Presidents of the two Houses representing three equal voices. Comparable to

---

[61] See n. 6 above.

Germany, the selection of the nominees is of course subject to political manipulations, but unlike Germany and the USA, their nomination is not submitted
to a vote in the houses. As a result of this, the presidents, and especially the
President of the Republic, can, *in extremis*, finally decide alone. Although this
procedure could be seen as a guarantee for the independence of the members
of the CC, these are very well aware that the French public is not used to this
kind of nomination in the legal branch. Any political faction can therefore
quite easily discredit one or another decision of the CC by simply recalling its
nomination procedure. In this context, the members of this court surely
remembered the harsh public and political criticism which followed the ECJ
AETR decision in 1971.[62] Although without any direct link with the
supremacy and direct effect doctrine, the vivid polemic which was triggered
off by the insight into the extent of integration through law must have been
impressive. All this might have led the members of the CC to consider that
their position was not strong enough to take over a leading role in the full
enforcement of Community law in France.

In any case, the CC had cleared the way for the two other courts. Let us,
in examing their reaction, begin with the inertness of the Conseil d'Etat.

Our first attempt to explain it can simply recall that none of the factors
which had determined the *Semoules* jurisdiction had become obsolete. Neither
had the CE's position within the institutional framework changed, nor had it
any reason now to consider that it could gain influence by subordinating itself
to Luxembourg. At this moment, it became quite obvious that the Conseil
d'Etat's position was hardly based on genuinely doctrinal foundations, for
otherwise, a pondering of the different doctrinal aspects would undoubtedly
have led to a change of its jurisprudence. On the one hand, French legal tradition protected laws as representing *"la volonté générale"*, but on the other,
the Constitution of 1958, adopted by the people in a referendum, clearly stated
that international treaties had supremacy, without making any difference
whatsoever between their former or latter character in relation to the treaty.
The CE therefore had to ponder between a purely praetorian rule and a clear
constitutional stipulation which had been confirmed by the people. The fact
that the CE decided to favour the creation of a court, namely the Matter doctrine, shows that its true reasons, at least since the CC decision in 1975, were
not of doctrinal dominance. Under these circumstances, its inertia cannot be
surprising.

Quite the opposite of the CE, the Cour de Cassation merely let four months
pass before it accepted the invitation of the French Constitutionnel Court. Its
Jacques Vabre decision[63] seems even more courageous if we remember that it
had quite heavy financial consequences for the French Treasury which had to
pay back an important sum to the coffee merchant who had filed the suit. In
our attempt to explain this "revolutionary" decision with extra-doctrinal

---

[62] Case 22/70, *Commission* v. *Council (AETR)*, 31 March 1971.
[63] See n. 14 above.

tools, the following discussion will focus on three different dimensions of explanation: institutions, people and finally perspective.

The institutional context within which the CCass is situated is quite the opposite of that described above concerning the CE. As already pointed out, the origin, formation and recruitment of the judges respectively serving in the CE and the CCass are very different. Just as much as these factors were of decisive importance to explain the CE's position, this dimension is surely also one of the main reasons for the progressive character of the CCass' jurisprudence. Understanding themselves as practitioners, the members of the magistracy always claimed to be led by two main preoccupations: to facilitate commerce and to protect the individual in his rights. This self-understanding must be completed by an observation concerning the magistrates' relationship with the State in general and political power in particular. In contrast to the CE, the magistrates, beginning with their training, do not have the feeling that their task receives the same recognition as that of the CE. This must not especially be based on ill will but simply on higher numbers and the consequently poorer cohesion of the magistracy as a corps: the CE is an elite corps concentrated in Paris, the magistracy a heterogeneous "melting pot" spread all over France. This—certainly unconscious—feeling of being less privileged than their administrative colleagues must then be combined with a certain distance towards government and politics. The notion of "national interest", an invisible pillar of the ENA curriculum, is absent from that of the Ecole de la Magistrature and can hardly be found in any defence speech before a civil court. It would seem, therefore, that the institutional position of the Cour de Cassation greatly favoured a swift endorsement of Community law.

Given its feeling of being second to the CE, the Community level offered itself as an instrument enabling the judicial branch not only to accomplish its task even better but also to gain an advantage over the CE.

A second important dimension concerns people involved in the process of change. Although a single individual of course only seldomly makes a difference in a matter of such importance, an especially convincing individual in the right moment can be of great significance. Although the secret nature of the deliberations makes it unable to present absolute proof, it seems very likely that the role played by the public prosecutor Touffait was decisive. Of fervent European conviction, the late Adolph Touffait had been a close friend of Pierre-Henri Teittgen, who himself was one of the pioneers of Community law in France. Together they had done a great deal for the promotion of the European idea in the field of law during a period which was not particularly favourable to such activity.[64] It was therefore extremely fortunate (if not deliberate) that the conclusions of the first case presenting the *lex posteriori* problem which the CCass had to decide after the Conseil Constitutionnel deci-

---

[64] Cf. de Gaulle's remark: "Of course one can jump on a chair like a kid crying 'Europe! Europe! Europe! but that doesn't lead to anything and that doesn't mean anything": radio-television interview on 14 December 1965.

sion of January 1975 were presented by Touffait. Hearing his exposition with eyes closed, one could for a moment have imagined oneself to be in the European Court of Justice: " . . . the reasoning the Court of Justice of Luxembourg (develops) such a coherent argumentation that its conclusions impose themselves".[65] Not only does Touffait completely endorse the reasoning of the ECJ concerning the necessity of direct effect and supremacy of Community law but he also bases his argument on a teleological interpretation of the EC Treaty by paraphrasing its articles 2 and 3. It should be remembered that his suggestion was to found the decision exclusively on the specific character of Community law. The fact that the court did not follow him on this point should not diminish his merits. It probably is no coincidence that, only one year later, Touffait took the first opportunity to go to Luxembourg as a judge at the ECJ. Despite the fact that he surely considered this change to be a promotion, there were some very political reasons for his departure. Not only for the financial reasons mentioned above, the reaction of the Government was unenthusiastic: on the one hand, the newly elected President Giscard d'Estaing was a declared supporter of the European idea, but on the other hand, the governmental bureaucracy (partly dominated by the Conseil d'Etat) was opposed to any abandonment of sovereignty. Also to the ears of a political public, Touffait's conclusion that "the operated transfer . . . in favour of the Community legal order . . . leads to a definitive limitation of (our) sovereign rights"[66] seemed tantamount to the end of France's sovereignty.

The reaction of the political class actually turned out to be a "time bomb": it took almost four years before the full extent of its anger became public. Lead by some Gaullist politicians and lawyers, the ECJ was compared with Stalin's revolutionary courts and the CCass considered as its accomplice:[67] "The Cour de Cassation has been contaminated by the virus of supranationality!"[68] We will return to the consequences of this uproar further below.

The fact that the CCass did not let this harsh criticism influence its jurisprudence leads us to the third element of our analysis: perspective. The Court's far-sightedness showed itself in two ways. First and foremost, the CCass had in mind the interests of French economic agents and citizens. In the case of the former, the impossibility of referring to certain Community regulation was bound to represent a serious economic disadvantage in comparison to their European competition. In the long run, this could have lead to a movement of forum shopping, combined with some delocalisations of head offices. Concerning the individuals, the problem was basically the same, only that in this case the stake was not economic competitivity, but the protection of civil rights. Would it be conceivable that in France, cradle of human and civil

---

[65] Conclusions Touffait, n. 16 above.
[66] *Ibid.*
[67] *Le Monde*, 20 September 1980, p. 9.
[68] *Le Monde*, 23 September 1980, p. 14.

rights, individuals would benefit from a poorer standard of protection than in the other countries of the Community? In the eyes of the CCass, traditionally a rampart against arbitrary state action, this perspective must have seemed quite unacceptable.

Another consideration could have been of a more "down to earth" nature. By fully enacting direct effect and supremacy, the scope of action open to the judicial magistrate would undergo considerable widening: from now on, any simple court could not only control all Acts of Parliament but also became what the EC Treaty had foreseen, the common judge of Community law. This extension of competence was indeed very tempting and offered exciting new perspectives on the work of France's judicial branch.

As a result, we can consequently credit the Cour de Cassation for having made the first, courageous step. Its position within the institutional context of the French legal system lead it to regard the full integration of Community law as a chance for increasing its own powers and improving its position within the system. Furthermore, its practical, non-doctrinal approach proved to be open-minded towards the strong European convictions of certain of its members. In this situation, the full endorsement of the two Community doctrines was the only possible solution for granting French citizens and economic agents the same rights as their European neighbours.

While the quite critical reception of the *Jacques Vabre* decision by political opinion did not influence the CCass, it did, however, lead to quite a threatening development.[69] During a public meeting organised by Michel Debré[70] (Gaullist, one of the main people responsible for the Assemblées decision against the European Defence Community, ex-Prime Minister and presidential candidate in 1974), the idea of a bill protecting laws against international treaties had been born. Taking advantage of Parliamentary negotiations concerning a "code of judicial organisation", the Gaullist MP M. Aurillac tabled the following amendment: "Jurisdictions can neither directly nor indirectly take part in the exercise of the legislative power, nor prevent or suspend the execution of regularly promulgated laws for any reason whatsoever".[71] To the great surprise of everybody, the amendment was accepted.[72] Fortunately, it was to be blocked by the Senate a few weeks later.

This episode gives an insight on the "public" acceptance of direct effect and supremacy in the early 1980s. Although these events only occurred four years after the *Jacques Vabre* decision, there can be no doubt concerning the direct link between the two affairs. One can furthermore presume that the criticism did not suddenly erupt but had been steadily building up within the political and administrative establishment. This provides us with a first answer to the

[69] See *Revue du Marché Commun*, (no 247), May 1981, pp. 245–7.

[70] See *Le Monde*, 21 October 1980, p. 9.

[71] *Journal Officiel Assemblé National*, débats, session on 10 October 1980, pp. 2634–44.

[72] It should be added that the only socialist to take part in the vote announced that he would use the time during which the amendment was under consideration by the Senate to study it "more carefully". See *Le Monde*, n. 67 above.

question why the Conseil d'Etat did not follow the CCass on the path of full compliance with the ECJ's *Costa* jurisprudence. The first reason for the continuing inertia of the CE indeed lies in its hope that Parliament would decide and thereby settle the difference between CE and CCass. This expectation first of all resulted from the CE's traditional belief in state and strong central power as described above. Furthermore, it also confirms our presumptions concerning the motivations of its *Semoules* jurisprudence; the fear of entering into conflict with the legislator. From this perspective, the CE would have more or less enthusiastically been able to accept any solution adopted by the Assemblée: if it had decided to allow courts to examine and, given incompatibility with a treaty, not apply national laws, the CE would at least have avoided a potential conflict with Parliament. If, on the contrary, the National Assembly had taken the legal decision to prevent the above, the CE could have continued its jurisprudence concerning the *lex posteriori*. In any case, its hesitant attitude would have had the merit of leaving the final decision to those who represented *"la volonté générale"*.

Consequently, growing Parliamentary resistance to the CCass' judicial politics of which the CE certainly had knowledge is liable to have made it persist in its refusal to follow the judicial branch. This explanation, however, only remains valid until the end of 1980, the date on which the Senate refused to accept the amendment of Mr. Aurillac. From then on, it should have been quite clear that a decision could not be expected from that side.

The only hope which then remained was that the Conseil Constitutionnel would change its jurisprudence and thereby accept control over the conformity of laws with the existing treaties.[73] Although some authors continued to criticise the CC's refusal to "stand up to its responsibilities", there was little chance that it would change a jurisprudence now five years old, frequently confirmed and in concordance with that of the CCass. Objectively, everything pointed in the direction that the only solution for the CE would be to modify its own point of view. Until this finally took place in 1989 with the *Nicolo* decision, a line of events lead the CE to understand that change was imperative.

This chain of events is presented here in as far as possible, chronological order. It may be added at this stage that we are far from proposing any deterministic approach to explain changes. It is certainly true that the motivation for the eventual shift in jurisprudence was pluricausal. All of the following aspects were of importance when the CE finally "broke the spell".

A first series of events finds its origin outside of France. In 1983, France was condemned for breach of Community law:[74] in application of a Community directive voted in 1972, a French law had amended the national tobacco monopoly, authorising the responsible minister to fix the retail price of every

---

[73] See Y. Galmot, n. 59 above.
[74] 21 June 1983, *Commission* v. *France*, *Rec.*, p. 2011, ECJ.

product. This, the ECJ held, was in contradiction to the goals of the above-mentioned directive. In an action brought by a tobacco-importing company, the CE was asked to annul a ministerial decision refusing the company the right to raise its prices for certain tobaccos. Based on the French law (incorrectly) transposing the Community directive into national law, the CE confirmed the legality of the Government's decision, and this despite the ECJ's decision of breach of EC law.[75] The law not having been modified by Parliament, France was a second time condemned in 1988.[76] This chain of verdicts was of course a direct consequence of the CE refusal to remind the French Government that it was not respecting its international commitments. It was only a matter of time until the next comparable case would come before the ECJ.

It is possible that at least the particular case just described was not a pure product of coincidence. The company which asked the CE to annull the Minister's refusal, the Societé International Sales, was one of the biggest importers of tobacco. If we then remember that the CE decision which confirmed the direct effect of Community directives in France was initiated by Philipp Morris and Rothmans, the existence of a concerted action seems possible. It could indeed be that certain very export- or import-oriented companies systematically attacked Government decisions they felt would be possibly contrary to Community law. The aim of this action would then have been to provoke such chain of verdicts, thereby steadily increasing the pressure on the French Government and on the CE.

Some resonances can be found in this context with the neofunctionalist theory on regional integration.[77] According to its premises, the above-mentioned tobacco industry would be part of an important number of pressure groups selfishly seeking economic advantages. A side product of their pressure would, however, be the incremental expansion of integration by functional spill-over: acting within an economic context already characterised by a high degree of integration in some sectors (e.g. lack of protected national markets in the EEC), fair competition henceforth depends on the existence of comparable legal constraints in every Member State. As the CE refuses to assure the correct application of Community directives, the legal context economic agents find in France is bound to be different from that of the rest of the Community. As soon as this difference is felt as being harmful to economic agents established in France, they will develop pressure in order to integrate the legal sector on the Community level. In our case, this means to assure the full supremacy and direct effect of Community law.

---

[75] C.E., 13 December 1985, *Rec. Lebon*, p. 377.

[76] Case 169/87, 13 July 1988, *Commission* v. *France*, *Rec.*, p. 2603.

[77] See Haas, *The uniting of Europe* (Stanfort: Stanfort University Press, 1958). For a recent study applying this theory to legal integration see Anne-Marie Burley and Walter Mattli, "Europe Before the Court: A Political Theory of Legal Integration", *International Organisation* 47 (Winter 1993), pp. 41–76, esp. pp. 52–6.

In any case and despite the lack of any concrete legal consequence of the above-mentioned verdicts, the CE must have increasingly become nervous. From this point of view, the two decisions opening certain possibilities for the direct effect of directives which the CE took at the end of 1984[78] could have been addressed to the ECJ as an "armistice" offer. The message could have been: give us some time to find our own way to assure full effect of Community law because the result is what really counts.

Taking into consideration the growing reception which the direct effect and supremacy doctrines received in the other Member States, there was little chance of this offer being accepted. Until the beginning of 1980, the CE had quite a valid argument for its refusal to endorse: not only in France were the judicial politics of the ECJ seen with a certain distrust. Two of its major partners, Germany and Italy, both had supreme courts which refused to fully comply with the ECJ's jurisprudence. This resistance, however, diminished more and more during the 1980s. In 1984, the Italian Constitutional Court in its *Granital* decision authorised lower judges to themselves declare a national law incompatible with a former treaty without beforehand referring the case to the Constitutional Court.

In Germany, the *Bundesverfassungsgericht* 1986 pronounced its famous *Solange II* decision, announcing that henceforth it would no longer control the constitutionality of Community legal acts, since the level of protection of the fundamental rights on Community level was comparable to that on a national level.[79] From this moment on, not only the Conseil d'Etat but also France were totally isolated.

Apart from the psychological effect of this isolation, it also lead to a growth of the discrepancy in treatment of the French nationals in comparison to other Member State citizens. This development became even more alarming when in 1985, the European Council decided to create a fully integrated Common Market. Even if the full dimension of change programmed by the Single European Act only became evident at the end of 1987 and the beginning of 1988, its impact on the CE's perception of European integration must have been considerable. From this moment on, the project of European unification was, for the first time in decades, once again on the top of the public agenda.

Reacting to the announcement of Jacques Delors that in ten years 80 per cent of economic law would be of Community origin, lawyers and students of law or economics started to study Community law. This of course had consequences on the activity of the courts. Not only did judges more often decide preliminary references to the ECJ but also the lawyers more frequently made use of Community law in the defence of their clients' interest. From 1987 onwards, the number of demands for preliminary rulings referred to the ECJ

---

[78] See nn. 37 and 38 above.
[79] BVerfG, 22 October 1986, *Solange II*.

by French lower courts stabilised to more than thirty a year whereas until 1986 the average was eighteen.[80]

All this added up to create supplementary pressure on the CE which must have begun to feel overrun by the events leading to the key date 1992. Apart from this—important—psychological effect, there also were solid economic reasons which, in advance of the Common Market made a full integration of Community law into French law paramount. How could the project of 1992 become effective if the almost three hundred directives intended to transform it into legal reality were not to be directly enforced by the Conseil d'Etat? That this problem is not of mere academic interest is proved by the fact that the Assemblée Nationale apparently shared the same preoccupation.

Obviously worried about the CE's intransigent and hostile position towards international and more specifically Community law, Parliament did not hesitate to let the CE know of its discontent: in 1987, it accepted the transfer of the competence for suits directed against the action of the newly created Conseil de Concurrence from the Conseil d'Etat to the Court of Appeal of Paris.[81]

The CE clearly considered this transfer as an unfriendly act which lead it to reconsider one of its motives for its *Semoules* jurisprudence. As mentioned above, one of the reasons for this jurisprudence had been that keeping Community law out of the way seemed to be in the well understood interest of the CE as a corps; it was, in other words, a question of power. To what extent, however, was it still possible under these circumstances to believe that the present jurisprudence was liable to add or even to preserve the CE status within the French judicial and political establishment? The pertinence and topicality of these questions were confirmed by additional Governmental pressure. In November 1988, the French Prime Minister asked the CE to undertake a "synthetic reflection on the possibilities of increasing the effort of adaptation of the French domestic law to the Community exigencies" in the "perspective of the imminent fulfilment of the large domestic market".[82]

Even if as a result of the above the CE was totally aware that it could no longer count on Governmental or Parliamentary support for its jurisprudence, it may have hesitated to act in accordance with the current political will. What would happen if it changed its position and the next Gaullist President and his Parliamentary majority would then be less enthusiastic for the European cause? Here again, we find the "*Canal*-syndrome" mentioned above. This fear was removed from the CE by a decision of the Conseil Constitutionnel in 1987, confirmed in 1989.[83] In its findings, the CC acknowledged that the

---

[80] European Court of Justice, *Annual Report 1991*, (Luxembourg: Office des Publications Officielles des Communautés Européennes, 1993), p. 136.

[81] *Journal Officiel*, 7 March 1987, p. 7391.

[82] Letter from the Prime Minister dated 21 November 1988, quoted by Y. Galmot, n. 59 above.

[83] C.C., 23 January 1987, J.O. 25 January 1987, p. 924. C.C., 28 July 1989, J.O. 1 August 1989, p. 9679.

existence of an administrative jurisdiction represented a "fundamental principle confirmed by the laws of the Republic", thus its existence was a rule of constitutional value.[84] From this moment on, Parliament had lost the power and competence simply to abolish the administrative branch of justice. Therefore, a repetition of the *Canal* decision would not newly endanger the very existence of the Conseil d'Etat.

At the end of 1988, the main reasons of the CE's *Semoules* jurisprudence had consequently become obsolete:

(i)   With Government and even Parliament urging it to change its jurisprudence, should the CE have been "more royalist than the king"? Did it make sense to protect the Assemblée against a development the High House was now energetically furthering?

(ii) In this situation, the members of the CE could also no longer hope to maintain and even less to add to their power within the French establishment. On the contrary, it was slowly drifting into isolation.

(iii) All of these elements were amplified by the new pro-European spirit which had taken hold of the entire Community. Standing aside in this situation was no longer appreciated as a particularly patriotic French attitude but rather as that of a "spoil-sport".

Under these circumstances, an objective mind would have considered change as the only way out, therefore imminent. The question then is to what degree the members of the CE were to be described as "objective minds". It is not our intention to underestimate the CE; there can be no doubt about the brilliance and intelligence united in this superb corps. However, a study on the extra-doctrinal reasons for legal change must strongly focus on the individuality of the actors concerned and the social constraints under which they act. In the case of the CE, this aspect is of great importance because we are dealing with quite a homogenous corps; this exerts strong social pressure on its members to act in accordance with the corps tradition, which consists in serving national interests. The last element of our explanation of change concerning the CE must therefore deal with the question of how the majority of the corps members came to believe that an enactment of the direct effect and supremacy doctrine would in the end serve the interests of France as a nation.

One of the keys to the understanding of this development may well lie in the evolution of the ENA's curriculum. Until the beginning of the 1980s, it was characterised by—to put it cautiously—a certain distance towards Community law. As a Sorbonne professor told us, the simple fact that European law courses existed must not be taken as a guarantor of Community friendliness. He himself had the following experience while giving some lessons on EC law at the ENA: having asked the administration to copy and distribute some documents drafted by the European Commission for the

---

[84] C.C., 23 January 1987, J.O. 25 January 1987, p. 924. C.C., 28 July 1989, J.O. 1 August 1989, p. 9679.

preparation of his next class, he was told by the Vice Director: "*Monsieur, ici, nous défondons les intérêts de la France!*" and the distribution was refused. As one can imagine, we have come a long way since then.

A first reason for a development of a more Community-friendly attitude within the ENA simply lies in the fact that the members of the CE could not possibly have remained completely immune to the (in some aspects) euphoric 1992 campaign. Becoming aware of the crucial lack of information on the Community as a whole and of the considerable influence of EC law in particular, seminars and meetings were organised all over France. Public organisations and private companies established posts for advisers in Community matters. Being a major pillar of the French establishment, the CE could not avoid coming more and more frequently into contact with Community law and with people who felt that this law was, after all, a good thing for France.

The most direct contact the CE had with European law stemmed from the delegation of an experienced Conseiller d'Etat to the ECJ. As one of the "major" Member States, France had the right to nominate two candidates for the ECJ, a judge and an Avocat General.

Since 1952, the French Government had thought it wise to nominate a member of the CE for the post of Avocat General. The organisation of the ECJ having been developed according to the blueprints of the CE, the belief was that a member of the administrative law branch would more easily fulfil this role specific to the French law system. According to this logic, the judicial branch provided the candidate for the post of judge. This division of tasks lasted until 1982, a year in which the Government took advantage of a third seat it had received for two years in order to swap the roles:[85] from now on, the CE nominated the judge, and the magistrates occupied the function of Avocat General. This "*rochade*" was the result of pressure on the part of the CE which had become increasingly unhappy with the *status quo*. Unexpectedly, the role of the public prosecutor in the ECJ had developed to be much less influential than that of the French original. In contrast to French courts, the European Court quite frequently did not follow the conclusions of the prosecutor who, again unlike the French model, never assisted in the final deliberation. Under these circumstances, the role played by nominated Conseillers d'Etat had proven to be tiring and of lesser influence than expected. As we have learned from magistrates, another reason for the CE's determination to occupy the position of judge was linked with its growing isolation in France concerning the endorsement of Community law. If it was not possible to convince the other French supreme courts not to follow the *Costa*-jurisprudence, it could at least try to influence the jurisprudence of the ECJ. The first member of the CE to be nominated for the post of judge at the ECJ was Yves Galmot, according to his *curriculum vitae* a typical product of the

---

[85] This third seat was accorded to compensate the effects of the Community expansion to include Greece and was occupied by Mrs. Simone Rozès.

French elite educational system.[86] During the six years Mr. Galmot was in office in Luxembourg, no remarkable shift in the *Costa* jurisprudence had occurred; it is, however, not certain that this can be said about Mr. Galmot's attitude towards the Conseil d'Etat's jurisprudence. As he said in his farewell speech in 1988: "I can assure you that after six years in Luxembourg I, as a Conseiller d'Etat, will never again see the French Public Law as before".[87] This is actually only one example for the impressive socialisation "device" the ECJ represents. In interviews conducted with all former French ECJ members, this was a feature they all agreed upon. The general opinion was that an institution, which today can already look back on (measured by its importance and degree of innovation) a tremendous jurisprudence, imposes itself on all new members. Even if the attitude of a newcomer towards Community law should be a critical one, he would in a short span of time be assimilated by the institution as such and by the older members. Consequently, the members of the ECJ tend eventually to become the best ambassadors of EC law in their countries of origin.

If we look at the chronology of events, this remark seems to be singularly true in the case of Y. Galmot: having left the Luxembourg court in October 1988, he was immediately reintegrated into the CE; one year later, the CE took its *Nicolo* decision. As members of the CE have told us, this is far from being a coincidence. As we have learned, Galmot had already been in frequent contact with the CE during his stay in Luxembourg in order to insist on the growing necessity to end the isolation into which the supreme court had manoeuvred itself.

It would be blunt determinism to pretend that a single individual finally decided a fifteen-year-old struggle. One should, however, consider that the case of Galmot was only the "tip of an iceberg". Together with younger colleagues such as Patrick Frydman and Bruno Genevois, Galmot was the most obvious indicator of change within the corps.

Also relevant to this issue is the significant influence of Marceau Long, vice-president of the CE since February 1987. Long had served as Secretary General to the French Government in the early 1980s and had been President of the French national carrier Air France. Also because of his professional background, he was widely regarded as a pro-European.

Here, our three sub-strands of explanation merge: a changed environment, henceforth favourable to European integration, a more pro-European training and finally the influence of the ECJ via its French judges. At this point, all was set for the two landmark decisions *Nicolo* and *Alitalia*. Given the developments

---

[86] Born in 1931, Galmot attended the most famous French High School, the Lycée Louis le Grand, before taking a degree in law and then acquiring his diploma at the Institut d'Etudes Politiques de Paris which directly lead him to the ENA, which he left in 1956. At the age of 32, he was a member of the CE.

[87] European Court of Justice, *Apercu des travaux de la Cour de justice et du Tribunal de première instance des Communautés Européennes en 1988 et 1989 et audiances solennelles 1988 et 1989* (Luxembourg: Office des Publications Officielles des Communautés Européennes 1990), p. 191.

described above, it is no coincidence that the two decisions were taken with an only eight-month interval as well as the fact that *Alitalia* lead the way. As we have seen, the problems the CE had and still has with the doctrine of direct effect are certainly of doctrinal character. The circumstances in which the problem presents itself do, however, leave some latitude for compromise; the *Alitalia* decision is situated within it. With supremacy, such a compromise seemed impossible: either the CE accepted it or it didn't! Therefore, the order in which the two decisions were handed down correspond to the amount of conviction needed to persuade the more sceptical members of the court that the time was ripe for change. Once this step was made, the extension of supremacy to Community regulations and directives was the next problem on the agenda. The CE probably felt that it would, now that full supremacy had been granted, have to deal with a considerable number of cases. It would undoubtedly have created an extremely complicated doctrinal and practical situation if the CE would have excluded the derived Community law from the benifit of supremacy.

Under these circumstances, it must have seemed a wiser solution to now draw back to an operational jurisprudence instead of deliberately opening the next field of conflict.

What still today remains to be done is the full enforcement of direct effect. As described above, the method employed by the CE which consists in always founding an action in court on the national regulation translating the Community directive is not only complicated but more important, it does not cover all possible situations. Here one can see the disadvantages of compromise: believing that it could apply direct effect to directives on the basis of national law only, the CE has built up a complicated and *in extremis* ineffective jurisprudence. It will now take a great deal of courage to abandon the initial path in favour of a clear alignment on the *Van Gend en Loos* jurisprudence.

Whatever the future development of this question will be, the analysis of the extra-doctrinal reasons for legal change has shown that the combination of a great number of very different pressure-creating factors were necessary, before the Conseil d'Etat realised that it could only gain by change. In our attempt to understand why the CCass shifted its jurisprudence into a Community-conforming direction almost fifteen years earlier than the CE, two reasons seemed to be of central importance:

(i)   The importance of the diverging education of the magistracy on the one hand and the CE corps was decisive. Placing the latter in the front row of the French establishment, their elite training lead them to feel particularly attached to the French central state. For the former, things were quite the other way around. Lesser public esteem, lesser cohesion as a corps and a more heterogeneous educational backround lead them to recognise at an earlier stage the chance of adding to their influence via Community law.

(ii) The consequence of this first element was that our two actors originally saw themselves on different steps of the ladder of a (judicial and political) French establishment. While for the CE any change in the *status quo* could only mean loss of influence, things were the other way around for the CCass. Their reaction to direct effect and supremacy was a flawless application of this insight.

As to the situation today, apart from the problem of the legal basis for the two doctrines, the only difficulties come from the Conseil d'Etat. As one author entitled a study on the courts' relation with Community law: " . . . *des progrès mais peut mieux faire*".[88]

The influence of doctrine on jurisprudence

The last issue to be discussed is intimately linked to the foregoing in as far as it also aims at explaining how change in jurisprudence takes place. While the previous section was open to a wide range of socio-cultural influences on judges and courts, this one will focus on a single potential source of influence on jurisprudence: doctrine.

Examining this question calls for a certain number of methodological remarks beginning with the definition of "doctrine". Even if it should be easy to admit the working definition that what we are talking about is the sum of scientific, published opinion concerning a field of science, the problem of knowing what to consider remains. Considering the great number of publications which deal with international, European and French constitutional law, a representative selection had to be made.

For the purposes of this chapter the pure teaching manuals were ruled out. Although doubtless of importance, their approach was purely descriptive and—except for the fact-creating power of regulation—therefore unlikely to have had any determining influence. Instead, the focus was placed on periodical publications. This choice had the advantage of giving us an impression of the dynamics of doctrine: how had the reaction to the ECJ's jurisprudence developed and was there a growing or maybe declining pressure on national courts to behave in a certain manner? The risk that this choice would lead us to ignore certain non-periodical publications which however directly concerned our subject were comparatively minor. If a book turned out to be of such importance, it would necessarily be discussed in the periodicals. The last methodological question concerned the choice of the periodicals, which was guided by two main criteria: the duration of its publication (as far as possible having begun before 1963 because of *Van Gend en Loos*) and the

---

[88] Kovar, "Le Conseil d'Etat et le droit communautaire: des progrès main peut mieux faire", *Dalloz chr.* (1992), p. 207.

importance accorded to Community matters. This lead to a selection of eight titles.[89]

Our analysis will proceed in two steps: first considering the way the French doctrine reacted to some major decisions of the ECJ; then, since the influence doctrine has had on the different supreme courts varies, examining them one by one. Before doing so, a few general remarks should be made concerning the doctrine's relation with Community law. As we know, the development of a distinct scientific domain of Community law is a recent phenomenon; as far as France is concerned, we find first signs for this as late as the end of the 1960s. This has two consequences: until today, the majority of the confirmed scientific specialists in Community law are people who originally either came from the field of domestic public law or from classical international law. Having abandoned their traditional field of studies, their professional existence henceforth strongly depends on a positive, expansive development of Community law. This can of course not remain without consequence on their work as scientists. Concerning this phenomenon, Anne-Marie Slaughter Burley speaks of an "identity of interest" between scholars and practitioners of Community Law.[90] In the worst case, this could be an elegant description of a voluntary blindness for the deficiencies of Community law, since otherwise public criticism on decisions of the ECJ is considered as "cutting the ground from under one's own feet". As we will see below, one of these possibilities could very well apply to France.

The second consequence of the only recent advent of EC law is that, apart from those directly specialised in it, ignorance dominantes. This lack of even quite basic knowledge lasted right up to the early 1980s.

This is one of the reasons why in 1963 and 1964, the two decisions founding the doctrines of direct effect and supremacy were almost ignored in the analysed French literature. Only two of the eight chosen publications- those specialised in international law—seemed to have realised the fundamental innovation represented by the courts *Van Gend en Loos* decision. In the *AFDI*, one of France's leading specialists in EC law quite simply notes that one will have to expect a difficult phase of transition.[91] A note in the *RGDI* seems more enthusiastic when it declares that the *Van Gend en Loos* decision "opens perspectives of which one cannot underestimate the importance".[92] All in all it must, however, be underlined that the reaction to this first fundamental decision was of benign neglect, and specialised publications like the *RMC*—

[89] *Revue du Marché Commun* (RMC), *Revue Trimesterielle de Droit Européen* (RTDE), *Gazette du Palais* (GP), *Actualité juridique* (AJ), *Revue Francaise de Droit International Public* (RFDIP), *Revue critique de Droit International Privé* (RDIP), *Annuaire Francais de Droit International* (AFDI) and *Revue Générale de Droit International* (RGDI); subsequently referred to in their respective abbreviation or as "analysed" (French) literature/publications/periodicals.

[90] Slaughter Burley, "Legal Research and the EC", *Journal of Common Market Studies* 31, no 3 (September 1993), pp. 391–400, 395.

[91] Boulouis, "Le juge intern et le droit communautaire", *AFDI*, (1963), pp. 736–78.

[92] Ampoux, "A propos de Van Gend en Loos", *RGDI*, (1964), pp. 110–57.

admittedly more tuned towards the purely economic aspects of the EEC—did not even mention the case.

The reaction to the 1964 *Costa* case was quite identical. While neutral analysis dominated in all publications, Boulouis added that one could begin to recognise "the essential lines of a doctrine for a Community based on law".[93]

The third and last decision to be discussed here in relation to the reaction of the French doctrine is the *AETR* case in 1971. Unlike the two former cases, the choice of this decision perhaps requires some explanation: two aspects are most significant here. First, the *AETR* case marked the end of the founding period of Community law. As Robert Lecourt, member and later President of the ECJ from 1963 to 1976 confirmed to us, the judges had clearly felt that this decision touched the furthest point to which they could go without endangering the whole legal edifice. Secondly, the political reaction set off by this decision in France represents the moment at which the broader French public became aware that something important was taking place in Luxembourg. For the first time in history, a decision of the ECJ found its way into newspaper articles of considerable size. In a first reaction, the puzzled journalist merely spoke of an "at first sight disconcerting decision".[94] Two weeks later, a "high-ranking international government agent" was to be heard on the subject in an article entitled: "Has the Court of Justice of Luxembourg exceeded its competence?"[95]

Under these circumstances, one could have expected a more extensive reaction in the specialised publications; this was, however, not to be found. In his traditional review of the ECJ jurisprudence, Boulouis simply ended a neutral description of the facts by noting that this decision would enter into the annals of Community jurisprudence.[96] Reacting to public discontent, Kovar remarked that the basically positive contribution of the *AETR* decision could be endangered by political resistance.[97] And yet the impact of this decision had been more important than printed opinion leads us to believe. It is for instance a "public secret" that Mr. Boulouis, pioneer of Community law in France and Professor of Community Law at the University Paris II Assas, started discreetly to distance himself from the ECJ's jurisprudence he felt was no longer in accord with the Treaties. There is, however, no trace of this alienation in his comments, which remain sober.

The overall lesson from this brief examination of the French doctrine's reaction to three decisive ECJ decisions is consequently first of all ignorance, and secondly neutral, cautiously positive description. It almost seems as if those more closely concerned with Community law did not wish to break the

---

[93] Boulouis, "Note sous Van Gend en Loos", *AFDI*, (1964), pp. 398–403.
[94] *Le Monde*, 3 April 1971, p. 37.
[95] *Le Monde*, 27 April 1971, pp. 19–20.
[96] Boulouis, "Note sous l'arrêt AETR", *AFDI* (1971), pp. 366–70.
[97] Kovar, "Note sous l'arrêt AETR", *RGDI* (1971), pp. 387–418.

silence for fear of the public reaction when confronted with the extent of legal integration.

The second part of this section will consist of an analysis of the influence doctrine had on the supreme courts. As mentioned above, the potential influence of doctrine strongly varies from court to court. This difference is essentially due to the distinct legal culture of each institution; for this, we can therefore refer to the previous section in which legal change was also explained by institutional culture.

Especially in the case of the Cour de Cassation, the doctrinal discussion of direct effect and supremacy, or of Community law in general, was of little importance when it took its *Jacques Vabre* decision. In compensation for the relative lack of doctrine, it must however be pointed out that the CCass is traditionally very sensitive to doctrinal discussions. Consequently, the fact that published opinion since *Van Gend en Loos* can be characterised as neutral to friendly could have confirmed the court in its intention to endorse community doctrines. For two reasons, however, its influence does not seem to have been decisive: first of all, the sparse place accorded to Community law in the analysed publications reflects the rank which Community law had within the doctrinal discussion. It can quite clearly be said that it was not a major topic. Its simple extent can therefore not have been enough to bring a supreme court to change jurisprudence. This appears to be even more true when recalling the reaction to *AETR*. The *Vabre* decision having been taken only four years later, the members of the CCass must still have remembered the public and political distrust towards Community jurisprudence expressed by the reaction in 1971. The court must therefore have known that an identical, maybe even stronger reaction could be expected if it decided to put the two doctrines into effect. Under these circumstances, the positive input caused by the doctrine was surely neither strong nor wide enough to counterbalance the negative one based on the establishment's political distrust towards integration by law.

If there has been an influence, it went rather the other way: the CCass lead doctrine to understand better the reasons for which the full enforcement of Community law was so important.

In the case of the Conseil d'Etat, the thesis that doctrine had little influence on the jurisprudence concerning Community law can also be defended, the argument, however, being the opposite to that concerning the judicial court. Once again because of its specific tradition, the CE is reputed to pay very little attention to the doctrine in general. This can already be deduced from the fact that in the Advocate General's conclusion, references other than those to the court jurisprudence are forbidden. As a Conseiller d'Etat explained, not only do the members of his corps simply not have the habit of looking at the doctrine, they also have a slight feeling of disdain for those who try to "understand" what they, the supreme court, intend to say. Had this been otherwise, the CE would probably not have maintained its conservative jurisprudence over so many years during which doctrine steadily increased its demands for realignment in the direction of the CE. Compared with the multitude of pressures the CE was subject to at the end of the 1980s, that caused by doctrine must have worried it the least.

Summing up, no direct, causal link between the supreme court's jurisprudence in Community matters and doctrinal pressure can be made, according to our analysis of French doctrine. Although doctrinal pressure, when it existed, generally went in the direction subsequently taken by the courts, there are no indications that this pressure was strong enough to have made the difference. If, as in the case of the CE, doctrine strongly argued in favour of a shift in jurisprudence, it merely represented one instrument within a whole orchestra.

3

Report on Germany

JULIANE KOKOTT

INTRODUCTION

This chapter mainly deals with the development of the jurisprudence of the German Federal Constitutional Court (Bundesverfassungsgericht) concerning the relationship between European Community law and the German legal order. The Federal Constitutional Court is the highest court in Germany. Its decisions are binding upon all other state authorities including all other courts. The Federal Constitutional Court's decisions handed down in a number of proceedings have the effect of statutes.[1] Therefore, the Federal Constitutional Court's approach to European integration is particularly relevant. Lower courts must and do observe Federal Constitutional Court's decisions. Different approaches by lower courts, like that of the Federal Tax Court (Bundesfinanzhof) can only be preliminary.

* I wish to thank Beate Rudolf for her invaluable assistance. The following abbreviations will be used:

AöR	Archiv des öffentlichen Rechts	EWS	Europäisches Wirtschafts- und
BAG	Bundesarbeitsgericht		Steuerrecht
BFH	Bundesfinanzhof	FAZ	Frankfurter Allgemeine Zeitung
BFHE	Entscheidungen des	JA	Juristische Ausbildung
	Bundesfinanzhofs	JuS	Juristische Schulung
BGH	Bundesgerichtshof	JZ	Juristenzeitung
BVerfG	Bundesverfassungsgericht	NJW	Neue juristische Wochenschrift
BVerfGE	Entscheidungen des	NVwZ	Neue Zeitschrift für
	Bundesverfassungsgerichts		Verwaltungsrecht
BVerfGG	Bundesverfassungsgerichtsgesetz	NZA	Neue Zeitschrift für Arbeitsrecht
CMLR	Common Market Law Review	RIW	Recht der internationalen
DÖV	Die öffentliche Verwaltung		Wirtschaft
DVBl	Deutsches Verwaltungsblatt	RUDH	Revue universelle des droits de
EFG	Entscheidungen der Finanzgerichte		l'homme
EJIL	European Journal of International	VVDStRL	Veröffentlichungen der
	Law		Vereinigung der Deutschen
EuGRZ	Europäische Grundrechte-		Staatsrechtslehrer
	Zeitschrift	ZaöRV	Zeitschrift für ausländisches
EuR	Europarecht		öffentliches Recht und
EuZW	Europäische Zeitschrift für		Völkerrecht.
	Wirtschaftsrecht		

[1] Cf. § 31 BVerfGG.

This chapter will show that although the case law of the Federal Constitutional Court has not developed in a completely consistent fashion, certain strands of reasoning can be detected. Traditionally, the focus has been on the question whether basic rights as guaranteed in the Basic Law are sufficiently protected under European Community law. The *Maastricht* decision of 12 October 1993[2] constitutes a major shift as it addressed the issues of sovereignty and *"Kompetenz-Kompetenz"*, thus exploring in detail the limits to the transfer of power to the European Communities. In the *Maastricht* decision, the German Federal Constitutional Court preserves to itself the competence to determine the limits of Community jurisdiction (*Kompetenz-Kompetenz*). In cases of drastic *ultra vires* acts of the Communities, the Federal Constitutional Court apparently would not accept the European Court of Justice as having the final and exclusive authority to interpret the founding Treaties and thus define the competences of the Communities.

In the examination of the Constitutional Court's case law prior to *Maastricht*, two main questions arise. First, to what extent did the Constitutional Court use the theory that national law and Community law constitute two autonomous legal orders, on which the ECJ founded the priority of Community law? Secondly, how did the Constitutional Court try to ensure an effective protection of basic rights within Community law? This part will also show how the Constitutional Court's case law paved the way for the *Maastricht* decision in using German constitutional law as the yardstick of the application of Community law in Germany. The controversial *Maastricht* decision directly addresses the problem of *Kompetenz-Kompetenz*. It is based on the traditional assumption that only sovereign states and not international or supra-national organizations may have *Kompetenz-Kompetenz*, that is the power to design their own competences. Because these and other controversial assumptions and statements are so fundamental to the relationship between national and supra-national law and for the co-operation between supra-national and national authorities or courts, this chapter analyses the *Maastricht* decision extensively.

This analysis explains the effects of the Constitutional Court's interpretation of democracy as the people's right to a parliament with substantive powers. It will also show how the Court endeavoured to uphold the Maastricht Treaty on European Union by giving its provisions a content compatible with the German Constitution. A central point in these considerations are the passages of the decision dealing with the monetary union, one of the most controversial parts of the Treaty within Germany before the judgment was handed down.

The last part of the chapter primarily undertakes an evaluation of the co-operative relationship between the Federal Constitutional Court and the ECJ. By this, the Constitutional Court wants to give a legal backing to the influ-

---

[2] 20 EuGRZ 429 *et seq* (1993); English text in 33 ILM 388 *et seq* (1994).

ence it tries to exert on the jurisprudence of the ECJ, especially as far as it concerns the progressive development of European law by interpretation of the founding Treaties. This section also elucidates the different sources of influence on the Constitutional Court's jurisprudence, the most prominent of which is "*La doctrine*", the academic community consisting of professors of public, European and international law including former and future justices. This predominantly legal discussion of foreign policy questions like the ratification of the Maastricht Treaty is a specific feature of contemporary Germany.

DOCTRINAL MATRIX

Constitutional law background

The questions of the relationship between European law and German constitutional law and of the relationship between the ECJ and national courts have centered around only a few provisions of the Basic Law. Prominent among them is the former article 24, para. 1 (now article 23 para. 1, second sentence) which provides for the transfer of sovereign powers to inter-governmental institutions by legislation.[3] All legislation has to respect the limits set by the

---

[3] Art. 24, para. 1 of the Basic Law reads: "The Federation may by legislation transfer sovereign powers to inter-governmental institutions".

In connection with the ratification of the Treaty of Maastricht, a new article 23 was adopted, which provides:

(European Union)

"(1) For the realization of a unified Europe, the Federal Republic of Germany cooperates in the development of the European Union which upholds democratic, social and federal principles, the rule of law and the principle of subsidiarity and which guarantees the protection of basic rights in a way which is basically comparable to this Basic Law. For this, the Federation may by legislation with consent of the Bundesrat (Federal Council) transfer sovereign powers. Art. 79 paras. 2 and 3 apply to the establishment of the European Union as well as to the alteration of its treaty basis and to comparable regulations, which modify or amend the content of this Basic Law or which facilitate such modifications or amendments.

(2) The Bundestag (Federal Chamber) and, through the Bundesrat (Federal Council), the Länder participate in matters of the European Union. The Federal Government has to inform the Bundestag (Federal Chamber) comprehensively and as early as possible.

(3) The Federal Government hears the Bundestag (Federal Chamber) before its participation in the legislation of the European Union. The Federal Government takes into account the opinion of the Bundestag (Federal Chamber) in its negotiations. Details shall be regulated by a law.

(4) The Bundesrat (Federal Chamber) has to be involved in the formation of the will of the Federation insofar as it would have to participate in a corresponding domestic measure or insofar as the Länder would be competent under domestic law.

(5) Insofar as interests of the Länder are affected in a field under the exclusive competence of the Federation or insofar as the Federation has otherwise jurisdiction, the Federal Government takes into consideration the comments of the Bundesrat (Federal Council). The opinion of the Bundesrat (Federal Council) has to be considered pertinently at the formation of the will of the Federation, if the legislative powers of the Länder, the establishment of their agencies or their administrative procedures are affected mainly; thereby, the responsibility of the Federation for the whole state will be respected. The Federal Government has to give its consent in matters which may lead to an increase of expenditures or a decrease of revenue for the Federation.

Constitution.[4] Changes to the Constitution are possible if approved by a majority of two-thirds of the Bundestag (Parliament) and of the Bundesrat (Second Chamber, composed of representatives of the states or "*Länder*").[5] However, the Constitution itself limits this power by the so-called "eternal guarantee clause". According to this provision, the Constitution cannot be changed as far as specified fundamental principles are concerned—notably the fundamental principles of individual basic rights.[6]

Since the Federal Constitutional Court is not an appellate court, its powers are limited to constitutional law questions. The yardstick to be applied depends on the procedure by which the Court has been accessed. The main decisions on the relationship of European law and German law have been handed down either by way of a constitutional complaint[7] or "concrete" norm control.[8] In a constitutional complaint anyone can ask the Court to find that an act of a German authority (including courts) violated the complainant's fundamental rights. No other reason for non-constitutionality of that act can

(6) If mainly exclusive legislative competences of the Länder are affected, the exercise of the rights pertaining to the Federal Republic of Germany as a member state of the European Union, shall be transferred from the Federation to a representative of the Länder nominated by the Bundesrat (Federal Council). The rights are exercised in cooperation with and in agreement with the Federal Government; thereby, the responsibility of the Federation for the whole state will be respected.

(7) Details on paras. 4 to 6 shall be regulated by a federal law with the consent of the Federal Council".

For critique of the new article 23 see R. Breuer, "Die Sackgasse des neuen Europaartikels (Art. 23 GG)", 10 *NVwZ* 417 (1994); see also R. Streinz, "Art. 23", in M. Sachs (ed.), *Grundgesetz, Kommentar* (1996).

[4] Art. 79, para.1 of the Basic Law: "This Basic Law can be amended only by laws which expressly amend or supplement the text thereof. In respect of international treaties the subject of which is a peace settlement, the preparation of a peace settlement, or the abolition of an occupation regime, or which are designed to serve the defence of the Federal Republic, it shall be sufficient, for the purpose of clarifying that the provisions of this Basic Law do not preclude the conclusion and entry into force of such treaties, to effect a supplementation of the text of this Basic Law confined to such clarification".

[5] Art. 79, para. 2 of the Basic Law: "Any such law shall require the affirmative vote of two thirds of the members of the Bundestag and two thirds of the votes of the Bundesrat".

[6] Art. 79, para. 3 of the Basic Law reads: "Amendments of this Basic Law affecting the division of the Federation into Länder, the participation in principle of the Länder in legislation, or the basic principles laid down in Articles 1 and 20, shall be inadmissible".

[7] Art. 93, para. 1 no. 4a: "The Federal Constitutional Court decides on constitutional complaints, which can be introduced by everyone alleging a violation of his/her basic rights or the rights contained in Arts. 20, para. 4, 33, 38, 101, 103, 104 by an act of public power".

[8] Art. 100, para. 1: "If a court considers unconstitutional a statute the validity of which is relevant to its decision, the proceedings shall be stayed, and a decision shall be obtained from the Land court competent for constitutional disputes if the constitution of a Land is held to be violated, or from the Federal Constitutional Court if this Basic Law is held to be violated. This shall also apply if this Basic Law is held to be violated by Land law or if a Land law is held to be incompatible with a federal law".

Art. 100, para. 1 concerns the procedure of "concrete" norm control whereas Art. 93, para. 1 no. 2 provides a procedure of "abstract" norm control.

Art. 93, para. 1 no. 2: "The Federal Constitutional Court decides in case of disputes or doubts concerning the formal or material compatibility of federal or state law with this Basic Law or the compatibility of the state law with other federal law at the request of the Federal Government, a state government or one third of the members of parliament".

be invoked. Through the procedure of norm control any court has to request the Federal Constitutional Court to rule on the constitutionality of statutory law, if the referring court is convinced that, by applying this norm in its decision, it would violate the Constitution. Decisions handed down in the procedure of norm control have the effect of statutes.[9]

Doctrinal Matrix before and after the *Maastricht* decision

The jurisprudence of the German Federal Constitutional Court has developed over a period of several years. Two intertwined strands of reasoning are evident prior to the *Maastricht* decision. The first is that the recognition of the autonomy of Community law is gradually eroded, despite the underlying concern of the Constitutional Court to ensure that lower courts respect the priority of Community law over national law. The second is the conviction that there are limits to the transfer of power by the Member States to the European Communities. Before the *Maastricht* decision, these limits were found in the basic rights guaranteed by the Basic Law. With that decision, the principles of democracy and sovereignty came into play. The Court's new assumption in *Maastricht* is that the integration process must, in a certain way, be controlled by the representatives of the people, i.e. by Parliament. This follows from the principle of democracy. At the current stage of integration, the Court still recognises the major legitimating function of the national Parliaments; the European Parliament only has a supporting legitimating function.[10] Therefore, integration must develop within the framework of the Treaties to which the national Parliaments have given their consent. *Ultra vires* acts would be "undemocratic" according to this logic. This new conceptional framework is different from the Court's approach as developed before *Maastricht*. Theoretically, the limits to Community jurisdiction have become narrower, because the German Federal Constitutional Court now generally reserves for itself the jurisdiction to declare ultra vires acts of the Communities inapplicable in Germany. In the *Maastricht* decision, the Court reversed its case law according to which only acts of German authorities are directly subject to constitutional complaints.[11] Now, also *ultra vires* acts of the Community may be challenged before the Federal Constitutional Court.

The earlier approach, according to which Community acts could not be directly challenged in German courts had led to a factual supremacy of Community law over national law. The Federal Constitutional Court maintains the supremacy of Community law in Maastricht emphasising its "co-operative relationship" with the ECJ. However, according to *Maastricht* the supremacy of Community law does not extend to *ultra vires* acts.

[9] § 31 BVerfGG.
[10] 33 ILM 420 (1994).
[11] See e.g. 22 BVerfGE 297 (1967); 37 BVerfGE 283 (1974).

Before *Maastricht*, the Federal Constitutional Court's concern was not generally *ultra vires* acts of the Communities, but only the basic rights as set forth in the German Basic Law. This refers to the famous "*Solange*" cases. Through *Solange* and other cases, the case law of the Federal Constitutional Court on basic rights and European integration gradually developed into a *de facto* concession to the ECJ of almost exclusive jurisdiction (*Solange II*). In the end, basic rights are no more a real limit to the ECJ's exclusive jurisdiction, because the ECJ itself protects basic rights sufficiently. Then came the *Maastricht* decision, in which the Federal Constitutional Court declared *ultra vires* acts of the Communities inapplicable in Germany. This is a shift away from the basic rights paradigm, even though the Federal Constitutional Court managed to review *ultra vires* problems, principles of democracy and rights to democratic elections in the framework of a *constitutional complaint procedure* concerning the Maastricht Treaty.

Thus, the *Maastricht* decision of 12 October 1993,[12] exceeds the basic rights approach of earlier cases. Within the procedure of constitutional complaints the Federal Constitutional Court, for the first time, deals with the guarantee of general, direct, free, equal and secret elections (article 38 of the Basic Law) as a subjective right. The Court ruled that this forbids the "weakening . . . of the legitimization of state power gained through an election, and of the influence of the exercise of such power, by means of a transfer of duties and responsibilities of the Federal Parliament, to the extent that the principle of democracy, declared as inviolable in Article 79, para. 3 in conjunction with Art. 20, paras. 1 and 2 of the GG, is violated".[13] Therefore, it was crucial to decide whether the German Parliament still had influence over the future development of the European Union. The Court found that Germany had only transferred limited powers to the European Communities by ratifying the Maastricht Treaty. Thus, the control of the Parliaments of Germany and the other Member States was preserved: the point of no return to a European state had not been passed. Consequently the Court reasoned, there was no violation of the complainant's right protected under article 38 of the Basic Law, and the Maastricht Treaty could be ratified by Germany.

DOCTRINE, JURISPRUDENCE AND BEYOND

Doctrinal shifts of the Federal Constitutional Court's jurisprudence and their possible causes

From a strictly doctrinal point of view, the case law of the Federal Constitutional Court has developed in a relatively consistent fashion. But there were shifts in the factual evaluation of the ECJ's function and ability to

[12] 20 EuGRZ 429 (1993), English version in 33 ILM 388 (1994).
[13] 30 ILM 395 (1994).

protect the basic rights (*Solange I* and *Solange II*) and to promote the integration process on the basis of and within the limits set by the founding Treaties.

The following section attempts to identify reiterated shifts in the jurisprudence and will try to offer some explanations for them. It will be shown that although the Court verbally recognised the autonomy of Community law in its first decision on the relationship between Community law and national law, the approach nevertheless remained within the concepts of international law. In particular, the question of the limits to a transfer of power pursuant to article 24, para. 1 of the Basic Law was already posed in 1967 and only culminated in the 1993 *Maastricht* decision, by which the Court reserved its right to control whether the development of Community law—be it by Community act or decision of the ECJ—constitutes a transgression of the revised founding Treaties.

From EC law as an autonomous legal order to qualification as international law

In its early cases dealing with the relationship of Community law and German law, the Court relied on the ECJ's position that Community law constituted an autonomous legal order.[14] The Federal Constitutional Court recognised the supremacy of Community law over national law, albeit in the form of "priority in application" ("*Anwendungsvorrang*"), and not "priority in validity" ("*Geltungsvorrang*").[15]

In *Solange I*, the Constitutional Court repeated that Community law formed an autonomous legal order flowing from an autonomous source. Thus, it was neither part of the national legal order nor international law. The Community is no state, specifically no federal state, but a community *sui generis* involved in the process of advancing integration. The Court further stated that the ECJ must determine the binding force, interpretation and observance of Community law. Also, the competent national organs must determine the binding force, interpretation and observance of the constitutional law of the Federal Republic of Germany. This, according to the Federal Constitutional Court, causes no problem as long as the two legal orders do not conflict with respect to their content. The ECJ and the Federal Constitutional Court, therefore, have a duty, according to the latter, to attempt to reach a consensus between the two legal orders in their jurisprudence.[16] However, in a case of conflict between domestic law and Community law, the Federal Constitutional Court qualifies and limits the supremacy of Community law over domestic law. It emphasised that the founding Treaties

---

[14] Cf. e.g. 22 BVerfGE 293, 296 (1967).

[15] Cf. e.g. 31 BVerGE 145 (1971).

[16] 37 BVerfGE 271, 278 (1974). See also Beutler/Bieber/Pipkorn/Streil, *Die Europäische Union* (1993), p. 104 *et seq* with further references to critical and approving comments on the decision.

do not bind the Federal Republic and the Member States in a unilateral way. This, in a way, foreshadows the co-operative relationship between the Federal Constitutional Court and the ECJ stressed in *Maastricht*. The organs of the Community are also bound to strive for resolutions of such conflicts that are consistent with peremptory norms of the constitutional law of the Federal Republic of Germany. The Court underlines that acknowledging this conflict does not constitute a Treaty violation. Rather, it triggers the Treaty mechanism within the European organs leading to a political solution of the conflict. In the case before it, the Court stated that as basic rights could be guaranteed on multiple levels it did not harm the Community if Member States guaranteed farther-reaching rights. Therefore, the Federal Constitutional Court considered itself not to be prevented from rejecting the priority in application of Community law in a given case. This amounts to a denial of the autonomy of Community law by subjecting it to national constitutional law, especially fundamental rights, under certain circumstances.

In the *Vielleicht-Beschluß* ("Maybe Decision") of 1979,[17] the logical consequence to this limitation of supremacy of EC law would have been to ensure the protection of basic rights procedurally by letting the Constitutional Court also control decisions of the ECJ. However, the Federal Constitutional Court shied away from this consequence in an obvious attempt to restrict *Solange I*. Recognising the need for uniformity in interpreting and applying Community law, the Constitutional Court decided that the EC Treaty requires full respect of the ECJ's interpretation of a Community law norm. Therefore, the Federal Constitutional Court denied its jurisdiction to declare Treaty provisions applicable in Germany with a meaning different from the interpretation given to them in a preliminary ruling by the ECJ.

There is no explicit reference to the autonomous character of Community law, although the Court could have used it as an argument in favour of exclusive competence of the ECJ to interpret EC law. This would have been in line with the distinction of competences between the ECJ and national courts made in *Solange I*. Instead, the Court referred to the object and purpose of the EC Treaty to argue that article 177 gives the ECJ the final say in the "reciprocal influences of national and Community legal order".[18] In a way, this emphasis on the interrelationship and mutual influences of the national and the Community legal orders qualifies the autonomous character of EC law. Thus, the Court in effect strengthened the position of the ECJ within Germany at the price of qualifying the principle of autonomy of Community law. Later decisions no longer refer any more to the autonomy of Community law.[19]

Although the main features of the *Solange II* case were identical to that of *Solange I* (allegations concerning the violation of basic rights by a German

---

[17] 52 BVerfGE 187 (1979).
[18] 52 BVerfGE 187, 200 (1979).
[19] BVerfG, Decision of 14 February 1983, 36 NJW 1258, 1959 (1983).

authority applying secondary Community law) the Court, this time, did not refer to the autonomy of the Community legal order. Instead, the perspective changed from the founding Treaties as the basis for the obligation of both the ECJ and national courts to avoid conflicts of their respective case law (*Solange I*)[20] to the German law transferring sovereign powers to the Communities as the final yardstick in deciding on the applicability of Community law contradicting German constitutional law.[21] Thus, the Constitutional Court reserved for itself the final say in the case of a conflict with the ECJ. *Solange II*, which recognised the ECJ as an effective guardian of fundamental rights, lays the doctrinal groundwork for Maastricht. A possible explanation of this shift is the fact that in *Solange II* the Constitutional Court also had to decide whether the ECJ was a "lawful judge" pursuant to article 101, para. 1 of the Basic Law. As the Court obviously wanted to reach that result in order to reinforce the obligation of courts to request a preliminary ruling according to article 177, it had to overcome the difficulty that the ECJ is not a national organ. Therefore, the Constitutional Court, again, heavily relied on the functional interplay between national courts and the ECJ.[22] Stressing the autonomy of the Community legal order would not have been compatible with this argument. The Court said:

> "The functional interplay of the Court of Justice of the European Communities with the courts of member states together with the fact, that the Founding Treaties—based on the ratification laws pursuant to Arts. 24 para. 1, 59 para. 2 s. 1 of the Basic Law, and the derived Commmunity law, adopted on the basis of the Treaties—are part of the domestic legal order of the Federal Republic of Germany and have to be observed, interpreted and applied by its courts, qualify the ECJ as a lawful judge pursuant to Art. 101 para. 1 s. 2 of the Basic Law, to the extent that the ratification laws of the Founding Treaties transfer jurisdiction to that court".[23]

In the two last-mentioned cases, the shift away from the paradigm of the autonomous legal order promoted the effectiveness of EC law. That the Court no longer referred to the "autonomy" of the Community legal order in these cases, cannot be understood as a move to a more nationalistic approach. However, the more extensively the Federal Constitutional Court has to deal with European integration, the more its international law approach to the new phenomenon of supra-nationality comes to the surface.

The Maastricht decision does not mention the autonomy of Community law. This can be explained by the issues in that case. The Court had to decide whether the Maastricht Treaty allowed for a transfer of power to the European Communities to an extent that would violate the individual's right to elect a German Bundestag with substantive powers. Consequently, it was

---

[20] 37 BVerfGE 27, 287 *et seq* (1974).
[21] 73 BVerfGE 339, 375 (1986).
[22] 73 BVerfGE 339, 367 (1986).
[23] 73 BVerfGE 339, 367 *et seq* (1986) (author's translation).

the extent of power transferred by the Treaty, not precisely the relationship of Community law and national law, that the Court had to deal with.

To conclude, the fact that the Federal Constitutional Court no longer refers to EC law as an autonomous legal order does not seem to express a different approach or a policy change of the Court towards European integration. Rather, the international law approach of the Court to EC law becomes explicit as soon as the Court deals more comprehensively with EC law. Moreover, the international law approach does not only underline the recent *Maastricht* judgment of the Kirchhof Court, but also the decisions of the Steinberger Court (e.g. *Solange I*) which are commonly considered as integration-friendly. German courts never really supported the theory that Community law flows from an autonomous source, even though early decisions of the Federal Constitutional Court speak of the "autonomy" of Community law.

From an expansive interpretation of article 24, para. 1 to a restrictive interpretation—the question of protecting human rights effectively

According to article 24 of the Basic Law, the Federation may by legislation transfer sovereign powers to inter-governmental institutions. In a 1967 case concerning constitutional complaints against Community regulations, the Court ruled that they were inadmissible since they were not directed against acts of German authorities.[24] Thereby, it recognised a *de facto* supremacy of Community law over national law.

As the Court held the constitutional complaints inadmissible, it could leave open the question whether and to what extent the Federal Republic of Germany had been able to exempt the Community organs from being bound by German basic rights when it had transferred sovereign powers under article 24, para. 1 of the Basic Law.[25]

In a 1971 decision, the Court only used article 24, para. 1 as an argument in favour of the obligation to recognize a judgment of the ECJ.[26]

It was in *Solange I*[27] that the Federal Constitutional Court for the first time touched upon the question of the limits of transferring sovereign powers under article 24, para. 1. The Court held that this provision does not allow legislation of the inter-governmental institution to change the basic structure of the Constitution on which its identity is founded. Such a change would require a constitutional amendment.[28] The basic rights belong to this basic structure. Therefore, the Court ruled that preliminary requests in the procedure of norm control were admissible and required after requesting the decision of the ECJ according to article 177 of the Treaty, "as long as Community

---

[24] See e.g. 22 BVerfGE 297 (1967).
[25] 22 BVerfGE 293, 298 *et seq* (1967).
[26] 31 BVerfGE 145, 174 (1971).
[27] 37 BVerfGE 271 (1974).
[28] 37 BVerfGE 271, 278 *et seq* (1974).

law does not contain a valid and formulated catalogue of basic rights established by a parliament which is equivalent to the catalogue of basic rights of the Basic Law".[29] The relevance of the stage of integration of the Community is underlined by the words "as long as". It is noteworthy that the Constitutional Court did not take into account the Nold decision of the ECJ[30] which had been handed down two weeks before the *Solange I* decision.[31] In the Nold decision, the ECJ emphasised that fundamental rights belonged to the general principles of law which it had to guarantee. Thereby, the European Court would be guided by the common constitutional traditions of the Member States. In *Nold*, the ECJ held that it could not consider legal acts incompatible with the fundamental rights recognised and protected by the constitutions of those states. The ECJ would also consider international treaties on the protection of human rights.

In the "*Solange I*" ("As long as" I) decision[32] the Court thus reserved the right to ensure, by way of norm control, that Community law as interpreted by the ECJ was applied in a manner not violating the fundamental rights contained in the Basic Law. It should be noted that in the case concerned, the Constitutional Court did not find a violation of fundamental rights.[33] The decision is named after the words of its operative part that norm control is admissible "as long as the integration process of the Community has not advanced to the point that the Community law also contains a valid and formulated catalogue of basic rights established by a parliament that is equivalent to the catalogue of basic rights of the Basic Law". However, the wording suggests a possible restriction of the Court's jurisdiction at a later stage. The decision was heavily criticised for making German basic rights a standard for the further development of Community rights.[34]

After *Solange I*, the Federal Constitutional Court shows more and more willingness to relinquish its control as to whether the application of Community law by German authorities may violate the basic rights. This more integration-friendly approach by the Federal Constitutional Court is a consequence of the ever-growing importance of fundamental rights in the ECJ's newer case law. At the same time, the Federal Constitutional Court's increasing willingness to accept the ECJ as an effective protector of the rights of the individual can be seen as a reaction to the heavy criticism met by *Solange I*.

---

[29] This is the operative part of the judgment (author's translation), 37 BVerfGE 271 (1974).

[30] *Nold* v. *Commission*, Case 4/73 [1974] ECR 491, ECJ.

[31] *Solange I* was handed down on 29 May 1974.

[32] 37 BVerfGE 271 (1974).

[33] The norm control was directed against a Community law rule which provided for the forfeiture of a deposit that had to be paid upon the granting of a licence for export or import of specified goods, if the holder did not make use of that licence. The complainant alleged that this rule violated his freedom of profession (art. 12 of the Basic Law).

[34] On criticism of *Solange I*, M. Hilf, "Solange II: Wie lange noch Solange?", 14 EuGRZ (1987), 1 with references.

The *Vielleicht-Beschluß* ("Maybe" decision) of 1979[35] is widely seen as a reaction to the criticism of *Solange I*. The case dealt with the application of articles 92 and 93 on subsidies of the then EEC Treaty by the Commission. The ECJ had interpreted these provisions as excluding the right of national courts to find a national subsidy incompatible with the EEC Treaty as long as the Commission has not taken a decision in that matter. The referring German court had seen this interpretation as violating the basic right to effective judicial protection as guaranteed by article 19, para. 4 of the Basic Law. The Federal Constitutional Court rejected that opinion because it considered itself to be bound by the ECJ's interpretation of Community law according to article 177. The Court stated that it did not have the power "to declare applicable for the territory of the Federal Republic of Germany norms of primary Community law with a content contradicting the content given to them by the ECJ".[36] Much more famous than this operative part of the decision is the *obiter dictum* which resulted in the name "Maybe" decision and which shows a certain willingness of the Court to reconsider *Solange I*:

"The Senate leaves open whether and possibly how far—maybe in view of the political and legal developments in the European area accomplished in the meantime— the principles of the decision of May 29, 1974 (37 BVerfGE 271 ff.) can be further upheld unrestricted".[37]

In the "Maybe" decision, the Federal Constitutional Court uses article 24, para. 1 of the Basic Law in an unusual way. In order to give reasons for declaring inadmissible the request for norm control, the Court stated that the requesting court had failed to allege that the German law transferring sovereign powers to the European Communities (act of accession or "*Zustimmungsgesetz*") was unconstitutional. As the Constitutional Court considered itself bound by the interpretation of Community law given by the ECJ, the constitutionality of this legislation could not be the object of a norm control.[38] By this way of reasoning, the Court upheld the view that article 24, para. 1 could be used to control whether the transfer of powers was within the constitutional limits prescribed by the Basic Law. At the same time, the Constitutional Court ensured respect of the decisions of the ECJ without materially departing from *Solange I*.

Subsequent decisions of the Court confirm its readiness, in principle, to relinquish its control in view of further development in the protection of basic rights in the Community. Although the two Eurocontrol decisions[39] do not

---

[35] 52 BVerfGE 187 (1979).

[36] 52 BVerfGE, 187, 200 (1979).

[37] 52 BVerfGE, 187, 202 *et seq* (1979).

[38] 52 BVerfGE, 187, 199 *et seq* (1979).

[39] 58 BVerfGE, 1 (1981); 59 BVerfGE, 63 (1981). Both decisions concerned constitutional complaints against the transfer of jurisdiction, the one to Belgian courts for all litigation concerning EUROCONTROL's fees, and the other the transfer of jurisdiction to the ILO's administrative tribunal for labour litigation concerning EUROCONTROL's permanent officials.

directly concern Community law, they show that the Court would loosen its requirements for transfer of sovereign powers under article 24, para. 1. It interprets that clause as an ensurance of effective protection of fundamental rights. However and this is important against the background of *Solange I*, the Court does not presuppose that the protection by an international organisation has to correspond to that under the Basic Law. These decisions open the door for *Solange II*.

In the *Mittlerweile-Beschluß* ("Meanwhile" decision)[40] the Court applied the standard spelled out by *Solange I* only to find that the regulation in question did not surpass the outer limits of article 24, para. 1 of the Basic Law. Specifically, it did not consider it necessary that Community law contained the requirement that there must be a democratically legitimised empowerment of the executive to legislate, a requirement under German law according to article 80, para. 1 of the Basic Law. Neither was it obligatory, in the Court's view, to have a rule similar to article 19, para. 1 of the Basic Law in the sense that a regulation interfering with a specific basic right must cite that right. Moreover, the Court deemed it useful to explicitly leave open whether, in the future, it will not exercise its jurisdiction "as long as on the Community level a sufficient protection in comparison with the basic rights of the Basic Law is generally guaranteed, in particular by the ECJ".

This was the position that the Court finally took in 1986 in the landmark *Solange II* decision ("As long as" II decision).[41] The constitutional complaint alleged a violation of the right to a lawful judge (article 101, para. 1)[42] by the Federal Administrative Court (*Bundesverwaltungsgericht*). That Court had declared legal the denial of an import licence to the applicant without either referring the question to the ECJ for a second time or instituting a procedure of norm control before the Federal Constitutional Court. As to the first point the Constitutional Court ruled that the ECJ was a "lawful judge" pursuant to article 101, para. 1 of the Basic Law. Therefore, individuals may force lower courts to request preliminary rulings under article 177 of the EC Treaty by filing a constitutional complaint. In the case before the Constitutional Court, however, the Federal Administrative Court's decision not to request a second preliminary ruling in the same question was not arbitrary and therefore not in violation of article 101, para. 1. The importance of the decision lies in the Court's reasoning concerning the second point, viz. the opinion proffered that the Federal Administrative Court should have referred the question to the Constitutional Court to decide on whether the regulation of the Commission on which the denial of the licence was based and its interpretation by the ECJ constituted a violation of German basic rights. The Court now recognised the protection of fundamental rights by the ECJ as being sufficient. Therefore, the Federal Constitutional Court would not exercise its jurisdiction over the

[40] 36 NJW 1258 (1983).
[41] 73 BVerfGE 339 (1986).
[42] The provision reads: "No one may be removed from the jurisdiction of his lawful judge".

application of secondary Community law serving as a legal basis for the conduct of German courts and authorities:

> "as long as the European Communities, in particular the Court of Justice of the Communities, generally ensures an effective protection of the basic rights against acts (*Hoheitsgewalt*) of the Communities, which basically corresponds to the protection of basic rights compelled by the Basic Law . . . Such requests for preliminary ruling under Art. 100 para. 1 of the Basic Law are consequently inadmissible".[43]

Solange II can be seen as the highest point of harmony and convergence between the German Federal Constitutional Court and the ECJ. After *Solange II* it was generally accepted that the positions of the Federal Constitutional Court and the ECJ had become rather close.[44]

This is true at least from a pragmatic result-oriented approach. On the other hand, *Solange II*, which is commonly understood as integration-friendly, clearly points to the international law basis of the Community. According to the Court, Community law is valid in Germany because the German ratification statute under articles 24, para. 1, 59, para. 2 of the Basic Law says so.[45] Therefore, the ECJ is a "lawful judge" insofar as the ratification statute has transferred to it the power to administrate justice. The Court then repeats that the transfer of power is limited by the basic structure of each Member State's constitution, on which its identity is founded.[46] In contrast to *Solange I*, the Court did not hold that the basic rights of the Basic Law as such were part of that fundamental structure. In *Solange II*, only the legal principles underlying the basic rights section of the Basic Law were called non-renouncable. This is an obvious attempt to limit the restriction to article 24, para. 1 to counter the criticism to *Solange I*. To defend its position, the Constitutional Court referred to the jurisprudence of the Italian Constitutional Court.[47]

It is striking that in *Solange II*, the German Federal Constitutional Court gave up the two requirements stated in the *Solange I* decision rendered twelve years earlier. In *Solange II*, the Federal Constitutional Court did not insist any more on a protection of the basic rights under the Basic Law in each individual case; nor did it request a codified catalogue of basic rights on the Community level. Rather, the Court set forth that, on the ground that there has been a development of the fundamental rights jurisprudence of the ECJ, the Common Declaration of the European Parliament, the Council and the Commission of the European Communities of 5 April 1977 on the respect of fundamental rights and the Declaration of the European Council on Democracy of 7, 8 April 1978, a minimum standard of substantial basic rights

---

[43] 73 BVerfGE 339, 340 (1986).
[44] Cf. Beutler/Bieber/Pipkorn/Streil, *Die Europäische Union* (1993), p. 106.
[45] 73 BVerfGE 339, 367 (1986). See also Streintz, *Bundesverfassungsgerichtlicher Grundrechtsschutz und Europäisches Gemeinschaftsrecht* (1989), p. 101.
[46] 73 BVerfGE 339, 375 (1986).
[47] 73 BVerfGE 339, 376 (1986).

protection is generally guaranteed, which meets the principal constitutional requirements of the Basic Law.[48] The Federal Constitutional Court noted thereby that the ECJ takes account of the European Convention on Human Rights and that it was not relevant that the Community as such was not a party to the European Convention on Human Rights.[49]

When the Federal Constitutional Court was called upon to decide whether the Federal Minister of Justice had to control the constitutionality of a judgment by the ECJ before giving the order for its enforcement,[50] it further confirmed the recognition of the ECJ's protection of human rights. The Court held that courts and agencies of the Federal Republic of Germany were neither entitled nor obliged to review acts of organs of the European Communities.[51] Therefore, it had to be left open whether the complainant was right in that the decision of the ECJ violated her basic rights.

However, the Federal Constitutional Court reserved its jurisdiction for exceptional cases. The Court said that it could be left open whether the challenged regulations of the Commission violated the complainant's basic rights, as neither the complainant's allegations nor the preliminary ruling by the ECJ showed that the Court of Justice was absolutely and generally unable or unwilling to recognise or protect her basic rights.[52] For this reason only, recourse to the German Federal Constitutional Court was inadmissible. In a way, *Solange II* is encouraging critique to the jurisprudence of the ECJ. As far as the basic rights of the individual are concerned, it is at least misleading to argue with the level of basic rights protection that the Community generally guarantees.

The Constitutional Court affirmed its *Solange II* jurisprudence in a constitutional complaint procedure the following year, when it reversed a judgment of the Federal Tax Court for not having requested a preliminary ruling by the ECJ.[53] The Court held that the Tax Court had violated the complainant's right to a lawful judge when denying the direct effect of the Sixth Directive[54] on the sales tax even though the ECJ had ruled in favour of direct effect on request of the lower tax court. But then, after the entry into force of the Single European Act in 1986, the Federal Constitutional Court, in a new composition, seems to follow again a slightly more reserved approach to the ECJ. In a 1989 decision, the Federal Constitutional Court mentions, without cause, the possibility of a constitutional complaint if the basic rights' standard compelled

---

[48] 73 BVerfGE 339, 386 (1986). Critically R. Streintz, *Bundesverfassungsgerichtlicher Grundrechtsschutz und Europäisches Gemeinschaftsrecht* (1989), p. 64. On the protection of fundamental rights by the European Court of Justice, J. Kokott, "Der Grundrechtsschutz im Europäischen Gemeinschaftsrecht", 121 AöR 599 (1996).

[49] BVerfG *ibid*. On accession of the EC to the European Convention on Human Rights, Court of Justice of the European Communities, Opinion 2/94 of 28 March 1996, (1996) 17 *Human Rights Law Journal* 51; see also Kokott/Hoffmeister, note, 90 *AJIL* 664 (1996).

[51] BVerfG, Decision of 10 April 1987, 14 *EuGRZ* 386 (1987).

[52] 73 BVerfGE 339, 387 (1986).

[53] 75 BVerfGE 223 (1987).

[54] *See* Art. 192 para. 2 of the Treaty Establishing the European Community.

by the Basic Law cannot be realised through recourse to the ECJ.[55] Even though not inconsistent with the logic and theory of *Solange II*, this statement may foreshadow a different policy of the Court.

In 1992, the basic rights jurisprudence of the Federal Constitutional Court was integrated into the Basic Law by amendment. According to the new article 23, the Federal Republic of Germany co-operates in the development of the European Union "which guarantees the protection of basic rights in a way that is basically comparable to this Basic Law". Article 23 furthermore requires that the European Union upholds democratic, social and federal principles, the rule of law and the principle of subsidiarity. The drafting of article 23 was heavily influenced by the Federal Constitutional Court's case law and by the academia. Article 23 is the expression of a more self-conscious Germany trying to set some conditions for integration. Moreover, the new integration article—article 23—requires a two-thirds majority for the establishment of the European Union and for Treaty amendments, whereas a simple majority was sufficient under the old article 24. The reason, probably, is that after the Second World War, Germany could be happy to be integrated in any international organisation; post-war Germany could only gain, not lose thereby. Thus, article 24 was to make international and supra-national integration easy, even though it could lead to a material change in the constitutional order. After the Second World War, there was no spectre of the waning state, of Germany losing control over major policy decisions affecting the people under its jurisdiction. In view of this new aspect, article 23 now requires a constitution-amending majority of two-thirds of the legislature. Germany's "conditions" on European integration are certainly also the attribute of a state more powerful and more influential on the international plane than it used to be. As Germany identifies itself with a specific type of "Rechtsstaat" (rule of law), where courts rather than politicians make important choices, it is the Federal Constitutional Court rather than the German representatives in the Council of Ministers which tries harder to influence the process of integration.

Solange I influenced the fundamental rights jurisprudence of the ECJ. In the recent *Maastricht* decision the Federal Constitutional Court warns the ECJ against being too dynamic in interpreting Community law. The rest of this chapter will not consider further basic rights as a potential limit to the priority of EC law, but address instead the problem of "*Kompetenz-Kompetenz*".

"Kompetenz-Kompetenz"

"*Kompetenz-Kompetenz*" means the legal power ("competence") to define one's own competence. Traditionally, it is relevant with regard to international courts and tribunals. It lies with the court as only it—and not the

---

[55] BVerfG, decision of 12 May 1989, 42 NJW 974 (1989). This is the so-called "*Wenn-nicht-Beschluß*" ("if not" decision).

parties to the dispute—is competent to interpret the declarations and conventions establishing its jurisdiction. *Kompetenz-Kompetenz* is also relevant in the law of international organisations. According to traditional concepts of state theory and of the law of international organisations, only states and not international organisations have *Kompetenz-Kompetenz*. International and supranational organisations only have the competences transferred to them by the member states. This theory of the only attributed competences of international organisations suggests that member states should be able to protect themselves against drastic *ultra vires* acts of the organisation. *Kompetenz-Kompetenz* with regard to the EC Treaty and the Maastricht Treaty concerns the question whether organs of the Community (e.g. the ECJ) or organs of Member States (e.g. the Federal Constitutional Court) are "competent" to decide in the last resort whether the Communities act within the competences transferred to it by the founding Treaties, or whether they act *ultra vires*. Within the "legal community" (*Rechtsgemeinschaft*) of the European Communities, *Kompetenz-Kompetenz* thus means "*quis judicabit?*" (who or which court decides?).

The 1987 decision of the Constitutional Court reversing the Federal Tax Court was the first to deal with article 24, para. 1 and the problem of *Kompetenz-Kompetenz*. In that decision, the Federal Constitutional Court approved of the law-making function of the ECJ as being compatible with the transfer of sovereign power under article 24, para. 1 of the Basic Law,[56] thus limiting its own power to review judgments of the ECJ. It rejected the view of the Tax Court that the jurisprudence of the ECJ concerning the direct applicability of directives transgressed its powers under the EC Treaty and was therefore not covered by the German ratification law.[57] As the EC Treaty does not give the Community unlimited jurisdiction, the Constitutional Court stated: "The Community is no sovereign state in the sense of international law with *Kompetenz-Kompetenz* over its internal affairs".[58]

In the *Maastricht* decision the question of *Kompetenz-Kompetenz* turned out to be much more crucial as the ratification of the Maastricht Treaty depended upon its outcome.

Who decides on adhesion to the European Union? As set forth, the case law of the Federal Constitutional Court until its *Maastricht* decision of 12 October 1993[59] essentially concerned the protection of basic rights. *Kompetenz-Kompetenz* rather was a secondary or underlying concern. The *Maastricht* decision, even though handed down in the framework of a constitutional complaint procedure, has a broader approach. It directly and primarily concerns the problem of *Kompetenz-Kompetenz*. According to article 38 of the Basic

---

[56] 75 BVerfGE 223, 241 *et seq* (1987).
[57] 75 BVerfGE 223, 241 *et seq* (1987).
[58] BVerfG *ibid.* at 242.
[59] 20 EuGRZ 429 (1993). English version in 33 ILM 388 (1994).

Law "the deputies to the German Bundestag shall be elected in general, direct, free, equal, and secret elections". The Federal Constitutional Court interpreted article 38 of the Basic Law for the first time as not only guaranteeing the formal right to general, direct, free, equal, and secret elections but also gave article 38 of the Basic Law a substantive content. The Court said that article 38 of the Basic Law guaranteed a subjective right of the individual to elect a German Bundestag with substantive powers:

> "1. Art. 38 GG (*Grundgesetz*) forbids the weakening, within the scope of Art. 23 GG, of the legitimisation of state power gained through an election and of the influence on the exercise of such power by means of a transfer of duties and responsibilities of the Federal Parliament, to the extent that the principle of democracy declared as inviolable in Art. 79 para. 3 in conjunction with Art. 20 paras. 1 and 2 of the GG, is violated".[60]

In the tradition of its basic rights jurisprudence, the Federal Constitutional Court takes up the limits of the integration power under article 24, now more specifically under article 23 of the Basic Law. The principles of basic rights and of democracy are both among the limits falling under the "eternal guaranty" clause of article 79, para. 3 of the Basic Law and are thus binding also for constitutional amendments in the framework of international or supranational integration. Earlier decisions of the Federal Constitutional Court focused on the basic rights limits, whereas the Maastricht decision takes up— and this is the change—the principle of democracy as a measure and limit for German co-operation in European integration. The rather unusual consequence is that now, at least theoretically, any citizen may challenge German ratification laws to international treaties that transfer sovereign rights to international organisations as undemocratic. The new interpretation of the right to vote thus leads to a kind of *actio popularis* with respect to important international or supra-national treaties. This may be understood as another example showing a German tendency to constitutionalise even foreign policy.

Thus, the German Federal Constitutional Court had to give its consent to the Maastricht Treaty. On the other hand, some scholars had requested a popular referendum. The argument was that ratification of the Maastricht Treaty was the beginning of a process that, by and by, would lead to a European Federation and thus the elimination of Germany´s sovereignty and status as a state. These scholars requested an anticipatory popular referendum, because participation of the people must take place before it is too late; before the point of no return in the development following the ratification of the Maastricht Treaty is reached.[61] This approach leads to the question whether

---

[60] *See also* full quotation, reproduced *infra* p. 98.

[61] Cf. D. Murswiek, "Maastricht und der pouvoir constituant", *Der Staat* 32, 161 (1993); H. Stöcker, "Die Unvereinbarkeit der Währungsunion mit der Selbstbestimmungsgarantie in Art. 1 Abs. 2 GG", *Der Staat* 31, 495 (1992); H. H. Rupp, "Muß das Volk über den Vertrag von Maastricht entscheiden?" 46 *NJW* 38 (1993); J. Wolf, "Die Revision des Grundgesetzes durch Maastricht, Ein Anwendungsfall des Art. 146 GG", 48 *JZ* 594 (1993).

and how far adhering to the European Union implies giving up Germany's statehood in the long run. Member States will not lose their statehood as long as the principle of the limited transfer of powers to the Communities applies. If, even by the ratification law to the Maastricht Treaty, only limited powers are transferred to the Communities, the further development of the Union remains in a way under the control of the Parliaments of Germany and the other Member States. According to this reasoning of the German Federal Constitutional Court, the competences transferred to the European Union must not permit an autonomous development towards a European federal state with *Kompetenz-Kompetenz*.

From its different approach, the Federal Constitutional Court dealt with the problem of the vanishing statehood of Member States. The Court finally reached the conclusion that *Kompetenz-Kompetenz* was still with Germany. The German Bundestag was still in control of major decisions. Therefore, the Court rejected the complainants' allegations that their constitutional right to vote for the German Bundestag was unduly weakened in contravention of article 38 of the Basic Law.

Ultra vires acts and "Kompetenz-Kompetenz". A clearly international law approach to the Communities and to the European Union underlies the *Maastricht* judgment as well as *Solange II*. Accordingly, Community law applies in Germany only because the German ratification laws to the founding Treaties say so. In the *Maastricht* decision, the Federal Constitutional Court makes its international law approach even clearer saying that "[t]he validity and application of European law is Germany derive from the order governing application of law contained in the Act of Accession".[62]

More important, in the *Maastricht* judgment, the Court draws drastic consequences from its international law approach to the Communities: similar to *ultra vires* acts of traditional international organisations, acts transgressing the competences transferred to the Communities by the founding Treaties are not binding in the domestic sphere, according to the Court:

> "If, for example, European institutions or governmental entities were to implement or to develop the Maastricht Treaty in a manner no longer covered by the Treaty in the form of it upon which the German Act of Accession is based, any legal instrument arising from such activity would not be binding within German territory. German State institutions would be prevented by reasons of constitutional law from applying such legal instruments in Germany. Accordingly, the German Federal Constitutional Court must examine the question of whether or not legal instruments of European institutions and governmental entities may be considered to remain within the bounds of the sovereign rights accorded to them, or whether they may be considered to exceed those bounds".[63]

---

[62] 33 ILM 395, 424 (1994); the German original version is reproduced in 20 EuGRZ 429, 439 (1993). *See also* the full quotation reproduced below p. 98.
[63] 33 ILM 388, 423 (1994).

The Federal Constitutional Court thus extends its jurisdiction over Community acts. In the pre-*Maastricht* era, the Federal Constitutional Court only asked whether the German ratification laws to the founding Treaties or German acts applying Community law transgressed the integration power under article 24 of the Basic Law; in particular, whether they violated the principle guarantees of basic rights. That meant that Community acts could only be challenged indirectly and with the allegation that they were not compatible with article 79, para. 3 of the Basic Law, i.e. that they violated the basic rights. Now, Community acts can be challenged directly before the Federal Constitutional Court with the allegation that they are not covered by the German ratification laws to the founding Treaties. *Ultra vires* acts of the Communities will be inapplicable in Germany. The standard is no longer article 24 (now article 23) of the Basic Law, along with article 79, para. 3. Rather, the standard for the Federal Constitutional Court, when judging Community acts, are now the German ratifications reproducing the founding Treaties. The potential for conflict with the ECJ is obvious. The European Communities have developed into a system where the ECJ is competent to interpret the treaties authoritatively. Relying on the basic right to vote and the democracy principle, the German Federal Constitutional Court has indirectly constitutionalised the interpretation of the founding Treaties.[64] According to the *Maastricht* decision, *ultra vires* acts of the Communities violate the constitutional right to vote for a German Parliament with substantial powers (article 38 of the Basic Law). If, however, the Federal Constitutional Court had not reserved itself some residual jurisdiction for grave conflicts between national and Community law, a European organ would authoritatively decide on the distribution of competences between Germany and the European Communities. Then, an argument could be made that *Kompetenz-Kompetenz* would lie with the Communities. This could apply, if, based on an ultradynamic jurisprudence of the ECJ, there would be no more effective check on the usurpation of powers by Community organs.

"Kompetenz-Kompetenz": *and democracy*. According to the conception of the German Federal Constitutional Court, *Kompetenz-Kompetenz* of the Federal Republic of Germany is a matter of democracy. The European Parliament, even after obtaining substantial competences through the Maastricht Treaty, still does not have legislative powers comparable to those of a national parliament in a democratic state. More importantly, according to the Federal Constitutional Court, granting more powers to the European Parliament

---

[64] According to E. Klein and U. Everling, this amounts to a violation of the EC Treaty, cf. E. Klein, "Diskussionsbeitrag" in Hommelhoff/Kirchhof, *Der Staatenverbund der Europäischen Union* (Heidelberg 1994), 103, 105; U. Everling, "Das Maastricht-Urteil des Bundesverfassungsgerichts und seine Bedeutung für die Entwicklung der Europäischen Union", 17 *Integration* 165, 171 (1994); for an opinion to the contrary see H. Gersdorf, "Das Kooperationsverhältnis zwischen deutscher Gerichtsbarkeit und EuGH", 23 *DVBl* 674, 683 (1994).

could not even remedy the so-called democracy deficit of the European Communities. On the contrary, the democratic legitimacy of the Communities lies with the national parliaments of the Member States. As there is not one European people, the European Parliament cannot provide the necessary democratic legitimisation of the Communities. Rather the peoples of the Member States provide the democratic basis through parliamentary control of their delegates to the Council of Ministers.[65] If, as the Court assumes, the indirect democratic legitimisation of Community power lies with the national delegates in the Council of Ministers, this could even be used as an argument against the further transfer of powers to the European Parliament at this stage. In its judgment, the Court refers to the extra-legal conditions for the functioning of democracy such as ongoing free interaction of social forces, interests and ideas.

"In cases where they do not already exist, actual conditions of this kind may be developed, in the course of time, within the institutional framework of the European Union . . . Within the community of States which is the European Union, democratic legitimisation is by necessity effected by the parliaments of the individual member states receiving information on the activities of the European institutions. To an increasing extent, in view of the degree to which the nations of Europe are growing together, the transmission of democratic legitimisation within the institutional structure of the European Union by the European Parliament elected by the citizens of the member states must also be taken into consideration. Even at the present stage of development, legitimisation by the European Parliament has a supportive function, which could be strengthened if the European Parliament were elected on the basis of a uniform electoral law in all member states pursuant to Art. 138, para. 3 of the EC Treaty and if its influence on the policy and law-making of the European Communities were to increase. The important factor is that the democratic foundations upon which the Union is based are extended concurrent with integration, and that a living democracy is maintained in the member states while integration proceeds. If too many functions and powers were placed in the hands of the European inter-governmental community, democracy on the level of the individual States would be weakened to such an extent that the parliaments of the member states would no longer be able to convey adequately that legitimisation of the sovereign power exercised by the Union. If the peoples of the individual States (as is true at present) convey democratic legitimisation via the national parliaments, then limits are imposed by the principle of democracy on an extension of the functions and powers of the European Communities".[66]

---

[65] Cf. also P. Badura, "Der Bundesstaat Deutschland im Prozeß der europäischen Union", in G. Ress/T. Stein (eds.), *Vorträge, Reden und Berichte aus dem Europainstitut—Sektion Rechtswissenschaft—der Universität des Saarlandes*, no 298 (1993), p. 18.; for a detailed analysis of the democratic deficit and of remedial measures G. Ress, "Über die Notwendigkeit der parlamentarischen Legitimierung der Rechtsetzung der Europäischen Gemeinschaften", in W.Fiedler/G. Ress (eds.), *Verfassungsrecht und Völkerrecht, Gedächtnisschrift für Wilhelm Karl Geck* (1989), p. 625 *et seq.*

[66] 33 ILM 395, 420 *et seq* (1994).

The national parliaments thus primarily provide for the democratic legitimisation of the Communities,[67] but the European Parliament has at least a
supportive function thus far.[68] In this respect, it is interesting to note that the
Austrian Parliament shares the opinion that accession to the European Union
considerably modifies the system of democracy in Austria. Therefore, the
Maastricht Treaty had to be subjected to a popular referendum in Austria.[69]

The Federal Constitutional Court generally recognises that the requirement
of a law made by Parliament as the basis for acts touching the position and
in particular the basic rights of the individual (*Gesetzesvorbehalt*; rule of law;
proviso of legality) cannot be applied in an equally strict manner to national
and supra-national acts. Otherwise, the international and supra-national integration provided for by the Basic Law would become impossible.[70] On the
other hand, the process of integration must remain sufficiently predictable.
This, again, concerns the question of who decides in cases of conflicts concerning the integration programme, which is laid down in the founding
Treaties and which binds domestic authorities and individuals on the basis of
the German ratification laws. The Federal Constitutional Court held that it
would decide under certain circumstances, but it said that it would exercise
its jurisdiction "in a co-operative relationship" with the ECJ.[71]

Interpreting the Maastricht Treaty to avoid "Kompetenz-Kompetenz" *of the
Communities.* According to the Federal Constitutional Court, accession to the
Maastricht Treaty is only compatible with the Basic Law, if the process of
integration remains sufficiently predictable and if no *Kompetenz-Kompetenz*
is transferred to the European Communities. The topic of *Kompetenz-
Kompetenz* is particularly treated in three contexts. Perhaps the least problematical point is article F, para. 3.

---

[67] For critique see: B.-O. Bryde, "Die bundesrepublikanische Volksdemokratie als Irrweg der
Demokratietheorie", in 5 *Staatswissenschaft und Staatspraxis* 305 (1994); for support see H. Klein,
"Europa—Verschiedenes gemeinsam erlebt", *FAZ* of 17 October 12 (1994) and G. Schuppert,
"Zur Staatswerdung Europas", in 5 *Staatswissenschaft und Staatspraxis* 35, 49 (1994).

[68] Assuming there is an indirect democratic legitimisation of the Communities through the
Council, it is problematical that the Council could hardly ever be dismissed in case its policy does
not reflect the will of the peoples. The Council could only be dismissed in the hypothetical case
that the peoples of all Member States would remove their governments at the same time.
Therefore, the Council of the European Communities is not subject to any meaningful political
control. (Cf. K. Doehring, "Staat und Verfassung in einem zusammenwachsenden Europa", 7
ZRP 98, 100 (1993); J. Kokott, "Deutschland im Rahmen der Europäischen Union—zum Vertrag
von Maastricht", 119 *AöR* 207, 215 (1994)). This shows that, in the long run, only the European
Parliament could provide a sufficient basis for a democratic European Union. It may seem problematical if, at a later stage, the German Federal Constitutional Court should decide again on
whether and at what stage of integration the extra-legal or specific privileged conditions for the
existence of one European people are fulfilled.

[69] Cf. *Bundesverfassungsgesetz über den Beitritt Österreichs zur Europäischen Union* (Federal
Constitutional Law on the Accession of Austria to the European Union), 1546 der Beilagen zu
den Stenographischen Protokollen des Nationalrates XVIII. GP, reprint of 12 April 1994.

[70] Cf. Judgment on the Maastricht Treaty, 33 ILM 395, 422 (1994).

[71] *Ibid.* at 396.

(*a*) Article F, para. 3 of the Treaty establishing the European Union does not give the Union a broad and unspecified competence. Article F, para. 3 of the Treaty establishing the European Union reads: "The Community provides itself the means necessary to achieve its aims and to implement its policies".

The German Federal Constitutional Court interprets article F, para. 3 of the Maastricht Treaty as follows:

"The requirement of sufficient statutory definition of the sovereign rights granted, and therefore of parliamentary responsibility for their granting, would, however, be violated if Art. F, para. 3 of the Maastricht Treaty were applied to grant exclusive competence (*Kompetenz-Kompetenz*) for jurisdictional conflicts to the European Union as a community of sovereign States. Art. F, para.·3 merely states the political intention that the member states forming the Union wish to provide it, within the scope of the required procedures, with the means necessary to attain its objectives and carry through its policies. If European institutions were to interpret and administer Art. F, para. 3 of the Maastricht Treaty in a manner which conflicts with its substance, which has been assumed into the German Act of Accession, such conduct would not be covered by the Act of Accession and would therefore not be legally binding within Germany, which is one of the member states. German institutions would be forced to refuse compliance with any legal instruments based upon an interpretation of Art. F, para. 3 of the Maastricht Treaty of this nature.

The very fact that there is no point in the Maastricht Treaty at which it is clear that the contracting parties have agreed to establish the Union as an independent legal entity with powers on its own, conflicts with the view that an exclusive competence for jurisdictional conflicts has been established. According to the interpretation applied by the Federal Government, the Union does not have a distinct legal personality either in terms of its relationship with the European Communities or of its relationship with the member states".[72]

The German Federal Constitutional Court thus sees article F, para. 3, notwithstanding its formulation, rather as a mere statement of political intention than as a binding norm. Also, the Federal Constitutional Court points out that the European Union is no subject of international law. The Federal Constitutional Court created a new legal term for the European Union, "*Staatenverbund*" (community of states). The term *Staatenverbund* apparently first appears in an article on European integration written by the reporting Justice Kirchhof shortly before he drafted the *Maastricht* decision.[73] This 1992 article already contains important principles of the *Maastricht* decision. According to the Federal Constitutional Court, the European Union is a "*Staatenverbund*", a community of states, which is distinguished from a "*Staatenbund*", a confederation of states on the one hand, and a "*Bundesstaat*", a federal state, on the other hand. Correspondingly, German doctrine continues to refer to the organs of the European Communities rather

[72] 33 ILM 388, 428 *et seq* (1994).
[73] P. Kirchhof, "Der deutsche Staat im Prozeß der europäischen Integration", in Isensee/Kirchhof (eds.), VII *Handbuch des Staatsrechts der Bundesrepublik Deutschland* 855, 879 *et seq* (1992).

than to the Council and the Commission of the European Union.[74] This corresponds to the legal situation, but not necessarily to practice. According to their own new regulations, the Council and the Commission have now turned into the Council and the Commission of the European Union.

The Federal Constitutional Court's interpretation of article F, para. 3 of the Maastricht Treaty apparently corresponds to the will of the contracting parties and to the treaty system.[75] Article F, para. 3 of the Maastricht Treaty thus does not transfer some broad and unspecified competence to the European Union.

(b) Germany may withdraw. There are two references to the possibility of withdrawal in the Maastricht decision. One is with regard to monetary union, the other is formulated more generally:

> "Therefore, even after the Maastricht Treaty has entered into force, the Federal Republic of Germany remains a member of an inter-governmental community (*Staatenverbund*), the authority of which is derived from the member states and has binding effect in German sovereign territory only if a German order governing application of law (*Rechtsanwendungsbefehl*) is issued in respect of it. Germany is one of the 'High contracting parties' (*Herren der Verträge* = masters of the Treaties) which have given as the reason for their commitment to the Maastricht Treaty, concluded 'for an unlimited period' (Art. Q), their desire to be members of the European Union for a lengthy period; such membership may, however, be terminated by means of an appropriate act (*gegenläufiger Akt*) being passed. The validity and application of European law in Germany derive from the order governing application of law contained in the Act of Accession. Germany is therefore maintaining its status as a sovereign State in its own right as well as the status of sovereign equality with other States in the sense of Art. 2, sub-para. 1 of the UN Charter".[76]

This passage of the *Maastricht* decision is not easy to interpret. The term "appropriate act being passed" or the act to the contrary (*gegenläufiger Akt*) grammatically refers to the Treaty establishing the European Union. But the clause appears in direct context of the statement about Germany as one of the "*Herren der Verträge*". German doctrine uses the term "*Herren der Verträge*" (masters of the Treaties) to show that Member States still control the process of integration and to deny a *Kompetenz-Kompetenz* of the Communities.[77] In this context, the term "appropriate act being passed" or act to the contrary (*gegenläufiger Akt*) does not only refer to a withdrawal of the Treaty establishing the European Union, but also to the three founding Treaties establishing the European Communities. Moreover, article O (accession to the Union) and article Q (indefinite validity) of the Treaty establishing the

---

[74] Cf. Schweitzer/Hummer, *Europarecht* 23 (1996); R. Streinz, *Europarecht* 40 (1996); but v. Bogdandy/Nettesheim, "Die Verschmelzung der Europäischen Gemeinschaften in der Europäischen Union", 48 *NJW* 2324 (1995).

[75] Cf. 33 ILM 388, 428 *et seq* (1994).

[76] *Ibid.* at 424.

[77] Cf. e.g. T. Oppermann, *Europarecht* 28 (1995).

European Union govern both membership and indefinite validity with regard to the Treaty Establishing the European Union and with regard to the founding Treaties of the European Communities. An isolated withdrawal from the Union is not provided for.

The passage on withdrawal from the Union (i.e. the Communities) is also ambiguous as to whether it refers to termination of the Treaties by mutual agreement or to the possibility of unilaterally renouncing them. A grammatical interpretation of the short passage reproduced above would rather lead to the conclusion that the Federal Constitutional Court only refers to the possibility of terminating the Treaties by mutual agreement. According to German doctrine, it is not self-evident that the High Contracting Parties may terminate the founding Treaties by mutual agreement. Several authors have concluded that the Communities have reached an integration standard that legally excludes even their dissolution by mutual agreement.[78]

The statement of the Federal Constitutional Court concerning withdrawal from the Communities may refer to the possibility that Germany, in an extreme situation, may unilaterally denounce the founding Treaties. Such an act would obviously violate article Q of the Treaty establishing the European Union, according to which the Treaty is valid for an indefinite period of time. Therefore, it is hard to assume that the Federal Constitutional Court may have envisaged such a unilateral step. But the passage on withdrawal from the Communities appears in the context and framework of explanations where the Court strongly emphasises Germany's remaining sovereignty and where the Court underlines that Community law is only valid within Germany because the domestic law says so. A contextual understanding of the statement on withdrawal from the Communities thus suggests that Germany, in a most probably theoretical and extreme situation, may leave the Communities without consent of the other Member States. As already mentioned, such an interpretation would violate the founding Treaties unless one considers drastic *ultra vires* acts of the Communities as a fundamental change of circumstances in the sense of article 62 of the Vienna Convention on the Law of Treaties.[79] The principle "friendliness to public international law" underlying the Basic Law (*Völkerrechtsfreundlichkeit des Grundgesetzes*)[80] rather hinders such an approach. On the other hand, we are here confronted with the fundamental question of "Who decides?" According to the Federal Constitutional

---

[78] Ipsen was probably the earliest taking this view. For references on the different views on the termination of the Communities by mutual agreement, see P. Huber, *Recht der Europäischen Integration* 49 and 76 (1996). Huber affirms a right to termination. According to Beutler, a termination by mutual agreement is illegal. B. Beutler, in Beutler/Bieber/Pipkorn/Streil, *Die Europäische Union* (1993), p. 7. But see R. Streinz, *Europarecht* 33 (1996).

[79] In this sense the explanations to the Austrian *Bundesverfassungsgesetz* (Federal Constitutional Law) on accession to the European Union. Cf. 1546 der Beilagen zu den Stenographischen Protokollen des Nationalrates XVIII. GP, reprint of 12 April 1994, p. 7. On fundamental change of circumstances, see p. 104 below.

[80] Cf. C. Tomuschat, "Die staatsrechtliche Entscheidung für die internationale Offenheit", in VII *Handbuch des Staatsrechts*, 483 (1992).

Court, the principle of democracy requires, at the present stage of integration of the Communities, that the final responsibility stays with the German Parliament. If the point of no return has already been passed and if a unilateral withdrawal from the Communities is legally excluded under all circumstances, then it is much harder to uphold the thesis of the final say and the final responsibility of the German Parliament. These reasons permit an understanding of the ambiguous passage of the Maastricht-judgment according to which a unilateral denunciation of the founding Treaties could be justified under national constitutional law as a last resort against too much integration by ultra *vires acts* of the Communities.

(*c*) Germany controls whether and under what conditions it enters the monetary union.[81]

(i) Monetary union and "*Kompetenz-Kompetenz*".

The establishment of a monetary union under a European Central Bank modifies the sovereignty of Member States fundamentally. Therefore, the Federal Constitutional Court considers it essential that Germany, i.e. the German Parliament, controls the transition to the monetary union. The Federal Constitutional Court tries very hard to interpret the Treaty in a way that does not automatically lead to monetary union; its position is that Germany—in particular the German Parliament—still controls the process of and the transition to the monetary union. This issue is not primarily linked to the relationship between national courts and the ECJ. However, it is most closely linked to the problem of *Kompetenz-Kompetenz* as it appears in the context of state theory and of the law of international organisations, that is to the question whether Germany stills controls the integration process. The Court tries to explain that Germany and not the European Commission or the Council of Ministers decides upon this major step of further integration. According to the Federal Constitutional Court, it is the German Parliament who attributes these further powers entailed by the monetary union to the Communities. Therefore, according to the logic of the Court, Germany still controls the integration process and has *Kompetenz-Kompetenz*.

But the Federal Constitutional Court's explanations on the monetary union also concern its relationship with the ECJ and its approach to EC law for several reasons: (1) the Court's statements on monetary union concern the distribution of power between Member States and Community organs, and this indirectly affects the distribution of power between the ECJ as a Community organ and national courts; (2) the Court interprets the Maastricht Treaty even though this falls into the exclusive competence of the ECJ; (3) the Court emphasises conditions for Germany's integration into monetary union, foremost the ability to withdraw, and thus limits the reach of Community law provisions.

---

[81] On the concept of the monetary union see M. Seidel, "Probleme der Verfassung der Europäischen Gemeinschaft als Wirtschafts- und Währungsunion", in J. F. Bauer/P.-C. Müller-Graff/M. Zuleeg (eds.), *Europarecht—Energierecht—Wirtschaftsrecht, Festschrift für Bodo Börner zum 70. Geburtstag* 417 (1992).

The following section shows how hard the Court tries to fit the provisions of the Maastricht Treaty on monetary union into its paradigm of German parliamentary control of the integration process.

(ii) Interpreting the provisions on monetary union to make them constitutional—an effort in co-operation.[82]

The Federal Constitutional Court had to ask whether the development leading to the monetary union was sufficiently anticipated by the ratification law to the Treaty establishing the European Union. If the Maastricht Treaty permitted a not sufficiently anticipated development beyond parliamentary control, this would violate the right to democratic participation derived from article 38 of the Basic Law. The Federal Constitutional Court tries to interpret the Treaty to make it constitutional. This is part of the German Court's "co-operative relationship" with the European Communities. Article 109j, para. 4 of the EC Treaty reads: "If by the end of 1997 the date for the beginning of the third stage has not been set, the third stage shall start on 1 January 1999". According to the Federal Constitutional Court, this provision should be considered as an objective rather than a date that can be legally enforced.[83] In principle, the ECJ is competent to interpret the articles of the Treaty. The statements of the Federal Constitutional Court are an emanation of Germany's remaining sovereignty and *Kompetenz-Kompetenz* as understood by the Constitutional Court. If the Maastricht Treaty would automatically lead to a monetary union and if Member States including Germany could not control whether the stability requirements were fulfilled, this would violate the principle of democracy.

According to article 5 of the EC Treaty, Member States are under a duty to facilitate the achievements of the Community's aims. The Federal Constitutional Court points out that the provision implies an obligation mutually to co-operate with the Communities as well as with the member states.[84]

According to the Federal Constitutional Court, the concern of the German Federal Parliament to reserve the right to make its own evaluation on the transition to the third stage of economic and monetary union, and therefore to resist any relaxation of the criteria for stability, may be based in particular on article 6 of the Protocol on the Convergence Criteria.[85] The convergence criteria to be fulfilled in order to reach the third stage of the monetary union are: the achievement of a high degree of price stability; the sustainability of the government financial position; the observance of the normal fluctuation

---

[82] On the following see J. Kokott, "Deutschland im Rahmen der Europäischen Union—zum Vertrag von Maastricht," 119 *AöR* 207, 227 *et seq.* (1994).

[83] Cf. 33 ILM 434 (1994).

[84] 33 ILM 434 (1994).

[85] Article 6 of the Protocol on the Convergence Criteria referred to in Article 109j of the EC Treaty reads: "The Council shall, acting unanimously on a proposal from the Commission and after consulting the European Parliament, the EMI or the ECB as the case may be, and the Committee referred to in Article 109c, adopt appropriate provisions to lay down the details of the convergence criteria referred to in Article 109j of this Treaty, which shall then replace this Protocol". Reproduced at 33 ILM 353 (1994).

margins provided for by the Exchange Rate Mechanism of the European Monetary System, for at least two years, without devaluing against the currency of any other Member State; and the durability of convergence achieved by the Member State and of its participation in the exchange rate mechanism of the European Monetary System being reflected in the long-term interest rate levels. According to article 109j of the EC Treaty the Council decides by a qualified majority, among other things, whether it is appropriate for the Community to enter the third stage and, if so, set the date for the beginning of the third stage. Thereby, the Council "takes due account of the reports" by the Commission and the European Monetary Institute on the convergence criteria specified in the Protocol on the Convergence Criteria. According to the already mentioned article 6 of this Protocol, the Council can only replace the convergence criteria laid down in the Protocol unanimously. From this requirement of unanimity, the Federal Constitutional Court concludes, in a complicated operation, that there can be no relaxation of the convergence criteria without German consent and thus not without substantial participation of the German Federal Parliament.

The Federal Court's reasoning is complicated and not totally convincing. The Council only has to take "due account" of the reports on the convergence criteria in the framework of its *majority decision* on entrance into the third stage (article 109j, para. 3 of EC Treaty). Moreover, as to the convergence criteria, we are dealing with economic facts. The evaluation of economic facts is not fully justiciable. It will also be important who decides. The Federal Constitutional Court tries very hard to minimise these imponderables and thus concludes that the German Federal Parliament has sufficient control with respect to the strict convergence criteria.[86]

Interpreting the provisions on the monetary union, the Federal Constitutional Court tried very hard to avoid conflicts between German constitutional law and European law (i.e. international law). Such conflicts could only be resolved by the precedence of either national or international/European law. European law requires precedence, but national constitutional law cannot totally give way to supra-national law as long as the Communities are not a Federal state with *Kompetenz-Kompetenz*. The interpretational endeavours of the Federal Constitutional Court have to be seen against this background. Once the Court had accepted the constitutional complaint alleging violation of the principle of democracy, it was feared that the Federal Constitutional Court might require the Federal Government to renegotiate the

---

[86] 33 ILM 436 (1994): "In conclusion, the Federal Republic of Germany is not, by ratifying the Maastricht Treaty, subjecting itself to an uncontrollable, unforeseeable process which will lead inexorably towards monetary union; the Maastricht Treaty simply paves the way for gradual further integration of the European Communities as a community of laws. Every further step along this way is dependent either upon conditions being fulfilled by the parliament which can already be foreseen, or upon further consent from the Federal Government, which consent is subject to parliamentary influence. Even after transition to the third stage, development of the monetary union is subject to foreseeable standards and thus to parliamentary accountability".

provisions on the monetary union or even to make a reservation as the United Kingdom and Denmark did. The Court's approach to interpret the provisions on the monetary union to make them constitutional was the alternative to these further reaching possibilities. It could be seen as an effort of the Federal Constitutional Court to co-operate in European integration.

(iii) Withdrawal from the community of stability.

The Protocol on the Transition to the Third Stage of Economic and Monetary Union underlines "the irreversible character of the Community's movement to the third stage of Economic and Monetary Union."[87] According to article 109l, para. 4 of the Treaty, the Council "shall adopt the conversion rates at which the currencies of member states shall be irrevocably fixed and at which irrevocably fixed rate the ECU shall be substituted for these currencies". This would suggest that at least a unilateral withdrawal from the monetary union is inadmissible.[88] For the Federal Constitutional Court, respect for the convergence criteria, which have to be understood strictly, is vital to the question of withdrawal. The Court states:

"The Maastricht Treaty sets long-term standards which establish the goal of stability as the yardstick by which the monetary union is to be measured, which endeavour, by institutional provisions, to ensure that these objectives are fulfilled, and which finally do not stand in the way of withdrawal from the Community as a last resort if it proves impossible to achieve the stability sought".[89]

and:

"This concept of the monetary union as a community of stability is the basis and object of the German Act of Accession. If the monetary union were not able to continually develop that stability existing upon transition to the third stage as provided by the mandate of stability which has been agreed upon, it would move away from the concept upon which the Maastricht Treaty is based".[90]

The future economic development cannot be predicted even if the Treaty and the relevant protocols contain many provisions on stability. Therefore, the Federal Constitutional Court takes into account the eventuality of failure of the community of stability. Especially the second passage quoted suggests the invocation of rules like fundamental change of circumstances, *clausula rebus sic stantibus* or frustration. According to article 62 of the Vienna Convention on the Law of Treaties:

[87] Protocol, reproduced at 33 ILM 355 (1994).

[88] But see C. Tomuschat, "Die Europäische Union unter der Aufsicht des Bundesverfassungsgerichts", 20 *EuGRZ* 489, 495, note 33 (1993). According to Tomuschat, denunciation of or withdrawal from the monetary union is admissible pursuant to article 56 of the Vienna Convention on the Law of Treaties. Article 56 reads: "(1) A treaty which contains no provision regardings its termination and which does not provide for denunciation or withdrawal is not subject to denunciation or withdrawal unless: (a) it is established that the parties intended to admit the possibility of denunciation or withdrawal; or (b) a right of denunciation or withdrawal may be implied by the nature of the treaty".

[89] 33 ILM 436 (1994).

[90] 33 ILM 437 (1994).

"a fundamental change of circumstances which has occurred with regard to those existing at the time of the conclusion of a treaty, and which was not foreseen by the parties, may not be invoked as a ground for terminating or withdrawing from the Treaty unless: (a) the existence of those circumstances constituted an essential basis of the consent of the parties to be bound by the Treaty; and (b) the effect of the change is radically to transform the obligations still to be performed under the Treaty".

These are very strict requirements. The rule on fundamental change of circumstances plays no role in State practice. Moreover, it would not be easy for Germany to maintain that a potential relaxation of the convergence criteria is a fundamental change of circumstances from an objective perspective. If, according to article 109j of the EC Treaty, Member States evaluate economic facts by majority, it seems natural that not necessarily the especially strict requirements of Germany will prevail. It would thus be difficult for Germany to withdraw from the monetary union unilaterally.

Whether it would be compatible with European and international law to withdraw from the monetary union by mutual consent is another question. The Protocol on the Transition to the Third Stage of Economic and Monetary Union underlines "the irreversible character of the Community's movement to the third stage of Economic and Monetary Union", and speaks against dissolution by mutual consent. The monetary union appears as an essential further development of the founding Treaties which are "concluded for an unlimited period".[91] On the other hand, the United Kingdom has made substantial reservations to the provisions on the monetary union.[92] By accepting these reservations, the other Member States showed that they consider these reservations as compatible with the object and purpose of the Treaty.[93] The better reasons probably speak for the admissibility of withdrawal from the monetary union by mutual consent. This is even true if one adheres to the view that withdrawal from the Communities by mutual consent is excluded on account of the stage of integration now reached.

The Federal Constitutional Court's explanations on withdrawal from the "community of stability" interpret the Treaty to make it constitutional. At the same time they underline the importance of strictly adhering to the convergence criteria. In this sense they could be understood as an appeal to the Community institutions and to the other Member States. The Federal Constitutional Court constitutionalised the convergence criteria; transgressing the convergence criteria would be an undemocratic *ultra vires* act. In the same judgment, the Court emphasised the Communities' duty to take the constitutional interests of the Member States into account. Thus, in a certain way,

---

[91] Cf. article Q of the Treaty establishing the European Union. Reproduced at 31 ILM 331 (1992).

[92] Cf. Protocol on Certain Provisions Relating to the United Kingdom of Great Britain and Northern Ireland, 33 ILM 355 (1994).

[93] Cf. article 19 of the Vienna Convention on the Law of Treaties.

even the Court's explanations on monetary union can be seen in the larger context of co-operation and dialogue between Community institutions and the Federal Constitutional Court.

Conclusion

The above shows that the importance of the *Maastricht* decision does not lie in a change of the jurisprudence of the Federal Constitutional Court on the problem of *Kompetenz-Kompetenz*. The Court did not doctrinally change grounds from the earlier decision involving *Kompetenz-Kompetenz*; in fact, it never recognised *Kompetenz-Kompetenz* as lying with the Community. What makes the *Maastricht* decision special is the detailed discussion of various provisions of the Maastricht Treaty to find out whether they constitute a transfer of *Kompetenz-Kompetenz* to the Communities, thus violating the Federal Parliament's prerogatives. The Maastricht decision can be seen as indicating how the Federal Constitutional Court may, in future, exercise an additional control over the development of Community law, notably whether Community organs have transgressed their authority.

The second point of importance is the Federal Constitutional Court's view of democracy as presupposing a parliament with substantive powers. This in turn requires that a transfer of sovereign powers to an inter-governmental organisation under the new article 23, para. 1 of the Basic Law is limited. Moreover, if the German Parliament empowered the European Communities unrestrictedly, Germany would lose its statehood[94] according to the traditional concept of sovereignty adopted by the Court. This is a consequence that the Basic Law in its present form does not provide for. A sovereign state is characterised by its *Kompetenz-Kompetenz*: if the Maastricht Treaty had given the European Communities *Kompetenz-Kompetenz*, this would have been unconstitutional under German law.[95] Therefore, in the reasoning of the Constitutional Court, reserving its right to review whether Community organs have acted *ultra vires* is a precondition to finding ratification of the Maastricht Treaty constitutional. The *Kompetenz-Kompetenz* of Germany as opposed to the *Kompetenz-Kompetenz* of the Communities implies, according to this logic, that national authorities, i.e. the Federal Constitutional Court, and not supra-national organs (i.e. the ECJ) decide on the applicability of *ultra vires* acts in Germany.

[94] For a more restricted view see K. Meessen, "Hedging European Integration: The Maastricht-Judgment of the Federal Constitutional Court of Germany", 17 *Fordham Int'l Law Journal* 490, 519 (1994): The loss of competences of the Federal Parliament can be compensated by an increase in the competences of the European Parliament.

[95] See also B. Kahl, "Europäische Union: Bundesstaat—Staatenbund—Staatenverbund", in 33 *Der Staat* 241, 246 *et seq* (1994).

The European Court and national courts

The German Federal Constitutional Court's "co-operative relationship" with the ECJ[96]

According to the founding Treaties, the ECJ decides authoritatively on the interpretation of Community law. However, this monopoly of the ECJ has been challenged and qualified by the highest national courts of some Member States claiming their jurisdiction to control whether Community acts remain within the constitutional authorisation. Pursuant to this approach by the Federal Constitutional Court, only acts within constitutional authorization benefit from the supremacy of Community law.[97] This conflicts with the position of the ECJ under Community law.

Until the *Maastricht* judgment, the Federal Constitutional Court held that it could only control the constitutionality of acts or emanations of the German government.[98] The Federal Constitutional Court reviewed the German implementation acts to acts of the Communities directly; the corresponding Community acts, however, were subject to an indirect control. The German Federal Constitutional Court reversed this jurisprudence in its judgment on the Maastricht Treaty saying:

> "Acts of the particular public power of a supranational organisation which is separate from the State power of the member states may also affect those persons protected by the basic rights in Germany. Such acts therefore affect the guarantees provided under the Basic Law and the duties of the Federal Constitutional Court, which include the protection of basic rights in Germany, and not only in respect of German governmental institutions (BVerfGE 58, 1, 27 reversed). However, the Federal Constitutional Court exercises its jurisdiction regarding the applicability of derivative Community law in Germany in a 'cooperative relationship' with the ECJ".[99]

According to the Federal Constitutional Court, "the ECJ guarantees the protection of basic rights in each individual case for the entire area of the European Communities; the Federal Constitutional Court can therefore limit itself to a general guarantee of mandatory standards of basic rights". Here, the Federal Constitutional Court refers to the already cited passage of *Solange II* saying that it was not shown that the ECJ was absolutely or generally unable or unwilling to recognise or protect the basic rights of the com-

---

[96] For a general evaluation see H. Gersdorf, "Das Kooperationsverhältnis zwischen deutscher Gerichtsbarkeit und EuGH", 24 *DVBl* 674 (1994).

[97] Cf. R. Streinz, *Bundesverfassungsgerichtlicher Grundrechtsschutz und Europäisches Gemeinschaftsrecht* 128 (1989).

[98] Cf. 58 BVerfGE 1, 27 (1981) EUROCONTROL.

[99] 33 ILM 388, 396 (1994). However, the author translated "*Abweichung von BVerfGE 58, 1, 27*" with "BVerfGE 58, 1, 27 reversed" instead of "notwithstanding BVerfGE 58, 1, 27" which is the ILM version.

[100] 73 BVerfGE 339, 387 (1986) and see p. 88 above.

plainant.[100] Thus, the Federal Constitutional Court tries to put its *Maastricht* decision in the tradition of the *Solange II* decision. The Federal Constitutional Court's ruling on the non-binding character of *ultra vires* acts must be seen in this relatively restrictive context. From the *Maastricht* decision, it should be clear that only the Federal Constitutional Court and no other German state authority can decide on the non-binding character of a piece of Community legislation,[101] and the Constitutional Court would do so only in exceptional cases.

The Federal Constitutional Court's *dictum* must not be misunderstood in the sense that, now, any German state organ, any court or any agency may challenge the validity of Community acts.[102] Such an approach would lead to the fragmentation of Community law. The context of the Court's statements on the non-binding force of *ultra vires* acts of the Communities leaves no room for an interpretation challenging the Federal Constitutional Court's monopoly on decisions regarding the validity of Community acts.[103]

The Federal Constitutional Court affirms that there is a mutual relationship of co-operation between the Communities and the Member States. Member States must not only fulfill their obligations under Community law. Rather, the Communities are also under a duty to take the constitutional interest of Member States into account. The fundamental rights jurisprudence of the ECJ is seen partly as a reaction to the German *Solange I* decision. The "co-operative relationship" with the ECJ is also directed toward the mutual influence of the European Court and of the constitutional courts of Member States. The ECJ may dislike this. But, against that, the Federal Constitutional Court points to the *Kompetenz-Kompetenz*, which is still with the Member States.

The concept of a co-operative relationship between the constitutional courts of the Member States and the ECJ is not new. Frowein, in 1976, diagnosed a co-operative relationship between the ECJ and the constitutional courts of Member States in the *mélanges* for the Federal Constitutional Court.[104] Many share the opinion that the German Constitutional Court's *Solange I* decision substantially influenced the fundamental rights jurisprudence of the ECJ.[105] In this respect, it should be noted that the co-operative relationship is not a one-way street. The "Maybe" decision is a clear example of how the Federal Constitutional Court responded in a positive way to the ECJ's growing human rights jurisprudence. This respect of the ECJ for

---

[101] Cf. 33 ILM 388, 423 (1994).

[102] But see C. Tomuschat, "Die Europäische Union unter der Aufsicht des Bundesverfassungsgerichts", 20 *EuGRZ* 489, 494 (1993).

[103] Cf. J. Kokott, "Deutschland im Rahmen der Europäischen Union—zum Vertrag von Maastricht", 119 *AöR* 207, 218–20 (1994).

[104] J. Frowein, "Europäisches Gemeinschaftsrecht und Bundesverfassungsgericht", in: C. Starck (ed.), *Bundesverfassungsgericht und Grundgesetz, Festgabe aus Anlaß des 25 jährigen Bestehens des Bundesverfassungsgerichts* 187, 212 (1976).

[105] Cf. n. 164 below; for the opposite view see U. Everling, "Das Maastricht-Urteil des Bundesverfassungsgerichts und seine Bedeutung für die Entwicklung der Europäischen Union", 17 *Integration* 165, 171 (1994).

the Constitutional Court's concern with human rights can be seen as an engagement in a co-operative relationship with the Constitutional Court, which constituted the underlying motivation for the latter's decision to recognize the ECJ's exclusive competence in interpreting Community law. The Federal Constitutional Court may have hoped to again influence the ECJ by "*Solange III*". This time, the Federal Constitutional Court's concern was not only fundamental rights, but more generally the dynamic activism of the Luxembourg Court. One might argue that here, as in the "Maybe" decision, the Federal Constitutional Court tries to establish a co-operative relationship with the ECJ to arrive at a division of competences between the two courts in order to preserve what is regarded as fundamental to the political system of Germany.[106]

The Federal Constitutional Court—last instance in disputes on foreign relations politics?

The Federal Constitutional Court is often reproached as taking over competences of other branches of government by setting detailed limits to future government action that leave little or no room to manoeuvre. Mindful of that criticism, the Court tried in the *Maastricht* decision to assure itself of wide support for its judgment while respecting the political decision taken by Parliament.[107]

The main way by which the Court sought support is its emphasis on the constitutionality of the envisaged monetary union. After the elaboration of the Maastricht Treaty, there was widespread fear within Germany that the monetary union would weaken the German currency. This special attachment of the German population to a strong currency stems from the historical experience of currency reforms in Germany entailing the loss of life-long earnings. In addition, the strength of the Deutsche Mark is considered by many as a achievement of post-war Germany which should not be given up lightly.[108] One should bear in mind that with the unification of Germany and the currency union preceding it, the population of the former German Democratic Republic experienced a devaluation, albeit nominal, of their earnings[109] while the population of the former Federal Republic feared inflation through a rise

---

[106] Cf. O. Schneider, "Der Vertrag von Maastricht vor dem Bundesverfassungsgericht", 3/1994 *Europablätter* 67, 78.

[107] For the—mainly positive—reactions to the decision see I. Winkelmann (ed.), *Das Maastricht-Urteil des Bundesverfassungsgerichts vom 12. Oktober 1993*, p. 61 *et seq* (1994).

[108] J. Wieland even goes so far as to say that "to the general public, the Mark is a foundation of the Republic which is perhaps more important than the Constitution itself", cf. J. Wieland, "Germany in the European Union—The Maastricht Decision of the Bundesverfassungsgericht", 5 *EJIL* 259, 260 (1994).

[109] Despite the fact that the lack of purchasing power of the East German currency (Mark der DDR) was notorious, the psychological impact of giving up one's currency was such as to prohibit a political decision in favour of economically sound exchange rates. One relevant factor may also have been that in the GDR the official exchange rate between the two German currencies had been 1:1.

in money necessary to cope with unification. Thus, political support for the anti-*Maastricht* forces grew. It was within this context that the Federal Constitutional Court rendered its *Maastricht* decision. This background explains why the Court elaborated in detail on the question of monetary union and why it emphasised the significance of the convergence criteria by making them a precondition for the constitutionality of the Maastricht Treaty.

The *Maastricht* decision is another good example of how the Federal Constitutional Court copes with the German tendency to constitutionalise foreign policy questions. Perhaps more than in other countries with a constitutional court, a defeated opposition will try to have the political decision overturned by the Constitutional Court. To some extent, this is due to the fact that the Federal Constitutional Court does not apply the "political question" doctrine. Every constitutional law question must be answered by the Court as long as the procedural requirements are fulfilled. Especially with the procedure of abstract norm control[110] (i.e. the control of the constitutionality of a norm unrelated to a concrete case before a court, which can be instituted by a political party constituting one-third of the MPs in the Bundestag) a law adopted can be subjected to constitutional scrutiny. Yet it is not only due to constitutional procedure that the Federal Constitutional Court is called upon to decide politically controversial questions. To a great extent, the national identity of post-war Germany is founded on and shaped by the Constitution. Instead of an identity based on the nation state, discredited by the Nazis, the Federal Republic of Germany developed a "constitutional patriotism" (*Verfassungspatriotismus*), i.e. a pride in the values protected by the Constitution and the established political system. The Basic Law is considered a major achievement in overcoming Germany's undemocratic past. Therefore, respect for the Constitution is indispensable and has to be ensured to prevent even the appearance of a relapse to that past. This concern is also the reason why the political discussion, especially in delicate questions, cannot focus openly on national interests, as they are seen as a return to mere power politics associated with Germany's recent history. Instead, the constitutionality of the measure envisaged is regarded as being decisive.

These are some of the reasons why the Constitutional Court has been called upon to decide the most controversial political decisions, such as the deployment of nuclear missiles within Germany in the 1980s, or more recently the participation of the German Bundeswehr in the United Nations' Somalia mission, or the engagement of the Bundeswehr in NATO actions concerning former Yugoslavia.[111] As to the *Maastricht* decision, the Court had to take into

---

[110] Article 93, para. 2: "The Federal Constitutional Court decides in disputes or cases of doubt concerning the formal or material compatibility of federal statutes or statutes of the Länder with this Basic Law . . . upon the application by the Federal Government, the government of a Land or one third of the members of the Federal Parliament".

[111] 90 BVerfGE 286 (1994).

account the widespread Euro-scepticism that had replaced the eu(ro)phoria of the 1980s. The judgment shows how the Court tried to steer a course between the two positions taken by the German public: on the one hand, the demands to declare the Maastricht Treaty not compatible with the Basic Law, so that at least a re-negotiation of the Treaty would have been necessary, and the position that the Treaty should be ratified without any conditions attached so that the development towards an "ever closer union" could continue. While respecting the political position taken by the German Parliament which had, through the ratification law to the Maastricht Treaty, opted in favour of the latter position, the Court nevertheless took the objections seriously by using them to ensure that major future changes in the conception of the division of competences between the European Communities and the Member States will be subjected to both parliamentary control and that of the Federal Constitutional Court.

The interplay of Community law and national law in the jurisprudence of other German courts

The jurisprudence of the Federal Constitutional Court has generally remained unopposed by other German courts. Courts have accepted the supremacy of Community law and the ECJ's exclusive competence to interpret Community law.[112] They widely make use of the procedure to request a preliminary ruling under article 177 of the EC Treaty. However, recently, the Federal Labour Court (Bundesarbeitsgericht) has begun to use this procedure to force the ECJ to reconsider decisions that even the traditionally employee-friendly Labour Court regards as being too far-reaching. In one case the Labour Court explicitly stated that it requested a preliminary ruling because it did not envisage that it would follow the jurisprudence of the ECJ. This refers to the case of *Bötel* in which the European Court had ruled that a part-time employee has to be paid for the time spent on the employees' council even though the meetings had taken place outside the employee's working hours.[113] That decision was heavily criticised by German scholars for not taking into account that under German law membership in the employees' council is a honorary, non-paid function. The ECJ's interpretation of EC law amounts to a change of character of that function.[114] The Labour Court shares this criticism of the ECJ; in its view, the European Court seems to have misunderstood the German law background.[115] In its request for a preliminary ruling in a simi-

---

[112] Cf. as recent examples BAG, Decision of 9 October 1991, 45 NJW 1125, 1127 (1992); 87 BVerwGE 154 (1990), 158; BGH (private law matter), Decision of 8 March 1990, 44 NJW 651, 652 (1991); BGH (penal law matter), Decision of 31 January 1989, 42 NJW 1437 (1989).

[113] Decision of 4 June 1992, Case No. C-360/90, 9 NZA 687 (1992).

[114] See for criticism, e.g. A. Junker, "Der EuGH im Arbeitsrecht—Die schwarze Serie geht weiter", 47 NJW 2527, 2528 (1994); W. Blomeyer, "Der Einfluß der Rechtsprechung des EuGH auf das deutsche Arbeitsrecht", 11 NZA 633, 637 (1994).

[115] BAG, Decision of 20 October 1993, 11 NZA 278, 279 (1994).

lar case, the Labour Court explicitly asked whether Community law prohibits the institution of an honorary membership in the employees' council.[116] This question is rightly translated by a critic as meaning "Do you really believe the *Bötel* decision is correct?"[117]

A second case in point is the case of *Paletta*. Several years in a row, the family of Mr. Paletta had fallen ill at the end of their holiday in their home town in Italy. His employer refused to pay the salary during the time of the employee's illness because he did not accept the Italian medical certificates produced by Mr. Paletta. The ECJ ruled that the medical findings are binding upon the employer if they are made by an authority of the employee's place of residence.[118] The strong criticism that this decision encountered was based on the fact that the ECJ seemed to exclude any effective means against abuse of the right to continued salary in the case of an illness.[119] Sharing this concern, the Federal Labour Court referred the same case to the ECJ again, explaining that this extensive interpretation of the ECJ's decision would amount to a violation of the principle of proportionality.[120] By submitting the same case to the European Court a second time, the critical attitude of the Federal Labour Court towards the ECJ is even more obvious than in the *Bötel* case.

This development can be seen as an attempt by the Labour Court to establish its own "co-operative relationship" with the ECJ. The Court attempts to enter into a dialogue on the interpretation of Community law by pointing out the municipal law background of a question and by stressing that the consequences of a chosen interpretation have to be taken into account. This reflects an increased sense of self-consciousness by the Labour Court, which does not see itself in an inferior position *vis-à-vis* the ECJ and which asserts its own right and obligation to ensure a coherent national legal system.

It should be noted that in the field of labour law the Federal Labour Court was not the first German court to use the procedure of preliminary ruling to harmonise national and European law. Already in 1991, two labour courts of first instance had requested the ECJ to reconsider its rulings dealing with the succession in labour contracts through the sale of an enterprise. Under German law, employees have the right to challenge the transfer of an enterprise.[121] According to the established case law of the Federal Labour Court, the legal consequence of that challenge is that the seller remains bound by the existing labour contract between the employees and the transferring enter-

---

[116] *Ibid.* at 278.

[117] A. Junker, "Der EuGH im Arbeitsrecht—Die schwarze Serie geht weiter", 47 NJW 2527, 2528 (1994).

[118] *Alberto Paletta et al.*, Case No. C-45/90, Decision of 3 June 1992, 45 NJW 2687 (1992).

[119] See, e.g. A. Junker, "Der EuGH im Arbeitsrecht—Die schwarze Serie geht weiter", 47 NJW 2527, 2527 (1994); W. Blomeyer, "Der Einfluß der Rechtsprechung des EuGH auf das deutsche Arbeitsrecht", 11 NZA 633, 639 (1994).

[120] BAG, Decision of 27 April 1994, 11 NZA 683 (1994).

[121] Sect. 613a of the Civil Code (*Bürgerliches Gesetzbuch*, BGB).

[122] See, e.g., Decision of 30 October 1986, 4 NZA 524 (1987).

prise.[122] The ECJ, however, held that despite the employee's challenge to the sale the seller is freed of any obligation under the existing labour contract.[123] Upon the referrals of the two lower labour courts, the ECJ distinguished its prior case law and in effect reversed its rulings as requested by the Federal Labour Court.[124]

As the criticism of the European Court's decisions mounts, one can expect that the Labour Court will continue its dialogue with the ECJ in this manner, especially in cases where the latter's decisions summarily abolish an elaborate and long-standing case law of the Federal Labour Court. A case in point could be the transfer of parts of enterprises. According to the jurisprudence of the ECJ, such a transfer takes place even when merely a task that used to be fulfilled by a single person is transferred to another enterprise.[125] The result is that the employee by law becomes an employee of the enterprise to which the task has been transferred. In contrast to the Federal Labour Court's case law, no additional condition has to be met, such as the transfer of specific means to fulfil the task or of the pre-existing organisational structure.[126] There are already calls for further requests for preliminary rulings to bring about changes or limitations of the European Court's interpretation in this matter.[127] A comparable situation is developing with regard to the ECJ's jurisprudence concerning factual discrimination. According to the ECJ, there is factual discrimination if a provision negatively affects a significantly higher percentage of women than of men and if it cannot be proved that there are objective reasons for this distinction.[128] The ECJ has, for example, extended the right to continued salary in case of illness to part-time workers who are mainly

---

[123] Case of *Berg et al.*, Cases No. C-144/87 and C-145/87, Decision of 5 May 1988, 7 NZA 885 (1990).

[124] Case of *Katsikas et al.*, Cases No. C-132/91, C-138/91, C-139/91, Decision of 16 December 1992, 10 NZA 169 (1993). Thus, a similar request under article 177 instituted by the Federal Labour Court (Decision of 21 May 1992, 3 EuZW 739 (1993)) became obsolete.

[125] Case of *Christel Schmidt/Spar- und Leihkasse der früheren Ämter Bordesholm, Kiel und Cronshagen*, Decision of 14 April 1994, 11 NZA 545 (1994). The case concerned a cleaning woman who was in charge of the premises of a small bank branch. The bank wanted to extend its general contract with a cleaning company to this branch as well. The cleaning enterprise offered Ms Schmidt to work for them, but she refused to do so because she considered the conditions of the new contract to be less favourable than those of the old contract. Therefore, she asked the courts to find that there was a transfer of a part of the bank's enterprise, so that her contract with the bank now extended by law to the cleaning company. But see more restrictively, Court of Justice of the European Communities, Case C-298/94 of 15 October 1996, *Henke/Gemeinde Schierke u. Verwaltungsgemeinschaft "Brocken"*, 7 EuZW 734 (1996); Case C-13/95 of 11 March 1997, *Süzen/Zehnacker Gebäudereinigung GmbH Krankenhausservice Lefahrt GmbH*.

[126] See. e.g. BAG, Decision of 4 March 1993, 11 NZA 260 (1994); further references in G. Röder/U. Baeck, "EuGH: Funktionsnachfolge als Betriebsübergang", 11 *NZA* 542, 543 (1994).

[127] BAG, Order of 21 March 1996, 8 AZR 156/96 (A), 8 EuZW 92 (1997). See also A. Junker, "Der EuGH im Arbeitsrecht—Die schwarze Serie geht weiter", 47 NJW 2527, 2528 (1994); G. Röder/U. Baeck, "EuGH: Funktionsnachfolge als Betriebsübergang", 11 *NZA* 542, 544 (1994). For the ECJ's reaction see now *Süzen* Case No. C-13/95, Decision of 11 March 1997, ECJ 1997, 1259.

[128] *Bilka*, Case No. C-170/84, Decision of 13 May 1986, 3 NZA 599 (1986).

[129] *Rinner-Kühn*, Case No. C-171/88, Decision of 13 July 1989, 7 NZA 437 (1990).

women,[129] and has ruled that the employer cannot renounce a contract with a woman on the grounds that her pregnancy (unknown at the time of conclusion of the contract) prevents her by law from fulfilling her contractual obligation to work at night[130] or from replacing another pregnant worker.[131] Critics of this case law see this as an attempt to realise social policy objectives—for which the Community does not have competence—through the labour law competences of the EC.[132] It is also feared that the increase in social benefits accorded to holders of part-time jobs will render these jobs too costly, especially for small enterprises. Hiring women might thus become an unbearable economic burden if there are no compensatory measures taken on the national level.[133] This might have the result that by increasing the legal protection of women, especially in part-time jobs, the number of such jobs will decrease, so that the aim pursued is thwarted by the means employed. These examples show that the impact of Community law on the German legal order is increasingly noticed, and that the legal community becomes aware of the potential of a "co-operative relationship" with the ECJ.

The one court that for a long time adhered to its own jurisprudence on the relationship of Community law and national law is the Federal Tax Court (Bundesfinanzhof). The first case relevant to this question was decided by the Tax Court in 1968.[134] The case concerned the legal consequences of a Community regulation within the Member States. Basing its reasoning on the ECJ's jurisprudence on the autonomous character of EC law, the Tax Court concluded that it was the task of the separate Member States' courts to resolve the conflict between the Community law norm and the national norm.[135] The Tax Court decided that there was only a priority in application, not in validity—a qualification shared by the Federal Constitutional Court in its 1971 decision. However, the Tax Court, again pre-empting the Constitutional Court's jurisprudence, indicated that in specific cases, provisions of the Basic Law, in particular basic rights, can hinder the application of a Community regulation.[136] As to the autonomy of Community law, the Federal Tax Court underlines that this "autonomy" is created by the transfer of powers to the

---

[130] *Habermann-Beltermann/Arbeiterwohlfahrt*, Case No. C-421/92, Decision of 5 May 1994, 11 NZA 609 (1994).

[131] *Webb/EMO Air Cargo AUK'S Ltd*, Case No. C-32/93, Decision of 14 July 1994, 11 NZA 783 (1994). However, the ECJ's decision might have been less employee-friendly, had the replacing worker's contract not been concluded for an unlimited period.

[132] W. Blomeyer, "Der Einfluß der Rechtsprechung des EuGH auf das deutsche Arbeitsrecht", 11 NZA 633, 638 (1994).

[133] Cf. B. Waas, "Zur mittelbaren Diskriminierung von Frauen in der Rechtsprechung von EuGH und deutschen Gerichten", 29 *EuR* 97, 100 (1994) and J. Kokott, "Zur Gleichstellung von Mann und Frau—Deutsches Verfassungsrecht und Europäisches Gemeinschaftsrecht", 41 *NJW* 1049 (1995). It remains to be seen, how far the ECJ will be willing to accept the protection of small enterprises as a justification of factual discrimination, as indicated in *Kirsammer-Hack/Nurhan Sidal*, Case No. C-189/91, Decision of 30 November 1993, EWS 61 (1994).

[134] 93 BFHE 102 (1968).

[135] BFH *ibid*. at 102, first operative paragraph.

[136] BFH *ibid*. at 108.

European Communities under article 24, para. 1 of the Basic Law. Therefore, the Tax Court considers itself obliged to control whether this transfer is valid under the Basic Law.[137] Although the Tax Court found no such violation of the Constitution, a veiled reference to the "eternal guarantee-clause" of article 79, para. 3 of the Basic Law shows what the Court intended as the standard to be applied. This jurisprudence was confirmed in a decision[138] shortly thereafter, and was accepted by lower tax courts.[139]

The extent to which the Federal Tax Court reserved its right to control the constitutionality of Community law became clear in the 1981 decision on the direct applicability of directives.[140] The Court rejected the ECJ's jurisprudence in that matter by arguing that the transfer of powers under article 24, para. 1 of the Basic Law did not include legislative competences in the field of turnover taxes. The direct effect of a directive on that tax would, however, amount to such a competence. Considering the wording of the EC Treaty as being clear, the Tax Court concluded that the pertinent jurisprudence of the ECJ was not valid within the German legal order. With this reasoning, the Court explicitly supported the position of the French Conseil d'Etat.[141] What the Court did, in fact, was not an interpretation of the German act of accession under article 24, para. 1, but of the EC Treaty itself. Thus, it encroached upon the exclusive domain of the ECJ. Despite the criticism that the decision encountered,[142] the Federal Tax Court repeated its position in 1985.[143] This time, it became clear that the Tax Court interpreted article 24, para. 1 of the Basic Law as allowing a transfer of powers to an inter-governmental institution only insofar as the future development of that institution is foreseeable.[144] This reasoning resembles that of the Federal Constitutional Court in the *Maastricht* decision and shows a certain uneasiness at the progressive development of Community law by the ECJ. The decision was rightly criticised because of disregard for the ECJ's exclusive competence under article 177 of the EC Treaty.[145] The decision of the Federal Constitutional Court of 1987,[146] by which it ruled that the Tax Court's decision not to request a preliminary ruling violated the right to a lawful judge, effectively ended this controversy.

[137]   BFH *ibid.* at 107.
[138]   93 BFHE 405 (1968).
[139]   See, e.g. FG Münster, Decision of 6 November 1968, 17 EFG 160 (1969); FG Hamburg, Decision of 30 January 1970, 18 EFG 263 (1970); FG Baden-Württemberg, Decision of 29 April 1970, 18 EFG 367 (1970).
[140]   BFH, Decision of 16 July 1981, 16 EuR 442 (1981).
[141]   BFH *ibid.* at 443.
[142]   Cf., e.g. E. Millarg, casenote to BFH Decision of 16 July 1981, 16 EuR 444 (1981).
[143]   143 BFHE 383 (1985).
[144]   BFH *ibid.* at 387.
[145]   Cf. S. Magiera, "Die Rechtswirkungen von EG-Richtlinien im Konflikt zwischen Bundesfinanzhof und Europäischem Gerichtshof", 38 *DÖV* 937, 940 (1985); C. Tomuschat, "Nein, und abermals Nein!," 20 *EuR* 364, 351 (1985).
[146]   73 BVerfGE 339 (1986).

However, the ECJ's "Banana Judgment"[147]—in the aftermath of the *Maastricht* decision by the German Federal Constitutional Court—encouraged new opposition by courts.[148] According to the Federal Tax Court, the European banana market order may violate supreme international law, i.e. the GATT and the WTO Agreement. German courts must review such violations, according to the Federal Tax Court, even though the ECJ affirmed the banana market order as corresponding to Community law. The Federal Tax Court quotes the *Maastricht* decision according to which German courts may not apply *ultra vires* acts of the Community.[149]

What remains is the question of the underlying reasons for the Tax Court's decisions. The distrust towards the ECJ's approach of "integration through law jurisprudence" has already been mentioned. Another reason seems to be a power struggle between the Federal Tax Court and the ECJ. In an early decision, the Tax Court had in a request for a preliminary ruling criticised the ECJ for demanding from national courts that they ensure the fulfilment of the EC Treaty through decisions in individual cases, although there were other means provided for by the Treaty.[150] This shows that the Tax Court did not want to be turned into a mere assistant to the ECJ but tried to reserve its own independence through exclusive competences for itself. Interestingly, although the Federal Constitutional Court overruled the Tax Court, it finally arrived at a similar position. Yet, the main difference between the jurisprudence of both courts is that the Constitutional Court limits its own control to extreme cases of *ultra vires* acts of Community organs.[151]

"La Doctrine" *and its impact on the Federal Constitutional Court*

The most important landmark decisions in Germany are *Solange I*, *Solange II* and the recent *Maastricht* decision, all by the Federal Constitutional Court. These decisions, even though not inconsistent, manifest different approaches to European integration. They can be explained in the context of the politico-

---

[147] Judgment of 5 October 1994, Case C-280/93, *Federal Republic of Germany* v. *Council* [1994] ECRI-4973, ECJ; see also judgments of 11 November 1995, Case C-466/93, *Atlanta Fruchthandelsgesellschaft mbH et al.* v. *Bundesamt für Ernährung und Forstwirtschaft*, 22 EUGRZ 605. The German Federal Constitutional Court seems to be slightly more open to the concerns of the banana importers, cf. Order of 25 January 1995—2 BvR 2689/94 et al.—, 22 EuGRZ 170 (1995). But see recently, European Court of Justice, C-68/95, 8 EuZW 61 (1997).

[148] VG Frankfurt, Orders of 24 October 1996—1 E 798/95 (V) a. 1 E 2949/93 (V), 8 EuZW 182 (1997); see also Federal Tax Court, Order of 2 April 1996—VII R 119/94, 7 EuZW 668 (1996).

[149] Cf. Federal Tax Court, Order of 9 January 1996, VII B 225/95, 7 *EuZW* 126, 128 (1996). On the controversy relating to the European banana market order, see also H.-D. Kuschel, "Wie geht es weiter mit der Bananenmaktordnung", 7 *EuZW* 645 (1996); A. Weber, "Die Bananenmarktordnung unter Aufsicht des BVerfG?", 8 *EuZW* 165 (1997).

[150] BFH, Decision of 18 July 1967, 2 EuR 360 (1967).

[151] However, Meessen maintains that today the Federal Constitutional Court regrets having overruled the Tax Court, see K. Meessen, "Hedging European Integration: The Maastricht-Judgment of the Federal Constitutional Court of Germany", 17 *Fordham Int'l Law Journal* 510, 520 (1994).

doctrinal contexts of their time and in the framework of the Federal Constitutional Court's "co-operative relationship" with the ECJ.

Solange I. The Federal Republic of Germany considers the protection of the basic rights guaranteed in the Basic Law as probably the major asset of the "new" post-Third Reich Germany.[152] After the Second World War, Germany somewhat lost its confidence in politics and in the legislature. The Federal Constitutional Court is to fill this vacuum. These are elements of the identity of post-war Germany and may help to explain the Federal Constitutional Court's requirement in *Solange I* that within the Communities a court must protect the fundamental rights of the individual guaranteed "in a valid and formulated catalogue of basic rights established by a parliament, which is adequate to the catalogue of basic rights of the Basic Law".[153] Until 1974, the ECJ had rather neglected the element of fundamental rights of the individual in its jurisprudence. The heavily criticised *Solange I* decision was a reaction to this deficit.

Solange I, on the other hand, was criticised for "Germanizing" the Communities—of putting them too closely under the restraints of the German Basic Law.[154] It was considered a backward decision, which might damage the process of integration.[155]

As opposed to the *Solange II* and the *Maastricht* decisions, *Solange I* was handed down as a split decision, with three out of eight justices dissenting.[156] According to the dissenting justices, basic rights are not only guaranteed by the Basic Law within the national legal order of the Federal Republic of Germany, but also by the legal order of the European Communities. No Member State can request that fundamental rights are guaranteed on the Community level in exactly the same way as under the national constitution.[157] Particularly, the ECJ ensures respect for the rule of law and the basic rights on the Community level, the dissenting vote says.[158] The dissenters read article 24 of the Basic Law regarding the transfer of sovereign powers in a way that forbids national authorities to review acts of the supranational organisation.[159] The legal order of the Communities is structurally congruent with the

---

[152] Cf. also W. Zeidler, former President of the German Federal Constitutional Court, "Wandel durch Annäherung—Das Bundesverfassungsgericht und das Europarecht", in Brandt/Gollwitzer/Henschel (eds.), *Ein Richter, ein Bürger, ein Christ, Festschrift für Helmut Simon* (1987), 727, 732 with reference to Rupp; E. Bülow, case note, 1 EuGRZ, 19 (1974).

[153] Cf. the *Solange I* decision, 37 BVerfGE 271 (1974), n. 16 above and accompanying text.

[154] Cf. J. Frowein, "Anmerkung zum Beschluß des BVerfG v. 23. Juni 1981 (Eurocontrol)", 9 *EuGRZ* 179 (1982); Fromont spoke of legal nationalism, cf. M. Fromont, case note, *Revue trimestrielle de droit européen* 333, 335 (1975).

[155] Cf. Ipsen, "Das Bundesverfassungsgericht löst die Grundrechtsproblematik, Zum 'Mittlerweile'-Beschluß des 2. Senats vom 22. Oktober 1986," 22 *EuR* 1, 5 (1987).

[156] Dissenting vote by Justices Rupp, Hirsch and Wand, 37 BVerfGE 291 (1974).

[157] *Ibid.* at 297.

[158] *Ibid.* at 292.

[159] *Ibid.* at 295.

German Constitution, according to the dissenters.[160] Therefore, the Federal Constitutional Court has no jurisdiction to review Community law on whether it is compatible with the Basic Law. The Federal Constitutional Court, the dissenters concluded, cannot rule on the validity or invalidity or the applicability or inapplicability of Community law within Germany. The dissenting vote in *Solange I* underlines the authors´ trust in the Community legal order. The dissenters do not raise the problem of *ultra vires* acts and *Kompetenz-Kompetenz*, perhaps assuming these problems are factually irrelevant.

It is interesting to note that, like the reporting judge in *Solange II*, one of the dissenters in *Solange I* was particularly internationally educated: Justice Rupp had been a research fellow at Harvard Law School and had been a fellow at the Kaiser Wilhelm Institute for Foreign and Private International Law, the predecessor of the Max Planck Institute.[161] This background explains his reluctance to accept a national law standard for actions of an international organisation.

The requirement of a *written* catalogue of basic rights was especially criticised. It was rightly maintained that other countries like the United Kingdom protected the basic rights effectively without such a written catalogue.[162] The condition of a fundamental rights protection modelled exactly upon the protection of basic rights in Germany could indeed hinder further integration. The Commission of the European Communities told the Federal Government that the decision of the Federal Constitutional Court raised grave concerns and that it put at risk a most important principle of the founding Treaties, i.e. the uniform application of Community law in all Member States. The Commission explicitly reserved its right to initiate a procedure against the Federal Republic of Germany for violation of the Treaties.[163]

Thus, *Solange I* was overwhelmingly criticised, both nationally and internationally. However, many who had criticised *Solange I* harshly later admitted that this decision had a positive influence on the development of the fundamental rights protection within the Communities.[164]

---

[160] But see the Austrian draft ratification law on the Treaty establishing a European Union. Accordingly, democracy in Austria is substantially modified by accession to the European Union. Therefore, a popular referendum is required.

[161] Justice Hirsch had been a MP of the Bavarian State legislature; of Justice Wand there is no information available.

[162] Cf. W. Zeidler, "Wandel durch Annäherung—Das Bundesverfassungsgericht und das Europarecht", in Brandt/Gollwitzer/Henschel (eds.), *Ein Richter, ein Bürger, ein Christ, Festschrift für Helmut Simon* 727, 732 (1987) with references.

[163] Cf. Zeidler *ibid.* 732. On the problem whether the grounds for decision of *Solange I* constitute a violation of the Treaty under article 169 of the EC Treaty, see M. Hilf, 35 *ZaöRV* 51, 60 (1975); Meyer equally suggests a procedure against the Federal Republic of Germany under article 169 of the EC Treaty, G. Meyer, "Anmerkung", 27 *NJW* 1704, 1705 (1974).

[164] Cf. H. Golsong, case note, 1 *EuGRZ* 17, 18 (1974); H. P. Ipsen, "Das Bundesverfassungsgericht löst die Grundrechtsproblematik, Zum 'Mittlerweile'-Beschluß des 2. Senats vom 22. Oktober 1986", 22 *EuR* 1, 5 (1987). See also M. Kloepfer, "EG-Recht und Verfassungsrecht in der Rechtsprechung des Bundesverfassungsgerichts", 47 *JZ* 1092(1988);

In the 1970s and 1980s, the ECJ further developed its fundamental rights jurisprudence.[165] The ECJ now also bases its judgments on the European Convention on Human Rights which all Member States of the European Communities approved.[166] As a reaction to these developments on the European plane and possibly also to the strong criticism of *Solange I*, the Federal Constitutional Court handed down its "Maybe" and "Meanwhile" decisions.[167] These decisions appeared to signal a peace-making between the Federal Constitutional Court and the ECJ.[168] They were steps towards the Court's approach in *Solange II*.

Thus, the doctrine did not follow the Federal Constitutional Court's reasoning in *Solange I*. The critique is mostly directed against the critical approach of the Federal Constitutional Court towards the Communities and towards the ECJ. Most scholars and the dissenters in *Solange I* share the opinion that basic rights are sufficiently guaranteed on the European plane. Critics feared that the integration process may be unduly impeded by the Federal Constitutional Court's approach. In *Solange I*, the Federal Constitutional Court, in a way, already touched the problem of *Kompetenz-Kompetenz* with regard to basic rights. This approach of the Federal Constitutional Court as such does not meet with critique. It is generally accepted that there must be some kind of a remedy against *ultra vires* acts of the Community encroaching on fundamental rights. Some authors, however, are of the opinion that there is a milder remedy that would be more in accordance with Germany´s international obligations. Rather than declaring Community acts that violate basic rights inapplicable in Germany, the German Government should use its influence within the Community organs so that these Community acts or the relevant Community law should be changed. These authors advocated that even Community law violating basic rights should be applicable in Germany temporarily such as not to endanger the uniform application of Community law.[169]

But, as already mentioned, most criticism of *Solange I* focused on the different factual evaluation of the protection of fundamental rights in and by the Communities and on the requirements for an effective protection of the indi-

---

J. Scherer, "Solange II: Ein grundrechtspolitischer Kompromiß, Zum Verhältnis von Gemeinschaftsrecht und nationalem Verfassungsrecht nach dem Solange II-Beschluß des BVerfG", 19 *JA* 483, 484 (1987).

[165] Cf. R. Streinz, *Bundesverfassungsgerichtlicher Grundrechtsschutz und Europäisches Gemeinschaftsrecht* 51 (1989).

[166] Cf. W. Zeidler, "Wandel durch Annäherung—Das Bundesverfassungsgericht und das Europarecht", in: Brandt/Gollwitzer/Henschel, *Ein Richter, ein Bürger, ein Christ, Festschrift für Helmut Simon* 727, 738 (1987).

[167] Cf. p. 86 et seq. above.

[168] Tomuschat commented on the "Maybe" decision with the statement: "peace in sight". C. Tomuschat, "BVerfG contra EuGH—Friedensschluß in Sicht", 26 *NJW* 2611 (1980).

[169] Cf. J. Frowein, "Europäisches Gemeinschaftsrecht und Bundesverfassungsgericht", in C. Starck, 2 *Bundesverfassungsgericht und Grundgesetz* 187 (1976).

vidual. Several authors voiced their hope that the Federal Constitutional Court might soon have the chance to overrule *Solange I*.[170]

Solange II. Several factors have influenced the change of the Court's approach from *Solange I* to *Solange II*. It might be relevant that the composition of the second Senate of the Court changed completely between *Solange I* and *Solange II*.[171] Moreover, the mid-1970s, the time of *Solange I*, was not a high time for integration.[172] The dollar-based Western monetary system had broken down in 1971; Member States had to fight against inflation; and they had to deal with the oil crisis. In contrast *Solange II* was handed down in October 1986 during a very integration-friendly period. The Single European Act, commonly acclaimed as a major step towards integration had been signed in February 1986 and had entered into force on 1 July 1987. The Single European Act stands for more integration, but still without the concerns which were raised from within the Member States with regard to Maastricht.

Primarily, *Solange II* appears as a reaction to the Federal Constitutional Court to an intensified fundamental rights jurisprudence of the ECJ.[173] *Solange II* also seems to be influenced by the harsh criticism met by *Solange I*. For in *Solange II*, the Federal Constitutional Court considerably relaxed its requirement for an effective protection of basic rights that meets the standards guaranteed under the German Basic Law.[174] For example, the Federal Constitutional Court no longer insists on the requirement of a *written* catalogue of fundamental rights. Likewise, the Federal Constitutional Court modifies its requirement of a binding catalogue of fundamental rights. For the European Communities are not formally a party to the European Convention on Human Rights.

Some call the recent *Maastricht* decision "*Solange III*".[175] Certainly, the *Maastricht* decision is less integration-friendly than *Solange II*. It points out that the *Kompetenz-Kompetenz* lies with Germany and that *ultra vires* acts of the Communities, for constitutional reasons, are inapplicable in Germany. In order to understand what could be understood as a step back to pre-*Solange*

---

[170] Frowein *ibid.* at 213.

[171] The following Justices were sitting in *Solange I*: Seuffert, v. Schlabrendorff, Rupp, Geiger, Hirsch, Rinck, Rottmann, Wand with Justices Rupp, Hirsch and Wand dissenting. *Solange II* was handed down unanimously by Justices: Zeidler, Niebler, Steinberger, Träger, Mahrenholz, Böckenförde, Klein and Graßhof.

[172] Cf. also J.-V. Louis, case note, 1 *EuGRZ* 20, 21 (1974).

[173] Similarly M. Kloepfer, "EG-Recht und Verfassungsrecht in der Rechtsprechung des Bundesverfassungsgerichts", 43 *JZ* 1089 (1988), 1093; M. Hilf, "Solange II: Wie lange noch Solange? Der Beschluß des Bundesverfassungsgerichts vom 22. Oktober 1986", 44 *EuGRZ* 1 (1987).

[174] Cf. R. Streinz, *Bundesverfassungsgerichtlicher Grundrechtsschutz und Europäisches Gemeinschaftsrecht* 61 (1989); M. Kloepfer, "EG-Recht und Verfassungsrecht in der Rechtsprechung des Bundesverfassungsgerichts", 43 *JZ* 1089, 1093 (1988); J. Scherer, "Solange II: Ein grundrechtspolitischer Kompromiß", 19 *JA* 483, 489 (1987).

[175] Cf. C. Tietje, "Europäischer Grundrechtsschutz nach dem Maastricht-Urteil, 'Solange III'?—BVerfG", 39 *NJW* 1993, 3047, 34 *JuS* 197 (1994).

II, it is important to analyse the reactions to *Solange II*. The above explanations of *Solange I* and *Solange II* suggest that *Maastricht* or *Solange III* again is a reaction to the case law and jurisprudence of the ECJ and possibly, to a lesser extent, to reactions to *Solange II* by "*la doctrine*".

Reactions to *Solange II* were more friendly but also less unanimous than the overwhelming criticism of *Solange I*. *Solange II* was generally praised by many German scholars, especially by scholars dealing primarily with Community law.[176] According to the former president of the Federal Constitutional Court, Wolfgang Zeidler, the Court demonstrated that it was able to react flexibly to changed factual and legal developments.[177] *Solange II* is integration-friendly in two respects. According to *Solange II*, the European Communities and, in particular, the jurisprudence of the ECJ, now guarantee protection of basic rights that are comparable to the standards guaranteed under the Basic Law. The Federal Constitutional Court only reserves its jurisdiction for the hypothetical case in which the ECJ should become generally and totally unable or unwilling to protect fundamental rights. Moreover, *Solange II* makes sure that lower courts co-operate with the ECJ. If lower courts do not request preliminary opinions from the ECJ in contravention of article 177 of the EC Treaty, this constitutes a violation of the basic right to a lawful judge pursuant to article 101, para. 1 of the Basic Law. The Federal Constitutional Court can now remedy violations of article 177 of the EC Treaty by lower German courts upon constitutional complaints alleging violation of article 101, para. 1 of the Basic Law.[178]

Criticism of *Solange II* was more on procedural grounds. The Court said that requests for preliminary rulings were "inadmissible" as long as the European Communities, in particular the jurisprudence of the ECJ, generally ensures an effective protection of basic rights against acts of the Community. But there is no procedure in which the Federal Constitutional Court could find out whether the general level of basic rights protection within the Communities was still "generally" sufficient.[179]

The Maastricht *decision or* "Solange III". While *Solange II* might be explained as a reaction to the harsh criticism of *Solange I*, this is less true for the *Maastricht* decision. Like *Solange II*, the *Maastricht* decision was handed down without dissenting votes. Four of the justices voting for *Solange II* in 1986 sat in the *Maastricht* court in 1993.[180] Thus, the *Maastricht* court had

---

[176] Cf. e.g. P. Kalbe, "Keine nationalen Rechtsmittel gegen Vorabentscheidungen des Europäischen Gerichtshofs, Anmerkungen zum Beschluß des BVerfG vom 22.10.1986—Solange II", 33 *RIW* 455 (1987).

[177] W. Zeidler, "Wandel durch Annäherung—Das Bundesverfassungsgericht und das Europarecht", in Brandt/Gollwitzer/Henschler (eds.), *Ein Richter, ein Bürger, ein Christ, Festschrift für Helmut Simon* 727, 741 (1987).

[178] On *Solange II*, see n. 21 above and accompanying text.

[179] Cf. J. Scherer, "Solange II: Ein grundrechtspolitischer Kompromiß", 19 *JA* 487, 489 (1987).

[180] Justices Mahrenholz, Böckenförde, Klein and Graßhof.

four new judges.[181] Moreover, Justice Steinberger was reporting for *Solange II*, whereas Justice Kirchhof was reporting for the *Maastricht* decision. Justice Steinberger is a particularly internationally educated lawyer. He spent a long time at American law schools, was a fellow with the Max Planck Institute for Foreign Public and International Law and a professor for international law and European law before becoming a Justice on the Federal Constitutional Court. Now, former Justice Steinberger is one of the directors of the Max Planck Institute for Foreign Public and International Law and teaches, among other subjects, international law and European law at the University of Heidelberg. Likewise, Justice Kirchhof is a professor at the University of Heidelberg. He teaches national public law and tax law. But these factors concerning the compositions of the *Solange II* court and the *Maastricht* court should not be overestimated. The *Solange II* decision was handed down unanimously, and there are no dissenting or even concurring votes to the *Maastricht* decision. However, the *Maastricht* decision ends with the unusual clause: "The following justices participated in the decision: Vice-president Mahrenholz, Böckenförde, Klein, Graßhof, Kruis, Kirchhof, Winter, Sommer". This leaves room for speculation. All the eight Justices participated in the decision, but whether there were dissenters and who and in what sense is left open. The *Maastricht* court wanted to create the appearance of unity with regard to the vital question of European integration.

The *Maastricht* decision concerns a completely new Treaty. Moreover, at the beginning of the 1990s, European integration again showed symptoms of a crisis.[182] In 1992, the Danish population in its first referendum voted against the Maastricht Treaty. This provoked a serious crisis for the Communities. Even after the second referendum, which turned out to be in favour of the Maastricht Treaty, Denmark adhered to the Union only with substantial reservations to the monetary union.[183] Likewise, the United Kingdom will not participate in the third stage of the monetary union.[184] The French referendum, with 51.05 per cent to 48.95 per cent, came out very narrowly in favour of the European Union. Within the German academic community, some authors were requesting a popular referendum as a precondition to accession to the Maastricht Treaty.[185] Similar to *Solange I*, the general context of the *Maastricht* judgment was thus characterized by some as a reservation against

---

[181] The new justices are: Justices Kruis, Kirchhof, Winter and Sommer.

[182] Cf. also M. Schröder, "Das Bundesverfassungsgericht als Hüter des Staates im Prozeß der europäischen Integration—Bemerkungen zum Maastricht-Urteil", 109 *DVBl* 316 (1994).

[183] Cf. Protocol on Certain Provisions Relating to Denmark, 31 ILM 356 (1992).

[184] Cf. Protocol on certain Provisions Relating to the United Kingdom of Great Britain and Northern Ireland, 31 ILM 355 (1992).

[185] D. Murswiek, "Maastricht und der pouvoir constituant", 32 *Der Staat* 98 (1993); H. H. Rupp, "Muß das Volk über den Vertrag von Maastricht entscheiden?" 39 *NJW* 433 (1993); H. Stöcker, "Die Unvereinbarkeit der Währungsunion mit der Selbstbestimmungsgarantie in Art. 1 Abs. 2 GG," 31 *Der Staat* 495 (1992); J. Wolf, "Die Revision des Grundgesetzes durch Maastricht, Ein Anwendungsfall des Art. 146 GG", 48 *JZ* 1993, 594 (1993).

too much integration. According to Meessen, the Federal Constitutional Court had stopped integration after it had already come to a standstill.[186]

Most importantly, several rulings of the ECJ could be considered as too far-reaching.[187] For example, in *Francovich*[188] the ECJ found a general principle of Community law that Member States had to pay damages for not implementing the directives of the Community. This meant damages for not enacting the respective statute. It is doubtful whether such a principle of damages for omissions of the legislature can be derived from the domestic legal orders of Member States. In another judgment,[189] the ECJ ruled that German employers had to accept medical certificates from other Member States. In the specific case, an Italian family of four had all fallen sick altogether during their yearly summer holiday in Italy, according to the certificate. Exactly the same had happened to that family during their summer holidays in the three previous years. In *Bronzino*, the Court said that, in order to get family benefits for grown-up children who are unemployed, it is not necessary that those children are available to a domestic placement service. Rather, the relevant provision in the German statute on availability to placement services "in the territory where this law applies" read together with the EC regulation on family allowances covers the placement services in all Member States.[190] In the *Kus* decision,[191] the ECJ had interpreted the resolution of the association council broadly in granting Turkish workers a right to stay in Germany. Environmentalists do not like the judgment of the ECJ forbidding Germany to collect tolls from trucks using the Autobahn, as Germany lowered its high automobile taxes at the same time.[192] The Community's protectionism against the so-called "dollar bananas"[193] is difficult to understand both for the German consumer and for lawyers.

Thus, the results of the ECJ's case law are subject to criticism. The German Federal Labour Court now openly criticises the ECJ's extensive interpretation of the prohibition of factual discrimination. Generally, the influence of the

---

[186] K. Meessen, "Maastricht nach Karlsruhe", 40 *NJW* 549, 554 (1994).

[187] That the Maastricht decision can be explained as an expression of the Constitutional Court's criticism is maintained by several authors, cf. J. Wieland, "Germany in the European Union—The Maastricht Decision of the Bundesverfassungsgericht", 5 *EJIL* 295, 263 (1994) and K. Meessen, "Hedging European Integration: The Maastricht-Judgment of the Federal Constitutional Court of Germany", 17 *Fordham Int'l Law Journal* 17 510, 520 (1994).

[188] *Francovich v. Italy*, Case C-6/90 of 19 November 1991, [1991] ECR 5357, ECJ; see also *Brasserie du pêcheur* and *Secretary of State, ex parte Factortame Ltd*, Case C-46/93 and C-48/93, [1996] ECR 1029; J. Kokott, note, in Oetker/Preis, *Europäisches Arbeits- und Sozialrecht*, Art. 215 No. 2, p. 56 (1996).

[189] *Alberto Paletta, Vittorio Paletta, Raffaela Paletta u. Carmela Paletta/Brenner AG*, Case No. C-45/90 of 3 June 1992, 38 NJW 2687 (1992). For details, cf. p. 111 above.

[190] *Bronzino v. Kindergeldkasse*, Case 228/88 and *Gatto v. Bundesanstalt für Arbeit*. Case 12/89, both of 12 February 1989, [1990] ECR 531 and 559. Cf. also J. Kokott, casenote, 84 AJIL 926 ff. (1990).

[191] Case No. C-237/91 of 12 December 1992, 48 JZ 836 (1993).

[192] Case No. C-195/90 of 19 May 1992, 3 EuZW 390 (1992).

[193] Cf. Case No. C-280/93 R of 29 June 1993, 4 EuZW 483 (1993); Case No. 286/93 of 21 June 1993 *ibid.* at 487.

ECJ in specific cases is to some extent seen as a danger for the consistency of the remaining codified law.[194] Various preliminary rulings of the ECJ lead to certain provisions of national codifications no longer applying or only applying in modified form, because they would otherwise hinder the "*effet util*" of Community law.[195] This may lead to an unequal treatment of similar situations depending on whether the case falls under the Court's ruling or under remaining codification. Moreover, different areas of the law, e.g. labour law, tax law and administrative procedural law, have their own consistencies. They have developed their own principles of justice specific to the particular field. The specialised (national) courts decide real cases and controversies applying those specific principles. The Anglo-American case law method distrusts abstract principles and underlines the importance of having the issues and conflicts of interest sharpened in a real case or controversy before the court.[196] The ECJ, to the contrary, is far away from the parties and from the real controversies. It decides according to abstract principles, in particular according to the one most important policy principle of "*effet util*", of promoting integration through law. The ECJ comes under heavy criticism by German labour lawyers in this respect. In an article called "The ECJ in Labour Law—the Black Series Goes on", the author states: "Reality is of no interest to the ECJ; the world only exists as will and illusion[197] to the Court".[198] Even when the ECJ adopts preliminary rulings, these often have a decisive impact on the case or controversy pending before the national court. If applied too extensively, the preliminary ruling procedure may conflict with the assumption that cases are best decided by courts familiar with the specific legal issues, the parties and the legal and social context of the particular case. The ECJ should be as mindful of this structural problem as is compatible with the principles of integration and of "*effet util*".

One distinguished author sees massive deficiencies with regard to an effective protection of basic rights. He called for a modification of *Solange II* and that individual complainants be able to challenge directly directives and regulations of the Communities before the Federal Constitutional Court.[199] This author thus predicted what would become possible after the *Maastricht* decision.

---

[194] Cf. "Berichte und Diskussionen zum Thema Deutsches und Europäisches Verwaltungsrecht auf der Tagung der Deutschen Staatsrechtslehrer in Mainz vom 6. bis 9. Oktober 1993", 53 *VVDStRL* 154 (1994).

[195] Cf. *Zuckerfabrik Süderdithmarschen/Hauptzollamt Itzehoe und Zuckerfabrik Soest GmbH/Hauptzollamt Paderborn*, Case C-143/88 and C-92/89, [1991] ECR 415.

[196] Cf. W. Fikentscher, 2 *Methoden des Rechts, Angloamerikanischer Rechtskreis* 452 and 462 (1975); W. Brugger, *Einführung in das öffentliche Recht der USA* 83 (1993).

[197] This is a reference to the famous work by the philosopher A. Schopenhauer, "Die Welt als Wille und Vorstellung" ("The world as will and illusion").

[198] A. Junker, "Der EuGH im Arbeitsrecht—Die schwarze Serie geht weiter", 40 *NJW* 2527 (1994).

[199] R. Scholz, "Wie lange bis 'Solange III'?", 36 *NJW* 941 (1990).

The *Maastricht* decision is a critical reaction to the dynamic jurisprudence of the ECJ.[200] This is clear from the following passage:

"If to date dynamic expansion of the existing Treaties has been based upon liberal interpretation of Art. 235 of the EEC Treaty in the sense of 'competence which rounds off the Treaty' (*Vertragsabrundungskompetenz*), upon considerations of the implied powers of the European Communities, and upon interpreting the Treaty in the sense of the maximum possible exploitation of the Community's powers ('*effet util*') (see Zuleeg, in von der Groeben/Thiesing/Ehlermann, *EWG-Vertrag*, 4th edn. (1991), Art. 2, Annotation 3), when standards of competence are being interpreted by institutions and governmental entities of the Communities in the future, the fact that the Maastricht Treaty draws a basic distinction between the exercise of limited sovereign powers and amendment of the Treaty will have to be taken into consideration. Thus interpretation of such standards may not have an effect equivalent to an extension of the Treaty; indeed, if standards of competence were interpreted in this way, such interpretation would not have any binding effect on Germany".[201]

These remarks may even be directed against the position taken by Manfred Zuleeg, the German judge at the European Court. The Federal Constitutional Court criticises Zuleeg for his advocacy of a dynamic expansion of the existing Treaties, probably having in mind some judgments on social policy drafted by that judge. The passage by Zuleeg in Groeben/Thiesing/ Ehlermann, which the Court cites, does not deal with "*effet util*" and implied powers.

Beyond doctrine

Post-war Germany still has identity problems. For example, it is much more difficult for German politicians to articulate national interests than for French politicians. In comparison, it is easier for Germany to make its voice heard as the advocate or guarantor of legal principles. Interests and aims which other Member States may implement politically tend to be constitutionalised in Germany.

France initiated the Luxembourg Accords requiring that the Council of Ministers decide unanimously whenever the national interest of a Member State is at stake. Germany tries to influence the shape of European integration through the judiciary in the name of the fundamental rights of the individual and of democracy.

The Solange *era*

The 1974 *Solange I* decision is the expression of a concern for human rights protection against acts of supra-national organisations which is at least under-

---

[200] See also C. Grewe, "L'arrêt de la Cour constitutionnelle fédérale allemande du 12 octobre 1993 sur le Traité de Maastricht: l'Union européenne et les droits fondamentaux", 5 *RUDH* 226, 231 (1993).

[201] 33 ILM 441 (1994).

standable. Until 1974, the ECJ had rather neglected the element of fundamental rights of the individual in its jurisprudence. The heavily criticised *Solange I* decision was a reaction to this failing. However, the Federal Constitutional Court probably went too far in promoting this legitimate interest when it required a written human rights catalogue enacted by a parliament and comparable to the standards set up by the Basic Law. Also, the Federal Constitutional Court ignored the beginnings of a fundamental rights jurisprudence of the ECJ.

Germany's post-war constitutional or human rights patriotism becomes clear when the Court says that Germany is constitutionally prohibited from giving up the fundamental traits of its Constitution, upon which the identity of Germany is founded. The basic rights of the individual are such a fundamental trait essential to the identity of the German state.[202]

The 1986 *Solange II* decision is a reconciliation with the ECJ which, meanwhile, had developed judge-made fundamental rights. But the Federal Constitutional Court also reduced its requirements and renounced a written catalogue of human rights adopted by a parliament. Such a catalogue of human rights does not exist, although it would be a major factor of European integration making it easier for the people to identify with the European Union.

Maastricht *and its aftermath*

Socio-political and economic context. The 1993 *Maastricht* decision was handed down in an era of "Euroscepticism". The ideal of peace had become less important as war among Western European states seems unthinkable. A reunified and more self-conscious Germany was accepted and integrated into the international community. Moreover, it became questionable whether more integration, especially through a European monetary union, will still promote economic welfare and growth. Through German reunification every German could feel that a currency union with economically weaker partners may decrease the living standard and income of the people living in the economically more powerful state. The disappearance of the Deutsche Mark, a symbol of economic stability, is not a perspective attractive to everyone in Germany (rather more so in France).

Thus, the Treaty on European Union constitutes a major and important further integration step without full support of the people and without the enthusiasm of the earlier European movement where the idea of peace was more vital. The latest programmes of the political parties no longer mention the European federal state as an aim. In this socio-political and economic context, the German Federal Constitutional Court dared to hand down its provocative *Maastricht* decision.

---

[202] Cf. 37 BVerfGE 271, 279 (1974).

"Kompetenz-Kompetenz" *and* ultra vires *acts*. As integration becomes more intensive, the Federal Constitutional Court has clearly formulated the question of principle: does the final say—or the *Kompetenz-Kompetenz*—rest with the European Union or the national states at this stage of integration? Or—in other words—are the Member States still the "masters of the Treaties" (*Herren der Verträge*), deciding whether to attribute new competences to the European Communities or not? Or can the European Communities themselves create new competences by an ECJ-inspired too dynamic interpretation of the Treaties?

These fundamental questions about the aim and direction of European integration are—in accordance with good German tradition—put into a constitutional, legal, quasi-positivistic framework. The German Federal Constitutional Court tries to answer the questions in a constitutional complaint procedure concerning the newly created individual right to democracy. Thereby, the Court becomes involved in an eminently political question: whether Germany can ratify the Treaty on European Union or not. The Treaty on European Union had the full support of the German Parliament; therefore, the Federal Constitutional Court could not have hindered Germany from adhering to it. Also, the Court had always underlined the mutual duty of co-operation of Member States and Community organs. In this framework, the Federal Constitutional Court interpreted the Maastricht Treaty to make it constitutional. This can be seen in particular from its restrictive interpretation of the provisions on monetary union.[203]

According to the Court, Germany (like the other Member States) still has *Kompetenz-Kompetenz*. The Treaty is constitutional, because Germany, in particular the democratically elected German Parliament, still controls the process of integration.

However, problems arise when European organs including the ECJ overstep the competences attributed to them by the founding Treaties. The democratically elected German Parliament consented to Community acts covered by the Treaties; *ultra vires* acts not covered by the will of the German Parliament violate the principle of democracy. The Federal Constitutional Court as the guarantor of basic rights takes on the role of defending the people against undemocratic *ultra vires* acts of the Communities. These are now directly subject to review by the Federal Constitutional Court.

Impact of the Maastricht *decision*. The Federal Constitutional Court's *dictum* that Community acts not covered by the German ratification law are inapplicable in Germany for constitutional reasons sounds like an invitation to criticise and to hold inapplicable even judgments of the ECJ. Lower labour courts in Germany have used the ECJ to implement their very employee-

---

[203] Cf. p. 101 et seq. above and Kokott, "Deutschland im Rahmen der Europäischen Union—zum Vertrag von Maastricht", 119 *AöR* 207, 227 (1994).

friendly policies against the Federal Labour Court. Some strange and controversial decisions resulted. Now, some lawyers and courts have started to suggest that some of these decisions are inapplicable in Germany.[204] There are several labour courts which are again requesting the ECJ to determine in preliminary proceedings under article 177 whether it really meant what it said on an identical or a similar problem in a case decided shortly before.[205] Generally, it has become more acceptable to articulate criticism of the ECJ and the EU. But this is also a consequence of the fact that more people deal with EC law now. The times have gone, when ECJ decisions were commented on only by integration-friendly international or European lawyers. Thus, the success of the integration process is accompanied by increased criticism of the ECJ.

The Federal Constitutional Court itself probably will not continue in the provocative manner of the *Maastricht* decision. The long awaited decision of 22 March 1995 on the television directive[206]—contrary to expectations—does not implement limits to integration flowing from German federalism. Rather it refers to the duty of the *Länder* to observe the European law binding upon the Federal Republic of Germany, and which the ECJ interprets authoritatively.[207] Otherwise, the decision on the TV directive concentrates on the duty to co-operate between the German Federation and the German *Länder*.

CONCLUSIONS

In its *Maastricht* decision, the German Federal Constitutional Court underlined its "co-operative relationship" with the ECJ. That the Federal Constitutional Court co-operates with the ECJ is true insofar as the jurisprudence

---

[204] Cf. Federal Tax Court, Order of 9 January 1996—VII B 225/95, 7 EuZW 126; Federal Tax Court, Judgment of 2 April 1996—VII R 119/94, 7 EuZW 668 (1996); VG Frankfurt a.M., Orders of 24 October 1996—1 E 798/95 (V) a. 1 E 2949/93 (V), 8 EuZW 182 (1997). The Hamburg tax court issued several orders on the inapplicability of the European banana order in Germany, see e.g. FG Hamburg, Order of 19 May 1995—IV 119/95 H, 6 EuZW 413 (1995); Federal Constitutional Court, Order of 26 April 1995—2 BvR 760/95, 6 EuZW 412 (1995); VGH Kassel, Order of 9 February 1995—8 TG 292/95, 6 EuZW 222 (1995). See also Bauer, "Outsourcing out? Anmerkung zum Urteil des EuGH vom 14.4.1994", 49 *BB* 1433, 1435 (1994). Similarly Buchner, "Verlagerung betrieblicher Aufgaben als Betriebsübergang i. S. von § 613a BGB", 47 *DB* 1417 (1994) and Blomeyer, *Anm. zu EuGH vom 14.4.1994*, EzA § 613 a No. 113; Kuschel, "Wie geht es weiter mit der Bananenmarktordnung?", 7 *EuZW* 645 (1996); Kuschel, "Die EG-Bananenmarktordnung vor deutschen Gerichten", 6 *EuZW* 689 (1995).

[205] BAG, 11 NZA 278 (1994) with regard to ECJ, Case C-360/90 of 4 June 1992, [1992] ECR 3589. See also ECJ, Case C-13/95 of 11 March 1997, *Ayse Süzen* v. *Zehnacker Gebäudereinigung GmbH Krankenhause-Service*, ECJ 1997, 1259 concerning a situation very similar to that underlying Case C-392/92, *Christel Schmidt* v. *Spar- und Leihkasse der früheren Ämter Bordesholm, Kiel und Kronshagen*, [1994] ECR 1311; BAG, Decision of 27 April 1994, 11 NZA 683 (1994) with regard to ECJ, case *Alberto Paletta et al.*, Case No. 45/90, Decision of 3 June 1992, 45 NJW 2687 (1992),]1992] ECR 3423. See p. 111 above.

[206] Dir. 89/552.

[207] 22 EuGRZ 125, 135 (1995).

of the Luxembourg Court is probably the major factor of influence for the German Constitutional Court's decisions concerning Europe and the problem of *Kompetenz-Kompetenz*.

"*La doctrine*" in Germany used to consist mostly of the opinions of law professors who specialise in Community law and international law. This academic community tends to find the Constitutional Court's approach too centred on domestic law. *Solange II* was drafted by a law professor specialising in Community law and international law. This was the decision most acclaimed and least criticised by German academia. Otherwise, scholarly opinion or "*la doctrine*" has been rather critical of the Federal Constitutional Court's judgments concerning the integration of Europe.

However, with respect to the *Maastricht* decision, publications by German scholars specialising in German public law have prevailed. These authors were generally critical of too much integration. They initiated the important discussion on the implications of a far-reaching integration. It was only after the Federal Constitutional Court had handed down its *Maastricht* decision that some German international lawyers and European law scholars came out supporting the process of integration and criticising the Federal Constitutional Court.[208] According to Frowein, by far the most critical commentator, the Federal Constitutional Court committed clear breaches of European Union constitutional law.[209] On the other hand, the *Maastricht* decision already has followers. The explanations to the Austrian law on accession to the European Union say explicitly that the Maastricht Treaty substantially changes democracy in Austria, that drastic *ultra vires* acts of the Communities are void and may even entitle Austria to withdraw under international law.[210] Generally, the *Maastricht* decision is well received. Politicians very much appreciated that the Federal Constitutional Court had permitted the ratification of the Maastricht Treaty. Interestingly, even many German European law scholars view the judgment as an important contribution to reconcile the various

[208] See recently J. Frowein, "Das Maastricht-Urteil und die Grenzen der Verfassungsgerichtsbarkeit—Summary: The Maastricht Judgment and the Limits of Constitutional Jurisdiction", 54 *ZaöRV* 1 (1994); D. König, Das Urteil des Bundesverfassungsgerichts zum Vertrag von Maastricht—ein Stolperstein auf dem Weg in die europäische Integration? 54 *ZaöRV* 17 ff. (1994).

[209] J. Frowein, "Das Maastricht-Urteil und die Grenzen der Verfassungsgerichtsbarkeit—Summary: The Maastricht Judgment and the Limits of Constitutional Jurisdiction", 54 *ZaöRV* 1, 15 (1994): "4. The Court commits a clear breach of European constitutional law when it authorizes German courts and administrative authorities to disregard European law where, according to these authorities, the organs of the Union or Community had no jurisdiction.

5. The Court stresses that Germany can, apparently unilaterally, withdraw from the Union. This is in clear violation of Union constitutional law.

6. The Court correctly explains that the establishment of the currency union is not an automatic matter although the treaty language seems to indicate this.

7. One may hope that the Court's statements which are in contradiction with European constitutional law will not become effective."

[210] Bundesverfassungsgesetz über den Beitritt Österreichs zur Europäischen Union, Explanations, 1546 der Beilagen zu den Stenographischen Protokollen des Nationalrates XVIII. GP, reprint of 12 April 1994, p. 7.

approaches to European integration. There is hardly any explicit criticism.[211] The *Maastricht* decision can be seen as an important contribution to reconciling the various approaches to European integration. It is also partly a compensation for the lack of a proper political debate on the implications of the Maastricht Treaty and the monetary union. Such a discussion took place too late and too superficially in Germany. This factor furthers ambiguous feelings in the population. The *Maastricht* decision takes away the basis for some of these ambiguous feelings and fears. This way, European integration is better accepted in the country.

In addition to the ECJ, "*la doctrine*" also influenced certain changes in the generally consistent case law of the Federal Constitutional Court.

---

[211] Cf. I. Pernice, 4 *EuZW* Editorial (1993); M. Herdegen, "Maastricht and the German Constitutional Court: Constitutional Restraints for an 'Ever Closer Union'", 31 *CMLR* 235 (1994); H. P. Ipsen, "Zehn Glossen zum Maastricht-Urteil", 29 *EuR* 1 (1994); Bleckmann/Pieper, "Maastricht, Die grundgesetzliche Ordung und die 'Superrevisionsinstanz', Die Maastricht-Entscheidung des Bundesverfassungsgerichts", 39 *RiW* 970 (1993).

4

The Italian Constitutional Court and the Relationship Between the Italian legal system and the European Union

MARTA CARTABIA

THE THEORETICAL BASES OF THE ITALIAN MEMBERSHIP TO THE EUROPEAN UNION

Before analysing in detail the case-law of the Italian Constitutional Court regarding the basic principles of the European integration—i.e. supremacy, direct effect and division of powers—it might be useful to recall that the Italian Constitutional Court approached the incipient European integration in 1957 with the same theoretical tools used in the Italian legal system to deal with the problems of international law. Even if during these 40 years of membership of the Community the case-law of the Constitutional Court has developed dramatically, the initial choice of setting community law in the frame of international law kept on influencing the relationship between Italy and the European Community. At the beginning Community law was considered as international law, partly because the very nature of the European Community and its peculiarity were not that evident, and partly because the Italian constitutional system did not provide specific provisions regulating the relationship with European law. During the years that followed these theoretical bases inherited from international law have been maintained as landmarks of the Italian path towards European integration, notwithstanding the changes which have taken place both in the European and in the Italian system. The original theoretical principles on the basis of which Italy entered the Community have been adapted little by little to the changing structure of European law without introducing any specific amendment to the Constitution.

The first of these theoretical principles is *dualism*. Like many other European countries, Italy has traditionally adopted dualism as the theoretical construct upon which the Italian relationship to international law is based.[1]

---

[1] In Italy, the first scholars who adopted the "dualist" position were D. Anzilotti, *Corso di diritto internazionale*, Rome, 1928 and S. Romano, *La pluralità degli ordinamenti giuridici e le loro relazioni*, in *L'ordinamento giuridico*, Firenze, 1945, 86 ss.

Under dualism European and national systems are separated. Each legal system is empowered to regulate its own field of competence, without interference from any other system. From the dualist point of view, Community norms are considered as emanating from a completely separate legal order, so that they do not take part in the national hierarchy of norms nor national norms are part of European hierarchy of sources of law. Under the dualist approach, the separation of attributions and the division of powers play the most important role in the relationship of the two legal systems, because the validity and the efficacy of each norm depends on whether it falls within the proper field of jurisdiction.

Considering its content, the dualist principle seems to be more respectful of the sovereignty of the "national-states" than the monist principle,[2] because according to the former each legal system is wholly autonomous within its field of jurisdiction. That's probably the reason why at the beginning it was quite natural for the Court to appeal to dualism in order to define the constitutional treatment of community law. That's probably the reason why at the present stage of European integration dualism still marks deeply the Italian relationship with Europe, although in recent decisions concerning Community law the Constitutional Court has taken a "soft version" of dualism.

The other important principle which conditions the legal treatment of Community law in Italy is the principle of *limitation of sovereignty*, established in article 11 of the Constitution. For want of specific constitutional provisions concerning the membership to the European Community, the Constitutional Court turned to article 11 of the Constitution as the constitutional basis for the Italian accession to the Community, even if that provision was originally addressed to the United Nations. Article 11 states that Italy can accept, at the same conditions of the other countries, those limitations of sovereignty that are necessary to take part to international organisations aiming at fostering peace and justice among nations. The European community was considered as one of these international organisations aiming at peace and justice, so that Italy consented to suffer a limitation of power on the basis of article 11 in order to build up European integration. But article 11 of the Constitution while opening the way to a transfer of powers to European institutions, it also marks the limits of the reduction of powers that can be imposed to national institutions: "limitation" of sovereignty cannot become "loss" of sovereignty; consequently article 11 of the Constitution consents to the membership of European integration as far as it does not imply a loss of sovereignty. And the Constitutional Court is demanded to watch over European integration in order to prevent it from overstepping the borders of limitation of Italian sovereignty.

---

[2] See H. Kelsen, *Il problema della sovranità e la teoria del diritto internazionale* (1920), translated by A. Carrino, Milano, 1989.

THE ITALIAN CONSTITUTIONAL COURT CASE-LAW CONCERNING THE SUPREMACY OF EUROPEAN LAW: FROM THE DENIAL OF SUPREMACY TO THE SUPREMACY UNDER CONDITION

As regards supremacy of European law, an important development occurred in the case law of the Italian Constitutional Court. The Court began in 1964 by asserting that Community norms should be considered as the legal equivalent of acts of Italian Parliament—that means that the Court began by denying the supremacy of Community law. At the other extreme, nowadays the Court recognizes that European norms prevail over all sort of national norms and can even depart from constitutional provisions, although they are not endowed with the same "value" of Italian constitutional norms (decision 31 March 1994, n. 117 and decision 8 June 1994, n. 224).

Constitutional case-law concerning supremacy of European norms could be split up in three periods: since 1964 to 1973; since 1973 to 1984; since 1984 up to now.[3]

The first one is the period of the "denial of supremacy". In the famous Costa/ENEL case (7 March 1964, n. 14, point 6) the Constitutional Court asserted that the relationship between Community norms and national norms was not different from every other relationship that occurs between two sources of law possessing the same binding authority. From the Court's point of view, there were no reasons to attribute to European norms a legal force superior to that possessed by the Italian Parliament's acts. *Lex posterior derogat priori* should be the principle regulating the relationship between Community and national norms. In other words, the Court held that where a national and an EC norm conflict, the one most recent in time should prevail over the older one, without regard to the origin of the norms. This meant that the Italian Parliament was completely unbound by Community norms: it could at any time enact a statute contrary to Community law. In the Costa/ENEL decision the Court went so far to assert that Italy could even abandon its membership of the Community by means of a simple act of Parliament. Of course if it chose to do so, it could be held responsible at the international level for infringement of the Treaty. However, from the constitutional point of view, nothing prevented Italy from abandoning the EEC.

These statements were unacceptable for the European Court of Justice because if every national Parliament had the authority to disregard Community norms, the power transferred to Community institutions would be rendered useless. It is worth remarking that in fact in the *same* case Costa/ENEL of 1964, the European Court of Justice established for the first time the doctrine of supremacy of Community law.

---

[3] This division of the Italian Constitutional Court case-law into three periods is due to F. Sorrentino, *La Costituzione italiana di fronte al processo di integrazione europea*, in "Quaderni costituzionali", 1993, 71 ss.

In that time, the two Courts took opposite positions.

It was only during the seventies that the Italian Constitutional Court accepted the doctrine of supremacy of European law (starting with decision of 27 December 1973, n. 183). This second period (1973–1984) was distinguished by the fact that the Constitutional Court held that the jurisdictional guarantee of supremacy of Community law should be judicial review of Italian legislation conflicting with European norms. It meant that only the Constitutional Court had the power to invalidate national norms infringing Community obligations. To be more precise, the Constitutional Court suggested that when a national norm inconsistent with Community law entered into force after the infringed Community norm, the case was to be referred to the Constitutional Court for judicial review. In fact the Court retained that the national norms conflicting with Community law indirectly infringed article 11 of the Constitution (30 October 1975, n. 232; 28 July 1976, n. 205 and n. 206; 29 December 1977, n. 163). In other words, the supremacy of Community law within the Italian legal system was guaranteed in two ways: where the infringed community norm was "more recent" than the national one, it would prevail in accordance with the rule *lex posterior derogat priori*, and it was up to ordinary judges to ensure the supremacy of community law; on the contrary, where the infringed Community norm was older than the national one, the Community norm would be applied only after a finding of unconstitutionality, enacted by the Constitutional Court.

The European Court of Justice was not at all satisfied with this "two-folded" judicial guarantee of supremacy of Community law; in particular it contested the monopoly of the Italian Constitutional Court in invalidating national norms subsequent to the infringed Community norms. Actually, in the Simmenthal case of 1978 the European Court of Justice held that every national judge, and in particular every ordinary judge, called upon to apply provisions of Community law is under the duty to give full effect to those provisions, without applying for constitutional review.

This divergence of view between the European Court and the Constitutional Court brought about a lively debate in Italy.[4] The main problem to accepting the European Court's point of view was that in the Italian legal system judges are submitted to the law (article 101 Const.): following the French tradition in Italy judges are conceived as *"la bouche de la loi"*, so that they are expected to apply the legislation, not to put it into question. To be more precise, as Professor Mezzanotte[5] pointed out, in the present constitutional system, Italian judges are submitted both to the *principio di legalità* (rule of law) and to the *principio di costituzionalità* (rule of the Constitution). Since judges are submitted to the "rule of law", they are bound to apply all the provisions enacted by the Parliament. However, since they are submitted also to the superior "rule of the Constitution", when they doubt the

---

[4] See AA.VV. *Il primato del diritto comunitario e i giudici italiani*, Milano, 1978.
[5] C. Mezzanotte, *Corte costituzionale e legittimazione politica*, Roma, 1984.

coherence with the Constitution of the acts of the parliament, they must suspend the process and refer the question to the Constitutional Court for judicial review. The only "judge" who is endowed with the power of invalidating legislation is the Constitutional Court.

Given this context it becomes clear that with the Simmenthal decision the Court of Justice of the European Community was demanding an important change in the role of judges; it was demanding the Italian legal system to depart from the basic constitutional principle that submits judges to the will of Parliament. As a demonstration of the *bouleversement* demanded by the Court of Justice it could be noticed that nobody of the "constitutional scholars" has ever doubted that the Constitutional Court was right in pretending that it was reserved to the Constitutional Court to invalidate national norms conflicting with Community law.[6]

It took about ten years before the Constitutional Court complied with the requirements stated by the European Court of Justice with regard to the judicial guarantee of supremacy of Community law. To tell the truth, the Constitutional Court was presented with several opportunities to change its doctrine and to conform to the European Court of Justice's Simmenthal decision. However more than once the Court avoided the problem, by declaring the questions inadmissible (see e.g. 26 October 1981, n. 176 and n. 177).

In the Granital decision of 1984 (8 June 1984, n. 170) the Court reviewed its precedents on conflict between Community and national norms and abandoned the rule requiring ordinary judges to refer questions of constitutionality in cases dealing with statutes inconsistent with Community law. The Court accepted that Community norms having direct effect should immediately prevail over national norms and should consequently be applied by ordinary (or administrative) judges, regardless of the time of their enactment. Faithful to the dualist approach, the Court stressed that Community law does not have the power to repeal national law. Nevertheless when the same concrete situation is governed by both Community and national norms, the latter is no longer relevant to the case and the judge should apply Community law, instead of the national one.

Granital's rationale suffers three kinds of limitations.

First of all it is intended to regulate conflicts between Community and national norms, provided Community norms have direct effect. In case of Community provisions lacking direct effect, conflicts with national norms are still within the exclusive jurisdiction of the Constitutional Court.

Second, Granital's rationale applies only in "preliminary rulings" before the Constitutional Court, that is only in those procedures in which a question of constitutionality arises during a process before an ordinary judge, because only in that case there is a judge who can ensure the direct effect of commu-

---

[6] See e.g. F. Sorrentino, *Corte costituzionale e Corte di Giustizia delle Comunità europee*, Milano, 1973; P. Barile, *Il cammino comunitario della Corte*, "Giurisprudenza Costituzionale" 1973, 2405 ss.

nity law; on the contrary Granital does not apply in the other procedures before the Constitutional Court, in particular in the "direct procedures" between the State and the Regions (see decisions n. 384 of 1994 and n. 94 of 1995), so that in these cases the Constitutional Court is still playing an important role in the European game, because it has the power to erase all the norms which conflict with Community law from the Italian legal system. This result—says the Constitutional Court—complies with the European Court of Justice's case law, because it has always asked the member States not only to give ordinary judges the power to enforce Community law having direct effect, but also to "clean" the legal system, by the elimination of all the laws which do not agree with the European law.

Third, the Constitutional Court maintains its competence whenever Community law is suspected to infringe the fundamental principles of the Italian constitutional order. In other words Community law is endowed with supremacy within the Italian legal system, "*sous reserve*" that it does not threaten the very fundamental constitutional principles on the basis of which the whole legal system is built up. This "reserve" flows from the idea of limitation of sovereignty, which implies that power is not completely transferred to the Community: *limitation of sovereignty* has to have some "counter-limits", otherwise it would turn into transfer or *loss of sovereignty* in favour of the Community. These counter-limits consist of the fundamental values of the constitutional system, like fundamental rights, the democratic principles, the unity of the State, and some other "organisational" principles. This doctrine of "counter-limits" loomed for the first time in 1965 (27 December 1965, n. 98), but it was explicitly stated by the Court in the Frontini case of 1973, recalled in the Granital decision of 1984, and developed in 1989, in the Fragd decision (21 April 1989, n. 232). Following this doctrine every judicial authority that is called upon to apply Community law, if it suspects that Community law could violate fundamental rights or other basic values protected by the Italian Constitution, shall apply to the Constitutional Court for judicial review of Community law (*rectius*: for judicial review of the Italian act of ratification of the Community treaties, specifically of that part of the act on which the contested Community norm is based). Up to now the Constitutional Court has never declared any Community provision unconstitutional. Nevertheless the Court has used this competence of ensuring the respect of fundamental values in order to suggest to the European Court of Justice that some European rules were hardly acceptable within the Italian legal system— it was the case of perspective decisions of the European Court of Justice, which appeared to conflict with the right of defence, guaranteed by article 24 of the Italian Constitution (Fragd 1989). A first impression over these cases involving counter-limits and fundamental values is that they constitute an opportunity for the Constitutional Court to co-operate,[7] rather than to enter

---

[7] For more considerations on this point see M. Cartabia, *Principi inviolabili e integrazione europea*, Milano, 1995.

into conflict, with the European Court of Justice, in order to work out the basic values of the European system.

To summarise, we can say that at present Italy has accepted by and large the supremacy of Community law and it guarantees it with methods that fully comply with the requirements stated by the European Court of Justice. However, in Italy supremacy of Community law is still under condition: first, Community law cannot be applied in Italy if it infringes the fundamental values of the Constitution; second in some recent decisions the Constitutional Court has stated that although Community provisions are endowed with the power to derogate from Italian constitutional provisions, they do not have the same binding power, nor are they subject to the same "legal treatment" reserved to constitutional norms (one can guess that the difference is in structure and content, rather than in formal authority). For example, whereas some years ago (decision of 19 November 1987, n. 399) the Constitutional Court had recognised to Community norms the powers to shift the borders of division of powers between the State and the regions in Italy—that means recognising to Community norms the same authority of constitutional norms, because regional powers are enumerated within the text of the Constitution (article 117)—last year the Court in an *obiter dictum* explicitly renounced that affirmation, by asserting that in any case Community provisions do not have the authority to influence the division of powers between State and regions (sent. n. 115 of 1993). More recently, in the decision n. 224 of 8 June 1994, the Court went back to the previous rationale and accepted that Community norms, as well as national norms that execute Community directives, can derogate to the constitutional provisions establishing the division of powers between the State and the Regions. It was the case of the regional powers concerning the bank system, that have almost been deleted by directive EEC/89/646.

Apparently, the Court presents an inconsistent case-law about the relations Community law and national constitutional law. But the shortcomings disappear in the rationale of the decision n. 117 of 31 March 1994 where the Court said that community norms cannot be qualified as having "constitutional value" because they belong to a separate legal system, although they are empowered to derogate to national constitutional provisions, providing they respect the basic fundamental values of the constitutional system. This rationale complies with the requirements of supremacy of Community law over constitutional law. Nevertheless Community norms are not considered as the equivalent of constitutional norms, because the structure and the content of the two kinds of norms are "incommensurable". In other words, Community norms are able to prevail over constitutional norms without pretending to take their place in the national system, and in any case, they cannot derogate to the fundamental principles of the constitutional system.

Supremacy of Community law is not absolute. The conditions imposed by the Constitutional court to the supremacy of Community law are fully justified from the Constitutional point of view. Nevertheless they might cause new conflicts with the European Court of Justice, considering that since the decision International Handelgesellschaft (1979) the European Court has established that supremacy means that Community law should prevail over every national norm, including constitutional provisions, with no limits.

THE ITALIAN CONSTITUTIONAL COURT CASE-LAW CONCERNING THE DIRECT EFFECT OF EUROPEAN LAW

As regards the direct effect of Community law, the Italian Constitutional Court seems to have plainly accepted the doctrines established by the European Court of Justice. I dare say that to some extent the Constitutional Court anticipated the Court of Justice in drawing some important consequences from the principle of direct effect. Although the principle of direct effect and the principle of supremacy of Community law are strictly connected, one could contend that the Italian legal system imposed much less resistance to the doctrine of direct effect than to the doctrine of supremacy of Community law.

The first decisions concerning direct effect of Community law were rendered during the 1970s and they aimed at forbidding the practice of reproducing Community regulations into acts of the Italian Parliament. This practice had been condemned several times by the European Court of Justice, mainly because it abridged the direct applicability of regulations. Complying with the requirements of article 189, as interpreted by the European Court, the Italian Court said that EC regulations cannot be transposed into Italian acts because their transposition would differ or condition the coming into force of Community regulations within the Italian legal system. Furthermore, such a transposition would change the nature of the source of Community regulations so that they would be binding in Italy as "national" acts: consequently their legal treatment would change, including the rules of interpretation and the authorities competent to verify their validity or to interpret them (dec. n. 183 of 1973; n. 232 of 1975; 206–206 of 1976).

As to the problem of defining the sources of Community law which can have direct effect within the national system, the Constitutional Court has adopted a generous attitude. Since 1985—notice: one year later the fundamental decision n. 170 of 1984 (Granital)—the Constitutional Court has been accepting that every source of Community law which responds to the characters established by the European Court of Justice can receive direct effect within the Italian legal order. So, in decision 23 April 1985, n. 232 the Court stated that decisions rendered by the European Court of Justice in proceeding *ex* article 177 of the EC treaty should be applied by ordinary judges and should immediately prevail over national norms having a different content. Subsequently, in decision 11 July 1989, n. 389 the Constitutional Court expanded the previous rationale, by asserting that every decision enacted by the European Court of Justice, both in proceedings *ex* article 177 and in other types of proceedings, like those described in article 169 of the EC treaty, should receive direct effect.

It goes without saying that the Constitutional Court accepted without any problem that directives can have direct effect, under the conditions fixed by the Court of Justice. And although the first decision that explicitly recognizes direct effect to directives is dated 1990 (decision 2 February 1990, n. 64, confirmed by decision 18 April 1991, n. 168) it could be surely affirmed that in cases even before those decisions Community directives were given direct effect in the Italian system.

Briefly, every source of Community law is susceptible of having direct effect, provided it complies with the requirements established by the European Court of Justice.

From this perspective the Italian system presents no problems with direct effect. However it is worth remarking that it is not completely clear which is the authority competent to declare the direct effect of Community norms. For example, in decision n. 168 of 1991 the Constitutional Court said that it shares with the European Court of Justice and with ordinary judges the competence to decide whether a directive has direct effect. The Court retained to have "faculty"—notice: not the duty—to refer the problem of interpretation of directives to the European Court of Justice, by means of preliminary rulings provided in article 177 of the Treaty. But up to now the Constitutional Court has never used the faculty and has always interpreted community law on its own, without asking the European Court for a preliminary interpretation. Moreover, in recent years the Constitutional Court has changed its mind about its relationship with the European Court of justice: in decision n. 537 of 1995, confirmed by decision n. 319 or 1996, the Court said that it cannot be qualified a "jurisdiction" for the purposes of article 177 CE, and consequently it is not in its power to apply to the European Court of Justice for preliminary rulings about the validity or the interpretation of Community law.[8] If the Italian Court will maintain this position, one could easily foresee that in the future it might happen that different Courts give different interpretations of the same provision and that new conflicts might arise between the European Court of Justice and the Italian Constitutional Court about the direct effect of Community law.

As regards the identification of the national authorities which are called upon to ensure direct effect to community norms, it is interesting to remark that at the same moment when the European Court of Justice was establishing the rule that not only judges, but also administrative authorities are imme-

---

[8] About this problem see F. Sorrentino, *Rivisitando l'art. 177 del trattato di Roma, Lo stato delle istituzioni italiane*, Milano, 1994, 637 ss.; M. Cartabia, *Considerazioni sulla posizione del giudice comune di fronte a casi di "doppia pregiudizialità", comunitaria e costituzionale*, "Foro italiano", 1997.

diately bound by Community provisions having direct effect (Costanzo case, 1989), the Italian Constitutional Court was pronouncing the same doctrine. Certainly the Italian Court was not informed of the forthcoming decision of the European Court of Justice, because although it usually takes into account the case law of the European Court when necessary to decide questions under its jurisdiction, there is neither direct communication nor exchange of information between the two Courts. Nevertheless on that occasion the two Courts were "in tune" and both decided for endowing administrative authorities, as well as judges, with the power of immediately applying Community law having direct effect, instead of the relevant national provision, which in this case has to be set aside (for the Constitutional Court see decision n. 389 of 1989).

Like in the Granital decision, also in this case the Constitutional court prompted a deep change in the Italian legal system. As I have already said, one of the general principles of the Italian legal system is the "rule of law: (*principio di legalità*), which requires all the administrative and executive authorities—including the Government—to be bound by the acts of Parliament. Moreover the Italian version of the "rule of law" requires that every competence of administrative or executive institutions is based on an act of the Parliament: the idea implied in the Italian version of the rule of law is that administrative authorities should be explicitly authorised by the legislator before exercising any kind of power. As a consequence, administrative authorities should find in the acts of Parliament the basis and the measure of the power that they are entitled to exercise. Therefore it is evident that within decision n. 389 of 1989 the Constitutional Court accepted that, as far as community law is concerned, the rule of law can be disregarded by administrative institutions. After that decision Community law can surrogate the acts of the Italian Parliament as to the requirements of the rule of law. This means that in practice administrative authorities can find the basis of their powers within community law, notwithstanding different rules prescribed by Italian law. In order to understand the importance of this doctrine, one should consider that the Italian decision making process of Community law is entirely granted to the Government, both in the ascending phase and in the descending one. By consequence, through Community law, the executive branch is now free to decide the measure of its power, almost without parliamentary control.

THE ITALIAN CONSTITUTIONAL COURT AND THE *KOMPETENZ-KOMPE-TENZ* PRINCIPLE

The Italian Constitutional Court has never had to tackle the problem of deciding which of the two legal systems—the European one or the Italian one—possess the "*kompetenz-kompetenz*". Nevertheless, one could suppose that in case the Court would say that the competence of deciding over the competence belongs to the States, and more precisely to the national supreme Courts.

To demonstrate this speculative affirmation it is necessary to turn our minds to the whole construct of the relationship between Italy and Europe adopted by the Constitutional Court. I contend that from the idea of limitation of sovereignty and from the dualistic principle it follows that the competence over the competence remains within the States' jurisdiction.

First of all, the Court has affirmed and reaffirmed several times that the European Community and the European Union are endowed only with the enumerated powers established in the Treaties, whereas Italy, as well as the other member States, is entitled to all the remaining competencies. In particular in decision n. 183 of 1973 (Frontini) the Court insisted that in order to give some normative power to the Community institutions the States transferred a part of their powers to the Community, on the basis of the precise division of competence established in the Treaty, following which the Community is allowed to intervene within the matters listed in parts II and III of the EC Treaty. In this decision, the idea of limitation of sovereignty (article 11 of the Constitution), implies that the "general" competence should belong to the States, whereas the Community should act within the limits established by the Treaty. Consequently, in the Court's view the Community does not have power to enlarge its field of jurisdiction on its own and its actions are valid so long as they remain within the borders prescribed by the Treaty. It is implied within the idea of limitation of sovereignty, on the basis of which Italy entered the Community, that it is the State that decides the measure of the power to be transferred to the Community and that controls the respect of the enumerated power established in the Community treaties.

Also the dualistic principle leads to a similar result. Let us take the "soft" version of the dualistic principle, enunciated by the Court in decision n. 170 of 1984 (Granital), which is still the leading case on the relationship between Italy and the European Community. The Court says: "There is a reference-point in the Court's construct of the relationship between community law and national law: the two systems are shaped as autonomous and distinct, although co-ordinate on the basis of the division of power established and guaranteed in the Treaty". Dualism—i.e. distinction and independence of the two systems—needs co-ordination, otherwise the two systems would not even enter into relations with each other, and co-ordination is based on the separation of powers described in the Treaty. Also dualism, as well as limitation of sovereignty, leads the Court to insist on the limits of the enumerated powers which belong to the Community on the basis of the Treaty. In this perspective it seems necessary that the competence over the competence belongs to the unity (i.e. the State) which is entitled to the general competence.

Moreover, in the latest decision of October 1993 concerning the Treaty of Maastricht, the *Bundesverfassungsgericht* explicitly affirmed that the Community does not have the *kompetenz-kompetenz* power and that the German constitutional court would control that Community acts fall within the European field of jurisdiction. What is interesting is that the German constitutional court arrived at this important affirmation on the basis of article 38 of the *Grundgesetz* which guarantees the right to vote: since the Court has the power and the duty to protect the inviolable "core of value" of the fundamental rights, including the right to vote, it follows that the protection of the right to vote of each citizen demands the Court to watch that the Community remains within the limits of its jurisdiction. These conclusions are all the more interesting for Italy, because the Italian constitutional court, like the German one, has always maintained the power of protecting the inviolable "core of value" of the fundamental rights. Possibly the Italian Court will join the German Court as regards the control over the limitation of powers that binds Community actions.

THE CONTRIBUTION OF "*LA DOCTRINE*" TO THE DEVELOPMENT OF THE ITALIAN CONSTITUTIONAL COURT'S ATTITUDE TOWARDS EUROPEAN INTEGRATION

Generally speaking, the attitude of the Italian constitutional "doctrine" towards the "Constitutional Court's path towards European integration" has been receptive. The development of the case-law of the Constitutional Court was seen as an increasing assent to the ideals of European integration, and scholars, who were generally well-disposed towards Europe, in most cases applauded the Court's compliance with the Community requirements.

After the Maastricht Treaty, "*la doctrine*" split up into two parties taking two distinct positions: whereas some scholars are enthusiastic about the European Union as laid out in the Maastricht Treaty,[9] some others are critical and would like the Constitutional Court to be more watchful towards European law.[10] The Maastricht Treaty seems to threaten some aspects of Italian constitutional architecture, because it enhances the role of "market"[11] in the economic system, and gives small place to the "social rights", which are protected by the Italian Constitution. As a consequence, the role of the Constitutional Court as the "guardian of constitutional values" becomes more urgent and more crucial in regards to Community law.

During the period before Maastricht, whereas constitutional scholars have generally only annotated and commented the decisions of the Constitutional Court, it is worth mentioning at least one case in which a constitutional essay has possibly influenced the case-law of the Constitutional Court concerning

---

[9] See e.g. G. Bognetti, *La Costituzione economica italiana*, Milano, 1995; G. Guarino, *Pubblico e privato nell'economia, La sovranità tra Costituzione e istituzioni comunitarie*, "Quaderni costituzionali", 1992, 21 ss.

[10] M. Luciani, *La Costituzione italiana e gli ostacoli all'integrazione europea*, in "Politica del diritto", 1992, 101 ss.

[11] The relations between the idea of "market" in the Maastricht Treaty and in the Italian Constitution is becoming a topic of the Italian "doctrine": see, among many other, P. Bilancia, *Modello economico e quadro costituzionale*, Torino, 1996.

Community law: in fact the Frontini decision of December 1973 seems to have drawn inspiration from a book published a few months before, both in the theoretical construct and in the practical results. It is the book by Federico Sorrentino, *Corte costituzionale e Corte di Giustizia delle Comunità europee*, vol. II, published in June 1973.

After analysing all the different constructs of the relationship between the member States and the Community proposed by the scholars, and after refusing all construct that presupposes a hierarchy between the two systems, the author assumes dualism and division of competence as the criteria that give to the relations between the two legal systems a persuasive and acceptable shape. In Sorrentino's view, dualism and separation do not lead to the indifference of the legal systems, because of some important rules of connection that link community law to national law. The most important of them is the rigid division of powers between national law and community law, after which national law cannot regulate those matters described in the treaty because they are reserved to the Community (once the Community has enacted its norms).

Having established this general principle, the author says that the way of resolving conflict between national and community law changes in each national legal system, because it depends on the system of sources of law that each State has adopted. For the Italian case he suggests the "two-folded" guarantee that has been adopted by the Constitutional Court in Frontini and that marked the Italian position throughout the 1970s: if a Community norm comes into force after a conflicting national norm, the former has the force to repeal the latter, so that each jurisdictional authority, called upon to apply that Community norm, has the power and the duty to make Community norms prevail over any different national provision. In the opposite case, when the national norm is subsequent to the Community one, the Italian legislator has infringed the division of power between the two systems and, by consequence it has infringed article 11 of the Constitution: the power of resolving the conflict between the two norms is then granted only to the Constitutional Court.

Given the peculiarity of the solution proposed it is hardly deniable that this book was at least taken into account by the Constitutional Court when deciding the Frontini case. After all the Frontini rationale was consonant with the constitutional principles governing the sources of law, the role of judges, the role of the Constitutional Court, and so on: the following position taken up by the Constitutional Court demanded, as we already said, deep changes within the constitutional system. No wonder, then, if the main contribution of the constitutional doctrine was concerned only with the Frontini decision.

In fact, it was only *after* the Simmenthal decision of the European Court of Justice that some of the constitutional scholars very cautiously suggested that the Italian system could find a way of adhering to the position of the European

Court of Justice.[12] In any case these suggestions seem to have been urged more by the necessity of resolving the conflict with the European Court of Justice than by constitutional precepts.

[12] See e.g. the contributions of P. Barile and G. Motzo, in *Il primato del diritto comunitario e i giudici italiani*, Milano, 1978.

5

Report on Italy

FRANCESCO P. RUGGERI LADERCHI

INTRODUCTION

Jean Victor Louis when commenting on a landmark judgment of the Italian Constitutional Court[1] quoted the following phrase from the opinion of A-G Lagrange in *Costa* v. *Enel*: "I do not for a moment consider that Italy, which has always been in the forefront amongst the promoters of the European idea, the country of the conference of Messina and of the Treaty of Rome, cannot find a constitutional means of allowing the Community to live in full accordance with the rules created under its common charter".

A similar kind of uneasiness would probably still be the natural reaction of an external observer towards the striking contradictions between the strong, if often illusory, Europeanism of Italian politics and the Italian people and the creeping mistrust of the Constitutional Court towards the supremacy of Community law[2] which is the *leitmotif* of thirty years of case law.

The search for a constitutional device by means of which the doctrines emanating from Luxembourg could be accepted in Italy has been more prolonged and difficult than A-G Lagrange expected. It would be very easy to say that the "euro-scepticism" experienced by the Italian Constitutional Court paralleled the experience of other supreme courts and that according to the famous dictum of Lord Devlin "enthusiasm is not a judicial virtue".

However, the reasons for the attitude of the Italian Constitutional Court seem to a certain extent to be peculiar to it. Similarly the doctrinal construction that led to a qualified acceptance of direct effect and supremacy

* I am indebted to Prof. Weiler and to all the participants in the research project who made comments on the paper on which this chapter is based. I am particularly grateful to A-G La Pergola and Professor Ferrari-Bravo for their views on the subject and to Eileen Sheehan for her invaluable help. The usual disclaimer applies.

[1] Annotation to 232/75, ICIC, [1975] *Giurisprudenza Costituzionale*, 3227.

[2] One could analyse this apparent contradiction under the conceptual categories proposed by Weiler in "The Dual Character of Supranationalism" [1981] YEL 268. It might be a fascinating exercise to prove that normative supra-nationalism would not work in Italy because of the strong political supra-nationalist drive. It is submitted that this is probably excessive. It is certainly true that one of the reasons for the apparent supra-nationalism of Italian politics and of public opinion is the fact that Community law was not taken very seriously by politicians. It was not considered as a source of "real" obligations.

in 1984[3] is very peculiar. This chapter will attempt to examine those peculiar reasons. These observations will be based on a non-doctrinal approach. A particular emphasis will be placed on taking an external point of view, namely by describing the foundations of the discourse of the legal actors rather than accepting the accepted wisdom as a point of departure. This approach is contestable according to the standards of Italian legal writers but it aims at providing some further elements of reflection.

In particular, we will consider the emergence of the doctrine of separation of the two legal orders in the early case law of the Constitutional Court. This doctrine is an element of continuity which has characterised the whole development of the case law. One cannot consider the constant reference to it simply as some kind of "fig-leaf" to cover the reversal of the Constitutional Court's attitude towards Community law. The following discussion will try to show that these doctrinal elements were so solidly entrenched in the mind of the actors of the play as to represent a fundamental element which explains the development of the action and the outcomes. A few observations will be made questioning the constant reference from the Constitutional Court to *Granital* as representing a proper description of the law to date. This long awaited and highly praised solution was probably too precious in the eyes of the Constitutional Court to be put openly into question.

The Court has not addressed the issue of *Kompetenz Kompetenz*. Nonetheless the theory of separation of legal orders in the case law of the Constitutional Court is based on the idea of competence. The debate initiated by the German *Maastricht* decision could pave the way to new developments in Italy, which will pose large theoretical and procedural dilemmas for the Constitutional Court. This will be briefly touched on in the concluding remarks.

BEYOND THE DOCTRINE

The actors—judges

The *"primadonna"* in the play is generally acknowledged to be the Constitutional Court. Other courts generally did not feel in a position to accept the doctrines emanating from Luxembourg on their own accord. The Constitutional Court's rejection of supremacy in *Costa* v. *Enel*[4] placed Community law outside the realm of private litigants and ordinary judges. It is interesting to note that for more than four years[5] following *Costa* v. *Enel* no preliminary references were made to the European Court of Justice.

---

[3] Constitutional Court decision 170/84, *Granital*, [1984] *CMLRev* 756, with annotation by G. Gaja.

[4] *Costa* v. *Enel e soc. Edisonvolta*, 7 March 1964, n. 14, *Foro Italiano* [1964] I, 465.

[5] The first article 177 procedure after *Costa* v. *Enel* and *Albatros* (Case 20/64, judgment of 4 February 1965, [1965] ECR 29) which was referred on 18 January 1964 (before *Costa* v. *ENEL*) has been *Salgoil* which was referred by an order of 9 July 1968.

Presumably litigants and judges had a tendency to assimilate the procedure for seeking preliminary ruling of the ECJ to the procedure for judicial review of legislation by the Constitutional Court.[6] As long as the alleged incompatibility of national law with Community law did not enable the former to be set aside, there was not much point in enquiring into such incompatibility.

The Italian administration itself was largely unaware of Community law and would apply it only after its transposition into administrative circulars or even statutes.[7]

The weight of the ordinary courts should not, however, be underestimated. In contrast to the situation in Germany, litigants do not have direct access to the Constitutional Court. The evolution of the case law was prompted by the orders from lower courts referring matters to the Constitutional Court. Moreover, in order for such references to be admissible, lower courts are required to outline the reasons why the question submitted is relevant for the solution of the case at hand and demonstrate that the doubts on the constitutionality of the statute subject to review are not manifestly unfounded.

Lower courts since the 1970s have been particularly enthusiastic in using the procedure of preliminary ruling to the ECJ. It is undeniable that the making of references to Luxembourg by *Pretori*[8] would feature at the centre of the attention of the world of lawyers. Their judgments which are normally not reported, would be published in important law journals. The approval of their analysis by the ECJ, would demonstrate that they are citizens of the world and that "they get Community law right" while the professors in the Constitutional Court or senior judges did not grasp the importance of Community law. The quest for notoriety might be a psychological explanation of the attitude of lower courts.

Lower courts in a number of cases cast doubts on the validity of the Community Treaties. Sometimes those doubts were only raised in order to present the Constitutional Court with some of the consequences of its previous statements and consequently make the case more difficult for the Constitutional Court and oblige it to accept certain principles of Community law.[9] In other cases, lower courts seemed eager to exacerbate the conflict between the Court in Rome and the one in Luxembourg and require the Constitutional Court to defend certain national principles against the incoming tide of Community law.

Judicial empowerment of lower courts is a very important element in a nondoctrinal analysis of the reception of supremacy. The fact that orders making an article 177 reference are not subject to appeal amplified the power of lower courts making references. Superior courts not only could not impede such references but would be bound by the answers coming back from Luxembourg.

However, the fundamental constitutional principle which states that courts other than the Constitutional Court are subject to Parliament made it impos-

---

[6] This could easily explain the framing of the references to the ECJ in terms such as "is the national provision xyz, compatible with article x of the Treaty?".

sible for the lower courts to accept supremacy without the endorsement of the Constitutional Court. Although lower courts played an important role, until *Granital* they remained behind the scenes acting through the intermediary of the Constitutional Court and of the ECJ. *Granital* was the "green light" to lower courts to apply Community law by their own motion, which they did with great enthusiasm although sometimes rather imprecisely. At other times lower courts' decisions reveal very deep knowledge of and reflection upon Community law. In the meantime lower courts kept prompting the Constitutional Court towards further evolution. The overly intellectual nature of the doctrine of *Granital* may possibly explain this search for more clear-cut solutions.

The absolute predominance of the Constitutional Court in the reception of Community law can also be explained by the lack of a doctrine of precedent in Italian law. It is only recently that lawyers have started studying and quoting in their pleadings case law.[10] The study of case law is still exceptional in Italian universities. Statute books were normally not annotated with case law. Even the judgments from the Corte Suprema di Cassazione were generally reported in extremely short abstracts prepared by a service of the Court (*Ufficio massimario*). There is no "*Commissaire du Gouvernement*" and the conclusions of Procuratore Generale in the Cassazione are never reported.

In contrast, the decisions of the Constitutional Court are binding on all courts. Once a statute is declared contrary to the Constitution it is as if the former were repealed. The Court's case law has over the years devised more sophisticated forms of judgments. It can declare that a piece of legislation is not contrary to the Constitution provided that it is interpreted in a certain way;[11] or even that it is contrary to the Constitution in as much as it can be interpreted in a certain way.[12] In a system in which—at least in theory—judges cannot make the law, the Constitutional Court can. One could say that the Constitutional Court has a true, albeit limited, legislative power.

---

[7] The habit of transposing regulations into national acts was condemned by the ECJ in *Variola*, Case 34/73, [1973] ECR 981, and in *Zerbone*, Case 94/77, [1978] ECR 99, and by the Constitutional Court in *Frontini*.

[8] *Pretori* are lower judges, often sitting in small provincial cities, who until very recently had extremely wide powers in both civil and criminal matters. They had a very important and nearly revolutionary role also in other fields of law. Judges in Italy are civil servants appointed following a very difficult national competitive examination at the end of their university studies. They form a very independent body within the State. Discipline, career and other organisational matters rest largely within the Consiglio Superiore della Magistratura, an independent constitutional organ whose members are appointed as to two-thirds by the judiciary and one-third by Parliament.

[9] This is probably the sense of the question submitted to the Court in *Frontini*.

[10] Administrative law is an exception to this general rule. The Consiglio di Stato developed the whole construction of judicial review.

[11] Ordinary courts could of course still interpret it differently, and even refer it again to the Court on the basis of such an interpretation. This happens sometimes. The Court would often discard these rebel references with an order declaring the question manifestly unfounded.

[12] This type of modification of the scope of a provision is on the contrary binding on every court.

Moreover, the Constitutional Court is much more open than other courts to policy arguments and even if it is at times extremely doctrinal, at least on the surface of its discourse, it tends to be less formalistic than other courts. This is not only due to its position in the system but also to the educational and professional background of the judges.

One-third of the judges are appointed by Parliament, another third by the judges in the civil supreme (Cassazione) and administrative supreme (Consiglio di Stato, Corte dei Conti) courts and the final third by the President of the Republic.[13] The members of the Constitutional Court are senior judges, lawyers and university professors. The particular attention that the Court pays to *la doctrine* is not surprising. The members appointed by Parliament and by the President of the Republic, often a law professor himself, are mostly law professors. The post of judge of the Court has enormous prestige and is probably the zenith in the *cursus honorum* of a lawyer.

Decisions are discussed orally amongst the judges and drafted by the judge *rapporteur*. No dissenting opinions exist and similarly to the ECJ, all decisions are considered unanimous. The main decisions concerning Community law have been drafted by academics with a background in international law. The personal theoretical approach of the drafter is a key element particularly as far as *obiter dicta* are concerned. The influence of *la doctrine* in those judgments is even greater as counsel for the parties were often famous law professors who based their pleadings on their theories.

Another element to take into consideration is the involvement of a limited number of people in the handling of Community law matters. The same individuals were lawyers or judges in the Constitutional Court and in the ECJ.[14] The Italian Government has systematically designated law professors as judges and Advocates General in the ECJ. Judges of the Constitutional Court and of the ECJ come from the same *milieu universitaire* and have all given their contribution to the debate on Community law.

Yet another factor which has certainly played a role is the Avvocatura dello Stato.[15] The Italian Government is in fact always represented in the ECJ by a special team in the Avvocatura dello Stato of Rome. The Avvocatura dello Stato of Rome plays an important function in Constitutional Court proceedings as well. This role is somewhat similar to the one of the Advocate General

---

[13] This is one of the few real powers of the President under the Constitution.

[14] Just as an example one could note that Nicola Catalano a former Avvocato dello Stato was a negotiator of the EC Treaty, a judge in the ECJ, he annotated *Costa v. Enel* in the *Foro Italiano* (the most important law journal for practitioners) and in the *Common Market Law Review*, he pleaded in a number of cases in front of the ECJ, and he was counsel for the private parties in the Constitutional Court case 232/75 *ICIC*; the other counsel for private parties in the action was Leopoldo Elia, who was going to be the President of the Constitutional Court at the time of *Granital*.

[15] The Avvocatura dello Stato is a very competent and respected body which forms part of the Italian administration. They are lawyers, working pretty much in the same fashion as private lawyers, entrusted with the representation of the State in civil and administrative proceedings in which the State is a party.

in the ECJ. However, the Avvocatura intervenes on behalf of the Government and invariably defends the legality of the statutes under review. The Constitutional Court takes account of these pleadings and often quotes them in its decisions.

The actors—*la doctrine*

Looking from a non-doctrinal point of view at the case law, one has to acknowledge that the main point of reference of the Constitutional Court was *la doctrine*. The public at large and the press did not pay much attention to the whole debate. *Granital* and *Frontini*, which were followed by a press conference given by the President of the Court—something extremely unusual— were in fact the only occasions in which public opinion was aroused. These cases were perceived as "steps towards Europe", something for which there was a generic, yet not much reasoned, praise and favour.

Lawyers and academics, in contrast, addressed the relationship between the Italian legal order and the Community's in endless debates, conferences and writings.[16] *Simmenthal* provided further stimulus towards the flowering of new theories. By and large *la doctrine*, like the Constitutional Court, found the supremacy of Community law *per se* unacceptable, at least in the terms of *Costa* v. *Enel* and *Simmenthal*, as decided by the ECJ. There has been constant attempts both by the Constitutional Court and *la doctrine* to make Community law work within the framework of generally accepted Italian doctrines.

It is impossible to give an account of the different theories. If one reads the first commentaries on *Costa* v. *ENEL* one realises that there were already a dozen or more different theories proposed by academics in order to solve the divergence between Rome and Luxembourg. When looking back over thirty years of debate it is very arbitrary to refer to specific contributions. Nonetheless there are certain approaches that are common to several authors. It is therefore still useful to refer to them.

It is not very difficult to conclude that the fact that the authors of these theories had a background of international or constitutional law played a certain role. The former would dilute Community law in international law while the latter would rely mainly on the constitutional rules granting supremacy, thus recognising supremacy only because of these rules.

As an example of the first approach one could look at the first pages of one of the most widely used Community law handbooks:[17]

---

[16] Just to have a sample of the quantity of theories one could look at the authors quoted by P. De Caterini in his note to *Frontini* in [1975] *Cahier de Droit Européen*, 115. After *Simmenthal*, *Il primato del diritto Comunitario e i giudici Italiani* (Milano, 1978).

[17] F. Pocar, *Diritto delle Comunità Europee*, 4th edn. (Milano, 1991), 2–3.

"The insufficiency of this approach [i.e. Community law as an autonomous body of law] to define scientifically 'community law' does not need a specific demonstration, in the light of the consideration that the legal phenomenon of the Community has its basis and its discipline in a set of norms belonging to international law and that the Community can only be seen as a part of international law".

Further:

"In this respect the statements of the Court of Justice in *Van Gend & Loos* and *Costa* v. *ENEL* are not convincing when they affirm that the EEC Treaty is more 'than an agreement which merely creates mutual obligations between the contracting states' and that it would be different from 'ordinary international treaties'. The EEC Treaty . . . on the contrary is an international treaty like any other, and it only creates a series of rights and obligations between the contracting states".

This kind of statement is not uncommon. They do not mean that the authors do not acknowledge supremacy, but simply that they would prefer the supremacy of EC law to fall within the framework of the general international law principle of supremacy of treaties. They would rather stress the traditional principle of *interpretation conforme* or other rules of construction[18] in order to avoid conflicts between domestic provisions and Community provisions.

A role has also been played by the set of theories based on article 10 of the Constitution.[19] These theories were put forward by international lawyers and never gained wide acceptance. Due to their intellectual fascination and to the prestige of Rolando Quadri, their main advocate, everybody felt obliged to discuss them even if only in order to discard them later. The Corte di Cassazione and the Constitutional Court discarded them only in *Frontini*. These theories, when compared to the "soft monism" of other international lawyers, can be seen as a radical form of monism. If Italy had accepted this approach it would have adopted a very similar if not more radical position towards Community law than the Netherlands.

Rolando Quadri's theory roughly goes as follows. Article 10 of the Constitution incorporates by reference general international law into the Italian legal system. The most important rule of general international law is *pacta sunt servanda*. Treaties are therefore incorporated into the national legal order. This theory was not however specifically elaborated in relation to Community law. Quadri himself adapted it to Community law stressing that the rules incorporated by article 10 would have supremacy over ordinary legislation. The rejection of this approach which appeared to most authors and presumably to the Constitutional Court as an unrealistic intellectual game and

---

[18] B. Conforti, another important international lawyer, stressed the fact that rules of Community law are *special* in relation to ordinary statutes. Hence conflicts should be solved with the rule of interpretation *lex specialis derogat generali*. See *Diritto Internazionale*, 3rd edn. (Napoli, 1987).

[19] Which reads as follows: "The Italian legal order conforms with the generally recognised principles of international law".

as using "a sledgehammer to crack a nut" is symptomatic of how deeply rooted dualism is in the Italian legal culture.

On the other hand one can see those authors who were more influenced by Constitutional law. Their position was closer to the position of the Court. Cartabia has pointed to the role played by the theories of Federico Sorrentino who is a professor of constitutional law. It is probably worth mentioning the role of the theories of Antonio La Pergola. When referring to his book[20] published in 1961, but written earlier, one would find much of what is said in the subsequent case law, and indeed in *Granital*, which was drafted by La Pergola himself. He very much developed the concept of the "atypical sources of law" in relation to the acts reproducing rules of international law in the internal legal order. "Atypical sources of law are ordinary acts which because of some specific constitutional guarantee cannot be modified by other ordinary acts. Although the whole theory is dualist La Pergola emphasised the practical irrelevance of choosing between monism and dualism.

The Constitutional Court never uses the term "dualism" which seems to have a negative and provincial flavour. It rather relies on the theory of the plurality of legal orders.[21] This theory is well established in Italian constitutional law tradition. Even if it can be traced back to the "Republic" of Plato, it finds its main expression in the writings of Santi Romano (1875–1947).[22] This reference remains mainly an attempt to grant cultural nobility to a dualist approach.

Dualism after all is too entrenched in the Italian legal tradition to be abandoned. There was, and there is, a fundamental doctrinal and political concern to avoid a perceived change of "grundnorm" as a result of its rejection.

On the other hand most people sooner or later realised that the contrast between the ECJ and the Constitutional Court on the status of Community law in Italy could not be sustained. Legal certainty is a very appealing objective for every lawyer. The contrast between the courts far from enhanced legal certainty. *La doctrine* shared the same concerns and the same *Weltanschauung* as the Constitutional Court and in order to heal the schism between Rome and Luxembourg, while respecting the Italian orthodoxy, suggested, discussed and invented solutions, with a fervour that probably was not matched in any other country.

Looking back at the case law, it is still worth repeating what a very influential commentator wrote in a note to *Granital*:

---

[20] A. La Pergola, *Costituzione e adattamento dell'ordinamento interno al diritto internazionale* (Milano, 1961).

[21] In Case 168/91 *Giampaoli* (below) the Court while restating *Granital* literally said "the fundamental principle (inspired by the doctrine of the plurality of legal orders) according to which the two legal orders, the Community and the State legal orders, are 'distinct and in the same time coordinated' ".

[22] See in particular *L'ordinamento giuridico* (1918).

"[The Constitutional Court] was obliged to negotiate a path between the inflexibility of the legal rules; the requirements of the process of integration, . . . the more or less discrete pressure from the Community Institutions, . . . the behaviour of the legislature and of the administration often incoherent and sometimes schizophrenic and in striking contradiction between a 'labial' Europeanism in permanent service and a different if not opposed behaviour; *the contrasting stimuli of a strongly involved* doctrine, *divided, unstable, verbose and maybe even confusing for the unbelievable quantity and variety of solutions imagined and reasons given.*"[23]

Cross-fertilisation

The experience of other countries, and of Germany in particular, has been very important for the Constitutional Court. The influence was important both at the doctrinal level and at the judicial policy level.

La doctrine has always been very open in every field of law to foreign models. In the nineteenth century the French model was absolutely dominant. This is quite understandable as the Italian civil code was little more than a translation of the Napoleon code. Nonetheless German *doctrine* later became extremely influential. The *"Begriffe Jurisprudenz"* first influenced Roman and civil law studies, then became the model to which Italian academics tried to conform in every field of legal studies. Despite the fact that the knowledge of the German language was not generally widespread it became a necessary tool for any respectful academic. The footnotes to every classic civil or public law handbook often quote more German than Italian authors.

The shift away from the French to the German model, particularly evident in the Civil Code of 1942, has been carefully studied by comparative lawyers with particular attention to private law. The attention to German model in the field of public law was possibly even more marked. It is probably more common to find references to Jellineck and Laband in Italian textbooks than in German ones. The Weimar Constitution was a very influential model in the drafting of the Italian Constitution. The fact that Italy and Germany were the only two founding Member States of the Community to have a Constitutional Court, ensured that it was natural for both *la doctrine* and the Court to look carefully to the German solutions.

The Court certainly found in the *Solange* case law support for the limits to Community law for protection of human rights that were set in *Frontini*. In the beginning these limits, it is submitted, had more to do with theoretical worries than with actual problems in the application of Community law in Italy. The fact that the whole question of human rights was so relevant in Germany was a very compelling reason for retaining these limits in Italy as well.

[23] A. Tizzano, "La Corte costituzionale ed il diritto comunitario: vent'anni dopo . . . " [1984] *Foro Italiano* I, 2063.

The importance of German examples is openly revealed in *Granital*, where the Constitutional Court itself acknowledges that one of the reasons for accepting the decentralised control of conformity of legislative acts with Community law was the fact that this type of control was accepted everywhere *including Germany*.

Other influences can also be found in different respects. *Granital* or at least its discourse, is based on the idea of *"pre-emption"*. The influence of American federal doctrines is not totally extraneous to this approach.

In a different manner one could also see some kind of cross-fertilisation between the ECJ and the Constitutional Court. The Constitutional Court could not be unaware of the dimensions of the conflict and was very careful whenever it entered the minefield of the relationship between national and Community law. This attention became of course more evident in the *post-Granital* case law. It has already been pointed out that the two courts were acting in the same *milieu*. It is submitted that the parallelism between the Constitutional Court case *Bolzano*[24] and ECJ case *Flli Costanzo*,[25] was far from being accidental.[26]

At a later stage the Constitutional Court even tried to "steer" the case law of the ECJ. The signal that was sent to Luxembourg with the *Fragd*[27] decision is very symptomatic.

In contrast, in minor cases, which were not perceived to contain large constitutional issues, the Constitutional Court did not only appear to forget the complicated doctrines that it devised in the *grands arrêts*, but at times misinterpreted Community law. It is possible to find *obiter dicta*, and at times actual decisions, completely at variance with the case law of the ECJ. In this respect the refusal to use the procedure for preliminary rulings to the ECJ becomes particularly regrettable.

The above-mentioned peculiarities of the Italian legal system are of course too simplistic to be "explanations" of the whole story. They are merely elements which from within the system seem too trivial to be taken into consideration. Looking at the system from outside, however, they are necessary factors in order to make sense of the Constitutional Court's case law and to limit, at least to a certain extent, the puzzled unease that A-G Lagrange, Jean Victor Louis and many other external observers experienced when faced with the Italian rebellion to Community law.

In the light of the foregoing it might be useful to go back to the history of the story and see how the elements just mentioned played a role.

---

[24] Case 369/89, *Provincia di Bolzano*, [1990] *Diritto Comunitario e degli scambi internazionali* 395.

[25] Case 103/88, [1989] ECR 1839.

[26] The Consitutional Court underlines the "quasi simultaneity" of the two decisions in Case 94 of 30 March 1995, *Rivista di Diritto Europeo* [1995] 473.

[27] 13 April 1989, n. 168, *Fragd*, [1990] *Foro Italiano* I, 1855.

LOOKING BACK AT THE "COMMUNITY PATH" OF THE CONSTITUTIONAL
COURT

The origin of the Constitutional Court's doctrines: a device used to avoid declaring the EC Treaty contrary to the Constitution

The background

Bruno de Witte has correctly pointed out that national courts when confronted with Community law had to face problems of different kinds. Only once the national courts had accepted that the Treaties had been lawfully ratified (membership), could they proceed to examine the effects of the Treaties and to solve the conflicts between the Treaties and national legislation (the "supremacy, direct effect" cluster).

This distinction is particularly true for the Italian Constitutional Court. The distinction between the different types of problems, is more logical than chronological. It is, however, undeniable that the solutions given to the problems of direct effect and supremacy and the choice of procedural means for granting supremacy have been influenced—nearly determined in hereditary manner—by the choices and the compromises made in order to accept the constitutional legality of the membership to the Communities.

The dualist constitutional orthodoxy and a plain reading of the Constitution seem to offer very little support to the legality under Italian constitutional law of the Community Treaties.

Treaties, like any other rule which is not created by the constitutional organs endowed with the power to create such rules, do not have any effect *per se* in the national legal order. It is a national act that either by reproducing them or by referring to them gives them effect. As Parliament cannot modify the Constitution by ordinary statute, it cannot ratify and implement by statute treaties which result in a modification of the Constitution, unless some express rule in the Constitution grants this power.

The Constitution of 1947 was a compromise, and to a certain degree the last compromise, between all the political forces that succeeded to power following the collapse of the fascist regime. Later, however, major choices, especially with regard to foreign policy and the inclusion of Italy in the Western block, were made in the face of opposition from the strongest Communist party in Western Europe.

A so-called constitutional statute (*"legge costituzionale"*), having the same force as the Constitution and hence the force to derogate from the latter, could not be passed in Parliament in order to implement the Community Treaties as it would had been impossible to achieve the required two-thirds majority of votes. It might seem banal, but all the theories and the Court's doctrines devised in order to affirm the legality of the statutes implementing the Treaties, are merely means to avoid the consequences of the original sin of not having used the special procedure of revision of the Constitution when implementing the Treaties.[28]

One should keep in mind that the Constitutional Court was not even in place at the time of the entry into force of the Treaty of Paris. Ordinary judges and the administration were to a large extent unacquainted with the idea of the supremacy of the Constitution over ordinary statutes. The Constitutional Court, once established in 1956, had to fight a long struggle to give effect to many principles of the Constitution that had been considered as merely "programmatic" as opposed to rules in the Constitution having binding effect.

One could be forgiven for thinking that at the time of ratification of the Treaties, the—probably well founded—doubts as to the legality of the means (an ordinary statute passed in Parliament) used to give effect to them, were merely some kind of doctrinal formalism. Nobody could seriously have imagined the Constitutional Court questioning such an important political choice.

A difficult start

A legal realist, at the time of the ratification of the EC Treaty, would never have predicted that any court on the basis of the Treaties founding the Common Market could have prevented Parliament from proceeding to the nationalisation of the electricity industry. Nationalisation of the industry was an enormous political issue and amounted to a major societal choice. It was perceived as a step towards a new economic model, refusing—to a certain extent—capitalism and was the result of a significant political shift.

In *Costa* v. *Enel* the Constitutional Court was not directly faced with the issue of the legality of the Treaties. The judge Conciliatore, when ruling on a cleverly "invented" case,[29] assumed (a) that the EC Treaty was properly ratified and executed by means of a statute, (b) that a statute contrary to the Treaty would be unconstitutional.

It is well known that the Constitutional Court declared that indeed the State is bound by the Treaties but only as a subject of the international legal order. A statute contrary to the Treaties would hence be considered as a violation of international law but would not lose its value as a statute. The Constitutional Court noted that article 11 of the Constitution[30] only means

---

[28] It is interesting to note that during the Parliamentary debates for the ratification of the Maastricht Treaty, which went largely ignored by the public at large, the extreme right and the extreme left considered that article 11 of the Constitution could not authorise the ratification of the Maastricht Treaty and a revision of the Constitution was needed. See F. Mirabile in "Ordinamento Costituzionale Italiano ed Integrazione Europea: aspetti problematici" *Rivista di Diritto Europeo* [1995] 313.

[29] L. Ferrari Bravo "L'issue de l'affaire Costa c. ENEL devant le Conciliatore de Milan", [1967] *Cahier de Droit Européen*, 194.

[30] Which reads as follows: "Italy condemns war as an instrument of aggression against the liberties of other peoples and as means for settling international controversies; it agrees on conditions of equality with other states, to such limitation of sovereignty as may be necessary for a system designed to ensure peace between Nations; it promotes and encourages international organisations having such aims".

"that under certain conditions, it is possible to enter into agreements which limit sovereignty, and that it is possible to implement them by an ordinary statute". However "article 11 has not given to the ordinary statute that implements the Treaty a superior effect to the one of any other statute".

To a certain extent the Italian Government itself caused the bold reaction of the Court of Justice in *Costa*. The case that came to the ECJ was not technically speaking the same that went to Rome, it was in fact a case pending before a different *Conciliatore*. The Italian Government nonetheless, relied on the decision of the Constitutional Court in order to argue the inadmissibility of the article 177 reference. It was argued that the questions were irrelevant insofar the national judge was bound to apply the statute creating ENEL and not the Treaty which was enacted previously. The ECJ prompted by A-G Lagrange reacted in—by now—well known words to that plea.

However, in *Albatros*, which was decided immediately thereafter, the ECJ seemingly took a more cautious approach. Perhaps to avoid further frontal clashes with national jurisdictions or perhaps because the French Government did not introduce arguments of the type used by the Italian Government, the ECJ merely interpreted some articles of the Treaty without dealing with their effects on the subsequent French legislation in question.

It is commonplace to stigmatise the solution chosen by the Constitutional Court and to compare it to the one proposed by the ECJ as a reaction to it. It is certain that the judgment of the Constitutional Court was hasty[31] and formalistic. One has the impression that the Court was not really interested in the process of European integration. The Constitutional Court seemed very annoyed at having to deal with something so important as the annulment of the nationalisation of the electricity industry as a result of Mr Costa's legal challenge to an electricity bill of 1925 liras (little more than one dollar at today's rate).

However, it must be said that at the time the legal effects of the Community obligations were not so clear cut and not only in Rome. It was often argued that article 5 of the EC Treaty showed that it rested upon the Member States to ensure the conformity of their legislation with Community law.[32]

Even the recognition of the legality of the Italian accession to the EC Treaty on the basis of article 11 was far from being a foregone conclusion. The article is drafted in very different terms both from article 55 of the French Constitution and from article 24 of the German Basic Law. It was argued that article 11 was drafted in order to enable Italy to adhere to the United Nations and that it could not be "recycled" and made applicable to the Community. Some authors claimed that the constitutional provision was merely programmatic and deprived of any legal value. Very respected and influential writers

---

[31] The Court calls the Commission "*ad hoc* Commission" or "Consultative Commission" and the ECJ "High Court of Justice".

[32] This then common argument was used also by the Italian Government in the ECJ in *Costa* v. *E.N.E.L.*

were still calling for the use of article 10 as a peg on which to hang Community law (Quadri's theory).

The applicability of article 11 of the Constitution to the Community Treaties, so as to enable their valid ratification and implementation by ordinary statute, was ascribed to Perassi.[33] During parliamentary discussions on the act of ratification of the ECSC Treaty the *rapporteur* (Ambrosini) referred to article 11 in order to counter the objections of those requesting the use of a special "constitutional statute". It was in fact Nicola Catalano that placed more emphasis than any other on article 11. He remained nonetheless extremely critical of the judgment of the Constitutional Court.[34] To his mind article 11 should have been interpreted so as to grant supremacy.

Further steps—San Michele *and the adoption of the theory of separation of legal orders*

The legality of membership of the Community in *Costa* v. *ENEL* remained an *obiter dictum*. The very limited effect that the Constitutional Court reasoning gave to article 11 left many questions open in respect of the legality of the Treaties. Private parties therefore, tried to contest the legality of the Treaties, in particular the legality of the ECSC Treaty in order to challenge, in the Italian courts, penalties imposed within the framework of the latter.[35] Some courts[36] in the wake of the decision of the Constitutional Court in *Costa* v. *ENEL* were able to discard the argument with a generic reference to article 11 of the Constitution, while others went on to assess the legality of the provisions of the Treaties.[37]

The tribunal of Turin on 19 December 1964[38] made a reference to the Constitutional Court. It expressed doubts both as to the legality of an ordinary statute as the basis for membership and as to the compatibility with articles 102 and 113[39] of the Constitution of the exclusive jurisdiction of the ECJ in the annulment and suspension of decisions of the High Authority. The tribunal, on the basis of the statement in *Costa* in accordance to which article 11 did not give any specific value to the rules deriving from the Treaty, argued that these rules could not validly derogate from the above-mentioned articles of the Constitution.

---

[33] *La Costituzione Italiana e l'ordinamento internazionale* (1952), now published in *Scritti giuridici* (Milan, 1958).

[34] See his annotation to *Costa* v. *Enel* in [1964] *Foro Italiano* I, 465; [1965] *CMLRev* 224.

[35] E.g. Tribunale di Napoli, 22 April 1964, *Societa Metallurgica di Napoli s.p.a.* v. *CECA*, *Rivista di diritto Internazionale Privato e Processuale* [1965] 110; Tribunale di Roma, 22 September 1964, *S.p.a. Acciaierie ferriere di Roma* v. *CECA, ibid.*, 116; Tribunale di Milano, 28 September 1964, *S.p.a. Meroni* v. *CECA, ibid.*, 121.

[36] Pretura di Roma, Order of 11 March 1964, *Giustizia civile* [1964] III, 130.

[37] Cases quoted in n. 35 above.

[38] The order is published in [1965] *Rivista di diritto internazionale privato e processuale*, 126.

[39] Which prohibit the creation of special courts and establish the principle of judicial protection.

The Constitutional Court case in *San Michele* was just another step in a long saga that saw a number of Italian iron scrap users contesting in two occasions, without success, High Authority decisions before the ECJ.[40] The Constitutional Court in its decision[41] assessed *ex professo* the legality of the Treaties and established a framework of reference for the subsequent case law. The Constitutional Court did not follow the suggestions of the parties to the main proceedings, which requested a general review of the conformity of the Treaty with the Constitution. The Constitutional Court referred to *Costa* in order to show that article 11 authorised membership.

The Constitutional Court firstly said that the constitutional guarantees deriving from the above-mentioned articles applied only to individuals as part of the domestic legal order. It continued by stating that the EC Treaty, which involved more states, formed a completely separate legal order. The Court further stated that the domestic legal order did not incorporate the Community legal order. The domestic legal order only recognised the international co-operation that is within the aims of the Community. Finally, the domestic legal order determined the cases in which the activity of the organs of the Community, within their respective competence, had internal effects. The determination of the internal legal effects had to take into account the inviolable principle of judicial protection.

The Constitutional Court finally decided that the prohibition in article 104 of the Constitution on the establishment of special courts is valid only in connection with the domestic legal order and cannot be applied to the organs of the ECSC because they are part of a "separate legal orbit" and are not subject to the sovereign powers of the Member States. The Constitutional Court went on nonetheless to decide that the rules of the Community were not in breach of the principle of judicial protection.

The *dictum* of the case is not extremely clear and looks very much to be a compromise. It is clear that the Constitutional Court refused to evaluate *en bloc* the legality of the statute implementing the EC Treaty. It stated that it would check only the compatibility of specific rules with the Constitution. Article 11 was hence definitely established as a valid legal basis for membership of the Communities. It was not clear however to what extent article 11 enabled the Treaty to derogate from the other substantive provisions of the Constitution.

The fundamental result of this case is the adoption of the theory of separation of the two legal orders. The theory was used mainly as a device in order not to apply the specific rules of the Constitution to the organs of the Community. The subsequent case law built upon this legal device.

---

[40] *San Michele and others* v. *High Authority*, Joined Cases 5–11, 13–15/62, [1962] ECR 449 and *San Michele and others* v. *High Authority*, Joined Cases 2–10/63, [1963] ECR 327.

[41] 27 December 1965 n.98 *Acciaierie S. Michele* v. *CECA*, [1966] *Rivista di diritto Internazionale privato e processuale*, 106.

One could try to read more into this case. In its theory of separation of the two legal orders the Constitutional Court seemingly hints to the idea of *Kompetenz-Kompetenz*. The effects of the activities of the organs of the Community are recognised in the internal order only within the limits of their sphere of competence. On top of this, before having effect in the internal order, Community acts should comply with human rights.

As a final remark about *San Michele* it is interesting to note that the Community was a party to the main proceedings and submitted observations to the Constitutional Court. In its observations the High Authority stressed that article 11 was the legal basis not only for membership but also for supremacy. Prof. Giuliano,[42] counsel for the Community, had already adhered to Catalano's theories. The Avvocatura while recognising the legality of membership through article 11 sustained the theory of the separation.

The first in-depth analysis: Frontini

It is well known that it was only in *Frontini*[43] that the Constitutional Court tried to spell out the principles contained in *San Michele*. For the first time the Constitutional Court ventured into a detailed analysis of the Community legal order. The tone rather than the theoretical framework is radically different from the previous decisions.

In their orders for reference to the Constitutional Court the Tribunal of Turin and Genoa contested the legality of the legislative power of the Community. The Constitutional Court declared that article 11 not only authorised membership but that in order not to deprive article 11 of any significance it should be interpreted as allowing the Treaties to derogate from the Constitution without recourse to the special procedure of amendment. It went on to analyse the Community system proving that it complied with the conditions of article 11.

In *Frontini* as in *San Michele*, the Constitutional Court on the one hand says that the provisions of the Italian Constitution are not applicable to the Community legal order and on the other hand it still goes on to demonstrate that the Community legal order offers analogous guarantees. If the theory of the separation of the orders is formally the *ratio* of these cases, it is clear that the Constitutional Court needed some policy arguments on which to base its judgment and it was convinced only by them.

Moreover, while addressing the alleged violation of the principle of judicial protection enshrined in the Constitution, the Constitutional Court does not even use the theory of separation but rather demonstrates that the Community system offers an equivalent level of protection.

---

[42] "Droit communautaire et droit interne des Etats membres" [1966] *Rivista diritto internazionale privato e processuale* 220.

[43] 27 December 1973 *Frontini e altro c. Ministero delle Finanze*, [1974] *Rivista di diritto internazionale privato e processuale*, 154.

The recognition of the direct effect of regulations[44] was used to counter an objection raised by the Avvocatura which claimed that the regulations in question could not be applied by the judges in the main proceedings as they were bound to apply the subsequent national legislation reproducing them. This recognition was based once again on the doctrine of separation of the two legal orders. The distinct legal orders are nonetheless co-ordinated according to the distribution of competences guaranteed by the EC Treaty. The State, having limited its sovereignty, could no longer intervene in the sphere of competence of the Community.

The famous reservation on human rights seems to have been made *ad abundatiam*. On the one hand the Constitutional Court says that the legislative competence of the Community is limited to economic relations and on the other hand that there are rules in the Treaty which guarantee that Community law will not conflict with the Constitution in the area of civil and political rights. Nonetheless, if article 189 of the EC Treaty was to be interpreted as allowing the Community to trespass in this area, the acts adopted on the basis of such an interpretation would be outside the scope of the limitations of sovereignty allowed by article 11.

This reservation was prompted by *la doctrine*. The so-called "counter-limits", that is to say the limits to the limitations of sovereignty, are material rules prohibiting the Community from violating human rights and the fundamental principles of the Constitution. The Constitutional Court bases its reasoning on the fact that the limitations on sovereignty are allowed only for the aims of article 11 and that the Treaty sets out concretely the limitations on national sovereignty.

The language used is the language of competence. In the decision the Constitutional Court noted that the legislative power of the Community is based on the precise allocation of competences. This construction, which is the most persistent element in the evolution of the case law, does not make things very clear in practice. The Treaty as a matter of fact establishes an allocation of competences that is far from clear and in many areas the Member States and the Community have concurrent competences. The doctrine of the Constitutional Court has been interpreted practically as meaning wherever there is an act of Community law it has precedence because it is in the Community sphere of competence.

The possibility that an act of the Community would be beyond the Community competence seemed in *Frontini* merely theoretical. The reservation was expressed in a short paragraph without much reasoning. Two different approaches were confused. When it said that the Treaty deals only with economic questions and does not interfere with political rights the Constitutional Court was referring, although quite roughly, to a real problem

---

[44] The order of the Tribunal of Genoa was in fact contesting the legality of the regulations only in order to obtain a declaration of their direct effect. See De Caterini, n. 16 above.

of allocation of competence. By framing the limit of human rights in the same terms the Constitutional Court irremediably confused the issues.

From Frontini *to* Granital: *a few remarks*

It is well known that the doctrine of the separation of the legal orders and the acceptance of supremacy and direct effect in *Frontini* were not a solution for all the problems. It was not outlined what the judge should do when faced with a clash between Community legislation and subsequent domestic provisions.

The *ICIC*[45] case law and the choice of centralising enforcement in the hands of the Constitutional Court was a solution which was not only approved by a large section of *la doctrine*, but seemed to many authors to be compatible with Community law and the principle of institutional autonomy of Member States. It had the enormous advantage of coming squarely within the accepted doctrines on the Constitutional system.

The Constitutional Court has continuously tried to systematise its case law. The whole system of "atypical sources" and the possibility of declaring a statute unconstitutional for breach of rules incorporated by reference by the Constitution is rather common. The review of constitutionality of statutes for indirect breach of the Constitution is a device used, *inter alia*, in relation to statutory instruments in breach of the authorising statute, for regional statutes in breach of national framework statutes and in all kinds of other instances. The *ICIC* doctrine put Community law in a similar, if not identical, constitutional position to the position of the agreement between the Catholic Church and the State, and in a partially analogous position to the position of the agreements with other Churches. Community law would have had the same constitutional position as international treaties on the treatment of non-nationals.

The reaction of the ECJ in *Simmenthal* to supremacy "*all'italiana*" was perceived in Italy by the majority of *la doctrine* as an abusive interference in the procedural autonomy of Member States. The Tribunal of Milan put the Constitutional Court in a very difficult position when it required it to declare the Treaty contrary to the Constitution in so far as Community law, as interpreted in *Simmenthal*, would be contrary to the fundamental principles of the Constitution.[46]

The Tribunal of Milan was basically requiring the Constitutional Court either to accept *Simmenthal* and the decentralised control or to take a clear position against it. The Constitutional Court found a clever escape route by stating that in the pending case there was no conflict between domestic and Community law: the questions by the Tribunal of Milan were therefore irrelevant.

---

[45] 232/75 *Industrie Chimiche Italia Centrale* [1975] *Giurisprudenza Costituzionale* 2211.
[46] 6 October 1981 n. 176 *Comavicola* [1982] *Foro Italiano* I, 359 note Tizzano.

To make such an equivocal decision the Constitutional Court took nearly three years. To take a clear position on the issue in the case of *Granital* the Constitutional Court took nearly five years. This is a hint of the conflicts in the Constitutional Court and the difficulties involved by the acceptance of decentralised enforcement of Community law. *Granital* presented itself to the Constitutional Court as the ideal case for the reversal of the previous case law. It was the State which invoked Community law against a statute.

It is clear that the Constitutional Court wanted to terminate the conflict with the ECJ. The policy reasons for accepting the change are set out quite overtly in the decision. The conflict with the European Court could not be sustained for too long. The fact that in all the other Member States of the Community a satisfactory solution was found was clearly a further stimulus. "Docket control" reasons should not be forgotten. Constitutional Court proceedings are long and cumbersome. The Constitutional Court had an enormous back-load of cases since the 1970s. Leaving lower courts to deal with Community law would have made things easier. Even if the solution of the conflict was very much sought after the Constitutional Court had to find a way to do it. As the drafter of the judgment once said "One does not divorce only because his wife spends too much".

Simmenthal required a movement away from the doctrine of *ICIC*. That scheme, after all, meant that Community law had supremacy because of article 11 of the Constitution. The *ICIC* doctrine was in fact the supremacy of article 11. However, the reasons for which the Constitutional Court could not accept, in *ICIC*, the supremacy of EC law *per se*, were still there.

There were two main obstacles to this acceptance. The first is that if one were to consider—as the Constitutional Court did—the conflicts between domestic and Community law as a conflict of competence and not as a hierarchical conflict of norms it would follow that domestic provisions in breach of Community law would only be in breach of the superior rule that defines the respective spheres of competence of the domestic and of the Community legislature. This superior rule is article 11. The conflict between statutes and rules in the Constitution—such as article 11—can be solved only by the Constitutional Court.

Beyond the doctrinal concern derived from the theoretic dualist model there is a more fundamental one. The acceptance of the superiority of Community law per se would have meant accepting a shifting of the "grundnorm". The Court felt that it was impossible to accept such a change as a result of the signing of the Treaty or even worse as a result of doctrines emanating from the ECJ.

The main result of *Granital* is showing that it was conceptually possible to solve the problem of supremacy without giving up the doctrine of *Frontini*. The effort to show that nothing much was changing is very evident throughout the whole judgment. It is clear that this was meant to obtain a *consensus* within the Constitutional Court. But it is more than that. The effort to stick to the model of separation and to show that the power of every judge not to apply domestic provisions conflicting with Community law was the logical consequence of *Frontini* is the response to the two above-mentioned fundamental concerns of the Constitutional Court.

Granital can be defined as direct effect without supremacy. The Constitutional Court pointed out in Granital, and repeated forcefully in *Giampaoli*,[47] that the judge who applies Community law and does not apply the conflicting national provisions is not qualifying the national provisions as unconstitutional or void due to a trespass on the Community competence. The judge only applies Community law within its sphere. The conflicting domestic provisions are in another sphere.

The division of spheres of competence is established by the statute implementing the EC Treaty and granted by article 11. This can explain the reservation of jurisdiction against statutes designed to attack the core principles of Community law. The Court seemingly considered that when Parliament changed the boundaries of the spheres of competence as established by the statute implementing the Treaty, the problem could no longer be solved by a reference to the respective spheres of competence. The only criterion for deciding on the legality of a 'denunciation' of the Treaties is the Constitution. The Constitutional Court considers the power to remove the limits to sovereignty the bottom line of sovereignty. Renouncing it would have been a change of "grundnorm": a revolution.

With *Granital* the Court considered that the conflict with the ECJ was solved and in the process a revolution was avoided. The Court was cheating when it said that the results of its new doctrines coincided with the requirements set by the ECJ. What was probably true is that they wanted the conflict to be solved once and for all.

SOME OBSERVATIONS ON THE POST-*GRANITAL* CASE LAW

It is submitted that there are at least three strands in the post-*Granital* case law. In one way or another they all depart from the nice construction of *Granital*.

Some cases extend the scope of the *Granital* doctrine. In doing so, the Court, especially in the cases that are perceived as being important, redefines in long *obiter dicta* the whole scheme of the relationship between the two legal orders. The Constitutional Court claims that its case law is a mere application of *Granital*. But effectively it extends its scope[48] and at times comes out with solutions which are not fully compatible with the requirements of

---

[47] Case 168/91 *Giampaoli* [1992] *Foro It.* I 660, with note by Daniele.

[48] This extension has avoided many of the inconsistencies of a strict reading of *Granital* with the requirements set by the ECJ. For a very convincing analysis of these inconsistencies see Barav "Cour Constitutionnelle Italienne et Droit Communautaire: le fantôme de Simmenthal", [1985] *Révue Trimestrielle de droit Européen* 313.

Community law, if not in the results in the reasoning. As an example the Constitutional Court stated that the rulings of the ECJ have direct effect[49] or that it is possible to legislate (through a referendum)[50] against Community directives in consideration of the fact that, given the directives direct effect, the legislation would be inapplicable.

However, this line of case law remains the most coherent even in the cases in which the departure from the doctrines of the ECJ or the open conflict is deliberate, as it was in *Fragd*.[51] The *"pouvoir reservé"* that the Court retained is some kind of security valve. Federico Sorrentino has recently shown[52] that this represents a sign of a situation in which notwithstanding the supremacy of Community law (which in the formal traditional analysis would mean that sovereignty has passed from the state to the Community) the final decision in critical cases ("exceptional cases" to use C. Schimitt's terminology used by Sorrentino) remains with the state.

All these cases could be considered logical developments of *Granital*. Even if the Constitutional Court does not accept supremacy in *Simmenthal* terms, the system works as if supremacy was there. Pre-emption makes the sphere of competence of the Community flexible. Hence, whenever there is a rule of Community law it is applied despite the conflicting national provisions.

In the early post-*Granital* cases, in particular, the Constitutional Court has been very careful in sending to lower courts the message that the control of legislation against Community law should be decentralised. To do so the Constitutional Court discarded even cases in which the conflict with Community law was not the only ground of unconstitutionality.[53]

What one may regret is the refusal of the Court to make article 177 references. The Court recognised that it had a faculty to make references for preliminary rulings to the ECJ in *Giampaoli*,[54] but it did not make use of it. Previously[55] the Constitutional Court sent a case for which an article 177 reference was needed back to the referring judge instructing him to make a reference to Luxembourg. This was certainly a cumbersome procedure but was not in flagrant breach of article 177, para. 3. Before *Giampaoli* one might have thought that the Constitutional Court was not a national court within the meaning of article 177. The acknowledgement by the Constitutional Court that it is entitled to make references to the ECJ makes it impossible for the Constitutional Court not to be considered a "court against whose decisions

---

[49] Case 113/85, BECA, [1985] *Giurisprudenza Italiana* 388 for article 177 rulings, and Case 369/89, *Provincia di Bolzano*, [1990] *Diritto Comunitario e degli scambi internazionali* 395, for article 169 rulings.

[50] Case 64/90, *Referendum on pesticides* [1990] *Diritto Comunitario e degli scambi internazionali* 445, [1991] *RTDE* 296.

[51] 13 April 1989 n. 232 *Fragd* [1990] *Foro Italiano* I, 1855.

[52] "La Costituzione Italiana di fronte al processo di Integrazione Europea" [1992] *Quaderni Regionali* 417.

[53] This is very clear in Case 113/85 BECA, [1985] *Giurisprudenza Italiana* 388.

[54] 18 April 1991 n.168 [1992] *Foro It.* I 660, with note by Daniele.

[55] Case 206/76, [1976] *Foro It.* I. 2298, with note by Tizzano.

there is no judicial remedy" within the meaning of article 177, *papra*. 3. There might be room for arguing this in relation to constitutional review proceedings upon reference, in which the ruling is only an *"incidente"* of other proceedings. It is clear however that the Constitutional Court is acting as a supreme administrative court in cases of conflict between State and regions. In these cases the Court gives a ruling without appeal at the end of a contentious procedure.

No other Constitutional Court makes article 177 references, but *Giampaoli* was meant to be a Community-friendly move and ended up by being a blatant violation of the Treaty.[56]

There is a second line of cases, particularly very minor ones, in which the Community law issues are sometimes not fully appreciated. The Constitutional Court sometimes showed itself to be careless. In Case 286/86, *Pulos*[57] while quoting *Granital*, the Court checked the conformity of Italian legislation with Community law, in a pure pre-*Granital* fashion. The case did not seem to fall under the reservation made for legislation affecting the core principles of the Treaties.

Another example is Case 172/89, *Solcio*[58] where the Court seems to say that external commercial policy is outside of the scope of EC competence. What is particularly striking in this line of cases is the wording of the Constitutional Court's *dicta*. At times they are completely at variance with *Granital*. L. Daniele[59] notes that *"De tels passage sont peut-être le signal d'une certaine fatigue intellectuelle de la part de la cour vis-à-vis d'une vision somme toute artificielle et pourtant difficile à maîtriser"*.

Finally there are the cases in which *Granital* simply cannot work. In particular the Constitutional Court is not satisfied with decentralised control in many cases. In an impressive line of decisions[60] on regional legislation in breach of a Community directive the Constitutional Court went on to rule on the issue itself rather than sending the case to the referring judges according to the *Granital* orthodoxy. It has been argued that the directive did not have direct effect. It might be true. Nonetheless it remains a whole area of law in which legislation in breach of Community law needs to be declared unconstitutional by the Constitutional Court rather than being disapplied.

In action brought by the State[61] for the annulment or for impeding the coming into force of regional legislation supposedly in breach of Community law,

---

[56] With an order of 29 December 1995 n. 536 *Messagero Servizi* [1997] *Dirito Comunitario Scambi Internazionali*, 163 The Court has reversed *Giampaoli* and instructed the referring judge to make an article 177 reference (see note 55) on the assumption that The Constitutional Court is not a 'national jurisdiction' within the meaning of article 177.

[57] [1987] *Giurisprudenza Costituzionale* 2309.

[58] Order 172/89 *Cantieri Nautici Solcio* [1989] *Giurisprudenza Costituzionale* 806.

[59] "Après l' arrêt Granital" [1992] *Cahier de Droit Européen*, 3.

[60] n.14/91 *Incampo*, n.117/91 *Edino Jancovits*; n. 213/91 *Benedetti and other*; n. 307/91 *Ragogna*, n. 306/92 *Locatelli*; all these judgments are summarized in [1994] *Rivista di diritto Europeo* 610.

[61] See in particular Case 384 of 10 November 1994, *Regione Umbria*, *Rivista di Diritto Europeo* [1995] 468 and Case 94 of 30 March 1995, *Regione Sicilia ibid*. 473.

the regions tried to rely on *Granital* in order to have the actions declared inadmissible. The Court was therefore obliged to distinguish *Granital*. The Court summarised the *Granital* doctrine and the theory of separation of legal orders. However, it made it clear that centralised control under *Granital* is not possible only because of the Italian procedural rule according to which only when a judge is obliged to apply a rule which is suspected to be contrary to the Constitution can he refer it to the Constitutional court.

Because of the direct effect of the Community rules the judge is not obliged to apply the conflicting Italian rules. These Italian rules are nonetheless contrary to the Constitution. Whenever this is procedurally feasible (i.e. when the case is brought directly to the Court by privileged applicants) the Constitutional Court is therefore bound to declare unconstitutional (annul) Italian rules contrary to Community law. In this context the court cited the obligations flowing from article 5 of the Treaty and the need for legal certainty.

THE PROBLEM OF COMPETENCE

It was argued above that the framework of the doctrines of the Constitutional Court is the concept of "competence". The Court does not necessarily use this word but it refers to the idea of competence. Since "the separate legal orbits" of *San Michele* the basic idea is that each legal order has its sphere of competence and cannot interfere with the other legal order.

In *Frontini* it is said that the distribution of these competences is established by the EC Treaty. The Constitutional Court has not built upon this, as it was more concerned with material limits to Community intervention. The fact that in *Frontini* the material limit of human rights was framed in terms of competence has probably misdirected the question.

In *Frontini* the Court apparently considered that should the EC Treaty be interpreted by the Community institutions as giving power to violate human rights it would be deprived of its effect in Italy. In the case of *Fragd* the Constitutional Court has applied for the first and only time this doctrine. If one looks more carefully one can even spot a further variation on the theme. One might have thought that a Community act violating human rights would be— according to *Frontini*—beyond the scope of the EC Treaty and hence beyond the scope of article 11 of the Constitution, being the fruit of an "aberrant" interpretation of the Treaty. In *Fragd* in order to put its power of control into practice the Constitutional Court had to bend once again its own doctrine. In order to have a peg on which to hang its reprobation of a doctrine of the European Court it had to decide whether article 177, as interpreted by the ECJ, fell under article 11 of the Constitution and not whether the "aberrant" ECJ case law on temporal effects of preliminary rulings fell under article 177 of the Treaty.

In the wake of the German *Maastricht* decision, can one expect the Court to control the legality of Community acts allegedly beyond Community competence, as established by the Treaty, but not contrary to a material rule deriving from the Italian constitutional order? The influence of the German model should never be underestimated.[62] There is nonetheless a big procedural problem. The Constitutional Court, according to its dualist model, can review only the statute implementing the Treaty. In other words it can review only Treaty articles and acts adopted on the basis thereof. The Constitutional Court in order to check the conformity with human rights of a regulation would actually assess the legality of article 189 of the EC Treaty in as much as it granted to the Council the power to enact the contested regulation. This is precisely what happened in *Fragd*.

This type of review procedure cannot work for *ultra vires* acts. To say that an act is beyond the competence of the Community means that it was not taken on the basis of the EC Treaty. The Constitutional Court would not find anything in the statute implementing the Treaty to be declared contrary to the Constitution.

Only decentralised control by every court could be possible in relation to *ultra vires* acts. It does not seem very likely that the Court would accept lower judges checking the legality of Community acts.

One can accept that under the dualist model of the Constitutional Court *Kompetenz-Kompetenz* is for the national courts, but should the Constitutional Court decide to exercise the control over competence, it will be blocked by a procedural deadlock.

It is submitted that the Constitutional Court will try to control even Community acts *ultra vires* according to the material criteria set out in *Frontini* and *Granital*.

The Constitutional Court took upon itself in the 1980s to overcome the doctrinal and philosophical barriers concerning the recognition of supremacy. There were several reasons for this. Certainly the Constitutional Court did not want to remain the *arrière-garde* of the world of lawyers in Europe. On top of that, the Court realised the necessity to grant effectivity to a legal system, the one of Community law, which, largely due to the inefficiency of the Italian administration, was not giving to Italian citizens and economic operators the rights to which they were entitled to.

The changing of the political inclination towards the Community together with a more realistic appreciation of the process of European integration, which is no longer considered as some kind of providential source of rights for the citizens and efficiency for the administration, as well as the coming of the *Bundesverfassungsgericht* to positions that recall a traditional legalistic perception of the process of European integration—which the Corte Costituzionale has never definitely abandoned—may lead to the development of the case law in new directions.

---

[62] Sorrentino has immediately drawn the attention on the implications for Italy of the approach of the *Bundesverfassungsgericht*. "Ai limiti dell'integrazione europea: primato delle fonti o delle istituzioni comunitarie?" [1994] *Politica del diritto* 189 also in *Scintillae Iuris-Studi in memoria di G. Gorla* (Giuffré, Milan, 1994).

6

Report on the Netherlands

MONICA CLAES AND BRUNO DE WITTE

The Netherlands do not seem to fit well with the experiences of other countries outlined elsewhere in this book. All commentators, both inside and outside the Netherlands, agree that the reception of the European Court's direct effect/supremacy doctrine has gone very smoothly in the Netherlands, without major doctrinal controversies or judicial hesitations. Comparative studies of the domestic reaction to the supremacy and direct effect doctrines do not dwell on this country, and quickly move to other, more interesting cases such as those of France, Italy, Germany or the UK. We will not challenge that view here; the constitutional setting of the Netherlands is indeed optimal if compared to those other countries. Yet, the reaction to the direct effect/supremacy doctrine has not been without some ambiguities. In the second part of this chapter, we will look into them, and hope to show that even in the Netherlands the reception of the European Court's doctrine has not gone without some distortions of the message from Luxembourg.

The first part of the chapter will deal with something else. Before looking at the reception of the direct effect/supremacy doctrines, we will look at their conception. Those doctrines did not appear out of the blue. The European Court had its own intellectual sources from which it derived the formulation of those doctrines, and those sources, apart from sparse references in the case law of international courts, were to be found in national law. The link between the direct effect doctrine and the American doctrine of self-executing treaties is well-known, but the "European" sources of the Court's doctrine are less completely explored. The constitutional law of the Netherlands is, arguably, one of its major sources of inspiration. The first part of the chapter will therefore deal with the contribution of the Dutch legal order to the emergence of the European Court's doctrine.

Direct effect and supremacy of international treaties in the Netherlands prior to *Van Gend en Loos*

For a long time, the Dutch Constitution did not contain any provisions on the relationship between international law and national law. In the absence of express constitutional provisions, this question (which started to appear of practical relevance towards the end of last century) was left to legal writing and to the courts for discussion and decision. In this respect, the Netherlands does not stand apart from the other European countries. However, the discussion gradually took a distinctive turn in the Netherlands. In the beginning of this century, a large-scale doctrinal controversy, involving the leading professors of constitutional and international law, took place about the contending theories of monism and dualism: were international treaties directly applicable (i.e., were they a direct source of rights and duties upon their entry into force or their publication) or did they first require transformation into Dutch law?[1] In 1906, the Hoge Raad—the Dutch Supreme Court—made a statement which was not entirely clear, but was generally interpreted as a rejection of the transformation doctrine.[2] It is worth noting that the Supreme Court used the argument that all treaties affecting the rights of Dutch subjects needed prior approval by Parliament, so that a subsequent act of transformation would not serve a discernable purpose.[3] From that time onwards, monism became the leading doctrine among Dutch authors; as for the courts, their attitude was summarised as follows by Erades: "despite the employment of vague, confusing or ambiguous terms in some judgments, Netherlands case law as it was when the 1953 Constitution became operative, treated international agreements as rules of international law binding internally, and not as rules of municipal law".[4]

A second controversy had developed by then, which was predicated upon the first. It dealt with the rank of international treaties, and more specifically with the primacy of international law over later statutes in the case of a conflict. There were no clear judicial statements about this; rather, like in other countries, Dutch courts tried to avoid the issue by adopting rules of construction aiming at interpreting national law in accordance with international treaties, and vice versa.

At a conference of the Dutch Association of Jurists in 1937, two conflicting views were proposed by the rapporteurs, both professors of international

---

[1] For a summary of the debate, see L. Erades, "International Law and the Netherlands Legal Order", in *International Law in the Netherlands* (1980) Vol.III, p. 375, at p. 394 *et seq.*

[2] H.R., 25 May 1906, W., 8383.

[3] See the translation of the relevant part of the Supreme Court judgment in Erades, n. 1 above, at p. 397.

[4] Erades, n. 1 above, p. 402.

law.[5] Telders acted as a late defender of the dualist approach, arguing that a treaty, after its publication, produced internal effect as a national norm with the same rank as a formal statute. His opponent Verzijl defended the monist doctrine, combined with full recognition of supremacy. He considered international and internal law to be part of one system, in which treaty law had a higher rank, and the judge had to disapply any conflicting national rules. At a vote concluding the 1937 conference, the majority of lawyers present preferred Verzijl's theory. Yet, Verzijl had to admit that the most likely attitude of Dutch courts (if a conflict could not be interpreted away) would be to make the later statute prevail over the earlier treaty. One of the reasons that made him think so was the attitude of courts in all other countries which made it unlikely that Dutch courts would take the bold step of affirming the supremacy of international law in the absence of any constitutional authorisation to that effect.

Such an authorization came in 1953 when, in the slightly euphoric post-war period, a series of new external relations clauses were inserted in the Dutch Constitution, all of them inspired by an internationalist spirit.[6] Article 66 now held: "Agreements shall be binding on anyone insofar as they will have been published".[7] Although those words do not say so explicitly, they were meant to confirm the dominant view that treaties could be directly applied by domestic courts. The article also resolved a doctrinal controversy among monists about the moment from which a treaty displays its domestic effect, by settling upon the date of publication rather than the date of entry into force. Though publication could still theoretically be seen as operating transformation of the international treaty into Dutch law, this view was never defended either by a court or by legal writers, so that from 1953 monism reigns without dispute in the Netherlands.

More importantly, article 65 resolved the controversy about the rank of international treaties by stating unambiguously: "Legal provisions in force within the Kingdom shall not apply if the application should be incompatible with agreements which have been published in accordance with Article 66 either before or after the enactment of the provisions". The essence of this provision lay in the word "before" which confirmed that a treaty could not even be set aside by *subsequent* national laws. This bold assertion had not been proposed by the Government but was inserted in the Constitution on the basis of an amendment voted by the Second Chamber with a narrow majority of 46 votes to 40.[8] Thus, it was Parliament itself that took the initiative of submitting its future statutes to judicial review of their compatibility with

---

[5] *Handelingen van de Nederlandse Juristen Vereeniging* (1937).

[6] For a complete analysis of those changes, see H.F. van Panhuys, "The Netherlands Constitution and International Law", (1953) 47 *American Journal of International Law*, 537.

[7] Translations of the 1953 Constitution are taken from van Panhuys, n. 6 above.

[8] The amendment is known as the *Serrarens amendment*, from the name of its author. Serrarens became, shortly afterwards, the first Dutch judge at the European Court of Justice.

treaties. This step is all the more striking if one considers that, in 1953 as today, there is no judicial review of the *constitutionality* of legislation in the Netherlands. Since 1953 therefore, treaties are more effectively enforceable than the Constitution.

The relationship between the Constitution and treaty provisions was dealt with in two articles. The notion "legal provisions in force in the Kingdom" in article 65 was deemed to include the Constitution, that must therefore give way to treaty provisions.[9] This was confirmed in article 60(3): "the judge shall not review the constitutionality of Agreements".

The rules formulated in articles 65 and 66 with regard to *treaties* were made applicable, by virtue of the new article 67, also to *decisions of international organisations*. This provision was inspired, among other things, by the recently signed Treaty on the European Coal and Steel Community.[10] Contrary to the Italian and the German post-war Constitutions, the Netherlands Constitution contains no provision concerning general principles of international law.[11]

The Dutch constitutional reform was greeted by professor De Visscher, in his course at the Hague Academy, as providing the most audacious solution to the question of the relation between international and domestic law.[12] In the Netherlands itself, a lonely voice rejected the new regime,[13] but its fundamental principles were never to be called into question by a significant number of either politicians, courts or legal authors.

Immediately after the 1953 revision, the Government set up a new advisory committee with the task of preparing some "technical" revisions of parts of the 1953 text that were considered infelicitous. Acting upon the recommendations of the committee, the Government introduced a new constitutional amendment bill which was adopted by Parliament in 1956.[14] One modification was the reversion of the sequence of the above mentioned provisions, as

---

[9] Handelingen EK, 1952–1953, 2700, no 63a (Memorie van Antwoord), p. 3

[10] The judicial competence to set aside conflicting national legislation was considered indispensible in the light of the proposed preliminary reference procedure in the ECSC Treaty. Such procedure would imply that the national courts must follow the judgments of the European Court and give them precedence over conflicting national legislation. The absence of judicial review would be incompatible with the preliminary rulings procedure; see L. F. M. Besselink, "De zaak-Metten: de Grondwet voorbij", *Nederlands Juristenblad*, 1996, 165, at 166, with references to the parliamentary proceedings.

[11] The Hoge Raad has excluded the application of articles 65 and 66 to such principles, HR, 6 November 1959, *Nyugat*, NJ, 1962, 2; the courts are not competent to review the compatibility of Dutch legislation with general principles of international law.

[12] P. de Visscher, "Les tendances internationales des constitutions modernes", in *Recueil des Cours* 80 (1952-II), 511, at pp. 569–70. Yet, the author added a warning: "*L'expérience seule établira si un système aussi progressiste n'est pas de nature à provoquer entre le pouvoir législatif et le pouvoir judiciaire des conflits politiques dont ce dernier pourrait être la victime*". The experience of the next 40 years showed that major conflicts did not arise, but that must be partly due to the fact that, as will be indicated below, the courts made smooth the sharp angles of the new regime.

[13] Duynstee, *Grondwetsherziening 1953* (1953).

[14] See H. J. van Panhuys, "The Netherlands Constitution and International Law", (1964) 58 *American Journal of International Law*, 88.

it appeared more logical to deal with domestic effect first (new article 65), and with supremacy after that (new article 66). A second change was not merely "technical": it introduced the condition of "binding on anyone" in both articles 65 and 66. The 1953 text, by its sweeping terms, might have given the impression that *all* agreements were to be enforceable by Dutch courts.[15] The intention was to restrict it to what were called, in the American doctrine, "self-executing treaties". In order to remove any doubt about this, article 65 was henceforth formulated as follows: "Provisions of agreements *which, according to their terms, can be binding on anyone* shall have such binding force after having been published".[16] The same qualification was added to the supremacy clause (now article 66): "Legislation in force within the Kingdom shall not apply if this application would be incompatible with *provisions of agreements which are binding on anyone* and which have been entered into either before or after the enactment of such legislation".

The words "binding on anyone" stem from the text of 1953; its article 66 expressly said that such general (and horizontal) obligation could only arise once a treaty was published. The clause was meant to protect citizens; they could only be bound by a rule if they could know it.[17] In the 1956 version, however, the same words are used to insert a supplementary condition for treaties to become binding in the domestic legal order, and for the judge to have the competence to disapply conflicting national legislation. This condition, rather than protect the individuals, makes it more difficult for them to assert the benefits provided for them by a treaty.

The binding effect and the supremacy of treaty provisions is henceforth made subject to the capacity of those provisions to be "binding on anyone". As mentioned above, the American doctrine of "self-executing" treaties inspired this. Yet, it is by no means clear when a treaty provision is capable of binding individuals. Which were to be the criteria to decide whether treaty provisions complied with that condition? Was it the wording of the provision (only those expressly conferring rights to individuals)? Was the intention of the contracting parties decisive? Or was it the possibility for courts to apply those provisions without the need for prior implementation by either the legislature or the executive?

The 1956 additions were presented by their authors as technical updates of the 1953 revision, as the self-executing criterion was, according to them,

[15] This was never the opinion of the Government. Already in 1953, the Government deemed both articles to be limited to "self-executing" provisions. In the Memorandum on the revision of 1953, the term "self-executing" was explained by the Government as meaning "provisions that according to their nature can be applied directly by the judge" and further as "provisions that are directly effective vis-à-vis the citizens", as opposed to norms of instruction addressed to the legislative and executive organs. The question whether a norm was directly effective or not was "in full confidence" left for the judge to decide, since this amounted to an interpretation of the provision: TK, 1952–1953, 2700, no 63a, p. 3.

[16] The newly inserted part is emphasised.

[17] Handelingen TK, 1951–52, 2374, no 11 (Memorie van Toelichting).

implied in the 1953 formulation. Yet, the fact of specifying this condition so openly could also be interpreted as an invitation to the courts to use that criterion as a means for restraining the disruptive effect of international treaties on the domestic legal order. That, at any rate, was what happened in the court practice of the late 1950s. The courts tended to shy away from their newly recognised power to review legislation on its compatibility with international treaties, either by relying on the rule of construction (interpreting national law in accordance with treaties, and vice versa) or by denying the self-executing nature of international conventions.[18] The first device is a natural attitude for courts, and one which is practised in many countries. The second device is more typical for the Dutch courts of that period, and was probably encouraged by the insistence of the Constitution (in its post-1956 version) that treaty provisions needed to be "binding on anyone" before they could be the basis for reviewing domestic legislation.

Slightly more than one year after the 1956 revision, the EC Treaty entered into force. In its early years of operation, several business companies sought to enforce the competition rules of that treaty, articles 85 and 86, before Dutch courts.[19] The general trend of those courts' judgments was that, in the absence of implementation rules to be issued by the organs of the Community under article 87 of the treaty,[20] articles 85 and 86 could not be regarded as "binding on anyone" and could therefore not be enforced in court.[21] There was also a debate on the underlying issue of whether the existence of direct effect was a matter of interpretation of Community law or of national law and related to this, which court was competent to decide on the matter. In *KIM Sieverding*,[22] Advocate-General Eyssen of the Hoge Raad held that it was a matter of domestic law.[23]

The Hague Court of Appeal took a different view and decided to suspend the proceedings in order to obtain a preliminary ruling of the Court of Justice on the proper interpretation of article 85 of the EC Treaty,[24] more particularly on the question of whether a contract between a German exporter and

---

[18] See M. Waelbroeck, *Traités internationaux et juridictions internes dans les pays du Marché commun* (1969), at pp. 250–1.

[19] This special interest for the competition rules was probably due to the fact that their enforcement was provisionally delegated, according to article 88 of the Treaty, to "the authorities in Member States", which could be seen to include the courts.

[20] Regulation No 17 of 1962 had not yet been adopted then.

[21] See the judgments mentioned in Van Panhuys (1964), n. 14 above, p. 102, footnote 65.

[22] Hoge Raad, 13 January 1961, K.I.M.-Sieverding, *S.E.W.* (1961) 324.

[23] The Hoge Raad quashed the judgment in question on grounds of national law and did not enter into the debate.

[24] Prior to this case, the Dutch courts had always assumed that article 85 could not be directly applicable. In this case however, one of the parties argued that under German law—applicable in the case—article 85 did produce direct effect. The Court of Appeal therefore decided that there were doubts as to the effect of article 85 in the national legal order. The Court held that whether or not it had direct effect was a matter of interpretation of the Treaty, and referred the question to the Court in Luxembourg.

Dutch importers was void by virtue of article 85(2).[25] This reference under article 177 EEC Treaty, in the *Bosch* case, was the first to be decided by the European Court of Justice.[26] Although the question whether article 85 had direct effect was not formulated *expressis verbis* by the Dutch court, it could seem to be implied in the question whether the contract was "void by virtue of article 85".[27]

One month after the judgment of the European Court, the Hoge Raad ruled on the appeal against the reference made.[28] The appeal was based on the same arguments as those developed by Advocate General Eyssen, that the direct effect issue had to be decided on the basis of domestic law. The Hoge Raad decided that: "as is clear from article 66, the question whether provisions of a Treaty bind the nationals of the Member States, is, at least for Dutch law, a question that can only be answered on the basis of interpretation of those treaty provisions". It was therefore a question which could properly be addressed by Dutch courts to the European Court of Justice. The Dutch Supreme Court thus cleared the way for a stream of preliminary questions.

But even before this acceptance of the jurisdiction of the Court of Justice by the Hoge Raad, the College van Beroep voor het Bedrijfsleven[29]—a specialised administrative court having jurisdiction in first and last instance in cases concerning industrial organisation and social and economic legislation—put five questions to the Court of Justice, the first of which read: "can articles 12 and 37(2) of the EC Treaty bind anyone, or are they addressed only to the Governments of the Member States, without the possibility for individuals to derive rights directly thereof?"[30] The College van Beroep was of the

---

[25] Preliminary Reference by the Hague Court of Appeal, 30 June 1961, in *Nederlandse Jurisprudentie* 1961, No. 375.

[26] *de Geus en Uitdenbogerd* v. *Robert Bosch GmbH et al.*, Case 13/61 [1962] ECR 45, ECJ.

[27] In its ruling in the *Bosch* case, the ECJ gave decisive importance to the adoption of Regulation 17 implementing articles 85 and 86, and implicitly denied the full direct effect of those articles prior to the date of adoption of the Regulation.

[28] *de Geus en Uitdenbogerd* v. *Robert Bosch GmbH et al.*, Hoge Raad, 18 May 1962, Nederlandse Jurisprudentie (1965), 115.

[29] College van Beroep voor het Bedrijfsleven, 10 January 1962, *S.E.W.* (1962) 65.

[30] According to Erades, the question was clearly inspired both by arts. 65 and 66 of the Constitution *and* by a "self-executing" theory borrowed from the Opinion of the Permanent Court of International Justice of 3 March 1928. The Government explained the terminology of the Constitution in its Memorandum to the revision of 1953 (TK, 1952–1953, 2700, no 63a, at p. 3): a provision that is binding on anyone is one that is self-executing (has direct effect *vis-à-vis* the citizens); it creates "objective rights" or obligations for individual citizens and is, by its terms, apt for application by the judge. Provisions that are not binding on anyone, are those addressed only to the law-making organs of the State (norms of instruction); they thus do not create rights and obligations for individuals; they are not self-executing. In the face of such provisions, the judge cannot set aside national legislation, because to do so would create a vacuum, a gap, that the judge could only fill by implementing an international obligation, thereby by-passing Government and Parliament. This is not part of the judicial function, and judicial review was thus to be restricted to self-executing provisions. A provision belongs to either one of the two categories made. The equation between distinct notions, made by the Government, did not work for the relevant articles of the EC Treaty in the case before the College van Beroep voor het Bedrijfsleven: the defendant had argued that *by their terms*, these articles did not create rights and

opinion that the determination of the self-executing nature of a provision was a question of interpretation of the Treaty which had to be made by the Court of Justice.

As the parties reached a settlement, the questions were withdrawn. But another Dutch court soon after made a reference which made the name of the applicant firm forever famous in Community law circles: *Van Gend en Loos*.

The Tariff Commission (a specialised administrative court), in the course of a dispute about an import tax, asked whether article 12 of the EEC Treaty had "internal effect, in other words whether individuals can directly derive rights from the article that are enforceable by the judge". The referring judge did not exactly frame his question in the terms used by the Constitution[31], although it is quite clear that the question was put in order to elucidate the application of the articles 65 and 66 of that Constitution.[32] Yet, what started as a request for help to the ECJ in the application of the Dutch Constitution— a request approved by the Hoge Raad in the *Bosch* judgment—became the occasion for the European Court to formulate its well-known doctrine on the direct effect of Community law which it addressed, beyond the obscure Dutch Tariff Commission, to all courts in all Member States of the Community.

The Influence of the Dutch legal order on the European Court's doctrine

At the conceptual level, there is hardly any doubt that the Netherlands have been an important testing-ground in the course of the 1950s (but even before that) for the principles of direct effect and supremacy as they were formulated by the European Court in the 1960s.

Also the *time and manner* by which the European Court's views were formulated may bear the stamp of Dutch influence:[33]

---

obligations, but since they only amounted to a prohibition, one could reasonably argue otherwise. According to the court, the question to which category a treaty provision belonged, was a question of interpretation which for the EC Treaty had to be decided by the Court in Luxembourg.

[31] Erades critised the Tariff Commission for confusing "internal effect" and "direct applicability", and for wrongfully identifying the former notion with a definition of "self-executing" borrowed from the Permanent Court of International Justice (L. Erades, *De verhouding van de rechtspraak van het Hof der Europese Gemeenschappen met die van de nationale rechters in de Lid-Staten* (Praeadvies, Mededelingen van de Nederlandse Vereniging voor Internationaal Recht, 1964), at p. 22).

[32] See L. Erades, n. 31 above, at p. 5: "The relation between the Arts. 65 and 66 of the Constitution and Art. 177 EEC has as a consequence that that Court has a specific task in the enforcement of the Dutch Constitution". And further: "Given the existence of the Arts. 65 and 66 of the Constitution, Art. 177 is more important for the Netherlands than for the five other Member States" (author's translation).

[33] The existence of this influence is testified by Donner, who was the Dutch judge in Luxembourg at the time of *Van Gend en Loos* v. *Nederlandse Belastingadministratie*, Case 26/62, [1963] CMLR 105 (and may have been instrumental in the Court's decision in that case): A. M. Donner in *Rechtsgeleerd Magazijn Themis* (1980), p. 354, at p. 359.

(a) The willingness of Dutch courts to refer preliminary rulings in the early days of the EEC[34] (which itself was a result of existing Dutch rules about the relationship between national and international law), the acceptance of the jurisdiction of the Court of Justice by the Hoge Raad, and the type of questions asked by the Dutch courts allowed the European Court to formulate its direct effect doctrine in *Van Gend en Loos*.

(b) The word "effect" in the expression "direct effect" was possibly borrowed from the preliminary question put by the Tariff Commission.[35] The question whether the Court of Justice wanted to indicate, by the use of those words, something different from the "direct applicability" mentioned in article 189 of the EC Treaty has puzzled commentators for many years.[36]

(c) Dutch law, through the questions referred, may have complicated the issue of direct effect by the terminology used. The Tariff Commission put the question of direct effect in terms of the creation of individual rights, probably because that is the pattern of the Dutch Constitution.[37] Direct effect was equated with the creation of objective rights (or obligations) for individuals, and the applicability by the judge. The Court of Justice followed this approach in *Van Gend en Loos* and seemed to equate direct effect with the creation of individual rights ("article 12 must be interpreted as producing direct effect and creating rights which national courts must protect"). The Court repeated the formula in numerous cases,[38] although the equation between direct effect and the creation of rights is deceptive, both for the national (procedural) law of many Member States and for Community law. It complicates the direct effect issue even today.[39]

Direct effect and the creation of rights do not always coincide, unless the term "right" is understood as comprising a procedural right to invoke the relevant provision. But this too seems artificial and needless in some cases.[40]

The rights issue obscures the direct effect issue, and this may, in the beginning, have been a direct consequence of the Dutch legal thinking on the subject.

---

[34] Ten out of the first thirteen references came from Dutch courts, see references in L. J. Brinkhorst, "De Nederlandse rechter en het gemeenschapsrecht", *S.E.W.* (1966), p. 65, at p. 83.

[35] The term "direct effect" (*"rechtstreekse werking"* or *"directe werking"*) was already used in the Netherlands. See e.g. the Memorandum of the Government to the constitutional revision 1953.

[36] A. M. Donner, n. 33 above, at p. 359; J. A. Winter, "Direct applicability and direct effect. Two distinct and different concepts in Community law", *C.M.L.Rev.* (1972), p. 425

[37] See n. 30 above.

[38] See for instance in *Salgoil*, Case 13/68 [1968] ECR 453: "Article 31 . . . lends itself perfectly to producing direct effect . . . *Thus* article 31 creates rights which national courts must protect".

[39] See for a discussion of this problem S. Prechal, *Directives in European Community law* (1995), at p. 124 *et seq*.

[40] For example in a *recours objectif*, review of the objective legality of a national rule. Direct effect can also be defined in terms of the applicability of the provision by the judge. A directly effective provision is a provision that is legally perfect and that can be applied by the judge. See S. Prechal, *Directives in European Community law* (1995), at p. 266 *et seq*, who defines direct effect as *the obligation of a court or another authority to apply the relevant provision of Community law, either as a norm which governs the case or as a standard for legal review.*

(d) The fact that the direct effect question was proposed and resolved in a separate case from the supremacy question (*Costa* v. *E.N.E.L.*) may be explained by the fact that the referring court in *Van Gend en Loos* did not need guidance about supremacy: if an EEC provision was declared to have direct effect, then it automatically had supremacy according to Dutch constitutional law. It remains debatable whether this initial distinction between direct effect and supremacy in the European Court's case law was a good or a bad thing, but it has certainly marked the later evolution in case law and legal thinking. (There are signs in more recent judgments of the European Court that the two principles are merging into an overarching principle of "effectiveness".)

(e) Article 66 of the Dutch Constitution, which made direct effect a condition for, and limit to, the supremacy of treaty provisions, was echoed by similar connections made in the European Court's case law. This is perhaps most evident in the later cases on the domestic effect of directives, where the review power of national courts was made dependent on the prior assessment of the direct effect of the directive. If such a connection exists between the case law of the European Court and Dutch constitutional doctrine, this would arguably be one of the more unfortunate influences of the latter. The fact that supremacy is limited to provisions with direct effect has been criticised, within the context of Dutch constitutional law, with the argument that those treaty provisions that need implementation by the domestic authorities (and do not, therefore, have direct effect) are more likely to be breached by national authorities and therefore more in need of judicial affirmation of their supremacy. That argument is also true for Community law. The supremacy of EC law is often more threatened when its provisions are not directly effective.

Direct effect and supremacy were however disconnected in a recent and controversial judgment, relating to Community law, of the Administrative Law (Judicial) Division of the Council of State, *Metten*, in which that court held that the principle of primacy of Community law also holds for provisions which are not directly effective. No reference was made in the judgment to the constitutional articles; instead, it based its conclusion on *Costa* v. *E.N.E.L.*, *Walt Wilhelm* and *Simmenthal*.[41]

(f) Another possible Dutch echo in *Van Gend en Loos* is even more speculative. It relates to the theoretical underpinnings of the doctrines of direct effect and supremacy of Community law. Judge Donner, president of the Court in the *Van Gend en Loos* case, was a Dutch Professor of constitutional law. In a handbook on Dutch constitutional law, published before the

---

[41] Administrative Law (Judicial) Division of the Council of State, 7 July 1995, *Alman Metten*, NJB-katern, 1995, 545; a translation in English of the judgment can be found in *Maastricht Journal of European and Comparative Law*, 1996, p. 179. *Costa* v. *E.N.E.L.*, Case 6/64, [1964] CMLR 425; *Wilhelm* v. *Bundeskartellamt*, Case 14/68, [1969] CMLR 100; *Simmenthal* v. *Amministrazione delle Finanze dello Stato*, Case 70/77, [1978] ECR 1453.

judgment in *Van Gend en Loos*, Donner reflected upon the relation between national law and treaty law as it stood *before* the revision of the Constitution of 1953 which decided the issue as a matter of positive law. Considering the situation of a conflict between an international treaty provision and a subsequent provision of national law, he wrote:

"My opinion was that when this situation occurs, the international act must be deemed to have precedence, not because it originates from a higher community of law,[42] but because, as Verzijl has put it, 'for the future the sovereign freedom of action of the state is limited and the legal possibility has been taken away to excercise its legislative function in full freedom, if he should try to do so' ".[43]

The author concluded from this that the judge had to review national legislation in the light of the treaty provisions and that he was obliged to give precedence to the rule of international law. In other words, the direct effect and supremacy of a treaty derive, in his view, from the fact that sovereign powers were transferred or limited by means of the treaty. The review power of national judges does not need to be expressly recognised by the Constitution; this power can only be denied by an express provision in the Constitution.

In *Van Gend en Loos*, the direct effect doctrine was founded on strikingly similar arguments. Judge Donner (and through him, a traditional current of thought from the Netherlands) may well have had a decisive influence on the doctrinal foundations of the European Court's case law on the relation between Community law and national law.[44]

THE RECEPTION OF THE EUROPEAN COURT'S DOCTRINE IN THE NETHERLANDS

There is a general consensus in the literature, since the 1960s, that with regard to the domestic status of EC law, the Netherlands "presents the least difficulty".[45] In view of the receptivity of the constitution to international treaty

[42] This was the opinion of a school of thought of which Krabbe was an exponent, who identified international law with supranational law, under the premise that national sovereignty is only a derivative from international law. International law has a higher rank in the hierarchy of norms, since it derives from "the wider community of law". For this school the acceptance of the competence of the judge to review national law was only a logical consequence of the character of international law.

[43] C. W. Van der Pot and A. M. Donner, *Handbook van het Nederlandse Staatsrecht*, (1962), at pp. 193–4.

[44] It is worth noting that the theoretical underpinnings in *Van Gend en Loos* were not essential for the case: as will be explained below, the "limitation of sovereignty" used by the Court as a basis for its direct effect doctrine has no bearing on the Dutch situation. In a Dutch case note on *Van Gend en Loos*, the theoretical "lecture" by the Court was accounted for as reaction to the political crisis in European integration caused by the failure of the accession negotiations with the United Kingdom (Samkalden, *S.E.W.* (1963) p. 107, at p. 108). Another reason for the Court to give this extensive description of the legal order of the Community was of course that in other Member States, there *was* a need for this approach in order to adopt the direct effect doctrine.

[45] C. J. Mann, *The Function of Judicial Decision in European Economic Integration* (1972), at p. 28.

law, the application of Community law did not require (as it did elsewhere) a painful reconsideration of established doctrine. The case law of the ECJ, so far, has always fitted into the Dutch system: the principle of direct effect, supremacy, interpretation of national law as in *Marleasing*, or even *Francovich* have never required the judges to re-arrange national law in a dramatic way. It all fits into the system of the Dutch Constitution and Dutch judges have accepted the doctrine of the European Court on those matters as the governing law.

Since 1956, the Constitution has been amended, but without any consequences for the relationship with Community law. As part of the general revision of the Dutch Constitution in 1983, the provisions on external relations were also modified. Only minor changes and shifts of emphasis occurred but the main lines of the 1953/1956 regime remained unaltered.[46] The existing provisions were re-numbered as article 93 (on domestic effect of treaties and international decisions) and article 94 (recognising the competence of the judge to set aside national law which conflicts with provisions of treaties and decisions that are "binding on anyone").

One may note, however, that the 1983 revision was not used for drafting a special provision relating to the European Communities. They continue to be covered by the global notions of "treaties" and "international organisations".

The constituents' view was that the articles 93 and 94 were to be applied to the Community treaties and to deal with the relationship between Community law and national law. In its advisory opinion on the proposed revision, the Council of State[47] warned the Government against the confusion that could arise for Dutch judges if one kept the words "binding on anyone" in the Constitution. Referring to a judgment of the European Court,[48] the Council of State reminded the Government of the fact that in the framework of Community law, the judge could be under a duty to review national legislation in the light of a directive. A directive is a "decision of an international organisation" that needs to be implemented by the national authorities and is not "binding on anyone" in the strict sense of the word. Therefore the wording of the Constitution might inhibit Dutch courts from enforcing EC directives to the extent required from them by the European Court. In the end the words "binding on anyone" were maintained in the Constitution. The Government referred to the *Bosch* judgment of the Hoge Raad, accepting the European Court's competence in the direct effect issue, and maintained that the Constitution offered sufficient leeway for the reception of the case law of the Court of Justice. Deleting the words "binding on anyone" would, according to the Government, be even more confusing, since judges may then

---

[46] E. A. Alkema, "Foreign Relations in the Netherlands Constitution of 1983", *Netherlands International Law Review* 1984, p. 307 (see his conclusion at p. 330).

[47] This institution, like its French model, has advisory and adjudicatory functions. Opinions given as part of its advisory function are not binding.

[48] *Verbond van Nederlands Ondernemingen* v. *Inspecteur der Invoerrechten en Accijnzen*, Case 51/76, [1977] ECR 113.

mistakenly think that they should change their whole attitude towards international treaties. Furthermore, outside the scope of Community law, the words were deemed necessary to refrain the judges from interfering with the competences of the other State organs, in cases where implementation was required by a treaty. But the Government indicated that provisions requiring implementation may sometimes be considered as "binding on anyone", with all the consequences (direct effect, supremacy) deriving from that qualification.

Yet, it is not clear whether the interpretation of the articles 93 and 94 is relevant at all to the question of the domestic effect of Community law. There are, in fact, two schools of thought on the question of the ultimate ground for the domestic effect of Community law: does it rest upon the constitutional articles presented above, or does it rather rest purely and exclusively on its autonomous character as defined by the European Court?

One might have thought that the Constitution would be the obvious basis. In most European countries, the Constitution is considered to deal, in an exhaustive manner, with the conditions and mode of application of legal rules on the country's territory.[49] There is even more reason to hold that view in the Netherlands, because the wording of its Constitution is so well adapted to the requirements of international cooperation and European integration.

Yet, one finds that most authors hold the view that the constitutional articles about the domestic effect of international treaties do not apply to *Community* law.[50] They argue that questions about the direct effect of Community law and its supremacy over national law (including the Constitution) have to be decided by the European Court and that Dutch judges are under an obligation to follow the ECJ's views as part of the general obligation of article 5 of the EC Treaty. That position has as its logical consequence (which is spelled out by some of those authors) that the Dutch constitutional system is entirely irrelevant in this matter;[51] *Luxembourg locuta, res finita.*

[49] See e.g. the characteristic statement by the German constitutional judge Kirchhof: "*Das Grundgesetz der Bundesrepublik Deutschland regelt Entscheidungs—und Geltungsgrund verbindlichen Rechts für seinen Anwendungsbereich abschliessend*" (P. Kirchhof, "Verfassungsrechtlicher Schutz und internationaler Schutz der Menschenrechte: Konkurrenz oder Ergänzung?", in *Europäische Grundrechte Zeitschrift* (1994), p. 16, at p. 18.

[50] F. C. L. M. Crijns, *Het Europees perspectief van het Nederlandse staatsrecht* (1989) at pp. 27–8; C. A. J. M. Kortmann, *Constitutioneel recht* (1990) at p. 155; J. G. Brouwer, *Verdragsrecht in Nederland* (1992) at p. 3; H. R. B. M. Kummeling and J. B. Mus, "De invloed van het gemeenschapsrecht op de nationale rechtsorde", in M. C. Burkens, H. R. B. M. Kummeling, *EG en de grondrechten* (1993) at p. 3; R. H. Lauwaars and C. W. A. Timmermans, *Europees gemeenschapsrecht in kort bestek* (1989) at p. 27; L. J. Brinkhorst and R. Barents, *Grondlijnen van het Europees gemeenschapsrecht* (1990) at p. 198; H. R. B. M. Kummeling, "De doorwerking van internationale normen, in het bijzonder EEG-richtlijnen, in de Nederlandse rechtsorde", in *Nijmeegs staatsrecht, Bundel opstellen aangeboden aan Mr H.J.M. Beekman* (1987) at p. 68; P. J. G. Kapteyn and P. VerLoren van Themaat, *Inleiding tot het recht van de Europese gemeenschappen* (1987) at p. 241.

[51] See e.g. A. Kellermann, "Supremacy of Community law in the Netherlands", *European Law Review* (1989), p. 175, at p. 176: the "Constitution does not play a role in the question of whether there is supremacy of Community law".

Only a few authors take a different view.[52] They admit that, for practical purposes, it does not matter which is the ultimate ground for the review power of the judge—in the end both constructions will normally lead to the same result—but they argue that when a judge disapplies national law he does so on the basis of the authorisation granted by article 94 of the Constitution. In using this constitutional power, the courts may be guided by the European Court's doctrine, but that Court's case law is not the origin of their power to review national legislation. It is striking that authors who invoke the provisions of the Constitution when discussing the internal effect of Community law are often criticised by their colleagues for doing so.[53] They face the objection that "in the light of Community law, these references to the Constitution are not correct".

The almost unanimous approval of "la doctrine" for the theory of the radical autonomy of EC law is not confirmed by the views of Government and Parliament when they enacted the constitutional amendment of 1983. It is clear from the Memoranda of the 1983 revision that the relevant articles of the Constitution do apply to Community law, even if they have to be enforced by the judge with due regard to the jurisprudence of the European Court of Justice. But this does not seem to worry "la doctrine". The theoretical question of the ultimate ground of the domestic application of EC law is quickly disposed of, with the argument that the question does not have practical relevance.

Authors of both schools hardly refer to Dutch judicial statements for supporting their views. This is not surprising, as the Dutch courts generally exercise their power of reviewing national law without indicating the legal basis for their action. This is perfectly in line with the pragmatic ("un-doctrinal") attitude of Dutch courts: if application of articles 93 and 94 of the Constitution leads to the same result as the application of the European Court's doctrine on the autonomy of EC law, why would judges want to stir up trouble by specifying the basis for their decision? In the 1960s, judges did refer to articles 65 and 66 (as they then were) as the origin of their competence to disapply national law conflicting with Community law.[54] This practice faded away without any "revolutionary" overrulings.[55] The reference to

---

[52] See e.g. L. F. M. Besselink, "Curing a 'Childhood Sickness'? On Direct Effect, Internal Effect, Primacy and Derogation from Civil Rights. The Netherlands Council of State Judgment in the Metten Case", *Maastricht Journal of European and Comparative Law*, 1996, p. 165; of the same author, "De zaak-Metten, de Grondwet voorbij", *Nederlands Juristenblad*, 1996, p. 165.

[53] See G. H. Addink, B. P. Vermeulen on a handbook written by I. C. Van der Vlies, *RegelMaat* (1992), p. 2; see A. Meij, "Synchronisatie van rechtsorden", *Publiek Domein*, 1991, at p.178 where he reacts to references to articles 92–94 made by Van Maarseveen.

[54] Tariff Commission, 12 November 1963, *U.T.C.*, 1964 n. 71; Tariff Commission, 21 December 1965, *U.T.C.*, 1966, n. 58; CBB, 16 June 1970, *AB*, 1971, 50.

[55] Advocate General Van Soest briefly discussed the issue in a tax case before the Hoge Raad (H.R., 5 January 1983, BNB (1983) 104). He cited from the leading textbook on Community law (P. J. G. Kapteyn and P. VerLoren van Themaat, *Inleiding tot het recht van de Europese Gemeenschappen*, 3rd edn. (1980), p. 33) that "in the construction suggested by the Court in

the articles was simply left out without being replaced by another basis: no mention was (and is) made of the European Court's judgments in *Van Gend en Loos, Costa v. E.N.E.L.* or *Simmenthal*; nor are there any theoretical considerations on the relation between national law and Community law and the corresponding competences of the judiciary.

An exception to the practice of omitting the reference to articles 93 and 94 was the Afdeling Geschillen van Bestuur,[56] one of the two adjudicatory branches of the Raad van State (Council of State).[57] When disapplying a rule of national law, the Afdeling Geschillen bases its competence to do so on article 94 of the Constitution. Again, annotators of those judgments reject the reference to the articles of the Constitution as being incorrect.[58]

Now, does it matter in practice whether the competence of the judge is derived from the Constitution or not? Most—if not all—authors think that it does not really matter. That was also the view of the Government, expressed at the time of the latest revision of the Constitution; it declared that as far as Community law was concerned, articles 93 and 94 should always be applied in accordance with the jurisprudence of the European Court. Any discrepancies between the Constitution and the European Court's doctrine could be removed by using this rule of construction.

This is probably true. The choice between the Constitution or the autonomous nature of Community law as the ultimate basis may not be relevant in practice at present. Yet, a Constitution can be amended and the Dutch Constitution could be modified and made less internationalist than it is now. In that situation, it would become important to know whether Dutch judges base their authority to enforce EC law directly on its nature or, rather, on an authorisation given by their Constitution. Such a constitutional change is unlikely, but not unthinkable. Only a few years ago, the Minister of Justice proposed the creation of a constitutional court. According to this proposal, that court would be competent, to the exclusion of ordinary courts, for reviewing the constitutionality of acts of Parliament, but also for reviewing

---

Costa/ENEL . . . a reference to arts. 65, 66 and 67 of the Constitution is superfluous. The question whether this construction can be used by the national judge is itself an issue of constitutional law". And he went on to say: "However this may be, the Dutch constitutional system accepts the said construction and it is therefore beyond any doubt that the provisions of EEC law that are, by their content, binding on anyone, prevail over national legislation". He concluded that even though directives are not binding on anyone, they can produce direct effects in the relation between an individual and the State.

[56] The Afdeling Geschillen van Bestuur no longer exists since 1 January 1994; the two adjudicatory branches of the Raad van State have been merged into one Afdeling Bestuursrechtspraak (Administrative Law (Judicial) Division).

[57] Raad van State, Afdeling Geschillen van Bestuur, 6 September 1990, *AB*, 1990, no 12; 11 November 1991, *AB*, 1992, no 50; 17 February 1993, *Milieu en Recht*, 1993, 305, casenote G. H. Addink.

[58] G. H. Addink, casenote under Raad van State, 17 February 1993, *Milieu en Recht* (1993) 305, at p. 307.

their compatibility with international treaties.[59] Nothing came out of that proposal as yet, but it shows that constitutional amendments affecting the domestic status of EC law are possible even in the Netherlands.

The issue has recently gained interest after a decision, mentioned before, of the Administrative Law (Judicial) Division of the Council of State, concerning the Rules of Procedure of the Council of the European Communities and the Netherlands Act on Open Government (*Wet openbaarheid van bestuur*).[60] Metten, a Dutch member of the European Parliament requested the Minister for Finance to give access to the minutes of a number of meetings of the Ecofin Council. The Minister refused access on the basis of the secrecy clause contained in the Rules of Procedure of the Council and its precedence over national law, and alternatively, on an exception provided for in the Act of Open Government. Metten appealed to the President of the Administrative Law (Judicial) Division, who rejected the claim on the basis of primacy of Community law. In its final judgment, the Division upheld the refusal on the same grounds. It based its decision on the *Costa* v. *E.N.E.L.*, *Walt Wilhelm*, *Simmenthal* and *Hormones* judgments of the Court of Justice and derived from them a very strong version of primacy, applicable also to non-directly effective provisions of Community law. According to the Division, the relevant Rule of Procedure constitutes a binding rule of Community law, which takes precedence over the Act on Open Government. To hold otherwise would detract from its *effet utile*. The Division's interpretation of supremacy is at least questionable in the light of the European Court's case law, and a reference for preliminary ruling appears to have been expedient. It is also questionable whether these consequences could be attached to the Rules of Procedure of the Council. Yet, the judgment is also debatable in the light of articles 93 and 94 of the Constitution, which make judicial control of the supremacy of international treaties conditional upon their being "binding on anyone", which must, in relation to Community law, be interpreted in accordance with the case law of the Court of Justice. However, nothing in the case law of the Court of Justice indicates that in a case such as the one at hand, precedence must be granted to the Council's Rules of Procedure. At first sight, the Division's interpretation of supremacy could appear to be a political decision, necessary in order to achieve a certain result, namely in order to be able to deny access to the documents concerned. However, that result could have

---

[59] The proposal of the Minister was fiercely criticised in legal writings and in the advice given to the Government by several professors of law. One of their critiques was that such a system would be contrary to the principle in *Simmenthal*. Does this comment imply that the constitutional rules would suddenly become relevant to Community law? If the constitutional rules are irrelevant, they can say anything: they are not applicable to Community law anyway. See "Op weg naar constitutionele toetsing in Nederland, De adviezen aan de regering", *N.C.J.M. Bulletin* (1992), at p. 235 *et seq*.

[60] Discussed in L. F. M. Besselink, "Curing a 'Childhood Sickness'? On Direct Effect, Internal Effect, Primacy and Derogation from Civil Rights. The Netherlands Council of State Judgment in the Metten Case", *Maastricht Journal of European and Comparative Law*, 1996, p. 165.

been achieved in another and more elegant manner. The Act on Open Government offers sufficient leeway to make exceptions to open government: access can be denied when the supply of information is outweighed by the interests related to the conduct of international relations with foreign states or international organisations. It seems that the Division really wanted to make a statement on the principle of precedence of non-directly effective Community law; moreover, the members of the Division were well aware of the principles of direct effect and supremacy: one of its members is a prominent scholar in European law and co-author of a standard work on Community law.[61]

THE QUESTION OF "*KOMPETENZ-KOMPETENZ*"

This question has never been addressed in court in the Netherlands. The legal literature does not spend much thought on it. The issue is briefly mentioned in a 1994 textbook, clearly under the influence of the "Maastricht" judgment of the German Constitutional Court, but is dealt with in disappointingly simple terms. The authors write that the European Community does not possess "*Kompetenz-Kompetenz*" because its powers are attributed by the Member States.[62]

For a closer consideration of this issue, one needs first to distinguish between the attribution of competences, and the exercise of those competences.

The *attribution of competences* to the EC institutions at the time of the adoption of the treaties, or of any amendments to them, is subject to the approval of the Dutch Government and Parliament. They also have the duty to examine whether such attribution is compatible with the Constitution. Unlike the situation in most other countries, incompatibility does not mean that the Constitution has to be modified (or the treaty left unratified); it merely triggers a different procedure of parliamentary approval with a qualified majority voting requirement corresponding to that for constitutional revisions.[63] Moreover, the Constitution does not expressly refer to a "hard core" of constitutional values to be preserved against encroachment by means of an international agreement. Once a treaty has been approved and ratified in proper constitutional fashion, it is expressly declared by the Constitution to be immune from judicial challenge.

This remarkably generous reception of international (and European) treaties does not provide an answer to the question of "*Kompetenz-Kompetenz*", which arises in the course of the *exercise of competences* once

---

[61] See R. H. Lauwaars and C. W. A. Timmermans, *Europees Gemeenschapsrecht in kort bestek*, 3rd edn. (1994).

[62] J. A. Hofman, J. W. Sap, I. Sewandono, *Beginselen van Europees Constitutioneel Recht* (1994), at p. 49.

[63] This does not mean that the approval of an unconstitutional treaty is tantamount to a constitutional revision. The procedure for constitutional revision requires a vote by two subsequent Parliaments (and thus an intermediate general election), whereas one qualified majority vote of Parliament is enough to approve an unconstitutional treaty.

they have been attributed to the EC in accordance with each Member States' constitutional requirements. Setting the limits to the exercise of competences is a matter of interpretation. But the power of interpretation is itself one of the powers attributed to one of the EC institutions, namely the Court of Justice. Acceptance, by the Member States, of article 164 of the EC treaty at the time of ratification implies their recognition of the Court's authority to interpret the Treaty and to decide whether or not the other EC institutions remain within the limits of their powers.

This "orthodox" account of the *Kompetenz-Kompetenz* issue is, as far one can tell, unchallenged in the Netherlands. No claims are made for preserving an ultimate checking power by national courts on the exercise of Community competences. Since the *Bosch* decision of the Hoge Raad in 1962, the jurisdiction of the European Court in interpreting Community law is generally accepted.

One may nevertheless try to imagine how a *Kompetenz-Kompetenz* question could be raised by an applicant (or defendant) before a Dutch court. First, the party would clearly not be allowed to challenge the constitutionality of the EC Treaty itself or of the Parliamentary act of approval. Both are immune from judicial review under article 120 of the Constitution. The party should show that a specific act of application of the EC treaty is (a) *ultra vires* and (b) because of this, creates a legal situation which is in clear contrast with a substantive provision of the Constitution. The court may then want to check the plausibility of those two propositions by referring to the European Court of Justice a preliminary question on the validity of the Community act (in answer to proposition (a)) and possibly a preliminary question on the interpretation of that act (in order to help elucidate proposition (b)). If the Court of Justice fails to give satisfactory answers to those preliminary questions, then, just conceivably, the Dutch court might "rebel" and impose its own views on the validity, or the applicability, of the Community act.

Yet, at present, there is no sign whatsoever that a Dutch court might go to such lengths. But then, no really fundamental issues of compatibility of EC law and the Constitution have arisen as yet.

BEYOND THE LAW: THE SEARCH FOR EXPLANATIONS

The prevailing attitude towards international and European law is one of striking receptivity in principle, combined with cautious pragmatism in the application.

The traditional openness of the Dutch legal system

As is clear from this chapter, the receptivity of the Dutch legal order towards Community law is part of the larger and longer story of its receptivity to international law. Explanations must therefore also look at this underlying internationalist attitude, rather than focus exclusively on European law.

Part of the explanation may be the historical tradition of the Dutch school of international law. It may be tempting to draw a straight line from Grotius' *Mare Liberum* to the radical version of *pacta sunt servanda* espoused by Dutch internationalist doctrine. Since Grotius' time, this idealist attitude was in the best national interest. The traditional receptivity to international rules, and willingness to co-operate with foreign nations is clearly in the interest of a small trading nation, that is too small to preserve its independence on its own, and needs open borders for its prosperity. This connection is appropriately made in the title of a study of the history of Dutch foreign policy, Voorhoeve's *Peace, Profits and Principles*.[64]

The receptivity to international law may be considered as the combined result of national interest and internationalist ideology. Dutch jurists and politicians often (even today) bring a missionary spirit to international relations. They pretend to contribute to world order by setting an example. Lofty principles are combined with a rather pragmatic application of those principles, without causing any real disruptions of the domestic legal order.

There seem to be no impediments against this openness in the Constitution, nor in the constitutional values underlying it. There seems to be no clear "Grundnorm".

When a number of other European countries decided, in the immediate post-war period, to adapt their constitution to the new requirements of international co-operation and European integration, they typically did so by clauses allowing for "limitations of sovereignty".[65] The creation of international organisations with often far-reaching powers was declared to be compatible with the preservation of national sovereignty (albeit in an updated form). Yet, the principle of sovereignty also indicates a limit which should not be overstepped and which may become meaningful with further progress of integration (cf. the post-Maastricht decisions in France and Germany).

There is no such thing in the Netherlands. The 1953 Constitution allowed treaties to confer "certain powers with respect to legislation, administration and jurisdiction" on international organisations.[66] The term "sovereignty" is not used. Indeed, that term is altogether absent from the Constitution of the Netherlands. As for legal doctrine, its view of the concept of sovereignty is ambiguous and fluctuating. In a leading textbook of constitutional law, it is said that the concept of sovereignty is of limited use; the author even adds, without further explanation, that the Dutch state is no longer sovereign with regard to the powers attributed to the EC![67] In an advisory opinion of 1984, dealing with the then controversial issue of the placing of nuclear missiles on

---

[64] J. J. C. Voorhoeve, *Peace, Profits and Principles, a Study of Dutch Foreign Policy* (1979).

[65] Cf. French, Italian, German Constitutions.

[66] Article 67 of the 1953 Constitution. Since 1983, article 92 of the Constitution.

[67] C. A. J. M. Kortmann, *Constitutioneel recht* (1990), pp. 46–7.

Dutch territory, the Council of State took a similarly cavalier view of sovereignty.[68] It held that the conclusion of any international agreement implied a loss of sovereignty and that, therefore, the concept of sovereignty could not provide guidance as to which international treaties were unconstitutional and therefore required approval according to a more exacting procedure than ordinary treaties. Treaties were only unconstitutional if they conflicted with specific constitutional provisions, not with some abstractly defined core that would go under the name of sovereignty or any similar term (contrast with the German Constitutional Court in the "Maastricht" decision!). As a consequence, the idea that there is an entrenched and untouchable "constitutional core" does not play a meaningful role in Dutch constitutional doctrine, and cannot act as a limit to the "incoming tide" of Community law.

A negative element of explanation (which is therefore difficult to prove) is the absence, in the Netherlands, of a centralised constitutional court which could set itself the task of protecting the core values of the Dutch Constitution (as such courts tend to do in other countries). Instead, there is a variety of autonomous courts (the Supreme Court being merely a sort of *"primus inter pares"*), none of which thinks of itself as the supreme guardian of the constitutional order. The Dutch constitutional context thus seemed ideal for the acceptance of monism, direct effect and supremacy.

Separation of powers and the judicial function

Yet, in another respect, the absence of a constitutional court—or any other form of judicial review of statutes—had a negative impact on the acceptance of the supremacy of international law. Article 131 of the Constitution read until 1983: "statutes are inviolable".[69] Admittedly, article 131 was designed only to deny the judges the power to review the *constitutionality* of statutes. But this conception of the position of judges in relation to the other State organs did influence the debate on the constitutional reform with regard to treaty law. It was precisely the reason why the Government had left article 65 (on the supremacy of treaty law) outside the initial proposal for the constitutional revision. In the Government's opinion it was the responsibility of Parliament, not of the judges, to ensure that no conflicts would arise between treaties and statutes, just as it was Parliament's responsibility to control the constitutionality of statutes. The Government saw no reason to make a distinction between the two situations with regard to the respective function of the State organs. As described above, the review power of the judges with regard to treaty law was introduced on the insistence of Parliament itself. This

---

[68] An English version of the central parts of the Opinion can be found in the *Netherlands Yearbook of International Law* (1984) 320.

[69] The article was amended and re-numbered in 1983. Article 120 now reads: "The judge will not review the constitutionality of statutes and treaties".

new competence was framed in a wording that could have suggested a change in the constitutional position of the judges in relation to the other State organs. But in 1956, the Government insisted on the introduction of the specification "binding on anyone" in the article on supremacy, in order to elucidate that the article did not give the judges the competence to interfere with the functions of the Government and Parliament where a treaty's provisions were addressed to the latter organs, and not to individuals.

Even after the introduction of articles 65 and 66, entailing an express empowerment of the judges to control the observance of international obligations—though limited to self-executing provisions—judges refrained from using this newly attributed power. The main reason probably lies in the fact that there was no experience with judicial scrutiny of statutes, due to the absence of a constitutional court and given the constitutional ban on judicial review. Articles 65 and 66 gave the judges competences which were in fact alien to a long constitutional tradition.[70] At the same time, article 131 remained unaltered. This brought the judges in an odd position: they could now set aside statutes thought to violate certain international obligations, but at the same time, the inviolability of these statutes against any judicial review of their constitutionality was maintained.[71] The judges probably felt reluctant to use their new competences and to review what were constitutionally described as "inviolable" statutes, not because they did not want to give more weight to international treaty obligations than to a national statute, but because these new competences, although constitutionally recognised, clashed with their traditional role. Only when encouraged by another, "supranational" court,[72] the Court of Justice, did the Dutch judges start to assume their new constitutional task.

Judicial empowerment?

When the Hoge Raad accepted that the direct effect issue was one of interpretation that, for Community law, could properly be addressed to the Court of Justice, it may well have felt relieved. This meant that, at least for the direct effect issue, it could share responsibility with another, "supra-national" court; and when that other court decided that a provision of the EC Treaty produced direct effect, the courts may have felt less "awkward" to set aside what in the national constitutional context were "inviolable" statutes.

The Court of Justice in *Van Gend en Loos* and *Costa* v. *E.N.E.L.* did not empower the Dutch judges in the sense that it obliged them to assume a new function (as was the case in Belgium) nor did it convince lower courts to do

[70] T. Koopmans, "Receptivity and its Limits: the Dutch Case" in *In Memoriam J. D. B. Mitchell* (1983), 91 at p. 94.

[71] *Ibid.*

[72] See Hoge Raad, *Bosch*, 18 May 1962, *N.J.* (1965), 115.

what was under the Constitution the exclusive competence of the supreme court of the land (as was the case in Italy): all Dutch courts already possessed these competences under the Constitution. But the fact that the Court of Justice in *Van Gend en Loos* accepted the role of "accomplice" may well have encouraged the Dutch courts to excercise their constitutionally recognized powers against the national legislature.

The comparative dimension as a factor in the explanation

One of the factors traditionally inhibiting Dutch courts and legal writing from shedding all reservations towards international law were the flaws in the general enforcement mechanisms of international law. Before the Second World War, this fact was particularly obvious. When presenting, in 1937, the reasons pleading for the recognition of supremacy by national courts, Professor Verzijl had to acknowledge the existence of what he called "practical reservations" against his view. If international law displayed genuine force in the international community, he would not have any doubts in defending its absolute supremacy.[73] But would it be wise for the Netherlands to act as the "Don Quichote of international law"[74] by enforcing international law to its fullest extent at a time (1937!) when so many other nations trampled its norms? On balance, he concluded that the Netherlands should do it: the fight for the building of a genuine international legal order was a matter which was too serious and important for humanity to permit desertion.[75]

Things appeared in a different light after the Second World War. The change in the legal climate, heralded by the UN Charter and the regional European agreements, as well as the examples of some other constitutions (notably the French) convinced the Dutch Parliament to inscribe the supremacy of international treaties into the Constitution. Yet, some of the old fears about "going it alone" had not disappeared. Van Panhuys, after presenting the radical innovations of 1953, commented: "it cannot be denied that a state accepting the new principle runs certain risks as long as its example has not been followed by all other civilized countries, but this should not be a reason for rejecting it".[76]

Those doubts may well account for the partial retreat effected by the 1956 amendments to the Constitution, and for the restrictive application of the new constitutional provisions by Dutch courts. Hence the importance of the European Court's case law also for the Dutch legal order. By diffusing the "Dutch approach" to the other countries of the EC (at least with reference to the *Community* treaties), the Court of Justice has ended the isolation of the

---

[73] Verzijl, (1937), n. 5 above, at p. 56.
[74] *Ibid.*, p. 57.
[75] *Ibid.*
[76] See Van Panhuys, n. 6 above.

Netherlands and has thereby helped the Dutch courts to take their Constitution seriously and to recognise the direct effect and supremacy of international treaties more bravely than before.

Judicial dialogue

Dutch courts seem never to allude to the jurisprudence of the national courts of the other Member States. However, rather than demonstrating an unwillingness on the side of the Dutch courts to be inspired by the judicial reasoning of their counterparts in other countries, this is probably due to the fact that the Dutch legal order offers all the necessary tools to comply with the requirements of Community law, in a dialogue with the European Court of Justice.

Ever since the Hoge Raad accepted the jurisdiction of the Court of Justice in the *Bosch* case, the Dutch courts have frequently made use of article 177.[77] But also in cases where no reference is made, the Dutch courts often refer to the case law of the Court of Justice, without ever doubting its jurisdiction or openly rejecting its judgments.

The Dutch courts are receptive to the message from Luxembourg, but seem not to need inspiration from their counterparts in other states. Conversely, the Dutch constitutional system appears to have exerted its influence on the case law of the Court of Justice, and through it on that of other Member States. But also more directly, the Dutch constitutional system may well have inspired the evolution of other national courts. References to the Dutch Constitution— although often very concise and sometimes presenting a too idyllic picture— can be found in many textbooks, articles and judgments.

But not only its principles, also its scheme may well have influenced other legal systems. In Belgium, for instance, Procureur-Général Hayoit de Termicourt proposed in his *mercuriale* of 1963, to distinguish between self-executing treaty provisions, which would take precedence, and non self-executing provisions, which would have to give way to national statutes. The distinction appeared convenient, because it gave the Cour de Cassation the possibility to adopt a new approach without having to overrule its earlier case law. Also, he said, only in the case of self-executing provisions would conflicts arise. There is no proof that Hayoit de Termicourt intended to copy the Dutch pattern,[78] but in an article of 1965, Waelbroeck[79] commented that "the

---

[77] In 1993, the Court of Justice answered 43 questions coming from Dutch courts. Only German courts referred more questions. See *Eleventh Annual Report on Monitoring the Application of Community Law* (1993), COM(94) 500, 417–18.

[78] Hayoit de Termicourt gave a short overview of the approach adopted in several other European countries.

[79] M. Waelbroeck, "Le juge belge devant le droit international et le droit communautaire", *R.B.D.I.* (1965) p. 348 at p. 356; P. Pescatore, case note on *Franco-Suisse Le Ski*, C.D.E. (1971) also points at the parallellism with the Dutch system.

fact that the Dutch Constitution makes the power to review national legislation in the light of treaty provisions conditional upon their being directly applicable, is no sufficient reason to adopt the same approach in Belgium".[80]

Likewise, there is a striking parallel with the approach of the European Communities Act of the United Kingdom which makes primacy of Community law over municipal law conditional upon direct effect, by reference to the concept of the "enforceable Community right".[81]

Legal pragmatism

A factor which is difficult to pin down but plays an important role, in our opinion, is the practical mind of Dutch jurists and politicians, and their aversion from theoretical constructions and disputes. In relation, more specifically, to this subject, there is a striking lack of interest for "constitutional fundamentals". Issues which inflame the minds of scores of constitutionalists in countries like Germany and Italy fail to attract controversy.

In this way, the doctrine of direct effect and supremacy of Community law have become so self-evident in the Netherlands that the controversies about the relation between Community law and national constitutional law, existing in other Member States, are difficult to explain to younger generations of lawyers.[82]

---

[80] Ganshof van der Meersch agreed with this point of view in a footnote in his *mercuriale* of 1968 (Ganshof van der Meersch, Réflexions sur le droit international et le revision de la Constitution, address given to the official reassembly of the Cour de cassation on 2 September 1968, *J.T.* (1968) 485 at pp. 493–4, and footnote 142); however, in his Opinion in the *Franco-Suisse le Ski* case he proposed direct effect as a condition for supremacy, since only then there is a conflict of norms (Opinion of Procureur-Général W. J. Ganshof van der Meersch in the case of the *Belgian State* v. *S.A. Franco-Suisse le Ski*, 27 May 1971, Cour de cassation).

[81] Pescatore, "The Doctrine of 'Direct Effect': An Infant Disease of Community Law", *E.L.R.* (1983) p. 155 at p. 157

[82] A. W. H. Meij, *Prejudiciële vragen van Nederlandse rechters en hun gevolgen*, Preadvies, Vereniging voor de vergelijkende studie van het recht van België en Nederland (1993) at p. 3.

7

Report on the United Kingdom

P. P. CRAIG

This chapter will consider certain constitutional aspects of the relationship between the EC and the United Kingdom. The analysis will be divided into the following sections. The initial section will focus on constitutional doctrine within the United Kingdom and the way in which this has been affected by our membership of the EC. There will then be a discussion of the way in which the *"Kompetenz-Kompetenz"* issue might be addressed in our courts. The third section will address some of the broader issues involved in the constitutional interchange between the United Kingdom and the EC, and will explore the reasons which underlie the doctrinal changes which have occurred.

CONSTITUTIONAL DOCTRINE WITHIN THE UNITED KINGDOM: THE IMPACT OF THE EC

The discussion within this section will focus on the reception of EC supremacy within the UK constitutional order, the way in which UK courts have responded to the doctrine of direct effect and their approach to preliminary rulings. It is clear that these issues are connected, but nonetheless, for reasons which will become apparent within the ensuing discussion, they are best treated separately.

Supremacy: the traditional debate in the United Kingdom

The supremacy of Community law has always represented a particular difficulty for UK constitutional doctrine, because of the doctrine of Parliamentary sovereignty. It is impossible to understand the case law on this issue without some brief background on the sovereignty debate within the United Kingdom.

Students, and indeed academics, are prone to characterise the current debate over sovereignty as a contest between the traditionalists, represented by Dicey/Wade, and upholders of the "New View", represented by Jennings/Heuston/Marshall. However, the species of argument used by Wade is, in fact, very different from that advanced by Dicey, and therefore it is the views of Professor Wade which will be considered in this section. No attempt will be made to consider the detail of the debate between Wade and the advocates of the New View. The author's own views on this can be found elsewhere.[1] The Wade view of sovereignty is captured in the following quotation:[2]

> "An orthodox English lawyer, brought up consciously or unconsciously on the doctrine of parliamentary sovereignty stated by Coke and Blackstone, and enlarged on by Dicey, could explain it in simple terms. He would say that it meant merely that no Act of the sovereign legislature (composed of the Queen, Lords and Commons) could be invalid in the eyes of the courts; that it was always open to the legislature, so constituted, to repeal any previous legislation whatever; that therefore no Parliament could bind its successors . . . He would probably add that it is an invariable rule that in case of conflict between two Acts of Parliament, the later repeals the earlier. If he were then asked whether it would be possible for the United Kingdom to "entrench" legislation—for example, if it should wish to adopt a Bill of Rights which would be repealable only by some specially safeguarded process—he would answer that under English law this is a legal impossibility: it is easy enough to pass such legislation, but since that legislation, like all other legislation, would be repealable by any ordinary Act of Parliament the special safeguards would be legally futile. This is merely an illustration of the rule that one Parliament cannot bind its successors. It follows therefore that there is one, and only one, limit to Parliament's legal power: it cannot detract from its own continuing sovereignty."

The Wade thesis has been vigorously challenged by the proponents of the New View, who have argued that manner and form provisions enacted in a particular statute would be binding, in the sense that a later statute dealing with the same subject matter could only alter the earlier statute if passed in accordance with the provisions of that earlier statute.[3]

The details of these arguments can be found elsewhere.[4] What is of relevance in the present context is the way in which the Wade form of argumentation has coloured the entirety of the current debate. It has allowed Wade, and the supporters of his view, to by-pass discussion as to the existence of any normative justification for the sovereign, unlimited, power of Parliament. The issue is conceived of in "technical" terms, relating to the content of the ultimate legal principle or rule of recognition ("top rule"), which might be said to exist within society at any one point in time. While it is recognised that there might be a different top rule from that which we are presently said to have, there is no argument put as to whether the current rule is normatively justifiable. As will be seen below this mode of thought has had implications

---

[1] P. P. Craig, "Parliamentary Sovereignty of the United Kingdom Parliament After Factortame" (1991) 11 *Y.B.E.L.* 221.

[2] H. W. R. Wade, "The Basis of Legal Sovereignty" [1955] *C.L.J.* 172, at p. 174.

[3] Sir I. Jennings, *The Law of the Constitution*, 5th edn. (1967), Ch. 4; R. F. V. Heuston, *Essays in Constitutional Law*, 2nd. edn. (1964), Ch. 1; G. Marshall, *Constitutional Theory* (1971), Ch. 3.

[4] Craig, n. 1 above.

for the way in which the sovereignty issue has been perceived in the context of the United Kingdom's membership of the EC.

This absence of any principled justification for the *status quo* is mirrored by the way in which the courts are said to go about their task as interpreters of the content of the top rule.[5] The courts will make a political choice at the point where the law "stops". There is no need for the courts to engage in a principled discourse as to the "correct" answer to this question at any particular point in time, since the issue is never perceived in these terms.[6]

Supremacy and the judicial response prior to *Factortame*

It is readily apparent that on the traditional view of sovereignty as represented by Wade the latest will of Parliament must predominate, and that this also entails the proposition that if there is an implicit clash between a later and an earlier norm then the latter is taken to be impliedly repealed by the former in the event of a clash between the two.

It is equally apparent that this view of sovereignty places UK law in danger of constant clashes with EC law. There can be two types of inconsistency or conflict between domestic law and Community law: intentional and inadvertent conflict. The latter is far more common than the former. It is clear that, even with the best will in the world, there will be inadvertent clashes between Community law and national law. These will often be simply the result of an "absence of fit" between complex Community provisions on a topic and those subsisting within national law. More intentional recalcitrance on the part of the Member States will be less common, though it is not by any means unknown. Supremacy was asserted by the European Court of Justice early in its developing jurisprudence,[7] and extended by later case law.[8]

How then have the UK courts responded to this problem? How have they coped with the absence of a ready accommodation between traditional ideas of sovereignty and membership of the EC? The jurisprudence of UK courts can be divided between cases which were decided prior to the seminal *Factortame* case, and the decision of the House of Lords in that case itself.

Prior to the decision in *Factortame* there were a number of differing strands within the UK jurisprudence. Three can be identified here.

---

[5] Wade, n. 2 above, p. 192.

[6] The form of argument presented by Wade has, somewhat paradoxically, influenced the mode of counter-argument utilised by the advocates of the New View. This is, in some ways, unsurprising, since they are reacting to the traditionalist view. This reactive posture has, however, a "price". It means that their counter-arguments are also conducted in a manner which minimises the import of any normative arguments which might be presented for the limitation of sovereign power. It might well be true that they would favour rights-based limits on governmental power, which would thereby further the cause of an empowered citizenry, but this is never the focus of their response.

[7] *Costa* v. *E.N.E.L.*, Case 6/64, [1964] ECR 585, 593.

[8] *Simmenthal*, Case 106/77, [1978] ECR 629.

One strand, albeit not the predominant one, was to apply traditional ortho-doxy on sovereignty undiminished to the context of clashes between national law and Community law. This is exemplified by the dicta in the *Felixstowe Dock* case[9] in which Lord Denning MR made it clear that if there were to be any conflict between UK law and Community law then it would have to be the latter which would fall. We can see here the consequences of the form of thought which characterises the traditional view of sovereignty in the United Kingdom. Precisely because this view was not dependent on any principled justification for the ascription of unlimited sovereign power to the current UK Parliament, it could be applied in the context of the United Kingdom's mem-bership of the EC without any thought as to whether it made sense in that area. It served to forestall reasoned analysis as to whether our membership of the Community was not, in reality, premised on assumptions which were incompatible with traditional sovereignty theory in its stark form.

The second, and dominant, line of cases sought to blunt the edge of any conflict between the two systems by the use of strong principles of construc-tion, the import of which was that UK law would, whenever possible, be read so as to be compatible with Community law requirements. This line of cases is exemplified by the decision of the House of Lords in the *Litster* case.[10] Forth Dry Dock became insolvent and went into receivership. In order to render the firm more attractive to potential buyers the employees were dismissed, the firm was sold, and the new buyer then took on new workers at lower rates of pay. Directive 77/187 was designed to protect employees in the event of a busi-ness transfer, and this was implemented in the United Kingdom by delegated legislation in the form of a statutory instrument. The object of the legislation was to protect employees who would otherwise have a claim of no value against an insolvent company. The protection, however, only operated when the employee was employed immediately before the transfer. The companies argued that, because of the dismissals prior to the transfer of ownership, the workers did not come within the UK statutory instrument. The House of Lords disagreed. Their Lordships reasoned as follows: if the UK statutory instrument were to be read by itself then the construction contended for by the defendant firms might have to be accepted. However, this statutory instru-ment was passed in order to effectuate the objectives of an earlier EC Directive, and it should, whenever possible, be construed in order to attain those objectives. This reasoning process emerges clearly in the following extract from Lord Oliver:[11]

"If this provision fell to be construed by reference to the ordinary rules of con-struction applicable to a purely domestic statute and without reference to Treaty obligations, it would, I think, be quite impermissible to regard it as having the same

---

[9] *Felixstowe Docks Railway Co. v. British Transport Docks Board* [1976] 2 CMLR 655, 664.
[10] *Litster v. Forth Dry Dock* [1989] 2 WLR 634.
[11] *Ibid.* at 657–8.

prohibitory effect as that attributed by the European Court of Justice to Article 4 of the Directive. But it has always to be borne in mind that the purpose of the Directive and of the Regulations was and is to 'safeguard' the rights of employees on a transfer and that there is a mandatory obligation to provide remedies which are effective and not merely symbolic to which the Regulations were intended to give effect. The remedies provided by the Act of 1978 in the case of an insolvent transferor are largely illusory unless they can be exerted against the transferee as the Directive contemplates and I do not find it conceivable that, in framing Regulations intending to give effect to the Directive, the Secretary of State could have envisaged that its purpose should be capable of being avoided by the transparent device to which resort was had in the instant case. *Pickstone* v. *Freemans plc* [1989] A.C. 66, has established that the greater flexibility available to the court in applying a purposive construction to legislation designed to give effect to the United Kingdom's Treaty obligations to the Community enables the court, where necessary, to supply by implication words appropriate to comply with those obligations . . . Having regard to the manifest purpose of the Regulations, I do not, for my part, feel inhibited from making such an implication in the instant case".

The strategy in cases such as *Litster* was to avoid characterising the fact situation in a way which would entail a direct conflict between Community and national law. The principle of construction described above was the device used to attain this end. On this view the traditional theory of sovereignty could be maintained, but the national court could avoid the reality of any conflict with Community law by reading national provisions in a manner designed to effectuate the dictates of EC law. This mode of reasoning gained added force given that the facts of *Litster* concerned the enforcement of directives as between individuals. Community law, as is well known, denies that directives have any horizontal direct effect, and only requires that the national court employs canons of construction in order to try and read national law to be in conformity with Community norms. Viewed in this way the reasoning of the House of Lords at one and the same time could remain within the formal model of traditional sovereignty, while also complying with the demands of Community law as to the force of directives as between individuals.

The third type of case which can be found prior to the decision in *Factortame* is one in which the court accepts, in principle, the idea of purposive construction set out above, but where it feels unable on the facts before it to read the UK legislation to be in conformity with the relevant EC norm. *Duke* v. *GEC Reliance*[12] provides an example of this type of case. In this instance the House of Lords felt unable to read the Equal Pay Act 1970 and the Sex Discrimination Act 1975 to be in conformity with the Equal Treatment Directive 1976 (76/207), more particularly because the plaintiff was seeking to rely on a construction of the Directive which had only become apparent from a decision of the ECJ given in 1986. The case has been criticised by writers in

[12] [1988] 2 WLR 359.

the United Kingdom.[13] It should, however, be borne in mind that the case turned on the provisions of a directive in a dispute between private parties. In the absence of any horizontal direct effect the national court therefore approached the case via the *Von Colson* principle.[14] The issue before the national court was *not* whether EC law could trump national law, but whether the provisions of a directive which did not have direct effect between these parties could lead to national legislation being construed as the applicant wished. The House of Lords felt that the domestic statutes could not be interpreted in this manner.

Supremacy and the *Factortame* litigation

The leading decision on the sovereignty issue is now *R* v. *Secretary of State for Transport, ex parte Factortame Ltd.*[15] The background to the case was as follows. The applicants were companies which were incorporated under UK law, but the majority of the directors and shareholders of these companies were in fact Spanish. The companies were in the business of sea fishing and their vessels were registered as British under the Merchant Shipping Act 1894. The statutory regime governing sea fishing was radically altered by the passage of the Merchant Shipping Act 1988 and the regulations made pursuant thereto. Vessels which had been registered under the 1894 Act now had to register once again under the new legislation. Ninety-five vessels failed to meet the criteria in the new legislation and they sought to argue that the relevant parts of the 1988 Act were incompatible with articles 7, 52, 58, and 221 of the EC Treaty.

Whether the 1988 statute was in fact in breach of EC law was clearly a contentious question. All the UK courts involved in the case agreed that a reference should be made to the ECJ under article 177. The question which remained for decision in the first *Factortame* case concerned the status of the 1988 Act pending the decision on the substance of the case by the ECJ. This decision might not be forthcoming for some time and if the applicants could not fish in this intervening period they might well go out of business. The applicants sought therefore either for the 1988 Act to be "disapplied" pending the outcome on the substance of the case before the ECJ; or that if this was not to be the case, and the Act remained in force to prevent them from fishing, then the Government should have to give an undertaking to provide compensation should the ultimate decision given by the ECJ be in the applicants' favour. In other words, if the court did grant an interim injunction to the Government to prevent the applicants from fishing, then the Government

---

[13] E. Scyszcak, "Sovereignty: Crisis, Compliance, Confusion, Complacency?" (1990) 15 *E.L.Rev.* 480.

[14] *Von Colson and Kamann* v. *Land Nordrhein-Westfahlen*, Case 14/83, [1984] ECR 1891.

[15] [1990] 2 AC 85.

should have to give a cross-undertaking to pay damages if they should lose in the main action before the ECJ.

The operative point of this judgment for the purposes of the present discussion concerned the availability of interim relief against the Crown. Their Lordships affirmed that, as a matter of domestic law, this was not available.[16] Lord Bridge then considered the applicants' argument that the absence of any interim relief against the Crown was itself a violation of Community law. Lord Bridge was unsure whether this was indeed required by EC law, but since the point was clearly contentious and of importance a preliminary ruling was requested from the ECJ. The ECJ was therefore in effect being asked to rule on whether a "gap" in the availability of administrative law remedies in UK law was itself a breach of EC law, at least insofar as this "gap" affected actions which had an EC element to them.

The ECJ decided in favour of the applicants.[17] The reasoning was founded on the earlier judgment in the *Simmenthal* case.[18] In that case, as is well known, the ECJ held that provisions of Community law rendered "automatically inapplicable" any conflicting provision of national law. The *Simmenthal* decision had given a broad construction to the idea of a "conflicting provision" of national law, interpreting it to cover any legislative, administrative or judicial practice which might impair the effectiveness of Community law.[19] With this foundation the ECJ in the *Factortame* case concluded that:[20]

> "the full effectiveness of Community law would be just as much impaired if a rule of national law could prevent a court seised of a dispute governed by Community law from granting interim relief in order to ensure the full effectiveness of the judgment to be given on the existence of the rights claimed under Community law. It follows that a court which in those circumstances would grant interim relief, if it were not for a rule of national law is obliged to set aside that rule".

The case then returned to the House of Lords to be reconsidered in the light of the preliminary ruling given by the ECJ, *R* v. *Secretary of State for Transport, ex parte Factortame Ltd (No 2).*[21] A number of interesting issues emerge from their Lordships' decision, including the availability of interim relief against the Crown. Suffice it to say for the present that their Lordships accepted that, at least in the area covered by EC law, such relief would be made available against the Crown. The present discussion will focus upon the approach taken by the House of Lords to the issue of sovereignty and the EC.

Factortame (No 2) contains dicta by their Lordships on the more general issue of sovereignty, and the reasons why these dicta are contained in the

---

[16] The House of Lords has now reconsidered this matter in *M* v. *Home Office* [1993] 3 All ER 537.

[17] *R* v. *Secretary of State for Transport, ex parte Factortame Ltd*, Case 213/89, [1990] 3 CMLR 867.

[18] *Amministrazione Delle Finanze Dello Stato* v. *Simmenthal SpA* [1978] ECR 629.

[19] *Ibid.*, paras. 22 and 23.

[20] [1990] 3 CMLR 867, para. 21.

[21] [1991] 1 AC 603.

decision are not hard to find. The final decision on the substance of the case involved a potential clash between certain norms of the EC Treaty itself, combined with EC rules on the common fisheries policy, and a *later* Act of the UK Parliament, the Merchant Shipping Act 1988, combined with regulations made thereunder. One aspect of the traditional idea of sovereignty in the United Kingdom has been, as noted above, that if there is a clash between a later statutory norm and an earlier legal provision the former takes precedence. The strict application of this idea in the context of the EC could obviously be problematic, since the ECJ has repeatedly held that Community law must take precedence in the event of a clash with national law.

Moreover, and this is of some importance, the House of Lords in *Factortame* could not avoid confronting the sovereignty issue directly. It could not fall back on principles of construction as it had done in earlier cases. This avenue was not open to it for two reasons. On the one hand, it is doubtful on the facts of the case whether national law could have been found to be in conformity with EC law by this device. On the other hand, the conflict in this instance was between national law and, *inter alia*, provisions of the EC Treaty itself. The ECJ has made it quite clear that in the event of such a clash, whether raised in an action between individuals or between an individual and the state, EC law trumps national law. The duty of the national court was not therefore confined to seeing whether national law might be read to be in conformity with Community law, as is the case in actions between individuals based on directives.

The dicta of the House of Lords in *Factortame (No 2)* are therefore clearly of importance. Lord Bridge had this to say:[22]

"Some public comments on the decision of the Court of Justice, affirming the jurisdiction of the courts of the member states to override national legislation if necessary to enable interim relief to be granted in protection of rights under Community law, have suggested that this was a novel and dangerous invasion by a Community institution of the sovereignty of the United Kingdom Parliament. But such comments are based on a misconception. If the supremacy within the European Community of Community law over the national law of member states was not always inherent in the EEC Treaty it was certainly well established in the jurisprudence of the Court of Justice long before the United Kingdom joined the Community. Thus, whatever limitation of its sovereignty Parliament accepted when it enacted the European Communities Act 1972 was entirely voluntary. Under the terms of the 1972 Act it has always been clear that it was the duty of a United Kingdom court, when delivering final judgment, to override any rule of national law found to be in conflict with any directly enforceable rule of Community law. Similarly, when decisions of the Court of Justice have exposed areas of United Kingdom statute law which failed to implement Council directives, Parliament has always loyally accepted the obligation to make appropriate and prompt amendments. Thus there is nothing in any way novel in according supremacy to rules of Community law in areas to which

[22] *Ibid.* at 658–9.

they apply and to insist that, in the protection of rights under Community law, national courts must not be prohibited by rules of national law from granting interim relief in appropriate cases is no more than a logical recognition of that supremacy".

It is clear that Lord Bridge was speaking in broad terms about the relationship between EC law and UK law. His dictum represents a general statement concerning the priority of Community law over national law in the event of a clash between the two. There are two foundations for this reasoning evident in the above dictum. One is essentially *contractarian*: the United Kingdom knew when it joined the EC that priority should be accorded to EC law, and it must be taken to have contracted on those terms. If, therefore, "blame" was to be cast for a loss of sovereignty then this should be laid at the feet of Parliament and not the courts. The other conceptual base for Lord Bridge's reasoning is *a priori* and *functional*: it was always inherent in a regime such as the Community that it could only function adequately if EC law could indeed take precedence in the event of a clash with domestic legal norms.[23]

Supremacy and Community law after *Factortame*

Space precludes a thorough analysis of the effects of the second *Factortame* decision on the traditional concept of sovereignty as it operates in the United Kingdom. This can be found elsewhere.[24] Certain conclusions can, nonetheless, be drawn quite briefly concerning supremacy in the context of the EC. Three may be mentioned here.

First, in strict doctrinal terms the decision means, at the very least, that the concept of *implied repeal*, under which inconsistencies between later and earlier norms were resolved in favour of the former, will no longer apply to clashes concerning Community and national law.

Secondly, if Parliament ever does wish to derogate from its Community obligations then it will have to do so *expressly and unequivocally*. The reaction of our national courts to such an unlikely eventuality remains to be seen. In principle two options would be open to the national judiciary. Either they could choose to follow the latest will of Parliament, thereby preserving some remnant of traditional orthodoxy on sovereignty. Or they could argue that it is not open to our legislature to pick and choose which obligations to subscribe to while still remaining within the Community.

---

[23] Lord Goff, who gave the leading judgment of the House of Lords, said less on this particular issue than did Lord Bridge. However, even Lord Goff did state, in the course of deciding whether to grant interim relief to the applicants, that the applicants had strong grounds for "challenging the validity" of the provisions relating to residence and domicile in the UK legislation, *ibid.* at 672, 674.

[24] P. Craig, "Sovereignty of the United Kingdom Parliament after Factortame" (1991) 11 *Y.B.E.L.* 221, and "Administrative Law, Remedies and the EEC" (1991) 3 *E.R.P.L.* 521.

The final point follows on from the second and provides some hint as to which of the two options the national court would adopt. The reasoning in *Factortame (No 2)* reflects a move away from certain of the assumptions underlying what is taken to be the traditional view of sovereignty as propounded by Wade. We have already seen that on this view the courts are making an unconstrained political choice when they reach the boundaries of the accepted legal norms, and we have seen also that this mode of reasoning was itself connected to the particular species of legal positivism which underlies the Wade thesis. Yet this is not how the court approached the matter in *Factortame (No 2)*. It neither regarded the decision on sovereignty as one which it was to make wholly divorced from Parliament's will; nor can its decision accurately be characterised as one of political choice by the judiciary at the point where the law "stops". The mode of reasoning utilised by the court is more accurately represented as being based on *principle*, in the sense of working through the principled consequences of the United Kingdom's membership of the EC. Both the contractarian and *a priori* arguments used by the court exemplify this style of judicial discourse.[25] Given that this is so one might hazard the guess that even in the unlikely eventuality of express derogation from Community law by Parliament, the courts would be minded to follow the second option mentioned above: to decide, very much in accordance with the reasoning in *Factortame (No 2)*, that while we remain within the Community we cannot simply pick and choose which norms to accept. This conjecture is however based on the assumption that the relevant substantive issue is one which does fall within the Community's competence. Where there are serious questions as to whether this is so matters may become more complicated. This issue will be examined more fully below.

Direct effect

In terms of direct effect itself UK courts have on the whole accepted ECJ rulings on this issue without compunction. They have not sought to contest a ruling by the ECJ that a Treaty article, regulation or directive fulfils the conditions in order for it to have direct effect, either in its entirety, or in relation to certain of its provisions. What is of particular interest in this respect is the controversial area concerning the direct effect of directives. It is well known that certain national courts have expressed reservations about whether directives have direct effect, either at all, or as between individuals. The UK Government, along with most other Governments of the Member States, subscribes to the view that the ECJ should not go beyond its holding in the *Marshall* case,[26] and should not give horizontal direct effect to directives. The national courts in the United Kingdom have not themselves expressed any

---

[25] For further discussion of this view of sovereignty more generally, see Craig, n. 1 above.
[26] *Marshall* v. *Southampton Area Health Authority*, Case 152/84, [1986] ECR 723.

view directly on the issue. What their reaction would be if the ECJ were to reverse the limitations expressed in *Marshall* will have to be seen, if and when the occasion arises. This issue will be considered further within the third section of this chapter.[27]

Preliminary rulings

The approach of the UK courts as to when a reference should be made to the ECJ for a preliminary ruling pursuant to article 177 has changed over the course of the last decade. The reasons for this change of attitude will be explored in due course.[28]

The initial stance was somewhat restrictive and this is reflected in Lord Denning MR's guidelines in *Bulmer* v. *Bollinger*.[29] In that case he laid down certain guidelines as to when a reference should and should not be made. Four such guidelines were set down as to when a ruling from the ECJ would be deemed to be necessary within the meaning of article 177: the decision on the question of Community law must be conclusive of the case; the national court might choose to follow a previous ruling of the ECJ on the same point, although it could refer the matter to the ECJ in the hope that it would give a different ruling; a reference could be declined on the grounds of *acte clair*; the facts should generally be decided first in order to determine whether a reference really was necessary. Even if a reference was necessary in the above sense a court still possessed a discretion whether to refer and should, said Lord Denning, bear in mind the following factors when exercising that discretion: it should be aware of the length of time which it takes to obtain a preliminary ruling; it should not overload the ECJ with too many references; it should not refer the case unless the point of Community law was important and difficult; it should be cognisant of the expense of a reference for the parties involved in the case; and it should take account of the wishes of the parties, and be hesitant to refer where one or both of the parties did not wish to do so. These guidelines have been cited on a number of occasions,[30] albeit not necessarily followed to the letter, and it is apparent from the tenor of the conditions set out above that they are not designed to encourage too ready a use of the reference procedure.

More recent cases have, however, adopted a more liberal approach as to when a reference should be made under article 177. The beginnings of the more liberal approach can be traced to the decision of Bingham J in the *Samex*

---

[27] See pp. 218–19 below.
[28] See pp. 220–21 below.
[29] [1974] Ch 401.
[30] See, e.g., *R* v. *Inner London Education Authority, ex parte Hinde* [1985] 1 CMLR 716; *R* v. *Her Majesty's Treasury, ex parte Daily Mail and General Trust plc* [1987] 2 CMLR 1; *R* v. *Pharmaceutical Society of Great Britain, ex parte the Association of Pharmaceutical Importers* [1987] 3 CMLR 951.

case.[31] In that case Bingham J cited the criteria from *Bulmer*, but then went on to point out that the ECJ was in a far better position than a national court to determine issues of Community law. He noted that the ECJ had an expert knowledge of Community law, a unique grasp of the differing language texts, and a greater familiarity with principles of purposive construction than did a UK national court. Bingham J's caveat to the Denning guidelines has subsequently been cited with approval.[32] Other cases have continued this more liberal trend. Thus in *Bethell* v. *SABENA*[33] Parker J stated that the Denning guidelines were not binding and could not fetter the discretion of the court as to whether it felt that a reference was necessary. While in cases such as *Polydor*[34] the court has been content to order a reference if this was felt to be *reasonably* necessary. This greater willingness to make a ruling has been matched by a greater wariness about applying the *acte clair* doctrine as a reason for declining to refer.[35]

"KOMPETENZ-KOMPETENZ": PRACTICE AND DOCTRINE

The issue of "*Kompetenz-Kompetenz*" raises the question of who is to decide the limits of Community competence. Clearly if the Community has no competence to act then its action will be *ultra vires* and there will be no question of its primacy over national law. However, in many instances the question will be whether the Community does indeed have competence to act and this will be dependent on the interpretation of the relevant Community provisions. It will therefore be crucial who is to decide the limits of Community competences. In addressing this issue the discussion will be divided into three parts: how far, if at all, does the national case law provide any clue as to how the matter will be resolved; how far does constitutional doctrine dictate an answer; and how are the courts in practice likely to approach this issue?

As to the first of these questions, the issue of *Kompetenz-Kompetenz* has never yet arisen in the UK context. The closest "clue" from existing case law is to be found in the form of words used by Lord Bridge in *Factortame (No 2)*. The dictum of his Lordship in that case is an acceptance of Community supremacy in the areas to which Community law applies. Now it is doubtful whether he had in mind any *Kompetenz-Kompetenz* problem when framing his judgment in these terms, but this phraseology is likely to be picked up by a future counsel eager to find some peg on which to hang the competence of the UK courts to resolve for themselves this issue. It should however be noted

---

[31] *Commissioners of Customs and Excise* v. *Samex* [1983] 3 CMLR 194, 209–11.
[32] See, e.g., *R* v. *Intervention Board for Agricultural Produce, ex parte the Fish Producers' Organisation Ltd* [1988] 2 CMLR 661, 676.
[33] [1983] 3 CMLR 1, 4–5.
[34] *Polydor* v. *Harlequin Record Shops* [1980] 2 CMLR 413, 428; *R* v. *Plymouth Justices* [1982] QB 863, 869; *R* v. *Inner London Education Authority* [1985] 1 CMLR 716, 728.
[35] See, e.g., *R* v. *Pharmaceutical Society* [1987] 3 CMLR 951, 971.

that even on its face Lord Bridge's dictum is ambivalent as to which court should determine the limits of Community competence. It merely states that UK courts will accept Community supremacy within the areas to which EC law applies, without indicating which court will decide the placing of the appropriate boundary lines.

What then should be the approach in terms of constitutional doctrine? This is an interesting and important question. Any answer must distinguish between the response which would be forthcoming based on traditional theory, and that which might be given based on the reasoning in *Factortame (No 2)*.

On the traditional view of sovereignty articulated by Wade the answer, logically, would be that it was for the existing Parliament, coupled with the national courts, to determine the ambit of Community competence *vis-à-vis* the United Kingdom. On this theory the latest Act of the UK Parliament would trump any other norm. If therefore Parliament passed an Act of Parliament which expressly made it clear that it did not accept Community competence within a certain area, then on this view the national courts would be duty bound to follow this expression of Parliamentary will. It would presumably also follow on this view that even if there were no such Act of Parliament the national courts should at the least be willing to listen to an argument that the Community did not possess competence on a particular issue. The argument for this approach on traditional theory would be as follows. An individual would argue before the national court that a national norm should be applied in preference to a Community measure, contending that the former should take precedence because the Community had no competence to take the relevant action. On this theory, the fundamental obligation of the courts is to apply the latest expression of Parliamentary will. Given that this is so, the latest expression of this will may be controlling, even if earlier in time than the Community norm, if it can be maintained that the Community does not have competence over the issue.

We have however already had occasion to note that the House of Lords' reasoning in *Factortame (No 2)* does not sit easily with the traditional view of sovereignty. What then would be the doctrinal answer to the *Kompetenz-Kompetenz* issue if we extrapolate from the reasoning actually used in that case? Lord Bridge's acceptance of Community supremacy was, as we have seen, founded on a mixture of contractarian, *a priori* and functional grounds. The implications of these arguments for the *Kompetenz-Kompetenz* issue are not particularly easy to disaggregate. One line of reasoning would be as follows.

The contractarian foundation for Community law supremacy is premised on the idea that it was clear when we joined that the EC claimed supremacy over national law, and therefore that we must be taken to have joined on these terms. Let it be accepted for the sake of argument that this also connoted an acceptance that the Community institutions would define the limits of

Community competence. Notwithstanding this, it could still be maintained that there must be some limits, which are consonant with the contractarian argument, to the ability of the Community institutions to define the scope of Community competences. Thus while the national court might readily accept the contractarian logic of Community supremacy and control over the ambit of Community competence within areas which are four-square within the EC's sphere, such as trade barriers, tariffs and the like, one might plausibly contend that there are also contractarian limits to this form of argument. If there were not then it would be incumbent on the national courts to accept any vision of Community competence propounded by, for example, the ECJ, however contentious that might be, and however novel an inroad it might be into what were previously accepted spheres of national competence.

A similar species of argument might be made concerning the *a priori* and functional aspects of the reasoning in *Factortame (No 2)*. These arguments express the idea that the very nature of the Community demands that EC law is supreme over national law, since otherwise the enterprise could never have worked. Let it be accepted once again that this carries with it an acceptance of the idea that the Community can define the scope of its competence within the core areas which make up the EC. It is, however, by no means so obvious that such arguments provide a "conceptual *carte-blanche*" to legitimate exclusive Community control over the definition of its competence in any and every sphere in which the Community may wish to act. Indeed it could be argued that the further that we move away from the core elements which make up the Community, even after the Treaty on European Union, the less strong do the *a priori* and functional arguments become.

Let us move on to the third of our questions. How are the national courts in the United Kingdom likely to react to the *Kompetenz-Kompetenz* issue if and when it comes before them? That it will do so at some stage is highly likely. The problem could surface in any one of a number of differing contexts: it could arise via a dispute as to the meaning of subsidiarity; it could become a live issue in the context of EC fundamental rights' doctrine being applied to national measures; or it could in the past take the form of a claim that provisions of the Social Chapter were being applied to the United Kingdom, indirectly if not directly. The response of the UK courts to any such challenge concerning the *vires* of EC action can only be guessed at here, and much will probably depend upon the precise form which any such dispute assumes.

The approach of the UK courts will probably be affected by the type of case in which the issue is presented to them: an assertion by the Community institutions that they will determine the limits of Community competence within an area which is four square within the EC's sphere, and where the only live question is as to the reach of that field, is likely to be treated differently to the Community's assertion of its capacity to decide conclusively on the limits of its competence within a controversial area of social policy.

In the former type of case it is doubtful whether UK courts would, in their present mood, wish to engage in any direct constitutional challenge to the authority of the ECJ to determine the limits of the Community's competence.

Even in the latter type of case one would expect the national courts to be cautious. There are a number of reasons for this. The breadth of areas over which the Community now has some form of power after the Treaty on European Union renders the prospect of an egregious lack of Community competence less likely than it was under the original EC Treaty. Moreover, the national courts have become more accustomed to the mode of reasoning employed by the ECJ, whereby the latter will not infrequently found its judgment on reasoning from first principle, coupled with reliance on broad statements to be derived from foundational provisions of the EC Treaty, such as article 5. Given that this is so, those who seek to argue that the Community is not competent to act, and that the national courts should define the ambit of the relevant provisions, will find that they have an uphill task. At the least one could expect a UK court to seek a preliminary ruling from the ECJ on the matter before deciding whether to proffer and prefer its own interpretation. Having said this one cannot rule out the possibility that a case may arise of this more controversial type in which the national court really does feel that the definition of Community competence adopted by the Community institutions is not warranted by the textual material or by the background theory of the EC Treaty. In such a case one can conceive of the national court either refusing to accept the interpretation of Community competence proffered by the ECJ, or, more mildly, engaging in a discourse with the ECJ in which it "encourages" it to think about the matter once again.

DOCTRINE, JURISPRUDENCE AND BEYOND

The explanation for change within any particular legal order is seldom one-dimensional. This is more particularly so when one is considering the rationale for judicial reaction to a new legal order which is being engrafted onto a domestic legal system. It should moreover be pointed out that the motivation for national judicial reaction to one aspect of EC law may well be different from that which operates in relation to a different doctrinal issue. The reasons for the judicial response to the new Community order are likely therefore to be eclectic, and the object of the discussion within this section is to consider what some of these reasons might be.

Judicial identity, national identity and biting the constitutional bullet

There is little doubt that the courts' attitude towards the Community is but one part of that particular country's more general approach towards the EC. It would clearly be wrong to suggest that changes or shifts in judicial stance towards Europe will always march hand in hand with that of the country in general. Identifying what the country as a whole feels about Europe at any one point in time is in any event often a complex task. Even if this national sense can be identified there may be a plethora of reasons why changes in judicial stance might not always match those of the country at large. Having said this it would also be mistaken to reject any connection between the two. The nature of this connection can be exemplified by considering the evolution of the courts' approach towards supremacy and the EC.

Let us consider the acceptance of EC supremacy in the *Factortame* litigation. There are a number of striking aspects in this saga of cases. One of the most interesting elements of the reasoning and result in *Factortame (No 2)* is in many ways the ease with which the House of Lords accepted EC supremacy. What serves to explain this? After all the traditional doctrine of sovereignty was always felt to be one of the major stumbling blocks to a thoroughgoing acceptance of Community law within the United Kingdom. Why did this constitutional bastion prove to be so easily surmounted? A number of reasons can be suggested, each of which may well provide part of the explanation.

One argument might assume the following form. It might be contended that the courts could reach the solution in *Factortame* precisely because this did not involve any breach of traditional Diceyan orthodoxy. On this view it would still be open to Parliament expressly to derogate from EC law, the assumption being that the national courts would then follow this latest manifestation of Parliamentary will. This will not do. The traditional theory of sovereignty as expounded in its modern form by Wade includes the idea of implied repeal which operates in the event of a clash between inconsistent norms. It is clear that this no longer operates in the context of a clash between national law and EC law. Moreover, as we have seen, it is by no means self-evident that the national courts would in fact follow an express derogation from EC law by Parliament on a specific issue, while the legislature still purports to keep the United Kingdom within the Community. The argument set out above is also defective because it wholly ignores the fact that, as has been shown, the reasoning actually used by the House of Lords does not sit easily with that to be found in what was the traditional orthodoxy.

A more promising line of argument would be to take seriously the reasoning which the court itself actually utilised in *Factortame (No 2)*. Lord Bridge's dictum in that case was a conscious and honest attempt to clarify an issue which had to be faced at some juncture. The motivation for biting the constitutional bullet at this stage is itself interesting, as is the structure of Lord Bridge's argument which can be broken down into two parts.

In the first part he begins by addressing an issue which was felt to be of concern by the judiciary: certain sections of the media had been contending that the precious mantle of sovereignty was being sacrificed *by the judiciary*. It is this which Lord Bridge sought to deny on behalf of the courts as a whole:

any diminution in sovereignty was not the result of judicial decisions as such, but rather the consequence of Parliament's decision to take us into Europe.

The second part of the dictum is then devoted to explaining *why* this was so. Here too the explanation is cogent. The contractarian and *a priori* arguments have been set out above, and there is no need to repeat them here. These arguments provide a convincing conceptual foundation from which to accept the supremacy of the EC legal order.

If we stand back from the details of this reasoning we can perhaps begin to appreciate some of the connections between the changes in legal doctrine and more general developments in relation to the United Kingdom's attitude towards the Community.

There is little doubt that there is still a debate within the United Kingdom as to the nature of the "Community" which should evolve over the next five or ten years. One only has to consider the disagreements over the Maastricht Treaty in order to appreciate the divisions which continue to exist on this issue. That such disagreements continue to exist should not, however, serve to mask the fact that the United Kingdom has been in the Community for over twenty years; that within this period Community law has become an increasingly accepted part of national law; and that the majority of the population accept, in general terms, the United Kingdom's membership of the Community as the political norm. Furthermore, the picture of the United Kingdom as a country holding up the pace of integration is in some ways a distorted one. UK political representations about the future nature of the Community are but part of a continuing dialogue which is to be expected in the evolution of an institution which has such a marked impact on our lives. Moreover, it should not be forgotten that the United Kingdom normally heads the league table of countries for the putting into effect of directives.

Viewed against this backdrop the legal reasoning and result in *Factortame* can be seen as an attempt by the judiciary to bring constitutional doctrine up to date with political reality. Whatever the future shape of the Community should prove to be, the present reality is that we are a member of it, that the decision to adhere to the Community was a political decision made in 1972, and that EC norms are an accepted part of UK law in the different substantive spheres in which the Community has competence. The reasoning in *Factortame (No 2)* is a recognition of this *status quo*. It represents a refusal to continue to shelter behind a traditional constitutional doctrine which, taken literally, coheres so badly both with the political fact of membership and the nature of the Community legal order. When viewed from this perspective the House of Lords' decision can be seen as a form of "constitutional catch-up": a modification of constitutional doctrine in order that it might better reflect the existing political reality of our membership of the EC. This is readily apparent from the two parts of the courts' reasoning outlined above. The first part passes the "buck" back to the political arm of government whose decision it was to take us into the Community. The second then identifies the conceptual reasons why this decision entailed the supremacy of the Community legal order. Whatever the future attitudes of our courts might be when presented with difficult issues of *Kompetenz-Kompetenz*, *Factortame (No 2)* gives the judiciary a more rational constitutional platform from which to conduct any such future dialogue with the Community institutions.

The balance of power between different branches of government: the not-so-hidden agenda

While the reasoning actually used in *Factortame (No 2)* does, therefore, furnish a convincing explanation, in and of itself, for the timing and acceptance of Community supremacy there is a broader argument which might serve to explain the way in which sovereignty was dealt with in that case. It is to this that we should now turn.

This broader argument would be as follows. Developments in constitutional doctrine do not take place in neat, water-tight categories. Changes which occur in one area will often be affected by more general judicial trends which are apparent in other parts of the constitutional system. It will be suggested that the willingness to alter constitutional orthodoxy in the context of sovereignty and the United Kingdom's membership of the EC was itself affected by a changing attitude on the part of the courts more generally towards the relationship between judiciary and legislature.

This change is most evident in relation to rights and judicial review. Traditional constitutional theory in the United Kingdom has been that we do not possess rights as such, but only residual liberties which are left to us after the sum of all limits to free speech and the like which have been imposed by the legislature have been taken into account. On this view Parliament can do anything which it wishes, and the courts will faithfully enforce the Parliamentary will. It is indeed this facet of sovereignty which has always been regarded as one of the main conceptual stumbling blocks to the entrenchment of a Bill of Rights in the United Kingdom. Traditional theory maintains that any such Bill of Rights would be susceptible to express or implied repeal by a later Act of Parliament, and that this would be so irrespective of whether the Bill of Rights was entrenched, requiring special majorities before it could be altered. Now this proposition has never actually been tested in the UK courts, because we have never been faced with such a situation. The cases which are cited in support of this proposition by those who propound the traditional view were not concerned with the scenario of an entrenched Bill of Rights, and are a weak foundation for the theory which is built upon them.[36] Whether the courts would in fact lay idle, mesmerised by traditional conceptions of sovereignty, should Parliament attempt any such transgression of a putative Bill of Rights is doubtful in the extreme.

[36] See Craig, n. 1 above.

What is, however, apparent is that the courts have of late begun to exert far more judicial control over exercises of discretion which interfere with fundamental rights. It is now clear that any such intrusion will be subject to more intensive scrutiny when the interest which is being affected is what would normally be termed a fundamental right. Now to be sure this has stopped short of full blooded constitutional review of primary legislation, in the sense that the courts have not arrogated to themselves the power to strike down primary legislation which contravenes well established rights-based limitations on governmental action. They have, however, signalled that they will construe such legislation narrowly where fundamental rights are at stake. These judicial developments have been accompanied by extra-judicial statements by a growing number of judges which either openly advocate the adoption of a Bill of Rights, and/or attest to the power of the judiciary to protect basic rights.

These developments can be briefly charted here. The House of Lords in *Brind* placed limits on the extent to which the European Convention could be used in the absence of incorporation. The decision, which concerned the legality of limits imposed on broadcasting by certain organisations, does nonetheless contain interesting dicta on the relevance of rights within the common law itself. Lord Bridge, having noted the absence of any code of rights in domestic law, then had this to say:[37]

"But . . . this surely does not mean that in deciding whether the Secretary of State, in the exercise of his discretion, could reasonably impose the restriction he has imposed on the broadcasting organisations, we are not perfectly entitled to start from the premise that any restriction of the right to freedom of expression requires to be justified and nothing less than an important competing public interest will be sufficient to justify it".

Lord Bridge went on to say that while the primary judgement as to whether the public interest warranted the restriction which had been imposed rested with the minister, the court could exercise a secondary judgement by asking whether a reasonable Minister could reasonably make that judgement on the material before him.[38] Lord Templeman reasoned in a similar manner. He held that freedom of expression is a principle of every written and unwritten democratic constitution; that the court must inquire whether a reasonable minister could reasonably have concluded that the interference with this freedom was justifiable; and that in "in terms of the Convention" any such interference must be both necessary and proportionate.[39]

The decision in *Brind* is by no means the only authority to advert to the relevance of rights for the purposes of public law adjudication. Other cases which are concerned with freedom of speech demonstrate a similar approach. In the *Spycatcher* case[40] Lord Goff, in delineating the ambit of the duty of

[37] R v. *Secretary of State for the Home Department, ex parte Brind* [1991] 1 AC 696, 748–9.
[38] *Ibid.* at 749.
[39] *Ibid.* at 750–1.
[40] A-G v. *Guardian Newspapers (No 2)* [1990] 1 AC 109, 283–4.

confidentiality, and the exceptions thereto, stated that he saw no inconsistency between the position under the Convention, and that at common law. This was further emphasised in *Derbyshire County Council* v. *Times Newspapers Ltd.*[41] Their Lordships held that, as a matter of principle, a local authority should not be able to maintain an action in its own name for defamation, since this would place an unwarranted and undesirable limitation upon freedom of speech. Lord Keith, giving judgment for the House, reached this conclusion on the basis of the common law itself and echoed Lord Goff's satisfaction that there was no difference in principle between the common law and the Convention.[42] The importance of rights was also underlined in *Leech*.[43] In that case the court when construing the validity of a rule which allowed a prison governor to read letters from prisoners and stop those which were inordinately long or objectionable, adopted the principle of interpretation that the more fundamental the right which had been interfered with, the more difficult was it to imply any rule-making power in the primary legislation.

Lord Browne-Wilkinson, writing extra-judicially, has endorsed such developments and would go further.[44] He accepts that there are limits as to how far the Convention can be relied upon in our courts. But he raises the question as to whether there is not a more general presumption against interference with human rights which is grounded in the common law.[45] This presumption should apply when there is ambiguity in the domestic provisions. It should, he argues, also be utilised where there is no ambiguity as such, but just general statutory language:[46]

> "There is respectable authority for the proposition that such general words, even though unambiguous, are not to be construed as to authorise interference with individual freedom unless Parliament has made its intention so to do clear by express provision or necessary implication".[47]

The potential inherent within the common law itself is the subject of a similar piece by Sir John Laws.[48] He draws a distinction between reliance upon the European Convention as a legal instrument *stricto sensu*, and reliance upon the contents of the Convention as a series of propositions which are either already inherent in our law, or can be integrated into it by the judiciary through the normal process of common law adjudication. He maintains that

---

[41] [1993] 1 All ER 1011.

[42] *Ibid.* at 1021.

[43] *R* v. *Secretary of State for the Home Department, ex parte Leech* [1993] 4 All ER 539.

[44] "The Infiltration of a Bill of Rights" [1992] *P.L.* 397.

[45] *Ibid.* at 404.

[46] *Ibid.* at 406.

[47] The authorities cited by Lord Browne-Wilkinson include *R. and W. Paul* v. *The Wheat Commission* [1937] AC 139; *Morris* v. *Beardmore* [1981] AC 446, 463; *Raymond* v. *Honey* [1983] 1 AC 1; *Marcel* v. *Commissioner of Police of the Metropolis* [1992] 2 WLR 50, approving [1991] 2 WLR 1118, 1124.

[48] "Is the High Court the Guardian of Fundamental Constitutional Rights?" [1993] *P.L.* 59.

it is not for the courts themselves to incorporate the Convention, since that would be to trespass upon the legislature's sphere, but the courts could legitimately pursue the latter approach. They could, argues Sir John Laws, consider the Convention jurisprudence as one source for charting the development of the common law, in the same way that the courts not infrequently make reference to decisions from foreign jurisdictions. One consequence of this would be a variable standard of review:[49]

> "the greater the intrusion proposed by a body possessing public power over the citizen in an area where his fundamental rights are at stake, the greater must be the justification which the public authority must demonstrate . . . It means that the principles [of review] are neither unitary nor static; it means that the standard by which the court reviews administrative action is a variable one. It means, for example, that while the Secretary of State will largely be left to his own devices in promulgating national economic policy . . . the court will scrutinise the merits of his decisions much more closely when they concern refugees or free speech".

One can now begin to perceive the connection between the courts' attitude towards sovereignty and the EC, and their approach to judicial review of legislation or exercises of discretion which impinge on fundamental rights. The willingness of the courts to compromise or modify traditional orthodoxy concerning supremacy and the EC must be seen against the backdrop of their greater readiness to subject legislation which impinges on rights to intensive scrutiny. It is true, as stated above, that the courts have not yet arrogated to themselves a power to invalidate primary legislation which encroaches upon fundamental rights. In this sense their jurisprudence on this issue can be formally squared with traditional orthodoxy; it can be perceived as merely the normal process of statutory interpretation which has always been demanded of the courts. Yet it is readily apparent that this reconciliation of current judicial behaviour with traditional views of the courts faithfully applying the latest expression of Parliamentary sovereign will is strained to say the least. In reality the decisions sketched above represent a shift in judicial attitude. The courts have made it increasingly clear that the sovereign expression of Parliamentary will is to be read with the sanctity of fundamental rights firmly in mind.[50] The willingness to surrender constitutional orthodoxy concerning sovereignty in the context of the United Kingdom's membership of the EC should, therefore, be seen as but part of a broader development in which the courts are now ready to place other types of constraint on the exercise of sovereign Parliamentary power.

One can of course speculate as to why this broader development has begun to occur in the last few years. This is itself an interesting question, to which there are a number of possible answers.

---

[49] "Is the High Court the Guardian of Fundamental Constitutional Rights?" [1993] *P.L.* 59 at 69.

[50] This development is reinforced by the decision to incorporate the rights contained in the ECHR.

In part it may well have been an indirect result of having had the same party in power in the United Kingdom since the late 1970s. The Conservative Government had introduced the most wide-ranging changes in the socio-economic-political arena since the post-war Labour Government. The UK system of government gives the governing party which has a workable majority a very significant degree of power. Images of elective dictatorship have been used to characterise this situation. The idea that the courts should act as some form of counterweight to relatively untrammelled executive power may well therefore have played some part in the increased judicial activism which has occurred.

In part this shift in judicial attitude towards sovereignty as it relates to both the EC and fundamental rights may itself be an indirect result of our membership of the Community. One consequence of such membership has been the growing interrelationship between domestic systems of public law. The existence of rights-based review in a number of other countries within the EC, albeit in differing forms, might well have influenced the UK courts to extend their own power in this respect.

A third type of factor in this sea change concerns personalities. It is not fortuitous that these developments have taken place at a time when the higher judiciary is filled with many who are in sympathy with this species of increased judicial oversight. Lords Woolf, Browne-Wilkinson, Mustill and Slynn have all made notable judicial or extra-judicial contributions to the changes noted above. In the Court of Appeal Simon Brown LJ and Glidewell LJ have had a significant impact. Amongst those lower in the judicial hierarchy Schiemann J, Sedley J and Laws J deserve special mention for their contributions. What is of interest in this respect is that a number of those who have been mentioned were, while at the Bar, the Treasury Junior. In this capacity they represented the Government in public law actions: Lord Bridge, Lord Woolf, Simon Brown LJ and Laws J were all Treasury Junior before being elevated to the bench. This has clearly not prevented them from being active participants in the developments charted above.

Judicial empowerment, national courts and new tasks

It is customary to think that acceptance of Community law supremacy represents a relative decline in national competence. And so it does if the focus remains on the political arm of national government, or at least the national legislature. However, a moment's thought will reveal that the acceptance of EC supremacy can also serve to empower a national judiciary, particularly in a country such as the United Kingdom where the courts do not normally have the formal power to attack primary legislation. The UK jurisprudence also provides a good example of how readily the national courts can embrace their new-found authority.

The *EOC* case[51] demonstrates the ease with which the highest national courts have slipped into their new role. The case concerned the compatibility of UK legislation on unfair dismissal and redundancy pay with EC law. Under the relevant UK law[52] entitlement to these protections and benefits operated differentially depending upon whether the person was in full-time or part-time employment. Full-time workers were eligible after two years; part-time workers only after five. The great majority of part-time workers were women and the Equal Opportunities Commission took the view that the legislation discriminated against women, contrary to article 119 of the ECTreaty and to certain Community directives. The EOC sought a declaration that the UK legislation was in breach of EC law. The case raised a number of issues which do not directly concern us here, including the extent to which the EOC had standing to raise the issue at all. The House of Lords found for the applicant. It held that the national legislation was indeed in breach of article 119 and the directives.

The reasoning of the House of Lords is instructive. Not only did it grant the declaration that the primary legislation was in breach of Community law. It also refused to take the opportunity to duck the issue afforded by the way in which the question was framed by the applicants. The EOC had sought to argue that the decision which should be subject to judicial review was not the primary legislation itself, but a letter from the Minister in which he had denied that the UK statute was in violation of Community norms. This way of framing the argument was doubtless based on the applicant's fear that the national courts might be wary of undertaking the novel task of actually declaring the primary legislation to be incompatible with EC law. The House of Lords declined to avoid the matter in this manner. As Lord Keith stated:[53]

> "The real object of the EOC's attack is these provisions themselves. The question is whether judicial review is available for the purpose of securing a declaration that certain United Kingdom primary legislation is incompatible with Community law".

Having affirmed that judicial review could be used in this manner, the House of Lords went on to make it crystal clear that this power to review primary legislation resided in national *courts*. It was not only the House of Lords itself which was to have this species of authority. The Divisional Court, which is two rungs lower in the UK judicial hierarchy, and is the court in which many judicial review actions begin, could itself exercise this power.[54] Now it might well be the case that such a court would feel loath to exercise this power unless the case was especially clear, preferring instead to leave such heady matters to the Court of Appeal or the House of Lords. Time will tell.

---

[51] *R v. Secretary of State for Employment, ex parte Equal Opportunities Commission* [1994] 1 All ER 910.

[52] Employment Protection (Consolidation) Act 1978.

[53] Above n. 51 at 919.

[54] *Ibid.* at 920.

The fact remains that such lower courts have the authority in formal terms to exercise this type of control.

Their Lordships did not therefore shrink from recognising and acting upon the reality of the dispute which was presented to them. The effect of the case is to affirm that the national courts can themselves issue a declaration that primary legislation is in breach of our Community Treaty obligations. The sanctity of such legislation from challenge *by the national courts* themselves was formally denied.

The readiness with which the UK national courts have accepted the responsibilities granted to them may well be telling in a more general sense. We have already seen in the previous section the connection between the modifications of constitutional supremacy doctrine *vis-à-vis* the EC and the growing assertiveness of the national courts in relation to rights-based matters. The same connection can perhaps be perceived in this context. If national courts are willing to assume the power to declare primary legislation incompatible with Community law, then, at the very least, it renders the prospect that they might assume a similar power in relation to legislation which infringes rights-based constitutional protections less novel or revolutionary.

The impact of legal culture: the common law method and the reception of Community law

The discussion thus far within this section has said little about the way in which the UK courts have responded to the concepts of direct and indirect effect. The formal response of the UK courts to these doctrines has been described above. It was argued that UK courts have had little or no difficulty in accepting rulings by the ECJ that a particular provision of the EC Treaty, or a regulation or a directive, should have direct effect, but that they have experienced rather more difficulty in deciding how far they can or should go in pursuit of the interpretative obligation required by *Von Colson/Marleasing* and indirect effect.

The impact of the legal culture which prevails in the United Kingdom may go some way to explaining this reaction to Community law. More particularly the nature of the common law method of legal reasoning may help us to understand why the national courts have reacted in this manner.

In many respects the common law mode of adjudication is *pragmatic* and *non-doctrinaire*. Even before the formal acceptance of EC supremacy in *Factortame (No 2)* the UK courts clearly acknowledged that they were part of a Community legal order, *and* that the ECJ was the proper court to pass judgment on issues concerning the interpretation of the EC Treaty. This of course included the seminal concept of direct effect. The UK Government might well argue before the ECJ that a certain provision should not have direct effect, but if the ECJ then came to the contrary view this would be applied by the

UK courts with equanimity. It is for this reason, amongst others, that any rebellion will be unlikely to emerge from the UK judiciary should the ECJ decide to change its mind and to accord horizontal direct effect to directives.

The nature of the common law method, however, also helps to provide part of the explanation for the difficulties which some courts have had with the idea of indirect effect and the scope of the interpretative duty which this entails. If courts in the United Kingdom are told that certain norms of the EC trump national law in the event of a clash, then the common law approach will be to analyse the respective norms, determine whether they do in fact conflict, and if so give prominence to the Community provision. Common law courts find the application of indirect effect more problematic. They realise that they are to read national law if at all possible to be in conformity with the directive. They realise also that in doing so they should apply rather different principles of construction and interpretation than if they had been construing a purely domestic measure. Yet it is clear that they perceive a real distinction between even this species of interpretation and what would amount to judicial re-writing of the relevant domestic norm, and they are not always sure how far they can go without crossing this line. Now it may well be the case that courts in other national jurisdictions have experienced similar difficulties with regard to indirect effect. The problem in the United Kingdom is nonetheless particularly apparent because common law courts are accustomed to writing lengthy judgments in which the relevant material will be dissected in order to decide whether two norms can be made to fit together even though there are differences between them; and because they take seriously the limit of their remit, which is to interpret and not to re-write.

There is another facet of the legal culture which prevails in the United Kingdom which is also worthy of mention in relation to the reception of Community law generally within this country. One of the abiding features of the common law method which is often stressed in judicial decisions is the *adaptability* of the common law to meet the demands of new situations. The ability of the courts to mould common law doctrine in order to cope with such situations is a constant theme throughout our legal history. This is particularly so if one takes account of concepts developed by equity as well as by the common law *stricto sensu*. The response of the national courts to supremacy, to direct and indirect effect, and to the preliminary ruling procedure can then be seen as exemplifying this feature of our mode of legal reasoning. In each of these contexts we can see the UK courts demonstrating the ability of the common law to adapt to meet the demands of Community law membership.

This is evident in substantive terms in the way in which traditional doctrines of sovereignty have been modified to accommodate Community law membership. It is apparent in procedural terms in the willingness of the national courts to embrace principles of interpretation and construction different from those which would be used within domestic litigation. It can also be seen in the greater readiness to refer under article 177 which is apparent in the post-*Bulmer* jurisprudence. On this more modern approach to article 177 we can see the UK courts accepting that they are part of a Community judicial hierarchy, in which it is natural that certain matters should be decided by the ECJ. No longer is the ECJ perceived as some distant "international court" to which recourse should be had only in exceptional circumstances.

These particular instances of adaptation by the common law may exhibit moreover a desire by the national courts in the United Kingdom not to be perceived as parochial. The judiciary does not wish to be seen to be attached to substantive or procedural norms which are ill-suited to the international arena in which the EC operates.

Judicial discourse: the vertical dimension

It is clear that the reception of Community law involves a dialogue between national courts and the ECJ. It is clear also that there are both substantive and procedural dimensions to this vertical discourse.

In substantive terms the dialogue between the ECJ and national courts may serve to indicate how far, for example, the latter are willing to accept the extension of Community doctrines to new areas. The reaction of some national courts to the possibility of giving horizontal direct effect to directives is one obvious instance of this in operation.

In procedural terms the discourse between the two judicial systems may become apparent in the extent to which the national courts are willing to use the reference procedure under article 177. It is worth dwelling a little on this issue for the very reason that our courts have evinced a change of attitude in this respect. The more liberal approach of UK courts when exercising their discretion to make a preliminary ruling has been considered above. The reasons for this shift in attitude are interesting.

The initial restrictive approach represented by the Denning guidelines in *Bulmer* cannot be divorced from the nature of Lord Denning MR himself. He was always somewhat ambivalent about the EC. It was Lord Denning who decided *Felixstowe Dock*, asserting the traditional view of sovereignty; it was Lord Denning who also gave a powerful opinion in *Macarthys* v. *Smith*,[55] to the effect that a clash between Community law and national law should be resolved in favour of the former whenever possible.

The Denning who promulgated the guidelines in *Bulmer* was cognisant of the power of the EC, but also mindful of what he perceived to be the proper division of authority between national courts and the ECJ under article 177:

---

[55] [1979] ICR 785, although Lord Denning MR did add the caveat that if Parliament deliberately passed an Act with the intention of repudiating the Treaty or any provision thereof, and so stated in express terms, then it would be the duty of the courts to follow such a statute, at 789.

it was for national courts to decide whether to refer, and the conditions on which to do so; it was for the ECJ to provide the interpretation of EC law on the point placed before it. The restrictive nature of the conditions listed in *Bulmer* were themselves indicative of three related themes: references were to be relatively exceptional, as opposed to being a normal adjunct of litigation within a new legal order; they were only to be made when the point really was felt to be necessary for resolution of the case; and even then other factors such as cost or delay might lead the court to decline to make a reference.

The more liberal approach to references which is apparent in current case law can be explained in a number of ways. One factor is quite simply that the UK courts have become more familiar with the EC legal system. A reference to the ECJ is no longer regarded as something exceptional, but as something quite normal. The national courts have come to think of themselves more in terms of being part of a Community judicial hierarchy, in which certain matters are naturally dealt with by the ECJ. The recognition of the expertise of the ECJ at dealing with Community legal problems, which is evident in cases from *Samex* onwards, is part and parcel of the same acceptance and familiarity with the Community legal order.

A second factor in the greater readiness to make a reference than hitherto may be related to the workload of the national courts. They have a heavy case load, and therefore the prospect of being able to send a case off to the ECJ when there appears to be a plausible point of Community law which may be reasonably necessary for resolving the case can be quite attractive. To be sure the case will of course return to the national court, but in all probability the ECJ will have answered a point which will be central to the resolution of the entire case.

A third factor which may be of importance in this respect is that many of the points of Community law which are raised in national courts involve some technical aspect of the regime on free movement of goods, the Common Agricultural Policy or the like. National judges will know little about these issues, nor will they regard them as matters which they must try and decide at all costs. Quite the contrary. They are often only too happy for such issues to be decided by the ECJ or the CFI.

A final reason why the national courts may be more willing to refer than hitherto is that the very fact of referral may enable the national court to have some input into the substantive doctrine which is being developed by the ECJ. For a national legal system to be too reticent about referring matters to the ECJ has an obvious price: the relevant system foregoes any influence which it might otherwise have on the way in which that area of policy evolves in the ECJ. To be sure it is by no means certain that the ECJ will always adopt the approach which the national court may present to it through its formulation of the questions. It is however clear that if a national judiciary consciously or unconsciously declines to allow cases to proceed under article 177, it is to that extent diminishing any influence which it might otherwise have over the evolution of Community doctrine.[56]

Judicial discourse: the horizontal dimension

The existence of the EC has undoubtedly led to an increase in horizontal judicial discourse as between the differing national courts of the Member States. This occurs in a number of ways.

One manifestation of this may be felt not to be a dialogue as such at all, but rather the cross-fertilization of legal doctrine from one system to another. Whether one chooses to regard this as but one sub-part of horizontal discourse or as something of a different nature is a contestable issue. Howsoever one chooses to characterise the matter it is clear that it has become of increasing importance in recent years. It can be seen at work in the way in which principles of administrative legality are evolving within the United Kingdom. The development of the principle of proportionality in this country has been influenced partly by its existence within Community law, and partly by the fact that it is recognised, in varying forms, within the national legal systems of a number of Member States. Similarly, when deciding on the meaning to be ascribed to a concept such as legitimate expectations, even in cases which are not themselves concerned with Community law, national courts will be more receptive than hitherto to arguments derived from both EC law and the legal systems of countries which are within the EC.

A second, and more indirect, manifestation of horizontal judicial discourse is the existence now of regular meetings between the House of Lords and the Conseil d'Etat in order to discuss issues of a broadly public law nature. Matters of Community law will feature within such discussion sessions.

Individual litigants, national courts and the ECJ

There is little doubt that particular litigants, whether in the form of individuals as such, or in the form of pressure groups, have played a significant part in the development of substantive Community law. The prospect of being afforded greater rights under Community law than would otherwise have been available under national legal rules has been a principal reason motivating such litigants. Such actions have normally been brought through the medium of article 177 and thus the national courts have been involved both at the inception of, and at the conclusion of, the case. One of the main substantive areas in which UK nationals have sought to employ Community law

---

[56] Having said all this it must be acknowledged that references from UK courts have been lower in number than from other Member States. Precisely why this has been so is itself an interesting matter for further investigation.

in this manner concerns employment law, gender equality and the like. Many seminal Community decisions on these matters have emerged from UK courts; *Marshall* and *Barber* are two such cases which spring readily to mind. There have, in addition, been many cases in the UK courts concerning social policy in which the judiciary has fashioned its constitutional and doctrinal response to the EC; *Duke*, *Litster*, *Macarthys*, and *EOC* all come within this category.[57]

There is little, if any, doubt that the national courts are aware of the strategic use which has been made of EC law in this and other areas. It is more difficult to gauge what the national judiciary "feels" about it. The general impression conveyed by the case law is that the national courts are content for litigants to be able to use EC law in this manner. Community law is regarded as part of national law and is, in this sense, at the disposal of any party arguing a case in the same manner as would be any other potentially applicable legal norm. Thus in the *EOC* case considered above, the House of Lords had no hesitation in allowing the EOC to take advantage of EC law to advance its case. Their Lordships were content to declare the relevant national law contrary to Community law without the necessity of a referral. Moreover, as we have already seen, the House of Lords also made it clear that lower courts could exercise this declaratory power.

It would be wrong to conclude that judges as a whole in the UK have any agenda in relation to social policy which they are attempting to advance in this manner. The UK judiciary would, I think, regard the approach outlined above as one which simply follows through the logic of adherence to the Community.

Having said this one should not forget the point which has been made above,[58] concerning the benefits which accrue to the national judiciary as a result of the type of review power which they now exercise in the Community context. Other things being equal the existence of this type of declaratory power can only render it easier for the UK judiciary to exercise an analogous species of review in relation to domestic norms which infringe what are felt to be rights-based limits on the scope of governmental authority.

Judicial composition and the role of individual judges

We have already had occasion to comment on the role which individual judges have played in the evolution of public law within the United Kingdom.[59] At a more general level the Community has begun to have some influence on the

---

[57] *Duke* v. *GEC Reliance* [1988] 2 WLR 359; *Litster* v. *Forth Dry Dock* [1989] 2 WLR 634; *Macarthys* v. *Smith* [1979] ICR 785; *R* v. *Secretary of State for Employment, ex parte Equal Opportunities Commission* [1994] 1 All ER 910.

[58] See pp. 216–17 above.

[59] See p. 216 above.

way in which our judges perceive the relationship between national law and Community law.

One manifestation of this is to be found in the fact that UK appointees to the ECJ may then return to senior positions in the national judicial structure. The most obvious example of this is Lord Slynn who is now a member of the House of Lords. The presence in the country's highest domestic court of a judge who has real expertise in Community law is likely to have a positive effect on the way in which EC doctrine is received within the United Kingdom.

Another way in which the attitudes of the national judiciary are being influenced by Community law is through visits to the ECJ. In the United Kingdom judges are appointed from the senior members of the Bar. Some may have had experience with Community law in practice. Others will not. The organisation of visits for national judges to the Court performs a valuable function. It enables the national judiciary to see the ECJ in action and to gain a more first-hand impression of the way in which it operates.

CONCLUSION

No attempt will be made to summarise the arguments which have been presented in this chapter. Suffice it to say for the present that on the doctrinal front Community law has had a marked impact on traditional constitutional orthodoxy. This impact may well, as we have seen, have important implications for areas of domestic law which are untouched by EC law. How the national courts within the United Kingdom will deal with the problems of *Kompetenz-Kompetenz* remains to be seen. The modes of argument which might be employed have been examined above.

It is readily apparent from the third section of the discussion that there are a number of factors which serve to explain the reception of EC law within the United Kingdom. These cannot of course be isolated. They interact with each other, often in a complex fashion. It is moreover clear that inquiries of this nature are of real importance if we are to gain a richer understanding of the relationship between the Community and the Member States.

PART II: COMPARATIVE ANALYSES

8

Explaining National Court Acceptance of European Court Jurisprudence: A Critical Evaluation of Theories of Legal Integration

KAREN ALTER

The European Court of Justice is one of the most influential legal and political institutions in Europe. While lawyers have followed the bold jurisprudence of the European Court for many years, the Courts substantial influence over national and European Community policy in the 1980s caught many political scientists (and politicians) by surprise. How had the European Court obtained the authority and the power to influence national policy? How had ECJ authority expanded to include issues thought to be part of the exclusive domain of national governments, including educational grants, advertising abortion services, mandating employee work councils, and government rules regulating equal pay for men and women?

These questions provoked an inter-disciplinary debate over the causes and consequences of legal integration, meaning the expansion and penetration of European Community (EC) law into the national legal and political systems (Burley and Mattli (1993); Garrett (1992); Garrett (1995); Garrett and Weingast(1993); Slaughter and Mattli (1995); Weiler (1991)). This debate has focused predominately on the role of the European Court of Justice in promoting legal integration, measuring advances in legal integration in terms of ECJ doctrine which extends the scope and reach of European law into the national legal orders. But this focus on the ECJ can be misleading. Legal integration is not simply the issuing of legal decisions which create new doctrine, but more importantly the acceptance of this jurisprudence within national legal systems and by national politicians.

While the European Court has played a decisive role in issuing expansive and important decisions on EC law, the linchpins of European legal system are really the national courts of the Member States. When the ECJ had to rely on the Commission or Member States to raise cases about EC Treaty infringements, the Court's docket was rather empty. With national courts sending questions about Treaty infringements to the ECJ, numerous potential Treaty violations have been brought to the ECJ. National courts also present the ECJ with opportunities to expand the reach and scope of EC law, opportunities which in all likelihood would not exist if the ECJ had to rely on Member States or the Commission to raise broad infringement charges. Indeed, most of the ECJ's major decisions expanding the reach and scope of EC law were made in cases referred to the ECJ by national courts. Because national courts now apply ECJ jurisprudence directly within the national realm, even over the objections of national politicians and administrators, ECJ decisions have gained an enforcement mechanism.[1] Disregarding an ECJ decision in a preliminary ruling case would mean that a government was disobeying its own courts, and sanctions available under national law can now be applied in the enforcement of EC law creating significant financial liabilities for non-compliance with EC law.

Because of national court support the largest political threat against the Court—the threat of non-compliance—is largely gone. In the face of clear violations of EC law, national governments anticipate that a negative Court ruling will be applied by national courts so that even the threat of bringing a legal case to the European Court can be enough to encourage compliance with EC law. Given the fundamental role played by national courts in the EC legal system, the real question raised by legal integration is not why the ECJ seizes the opportunities presented to it to enlarge its jurisdictional authority and political power, rather why national courts give the ECJ the opportunity to expand its powers, even goading the ECJ to expand the reach and scope of EC law, and why national courts enforce EC law against their own governments.

The research project on which this chapter is based, "The European Court and the National Courts—Doctrine and Jurisprudence: Legal Change in its Social Context" represented part of an emerging scholarship which shifts the focus to the role of national courts in the process of legal integration. The project examined legal integration of the ECJ's doctrine of EC law supremacy. The project sought to go beyond simply recounting and analysing national court jurisprudence and doctrine, actually trying to explain changes in national legal doctrine and national court behaviour. The contributions to the project offer important evidence which can be used to evaluate the prevailing explanations of legal integration and to move the debate forward.

This chapter classifies alternative explanations of legal integration offered in the EC legal literature, focusing specifically on how different theories explain national court participation in legal integration, and evaluates the explanations in terms of evidence presented in the national reports, supple-

---

[1] Until the recent Maastricht Treaty reform ECJ decisions lacked sanctioning powers and thus there was no mechanism to enforce or coerce compliance with European Court decisions. The new enforcement mechanism is yet to be used, but recently the Commission asked to fine Italy and Germany for non-compliance with ECJ decisions.

mented by evidence gathered in the author's own research. While arguments from the country reports are used to evaluate alternative explanations of legal integration, an important caution must be noted. Participants in the project were asked to go "beyond doctrine", by "speculating" on the causes of judicial behaviour. In general, the empirical evidence offered to support the causal inferences made by the authors was scant. A significant burden of proof is still needed to turn all of the speculations in the national reports into empirical evidence. While the evidence is not perfect, it represents some of the only empirical information we have on legal integration in the national realm. The national reports can help us refine hypotheses, think more systematically and critically about what type of explanations are being offered, and what type of evidence could more definitively support or refute different arguments. What emerges from this is a strong questioning of the dominant explanations of legal integration prevalent in the literature and often accepted at face value by both practitioners and scholars. The chapter pushes and challenges political scientists and legal scholars to offer precise arguments about both judges and politicians in order to increase the explanatory power of the different hypotheses, and raises agendas for future research.

By way of conclusion, examination is made of what the explanations of legal integration can tell us about the future of legal integration in Europe and about the prospects of generalising from the European experience to other international contexts. The conclusion asks two questions: (1) Can legal integration proceed in light of the heightened vigilance and lack of political support for ECJ activism? and (2) Can the experience of legal integration in Europe be generalised to other international contexts?

ALTERNATIVE EXPLANATIONS OF NATIONAL JUDICIAL BEHAVIOUR IN LEGAL INTEGRATION

The literature on legal integration has offered four types of explanation of legal integration: a legalist explanation, a neo-realist explanation, a neo-functionalist explanation, and an inter-court competition explanation.[2] This section summarises the explanations of legal integration offered in the literature, assessing them in light of the "evidence" offered in the country reports, supplemented by the author's own research. As the alternative explanations are reviewed, I focus on how each theory explains national judicial behaviour in the process of legal integration, that is when and why courts apply European law in the national context and when and why EC law expands into new areas of law and policy; and on what each explanation has to say about the role of politicians in influencing judicial behaviour and thus legal integration. The

---

[2] Included is the author's own explanation of legal integration developed in the dissertation *The Making of a Rule of Law: The European Court and the National Judiciaries* (M.I.T. Department of Political Science, June 1996).

methodology of the national reports does not allow for a systematic testing of alternative explanations, but the national reports do supply enough evidence to raise serious questions about the most prevalent arguments and to gain a greater understanding of the legal and extra-legal forces influencing the process of legal integration.

Legalism: legal logic and legal reasoning as the motor of legal integration

Legalist approaches explain judicial behaviour in legal integration based on legal logic and legal reasoning. EC law is seen as having an inherent legal logic which creates its own internal dynamic of expansion, compelling the ECJ to render legal decisions which promote integration, and compelling national courts to apply the ECJ's jurisprudence.[3] Legalist explanations see the European Court as driving the process of integration through key integrative legal decisions which, by virtue of their authoritative force, transform the context in which political and legal integration proceeds. According fundamental importance to the compelling nature of the ECJ's legal doctrine, legalist approaches see national judiciaries as having been convinced by legal arguments of the validity of the supremacy of EC law over national law, and of the importance of national courts applying the supreme EC law in their jurisprudence. Explaining national court refusal of ECJ jurisprudence as unintended mistakes, the legalist approach implies that misunderstandings or a lack of information on the part of national judges are really the only factors hindering the process of legal integration at the national level, the assumption being that once properly informed, national judges will dutifully refer cases and apply EC law as directed by the ECJ. While ECJ justices are the strongest proponents of this position, similar arguments have been voiced in the legal articles explaining ECJ decisions, national court decisions and national jurisprudence on EC law. Indeed most European lawyers are trained to examine EC law from the legalist perspective and legalism remains the dominant paradigm for analysing legal integration in Europe.

The legalist account of legal integration implies that the Court's jurisprudence shapes national court behaviour because of its compelling nature and clear legal logic. But clearly many national courts and national judges have not been convinced by the ECJ's doctrine on EC law supremacy, despite having understood the reasoning, despite having been told of the importance of ECJ jurisprudence by Justices in Luxembourg, and despite the numerous arti-

---

[3] More nuanced legalist explanations acknowledge some voluntarism and activism in the ECJ's legal decisions, and allow for extra-legal forces to influence the process of legal integration including political considerations (Mancini (1989); Tomuschat (1989); Weiler (1994)). But even these legalist accounts cling strongly to a claim regarding a legal logic of EC law, if based only on a functionalist legal theory of *effet utile*, which implies that the ECJ virtually had to make legal decisions promoting the process of integration, lest the EC legal system become completely ineffective and unworkable (Cappelletti, Seccombe, and Weiler (1986) 30; Lecourt (1991)).

cles and lectures by legal scholars writing in support of ECJ jurisprudence. The significant and sustained challenges to European Court doctrine within national judiciaries imply that it is not just ignorance which creates national judicial reticence in participating in the preliminary ruling process and accepting ECJ jurisprudence. Indeed it is interesting to note that the national reports give very little credit to ECJ reasoning as having convinced national judges of the supremacy of EC law. Both the Belgium and the Dutch reports imply that the finding of a national constitutional basis for EC law supremacy was the culmination of long national doctrinal trends which pre-dated the ECJ's supremacy jurisprudence, thus the national doctrinal change did not come about because of the ECJ's legal argumentations *per se*. In the German report, Kokott says expressly that "German courts never really supported the theory that Community law flows from an autonomous source" (see Ch 3, Report on Germany, p. 86) and the Italian report notes that neither *La doctrine* in Italy nor the Italian judiciary have been convinced by the Court's *Costa* and *Simmenthal* jurisprudence (see Ch 5, Report on Italy, pp. 148, 152). Indeed every national judiciary examined in the study rejected the legal basis for EC law supremacy offered by the ECJ, insisting instead on a national constitutional basis for EC law supremacy.[4]

Formal legalism which uses only legal logic and legal reasoning to explain national court behaviour can be easily rejected given the evidence on national judicial experiences of legal integration. But more nuanced legalism is harder to reject. Clearly most ECJ decisions are seen as authoritative, and there is a great deal of respect for the European Court. Thus at some level the ECJ's jurisprudence has been accepted as being if not entirely legally convincing at least legally plausible and authoritative. At the same time, there remains much about the national experiences of legal integration within Member States which even a more nuanced legalism can not explain, such as the significant time lags in the acceptance of EC law supremacy by national courts, the significant variation in the national experiences in accepting EC law supremacy, and the continued variation in national court behaviour *vis-à-vis* ECJ doctrine. The legalist literature has offered a host of *ad hoc* "explanations" of this cross-national variation, such as the influence of dualist doctrine on national judiciaries (Bebr (1981)), the lack of a tradition of judicial review in some Member States (Maher (1994); Vedel (1987)), the lack of a federalist or constitutional model (Cappelletti and Golay (1986)), problems of diffusing information across national judiciaries, old habits embedded in judges not used to the new and strange EC law (Meier (1994) ; Pescatore (1970)), legal parochialism and judicial nationalism (Abraham (1989) 170–1). But none of these

---

[4] The one possible exception may be the Netherlands, but even there Claes and De Witte acknowledge that while academics insist the basis for EC law supremacy is the special nature of the EC legal system, most national judges are silent on the legal basis for EC law supremacy, and national politicians and the Council of the State explicitly reject an extra-constitutional basis for EC law supremacy.

conditions consistently holds true. Doctrinally dualist Germany had an easier time accepting EC law supremacy than doctrinally monist France. The Netherlands and Belgium, which also lack traditions of judicial review, have also had less trouble than France. Generational and information diffusion explanations fall short when accounting for the 1993 decision of the German Constitutional Court which was more reticent on the issue of EC law supremacy than its "*Solange I*" decision issued 20 years earlier.[5] And in France, despite common legal traditions, the three different branches of the legal system for many years adopted different doctrinal stances regarding EC law (Vedel (1987)). It is not a matter of the need to explain lags and variation for explanation sake, rather the variation in itself implies that there are important extra-legal factors influencing legal interpretation and legal integration in Europe which legalist analyses are not considering.

While national judiciaries clearly did not find ECJ doctrine inherently compelling, the national reports referred to a "dialogue" where the ECJ worked with national judiciaries to develop legal doctrine which both sides could accept, thus to accommodate each others' jurisprudence on key points. Clarence Mann was one of the first legal scholars to note that the preliminary ruling procedure provided an important mechanism for "judicial dialogue", allowing national courts to challenge and try to influence ECJ jurisprudence with which they disagreed and the ECJ to "seek support" for its jurisprudence (Mann (1972)). Legal scholars have noted examples where ECJ jurisprudence influenced national jurisprudence (Mann (1972)), and they have also found instances where dialogue with national judges influenced the ECJ to adjust its jurisprudence to what national courts were willing to accept (Mancini and Keeling (1992); Morris and David (1987); Rasmussen (1984)). Indeed the desire to "dialogue" with the ECJ and influence EC jurisprudence was seen as a positive incentive for national courts to work with the ECJ, and the goal of initiating a dialogue with the ECJ was used to "explain" some national judicial behaviour (for example see Ch 3, Report on Germany, p. 113 and Ch 5, Report on Italy, p. 149). While still within the legalist tradition, an argument about judicial dialogue and accommodation as the basis for legal integration challenges the notion that law develops from some internal and apolitical logic in the texts, and opens the possibility that multiple—although not infinite—legal interpretations and legal consensus points can exist. This raises the question of what makes consensus regarding EC law shift, and why consensus shifts differently in different countries? The question for this project is why did legal consensus in *all* Member States shift to doctrines compatible with the supremacy of EC law?

While many scholars mentioned the importance of judicial dialogue between national courts and the ECJ, most of the national reports analysed

---

[5] BVerfG "*Solange I*" 2 BvL 52/71 decision from 29 May 1974; BVerfGE 37, p. 271; [1974] 2 CMLR 540–69; BVerfG "*Maastricht decision*" of 12 October 1993, 2 BvR 2134/92 and 2 BvR 2159/92.

national legal doctrine as an artifact of a national legal dialogue in the context of the larger domestic political system. Indeed the contrast between the national reports and the majority of writings by EC law specialists is noteworthy. EC law specialists tend to assume that ECJ jurisprudence will be accepted by national courts and dismiss incongruent national jurisprudence as unintended or misinformed mistakes. For EC law specialists, the national reports in the project on *Legal Change in its Social Context* point to the need to give greater consideration and significance to how national courts interpret, apply and challenge ECJ jurisprudence. But the national reports had their own version of myopia. They lost sight of the role of the ECJ in the process of legal integration, in some cases giving the ECJ almost no credit at all for influencing national doctrine. More work is needed to bridge this disconnection between a national doctrinal focus and an ECJ doctrinal focus. In other words, a promising direction for legalist analysis to go would be to investigate more this interactive "dialogue" legal scholars refer to. The snippets of evidence provided by legal scholars imply that a dialogue does exist and that it is important in facilitating legal integration and in shaping European Court jurisprudence. But it is unclear how the dialogue shapes legal interpretation at the EC level or at the national level. Examination of a sustained legal dialogue across legal cases and across national legal systems, could help us understand how legal interpretation and legal dialogue contribute to legal integration. In addition, by looking at how doctrine emerges and changes across time one can also gain insight into the extra-legal factors which shape legal interpretation.

Another weakness with the legalist approach is that legalist analysis often forgets that politicians are part of the process of legal integration, dismissing political objections as simply misinformed and seeing a very limited role for politicians in shaping legal integration. In the legalist paradigm, politicians influence the process of legal integration when they write legislation, thus politicians are credited with opening the door to expansive legal interpretation of the legislation. But politicians are given virtually no role in influencing legal interpretation of the legislation. Indeed Martin Shapiro called legalist analysis of European integration "constitutional law without politics" where the Community is presented:

> "as a juristic idea; the written constitution (the treaty) as a sacred text; the professional commentary as a legal truth; the case law as the inevitable working out of the correct implications of the constitutional text; and the constitutional court (the ECJ) as the disembodied voice of right reason and constitutional teleology" (Shapiro (1980)).

The national reports opened the door for politicians to influence legal interpretation and legal integration. The chapter 5, Report on Italy, notes that Government lawyers help shape legal interpretation through their participation in the legal process, and at different points the other national reports noted the effects of political influence on national court interpretation. But no attempt was made to think systematically about how and when politicians influence legal interpretation and legal integration. Indeed, often in the legal literature positive developments in legal integration are explained in legalist terms, while "politics" is used as a residual category to explain the failure of a court to follow the logic of EC law or the refusal of ECJ jurisprudence by a national court. If political factors are influencing judges to contort sound legal reasoning, then we should be able to see the influence of these factors more systematically across cases. By examining when and why political factors influence some legal decisions and not others, we can gain a greater understanding of the conditions under which political factors will and will not influence judicial decisions.

Legalist accounts can provide rich and detailed commentary on the process of doctrinal change. While much of the Continental legal scholarship strips politics from legal analysis whenever possible, more nuanced legalist analysis—such as the country reports in the research project on *"Legal Change in its Social Context"*—examines law within a political context, thereby offering an account of the numerous legal, sociological and political factors influencing legal integration. But even these accounts could be improved by focusing on how national courts and the ECJ shape each others jurisprudence in the process of legal integration, by using variation across countries and across time as a tool to gain a better understanding of how extra-legal forces influence the process of legal interpretation, and by examining the influence of extra-legal forces more systematically across cases and across time.

Neo-realism: national interest as the motor of legal integration

Neo-realism explains judicial behaviour in terms of national political and economic interests. In its strongest form, the neo-realist argument claims that legal decisions at the EC level and at the national court level are shaped by national interest calculations (Garrett (1992); Garrett (1995); Garrett and Weingast (1993)). The ability of national governments to influence court behaviour comes from the tools politicians have to define the jurisdiction of courts, manipulate appointments, and ignore unwanted jurisprudence. Garrett and Weingast argue:

> "Embedding a legal system in a broader political structure places direct constraints on the discretion of a court, even one with as much constitutional independence as the United States Supreme Court. This conclusion holds even if the constitution makes no explicit provisions for altering a court's role. The reason is that political actors have a range of avenues through which they may alter or limit the role of courts. Sometimes such changes require amendment of the constitution, but usually the appropriate alterations may be accomplished more directly through statute, as by alteration of the court's jurisdiction in a way that makes it clear that continued undesired behavior will result in more radical changes. The principal conclusion

... is that the *possibility of such a reaction drives a court that wishes to preserve its independence and legitimacy to remain in the arena of acceptable latitude*" (Garrett and Weingast (1993) 201–2 emphasis in the original).

Few would dispute that judges must keep their jurisprudence within some acceptable range, but this statement in itself does not mean much—after all there are political and legal limits for *every* public actor. The real questions are what defines the "acceptable" range of judicial behaviour and how much latitude do judges have. Garrett and Weingast see national interest as defining the acceptable range of judicial behaviour, and see all courts, and especially the ECJ, as having very limited latitude. Indeed Garrett goes so far as to assert that the need to elicit voluntary compliance with its decisions makes the ECJ strategise and calculate to ensure that its jurisprudence reflects and promotes the economic interests of the dominant Member States (Garrett (1992), (1993), (1995)).

Some national reports found a relationship between national interest and the acceptance of EC law supremacy. Claes and De Witte noted that in the Netherlands:

"The traditional receptivity to international rules, and willingness to cooperate with foreign nations is clearly in the interest of a small trading nation that is too small to preserve its independence on its own, and needs open borders for its prosperity" (Ch 7, Report on the Netherlands, p. 189).

While not making a link to national interest *per se*, in the United Kingdom Report (Ch 7) Craig noted that in accepting the logical conclusion of EC law supremacy in the *Factortame* case, British judges were mainly bringing their jurisprudence "within political reality". But statements such as these are a far cry from the assertion that fickle national interest calculations directly shape national jurisprudence and ECJ jurisprudence (Garrett (1995); Volcansek (1986)). Such an inference is, however, drawn in the French Report (Ch 2) where Plötner saw a relationship between the changing identification of national interest by the French Government in the mid-1980s and the changing Conseil d'État jurisprudence on EC law supremacy (Ch 2, Report on France, p. 68). Plötner even speculated that certain economic interests could lobby to obtain legal outcomes which reflected their interest, although beyond the insight that interest groups used the legal process to promote their interests there is no evidence that interest group lobbying directly shaped legal interpretation or judicial behaviour in France. The author of the German report also saw changing political enthusiasm for EC integration as explaining in part the legal swings of the Federal Constitutional Court between the *Solange I* (1974), *Solange II* (1986) and *Maastricht* (1993) decisions.

Underpinning the different analyses of how national courts respond to political pressure is a fairly loose conception of how national interest is constituted, and how political pressure influences judicial decisions. Neo-realism as a paradigm conceives of states as unitary actors with given and definable national interests which are systemicly defined (although how systemic forces translate into national interest is greatly under-specified, making the national interest definitions in most neo-realist work extremely fungible). The national reports did not assume such unitary definitions of national interest, nor did they assume that national interests *vis-à-vis* other international actors were the main force shaping judicial positions. Instead, at different times it was implied that public opinion and domestic political divisions were creating political pressures on national judiciaries. The German Report (Ch 3), for example, noted that public opinion played a role in the Constitutional Court's *Maastricht* decision and the Belgium report argued that the domestic conflict between the Walloons and the Francophones came to be a force influencing national positions on EC law supremacy.[6] But the variables of public opinion and domestic conflict were not examined across time and across a body of cases, so that the appeal to different political arguments was *ad hoc*.

While there are different anecdotal accounts of political forces influencing judicial decisions at different times, there is currently no consistent evidence which supports the neo-realist assertion that national interest or political concerns are shaping judicial behaviour. Indeed variation in national court jurisprudence on EC law is not easily or consistently explainable by political preferences, so that maintaining a neo-realist argument in practice requires very loose and fungible interpretations of national interest. For every action one can find a political rationalisation to "explain" an outcome. But in using an *ad hoc* approach, neo-realist arguments become nothing more than counter-factual re-interpretations of political interests, losing all predictive or explanatory power.

There is also considerable evidence that national politicians were quite upset with national court enforcement of EC law supremacy, and one can find quite a few examples where politicians actually tried to reverse national legal doctrine by political fiat, but failed. An examination of such an attempt reveals limitations to the neo-realist argument. In 1981 French politicians voted overwhelmingly to re-assert a ban on judges practising judicial review. The "Aurillac amendment" was a political reaction to an unwanted legal decision made by the highest French civil court, the Cour de Cassation. In the *Vabre* case, the Cour de Cassation had reversed historic national legal practice and refused to apply a Government law which had been passed in contradiction to existing EC law.[7] The Parliamentary debate surrounding the

---

[6] These propositions about the influence of public opinion and domestic politics on national judicial positions are not neo-realist *per se*, and in many ways they challenge the narrow internationalist conception of how national positions on international phenomenon emerge. But for our purpose here they can be seen as broadly conceived arguments about how political perceptions of national interest influence judicial positions. Indeed Mary Volcansek folded these numerous domestic political factors into her national interest calculations to explain changes in national judicial positions based on changes in national interests (1986).

[7] *Administration des Douanes* v. *Societe Cafes Jacques Vabre and J. Weigel et Compagnie S..r.l.* Cour de Cassation (France) decision of 24 May 1975, [1975] 2 CMLR 343.

Aurillac amendment made it clear that it was politically unacceptable for a court not to follow the will of Parliament, and that the *Vabre* jurisprudence should be reversed. In a debate, representative M. Aurillac argued that with the *Vabre* jurisprudence "the Cour de Cassation contorted one of the foundations of French law—the prohibition against tribunals getting involved in the exercise of legislative powers". Aurillac suggested an amendment to a law under debate which would re-assert the ban on judges conducting judicial review and send a clear message to the Cour de Cassation. The Minister of Justice agreed with the goal of the amendment, arguing:

> "if the judge takes upon himself the authority to refuse to apply a law under the pretext that he estimates that (the law) was contrary to an international accord, in the case where that law was subsequent to the accord in question, that would imply that the judge is assuming the right to disregard a law, thus scorning the will of the parliament . . . This could clearly not be accepted by the national representation".

It was also made clear that both the Parliament and the Government preferred the doctrinal position of the Conseil d'État as far as the supremacy of EC law over French law was concerned. The Ministry of Justice continued:

> "One could think that the Conseil d'État better respected the provisions of the law of 1790 . . . than the Cour de Cassation . . . The government could not be anything but favourable to the [Auriallac] amendment".[8]

The amendment passed overwhelmingly in the National Assembly (Buffet-Tchakaloff (1984) 343–4).[9] But it died in the Senate because it was seen as being clearly unconstitutional. Not only was the *Vabre* jurisprudence maintained by the Cour de Cassation, but the Conseil Constitutionnel and the Conseil d'État eventually came over to the Cour de Cassation's position.

How can we interpret this failed political attempt to shape judicial behaviour? It has been argued that the failure of politicians to use political tools to overrule ECJ jurisprudence means that politicians at some level support legal integration (Garrett (1995); Garrett and Weingast (1993); Rasmussen (1986)). But support implies an actual preference for a given outcome. Given the vote in the national assembly, and the Government's unconditional support for the amendment, clearly a majority of French politicians preferred the Conseil d'État jurisprudence and did not want the Cour de Cassation to continue accepting the supremacy of EC law. But the French legislative rules, including the requirement that the Senate also pass the amendment, and the likelihood that a Senate decision in favour of the Aurillac amendment would be appealed to the Conseil Constitutionnel, effectively killed the legislative attempts to reverse the Cour de Cassation's jurisprudence. Rather than encouraging national courts to adopt a legal interpretation which the politicians preferred, the failed Aurillac amendment revealed that politicians' threats against the

[8] J.O. Ass. Nat. Deb. 9 October 1980, p. 2644.
[9] J.O. Ass. Nat. Deb. 9 October 1980, pp. 2634–44.

national judiciary were empty and their formidable tools of judicial influence of little consequence. I have focused on one failed political attempt to sanction courts for behaviour they did not like, but there are numerous other examples where politicians failed to reverse unwanted national court and ECJ jurisprudence (indeed the Belgium Report (Ch 1) refers to an event very similar to the Aurillac Amendment).

The neo-realist scholarship relies a great deal on deductive reasoning to support its conclusions, but such reasoning is simply not supported by the evidence on legal integration. It is difficult to construct a consistent positive account of how national interest calculations influence judicial behaviour across cases, and the evidence that politicians have tried and failed to influence national judicial behaviour implies that there is much more autonomy for judges than neo-realist scholarship acknowledges. While there certainly is a great need for scholars to increase the focus on how political actors and political factors influence judicial decisions and legal integration, there is little to imply that focusing on national interest definitions *per se* will increase our understanding of how politics influence the process of legal integration. This points to the need to refine neo-realist hypotheses, and perhaps to focus more systematically on domestic political factors. The national reports raise a host of domestic political factors worth considering, such as public opinion, Parliamentary debates, and regional and inter-group politics. One could also consider how inter-institutional politics such as struggles between Parliaments and executives, as well as party politics, influence legal integration.

Neo-functionalism: self-interest of litigants, judges and legal scholars as the motor of legal integration

Neo-functionalism focuses on the interests of individual legal actors in order to explain judicial behaviour in legal integration. The neo-functionalist explanation claims that the EU legal system has expanded and prospered by creating individual incentives to motivate actors within EU institutions and within national legal systems to promote legal integration. Burley and Mattli argue that the ECJ put into place a structure which allowed the pursuit of self interest to drive the process of legal integration:

> "The Court . . . created . . . opportunities, providing personal incentives for individual litigants, their lawyers, and lower national courts to participate in the construction of the community legal system. In the process, it enhanced its own power and the professional interests of all parties participating directly or indirectly in its business" (Burley and Mattli (1993) 60).

The Court's incentive structure gave national legal actors a "direct stake" in continued legal integration, so that promoting legal integration advanced the financial, prestige or political power of national legal actors: individual

European citizens got new rights and legal tools to promote their own interests through legal integration; lawyers specialising in EC law got more business through the growth and expansion of EC law; legal scholars supported legal integration through favourable doctrinal writings which parenthetically increased the demand for university professors to teach EC law and enhanced individual career prospects within the legal services of the European Union and the ECJ itself; national judges referred cases to the ECJ because it offered them a chance to practice judicial review, a practice involving more interesting legal questions, and a practice which gives national judges more power *vis-à-vis* politicians, and which gives lower court judges the power to conduct the same type of review as higher court judges or constitutional court judges; and the ECJ enhanced its own prestige and authority through its far-reaching decisions. Haas's conception of neo-functionalism implied that actors' identities and loyalties would actually shift through the process of integration and that their interest would be permanently melded with the larger process of integration (Haas (1958); Haas (1961); Haas (1964)). Burley and Mattli do not explicitly go as far, although they don't offer any reason to think that actors might stop seeing an interest in further legal integration, and they do imply that national legal actors pursuing their interests within the EC legal framework will always lead to increasing legal integration.[10]

The main incentive for national courts to embrace EC law was the empowerment it offered them by allowing national judges to conduct judicial review. Some national reports imply that national judges embraced EC law because they gained new powers of judicial review through legal integration. In the French report Plötner claimed that the Cour de Cassation gained the right to control Acts of Parliament through legal integration, offering "exciting new perspectives on the work of France's judicial branch" (Ch 2, Report on France, p. 62). In the United Kingdom Report (Ch 7) Craig argued that the House of Lords gained a new power to attack primary legislation through EC legal integration. In the Belgium Report (Ch 1) Bribosia also argued that judicial review was a new power introduced by EC law supremacy. While these authors assert that national judges have been empowered through EC law, there is an empirical question of how we would know that national judges have been empowered by EC legal integration? In most of the general judicial politics literature, the increased role and influence of national judiciaries is explained by factors not relating to European legal integration—explanations such as the experience with Fascism in the Second World War (Cappelletti (1989)), the corruption investigations in Italy, and legislative politics in France (Stone (1992)). Indeed in the United Kingdom Report Craig argued that while EC law supremacy had

---

[10] Burley and Mattli argue: "In neo-functionalist terms, the Court created a pro-community constituency of private individuals by giving them a direct stake in the promulgation and implementation of community law. Further, the Court was careful to create a one-way ratchet by permitting individual participation in the system only in a way that would advance community goals" (p. 60).

some impact on the movement of British judges towards conducting judicial review, there was a much larger and ultimately more influential process of judicial consensus change going on in Britain, so that EC legal integration could not be credited with shifting judicial conceptions of national sovereignty so as to permit judicial review (Ch 7, Report on the United Kingdom, p. 215–16).

While empowerment is clearly a factor influencing judicial behaviour, it is not clear that all legal actors see themselves as empowered through EC law or EC legal integration or that all judges aspire to conduct judicial review. Many if not the majority of potential plaintiffs, lawyers and judges choose not to invoke European legal arguments, even though such arguments would arguably advance their interests. And although the French Conseil d'État lacked the power of judicial review of Parliamentary Acts, it nonetheless refused this new power by not embracing the supremacy of EC law for twenty-five years. To the extent that Burley and Mattli are right that actors can promote their interests through the EC legal process, a real question exists as to why many legal actors do not do so.

The insights that legal integration is not about "zero-sum trade-offs" between national judicial authority and ECJ authority (Weiler (1991)), and that numerous legal actors actually gain through legal integration is very important. But it is not the case that legal integration is strictly about mutual empowerment and "win-win" situations. Like all political processes, there are winners and losers in the process and to say that certain actors win is not to explain why the winners win over losers, or why the losers accept their loss. Many high courts have found their supreme influence over national law to have been diminished because of EC law supremacy, and politicians have also been angered by ECJ activism as well as by national court application of ECJ jurisprudence. That some actors gain through legal integration cannot explain why those actors which saw themselves as net losers in the process accepted the outcome of legal integration.

In many respects, the neo-functionalist argument of Burley and Mattli is legalist argument with a theory of interests of legal actors grafted on to it. In its reliance on legal logic and functional spillovers to explain the expansionary motor of legal integration, it suffers from the same problems as the legalist argument: it is unable to explain significant time lags, variation in legal integration within countries and cross-national variation in legal integration. It also cannot explain periodic reverse trends in legal integration, that is when legal integration is not a one-way ratchet of increasing expansion and penetration of EC law into the national legal realm and when national courts refuse to accept ECJ jurisprudence.

Unlike legalist analyses, however, neo-functionalism takes head on the issue of explaining political acquiescence to legal integration. Political acquiescence is explained through the incremental nature of the legal integration which "upgrades common interests" making little steps in integration seem tolerable, and refusing the little steps seem disproportionately severe. Burley and Mattli argue that the technical nature of law provides a "mask" and a "shield" which limits the ability of politicians to influence legal integration, implying that in most cases the political process does not influence the legal process of integration because it is unable to pierce the shield of law. They acknowledge that in certain circumstances the mask and shield can be pierced by politics, and politicians can use legal terms and political tools to hamper and constrain the process of legal integration. But other than asserting that politicians can influence the process of legal integration Burley and Mattli provide little insight into *when* or *how* this may happen.

These weaknesses aside, neo-functionalism shifts the focus of legal integration to the various national legal actors involved in the process of legal integration, showing that the mutual pursuit of self interest fundamentally contributed to the process of legal integration. While underspecified in its account of why national actors pursuing self interest facilitated legal integration, neo-functionalist analysis represents a significant advance in the debate over legal integration.

Inter-court competition explanations: bureaucratic politics as a motor of legal integration

The author's own work has been developing an "inter-court competition" explanation of when and why judges participate in legal integration. This explanation is really a version of a bureaucratic politics explanation, drawing on the insight that courts—like all bureaucracies—have their own interests which they pursue within the constraints imposed by politicians and legal rules. The inter-court competition explanation claims that different courts have different interests *vis-à-vis* EC law, and that national courts use EC law in bureaucratic struggles between levels of the judiciary and between the judiciary and political bodies, thereby inadvertently facilitating the process of legal integration. This explanation differs from the neo-functionalist explanation in that national judges do not have a stake in promoting legal integration, so that their behaviour fluctuates between acting in ways which facilitate legal integration and acting in ways which undermine legal integration. Examining courts as bureaucracies and sub-bureaucracies with their own interests and bases of institutional support can offer considerable insight into why some courts more readily accepted EC law supremacy, the conditions under which certain courts will see an interest in further legal integration, and the conditions under which—and thus the extent to which—politicians will be able to control legal integration. Thus looking at courts as bureaucracies is also a good way to think about the origins of the current system as well as the limits on legal integration.

Like Burley and Mattli (1993) and Weiler (1991), the inter-court competition argument starts from the insight that some courts gain from legal integration, but it identifies different, indeed competing interests for lower and higher courts with respect to legal integration. It is the difference in lower and higher court interests which provides a motor for legal integration to proceed. Lower courts can use EC law to get to legal outcomes which they prefer, either for policy or legal reasons, by using an appeal to the ECJ to challenge established jurisprudence and to circumvent higher court jurisprudence. Lower courts can also magnify the influence of their jurisprudence by making references to the ECJ, eliciting journal articles on decisions which otherwise would not be reported and making their legal decision binding on other courts. But lower courts do not always see appealing to the ECJ as in their interest. As I have argued elsewhere, the ECJ is like a second parent in a battle where parental permission wards off a potential sanction for misbehaviour—if the lower court does not like what it thinks "Mom" (the higher court) will say, it can go ask "Dad" (the ECJ) to see if it will get a more pleasing answer. Having "Dad's" approval increases the likelihood that its actions will not be challenged. If the lower court does not think it will like what "Dad" will say, it simply does not ask. Lower courts can also play high courts and the ECJ off against each other to influence legal development in a direction they prefer (Alter (1996a)).

Higher courts, on the other hand, have an interest in thwarting the expansion and penetration of EC law into the national legal order. Having supreme influence over both the development of national law and the execution of public policy in the national realm, high courts are threatened by the existence of the European Court as the highest court on questions of European law, and by the principle of EC law supremacy since the supremacy doctrine gave the European Court jurisdictional authority over national legal interpretation which would normally be the exclusive domain of national high courts. In general, high courts have a preference to limit the doctrinal and substantive expansion of European law so as to limit the areas where the ECJ will become a higher court and they will be subjugated. Thus high courts refer relatively few questions of interpretation to the European Court, and virtually no questions which could allow the European Court to expand the reach of European law into their own sphere of jurisdictional authority. High courts protest and challenge ECJ doctrine when it infringes on their own jurisdictional authority and hence implies a *de facto* subjugation to the ECJ on important aspects of national law, and when ECJ doctrine would undermine the influence of the national court within the national legal and political system. High courts also try to limit lower court references to the ECJ when these references will allow the ECJ to make a ruling with which the higher court disagrees.[11] So if an EC

---

[11] For example the Italian Constitutional Court ruled a reference to the ECJ regarding the supremacy of EC law to be invalid (Bermann et al. (1993) 193). The Bundesfinanzhof tried to limit the direct effect of EC law regarding turnover equalization taxes (Alter (1996b)). The Bundesfinanzhof and the Conseil d'État both overruled references to the ECJ based on the direct effect of directives (BFH Kloppenburg I V B 51/80, decision of 16. July 1981; *Europarecht* 1981, p. 442, [1982] 1 CMLR 527–31; *Minister of Interior* v. *Daniel Cohn-Bendit*, French Conseil d'État, 22 December 1978, [1980] CMLR 545–62. This strategy is limited in that not all decisions to make references are appealed to higher courts, so that references can and do slip through.

legal doctrine specifically subjugates a high court to the ECJ, the high court often refuses the doctrine and tries to block other national courts from incorporating the doctrine into national legal practice.[12]

These static judicial preferences create a dynamic propelling legal integration forward allowing lower courts, in the end, to cajole higher courts to accept the supremacy of EC law over national law. Briefly, the argument runs that lower courts made references to the ECJ to challenge existing jurisprudence or to challenge high court decisions. Because of the actions of lower courts, EC law expanded and EC law came to influence national jurisprudence. As the legal questions were appealed up the national judicial hierarchies, higher courts were put in the position of either quashing ECJ doctrine or accepting it. High courts freely accepted ECJ jurisprudence so far as it did not encroach on their own authority. When the ECJ encroached too far in their own jurisdictional authority, high courts rejected the aspects of ECJ doctrine which undermined their autonomy. But the actions of the lower courts came to actually shift the national legal context from under the high courts. Lower courts eventually ignored higher court attempts to limit the reach of EC law, making references to the ECJ anyway and applying EC law. Those high courts which did not find their influence diminished by certain aspects of ECJ doctrine also accepted this jurisprudence. At a certain point it became clear that obstructing higher courts had failed to block the expansion and application of EC law within the national legal system, so that continued opposition created legal inconsistency and limited the high court's ability to influence legal interpretation at all. Because so much national law touched on EC law, and so many lower courts were following the ECJ rather than their own high courts, opposition to ECJ jurisprudence lost all influence and effectiveness. National high courts repositioned themselves to the new reality, reversing their jurisprudence which challenged EC law supremacy and adjusting national constitutional doctrine to make it compatible with enforcing EC law over national law. But they did not accept the ECJ's legal reasoning, making the continued enforcement of EC law supremacy a national constitutional issue under the

[12] While lower courts and higher courts in general have divergent interests with respect to EC legal integration, the classificatory distinction between "low" and "high" courts should not be drawn too starkly. Not all high courts share the same interests with respect to a given ECJ doctrine, and an ECJ doctrine which threatens one high court may not threaten another—it depends on the jurisdictional authority of each high court. In addition, there are some issues where an ECJ decision helps bolster the influence of national high courts; if a high court wants to challenge the validity of an EC law, a favourable decision of the ECJ bolsters their position with respect to EC organs and national governments. If high courts want to assert new powers within the national legal system, a statement by the ECJ that these new powers are consistent with EC law can bolster their position with respect to political bodies. Finally, if a high court does not want to be challenged by lower courts, a willingness to refer questions which clearly fall under the ECJ's jurisdictional authority can convince lower courts to rely on the court of last instance to refer relevant questions to the European Court, passing up opportunities to make a reference themselves. To bring back the analogy used earlier, such a tactic convinces the lower court that "Mom" and "Dad" will decide together so that there is no advantage to making the extra effort to appeal to "Dad" first.

control of national courts, and leaving open avenues through which they could refuse the authority of the ECJ in the future without contradicting their jurisprudence on EC law supremacy (Alter (1996b)).

The ECJ played an important role in the process of inter-court competition, by being a willing participant in challenges to traditional national jurisprudence and higher courts, even authorising and telling lower courts to ignore the jurisprudence of their higher courts. The ECJ also co-ordinated lower courts through its jurisprudence so that legal integration proceeded similarly in all national contexts. Through the bureaucratic struggles within national judiciaries, national courts created a basis of political power for the ECJ (Alter (1996a)), but national courts also created significant limits on the process of legal integration. The author's dissertation gives evidence to support this argument, explaining how competitive struggles between national courts, and between national courts and the ECJ shaped the process of legal integration in France and Germany. In this chapter, the focus will be only on the "evidence" made in the national reports to support this argument about the interests of national courts in the process of legal integration and about how competition between courts shaped judicial positions regarding EC law.

National reports note many examples where competition between courts was shaping judicial behaviour. In the German report, Kokott notes that national judicial behaviour is significantly influenced by the competitive position of national courts *vis-à-vis* each other and *vis-à-vis* the ECJ. She explains one Federal Tax Court decision challenging ECJ jurisprudence saying that "The Tax Court did not want to be turned into a mere assistant to the ECJ but tried to reserve its own independence through exclusive competences for itself" (Ch 3, Report on Germany, p. 117). Kokott also argued that the Federal Labour Court's recent challenge to ECJ jurisprudence "can be seen as an attempt by the Labour Court to establish its own 'co-operative relationship' with the ECJ . . . reflect[ing] an increased sense of self-consciousness by the Labour court, which does not see itself in an inferior position *vis-à-vis* the ECJ and which asserts its own right and obligation to ensure a coherent national legal system" (Ch 3, Report on Germany, p. 113).

In the French report, Plötner argued that the Conseil d'État's intransigence to EC law supremacy was shaped by its own interests, which in turn were derived from the Conseil d'État's institutional context within the French legal and political system. He argued that:

> "[u]p to 1958 the [Conseil d'État] had the monopoly of interpreting public and constitutional law in France. Furthermore it participated in the elaboration of all legal norms. This had placed the Conseil d'État in the very core of the French political system. From 1958 onwards, this predominance was under attack: the first assault consisted of the creation of the Conseil Constitutionnel . . . The [Conseil d'État]'s position was further threatened when it finally became obvious in Paris that there was court in Luxembourg which actually had the competence to intervene in what seemed to be French domestic affairs . . . This might have led its members to con-

sider supremacy and direct effect as another threat to the *status quo* which for them was still, after all, quite favourable. Even if full enforcement of Community law was unlikely to substantially endanger their position, the awareness of a certain precariousness of their situation led the corps as such to defend their '*acquis*' in quite a static manner" (Ch 2, Report on France, p. 57).

Comparing the Cour de Cassation's institutional position *vis-à-vis* that of the Conseil d'État, Plötner argued that the Cour de Cassation has an inferiority complex from its training and background. "Given its feeling of being second to the [Conseil d'État], the Community level offered itself as an instrument enabling the judicial branch not only to accomplish its task even better but also to gain an advantage over the Conseil" (Ch 2, Report on France, p. 60).

In the Belgium Report (Ch 1), Bribosia was perhaps the most blunt of all. He argued that the latest changes on EC law supremacy doctrine in Belgium comes from a struggle between the three highest courts over their jurisdictional authority. The Cour de Cassation is jealous of the new powers of the Conseil d'État and the Cour d'Arbitrage, and wants to ensure that it can review national law in light of international law, and the Cour d'Arbitrage defends the supremacy of the Constitution over international law in order to protect its own authority (Ch 1, Report on Belgium, p. 34).

The Italian Report (Ch 5) discusses the varying lower court support for legal integration, and how lower courts pushed the Constitutional Court to change its opposition to EC law supremacy. Laderchi writes:

"Lower courts in a number of cases cast doubt on the validity of the Community Treaties. Sometimes those doubts were only raised in order to present the Constitutional Court with some of the consequences of its previous statements and consequently to make the case more difficult for the Constitutional Court and oblige it to accept certain principles of Community law. In other cases lower courts seemed eager to exacerbate the conflict between the Court in Rome and the one in Luxembourg and require the Constitutional Court to defend certain national principles against the incoming tide of Community law" (Ch 5, Report on Italy, p. 149).

Finally, Claes and De Witte hypothesised that if there were a constitutional court in the Netherlands, Dutch legal doctrine on EC law supremacy might be different (Ch 6, Report on the Netherlands, p. 190). This observation lends credence to a point made at the workshop discussions in Florence—perhaps the largest determining factor on whether there exists national doctrine which challenges the ECJ's authority to expand its own jurisdictional authority at will (*Kompetenz-Kompetenz*) was whether or not there was a constitutional court in that country which was seeking to protect national constitutional guarantees and its own judicial independence.

The inter-court competition explanation offers a parsimonious explanation of national judicial behaviour in the process of legal integration, which can apply across courts and across borders. The explanation can also account for why the actions of a few lower courts in the national context led to a fundamental change in the entire national legal context and a shift in national court jurisprudence *vis-à-vis* EC law throughout the national judiciary. By itself, however, it does not explain how politicians influence the process. I supplement it with an argument about the conditions under which politicians will influence judicial behaviour. This develops the argument alluded to earlier in discussion of the neo-realist explanation, and shows how institutional rules kept national politicians from being able credibly to threaten either national courts or the ECJ into obedience.[13] Each failure to sanction the ECJ or national courts for unwanted judicial activism only exposed political impotence, giving the ECJ and the national courts a "green light" to proceed with legal integration. But the institutional barriers are not insurmountable, and I develop an explanation of the conditions under which politicians have greater influence over judicial behaviour in legal integration, (Alter (1998)).

It should be pointed out that the inter-court competition draws much from the insights of the other explanations of legal integration. But while it shares certain aspects in common with alternative explanations, there are important differences. Like the neo-functionalist explanation, this explanation argues that the EC legal system empowers some legal actors which helps explain why they act in ways which promote legal integration. But this empowerment is more limited than in the neo-functionalist explanation, and does not always work in the direction of furthering legal integration. This argument also sees bureaucratic politics as significantly influencing where, how and when EC law expands into the national legal realm. Because of these differences, the inter-court competition argument leads to very different conclusions about how legal integration works and how politics influences the process of legal integration. Spillover and legal logic is not seen as driving legal expansion, rather inter-court competition is seen as pushing legal expansion. The explanation also sees a real divergence between ECJ and national court interests. The ECJ is significantly constrained by national court willingness to apply its jurisprudence so that legal integration is by no means an ever-expanding process. The disconnection between the process of legal integration and the process of political integration also means that politicians will have limited influence and control over the expansion and penetration of EC law into the national realm.

CONCLUSION: LEGAL INTEGRATION IN A COMPARATIVE POLITICAL
PERSPECTIVE

This chapter has sought to bring a theoretical focus to the task of explaining national court behaviour in legal integration, and thus to explaining doctrinal

---

[13] See Alter (1998).

change within national legal systems. While not claiming that judicial behaviour can be encapsulated by a single factor, a theoretical approach puts a premium on identifying the most important and generalisable factors shaping national judicial behaviour *vis-à-vis* EC law across cases. For the legalist explanation, the most important factor shaping judicial behaviour is legal logic and legal reasoning. For neo-realism, the most important factor shaping judicial behaviour is national interest, although how national interest is defined or measured is underspecified. For neo-functionalism and the inter-court competition explanations, the most important factors shaping judicial behaviour are the interests of the judges and the courts themselves, but each of the explanations defines court interests differently. To identify which factors are most important is not to say that other factors do not matter, and indeed if anything this analysis of alternative explanations of legal integration revealed that many of the narrow forms of the different explanations must be rejected and that none of the explanations can adequately explain all judicial behaviour on its own.

While all of the theories of legal integration examined here had significant weaknesses, identifying the most important factors is still necessary if we want to understand larger and more general issues raised by legal integration. By identifying specific and generalisable forces shaping the process of legal integration in all Member States, we can better understand the limitations of legal integration, as well as the possibility of generalising the experience of European legal integration to other international contexts. Furthermore, only by identifying the conditions which allowed legal integration to proceed in the first thirty-five years of legal integration, can we understand why legal integration is perhaps more polemic these days.

Two of the largest questions raised by legal integration today are: can legal integration proceed in light of the apparent lack of political support for ECJ activism and can the experience of legal integration be generalised to other international contexts? By way of conclusion, I would like to examine what the national reports and the different explanations of legal integration imply about pre-conditions or permissive conditions which facilitated legal integration in the first thirty-five years.

Political support as a pre-condition for continued legal integration?

Legal integration is necessarily an outcome of a political process. National governments drafted the initial Treaties which put the Court in place and which created rules to guide the process of economic integration. National governments also play a decisive role in passing legislation and co-ordinating the implementation of EC law in the national realm. At the same time, there are some aspects of legal integration which can proceed without positive political action, indeed at times despite the desire of national governments. There has been an ongoing debate over whether or not continued positive political support is a necessary pre-condition for legal integration to proceed once the legal rules are put in place (Burley and Mattli (1993); Garrett (1992); Garrett (1995); Garrett and Weingast (1993); Slaughter (1995)).

The national reports note that judges are sensitive to political concerns in making judicial decisions, but this does not means that politicians must support judicial actions in order for legal integration to proceed. This chapter examined the experience of France in the Aurillac Amendment, and the Belgium Report (Ch 1) also discussed Parliamentary attempts to influence legal interpretation. In both France and in Belgium political amendments sanctioning national courts passed with overwhelming majorities in their assemblies. The fact that such attempts were made shows that there was a lack of political support for national courts controlling the compatibility of national law with international law. The fact that these attempts failed shows that national courts had significant room for manoeuvre, independent of the wishes or interests of political bodies.

At the EC level there have also been attempts by politicians to sanction the ECJ for its activism. Hjalte Rasmussen's work has noted quite a few cases—dating back to 1968—of political attacks against the Court in the Council, and failed political attempts to sanction the ECJ (Rasmussen (1986)). Politicians clearly are not helpless to influence legal integration, but the mere existence of tools of influence does not mean that politicians control judicial action (Alter (1998)). The failure of these political efforts to stem the legal integration tide implies that positive political support is not a necessary condition for legal integration to proceed. The question which remains is whether the current period is fundamentally different from previous periods of legal integration, so that a lack of political support today would have a different implication than a lack of political support twenty years ago.

It is also possible that while judges may not need political support to issue controversial decisions, they may need political support in order to have their jurisprudence transformed into policy. Judicial decisions apply to individual cases only, and while there is no hint that political bodies or administrators have ignored judicial decisions regarding EC law, there is also limited evidence that politicians and administrators are applying individual decisions beyond specific legal cases. As I have argued elsewhere, judicial decisions can not be assumed to create policy outcomes (Alter (1994)). Thus there is a need to investigate further the extent to which judicial decisions need political support to make the jurisprudence part of national policy, and when judicial decisions come to influence national policy.

Preliminary ruling system and the ECJ as a pre-condition for legal integration?

A new debate is bubbling up over whether legal integration in Europe is generalisable to other international contexts. Anne-Marie Slaughter and other scholars of liberal international relations theory have hypothesised about institutional and ideological conditions found in liberal democracies which could facilitate the creation of a transnational legal consensus on principles of international law, in contexts much broader than that of economic integration and of the European Union (Slaughter (1995)). Such approaches raise directly the question of what conditions in Europe made legal integration possible, or perhaps more probable.

The discussion of the *legalist* explanation, included discussion of the legal accommodation created through a dialogue between the ECJ and other Member States. The European legal system has mechanisms which greatly facilitate such a dialogue. The preliminary ruling procedure allows for national courts and the ECJ to interact directly with each other on specific legal issues. Furthermore, the European Court is an important co-ordinator and organising centre for a cross-national dialogue, allowing for controlled exchanges on specific and concrete issues as opposed to "free-for-alls" on an unlimited range of issues. It is unclear if the institutional mechanisms in the EC legal system and the existence of an ECJ are merely permissive conditions facilitating legal integration in Europe, or if they are actually pre-conditions for the increased expansion and penetration of international law into national political systems.

The inter-court competition explanation suggests that the institutional mechanisms of the EC legal system might indeed be a pre-condition for legal integration. European higher courts did not necessarily have an interest in promoting international legal integration, but the preliminary ruling system allowed lower courts to invoke the authoritative ECJ in their competitive battles with each other. References were often sent to the ECJ because the ECJ could lend credibility to the legal interpretations of national courts. Lower courts could use the preliminary ruling system to circumvent the higher courts because the ECJ gave them a legally defensible basis to do so. With ECJ support, lower court actions were able to shift the domestic political context so that opposition to ECJ jurisprudence no longer served the interests of higher courts, and so that higher courts gained an incentive to participate in the process of legal integration (though not necessarily through references to the ECJ). If there were not a preliminary ruling system, it is probable that lower courts would never have ventured into the uncharted legal territory as far as they did. Even if they had ventured, without the preliminary ruling mechanism, it is unlikely that lower court voyeurs would have been so successful in permeating the larger national—let alone transnational—legal context. Thus lower court access to the ECJ might be an important pre-condition for significant expansion of ECJ doctrine, and for the permeation of this law throughout national legal systems. The absence of a mechanism to allow for inter-court competition in the international context, and the absence of the ECJ to confer authority and to co-ordinate this inter-court competition, might undermine if not preclude the emergence of a significant transnational international consensus on issues of international law.

Other possible mechanisms to facilitate transnational legal integration exist, however. Joseph Weiler has suggested that the acceptance of legal norms by courts in one country can create a sort of peer pressure on other courts which extends over boarders (Weiler (1994)). National reports noted examples of cross-national judicial influence, where national advocates or judges noted their international isolation as one of the reasons why they should change their jurisprudence. However, it is clear that some national high courts maintained opposition to ECJ jurisprudence for many years despite the acceptance of ECJ jurisprudence by courts in other countries, raising the question of how much cross-national peer pressure was a factor in national doctrinal change.

At the same time, if it is true that legal doctrine develops and changes through dialogues, the increasing dialogues of legal communities (including scholars, lawyers and judges) across legal borders could facilitate doctrinal change within different national settings. Slaughter's work implies that this transnational dialogue can facilitate a convergence of legal interpretation across borders, at least in liberal democratic countries. Increasingly, there are exchanges between high courts of democratic countries, and the process of integration, as well as the computer and information revolution, is making it easier to learn about the jurisprudence of courts in other countries on certain legal issues. Thus one could argue that other mechanisms of dialogue are being developed. But can these mechanisms fill the same dialogue role as the preliminary ruling system in the EC legal system? It is often joked that putting more lawyers in a room only creates more disagreement—can a transnational legal consensus on issues of international law actually emerge? How stable would such a consensus be? Where and under what conditions might we expect to see international legal consensus fray? This last question raises a real issue in the EC context, highlighted by the different national reports: does it matter that national courts continue to have divergent legal bases for EC law supremacy?

The success of legal integration within the international context of the European Union raises many questions for scholars more generally interested in international institutions and international relations. This chapter has suggested that the key to understanding legal integration in Europe is explaining the actions of national courts. It examined alternative explanations of national judicial behaviour in legal integration, and raised questions about the need of political support to facilitate legal integration and the generalisability of the European experience in legal integration to other international contexts.

While the chapter did not venture much beyond a review of the dominant literature on legal integration, it suggested avenues of research which could advance the theoretical debate and enhance our understanding of the legal and political forces shaping the application and adherence to European law within the European Member States.

REFERENCES

ABRAHAM, R. (1989), *Droit international, droit communautaire et droit français*, Le Politique, L'Economique, Le Social (Paris: Hachette).

ALTER, K. and AITSAHALIA, M. (1994), "Judicial Politics in the European Community: European Integration and the pathbreaking Cassis de Dijon decision." *Comparative Political Studies* (24), 535–61.

ALTER, K. (1996a), "The European Court's Political Power" 19 *West European Politics* (3), 458–87.

——(1996b), "The Making of a Rule of Law: The European Court and the National Judiciaries" (Dissertation in Political Science, Massachusetts Institute of Technology).

——(1998), "Who are the Masters of the Treaty?: European Governments and the European Court of Justice", *International Organization* (Winter).

BEBR, G. (1981), *Development of Judicial Control of the European Communities* (The Hague: Martinus Nijhoff Publishers).

BERMANN, G., GOEBEL, R., DAVEY, W. and FOX, E. (1993), *Cases and Materials on European Community Law, American Casebook Series* (St. Paul: West Publishing Co.).

BUFFET-TCHAKALOFF, M.-F. (1984), *La France devant la cour de justice des communautés européennes* (Aix-en-Provence: Presses universitaires d'Aix-Marseille).

BURLEY, A.-M. and MATTLI, W. (1993), "Europe Before the Court", 47 *International Organization*(1), 41–76.

CAPPELLETTI, M. (1989), *The Judicial Process in Comparative Perspective* (Oxford: Clarendon Press).

——and GOLAY, D. (1986), "The Judicial Branch in the Federal and Transnational Union: Its Impact on Integration" in *Methods, Tools and Institutions: Political Organs, Integration Techniques and Judicial Process*, M. Cappelletti, M. Seccombe and J. Weiler (eds) (Berlin: Walter de Gruyter), 261–348

——SECCOMBE, M. and WEILER, J. (1986), "Integration Through Law: Europe and the American Federal Experience—A General Introduction" in *Integration Through Law: Europe and the American Federal Experience Book 1*, M. Cappelletti, M. Seccombe and J. Weiler (eds) (Berlin: Walter de Gruyter), 3–68

GARRETT, G. (1992), "The European Community's Internal Market", 46 *International Organization* (2), 533–60.

——(1995), "The Politics of Legal Integration in the European Union", 49 *International Organization* (1), 171–81.

——and WEINGAST, B. (1993), "Ideas, Interests and Institutions: Constructing the ECs Internal Market", in *Ideas and Foreign Policy*, J. Goldstein and R. Keohane (eds) (Ithaca: Cornell University Press), 173–206.

HAAS, E. (1958), *The Uniting of Europe* (Palo Alto: Stanford University Press).

HAAS, E. (1961), "International Integration: The European and the Universal Process", 15 *International Organization* (Summer), 366–92.

—— (1964), *Beyond the Nation-State: Functionalism and International Organization* (Stanford CA: Stanford University Press).

LECOURT, R. (1991), "Quel Eut été le Droit des Communauts sans les arrêt de 1963 et 1964?" in *Mélanges en Hommage Jean Boulouis: L'Europe et le Droit* (Paris: Edition Dalloz), 349–61.

MAHER, I. (1994), *The Common Law Courts as Community Courts* (paper presented at the 2nd ECSA World Conference, May 1994, Brussels).

MANCINI, F. (1989), "The Making of a Constitution for Europe", XXIV *Common Market Law Review* 595–614.

—— and KEELING, D. (1992), "From CILFIT to ERT: The Constitutional Challenge Facing the European Court" 11 *Yearbook of European Law* 1–13.

MANN, C. J. (1972), *The Function of Judicial Decision in European Economic Integration* (The Hague: Martinus Nijhoff Press).

MEIER, G. (1994), "Der Streit um die Umsatzausgleichsteuer aus integrationspolitischer Sicht", *Recht der Internationalen Wirtschaft* 3/94.

MORRIS, P. E., and DAVID, P. W. (1987), "Directives, Direct Effect and the European Court: The Triumph of Pragmatism" *Business Law Review* (April, May) 116–18, 135–6.

PESCATORE, P. (1970), "L'attitude des juridictions nationales à l'égard du problème des effets direct du droit communautaire", *Revue trimestrielle de droit européen* (2), 296–302.

RASMUSSEN, H. (1984), "The European Court's Acte Clair Strategy in C.I.L.I.T. or Acte Clair, of Course! But what does it Mean?" *European Law Review* 242–59.

—— (1986), *On Law and Policy in the European Court of Justice* (Dordrecht: Martinus Nijhoff Publishers).

SHAPIRO, M. (1980), "Comparative Law and Comparative Politics", *Southern California Law Review* 53.

SLAUGHTER, A.-M. (1995), "International Law in a World of Liberal States", *European Journal of International Law* 6.

—— and MATTLI, W. (1995), "Law and politics in the European Union: a reply to Garrett", 49 *International Organization* (1), 183–90.

STONE, A. (1992), *The Birth of Judicial Politics in France: The Constitutional Council in Comparative Perspective* (New York: Oxford University Press).

TOMUSCHAT, C. (1989), "Les rapports entre le droit communautaire et le droit interne allemand dans la jurisprudence récente de la court constitutionnelle allemande", *Cahiers de droit européen* 163–78.

VEDEL, G. (1987), *L'attitude des juridictions françaises envers les traités européens* (Vol. Europa-Institut der Universitt des Saarlands).

VOLCANSEK, M. (1986), *Judicial Politics in Europe* (Vol. 7, *American University Studies Series X Political Science*, New York: Peter Lang Publishers).

WEILER, J. (1991), "The Transformation of Europe" 100 *Yale Law Journal* 2403–83.

—— (1994), "A Quiet Revolution—The European Court of Justice and its Interlocutors", 26 *Comparative Political Studies* (4), 510–34.

9

The Role of National Courts in the Process of European Integration: Accounting for Judicial Preferences and Constraints

WALTER MATTLI AND ANNE-MARIE SLAUGHTER

INTRODUCTION

The European Court of Justice is in fashion, at least in academic circles. Hailed as the creator of the Community legal system and the constitutionaliser of the EC Treaty, the ECJ is no longer the specialised province of European law experts.[1] This renewed interest is particularly evident among political scientists, who long ignored the Court as a technical and largely irrelevant institution. In the last four years the literature on the Court has dramatically expanded, nourishing a lively debate between neofunctionalists and intergovernmentalists and spawning a new generation of dissertation research and detailed country studies of the relationship between the ECJ and national courts. All students of legal integration now agree that the Court is not only an important actor in the process of European integration but also a strategic actor in its own right.

It was not always so. In the 1980s and early 1990s legal scholars such as Eric Stein, Francis Snyder, Martin Shapiro, Hjalte Rasmussen, and, most notably, Joseph Weiler, called for an interdisciplinary approach to EU law, or at least for the examination of EU law in political, economic and social context. On the political science side, Mary Volcansek had revived the pioneering tradition of Stuart Scheingold in developing an impact analysis of European judicial politics, focusing particularly on the relationship between the ECJ and national courts.[2] Nevertheless, the overwhelming majority of political scientists studying and writing about the European Union still gave the Court very short shrift.

The new interest in the Court was sparked in large part by the unexpected reinvigoration of European integration itself, beginning with the Single

---

[1] A note on terminology. We use "EC" or "the Community" when referring to the construction of the legal system of the European Union, as the Court's landmark cases were all decided before the metamorphosis of the EC into the EU. We use "EU" to describe the Community today.

[2] Mary Volcansek, *Judicial Politics in Europe: An Impact Analysis* (New York: Peter Lang, 1986).

European Act in 1986 and the drive toward the completion of the single market in 1992. In discovering that regional integration was no longer obsolete, political scientists also became aware of what lawyers had known for some time—that legal integration had significantly outpaced economic and political integration. Moreover, the Court became the poster child for a revival of neofunctionalism. At a time when the Single European Act was being described as an inter-governmental bargain,[3] we argued that the Court's success in constructing an effective Community legal system was best explained in neofunctionalist terms.[4]

Scholars have challenged the neofunctionalist explanation of legal integration from two different directions. First is the intergovernmentalist or neorealist claim that the ECJ has actually had little independent or unforeseen impact on European integration; that although straying occasionally, it has acted largely as the faithful agent of Member State interests.[5] In response, we challenged the empirical evidence of congruence between ECJ decisions and Member State interests. More fundamentally, we questioned the identification of state "interests" as unitary economic interests. From this perspective, the value of a neofunctionalist analysis is its emphasis on microfoundations, on specifying the interests of particular actors in the process of European integration.

The second challenge to the neofunctionalist explanation of European legal integration concerned its teleological quality. Just as Haas's original neofunctionalist analysis waxed and waned with the fortunes of the Community itself, so too do neofunctional dynamics seem less compelling in 1996 than in 1992. Neofunctionalism seems to be a tale tailored for success, an account of how different actors can overcome obstacles to achieve a common goal. It is less a theory of when integration will and will not happen than a description of the process of how it does. To understand when the conditions favourable to this process are most likely to occur, we need a theory of interest formation.

In response to these challenges, and to a crop of new data, we propose to reexamine the neofunctionalist framework we put forward. Much of the empirical evidence that has emerged in the interim confirms the value of this framework in terms of its identification of the key actors in the legal integration process, their motives, the dynamics of their interaction, and the context in which they operate. EU lawyers themselves are increasingly willing to

---

[3] Andrew Moravcsik, "Negotiating the Single European Act: National Interests and Conventional Statecraft in the European Community", *International Organization* 45 (1991), 19–45.

[4] Anne-Marie Burley and Walter Mattli, "Europe Before the Court: A Political Theory of Legal Integration", *International Organization* 47 (Winter 1993), 41–76; also Walter Mattli and Anne-Marie Slaughter, "Law and Politics in the European Union", *International Organization* 41 (Winter 1995), 183–90.

[5] Geoffrey Garrett, "International Cooperation and Institutional Choice: The European Community's Internal Market", *International Organization* 46, 533–60; *id.*, "The Politics of Legal Integration in the European Union", *International Organization* 49. no. 1 (1995), 171–81.

acknowledge the existence of a closely constructed network of sub- and supra-national actors acting within an insulated and self-consciously constructed "community of law". At the same time, the limits of the initial framework are also now becoming clear. This chapter seeks to address some of those limits in ways that we hope will contribute to further research.

In the context of European legal integration, we originally argued that sub-national actors (private litigants, their lawyers, and lower national courts) cooperated with the ECJ in the construction of the EC legal system. We paid relatively little attention, however, to the specific motives animating these actors, beyond the broad assertion that they were generally pursuing their self-interest. Such generalisations cannot explain the considerable variation in the timing and the extent of acceptance of key doctrines of EC law among different national courts (see Figure 1).

We argue in this chapter that a theoretical account capable of explaining variation in the pace and scope of European legal integration among different Member States must disaggregate the state itself. The standard neofunction-alist model assumes that the "state" is a monolith, to be circumvented and influenced by coalitions of sub- and supra-national actors. Yet closer exami-nation of the actual process of integration, with starts and stops, as well as national variation, reveals courts, legislatures, executives, and administrative bureaucracies interacting as quasi-autonomous actors. Each of these institu-tions has specific interests shaped by the structure of a particular political sys-tem, the need to perform specific socio-political functions such as judging or legislating, and the demands of specific political constituencies.

In lieu of standard models of the unitary state, the picture that emerges is one of "disaggregated sovereignty", an image of different governmental insti-tutions interacting with one another, with individuals and groups in domestic and transnational society and with supra-national institutions.[6] This picture is closer to general liberal theories of international relations than it is to any particular account of European integration.

Therefore, what is needed is a more nuanced specification of the interests (preferences) of the actors involved in the process of integration. We offer such an account based on the six reports presented in this volume. The reports exam-ine the process of reception of the supremacy and direct effect doctrines in Belgium, France, Germany, Great Britain, Italy, and the Netherlands. However, a refinement of the specification of the interests is not enough; it must be com-plemented by a careful study of the constraints that actors face when pursuing their preferences. We analyse these constraints in the context of specific con-ceptions of judicial identity and the constraints imposed by legal legitimacy and democratic accountability. The next generation of scholarship on EC legal integration, as with European integration more generally, will require far more

---

[6] Anne-Marie Slaughter, "International Law in a World of Liberal States", *European Journal of International Law* 6 (1995), 503–38; *id.*, "The Real New World Order", *Foreign Affairs* Vol. 76, No. 5 (Sept/Oct 1997), pp. 183–197.

Figure 1: Summary of time of reception of Community doctrines by the Member States

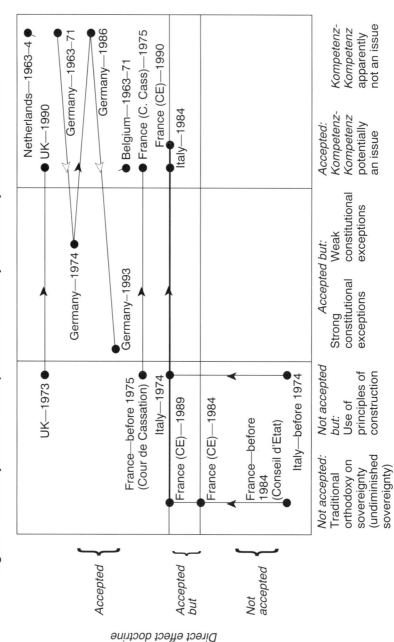

nuanced attention to the identification of both interests and constraints. Such a task demands that we move away from contending paradigms such as realism and neofunctionalism and toward the development of mid-range hypotheses that are both theoretically sophisticated and empirically informed.

THE ROLE OF NATIONAL COURTS IN EC LEGAL INTEGRATION

In our original account, drawing on the work of legal scholars such as Joseph Weiler, we identified the article 177 procedure in the EC Treaty as providing a framework for links between the European Court of Justice and subnational actors—private litigants, their lawyers, and lower national courts.[7] More specifically, we noted the Court's efforts to make European law attractive to individual litigants and their lawyers through its case law and its efforts to educate and appeal to national judges through tactics ranging from weekends in Luxembourg to tacit offers of a judicial partnership. A number of the national reports offer additional evidence for this picture. The judges of lower Italian courts, for instance, were assertedly motivated by a desire to have their cases referring issues to the ECJ "feature at the center of the attention of the world of lawyers".[8] This notoriety resulted from approval of their analysis by the ECJ, in the face of the apparent ignorance of EC law on the part of many law professors and higher court judges.[9]

The French Report (Ch 2) also highlights the potential importance of the socialisation of individual national judges through a tour on the ECJ. Plötner tells the tale of Yves Galmot, the first member of the French Conseil d'Etat nominated as a judge on the ECJ, who was sent off to Luxembourg with the expectation that he would hold the line against judicial activism at the European level. A year after he returned to the Conseil d'Etat—thoroughly converted to Community doctrines—the Conseil took its famous *Nicolo* decision that implicitly authorised judges to make treaties prevail over national law.[10] Much of the remaining time is spent in each other's company.[11] More

[7] Burley and Mattli, "Europe Before the Court: A Political Theory of Legal Integration", (n. 4 above); Mattli and Slaughter, "Law and Politics in the European Union" (n. 4 above). See also: Hjalte Rasmussen, On *Law and Policy in the European Court of Justice: A Comparative Study in Judicial Policy-making* (Dortrecht: M. Nijhoff, 1986); Martin Shapiro, "The European Court of Justice", in Alberta Sbragia, (ed.), *Euro-Politics: Institutions and Policymaking in the New European Community* (Washington, D.C.: Brookings Institution, 1991); Joseph Weiler, "The Community System: The Dual Character of Supranationalism", *Yearbook of European Law* 1 (1981); *idem*, "Community, Membership and European Integration: Is the Law Relevant?" *Journal of Common Market Studies* 21 (1983); *idem*, "The Transformation of Europe", *Yale Law Journal* 100 (1991); Jean-Paul Jacque and Joseph Weiler, "On the Road to European Union—A New Judicial Architecture. An Agenda for the Intergovernmental Conference", *Common Market Law Review* 27 (1990), 185.

[8] Ch 5, Report on Italy, p. 149.

[9] *Ibid.*

[10] Ch 2, Report on France, p. 68–9.

[11] "A Law Unto Many", *Financial Times*, 3 April 1995) p. 15.

generally, many of the country studies emphasise the small size and relatively close knit character of the legal community in each country, forged by ties of education, socialisation, and professional mobility between the professoriate, private practitioners, and the judiciary.

To the extent that we focused on national courts as independent participants in this community of sub- and supranational legal actors, we argued that they were motivated largely by self-interest, borrowing Joseph Weiler's concept of "judicial empowerment".[12] A number of scholars have argued convincingly that this analysis is too crude.[13] It does not specify what power judges seek, nor how they were able to obtain it through acceptance of the authority of the ECJ. We also conflated the professional and personal interests of individual interests with the institutional interests of judges.[14] Finally, such a general concept cannot explain differences in the rate of acceptance of critical ECJ doctrines such as direct effect and supremacy among different courts within the same national legal system. Nor can it account for limits to integration. A much more precise specification of judicial interests is needed, as well as of the constraints on the pursuit of those interests.

Borrowing from our critics, and drawing on the data presented in the country studies, we offer a more refined and differentiated definition of the kinds of power that courts actually seek. First is the power of judicial review to establish the validity of national legislation, which is an increase in power with respect to national legislatures. Some national courts, notably constitutional courts, already exercise this power within their domestic legal systems; others gained this power with respect to at least some subset of national statutes in partnership with the ECJ. Second is the pursuit of institutional power and prestige relative to other courts within the same national judicial system. Here we draw primarily on the work of Karen Alter, who has developed an "inter-court competition" approach to explain European legal integration. Third is the power to promote certain substantive policies through law. In other words, where European law and national law promote different policies or have different distributional effects with respect to a particular class of litigants, a national judge may have the opportunity to achieve the result that she favours through the application of European law.[15]

---

[12] Burley and Mattli, "Europe before the Court", (n. 4 above) p. 63.

[13] See Alter, Ch 8 above, "Explaining National Court Acceptance of European Court Jurisprudence: A Critical Evaluation of Theories of Legal Integration"; *idem*, "The European Court's Political Power" *West European Politics* 19/3 (July 1996), pp. 458–487.

Alec Stone also comments on the limitations of the neofunctionalist model as we originally formulated it, particularly with its inability to explain limits to integration (see Stone, "Constitutional Dialogues in the European Community", (European University Institute, Florence, working paper, 1996), p. 11).

[14] Stone, "Constitutional Dialogues in the European Community", (n. 13 abve) p. 8.

[15] Let us emphasise here that this point does not rely on a model of judges "making" the law, in the sense of simply voting their policy preferences. On the contrary, the assumption is that a national judge who conscientiously seeks to apply the law as written or interpreted will not vote her policy preferences where they appear to conflict with that law unless she can achieve the result

A noteworthy aspect of this refinement of judicial interests, or preferences, is that each factor may explain resistance to as well as acceptance of EC law. Courts that already exercise the power of judicial review, for instance, are likely to perceive the "parallel" exercise of that power by the ECJ regarding matters of European law as a threat. Alec Stone emphasises this tension in light of the particular incentives facing national constitutional courts, typically the only European courts entitled to engage in any form of judicial review.[16] Similarly, the inter-court competition model posits that courts that already enjoy substantial prestige and power relative to other courts within the same national legal system are likely to object to the extension or even transfer of that power elsewhere in the system; they may thus reject EC law for the same reasons that their counterparts accept it. Finally, the congruence of EC law with a particular set of substantive legal outcomes in different issue areas can produce opposition from national courts who favour the outcomes produced by the application of national law as easily as it can marshal support from judges who would like to see a change in national law.

The following subsections discuss each of these strands of judicial interests in turn, drawing on evidence from the country studies. The result is a more nuanced and sophisticated understanding of "judicial empowerment". Note, however, that this typology is inevitably stylized. A quest for power has both personal and professional aspects. It reflects a universal desire for individual recognition and acknowledgment by others as well as an instrumental effort to acquire the means to achieve specific goals. *Judicial* empowerment is likely also to partake of the ideals of the judiciary, closely allied with both the idea and the ideal of the rule of law. Self-images forged in this crucible include courts as protectors of the weak, as impartial dispensers of justice, as checks on the abuse of power by their fellow branches of government, and as guardians of social order through faithful application of the law as written and—occasionally—as felt.

The categories we advance here cannot capture this complexity. Our specification of both judicial interests, and, in the following section, the constraints attendant on the pursuit of those interests, are efforts to isolate specific elements of this mix as part of a more generalisable model.

Judicial preferences

Judicial review

A number of the country studies offer evidence of a link between acceptance of EC law through adoption of the doctrines of direct effect and supremacy

---

she favours by a legitimate legal route. Following European law within a framework in which a tribunal consented to by the national government has interpreted and applied it to trump national law offers such a route.

[16] Stone, "Constitutional Dialogues in the European Community", (n. 13 above) pp. 10–15.

and a desire to exercise some judicial review powers. In the Netherlands, for example, Parliament amended the Dutch Constitution in 1956 (introducing articles 65 and 66), giving national courts the power to review legislation for its compatibility with international treaties. This new power was at odds with a long tradition that banned judicial review of the constitutionality of legislation. Judges could now set aside statutes that violated international obligations, but at the same time, the inviolability of these statutes against any judicial review of their constitutionality was maintained. In the beginning the judges remained reluctant to use their new powers. Only when encouraged by the European Court of Justice did they assume their new task. Claes and de Witte note that in the landmark *Van Gend en Loos* case, the ECJ's willingness to accept the role of "accomplice" in *Van Gend* encouraged Dutch courts to exercise their constitutionally recognised powers against the national legislature.[17]

The British situation is similar to the Dutch in that the doctrine of Parliamentary sovereignty preempted any courts from attacking primary legislation. With the formal acceptance of EU supremacy in the *Factortame* case of 1990, however, national courts were granted the right to set aside primary legislation that violated Community obligations. Craig notes that "the UK jurisprudence provides a good example of how readily the national courts can embrace their new found authority".[18] Perhaps the best example, however, of the way in which a desire to exercise judicial review shaped acceptance of direct effect and supremacy comes from the Italian experience. As told by Ruggieri Laderchi, the Italian story is a drama with three principal characters: the ECJ, the Italian Constitutional Court, and the lower courts. Again aided and abetted by the ECJ, lower court judges understood that supremacy afforded them the opportunity to control Italian national legislation for consistency with Community law. The Italian Constitutional Court understood equally well that its prerogative of exclusive constitutional review was in jeopardy and sought to supervise the application of EC law in the face of contrary national legislation by the lower courts. Only in the 1980s, after it perceived that it was lagging behind the supreme courts of virtually all other Member States, did it finally accept supremacy more or less on the ECJ's terms.[19]

In France, the monopoly of interpretation of public and constitutional law belonged to the Conseil d'Etat until 1958. In that year, the power to review the constitutionality of legislation passed to the newly-established Conseil Constitutionnel. This body decided in 1975 to abstain from examining the

---

[17] Ch 6, Report on the Netherlands, p. 192, discussing *Van Gend en Loos v. Nederlandse Administratie der Belastingen*, Case 26/62 [1963] ECR 1.

[18] Ch 7, Report on the United Kingdom, p. 216.

[19] Ch 5, Report on Italy, p. 000. Alec Stone also recapitulates this story with a particularly attentive eye to the desire of the Italian Constitutional Court to preserve its prerogative of constitutional review. (See Stone, "Constitutional Dialogues in the European Community", (n. 13 above) pp. 10–11.)

conformity of international treaties with national laws. The Conseil d'Etat—a particularly elitist group of French civil servants—considered any interference by the ECJ in French domestic affairs as a direct menace to its administrative and political power and chose therefore to ignore the ECJ.[20] Not so the Cour de Cassation. It decided only four months after the Conseil Constitutionnel's refusal to review legislation on its compatibility with international treaties to accept the supremacy doctrine in the landmark *Jacques Vabre* case.[21] Up to that point, the Cour de Cassation had followed the famous "Matter" doctrine, requiring judges to avoid conflicts between domestic law and international obligations using rules of construction; but if such avoidance was impossible, judges had to enact national law for they "cannot know other will than that of the law".[22]

What motivated the Cour de Cassation to abandon the "Matter" doctrine? Plötner argues in favour of the judicial review thesis. He writes: "From now on, any simple court could not only control all acts of parliament but also became . . . the common judge of Community law".[23]

Judicial competition

Karen Alter has developed an "inter-court competition" model to explain variations in the scope and pace of national court acceptance of the doctrines of direct effect and supremacy.[24] She argues: "different courts have different interests *vis-à-vis* EC law . . . national courts use EC law in bureaucratic struggles between levels of the judiciary and between the judiciary and political bodies, thereby inadvertently facilitating the process of legal integration".[25]

[20] Plötner writes: "[To] keep . . . Community law out of the way seemed to be in the well understood interest of the Conseil d'Etat; it was . . . a question of power" and, "While for the Conseil d'Etat any change in the status quo could only mean loss of influence, things were the other way around for the Cour de Cassation. Their reaction to Direct Effect and Supremacy was a flawless application of this insight". (See Ch 2, Report on France, p. 66.)

[21] Alec Stone argues that the Cour de Cassation was not necessarily waiting for "permission" from the Conseil Constitutionnel. As he reminds us, the lower court decision that was being appealed in *Vabre*, refusing to apply French law in violation of the EC Treaty, had been decided in 1971. (See Stone, "Constitutional Dialogues in the European Community", (n. 13 above) p. 12.)

[22] Ch 2, Report on France, p. 45. Similar doctrines were in place in most other Member States of the European Union prior to their acceptance of EU supremacy. In UK jurisprudence, for example, the predominant strand before *Factortame* sought to "blunt the edge of any conflict between the two sytems by use of strong principles of construction, the import of which was that UK law would, whenever possible, be read so as to be compatible with Community law requirements . . . On this view the traditional theory of sovereignty could be maintained". See Ch 7, Report on the United Kingdom, p. 198–9. The Dutch situation is discussed in Ch 6, Report on the Netherlands, p. 171.

[23] Ch 3, Report on France, p. 63.

[24] See Alter, "The Making of a Rule of Law: The European Court and the National Judiciaries", unpublished dissertation, Department of Political Science, MIT, June 1996; and *idem*, "The European Court's Political Power (above n. 13);" and *idem*, Ch 8 above, "Explaining National Court Acceptance of European Court Jurisprudence: A Critical Evaluation of Theories of Legal Integration".

[25] Alter, Ch 8 above, p. 241.

The exercise of judicial review involves a "horizontal" competition between courts and legislatures, allowing a judge to invoke the higher law of the constitution or a treaty as a bar to enforcement of a particular legislative product. Pure inter-court competition, on the other hand, can occur both horizontally, between high courts each charged with superintending a different body of law, and "vertically", between higher and lower courts within different branches of a national court system.

The country studies contain substantial evidence for the inter-court competition model, as Alter documents.[26] The model is particularly appropriate to Germany, as benefits to lower national courts from integration are less apparent in Germany than in most other member states. The power to conduct judicial review was already present in the German legal system and cannot be seen as a new introduction of the EC legal system.[27] Vertical competition between lower and higher courts offers a better account of the incentives propelling German courts to accept direct effect and supremacy. But the model also offers a convincing framework within which to analyse variation in other Member States. Indeed, it dovetails with Alec Stone's emphasis on the competition between constitutional courts and other national courts, another important chunk of the story.

Judicial interests flowing from inter-court competition reflect interests in relative judicial power—power and prestige relative to other courts within the same national legal system. These interests may intersect interests in gaining the power of judicial review; in national legal systems in which some courts exercise judicial review while others do not, for instance, those courts lacking the power under the national system may seek to equalise their status with other national courts by arrogating the power to review national law for compatibility with EC law in partnership with the ECJ. For instance, Plötner argues that the Cour de Cassation's institutional position *vis-à-vis* the Conseil d'Etat improved greatly with its swift endorsement of EC supremacy.[28] Such competitive interests may also intersect with interests in promoting particular substantive policies, to the extent that a lower national court disagrees with a higher national court on a particular set of doctrinal outcomes and seeks to leapfrog that higher court by reference to the ECJ. It is to the interests in promoting substantive policies that we now turn.

Promotion of substantive policies

Jonathan Golub has recently demonstrated the ways in which a desire to shape specific policy outcomes may motivate national courts to limit the number of references to the ECJ. He shows that British courts have been reluctant to make references in cases in which the environmental protection require-

---

[26] *Ibid.*, p. 241.
[27] See Alter, "The Making of a Rule of Law", (above n. 24) Ch 2, pp. 16–55.
[28] Ch 2, Report on France, p. 62.

ments in EC law are less stringent than in British environmental law.[29] Golub seeks to explain patterns of references, not acceptance of the doctrines of direct effect and supremacy. But other analysts of the reception of Community law by national courts have similarly pointed to judicial policy preferences as an explanatory factor. For Stone, a court has an "interest in using its decisions to make good policy".[30] Alter notes that "lower courts can use EC law to get to policy outcomes which they prefer, either for policy or legal reasons".[31]

How are we to identify and assess judicial policy preferences? The question has long bedeviled students of judicial politics, who have been singularly unsuccessful at generating an algorithm that can help predict the political attitudes of individual judges.[32] It is much easier to demonstrate a correlation between the political posture of a particular judge and a particular set of judicial outcomes than to identify which judge will favour which policies.

This uncertainty is multiplied in the present context by the difficulty of predicting how acceptance of direct effect and supremacy will affect outcomes in individual cases. Suppose, for instance, that a British judge favours high levels of environmental protection. At a given moment, EC directives and ECJ interpretations of those directives might mandate higher levels of environmental protection than British law. Yet those directives could change, as could the composition or disposition of the ECJ. Further, the acceptance of direct effect and supremacy cannot be limited to a particular class of cases. EC law and the ECJ's interpretation of that law could contradict the same national judge's policy preferences with regard to state subsidies for particular industries, gender discrimination, immigration law, or any other substantive area.

But why cannot an individual national judge accept direct effect and supremacy and then control the actual application of EC law simply by manipulating references? Golub's findings suggest that British courts may be pursuing this strategy. However, courts' ability to pick and choose cases to refer will be progressively limited both by the pressure of individual litigants and lower courts, as well as by the overriding need for minimum consistency and coherence in the law itself. Once a court has declared that EC law is supreme over national law, litigants will cite favourable doctrines of EC law and appeal national court decisions that do not follow those doctrines where they clearly apply to the facts in a particular case. Lower courts will similarly seek clarification in cases of apparent conflict between EC and national law. And to the extent that higher national courts refuse to provide such clarification, or selectively apply EC law in individual cases, the resulting patchwork will endanger the legitimacy of the national legal system.

[29] Golub, "The Politics of Judicial Discretion: Rethinking the Interaction between National Courts and the European Court of Justice", *West European Politics* 19/2 (April 1996), pp. 360–385.
[30] Stone, "Constitutional Dialogues in the European Community", (n. 13 above) p. 26.
[31] Alter, Ch 8 above, p. 242.
[32] See Martin Shapiro, *Courts: A Comparative and Political Analysis* (University of Chicago Press: 1981), p. 29.

Such pressure from litigants and the requirements of the legal process are more properly classified as constraints, as discussed below. For purposes of analytical clarity, a judge's preferences regarding any individual case or class of cases will be a compound of views on a range of substantive issues: highly individualised preferences over specific policy outcomes combined with more general preferences concerning modes of statutory interpretation, the optimal relationship between courts and the legislature, and the need to protect specific classes of litigants. These preferences will then be tempered by a need for consistent, coherent, generalizable rules. It is important to note, however, that legal education, training, and socialization often results in the internalisation of the constraints of clarity and predictability as independent preferences. Judges will thus often refer to these attributes as goals that they seek to pursue in upholding the "rule of law".

Returning to the question of preferences concerning direct effect and supremacy, it is still possible to identify situations where accepting direct effect and supremacy may on balance advance a judge's substantive policy preferences. First, some number of national judges may simply favour European integration and would see participation in the construction of the European legal system as an important step in that direction. Secondly, a national court might have a particular "constituency", such as workers or traders, that will be systematically advantaged by EC law. Plötner appears to provide such an example, noting that the judges of the Cour de Cassation "had in mind the interests of French economic agents and citizens" in a way that the members of the Conseil d'Etat did not. These judges "realized that the impossibility of referring to certain Community regulation was bound to represent a serious economic disadvantage in comparison to their European competition and that it might also hamper the protection of civil rights".[33] Kokott's study also suggests a similar dynamic with respect to the willingness of German labour courts to make references to the ECJ on the assumption that EC law would be more "employee-friendly" than national law, although she points out that the ECJ has recently gone too far in this regard.[34]

Overall, however, such examples are few, hard to prove, and easy to challenge. Courts typically do not have readily identifiable constituencies;[35] further, it is very difficult to predict the ultimate effect of acceptance of any legal doctrine. It is far more likely that a judge's preferences for coherence, consistency, and generalisability will produce a preference for direct effect and supremacy in situations in which other national courts have already accepted

---

[33] Ch 2, Report on France, p. 61.

[34] Ch 3, Report on Germany, p. 112.

[35] It might be argued that courts regard minorities as their special concern; more generally still, that courts tend to favour "the little guy", individuals against corporatist entities, "David" against "Goliath". While it is true that the early cases in which national courts accepted direct effect and supremacy tended to involve presumptively weak individuals fighting for their rights against the state customs apparatus or some similar bureaucracy and seeking to enlist Community law on their side, such plaintiffs cannot readily be identified as part of a defined constituency.

these doctrines, creating a patchwork that can now only be remedied by universal acceptance. Plötner's discussion of the Cour de Cassation, for instance, assumes that national judges across Europe were already applying EC law. The Italian Constitutional Court explicitly noted in accepting supremacy in the 1980s that other high courts across Europe, including Germany, had already taken this step.[36] Indeed, the phenomenon of "judicial cross-fertilization" identified in many of the country studies—meaning instances in which courts of one nation refer to the decisions of another—may be understood not only as a pure intellectual exchange and as a risk minimisation strategy with respect to incurring obligations already accepted by other Member States,[37] but also as recognition of the need to harmonise European law as law.

In sum, judicial preferences over specific policy outcomes are unlikely to be sufficiently generalisable to explain initial acceptances of direct effect and supremacy, although they may nevertheless be relevant to explaining or understanding the outcome of any particular case. Preferences for consistency and coherence across a body of rules are generalisable and may provide motives for acceptance of direct effect and supremacy. But they are more likely to operate at the end rather than the beginning of the first stage of constructing an EC legal system. Kokott points to the German Labour Court's "right and obligation to ensure a coherent legal system" as the driving factor behind a new phase of references to the ECJ, which she reads as inviting the ECJ to change its case law to conform better to the realities of national labor conditions and the specific contours of national law.[38]

CONSTRAINTS ON THE PROCESS OF LEGAL INTEGRATION

In the end, even the most precise specification of the preferences of individual litigants and national courts provides an incomplete account of the legal integration process. It is simultaneously necessary to identify the constraints operating on these actors in their pursuit of their preferences. As outlined above, different courts within different national legal systems have different preferences. However, to the extent that we observe variation in the timing and scope of acceptance of EC legal doctrines by national courts that should have roughly the same preferences (two national constitutional courts, for instance) those differences are likely to flow from the relative constraints that those courts face in pursuing their preferences. We discuss these constraints as they operate on national courts in terms of a more refined conception of judicial identity.

---

[36] Ch 5, Report on Italy, p. 156.
[37] Joseph Weiler, "A Quiet Revolution: The European Court of Justice and its Interlocutors", *Comparative Political Studies* 26 (1994).
[38] Ch 3, Report on Germany, p. 113.

In our initial analysis we focused principally on one very general, albeit fundamental, aspect of judicial identity: the self-conception of courts in countries upholding the rule of law as non-political actors.[39] These courts universally conceive of themselves as agents and servants of the law, and thus as participants in a specialised normative discourse with other courts. Their receptivity to participation in a dialogue with the ECJ depends in part on their perception of it as a court like themselves, as a fellow member of "a community of law".[40] This conception of judicial identity as fundamentally non-political was crucial to our "mask of law argument". Political considerations attach to judicial decisions and may motivate these decisions at the margin. Nevertheless, overt political arguments are illegitimate; actions must be justified with reference to generalisable principles and in a technical discourse that imposes its own constraints.[41] Law thus operated as a mask to conceal the full political import of the ECJ's decisions.[42]

In this account, judicial identity helped to insulate the pursuit of judicial preferences from political interference; it thus functioned primarily to facilitate the pursuit of those preferences as protected participants in a "community of law".[43] We paid less attention to the ways in which a particular conception of judicial identity in liberal democracies committed to the rule of law can function as a constraint on the pursuit of judicial preferences. A closer examination of the constraints flowing from this conception of judicial identity reveals parameters that can vary across countries. Identification and exploration of these constraints thus provides a critical piece in an account of variation in the acceptance of the foundational doctrines of the EC legal system across national courts.

A court in a liberal democracy is charged with interpreting and applying the law without regard to the judge's own political preferences, the power and political preferences of the parties appearing before her, or the power and political preferences of any other branch of government with an interest in the case. Two principal constraints shape this process of rule interpretation and application. First is the constraint of minimum fidelity to the demands of legal discourse: "the language of reasoned interpretation, logical deduction,

---

[39] Burley and Mattli, "Europe Before the Court", (n. 4 above) pp. 74–5.

[40] We did not use this term in our original article, but Slaughter has subsequently used it to describe the type of relationships between courts that we described through the neofunctionalist lens. See Anne-Marie Slaughter, "A Typology of Transjudicial Communication", *University of Richmond Law Review* 29 (1994), 99–137, at 133.

[41] This point remains valid with regard to the way in which national courts can exercise their policy preferences through the choice of either EC or national law. To say that judges can use EC law to advance their individual policy preferences is not to say that they do not remain constrained by the demands of legal reasoning in either case.

[42] It was this insight that led us to conclude that "sophisticated legalists", such as Joseph Weiler, who offered an account of the evolution of legal doctrine "in political context", ultimately provided the best account (see Burley and Mattli, "Europe Before the Court", (n. 4 above) pp. 75–6.)

[43] *Ibid.*, p. 70.

systemic and temporal coherence . . . ".[44] Reasoning and results that do not meet these requirements may be challenged as "unfounded in law", or as indicative that a court is acting *ultra vires*—in excess of its mandate.

Second is a constraint of minimum democratic accountability: the requirement that a court not stray too far from majority political preferences.[45] At first glance, this constraint may seem completely at variance with the conception of courts as non-political actors. By definition, surely, courts are *not* accountable to voter preferences. A closer look, however, reveals that although judges are not and cannot be directly accountable to the voters, and indeed are specifically safeguarded by guarantees of life tenure and prohibitions on judicial salary reduction from feeling the full effects of electoral disagreement with their decisions, judicial decisions that consistently and sharply contradict majority policy preferences are likely to undermine perceptions of judicial legitimacy and can result in legislative efforts to restrict or even curtail judicial jurisdiction—the scope of judicial power over particular classes of cases.[46] An astute judge will anticipate these reactions and seek to avoid them.

Yet if a court is constrained by the demands of legal reasoning and discourse, how can it "choose" to decide more or less in line with majority preferences? In many cases the choice will be clear: the weight of text and precedent, the elemental requirements of precision, clarity, and determinacy in rule interpretation and application, or the potentially disastrous social, political, or economic consequences attendant on one of the proffered readings of a textual provision as compared to another, leave little room for doubt as to the correct "legal" outcome. In such cases, should the judicial outcome diverge from majority preferences, then it is up to the legislature to change the law. In other cases, however, the sides are much more evenly matched. The text may be genuinely ambiguous, legislative intent murky, the option of a clear and determinate rule equally available on both sides, equal prospects for creating a cascade of evils or a cornucopia of benefits however the court comes out. In these cases—hard cases, close cases, frequently very important cases—judicial outcomes that consistently or persistently stray too far from perceived majority opinion in a particular country, whether expressed through the legislature or not, are likely to trigger suspicions that judges are substituting their own policy preferences for those of "the people".

Both these constraints—the demands of legal discourse and democratic

---

[44] Joseph Weiler, "*A Quiet Revolution*", (n. 37 above) p. 521.

[45] This constraint will not operate in cases involving the protection of minority rights where the national constitution explicitly enjoins courts to protect minorities from majority decisions infringing on their fundamental rights.

[46] Consider the proposals floated at Maastricht and by some parties prior to the 1996 IGCC to curtail the jurisdiction of the ECJ. See Alter, "The Making of a Rule of Law", (above n. 24) Ch 6, pp. 282–5; Kevin Brown, "Government to Demand Curb on European Court", *Financial Times*, 2 February 1995 at p. 10; Anthony Arnull, "Judging the New Europe", *European Law Review* 19 (February 1994), p. 13.

accountability—are likely to vary from country to country. The sources of this variation are three:

(1)   variation in national policy preferences concerning the desirability of European integration;
(2)   variation in "national legal culture"; and
(3)   variation in specific national legal doctrines.

In the first category, a national court that readily accepts direct effect and supremacy will face less of a challenge to its legitimacy in a polity where public support for European integration is generally strong than in one with a split in public attitudes. In the second category, the demands of legal discourse will vary depending on the nature and strength of the links between the legislature and the judiciary and different styles of legal reasoning. Some national legal cultures prove more hospitable to national judicial participation in the EC legal system than others. In the third category, doctrines governing the relationship between national and international law, the specific function of particular national courts, and the definition and operationalisation of national sovereignty pose particular obstacles within national legal discourse and may themselves reflect majority preferences. The remainder of this section explores the ways in which factors in each of these categories produced variations in the constraints facing different national courts.

National policy preferences

As discussed above, the case studies show that the rate of acceptance of supremacy doctrine in particular, and to a lesser extent direct effect, generally track national attitudes toward European integration. Figure 1 shows that the first countries to accept the doctrines of direct effect and supremacy were the Netherlands, Germany, and Belgium, followed by Italy, France, and Great Britain, in that order.[47] No surprises here; an observer ignorant of EC law and national legal doctrine but knowledgeable about relative political support for the EC in these various countries is likely to have predicted a similar sequence. It is possible, of course, that national judges simply shared the prevailing attitudes toward European integration held by their fellow citizens and interpreted the law accordingly. We cannot know without interviewing individual judges, who would in any event be reluctant to confirm such speculation. However, such evidence is unnecessary insofar as the democratic account-

---

[47]   It should be noted that direct effect and supremacy were accepted at different times by each country, with often an appreciable lag concerning acceptance of supremacy. The Netherlands quickly accepted both doctrines in 1963/64; Germany accepted direct effect in 1963 and partial supremacy in 1971, with subsequent modifications; Belgium accepted direct effect in 1963 and supremacy in 1971; Italy accepted direct effect in 1974 and supremacy unreservedly in 1984; the highest French private law court (Court de Cassation) accepted direct effect and supremacy in 1975, although the highest administrative court (Conseil d'Etat) held out until 1990; Great Britain accepted direct effect in 1973, upon its accession to the Community, but did not accept supremacy until 1990. This account omits other variations among different courts within these various national systems.

ability thesis would lead to the same result. Based on our assumption that national judges across countries shared uniform preferences concerning the advantages and disadvantages of entering into a partnership with the ECJ, the pursuit of these preferences would be constrained by the need not to allow their decisions to diverge too far from majority political preferences.

Behind the aggregate statistics presented in Figure 1 are a number of stories linking judicial outcomes with national policy preferences concerning European integration, policy preferences that are themselves derived from a composite of historical, geographical, and political factors. Hervé Bribosia, author of the Belgian case study, notes that Belgium's size and export-dependent economy produce favourable national attitudes toward European integration, a factor that he adduces as a partial explanation for the willingness of the Belgian Cour de Cassation (the highest private law court) to take a high profile stance accepting supremacy in 1971.[48] Monica Claes and Bruno De Witte, writing on the Netherlands, are even more explicit. They trace Dutch support for the direct enforcement and application of international treaties back to Hugo Grotius's magisterial seventeenth-century treatise on the freedom of the seas, locating these attitudes in small size and dependence on open borders for economic prosperity: "[T]he willingness to cooperate with foreign nations is clearly in the interest of a small trading nation that is too small to preserve its dependence on its own and needs open borders for its prosperity".[49] It is no coincidence that ten out of the first thirteen references to the European Court of Justice came from Dutch Courts.

On the other side of the ledger, Paul Craig observes that the reluctance of British courts to accept supremacy was but "one part of [Britain's] more general approach toward the EC".[50] However, he argues further that the view of Britain as consistently seeking to slow the pace of integration is distorted, that the majority of the British population accept EC membership as the political norm, and thus that the House of Lords simply sought "to bring constitutional doctrine up to date with political reality" when it finally accepted supremacy in 1990.[51]

If judges are constrained by majority preferences, however, how then is the construction of the European legal system even a puzzle? What of our story that the system was built by the ECJ and national judges, lawyers, and litigants against the wishes, or at least behind the backs of, Member State Governments? Are we not now advancing a version of Garrett's claim that the ECJ was able to do its job because both its substantive decisions and the legal apparatus it created to enforce them advanced the interests of the states that created it? The answer, of course, is no. But to advance our argument at this

---

[48] Ch 1, Report on Belgium, p. 32.
[49] Ch 6, Report on the Netherlands, p. 189. See also J. J. C. Voorhoeve, *Peace, Profits and Principles: A Study of Dutch Foreign Policy* (Boston: Nijhoff, 1979).
[50] Ch 7, Report on the United Kingdom, p. 209.
[51] *Ibid.*, p. 211.

level we must move beyond a unitary conception of the state. Our argument, in essence, pits courts and national executives against each other not in deciding whether to support further European integration (a decision ultimately up to the electorate) but in determining the balance of power among governmental institutions in an integrated Europe.

If we assume that the Member States of the European Union are arrayed along a spectrum in terms of favourable attitudes toward integration, attitudes broadly determined by the electorate as a reflection of economic interest, historical experience, and geopolitical position, we can nevertheless imagine alternative architectures for an integrated Europe that would be relatively more or less favourable to the interests of national executives, legislatures, and courts. For instance, a Union that required provisions of the EC Treaty to be implemented by decisions of the Council of Ministers, which in turn imposed obligations on national executives and legislatures to pass directives implementing these decisions at the national level, affords much more power to national executives than a structure in which Treaty provisions can be directly implemented through national courts. There is thus no contradiction between our original (and continuing) assertion that national courts did not follow the preferences of national executives in accepting direct effect and supremacy and our recognition that *both* national courts and national executives are more or less constrained by majority preferences concerning European integration.

The country studies provide considerable evidence for both these propositions. Relative to one another, national courts in all countries accepted direct effect and supremacy in keeping with the general attitudes of the electorate toward European integration: the Dutch first, the British last. At the same time, the Dutch Supreme Court accepted both these doctrines within a year after the Dutch executive argued fervently against the interpretation of the EC Treaty that gave rise to them in the landmark case of *Van Gend en Loos*.[52] In France the highest private court accepted direct effect and supremacy fifteen years before the highest administrative court, the Conseil d'Etat, which plays the dual role of adviser to the executive and most closely identifies with what it perceives to be the executive's interests. In Germany the executive unsuccessfully sought to intervene in the judicial process on the side of the highest financial court against a decision of a lower financial court mandating compliance with an ECJ judgment on the basis of supremacy.[53] The stakes in these cases concerned less the desirability of European integration *per se* than a struggle over which domestic branch of government would control decisions over the pace, scope, and manner of integration within the broad outlines of the Treaty.

This inter-branch struggle, however, does not always cut in favour of increased integration. A case in point is the relationship between the German

---

[52] *N.V. Algemene Transport & Expeditie Onderneming Van Gend en Loos* v. *Nederlandse Administratie der Belastingen*, Case 26/62, [1963] ECR 1.

[53] See Alter, "The European Court's Political Power" (above n. 13).

constitutional court, the German government, and the ECJ. Like the German Government, which has long perceived itself as a "motor of integration", the German Constitutional Court has sought to develop a special relationship with the ECJ, generally supporting the creation of the EC legal system but periodically applying the brakes by insisting that the ECJ develop Community-wide protections for human rights or, more recently, insisting on delimiting a core area of national sovereignty. The German court's contributions to this dialogue reflect *its* assessment of a number of different factors: the requirements of domestic constitutional law, the proper interpretation of the EC Treaty, and the mood of the people, among others. This assessment may overlap with the German Government's position, but may also diverge in ways that can bring the legal and the political branches into conflict. Thus, regarding its recent *Maastricht* decision, in which a German legislator challenged the Maastricht Treaty as a violation of the German Constitution, the Federal Constitutional Court essentially found for the Government by upholding the constitutionality of the Treaty. However, as Juliane Kokott explains: "[T]he Court tried . . . to assure itself of wide support for its judgment" by taking account of rising opposition to monetary integration among the German people in emphasizing the many strict preconditions for monetary union embedded in the Treaty, preserving the right of withdrawal from the monetary union should it prove to be unstable, and upholding the right of the German people to be represented by the German Parliament rather than the European parliament.[54]

These constraints may prove tighter than Kohl and his successors would like in pushing for monetary union as the bargaining chip with which to achieve widening of the Community. More generally, however, the Federal Constitutional Court has created a legal situation that will allow and may even spur Germany's negotiating partners to customise their acceptance of Community law. The Court emphasised that the Member States remained "masters of the treaties", thereby denying Community institutions complete supra-national authority. In the legal sphere, the Court translated this principle into a claim that it retained the power to determine the scope of Community competence. The ECJ would remain supreme with regard to the interpretation and application of Community law, but the Federal Constitutional Court would determine the scope of that law. Should the supreme courts of other EC members follow suit, the uniform administration of EC law, and the bargaining that now depends on the assumption that the deals struck will be uniformly enforced, could be imperiled.

National legal culture

Judges are products of specific national legal systems. Their training within particular systems gives rise to a set of professional values attitudes that overlay, mediate, and temper their political instincts. They not only learn a body

---

[54] Ch 3, Report on Germany, p. 110.

of national legal rules, but also absorb specific features of their national legal culture. At the core of this culture are particular modes of legal reasoning—formal versus pragmatic, deductive versus inductive, abstract versus contextual—that give rise to a distinctive style of framing and resolving legal questions. Other features of national legal culture include a particular understanding of the role of courts in relation to legislative bodies, differing specifically on the extent to which judges "make" law in the process of interpretation and application of legislative provisions and the extent to which they can fill the gaps in those provisions.

Even wider is the gap between common law judges, who elaborate rules without legislative guidance based on the doctrine of precedent, and civil law judges, whose only source of authority flows from national legal codes. Yet both systems contain room for yet a third feature of national legal culture: relative judicial activism or restraint. How far should a judge depart from a previous decision, or from the strict letter of a particular statute? Individual judges within a particular national legal system can differ on this question, of course, but an entire national legal culture—due largely to the influence of national history and tradition—can lean in one direction or the other. Finally, national legal culture may reflect national legal structure: different types of federalism, as in Belgium or Germany, or systems divided into substantively specialised courts (labour courts, tax courts, constitutional courts) in which each court develops its own tradition of protecting a specific set of interests.

These features of national legal culture ultimately condition the relationship between national courts and a supra-national tribunal. The development of "a community of law", requires that the participants recognise one another as equivalent legal actors speaking a common language and sharing a common legitimacy. Nevertheless, the forging of such a relationship between specific national courts and the ECJ depended on a number of preconditions. Judicial preferences, constrained by national political attitudes toward integration, created a predisposition; ECJ decisions provided the opportunity by creating the doctrinal "hook". But an additional factor constraining or facilitating the establishment of this relationship—particularly the acceptance of the legal hierarchy between the ECJ and national courts created by the doctrine of supremacy—was the relative "fit" between the two legal systems, a fit optimised by traits of national legal culture.

A core element of national legal culture is the delimitation of the scope of judicial relative to legislative power. All the members of the EU uphold the general liberal principle of a division between the legislative and the judicial power; however, its implementation in each country is historically and culturally conditioned. A principal indicator of this distribution of power is recognition of the principle of judicial review, even if it is exercised only by constitutional courts. The existence of judicial review anywhere in the national legal system embodies recognition of a higher law constraining the will of the people as expressed through the legislature. On this dimension, it is not surprising that German and Italian courts, from national legal systems that have judicial review, were quicker to recognize supremacy than French and British courts, which have traditionally been wholly deferential to the national legislature.[55] On the other hand, countries that do not have judicial review, such as the Netherlands, can nevertheless recognise supremacy as the result of the will of the legislature expressed either in the Constitution or the Treaty itself. This is the route that was ultimately taken by both British and French courts.[56]

Legal culture is also conditioned by the specific historic role of courts within a particular society. Here German and Italian courts face specific constraints that other courts do not. The constitutional courts in both countries are specifically charged with safeguarding individual rights and the rule of law against the revival of fascism. In the German case, the commitment to *Verfassungspatriotismus*, or constitutional patriotism, results in the Constitutional Court's unusual willingness to decide cases with important foreign policy implications. According to Juliane Kokott, this willingness flows from the renewed German commitment to the *Rechtstaat* in the wake of the Second World War—no questions are above or beyond the law. The Constitutional Court thus conceives itself as an equal participant with the political branches of the German Government in the process of European integration.[57] At the same time, however, the Court's primary commitment to individual rights and the preservation of German democracy has led it to apply the brakes to that process in ways that may well constrain the German Government's pursuit of its perception of the national interest.[58]

A third element of national legal culture concerns style of legal reasoning. Writing about Britain, Paul Craig notes that the "common law mode of adjudication is *pragmatic* and *non-doctrinaire*".[59] He argues that these characteristics allowed British courts early on to "acknowledge . . . that they were part of a Community legal order, and that the ECJ was the proper court to pass judgment on issues concerning the interpretation of the EC Treaty".[60] This acceptance included the doctrine of direct effect. At the same time, however, he asserts that the common law method helps explain why British courts had difficulty with the doctrine of indirect effect, which required them to read national legislation to be in conformity with an EC directive even when the national legislature has not implemented the directive directly. The trick is to perform this feat of construction without actually rewriting the statute, often a difficult task. The common law requirement, unlike in civil law countries,

---

[55] See Ch 2, Report on France, p. 42.
[56] See Bruno De Witte, "The European Court and National Courts—The Role of the Principle of Sovereignty", (unpublished manuscript, March 1995).
[57] Ch 3, Report on Germany, p. 92.
[58] *Ibid.*, p. 112.
[59] Ch 7, Report on the United Kingdom, p. 218.
[60] *Ibid.* 218.

that courts write lengthy opinions explaining their reasoning to reach a particular result tends to highlight this tension in ways that lead British courts to stop short of the result desired by the ECJ.[61]

National legal doctrine

In the most general sense, to say that national judges are constrained by national legal doctrine is to say that courts are constrained by the shape and specific form of national law. Legal doctrines frame particular issues: for an American judge a question concerning abortion must be understood in terms a right of privacy or perhaps of a question of equal protection of the laws; for a German judge it must be analysed in terms of specified textual rights to life and to human dignity.[62] They also provide the baselines against which the legitimacy of a particular judicial decision can be measured, in terms of linguistic, logical, and teleological consistency with stated principles or precedents. Specific doctrines can thus provide either obstacles or channels to achieving particular results, particularly when a national court faces the task of harmonising a new set of doctrines laid down by another court outside the national legal system with long-standing national doctrinal traditions and formulations. The resulting constraints, where they exist, are likely to act more as temporary checks than absolute bars, as courts identify various incremental strategies to mesh apparently conflicting principles or to graft new doctrinal formulations onto old.

To some extent, particular national legal doctrines simply reflect and codify aspects of national history and culture that define the role of courts within a particular national legal system. The best example in this category is the "eternal guarantee clause" (*Ewigkeitsklausel*) in the German Constitution, which prohibits amendment of the constitution to abridge fundamental individual rights.[63] The German Constitutional Court thus had strong textual support for its claim that the Maastricht Treaty could only be consistent with the German Constitution to the extent that it did not abridge the fundamental rights of German citizens.[64]

A less obvious way in which national legal doctrine can shape judicial identity in ways that can constrain national courts in accepting direct effect and supremacy concerns the distinction between "monism" and "dualism": between a conception of the national legal order existing as an integrated part of the international legal order and a conception of two distinct legal orders

---

[61] Ch 7, Report on the United Kingdom, p. 219.

[62] See David Currie, *The Constitution of the Federal Republic of Germany* (Chicago: The University of Chicago Press, 1994), pp. 310–14.

[63] Ch 3, Report on Germany, p. 116.

[64] The controversy, of course, concerned its definition of those basic rights. It interpreted the right to vote, guaranteed in article 38 of the German constitution, as entitling German citizens to an undiluted voice in the German Parliament. It thus blocked further transfer of law-making power to the European Parliament in the absence of the development of a genuine German "people".

in which rules from the one must be "translated" into the other through specified processes to have any legal effect. The Netherlands has the strongest
tradition of monism, leading the Dutch Supreme Court to declare in 1906 that
treaties were directly applicable in Dutch law without "transformation" or
transposition into national statutes by the Dutch parliament.[65] This tradition
made it particularly easy for Dutch courts to accept direct effect of EC law in
the wake of *Van Gend en Loos*. Italy, on the other hand, has a centuries-old
dualist tradition, referred to in Italian law as the "plurality of legal orders".[66]
After the Second World War, this tradition became linked with the primacy
of the Italian constitution.[67] The Italian case study documents the ways in
which the dualist approach hampered acceptance of EC law supremacy by the
Italian Constitutional Court for decades.[68]

A final example of the interrelationship between specific national legal doctrines and judicial perceptions of their ability to act as autonomous actors
concerns different national conceptions of "sovereignty". Bruno de Witte documents the role of the "principle of sovereignty" in all the countries under
consideration as a principle "known to all the legal systems under review" and
that "can be considered part of the common traditions of European constitutional law".[69] Nevertheless, its different treatment within these national legal
systems strongly affected relative receptivity to acceptance of direct effect and
supremacy, as well as, more recently, acceptance of the Maastricht Treaty.

In France, Belgium, and the Netherlands, constitutional provisions and doctrinal traditions recognising the primacy of international treaty law (another
facet of a monist tradition) has meant that the absolute supremacy of EC law
could be accepted as international law without a perceived infringement of
national sovereignty. In Germany and Italy, by contrast, international treaties
are regarded as comprising part of a separate legal order, which cannot alter
fundamental aspects of the national legal order. In both these countries
supremacy was ultimately accepted on the basis of a specific constitutional
provision authorising membership in the Community. The difficulty is that the
constitutional courts in both countries interpret these specific constitutional
provisions as containing their own implied limits embedded elsewhere in the
national constitution, limits that can be asserted as necessary *against*
European Community law. The result is ultimately a *conditional* acceptance
of supremacy, reserving a core of absolute power for the national courts contrary to the doctrine of the ECJ itself.[70] The German Constitutional Court
reasserted this power in its *Maastricht* decision, in ways that will shape the
next stage of development of the EC legal system.

---

[65] Ch 6, Report on the Netherlands, p. 172.
[66] Ch 5, Report on Italy, p. 154.
[67] *Ibid.*, p. 155.
[68] *Ibid.*, see also De Witte, "The Role of the Principle of Sovereignty", (n. 56 above) p. 15.
[69] De Witte, "The Role of the Principle of Sovereignty", (n. 56 above) p. 1.

CONCLUSION

The explosion of literature on the ECJ has provided important new data and analytical insights in the context of a flourishing theoretical debate. The neo-functionalist model continues to provide a remarkably accurate account of the process of legal integration, with its emphasis on a community of sub- and supra-national actors pursuing their self-interest in a nominally apolitical context. However, the model must be refined and coupled with more precise specifications of the interests driving participants in the process and the constraints they face in pursuing those interests. These participants include both state and social actors as well as the ECJ. This chapter has sought to draw on the new literature to specify those interests and constraints, taking a preliminary look at the types of litigants most likely to use the ECJ and parsing the motives of national courts in accepting or rejecting the doctrines of direct effect and supremacy.

In addition, a genuine theory of legal integration must move beyond the assumption of a unitary state, taking account of differences between different levels of courts as well as between courts and other state institutions. Courts are not just the relevant "face of the state" for purposes of legal integration; they are quasi-autonomous actors in the wider integration process. A full explanation of this process thus requires combining the neofunctionalist framework with a model of the disaggregated state.

The result moves away from neofunctionalism *per se*; it may be time to leave such labels behind. The rich empirical data presented in this volume challenges scholars to forsake contending paradigms and to concentrate on developing more specific hypotheses that can account for variation in the legal integration process across countries and among courts within a particular national legal system. The precondition for such hypotheses, however, is a more precise specification of the incentives and constraints facing all the different actors in the process: individuals, supra-national institutions, and the contending branches of domestic governments. Further, the findings in this volume must be combined with findings concerning the variation of such incentives and constraints in different issue areas, such as labour law, competition law, and environmental law.[71] The result will not be a comprehensive single theory of legal integration, but a better understanding of the richness and complexity of the ECJ's achievement.

[70] De Witte, "The Role of the Principle of Sovereignty", (n. 56 above) p. 18.

[71] The European University Institute is currently sponsoring a series of papers by a multinational team of researchers on the relationship between national courts and the ECJ in the field of labour law. Preliminary papers on the impact of EU rules and ECJ decisions interpreting those rules on British and German national law have already generated very interesting findings about the motives of national courts, the significance of a pre-existing body of national law directly conflicting with EU law, and specific litigation strategies of state and private parties opposed to EU law. This project is being led by Professor Silvana Sciarra.

10

Sovereignty and European Integration: the Weight of Legal Tradition

BRUNO DE WITTE

INTRODUCTION: THE MEANINGS OF SOVEREIGNTY

The relation between European legal integration and the fundamental principles and values of the constitutions of the Member States is far from settled. This question, which was neglected for some time, has resurfaced strongly in recent years, due in particular to the vicissitudes of the national ratification procedures of the Treaty on European Union.[1] This new stage of the integration process has been, for all the Member States, the most obvious and immediate challenge to the constitutional *status quo*. Questions have been raised such as whether EC law should have primacy over national constitutional law, whether the European Court of Justice or national supreme courts should have final authority over the limits of EC competence, and whether there are constitutional limits to further moves of European integration beyond "Maastricht".

This article will examine, from a comparative perspective, one concept which is at the heart of this debate but whose role has hitherto been insufficiently acknowledged in legal writing on Community law, namely the concept or principle of *sovereignty*.[2] The concept of sovereignty is a product of the legal imagination and, beyond that, of a political ideology emerging in a particular territorial and historical context. That context is sometimes described as the "Westphalian model" which is marked by the coexistence of independent nation states. "Independence", wrote Dionisio Anzilotti, "is really no more than the normal condition of States according to international law; it

---

[1] The constitutional reforms and judicial rulings caused by the Maastricht Treaty in the single countries of the European Union have received ample attention in the journals of European and constitutional law. Two monographs may be specially mentioned here; although they primarily examine the constitutional position in the author's own country, they also offer a very valuable *comparative* analysis of the relation between Community law and national constitutional law: P. Pérez Tremps, *Constitución española y Comunidad Europea* (Civitas, 1994); Th. de Berranger, *Constitutions nationales et construction communautaire* (LGDJ, 1995).

[2] The term "concept" will be used when dealing with sovereignty as a legal philosophical construct, and the term "principle" when dealing with sovereignty as an element of positive constitutional law.

may also be described as sovereignty (*suprema potestas*) or external sovereignty, by which is meant that the State has over it no other authority than that of international law".[3] A pragmatic view was taken by the Permanent Court of International Justice in the case of the steamship *Wimbledon* in what has become the *locus classicus* of the modern international law doctrine of sovereignty:

> "The Court declines to see in the conclusion of any Treaty by which a State undertakes to perform or refrain from performing a particular act an abandonment of its sovereignty. No doubt any convention creating an obligation of this kind places a restriction upon the exercise of the sovereign rights of the State, in the sense that it requires to be exercised in a certain way. But the right of entering into international engagements is an attribute of State sovereignty".[4]

On this flexible view of sovereignty, which is far removed from an absolute concept of sovereignty allowing states to act as they please, the decision of a state to adhere to an international organisation is also an attribute of state sovereignty, even though that organisation might possess the power to adopt rules which are binding for the Member States. Thus, the United Nations Charter certainly gives far-reaching powers to the institutions of the UN (particularly to the Security Council) and yet, the Charter purports to be based on the *sovereign equality* of states.[5]

There is no reason, at first sight, why the European Community would be different from other international organisations in this respect. It is also based on the conclusion of treaties by states that did not abandon their sovereignty but freely accepted a restriction on the exercise of sovereignty. Yet, because the European Community treaties impose more far-reaching restrictions on states than any other international convention, they have revealed the deep constitutional problems laying beneath the deceptively smooth sovereignty formulas used in the practice of international law.

Indeed, the "external" sovereignty of states, as Anzilotti calls it, together with many other writers, is the reflection of a more deeply-rooted ideological construct: that of *internal sovereignty*. This is a central element of the constitutional doctrine of most, if not all, European states which could loosely be defined as the *ultimate source of legal authority within a state*.[6] "External" and "internal" sovereignty may be distinguished for the sake of clarity, but they

---

[3] Individual Opinion in the *Austro-German Customs Regime* case, PCIJ Ser. A/B no. 41 (1931), 57.

[4] Case of the *S.S. Wimbledon*, PCIJ Ser. A no. 1 (1923) 25.

[5] For a lucid treatment of the historical development and present meaning of sovereignty in international law, see L. Wildhaber, "Sovereignty and International Law" in R. St.J. Macdonald and D. M. Johnston (eds), *The Structure and Process of International Law* (Nijhoff, 1983) 425.

[6] This is a *loose* definition because it does not claim to possess validity as a matter of positive constitutional law of any particular state. In fact, constitutions do not always define what they mean by sovereignty, and courts and political institutions often use the term without defining its precise meaning.

are two dimensions of one and the same concept. This Janus-like character of sovereignty has been there from the beginning. The first developed theory of sovereignty, offered by Jean Bodin,[7] provided philosophical ammunition to the affirmation of the authority of the French kings both *internally* (against the feudal nobles) and *externally* (against the "supra-national" pretensions of papacy and empire). Today, one can say that external sovereignty is but a reflection or "logical consequence"[8] of internal sovereignty. Because "internal" sovereignty is seen to belong to a particular institution (the King, or the Parliament) or a specific collectivity (the people or the nation) within the framework of a particular state, that state as a whole partakes of this ultimate authority in its relation with the outside world. The holder of internal sovereignty is also the holder of external sovereignty; but, through the legal fictions employed by international law, external sovereignty is attributed to the state as a whole without addressing the question which institution or collectivity, within the state, is the ultimate bearer of authority.

That question used to be very controversial in earlier centuries. At the time of Bodin and Hobbes, sovereignty was held by the person of the monarch, and the term "sovereignty" is particularly well fitted for attribution to a single person. Since then, in the constitutional thinking of every European state, the ultimate authority has been withdrawn from the person of the Head of State but the concept of sovereignty has been preserved. The original conception was transformed in a different way in Britain and on the European continent. In the British tradition, sovereignty is located in an *institution*: first the "King in Parliament" and then, after a long struggle for supremacy during the seventeenth century, the Parliament alone took over the former supremacy of the monarch;[9] the concept of popular sovereignty never secured acceptance in mainstream constitutional doctrine.

On the other hand, *popular sovereignty* became the dominant model in all continental European countries, under the influence of the American and French Revolutions of the late eighteenth century. In seeking an ideological basis for their opposition to the colonial power, the North American revolutionaries were led to reject the sovereignty of the (British) Parliament, and adopted instead the doctrine of the sovereignty of the people.[10] The French

---

[7] The first genuine theory of *souveraineté* (as opposed to the mere use of the term) is commonly attributed to Bodin in his *Six livres de la République* (1576). The term, with the meaning attributed to it by Bodin, spread with striking rapidity to other European languages.

[8] A. Bleckmann, "Article 2(1)" in B. Simma (ed.), *The Charter of the United Nations. A Commentary* (Oxford UP, 1994) p. 77, at p. 79.

[9] Wade and Bradley, *Constitutional and Administrative Law*, 11th edn (Longman, 1993), p. 65 *et seq.*

[10] That doctrine had, in turn, its philosophical roots in English political philosophy of the seventeenth and eighteenth century (see E. S. Morgan, *Inventing the People—The Rise of Popular Sovereignty in England and America* (W. W. Norton & Company, 1989)). Therefore, one might say with some exaggeration that the doctrine of popular sovereignty became dominant in all Western countries except the one in which it was born.

Revolution hesitated between *national* and *popular* sovereignty,[11] but the ideological opposition between those two concepts faded with the introduction of universal suffrage and today article 3 of the French Constitution operates a delicate synthesis between both views by stating: "*La souveraineté nationale appartient au peuple*".[12] The French and North-American model spread throughout the European continent in the course of the nineteenth and twentieth centuries.[13] Today, the sovereignty of the people is affirmed, explicitly or in circumlocutions, by the Constitutions of most Member States of the European Union, often in one of their very first articles.[14] In addition, many of their Preambles solemnly state (following the model of the famous American "We the People" formula) that the Constitution as a whole emanates from the people, whose constituent power and ultimate authority is thus affirmed.[15] The principle of popular sovereignty is the apex of the constitutional systems of most European states;[16] it acts, to borrow the language of H. L. A. Hart, as the *rule of recognition* within those legal orders.[17]

Popular sovereignty is thus firmly entrenched in constitutional law, but it is also (according to many political and legal commentators) utterly empty. It seems to offer little or no value for explaining the effective functioning of today's constitutional systems. In the countries of continental Europe, the "people" may well formally hold the ultimate authority in the state but it is barred from the immediate exercise of state power. Although both the French and German Constitutions (to mention only those two) state that the people can exercise its sovereignty by voting for Parliament and by a direct expression of their will, the French constitutional system offers only some very constrained opportunities for the citizens to express their will directly by referendum, and the German Basic Law none at all. Switzerland remains,

---

[11] On the debate between the supporters of national sovereignty and those of popular sovereignty, during the French Revolution, see K. M. Baker, "Souveraineté", in F. Furet and M. Ozouf (eds), *Dictionnaire critique de la révolution française—Idées* (Flammarion, 1992) p. 483, at 492 *et seq*. On the later evolution of the debate, see G. Bacot, *Carré de Malberg et l'origine de la distinction entre souveraineté du peuple et souveraineté nationale* (CNRS, 1985).

[12] The term *national sovereignty* continues to be frequently used in a different sense, namely as an equivalent for *state sovereignty*, that is, the external face of sovereignty which appears in the language of international law and international relations.

[13] See the comparative survey by C. Grewe and H. Ruiz Fabri, *Droits constitutionnels européens* (Presses Universitaires de France, 1995), p. 207 *et seq*.

[14] The term "sovereignty" is used expressly by the Constitutions of Spain (art. 1), Italy (art. 1), Portugal (art. 3), Luxembourg (art. 32) and France (art. 3 of the Constitution, but see also article 3 of the Déclaration des Droits de l'Homme which is part of positive constitutional law). Circumlocutions of the type "all power emanates from the people" are used in the Constitutions of Belgium (art. 25), Germany (art. 20.2), Greece (art. 1) and Ireland (art. 6).

[15] See the comparative analysis of texts proposed by P. Häberle, "Die verfassunggebende Gewalt des Volkes im Verfassungsstaat—eine vergleichende Textstufenanalyse", *Archiv des öffentlichen Rechts* (1987) 54.

[16] Among the 12 "old" Member States of the EU, and setting apart the United Kingdom, there are two Constitutions from which the concept of popular sovereignty is absent: those of Denmark and the Netherlands.

[17] H. L. A. Hart, *The Concept of Law*, 2nd edn (Clarendon Press, 1994), pp. 100–10.

perhaps, as the sole European country where popular sovereignty takes the shape of a direct right for the electorate to abrogate legislation and to enact or reject constitutional amendments.[18]

While popular sovereignty may seem little more than a legal fiction from the point of view of the *internal functioning* of constitutional systems, it continues to have important legal consequences in *international constitutional law*, that is, that part of constitutional law which deals with the external relations of the state and the domestic effect of international law. The fiction of popular sovereignty can easily accommodate the fact that all state power is exercised by political institutions that act in the name of the people and are accountable to the electorate (directly or through the intermediary of an elected Parliament), but it can less easily accommodate the exercise of power by *international* institutions that do not act in the name of the people of a single nation and are not, or only very remotely, accountable. This is the reason why the European Community cannot easily be integrated within the traditional account of popular sovereignty. This also explains why the principle of sovereignty may be used, and is being used by several constitutional courts, as an *instrument for regulating the pace of European legal integration*, for drawing the border between acceptable and impalatable advances of European law.

This chapter will examine the role played by the concept of sovereignty in building the relationship between the Community legal order and the legal order of its Member States. The concept of sovereignty had to be adapted in order to allow the states to set up or join the European Communities, but that concept has continued to hamper the full reception of Community law within the domestic legal orders of its Member States. Although a "peaceful coexistence" between state sovereignty and European integration was gradually developed in the course of the years, thanks mainly to the creative efforts of European and national courts, the new stage of European integration reached with the adoption of the Treaty on European Union upset this careful balance and led to a new doctrinal conflict in the 1990s, which has not been adequately settled yet, between sovereignty and European integration.

SOVEREIGNTY AND THE DEMANDS OF COMMUNITY LAW:
THE DEVELOPMENT OF "PEACEFUL COEXISTENCE" (1945–1990)

Limitation of sovereignty as the constitutional basis of EC membership

When, after 1945, it was agreed to create European and universal organisations with effective powers for the preservation of international peace and security, the attribution of such powers was seen to depart from the existing

---

[18] For a short analysis of the instruments of direct democracy in Switzerland, as compared to other European states, see C. Grewe and H. Ruiz Fabri, *Droits constitutionnels européens*, at 254.

constitutional division of powers (which was a division of powers between *national* institutions) and, therefore, to require a specific constitutional arrangement allowing for such a derogation for the purpose of international co-operation.

The constitutional connection between the (old) principle of popular sovereignty and the (new) attribution of powers to international organisations is most clearly illustrated by the Belgian Constitution. Its article 25 (now renumbered as article 33) enunciated, since 1831, the principle of sovereignty in the following terms: "All powers proceed from the Nation. They are exercised in the manner laid down by the Constitution".[19] In 1970, in order to suppress constitutional misgivings about the fact that State powers had been attributed to the European Communities,[20] a new article 25bis (now article 34) was inserted immediately after article 25, stating that "[t]he exercise of delimited powers can be attributed by treaty or by law to institutions of public international law".[21] The place of this amendment in the text of the Belgian Constitution is to be explained by the doctrinal position that the attribution of powers to international organisations, such as the European Communities, had to be seen as a *qualification* of the principle of sovereignty.[22] On the other hand, it is also made clear that the attribution of powers does not amount to a partial abandonment of sovereignty; only the *exercise* of those powers can be transferred to the international institution, which implies that they can return to the institutions of the state upon termination of the treaty or some other event in the future.

This cautious approach—accommodation of the principle of sovereignty to the needs of international co-operation, but preservation of its existence—has marked the constitutional evolution of most other Member States of the European Communities. The evolution had started in the years immediately after the Second World War. In France, Italy and Germany, the post-war restoration of democracy was accompanied by the recognition, in their new Constitutions, that effective international organisation was necessary in order to prevent new wars and to avoid the excesses caused by unbridled State sovereignty. Each of those three Constitutions contained a provision permitting limitations of sovereignty or transfer of sovereign powers to international institutions.

In France, paragraph 15 of the Preamble of the Constitution of the Fourth Republic adopted in 1946 (and which is still part of positive constitutional

---

[19] In the French version of the Constitution: "*Tous les pouvoirs émanent de la Nation. Ils sont exercés de la manière établie par la Constitution*".

[20] Those misgivings had been expressed in legal writing, but not by courts. The Acts authorising membership of the European Communities were, like all other legislative acts, immune from judicial review in Belgium at the time.

[21] In French: "*L'exercice de pouvoirs déterminés peut être attribué par un traité ou par une loi à des institutions de droit international public*".

[22] On the context of the adoption of article 25bis, see J. V. Louis, "L'article 25bis de la Constitution belge", *Revue du marché commun* (1970) 410.

law[23]) stated that "subject to reciprocity, France consents to limitations of sovereignty necessary for the realisation and the defence of peace."[24] Article 11 of the Italian Constitution of 1948 declares in strikingly similar terms that "Italy may consent, on equal terms with other States, to limitations of sovereignty necessary to establish an order ensuring peace and justice among nations, and it will favour international organisations which have that aim".[25] Article 24(1) of the German Basic Law of 1949 expresses the same intention in active, rather than passive, wording: "The Federation may by legislation transfer sovereign powers to intergovernmental institutions".[26]

The model set in the post-war years by the three leading Member States of the European Communities, of adopting special constitutional provisions on international co-operation, was followed, somewhat later, by their smaller partners. The Netherlands adopted a constitutional amendment in 1953 (article 67 of the Constitution, now renumbered as article 92), and Luxembourg in 1956 (article 49bis). Most of the countries joining the European Communities subsequently have adopted constitutional provisions similar to those of the original Six.[27]

On a global view of all those constitutional authorisations to limit sovereignty for the sake of international co-operation,[28] it is striking how few actually mention the European Communities in so many words. Most of the texts refer to membership of *international organisations* in general.[29] The constitutional silence about the European Communities is comprehensible for the "old" post-war documents, but, for the countries joining the European Community when it was in full operation, the failure to come openly to terms with the vast constitutional implications of European integration is rather surprising. Yet, despite their diverging and often too laconical formulation, all those constitutional provisions have served the same practical purpose of allowing the country's membership of an organisation such as the European

---

[23] The Preamble of 1946 is incorporated by reference in the first paragraph of the Preamble of the present Constitution of 1958. Both Preambles are part of the "*bloc constitutionnel*" which is binding law for all French authorities (see Th. Renoux and M. de Villiers, *Code constitutionnel* (Litec, 1994) at p. 9).

[24] "*Sous réserve de réciprocité, la France consent aux limitations de souveraineté nécessaires à l'organisation et à la défense de la paix*" (translation taken from S. E. Finer, V. Bogdanor, B. Rudden, *Comparing Constitutions* (Clarendon Press, 1995) at p. 212).

[25] "*L'Italia . . . consente, in condizioni di parità con gli altri Stati, alle limitazioni di sovranità necessarie ad un ordinamento che assicuri la pace e la giustizia fra le Nazioni; promuove e favorisce le organizzazioni internazionali rivolte a tale scopo*".

[26] "*Der Bund kann durch Gesetz Hoheitsrechte auf zwischenstaatliche Einrichtungen übertragen*".

[27] Danish Constitution, article 20(1); Irish Constitution, article 29(4); Greek Constitution, article 28(2) and (3); Spanish Constitution, article 93; Portuguese Constitution, article 7(5).

[28] For a comparative analysis of those provisions, see Th. de Berranger, *Constitutions nationales*, at pp. 38–123, and N. Lorenz, *Die Übertragung von Hoheitsrechten auf die Europäischen Gemeinschaften* (Lang, 1990). See also the brief survey by A. Cassese, "Modern Constitutions and International Law", 192 *Recueil des Cours* (1985-III) at 413–18.

[29] The exception is article 29, s. 4, sub-s. 3 of the Irish Constitution which refers directly, and exclusively, to the European Communities.

Community with its own institutions exercising legislative, executive and judicial powers.

Among those "integration clauses", there is an obvious semantic difference between the "Belgo-German" formula allowing for *attribution* of powers or *transfers* of sovereign rights and the "Franco-Italian" formula allowing for *limitations* of sovereignty. The Greek Constitution is the only one providing for both these formulas in two subsequent paragraphs of article 28. One should not attach too much importance to those different formulations. There may, indeed, be international treaties which result in limitations of the freedom of states but which do not attribute powers to international institutions. But in the case of the European Communities, the limitation of sovereignty has been accompanied by the attribution of powers to international institutions, and those two operations are inseparable. This connection was emphasised by the European Court of Justice in its *Costa* v. *E.N.E.L.* judgment of 1964. In the course of its argument in favour of the primacy of Community law, the Court stated:

> "[b]y creating a Community of unlimited duration, having its own institutions, its own personality, its own legal capacity and capacity of representation on the international plane and, more particularly, real powers stemming from a *limitation of sovereignty or a transfer of powers* from the States to the Community, the Member States have *limited their sovereign rights* and have thus created a body of law which binds both their nationals and themselves".[30]

In the conclusion of its demonstration, the Court restated the same view:

> "The transfer by the States from their domestic legal system to the Community legal system of the rights and obligations arising under the Treaty carries with it a permanent limitation of their sovereign rights, against which a subsequent unilateral act incompatible with the concept of the Community cannot prevail".[31]

The connection made by the European Court was approvingly quoted by the Spanish Constitutional Tribunal in its "Maastricht" Declaration of 1992 for the purpose of interpreting the integration clause of the Spanish Constitution:

> "Article 93 permits the granting of the right to 'exercise powers derived from the Constitution' which will involve (and has already involved) the specific limitation or restriction for certain purposes, of the powers and competences of the Spanish

---

[30] *Costa* v. *E.N.E.L.*, Case 6/64, [1964] ECR 585, at 593–4. The English text of the judgment is, of course, a later translation. The word "sovereign" is less prominently present in the original versions of the judgment. The French version is as follows: "*en instituant une Communauté . . . dotée de pouvoirs réels issus d'une limitation de compétences ou d'un transfert d'attributions des Etats à la Communauté, ceux-ci ont limité, bien que dans des domaines restreints, leurs droits souverains*".

[31] This time, the word "permanent" is added. In the context of the judgment, which deals with the primacy of EC law, the word "permanent" probably means that the limitation of sovereignty accepted by the Member States upon accession to the EC cannot be taken back subsequently by denying precedence to the Treaty which they have freely accepted.

public authorities (limitation of 'sovereign rights' in the expression of the Court of Justice of the European Communities in *Costa v. ENEL . . .*)".[32]

Thus, the Spanish Court accepted that the "attribution of powers" allowed by the Constitution implies the acceptance of a "limitation of sovereignty". Conversely, where the French and Italian Constitutions speak of "limitations of sovereignty", what is meant is not merely the capacity to enter international agreements which are binding for the state ("limitations of sovereignty" in the generic sense used in the *Wimbledon* case by the Hague Court) but also the creation of international institutions exercising powers which are "normally" reserved for state institutions.

One may therefore conclude that, in post-1945 Western Europe, a doctrinal compromise emerged, which is common to the various states, between the traditional concept of state sovereignty and the new needs of international co-operation and European integration. This common European doctrine may be enunciated as follows: sovereignty continues to reside in the people and is to be exercised primarily by the institutions of the state.[33] This exercise of sovereign powers may be dispersed horizontally, among the central institutions of the state (the legislative, the executive and the judiciary),[34] but there is no conceptual obstacle against its vertical dispersion, allowing sub-national institutions (such as the *Länder* in Germany) to participate in the exercise of sovereign powers. Similarly, thanks to the post-war constitutional innovations, the exercise of state powers may henceforth be attributed to international institutions such as the European Community. As a result, action by the European Community "somehow appears as another mode for the Member States to assume their own sovereignty, not any longer through autonomous, but through common decision-making".[35] From this perspective of the *joint exercise of sovereignty*,[36] the institutions of the European Union are, as it were, acting on behalf of the various sovereign peoples of the Member States. Yet, and this remained firmly established in constitutional doctrine, nothing has changed in the basic rule that *sovereignty itself continues to reside in the people* and may therefore not be *alienated*, either wholly or in part, by the institutions of the state.

[32] Spanish Constitutional Tribunal, Case No. 1236/92 of 1 July 1992; English translation by A. Oppenheimer (ed), *The Relationship Between European Community Law and National Law: The Cases* (Cambridge UP, 1994), p. 712, at p. 726.

[33] See, for illustrations, article 3 of the French Constitution: "*La souveraineté nationale* appartient *au peuple qui* l'exerce *par ses représentants et par la voie du référendum*" (emphasis added), and article 1, second sentence, of the Italian Constitution: "*La sovranità* appartiene *al popolo, che la* esercita *nelle forme e nei limiti della Costituzione*" (emphasis added).

[34] Thus, the principle of separation of powers is reconciled with the seemingly absolute principle of popular sovereignty.

[35] K. Lenaerts, "Constitutionalism and the Many Faces of Federalism", 38 *American Journal of Comparative Law* (1990) 205, at 231.

[36] This expression was often used by the former President of the Commission, Jacques Delors. See for instance his "Bruges speech": J. Delors, "Address at the College of Europe, 17 October 1989", reprinted in B. F. Nelsen and A. Stubb, *The European Union. Readings on the Theory and Practice of European Integration* (Lynne Rienner Publishers, 1994) p. 51, at pp. 53, 56 and 58.

This compromise allowed all Member States, *at least at the time of accession to the European Communities*, the precarious preservation of the traditional unitary concept of sovereignty while at the same time allowing for the incipient "integration of sovereignties"[37] imposed by post-war political developments in Europe.

Yet, behind this harmonious view of things, there is a major conceptual problem. As sovereignty was traditionally defined as the ultimate source of any particular exercise of legal authority by state institutions, how could this account for the unprecedented situation in which power was exercised by supra-national institutions without any direct control by the states, particularly in cases where Community acts can be adopted by majority vote, against the views of those members of the Council and the European Parliament who can be said to represent the people of a particular state? Is it not an artificial contrivance to bring this institutional mechanism under the heading of the "common exercise of State sovereignty"?

This problem will be discussed further in the concluding section. But, despite its fictional nature, this is the view which has prevailed in the constitutional doctrine of the Member States of the European Union until now. Nor has this view been openly challenged by the European Court of Justice. On the whole, that Court has remained remarkably silent on the subject of sovereignty and has not made any attempt at formulating a comprehensive theory about the place of (state) sovereignty within the framework of European integration. The word "sovereign" appears, as was mentioned above, in its *Costa* judgment of 1964, and also in a few other landmark cases. In those cases, the formula most commonly used was that the Member States had "limited their sovereign rights".[38] At one point in the *Van Gend en Loos* judgment of 1963, the Court took a slightly different approach and described the Community institutions as being endowed with "sovereign rights".[39] Thus, borrowing from the constitutional texts of the principal Member States of the early EEC, the Court mainly uses the "Franco-Italian" formula of the limitation of the Member States' sovereign rights, but it also refers, at least once, to the "German" formula of the endowment of the Community with sovereign rights. But even the latter expression does not justify the claim that the ECJ would have required a "true transfer of sovereignty"[40] or that it

---

[37] This expression was used, in the first line of his course at the Hague Academy, by P. De Visscher, "Les tendances internationales des constitutions modernes", 80 *Recueil des Cours* (1952-II), 511.

[38] Apart from *Costa*, n. 30 above, see also *Van Gend en Loos*, Case 26/62, [1963] ECR 1, at 12; Opinion 1/91, *Agreement on the European Economic Area*, [1991] ECR I-6079, at 6102 (quoting from *Van Gend en Loos*).

[39] The relevant French words are: " . . . par la création d'organes qui institutionnalisent des *droits souverains*"; in German: "*in der Schaffung von Organen, welche* Hoheitsrechte *übertragen sind*" (emphasis added).

[40] T. C. Hartley, *The Foundations of European Community Law*, 3rd edn (Clarendon Press, 1994), at p. 239.

would have repeatedly stated that such a transfer had effectively taken place.[41]

The ECJ has not genuinely tried to construct its own alternative doctrine of sovereignty, to be opposed to the traditional views obtaining in the constitutional law of the Member States. The European Court, as the traditional champion of European integration, may well have viewed the doctrine of state sovereignty as inimical to integration, but it has not sought to mount a frontal attack against the doctrinal consensus existing at the national constitutional level. It has only required from its direct interlocutors, the national courts, that the venerable doctrine of sovereignty should not interfere with the practical exigencies formulated in *Van Gend en Loos* and *Costa*: the recognition of the direct effect and primacy of Community law within the domestic legal order of the Member States. Yet, as will be shown in the next section, sovereignty inevitably casts its shadow on this matter of the reception of Community law.

Sovereignty as a limit to the reception of Community law

The use, in *Van Gend en Loos* and *Costa*, of wording similar to that employed in the constitutions of the leading Member States (at that time) was probably not coincidental. The argument of the limitations of sovereignty was only one of the many which the European Court used to justify the need to recognise the domestic effect and primacy of Community law, but it was a strategic argument as it invited national courts to make use, if necessary, of their Constitutions' integration clauses for furthering the application of EC law.

In the four monist countries among the original Six, namely France, Belgium, Luxembourg and the Netherlands, the direct effect and primacy of EC law was recognised without recourse to the "limitations of sovereignty" clause. Community law was, rather, given the benefit of the primacy which the Constitutions (explicitly or not) recognized to the directly effective provisions of *all* international agreements (whether or not they involved "limitations of sovereignty").[42]

---

[41] D. Obradovic, "Community Law and the Doctrine of Divisible Sovereignty", *Legal Issues of European Integration* (1993), 1, at 7. There is one little-known ruling in which the European Court seems to go further by implying that the Member States had transferred part of their *sovereignty*—and not just sovereign rights—to the Community. In that case, Euratom Ruling 1/78, the Court held that "[t]o the extent to which jurisdiction and powers have been conferred on the Community under the EAEC Treaty, the Member States . . . are no longer able to . . . impose conditions on the exercise of prerogatives which thenceforth belong to the Community and which therefore *no longer fall within the field of national sovereignty*" (Ruling 1/78, [1978] ECR 2151, at 2178). In the absence of arguments and of confirmation in later rulings, this phrase must be considered as a loose description rather than as a conceptual innovation.

[42] The fact that the "limitations of sovereignty" clauses were not used in those countries as a basis for the reception of Community law does not mean that those countries' Constitutions and courts have *unreservedly* accepted the supremacy of Community law, but that is a different story.

In Italy and Germany, however, the actual duties imposed on national courts by *Van Gend en Loos* and *Costa* went well beyond what the mainstream constitutional doctrine, at that time, was prepared to accept in terms of the domestic operation of international treaty law. Yet, the European Court suggested, by using the argument of limitation of sovereignty and attribution of competences, that the German and Italian courts might, with some creativity, find the constitutional resources needed for recognising the primacy of Community law.

The message, in *Costa*, was primarily addressed to the Italian Constitutional Court. That Court had, in its own *Costa* decision a few months earlier, taken a very different view. It had held that there is no logical link between the constitutional clause allowing for limitations of sovereignty in favour of international organisations (article 11 of the Italian Constitution) and the question of the domestic status of the rules produced by such international organisations. It affirmed that article 11 did not cause any deviation from the existing rules about the efficacy in national law of international obligations contracted by Italy, and that therefore a later Act of Parliament should prevail over Community law, which was exactly the opposite of the European Court's position in *Costa*.[43]

Yet, in the course of the years, the Italian Constitutional Court has let itself be convinced by the European Court's view (and by that part of legal writing which supported the message coming from Luxembourg) and has gradually come to recognise the supremacy of Community law over national legislation, on the basis of its special nature which distinguishes it from other international treaties.[44] Article 11 became the constitutional peg on which to hang the primacy of Community law, or, to quote another frequently used metaphor, the instrument piercing the barrier of dualism and allowing Community law to have direct effect and primacy within the Italian legal order. Thus, one of the "limitations of sovereignty" allowed by article 11 is that the legislator should accept that its statutes are no longer enforceable by the courts when they are incompatible with Community obligations.

There are several difficulties with this doctrinal construction but it has, since *Granital*,[45] generally achieved its purpose of ensuring the enforcement of European Community law obligations by Italian courts. Yet, at the same time the Constitutional Court has consistently held that those limitations of sovereignty can never go as far as to nullify sovereignty itself; there are "counter-limits" (*controlimiti*) formed by the fundamental principles of the Italian constitutional order, against which EC law cannot prevail. Article 11 allows for implicit derogations to "ordinary" rules of the Constitution, but it

[43] Constitutional Court, judgment of 7 March 1964, n. 14, *Foro Italiano* (1964) I, 465.

[44] The evolution is described by M. Cartabia, "The Italian Constitutional Court and the Relationship Between the Italian Legal System and the European Community", 12 *Michigan Journal of International Law* (1990) 173.

[45] Italian Constitutional Court, Decision No. 170 of 8 June 1984, *S.p.a. Granital v. Amministrazione delle Finanze dello Stato* (summarised, with an annotation by G. Gaja, in (1984) *Common Market Law Review* 756).

cannot allow the European Community to derogate from the "fundamental" principles of the Italian constitutional order. When *state* institutions exercise sovereign powers, they must respect the fundamental values and principles of the Constitution; one cannot accept a complete renunciation of those values and principles when powers are attributed to the *European* institutions. In its *Fragd* ruling of 1989, the Court went so far as to state that it could control the consistency of *individual* rules of EC law with the fundamental principles of the Italian Constitution, particularly (but not only) in the field of human rights.[46] The Court did not use that power, neither in *Fragd* nor in subsequent cases, but it is clear that there is no place, in this scheme of thought, for a recognition of the absolute primacy of Community law.

At the time of *Van Gend en Loos* and *Costa*, the position in *German* constitutional law was very similar to that in Italy.[47] The dominant doctrine of dualism meant that European Community law, like any other form of international treaty law, could not prevail over later statutes enacted by the German Parliament. But, in the interpretation of article 24 of the German Constitution given to it by the Constitutional Court since the late 1960's, that article has come to play exactly the same role as article 11 of the Italian Constitution. Its explicit and primary function is to allow for membership of international organisations with such incisive powers as those of the European Communities; but its implicit and secondary function has become to serve as the constitutional basis for the recognition of the direct effect and supremacy of Community law.

Yet, article 24 does not allow for an absolute and limitless primacy of Community law. The German Constitutional Court has developed a theory of "counter-limits" which it formulated in its *Solange I* and *Solange II* judgments of 1974 and 1986.[48] Referring expressly to the doctrine of its Italian counterpart, the Karlsruhe Court held, in both cases, that article 24 does not allow transfers of sovereign rights that would "abandon the identity of the German constitutional order by breaching its fundamental structures".[49] What

---

[46] Decision No. 232 of 21 April 1989, *S.p.a. Fragd* v. *Amministrazione delle Finanze* (English text in A. Oppenheimer (ed), *The Relationship between European Community Law and National Law—The Cases* (Cambridge UP, 1994), at p. 653). Formally speaking, the Court, in such cases, would not be reviewing Community law directly but the Italian act of ratification of the EEC Treaty; that act would be declared unconstitutional to the extent that it allowed the EC to breach fundamental principles of the Italian constitutional order. On the implications of the *Fragd* case, see G. Gaja, "New Developments in a Continuing Story: The Relationship between EEC Law and Italian Law", (1990) *Common Market Law Review* 83, at 94; M. Cartabia, "The Italian Constitutional Court", (n. 44 above) at 181.

[47] See, e.g., H. J. Schlochauer, "Das Verhaltnis des Rechts der europaischen Wirtschaftsgemeinschaft zu den nationalen Rechtsordnungen der Mitgliedstaaten", *Archiv des Volkerrechts* (1963) 22.

[48] *Solange I*, BVerfGE 37, 271 and Oppenheimer, *The Relationship*, (n. 46 above) at 440; *Solange II*, BVerfGE 73, 339 and Oppenheimer, at 462.

[49] "*Die Ermächtigung aufgrund des Art.24 Abs.1 GG ist indessen nicht ohne Verfassungsrechtliche Grenzen. Die Vorschrift ermächtigt nicht dazu, im Wege der Einräumung von Hoheitsrechten für zwischenstaatliche Einrichtungen die Identität der geltenden Verfassungsordnung der Bundesrepublik Deutschland durch Einbruch in ihr Grundgefüge, in die sie konstituierenden Strukturen, aufzugeben*" (BVerfGE 73, 339 at 375).

this enigmatic formula exactly means has been a subject of considerable controversy among German lawyers. According to a "pro-European" interpretation, the clause does not so much act as a *limit* to European integration, but rather as an indication of the *direction* in which Community law should develop; the substantive values underlying the German Basic Law, referred to by the Court, could be achieved in similar fashion within the European Community. If the EC legal order would further develop legal guarantees for fundamental rights and would become more democratic, then national constitutional values would be part and parcel of the Community legal order, and the German Constitutional Court would no longer need to subject its acceptance of the primacy of EC law to any qualifications.[50]

However, there was also a rather different, sovereignty-inspired interpretation of the *Solange* cases, which was proposed most prominently in the extra-judicial writings of a member of the Constitutional Court, Paul Kirchhof. In his interpretation, the *Solange* reservation was primarily (though not exclusively) inspired by the wish to protect state sovereignty against the "incoming tide" of Community law. He argued, rather plausibly, that the guarantee of the *identity* of the German constitutional order must mean, at the very least, that the German Parliament is not allowed to *put an end to the German state* by transferring sovereignty to a newly-created European federal state. That view is further confirmed by a look at article 79(3) of the German Constitution—the so-called *Ewigkeitsklausel*—which sets apart some fundamental provisions of the *Grundgesetz* as being unalterable by constitutional amendment. Among those intangible provisions referred to in article 79(3) is article 20 of the Constitution which declares, in its first paragraph, that the Federal Republic of Germany is a democratic and social federal state and, in its second paragraph, that all state powers emanate from the people ("*Alle Staatsgewalt geht vom Volke aus*").[51] This, again, presupposes that Germany may not cease to be a sovereign state and become part of a European federation.[52] According to this interpretation of the *Solange* case law, the Constitutional Court had indicated, implicitly but clearly, that it intended to protect the existence of the German state and the principle of popular sover-

---

[50] This view was expressed, for instance, by W. von Simson and J. Schwarze, *Europäische Integration und Grundgesetz. Maastricht und die Folgen für das deutsche Verfassungsrecht* (de Gruyter, 1992) at p. 66.

[51] Article 20 of the *Grundgesetz*: "(1) The Federal Republic of Germany is a democratic and social federal state. (2) All state authority emanates from the people. It shall be exercised by the people by means of elections and voting and by specific legislative, executive and judicial organs".

[52] This implication of article 20(1) was strongly insisted upon by Paul Kirchhof in his "Der deutsche Staat im Prozess der europäischen Integration", in J. Isensee and P. Kirchhof (eds), *Handbuch des Staatsrechts der Bundesrepublik Deutschland*, Vol. VII (1992) p. 855, at p. 883: "The core content of this provision [namely Art. 20(1)] is 'the Federal Republic is a State'. The addition of the democratic, federal and social characteristics of that State may occasionally lead one to consider the primary statement—the guarantee of statehood—to be self-evident. That primary statement, however, becomes meaningful in the present discussion of whether to change the Community into a European Union with the character of a federal State".

eignty against their abridgment by Acts approving international treaties. The full implications of this view would become clear subsequently in the *Maastricht* judgment of the German Constitutional Court, on which Kirchhof, as judge *rapporteur*, exercised considerable influence.[53]

Thus, the clauses about limitation of sovereignty have been given by the Italian and German Constitutional courts a closely similar interpretation in the context of European integration. Those clauses have a double role. On the one hand, they allow for the smooth integration of EC law into the national legal system, discarding dualist doctrine for the exclusive benefit of EC law and ensuring the direct effect and supremacy of EC law in all "normal" situations. On the other had, the sovereignty clauses allow the constitutional courts of those two countries to protect what they consider to be the "core" of the Constitution against any encroachments of Community law; in this way, those courts continue to assume what they conceive as their function, that of being the guardian of the Constitution against both internal and external threats.[54]

In the discussion so far of a "Europe-wide" doctrine of limitation of sovereignty, one country has been absent: the *United Kingdom*. In the absence of a written constitution, there was no need for a constitutional amendment allowing for the vesting of state powers in the European institutions. More fundamentally, as sovereignty was seen to be located in a particular institution, the Parliament, rather than the people as a whole, any limitations of sovereignty involved in membership of the Community merely required a simple Act of Parliament (the European Communities Act 1972) without the need for prior "constitutional authorisation" as in other countries. Whereas the principle of the sovereignty of Parliament made *membership* of the European Communities a constitutional non-issue, it caused immediate concern for the negative implications it might have for the *reception* of Community law within the British legal order. The threat seemed to result directly from Dicey's classical definition: "the principle of Parliamentary Sovereignty means nothing more nor less than this, namely, that Parliament . . . has, under the English constitution, the right to make or unmake any law whatever; and, further, that no person or body is recognised by the law of England as having a right to override or set aside the legislation of Parliament".[55]

But today, more than twenty years after Britain's accession to the European Communities, this threat has not materialised and Dicey's definition is no longer a full statement of the law as it stands. In its remarkable *Factortame*

---

[53] See p. 295, below.

[54] The situation in *Spain*, despite its monist tradition, may not be that different from Italy and Germany. Primacy of Community law is based on the "attribution of powers" clause of article 93 and is also subject to constitutional limitations. It is not clear to what extent the Constitutional Tribunal is prepared to enforce those constitutional reservations against EC law. See P. Pérez Tremps, *Constitución española y Comunidad Europea*, at p. 127 *et seq.*

[55] Dicey, *Introduction to the Study of the Law of the Constitution*, 10th edn (Macmillan, 1959), at pp. 39–40.

judgment of 1990, the House of Lords has formally established the precedence of Community law over later statutory norms. In his speech in the *Factortame* case, Lord Bridge denied (against what he described as allegations by the media) that the judiciary were sacrificing sovereignty by recognising the primacy of European Community law. He cleverly argued that Parliament itself had ordered the courts to make Community law prevail over Acts of Parliament.[56]

Factortame shows "how smoothly", in Britain at least, "the courts may discard fundamental doctrine without appearing to notice"; according to Professor Wade, the "only remnant of the old unqualified sovereignty is Parliament's ability to legislate in deliberate breach of the Treaty";[57] and even then, it is not altogether certain that the courts would follow suit.[58]

The smooth acceptance by British courts of the European Court's doctrine on direct effect and primacy, despite the initial fears about British legal insularity, show that British-style Parliamentary sovereignty may be less intractable than originally feared,[59] and perhaps less threatening, for the uniform application of EC law, than some national brands of continental-style popular sovereignty. If sovereign powers are located in an institution, rather than an abstract entity, then any limitations of sovereignty can be decided by that institution alone, without further need for delicate constitutional balancing or complicated constitutional revisions. Also, a type of sovereignty like that obtaining in Britain may more easily be conceived as shifting—from one (national) to another (European?) institution—than the abstract concept of popular sovereignty.

To conclude this section, it appears that in a number of Member States, the supreme courts, rather than accepting the absolute supremacy of EC law which the European Court of Justice requires them to do, have established a fine-tuned legal balance between the requirements of European integration and state sovereignty; generally speaking, there has not been a smooth harmonisation of the principle of sovereignty with the legal requirements of

---

[56] "If the supremacy within the European Community of Community law over the national law of member states was not always inherent in the EEC Treaty it was certainly well established in the jurisprudence of the Court of Justice long before the United Kingdom joined the Community. Thus, whatever limitation of its sovereignty Parliament accepted when it enacted the European Communities Act 1972 was entirely voluntary" (*R v. Secretary of State for Transport, ex parte Factortame Ltd (No 2)*, [1991] 1 All ER 70, at 107–8.

[57] Both quotations from H. W. R. Wade, "What has Happened to the Sovereignty of Parliament?", (1991) *Law Quarterly Review* 1, at 4 and 3.

[58] Doubt on this point is expressed by Finer, Bogdanor and Rudden, *Comparing Constitutions*, at 47; Hartley writes that Parliament could always, albeit as a last resort, repeal the European Communities Act itself: "ultimate sovereignty still rests with Parliament: Community law prevails only because Parliament wants it to prevail. Parliament could always repeal the European Communities Act and then Community law would cease to have effect in the United Kingdom" (T. C. Hartley, *The Foundations of European Community Law*, at 263).

[59] For a detailed examination of the implications of *Factortame* for the sovereignty debate in Britain, see P. P. Craig, "Sovereignty of the United Kingdom Parliament after *Factortame*", (1991) 11 *Yearbook of European Law* 221, at 243 *et seq.*

European integration, but rather a "peaceful coexistence" whose maintenance is in the hands of the political and judicial institutions of the Member States.

The year 1990 can retrospectively be seen as the high-water mark of European legal integration. After the *Nicolo* decision of the Conseil d'Etat in 1989 and the *Factortame* judgment of the House of Lords in 1990, the primacy of Community law over national law seemed solidly affirmed in all Member States. State sovereignty was not much heard of any more. Even in the United Kingdom, the seemingly intractable principle of Parliamentary sovereignty had effectively been "tamed" on the basis of the creative constitutional doctrine developed by the House of Lords. Speculations about constitutional reservations to the full reception of Community law seemed confined to Germany and Italy and could appear more as symbolic gestures than as effective threats to the uniform application of EC law.

Yet, the negotiation and adoption of the Treaty on European Union, during the year 1991, and above all the national debates on its ratification, during 1992 and 1993, put this *modus vivendi* under strain. They revealed the potentially conflictual nature of the relation between constitutional law and European law[60] and gave renewed vigour to the debate on the legal implications of state sovereignty in the context of European unification.

SOVEREIGNTY AND THE EUROPEAN UNION:
AN UNAVOIDABLE CONFLICT?

The reassertion of state sovereignty in the aftermath of "Maastricht"

In the political debate about "Maastricht", a commonly used argument was that the Treaty on European Union contained such an extensive transfer of powers that the sovereign statehood of the Member States was called into question. The new transfer of state powers made at Maastricht, when seen in conjunction with earlier developments such as the Single European Act, caused a critical change in the nature of the European Union—which was now becoming a federal state without this being mentioned—and of its Member States—which were relinquishing their sovereignty without noticing. That interpretation of "Maastricht" remained a minority view in legal circles, but one could at least argue that the existing integration clauses of the national Constitutions, which had allowed the various states to *enter* the Community were, because of their generic character, no longer suited as a constitutional basis for the mature form of European integration represented by the Treaty on European Union.

---

[60] "*L'affaire de la ratification du Traité de Maastricht a été un révélateur puissant de cet état de concurrence ou même de confrontation entre normes constitutionnelles et normes internationales*" (L. Favoreu, "Le contrôle de constitutionnalité du Traité de Maastricht et le développement du 'droit constitutionnel international'", *Revue générale du droit international public* (1993) 39, at 42).

In several Member States, though not in all, the ratification of the treaty on European Union formed the occasion to confront constitutional problems which were not entirely new but had been ignored or minimised earlier on. More specifically, the ratification debate revealed in some countries the considerable obstruction power of the principle of sovereignty. The theme of sovereignty took pride of place in the French constitutional debate; it also inspired, less directly but more insidiously, the *Maastricht* ruling of the German Constitutional Court of 1993; and finally, in several other Member States where the Constitution was not modified for the purpose of the Treaty on European Union and where supreme courts were not asked for their views on the matter,[61] the principle of sovereignty threatens to disrupt, at some future occasion, the "peaceful coexistence" between Community law and constitutional law.

In *France*, sovereignty had been for some time already the pivotal concept in the Conseil Constitutionnel's case law on the constitutionality of international conventions concluded by the French Government, and this was confirmed by the ruling of the Conseil in April 1992 in response to a request from the President of the Republic to examine the constitutionality of the Maastricht Treaty.[62]

The Conseil Constitutionnel had been confronted with the compatibility of Acts of EC law with the Constitution on one previous occasion, when in 1976 the French Act approving the organisation of direct elections to the European Parliament was challenged.[63] While denying that there had been a breach of the Constitution, the Conseil had added a few *obiter dicta* which were generally interpreted as showing distrust towards the integration process. It made the famous distinction between *limitations of sovereignty*, which were expressly accepted by the Preamble of the 1946 Constitution (itself incorporated in the 1958 Constitution) and *transfers* of part or the totality of sovereignty which were not allowed.[64]

---

[61] For a comparative survey of the constitutional implications of the Treaty on European Union, see H. Henrichs, "Der Vertrag über die Europäische Union und seine Auswirkungen auf die Verfassungen der Mitgliedstaaten", *Die Öffentliche Verwaltung* (1994) 368. On the ratification procedures in the single countries, see the surveys in (1993) *European Law Review*, at 228, 356, 448 and 541; and (1994), at 94.

[62] For a global view of the "Maastricht" Decisions of the Constitutonal Council, and the intervening reform of the Constitution, see, among others: P. Oliver, "The French Constitution and the Treaty of Maastricht", *International and Comparative Law Quarterly* (1994) 1; L. Favoreu, "Le contrôle de constitutionnalité du Traité de Maastricht et le développement du 'droit constitutionnel international'", *Revue générale du droit international public* (1993) 39; C. Grewe and H. Ruiz Fabri, "Le Conseil constitutionnel et l'intégration européenne", *Revue universelle des droits de l'homme* (1992) 277.

[63] It should be noted that neither the ECSC Treaty nor the EEC Treaty nor the Single European Act had been subjected to a similar constitutional control.

[64] "*Considérant que si le préambule de la Constitution de 1946, confirmé par celui de la Constitution de 1958, dispose que, sous réserve de réfiprocité, la France consent aux limitations de souveraineté nécessaires à l'organisation et à la défense de la paix, aucune disposition de nature constitutionnelle n'autorise des transfers de tout ou partie de la souveraineté nationale à quelque organisation internationale que ce soit*" (Decision of 29–30 December 1976, *Assemblée européenne*, J.O. 31 December 1976, p.7651, second recital).

That distinction proved to be too crude, and it was gradually displaced, in rulings of the Conseil dealing with other international treaties, by a distinction between constitutional and unconstitutional limitations of sovereignty; the latter were those affecting the *conditions essentielles d'exercice de la souveraineté nationale*.[65] This was also the standard chosen by the Constitutional Council in its *Decision on the Maastricht Treaty*. For the first time, it decided that a treaty did indeed affect the essential conditions for the exercise of sovereignty, in two different fields corresponding to the traditional *domaines de souveraineté* of control of money and of territory: the provisions of the EU Treaty about economic and monetary union and the provision of the new article 100C of the EC Treaty on a common visa policy were declared to affect the essential conditions of sovereignty. In addition, the new article 8B of the EC Treaty recognising for citizens of the EU the right to vote and stand for local elections throughout the EU was found to be in direct contradiction of the Constitution.

In order to eliminate the incompatibilities found by the Constitutional Council, a constitutional amendment was enacted by both houses of the French Parliament, meeting together as the Congrès, on 23 June 1992. The revision gave formal authorisation to membership of the European Union (new article 88-1) and specifically enshrined in the text of the Constitution the elements of the Maastricht Treaty with which the Conseil Constitutionnel had found fault (Articles 88-2 and 88-3). It may seem strange that Treaty clauses that had been considered to affect the *essential* conditions of sovereignty could be, as it were, incorporated within the French Constitution without modifying any of the other parts of that Constitution.[66] This paradox was seen, by some, as a logical contradiction: if one accepts that a simple amendment of the Constitution may authorise breaches of essential conditions of national sovereignty, this is tantamount to accepting that sovereignty itself can be disposed of by the constitutional legislator. That was one of the questions submitted by a group of Senators of the (then) opposition to the Conseil Constitutionnel in the early Summer of 1992. They argued that, despite the insertion of the new provisions, the Treaty on European Union was still incompatible with the French Constitution and particularly with the principle of national sovereignty. In its Maastricht II ruling, the Conseil Constitutionnel rejected the application and held that the constitutional legislator is 'sovereign', which is a somewhat awkward way of affirming the full discretion of

---

[65] On the constitutional review of international agreements prior to the "Maastricht" Decision, see J. Rideau, "Constitution et droit international dans les Etats membres des communautés européennes—Réflexions générales et situation française", *Revue française de droit constitutionnel* (1990) 259, at pp. 268–89; also P. Oliver, "The French Constitution", (n. 62 above) at 5–11. For special attention to the Conseil's doctrine of *sovereignty*, see F. Luchaire, "Le Conseil constitutionnel et la souveraineté nationale", *Revue du droit public* (1991) 1499.

[66] For a discussion of this method of "*révision-adjonction*", see C. Grewe, "La révision constitutionnelle en vue de la ratification du traité de Maastricht", *Revue française de Droit constitutionnel* (1992) 413, at 420.

the Congrès to modify the Constitution as it wishes,[67] and of denying that the principle of sovereignty embodied in article 3 of the Constitution possesses an intangible or supra-constitutional status.[68]

The pragmatic attitude displayed by the Conseil in Maastricht II, combined with the limited scope of its Maastricht I finding of incompatibility, may justify the evaluation that those rulings "should not in any sense be regarded as hostile to Community law or international law".[69] On the other hand, any future expansion of Community powers (say, in the field of defence) or of the supranational character of its decision-making process (say, by a shift to majority voting in the EC Council in some "sensitive" field) will most probably be submitted to the Conseil Constitutionnel in order to check whether the essential conditions of the exercise of sovereignty have been affected. Due to the vagueness of this concept, it is difficult to predict whether such a check would open the way to a procedure for constitutional amendment and a referendum, whose outcome is even more unpredictable.

It should further be noted that the "European integration clause" of article 88(1), which has now replaced paragraph 15 of the Preamble of 1946 as the constitutional basis for French membership, is very much inspired by the classical conception of sovereignty: "*la République participe aux Communautés européennes et à l'Union européenne, constituée d'Etats qui ont choisi librement, en vertu des traités qui les ont instituées, d'exercer en commun certaines de leurs compétences*". This can be seen as a confirmation of the traditional legal fiction that, when the European Community institutions exercise their powers, they are, constitutionally speaking, acting on behalf of the sovereign peoples of the Member States. For the time being, French sovereignty has not been abandoned, nor transferred, but is merely "exercised in common" with other states within the institutional structure of the European Union.[70]

Similarly, the new article 23 of the *German* Basic Law, adopted in December 1992 in order to clear the way for ratification of the Maastricht Treaty, codified the Constitutional Court's earlier case law on the constitu-

---

[67] It must only respect the revision *procedure* and one *substantive* limitation contained in article 89 which states that the "Republican form of government may not be the object of a revision" (*Maastricht II*, Decision no. 92–312 of 2 September 1992, in *Revue du droit public* (1992) 1610, at 1613).

[68] This doctrine, which is based on the theory that a constitutional revision is the direct expression of the people's sovereignty, is expounded in full detail by G. Vedel, "Souveraineté et supra-constitutionnalité", *Pouvoirs* no 67 (1993) 79. The contrary view, that sovereignty *is* an intangible constitutional principle (and that ratification of the Treaty of Maastricht can therefore only be explained as a "constitutional revolution", changing the legal nature of the French state), is defended by O. Beaud, *La puissance de l'Etat* (Presses Universitaires de France, 1994), at pp. 457–91. For a short *comparative* discussion of this point, see C. Grewe and H. Ruiz Fabri, *Droits constitutionnels européens*, at p. 61.

[69] P. Oliver, "The French Constitution", (n. 62 above) at 23.

[70] According to C. Grewe (n. 68 above), "*La révision constitutionnelle*", at 431, Article 88-1 "*vise à empêcher toute 'dérive fédérale' de l'Europe en rappelant que les Communautés européennes sont composées d'Etats. La souveraineté demeure par conséquent nationale, elle ne devient pas européenne*".

tional limits to European integration and, for the future, it affirmed the constituent power's will to erect a constitutional barrier for the protection of the fundamental values of the German legal orders in the perspective of new attributions of powers to the European Union.[71] It states that the Federation may by legislation transfer sovereign powers (*Hoheitsrechte*) for the development of the European Union "which is bound to democratic, law-governed, social and federal principles, and to the principle of subsidiarity and which guarantees a protection of basic rights essentially comparable to that of this Basic Law". It is added that for the establishment of the European Union and any future changes to it, the procedure for constitutional amendment shall be followed (as delineated in article 79, para. 2) and that no modifications may be made to the fundamental principles covered by the *Ewigkeitsklausel* of article 79, para. 3. As a result of the 1992 reform, the German Constitution now contains express substantive limits to European integration.

The new article 23 immediately served as the basis for the Parliamentary approval of the Treaty on European Union. Yet, the constitutional position of that Treaty was not yet secured. The Act approving the Treaty was challenged before the Constitutional Court, which rendered its judgments in the *Maastricht* case (or *Brunner* case, as it is sometimes called after the only applicant whose claim was found admissible) in October 1993.[72] In its judgment, the Court undertook a full examination of the compatibility of the Treaty with the German constitutional system, as if the new article 23 of the Constitution, which was intended to remove any constitutional misgivings, had never been enacted.[73]

Superficially, the Constitutional Court seems to be concerned above all with the need to protect fundamental rights and to guarantee the democratic nature of the European integration process. Yet, it is submitted that the "hidden core" of the judgment is the wish to protect the *sovereignty* of the German state. It is true that the claim that the Treaty on European Union formed a breach of national sovereignty, which had been raised in the application, was declared inadmissible by the Constitutional Court because the

---

[71] J. V. Louis, in *Commentaire Mégret: le droit de la CEE*, Vol. 10, 2nd edn (Edit. de l'Univ. de Bruxelles, 1993), at 569.

[72] BVerfGE 89, 155; English translation of the judgment in [1994] 1 CMLR 57. There is already an immense literature on "Maastricht and the German Constitution", which I cannot fully list here. Contributions *prior* to the October 1993 judgment are conveniently listed in U. Everling, "Überlegungen zur Struktur der Europäischen Union und zum neuen Europa-Artikel des Grundgesetzes", *Deutsches Verwaltungsblatt* 1993, 936, n. 2. A representative list of commentaries of the judgment itself can be found in U. Everling, "Bundesverfassungsgericht und Gerichtshof der Europäischen Gemeinschaften nach dem Maastricht-Urteil" in A. Randelzhofer, R. Scholz, D. Wilke (eds), *Gedächtnisschrift für Eberhard Grabitz* (C. H. Beck, 1995) 57, n. 5. Annotations of the judgment in English by Crossland in *European Law Review* (1994) 206 and by M. Herdegen in *Common Market Law Review* (1994) 235.

[73] On the Court's lack of recognition of the constitutional legislator's clearly expressed will, see C. Tomuschat, "Die europäische Union unter der Aufsicht des Bundesverfassungsgerichts", *Europäische Grundrechte Zeitschrift* (1993) 489, at 492–3. It contrasts with the deference shown by the Conseil Constitutionnel in its *Maastricht II* decision.

Verfassungsbeschwerde procedure only allows for claims based on a breach of individual rights, and not of structural rules of the Constitution.[74] Yet, the deep doctrinal structure of the judgment is formed by what one commentator defined as a "rediscovery" of sovereignty by the *Bundesverfassungsgericht*.[75] Ostensibly, the constitutional standard by which the Maastricht Treaty is judged is the right to vote, recognised in article 38 of the Constitution. But this provision is given a very wide, and entirely unprecedented, interpretation by the Court. It becomes, in the Court's view, a right to *participate, through the vote, in the legitimation of state power*. Through the door of the individual right to vote, the Court brings in the structural principle of *popular sovereignty* as the constitutional standard by which to judge the Treaty on European Union.

The core of the individual right to vote is part of those fundamental principles which, according to the Court's established case law, had to be preserved in the course of the European integration process. This core guarantee implies, first, that the German Parliament must continue to play a meaningful role in the legitimation of Community decision-making, and secondly, that the competences exercised by the Community institutions must be clearly defined and are subject to control by the Constitutional Court itself. Thus, in what can be qualified only as a breath-taking doctrinal *parcours*, the Court starts from the fundamental right to vote and ends by affirming its own power to control whether EC acts might be *ultra vires*.

Already before the 1993 ruling, there was no doubt that the democratic principle was one of those core principles which the Constitutional Court was prepared to protect against encroachments by the Community institutions. But many writers optimistically thought that the penetration of "constitutional" values such as respect for fundamental rights and democratic legitimation in the European Community legal order would gradually dispel any concern which national courts might have about the respect by the Community for fundamental values.[76] The *Maastricht* judgment makes clear

---

[74] Had a constitutional challenge to Maastricht been brought by a political institution (say, one of the *Länder*), then the Court might have had to deal squarely with the sovereignty issue.

[75] J. A. Frowein, "Das *Maastricht*-Urteil und die Grenzen der Verfassungsgerichtsbarkeit", *Zeitschrift für ausländisches öffentliches Recht und Völkerrecht* (1994) 1, at 5. In the commentaries of the judgment, the sovereignty issue is given very uneven attention. Among those who emphasise its central role in the judgment are: J. Kokott, "Deutschland im Rahmen der Europäischen Union—zum Vertrag von Maastricht", *Archiv des öffentlichen Rechts* (1994) 207; W. Schroeder, "Alles unter Karlsruher Kontrolle? Die Souveränitätsfrage im Maastricht-Urteil des BVerfG", *Zeitschrift für Rechtsvergleichung* (1994) 143. See also, in English, M. Herdegen, "Maastricht and the German Constitutional Court: Constitutional Restraints for an 'Ever Closer Union'", *Common Market Law Review* (1994) 235, at 241; and in French, D. Hanf, "Le jugement de la Cour constitutionnelle fédérale allemande sur la constitutionnalité du Traité de Maastricht", *Revue trimestrielle de droit européen* (1994) 391, at 421.

[76] See, for instance, the perspective of a growing "constitutional homogeneity" between the national and European legal order drawn by R. Bieber, B. Kahil-Wolff, L. Muller, "Cours général de droit communautaire", *Collected Courses of the Academy of European Law*, Volume III, Book I (1994) 49, at 59.

that what is meant by democracy, in the eyes of the *Bundesverfassungsgericht*, is that any power (either national or European) exercised over German citizens must be legitimised by the German Parliament as the direct emanation of the German *Staatsvolk*.[77] The Constitution requires there to be a *German democracy*;[78] it does not allow for a truly *European* democracy.

In its judgment, the Court confirms very clearly the post-war constitutional "compromise": the exercise of powers by the European Community institutions is based on constitutional authorisations made by Member States that have preserved their sovereignty.[79] In his extra-judicial writings, judge Kirchhof has insisted on this point by adding that a true transfer of sovereignty would mean that a European (federal) state is being created; this has not happened with the Treaty on European Union and cannot happen as long as the present Constitution is in force. Some writers have argued that such a fundamental change could be decided by the German people themselves in the form of a complete revision of the Constitution,[80] but Kirchhof discards even this possibility by stating that such a constitutional "revolution" presupposes the existence of a "European people" to which sovereignty can be transferred, and that such a European people does not exist now and will not exist in the foreseeable future.[81]

[77] "If sovereign rights (*Hoheitsrechte*) are granted to international institutions, then the representative body elected by the people—the German Bundestag—and along with it the citizens entitled to vote, necessarily lose some influence on the processes of political will-formation and decision-making . . . The democratic principle . . . does not prevent the Federal Republic of Germany from becoming a member of a community of States (organised on a supranational basis). But it is a precondition for membership that a legitimation and an influence proceeding from the people is also secured inside the federation of States (*Staatenverbund*) . . . If the [European] Union carries out sovereign tasks (*hoheitliche Aufgaben*) and exercises sovereign powers (*hoheitliche Befugnisse*) for those purposes, it is first and foremost the national peoples of the Member States who, through their national parliaments, have to provide the democratic legitimation for its so doing": (German Constitutional Court, *Maastricht* judgment of 12 October 1993, BVerfGE 89, 155, at 182–3; translation taken from [1994] 1 CMLR 57, at 85–6; with the German original of some crucial expressions; it must also be mentioned that the translation "federation of States" for the German *Staatenverbund* is not correct).

[78] The ambiguity of the Court's doctrine, with its emphasis on *democratic* values but embedded in a *national* framework, may explain the very different reactions provoked by its judgment among foreign commentators. Positive comments insist on the first element, that of democracy (see e.g. M. Cartabia, "Il pluralismo istituzionale come forma della democrazia sovranazionale", *Politica del Diritto* (1994) 203; R. de Lange, "Het Bundesverfassungsgericht over het Verdrag van Maastricht: een nieuw Solange?", *SEW* (1994) 418), whereas negative comments insist on the state-centred and nationalistic overtones (see e.g. T. Koopmans, "Rechter, D-mark en democratie; het Bundesverfassungsgericht en de Europese Unie", *Nederlands Juristenblad* (1994) 245; A. Gattini, "La Corte costituzionale tedesca e il Trattato sull'Unione europea", *Rivista di diritto internazionale* (1994) 114).

[79] "Die Wahrnehmung von Hoheitsgewalt durch einen Staatenverbund wie die Europäische Union gründet sich auf Ermächtigungen souverän bleibender Staaten . . . " (BVerfGE 89, 155, at 186).

[80] See e.g. R. Streinz, "Das Maastricht-Urteil des Bundesverfassungsgerichts", *Europäische Zeitschrift für Wirtschaftsrecht* (1994), 329, at 332; T. Schilling, "Die deutsche Verfassung und die europäische Einigung", *Archiv des öffentlichen Rechts* (1991) 32, at 65.

[81] P. Kirchhof, "Der deutsche Staat im Prozess der europäischen Integration", in *Handbuch des Staatsrechts der Bundesrepublik Deutschland*, Volume VII, at 882 onwards.

This solemn reaffirmation of the principle of popular sovereignty, in which the "people" is equated with the *Staatsvolk*, reveals that when the Constitutional Court defends the fundamental principles of the constitutional order, it defends not merely the *universalist* principles of democracy, rule of law and fundamental rights but also the *identity* of the constitutional order as that of a particular state; another name for that is state sovereignty.

It would be a misconception to see all this as creating a specifically *German* obstacle on the road to European integration. In the United Kingdom, the principle of sovereignty of Parliament is tamed but not eliminated and continues to attract support in public opinion. In France, as was mentioned before, the post-Maastricht text of the Constitution is very much inspired by the traditional view of sovereignty and the same can be said about the new article 7(6) of the Portuguese Constitution which may have been partially inspired by the French revision.[82]

It is also far from excluded that the "rediscovery" of sovereignty by the German Constitutional Court might find emulation among its counterparts in two other large states of the European Union, Italy and Spain. In *Italy*, no institution or private person has challenged the constitutionality of the Act incorporating the Treaty of Maastricht, so that the Constitutional Court was not called upon to apply its existing doctrine to the new situation arising from Maastricht.[83] Yet, a close analysis of its case law in EC and other matters shows that the Court's theory of "counter-limits" is also inspired by its concern to protect state sovereignty. Powers whose exercise has been attributed to the Community institutions do not escape control; rather, the Constitutional Court considers it as its duty to exercise control so that they are not misused so as to threaten the fundamental principles of the Italian legal order. The dominant doctrinal position, like in Germany, is that a European state cannot be legitimately created as long as the present Italian Constitution is in force,[84] although a "revolutionary" *coup* establishing the United States of Europe might perhaps be greeted with more sympathy here than in Germany.

In *Spain*, the Constitutional Tribunal was, like its French counterpart, called to review in 1992 the constitutionality of the Treaty on European Union, but its remit was restricted by the Government to one single provision of the Treaty: article 8B, dealing with the European citizens" right to vote and

---

[82] "Portugal may, on condition of reciprocity, with respect for the principle of subsidiarity and with the goal of establishing economic and social cohesion, pool, on the basis of a treaty, the exercise of the powers necessary for the construction of the European Union". On the constitutional reform of 1992 in Portugal, see J. Miranda, "La constitution portugaise et le traité de Maastricht", *Revue française de droit constitutionnel* (1992) 679.

[83] For a doctrinal essay on the question whether specific provisions of the TEU breach fundamental principles of the Italian constitutional order, see M. Luciani, "La Costituzione italiana e gli ostacoli all'integrazione europea", *Politica del Diritto* (1992) 557, at 578–88.

[84] M. Luciani, "La Costituzione italiana e gli ostacoli all'integrazione europea", *Politica del Diritto* (1992) 557, at 589.

be elected at local elections. This article was seen to be in direct contrast with the text of the Spanish Constitution, so that the Tribunal did not need to embark on a more wide-ranging review such as that undertaken by the French and German courts. Yet, the Tribunal insisted, in its Maastricht Declaration, on the fact that article 93 of the Constitution allowed only for the transfer of the *exercise* and not of the *ownership* of state powers, which is an implicit confirmation of the traditional doctrine of state sovereignty.

Sovereignty: resilient or obsolete?

Sovereignty is certainly part of the stock of legal principles which are common to the countries of Western Europe. Yet, there is perhaps less common ground today than fifty or even twenty years ago. Sovereignty is a legal concept which continues to have practical consequences in structuring, from the national constitutional perspective, the relation between European Community law and the national legal orders, but its meaning and importance vary considerably. The debate on the Treaty on European Union has started a new phase of turmoil in the legal analysis of European integration, and the concept of sovereignty is playing a key role in this debate which should be acknowledged by both its defenders and its opponents. The outcome of the debate is uncertain. On the one hand, it appears that the continuing expansion of the reach of European integration, combined with a certain disenchantment in public opinion, has lent new force to national sovereignty. On the other hand, an increasing number of legal scholars argue that the reality of European integration should lead to rethink entirely, or even abandon, the concept of sovereignty.

The classical conception of sovereignty has found a powerful advocate in the German Constitutional Court. Its *Maastricht* judgment has been criticized because of its "antiquated" conception of state and sovereignty,[85] but it shows that the doctrine of popular sovereignty continues to have a compelling inner logic which sets clear limits to the scope of integration. In this vision, the sovereignty of the people remains the, almost metaphysical, normative origin of all governmental power and provides legitimacy to all national and international authorities by means of an "uninterrupted chain of democratic legitimation".[86] The national Parliaments are the first link in this chain; the institutions of the European Union can also find their place along this chain, but they should not be allowed to break it.

[85] C. Tomuschat, "Die Europäische Union unter der Aufsicht des Bundesverfassungsgerichts", at 496; T. Koopmans, "Rechter, D-mark en democratie"; J.A. Frowein, "Das *Maastricht*-Urteil"; J. Schwarze, "Europapolitik unter deutschem Verfassungsrichtervorbehalt", *Neue Justiz* (1994) 1, at 3.

[86] This expression was used, extra-judicially, by another of the judges participating in the *Maastricht* judgment: E.W. Böckenförde, "Demokratie als Verfassungsprinzip", in *Handbuch des Staatsrechts*, Vol.I (1987) 887, at 894.

The misgivings about the traditional doctrine start from the pragmatic consideration, buttressed by the analysis of the integration process by political scientists, that formal sovereignty cannot exist in the absence of the effective capacity of states to adopt an autonomous course of action, a capacity which the Member States of the European Union have lost to a smaller or greater extent.[87] Political power is now disaggregated between many institutions both at the national and at the European level. Is the legal fiction that all those powers emanate from a unique source—the people of the nation-state—and that they remain subject to its control, still tenable? Is a legal concept which has become so far removed from the political reality of Western Europe worth preserving?

The efforts made in the various countries to accommodate the time-honoured doctrine of sovereignty, which have been described in earlier sections of this chapter, often lead to theoretical doctrinal "solutions" which seem more like dancing on a doctrinal tightrope.

Some authors have argued for years that one could not account for the legal innovation brought by the European Community by cautiously adapting the old principles; one rather needed to abandon the traditional concept of a unitary and indivisible state sovereignty and revive the alternative doctrine of *divided sovereignty*. That doctrine's philosophical pedigree is as respectable as that of the classical Bodinian concept of indivisible sovereignty.[88] It had been the vogue, in parts of the nineteenth century, in federal states like the USA, Germany and Switzerland,[89] but had almost disappeared from the philosophical and constitutional scene since the beginning of the twentieth century. Even in federal states, sovereignty is held to be residing in the people of the country as a whole (the *Staatsvolk*);[90] this is even true for Switzerland despite the fact that its Constitution refers to the "sovereignty" of the cantons.[91]

Would it be appropriate to resurrect the doctrine of divisible sovereignty in the late twentieth century context of European integration? A positive answer came, some twenty-five years ago already, from the then European Court judge Pierre Pescatore,[92] and the theory is currently defended, among others,

[87] For a recent assessment, see W. Wallace, "Rescue or Retreat? The Nation State in Western Europe, 1945–93", *Political Studies* (1994) 52.

[88] For most of the seventeenth and eighteenth century, the theory of the divisibility of sovereignty dominated in many parts of Europe; see J. H. Franklin, "Sovereignty and the Mixed Constitution: Bodin and his Critics", in J. H. Burns (ed), *The Cambridge History of Political Thought 1450–1700* (Cambridge UP, 1991) 298. But Rousseau insisted heavily on the indivisibility of sovereignty and his views would prove to be highly influential on later thinking (J. J. Rousseau, *Le contrat social* (1762), Livre II, Chapitre II, which is entitled "*Que la souveraineté est indivisible*").

[89] See references in L. Wildhaber, "Sovereignty and International Law", (n. 5 above) at 432–4.

[90] See, on this point, the comparative analysis offered by G. De Vergottini, "Stato federale", *Enciclopedia del Diritto* XLIII (1990) 831, at 835.

[91] According to a leading textbook of Swiss constitutional law, the cantons do not have true sovereignty as their competences are at the mercy of the federal government (U. Häfelin and W. Haller, *Schweizerisches Bundesstaatsrecht* (Schulthess, 1988), at 53.

[92] P. Pescatore, "L'apport du droit communautaire au droit international public", *Cahiers de droit européen* (1970) 501, at 502–11.

in J. V. Louis' widely translated and influential work on the *Community Legal Order*.[93]

Those authors have sought arguments for this alternative view in the text of the German Constitution and the case law of the European Court of Justice. The reference, in article 24 of the German Basic Law, to the possibility of transferring sovereign powers was offered by judge Pescatore as an indication that it made constitutional sense to speak about a (partial) transfer of sovereignty to the European Community, and that sovereignty should henceforth be seen as a bundle of powers that can be divided between levels of government. Yet, in coming to this conclusion, Pescatore relied rather heavily on the usual English (and French) translations of article 24 of the *Grundgesetz* which render as "sovereign powers" (or "*droits souverains*") the German term *Hoheitsrechte*. *Hoheitsrechte* are the form in which sovereignty is exercised, but should not be confused with sovereignty itself, for which the German language has the different term of *Souveränität*. Article 24 of the German Constitution therefore meant that *Hoheitsrechte* (which can be translated as "sovereign rights" for lack of a better term in English) could be attributed to international institutions, just as they can be attributed to the *Länder* institutions,[94] but was not seen by German constitutional lawyers, neither then nor later, as permitting the transfer of a *portion* of *Souveränität* which remains, indivisibly, with the German people.[95]

As for the European Court's rulings in *Van Gend en Loos* and *Costa*, they do not seem to warrant the conclusion that the European Court really wanted to put forward a new doctrine, based on the divisibility of sovereignty, in opposition to the established doctrines in the Member States' constitutional law.[96]

The theory of divisible sovereignty cannot easily be reconciled with the logical structure of the term "sovereignty". If "sovereignty" denotes the *ultimate* authority within a particular territory, then it seems more logical to conceive of this ultimate authority as being held by one institution or collectivity than that it should be dispersed among several institutions. If sovereignty is divided, it loses its distinguishing trait.

A way around this difficulty is not to try to build an *alternative*, more Europe-friendly doctrine of sovereignty, but rather to *abandon* the concept of sovereignty altogether in the legal-constitutional discourse on integration.

---

[93] J. V. Louis, *The Community Legal Order*, 2nd edn (Office for Official Publications of the EC, 1990), at 11 *et seq*. See also R. Barents and L. J. Brinkhorst, *Grondlijnen van Europees recht*, 6th edn (Samsom H. D. Tjeenk Willink, 1994), at 433.

[94] The term *Hoheitsrechte* is, in fact, commonly used for describing the constitutionally-protected competences of the *Länder*. See, for example, the new (post-Maastricht) article 24(1)(a) of the *Grundgesetz*.

[95] This is the absolutely dominant view in German constitutional writing. See H. Mosler, "Die Übertragung von Hoheitsgewalt", in J. Isensee and P. Kirchhof (eds), *Handbuch des Staatsrechts der Bundesrepublik Deutschland*, Vol. VII (1992), 599, at 615.

[96] See p. 000 above.

Several authors, in different countries, have recently made short but intriguing suggestions of this nature. Their view seems to be that, in the relation between the states and the Community, neither of the two has *Kompetenz-Kompetenz* or ultimate authority, and that, therefore, the concept of sovereignty has lost its explanatory value in the present state of European legal integration.[97]

One would like to be convinced by the arguments offered, but the conclusion, that sovereignty is neither here nor there but dissolved in thin air, is rather troublesome. How should one order the complex web of legal relationships in Europe today *without* the help of the principle of sovereignty determining where final authority, in the case of conflict, lies.[98] Moreover, to state that in the relation between the Community and its Member States, either side lacks final authority, may not be entirely correct. Rather, article N of the EU Treaty shows, both by its wording and by the recent application of the similarly worded article 236 of the EEC Treaty on the occasion of the Treaty on European Union, that the ultimate authority lies with the intergovernmental conference of the Member States of the Union and the national constitutional bodies that must ratify their operation. Could it be that sovereignty lies with the peoples of the European Union taken together, rather than with each of those peoples separately? That might be a heretical statement for the German Constitutional Court, but the Russian Constitution of 1993 shows that it can make constitutional sense to attribute sovereignty to a *multinational people*.[99]

---

[97] J. A. Frowein, "Das *Maastricht*-Urteil", (n. 85 above) at 7; T. Koopmans, "Rechter, D-mark en democratie", (n. 78 above) at 249; T. Ohlinger, "Verfassungsfragen zwischen Brussel und Wien", *Revue européenne de droit public/European Review of Public Law* (1993) 143, at 170; the most elaborate recent critique of the concept of sovereignty is by N. MacCormick, "Beyond the Sovereign State", *The Modern Law Review* (1993) 1; and *id.*, "Sovereignty, Democracy, Subsidiarity", *Rechtstheorie* (1994) 281.

[98] See e.g. J. Kokott, "Deutschland im Rahmen", (n. 75 above) at 232: "It cannot, and should not, be possible that, in the case of a conflict, two legal orders have both final responsibility. The citizen would be the victim of this".

[99] Preamble of the Constitution of the Russian Federation: "We, the multinational people of the Russian Federation, . . . adopt the Constitution of the Russian Federation"; and article 3(1): "the holders of sovereignty and the sole source of authority in the Russian Federation are its multinational people." (translation taken from Finer, Bogdanor, Rudden, *Comparing Constitutions*, at 245).

11

Constitutional Dialogues in the European Community

ALEC STONE SWEET

INTRODUCTION

The convenors initiated "The European Court and National Courts—Doctrine and Jurisprudence" project in order to focus scholarly attention on a crucial but understudied component of European legal integration: the reception and implementation of EC law by national jurisdictions. A series of national reports have been produced, each of which traces how one national legal system accommodated the European Court of Justice's jurisprudence of supremacy. This jurisprudence constitutionalised the founding Treaties, and with the Treaties, the European Community. In addition, reporters were asked to describe (or ponder the potential for) the emergence of a jurisprudence, developed by national courts from national sources of law, capable of controlling the legal limits of European integration (an aspect of *Kompetenz-Kompetenz*). These reports demonstrate why an exclusive focus on the ECJ's case law gives us an incomplete, and at times erroneous, picture of the dynamics of constitutionalisation. The construction of a constitutional, "rule of law" Community has been a participatory process, a set of constitutional dialogues between supra-national and national judges.

This chapter presents a preliminary evaluation of these dialogues.[1] The first part will be an examination of the central tenets of the European Court's constitutional jurisprudence, before turning to existing scholarly approaches to the construction of the EC legal system. There then follows an elaboration on two linked sets of constitutional dialogues, or sites of ongoing inter-institutional interaction. The first is a set of intrajudicial dialogues between

[1] This chapter originally appeared as EUI Working Paper RSC No. 95/38, and is published here without substantial revision. Subsequent research in this area includes: Alec Stone Sweet and Thomas Brunell, "Constructing a Supranational Constitution: Dispute Resolution and Governance in the European Community", *American Political Science Review* (forthcoming 1998); Alec Stone Sweet and James A. Caporaso, "The European Court and Integration", *Revue française de science politique* (forthcoming 1998); and Alec Stone Sweet and Thomas Brunell, "The European Court and the National Courts: A Statistical Analysis of Preliminary References, 1961–1995, *Journal of European Public Policy* (forthcoming, 1998). The author is grateful to the National Science Foundation (Award No. SBR 94-12531) for its support of the project, "Constructing a Supranational Constitution" (1994–97).

the ECJ, conceived as a supra-national constitutional court, and national judges on the primacy of EC law in national legal orders. The second is the dialogue between the ECJ, national courts, and national legislators in the making of public policy.

CONSTITUTIONALISING THE TREATY SYSTEM

By "constitutionalisation" is meant the process by which the EC Treaties evolved from a set of legal arrangements binding upon sovereign states, into a vertically-integrated legal regime conferring judicially enforceable rights and obligations on all legal persons and entities, public and private, within EC territory. Put differently, it is the process by which the sources of EC law—the Treaties, secondary legislation, and the jurisprudence of the ECJ—have penetrated into national legal systems, and are enforced as law in proceedings before national judges. Two points deserve emphasis. First, constitutionalisation was neither preordained by the Treaties, nor an unforeseen consequence of them (e.g., a result of functional spillover). Rather, judicial will—the consistent interpretation, in the jurisprudence of the European Court, of the nature of EC legal norms and of the place of those norms within the legal system—provided the catalyst. Any account of constitutionalisation must begin with this jurisprudence. Secondly, the level of constitutionalisation can only be measured, at any given moment or across time, by how national courts have actually received this jurisprudence. The study of Community law is thus, *per force*, the study of comparative law. Put baldly, we can not begin to understand the constitutionalisation process until we take the second point as seriously as we do the first.

The process of constitutionalising the treaty system

What is innovative—what is constitutional—about the ECJ's jurisprudence is that it requires national judges to apply EC law as if it were an integral part of the national legal order. Simplifying, there have been two waves of constitutionalisation. In the 1962–79 period, the Court secured the core, constitutional principles of supremacy and direct effect. The Court made these moves despite the declared opposition of the Member States.[2] The *doctrine of supremacy* lays down the rule that in *any* conflict between an EC legal norm and a norm of national law, the EC norm must be given primacy.[3] Indeed, according to the Court, every EC norm, from the moment it enters into force, "renders automatically inapplicable any conflicting provision of . . . national

---

[2] Eric Stein, "Lawyers, Judges, and the Making of a Transnational Constitution", (1981) 75 *American Journal of International Law* 1–27.

[3] *Costa*, Case 6/64, [1964] CMLR 425.

law".[4] The *doctrine of direct effect* holds that provisions of EC law can confer on individuals rights that public authorities must respect, and which must be protected by national courts. During this period, the ECJ found that Treaty provisions[5] and directives[6] were directly effective, and the Court strengthened the direct effect of regulations.[7] As a consequence of the jurisprudence of direct effect, individuals and companies are empowered to sue Member State Governments or other public authorities for either not conforming to obligations contained in the Treaties or regulations, or for not properly transposing provisions of directives into national law. The jurisprudence of supremacy prohibits public authorities from relying on national law to justify their failure to comply with EC law, and requires national judges to resolve conflicts between national and EC law in favour of the latter. The ECJ thus constituted a Community legal order on the basis of a sophisticated monism, demanding that the orthodoxies of dualism, like *lex posteriori derogat leggi priori*, give way.[8]

In the second wave, the Court supplied national judges with enhanced means of guaranteeing the effectiveness of EC law. In 1983, the *doctrine of indirect effect* was established, according to which national judges must interpret national law in conformity with EC law.[9] The Court subsequently ruled that when a directive has either not been transposed or has been transposed incorrectly into national law, national judges must interpret existing national law to be in conformity with the directive.[10] The doctrine empowers national judges to rewrite national legislation—an exercise called "principled construction"—in order to render EC law applicable in the absence of implementing measures. Once national law has been so (re)constructed, EC law (in the guise of the national rule) can be applied in legal disputes between private legal persons (i.e., non-governmental entities). Thus, indirect effect

---

[4] *Simmenthal*, Case 70/77, [1978] ECR 1453.

[5] *Van Gend en Loos*, Case 26/62, [1963] CMLR 105.

[6] *Van Duyn*, Case 41/74, [1974] ECR 1337.

[7] Regulations are the only class of EC legislation recognised by the EEC Treaty to be "directly applicable". The ECJ has strengthened this applicability by, among other things, declaring that national implementing measures are "contrary to the Treaty" if they "have the result of creating an obstacle to the direct effect of Community Regulations", e.g., *Commission* v. *Italy*, Case 39/72, [1973] ECR 161.

[8] Simplifying, according to monist theories, international law and national law are part of a single hierarchy of norms, wherein international law is superior to national law. In dualist theories, international law and national law are conceived as separate legal orders, to be coordinated by national constitutional law. Although there are exceptions (discussed below), European legal systems have traditionally tended toward dualism: treaty law enters into the national legal order only after having been transposed—ratified—by a statute passed by the legislature. Once transposed, legislation and treaty law possess equivalent status, since they are produced by equivalent acts of the legislature. The juridical relationship between these two legislative acts is traditionally governed by the doctrine of *lex posteriori*, which states that when an irresoluble conflict between two otherwise equivalent legal norms arises in the context of a legal dispute, the judge must resolve the dispute by applying the most recently produced law. Thus, in a conflict between a statute adopted *after* the ratification of a treaty provision, the judge must refuse to apply the treaty law on the grounds that Parliament's latest word on the matter is controlling.

[9] *Van Colson*, Case 14/83, [1984] ECR 1891.

[10] *Marleasing*, Case C-106, 89, [1992] CMLR 305.

substantially reduces the problem that the Court's doctrine of direct effect only applies to disputes between a private person and a governmental entity. Finally, in 1990, the Court declared the *doctrine of governmental liability*.[11] According to this doctrine, a national court can hold a Member State liable for damages caused to individuals due to the failure on the part of the Member State to properly implement or apply a directive. The national court may then order Member States to compensate such individuals for their losses.

In summary, the ECJ's jurisprudence of supremacy *imagines* a particular type of relationship between the European and national courts: a working partnership in the construction of a constitutional, "rule of law" Community. In that partnership, national judges become agents of the Community order— they become *Community judges*—whenever they resolve disputes governed by EC law. The Court *obliges* the national judge to uphold the supremacy of EC law, even against conflicting subsequent national law; *encourages* her to make references concerning the proper interpretation of EC law to the Court; and *empowers* her (even without a referral) to interpret national rules so that these rules will conform to EC law, and to refuse to apply national rules when they do not. The ECJ has derived as much from the doctrine of supremacy.

Understanding constitutionalisation

Two deep, yet unresolved, mysteries accompanied the constitutionalisation process. First, why would the Member States acquiesce in such a profound, structural transformation of the Community's legal order? In declaring the doctrines of supremacy and direct effect, the Court had, after all, radically rewritten the Treaties (the Treaties contain neither supremacy clause nor textual support for the direct effect of Treaty provisions and directives). Further, the Court had accomplished this revision without overt Member State support, at a time when Member State Governments, *via* the Luxembourg compromise, had sacrificed progress on economic integration in order to preserve the essential inter-governmental elements of the Community. Our project is animated by a second mystery: why would national judges be willing to accept the ECJ's vision of a Community legal order? The Court's jurisprudence, after all, requires profound changes in the role and function of the national courts. To accept supremacy, for example, is to abandon, in every domain governed by EC law, the prohibition on judicial review of legislation—a Continental orthodoxy in place in every legal system under study in this project—as well as deeply entrenched *lex posteriori* solutions to coordinating international and national law. Although we do not have a theory of legal integration capable of solving either mystery, existing approaches to understanding European legal integration provide some guidance.

---

[11] *Francovich*, Joined Cases C-6/90 and C-9/90, [1992] IRLR 84.

Implementing the law

Simplifying a great deal, two types of legal scholarship dominate the field: (a) doctrinal analyses of the ECJ's case law, and (b) single-country, doctrinal analyses of the reception of that case law by national courts. In the first, scholars have worked to synthesise and publicise the Court's jurisprudence. Because the Court's jurisprudence is designed to ensure the unified application of EC law, the approach implicitly assumes that there will be a cross-national unification of doctrine and practice, and treats resistance to constitutionalisation on the part of national judges as anomalous, deviant behaviour. Yet, as the national reports document, such resistance has been a permanent feature of the Community's legal order. In the second, scholars assume that national law—and especially the judicial interpretation of constitutional provisions governing the relationship between municipal and treaty law—mediates the reception of EC law and the ECJ's jurisprudence. National deviance from the blueprint laid down by the European Court is treated as normal rather than pathological, to the extent that the blueprint conflicts with the national constitutional law of treaties. The approach suggests that even if we maintain a formal legal-doctrinal perspective (ignoring factors external to the law), we have no reason to presume that in a conflict between an EC norm and a subsequent national statute, national judges would follow supra-national precepts, newly constructed by the ECJ, rather than long-lived precepts developed and curated by national judges. Although often in conflict, both perspectives are valuable in their own right: the first provides us with a clear benchmark for measuring compliance with the dictates of EC law; the second provides us with data on the extent of that compliance. Taken together, these approaches signal to us that the process of constitutionalisation, being the enmeshment of two legal systems, will likely be one of conflict, compromise, and accommodation. That advantage stated, neither can predict the patterns of accommodation that have actually emerged.

Implementing the preferences of the Member States

This is an approach most explicitly elaborated by Garrett, who employs a "modified structural realist" (political science-international relations) approach[12] to the EC legal system.[13] Garrett notices that the EC is a regime unique in the world, possessing a capacity to generate legal norms which are both binding among and within the Member States. He notices, further, that these norms are capable of being enforced by courts at both the national and supra-national levels. Both of these findings conflict with fundamental

---

[12] For a survey of international relations theory relevant to the EC and international law and institutions more generally, see Alec Stone, "What is a Supranational Constitution?: An Essay in International Relations Theory", *Review of Politics* 56 (1994), 441–74

[13] Geoffrey Garrett, "International Cooperation and Institutional Choice: The EC's Internal Market", *International Organization* 46 (1992), 533–60.

precepts of his theory, which do not easily (if ever) allow for a meaningfully autonomous role for institutions and law in international affairs. Garrett resolves this tension by arguing that the development of the legal system was "consistent with the interests of the member states", and especially the most powerful of them. By providing a relatively cheap system of monitoring compliance and reducing the incentives of non-compliance, the system is an unusually sophisticated means of reducing bargaining and information costs in an unusually complex, multi-sectoral international regime. Although virtually no evidence is marshalled to support the claim, Garrett asserts that the ECJ, in its case law, codifies the policy preferences of the dominant Member States, thus reinforcing their dominance. The advantage of the approach is that it brings the political world—governments, national interests, and policy choices to be made—into the picture. Garrett's account is nonetheless riddled with problems (the approach has been strongly criticised elsewhere[14]), and nothing in it helps us to understand ECJ-national court interaction. Under his assumptions, we would at least expect that national courts would refuse to apply an EC norm if the Government or legislature signalled to the courts that it ought to apply conflicting national norms. But we know that all national courts have embraced supremacy and direct effect, in one guise or another, and regularly apply EC norms over conflicting, subsequently-enacted national norms.

Pursuing judicially-bounded interests

Building on the insights of legal scholarship,[15] Slaughter and Mattli have proposed an ingenious solution to both mysteries.[16] The answer to the first, they argue, is that legal processes are conducted in an insular, specialised discourse meaningfully distinct from the "normal", power and interest-based language of politics and political science. Put baldly, Governments simply did not understand what was happening until it was too late, presumably, until the costs of changing the system had risen to unacceptably high levels. Their account of the reception of the ECJ's doctrines by national courts is a dynamic and process-oriented. Simplifying, the EC legal system resembles a machine, animated by self-interested actors operating both above and below the nation state.[17] Litigation of EC law provides fuel for the machine. Litigators are seek-

[14] See Walter Mattli and Anne-Marie Slaughter, "Law and Politics in the European Union: A Reply to Garrett", *International Organization* 49 (1995), 183–90.

[15] Especially Stein, n. 2 above; Joseph H. H. Weiler, "The Community System: The Dual Character of Supranationalism", *Yearbook of European Law* 1 (1981), 268–306; Joseph H. H. Weiler, "The Transformation of Europe", *Yale Law Journal* 100 (1991), 2403–83.

[16] Anne-Marie Burley (now Slaughter) and Walter Mattli, "Europe Before the Court: A Political Theory of Legal Integration", *International Organization* 47 (1993), 41–76.

[17] The supranational equivalent of the "jurisprudential transmission belt" that is at the heart of European constitutional politics. See Alec Stone, "Governing with Judges", in J. Hayward and E. Page (eds.), *Governing the New Europe* (Oxford: Polity); Alec Stone, "Judging Socialist Reform: The Politics of Coordinate Construction in France and Germany", *Comparative Political Studies* 26 (1994), 443–69.

ing to force governments to comply with EC law, or to obtain redress for damages suffered as a result of non-compliance. National judges have an interest in referring these cases to the ECJ to the extent that the system will provide them with powers (of judicial review, for example) that they would not otherwise have. The ECJ encourages such referrals as a means of strengthening its own position by facilitating the penetration of EC law into the national legal order. Thus, the EC legal system functions to mutually legitimise, and thus mutually empower, judicial authority at both the national and supra-national levels. Finally, the machine creates its own momentum, as an ever expanding jurisprudence opens up both EC and national law to ever more litigation.

Sensitive to the social agency of law, to the complex interactions of official and non-official actors, and to the power of judicial process to socialise, the approach is an indispensable starting point for any serious research on European legal integration. Nevertheless, it is just as clear that the model distorts the constitutionalisation process in important ways. According to Slaughter and Mattli, for example, the institutional interests of courts (or the self-interest of judges) work in only one direction: toward an ever-deepening legal integration. Yet as the reports make clear, powerful disincentives to cooperating with the ECJ are also present.

Deriving propositions In the absence of systematic, cross-national research on the reception of EC law and the jurisprudence of the European Court by national courts, we should not expect that any of the approaches surveyed can adequately explain the dynamics or mechanics of legal integration processes in the EC. Nor was our project designed to adjudicate among these approaches. Existing explanations can be extraordinarily valuable nonetheless, to the extent that they can be distilled into a set of propositions which are: (1) capable of generating research questions; (2) useful in analyzing and evaluating data; (3) falsifiable. Four such propositions may be derived as follows:

(1a)   Proposition 1a: legal integration processes, driven by the pedagogical authority of the ECJ's jurisprudence, will ultimately result in a relatively coherent and unified legal system across institutional and national boundaries. Whatever doctrinal variance has existed will continue to narrow over time, in the direction of a more or less unified position.

(1b)   Proposition 1b: the more a national constitution provides for the supremacy of international law over national law, the more likely it will be for national courts to implement the ECJ's constitutional vision as pronounced.

(2)   Proposition 2: the ECJ's case law codifies the preferences of the dominant Member States, and will thus be faithfully implemented by the national courts. If, however, Governments enact legislation that conflicts with prior EC law, the national courts will give national law effect.

(3)   Proposition 3: the interaction of self-interested litigators and judges will unify and render increasingly effective the EC legal system. The number of EC law cases in each system will rise not fall, the jurisprudence of constitutionalisation will advance not retreat, and judicial control over national policy outcomes will deepen in old areas and widen in new areas touched by EC law.

These propositions will be evaluated, in light of the national reports and other research, in the two sections which follow. Propositions 1a and 1b direct our attention to an ongoing *doctrinal* dialogue between the ECJ and national courts as to the nature of the EC polity. Propositions 2 and 3 direct our attention to the policy-making impact of constitutionalisation. In the third section below, this impact is largely conceived as a set of *policy* dialogues.

CONSTITUTIONAL DIALOGUES: THREE PROBLEMS OF SUPREMACY

The ECJ broadcasted its vision of a constitutional order to national legal systems in the form of the doctrines of supremacy and direct effect. Not only had the ECJ consciously targeted an audience, that of national lawyers and judges but, over the past three decades, its message has been a remarkably consistent one. National courts did not just receive this message passively, but talked back, fully conscious that their response would be registered by the European Court. The national reports provide detailed assessments of the national responses to the supremacy-direct effect cluster in six Member States. What is clear from the reports is that legal integration processes have been driven as much by intra-judicial *conflict* as they have been by *cooperation*. Three interrelated, but nonetheless analytically separable, doctrinal "problem" areas have structured these interactions: (1) the problem of constitutional review, (2) the problem of fundamental rights, and (3) the problem of *Kompetenz-Kompetenz*. These interactions have in turn produced a wide reaching supremacy doctrine, induced the construction an enforceable charter of rights for the Community, and provoked a still unsettled controversy about the nature and legitimacy of the EC polity.

Supremacy and the problem of constitutional review

The supremacy doctrine evolved out of a delicate, often conflictual, dialogue between the Italian Constitutional Court (ICC) and the ECJ. As the Italian Report (Ch 6) documents, the evolution of the Italian constitutional law of treaties and the doctrine of supremacy have gone hand in hand. The story begins in 1962, when Mr. Costa went on trial for refusing to pay a three dollar electrical bill in protest at the nationalisation of electrical companies in Italy. Costa, a shareholder in one of the companies expropriated, defended himself on the grounds that the nationalisation violated article 37 of the EEC Treaty (which seeks to ensure that "national monopolies" are not managed in a discriminatory manner). The trial judge referred the matter both to the ECJ and the ICC.

The Italian Court, which disposed of the case first, was faced with determining the relative primacy of two sets of constitutional provisions. The first governs the relationship between international and national law: article 10 provides that "the Italian legal order conforms to the general principle of international law", and article 11 authorises the state to "limit" its sovereignty in order to "promote and encourage international organisations" like the EC. The second, article 80, states that treaty law enters into force upon an Act of Parliament. In its decision, the ICC declared that because treaty law possesses the same normative value as legislation, the *lex posteriori* rule controls, and Costa lost his case.[18] Five months later, the ECJ rejected Costa's claim as unfounded, at the same time announcing the doctrine of supremacy.[19] The decision repudiated all national *lex posteriori* doctrines to the extent that they inhibit the effective application of EC law.

Ignoring the ECJ's jurisprudence, the ICC let stand its position on *lex posteriori* until its 1977 ruling in *Società industrie chimiche* (ICC 1977). Simplifying, whereas in *Costa* the ICC had allowed article 80 to govern the case, in *Società industrie chimiche* it shifted control to articles 10 and 11. At this point, however, the ICC's conception of constitutional review got in the way. Arguing that the prohibition of judicial review prohibited the direct enforcement of treaty law against subsequent, conflicting legislation, the Court declared that judges would only be permitted to abandon the *lex posteriori* rule upon authorisation by the ICC, that is, after a preliminary reference. Thus, in the cases where the supremacy doctrine comes into play, the applicability of EC law would be subject to the enormous delays attending Italian constitutional review processes. From the perspective of EC law, directly applicable rights would be held hostage to an idiosyncratic, national procedure.

Some Italian judges, apparently hoping to gain a measure of autonomy from the ICC, worked to undermine this jurisprudence. The crucial case involved the importation of French beef into Italy by the Simmenthal company. In 1973, Italian customs authorities billed Simmenthal nearly 600,000 lire to pay for mandatory health inspections of its meat as it crossed the border. The border inspections, mandated by legislation passed in 1970, conflicted with the EEC Treaty and with two EC regulations dating from the 1960s. Simmenthal challenged the border inspections in an Italian court, which referred the matter to the ECJ. The European Court,[20] ruled that the border inspections violated principles of free movement and EC regulations,

---

[18] ICC decisions mentioned here are reported in the Italian Report (Ch 5).
[19] *Costa*, Case J 6/64, [1964] CMLR 425.
[20] *Simmenthal* v. *Minister for Finance* (*Simmenthal I*), Case 35/76, [1976] ECR 1871.

and authorised the Italian judge to order the Italian Government to return Simmenthal's payment. The Italian Government appealed the judge's order, partly on the grounds that only the ICC could authorise an Italian court to set aside national legislation, whereupon the judge requested the ECJ to declare the ICC's *Società industrie chimiche* jurisprudence incompatible with the supremacy doctrine! The European Court (*Simmenthal II*, ECJ 1978) agreed,[21] declaring that EC norms, from their entry into force, become immediately enforceable in every courtroom throughout the Community. Consequently, "any provision of a national legal system and any legislative, administrative, or judicial practice which might impair the effectiveness of Community law"—such as a mandatory concrete review process—"are incompatible with . . . *the very essence* of Community law".

The ICC let stand its *Società industrie chimiche* jurisprudence for nearly a decade. Finally, in *Granital* (ICC 1984), the Italian Court ruled that EC law is directly applicable by ordinary judges, without a preliminary reference to the ICC.[22] In its decision, the ICC was careful to stress that the Italian constitution and not the ECJ governed the relationship between Community law and national legislation, and that, contrary to the European Court's vision of things, the European and national legal orders are "independent and separate" of each other.

In this saga, both the ECJ and the ICC have remained stubbornly attached to their own "inalienable conceptual orders".[23] Nevertheless, the ICC has been forced to adapt far more than has the European Court. The European Court, for its part, has refused to back down, using its interactions with the ICC to clarify and extend its message. Cross-nationally, it has been in those states where constitutional review by constitutional courts exists—France, Germany, and Italy—that supremacy has proved to be the most problematic.

In France, despite what looks on the surface to be friendly terrain, the story is one of confusion. The constitution of 1958 is resolutely monist, article 55 declaring that treaty law is both part of French law and superior to statute. Given the fragmentation of the legal system, it is unsurprising that each of France's three autonomous high courts would have to take a position on article 55 and its relationship to supremacy. In 1975, in a decision having no relationship to EC law, the Constitutional Council ruled (contrary to the ICC's position) that constitutional review and the review of the conformity of national legislation with treaty law were inherently different juridical exercises, and that its powers were limited exclusively to constitutional review.[24] This decision is now commonly read as constitutional authorisation, granted

---

[21] *Simmenthal v. Commission* (*Simmenthal II*), Case 92/78, [1978] ECR 1129.
[22] The ICC finessed the constitutional review issue, ordering judges simply to ignore national law conflicting with antecedent EC law.
[23] Ami Barav, "Cour constitutionnelle italienne et droit communautaire: le fantôme de Simmenthal", *Revue triméstérielle de Droit européenne* 21 (1985), 314.
[24] Reported in Ch 2, Report on France, p. 43.

by the Council to the judiciary, to accept supremacy. Although the interpretation has found its way into Jens Plötner's Report on France (Ch 3), it should be resisted or at least relativised. The fact is that the civil courts needed no such authorisation. In *Vabre*, four years *before* the Council's ruling, a Paris trial court had set aside certain customs rules, adopted in a law of 1966, that effectively taxed imports from other EC countries more than the same products produced in France.[25] The French administration had argued that the civil courts could not apply EC Treaty law without overruling the *lex posteriori* rule and thus "making of themselves judges of the constitutionality of laws". The trial court disagreed, basing its decision on both article 55 and the autonomous nature of EC law. The ruling was upheld by the Paris court of appeal and by the high civil court, the Cour de Cassation.

France's administrative courts refused to accept supremacy until 1989 in *Nicolo*.[26] Before *Nicolo*, the position was that while article 55 provided for the supremacy of treaty law over statute, the administrative courts could not enforce this supremacy, because (1) judicial review was prohibited, and (2) the authority to set aside legislation conflicting with a constitutional provision rested exclusively with the Constitutional Council. In *Nicolo*, the Council of State simply empowered the administrative courts to enforce article 55, while avoiding mention of the ECJ, the status of Community law, the *Vabre* line of decisions, or the Constitutional Council's jurisprudence on article 55. Further, in *Nicolo* the the Council of State's legal advisor went out of his way to criticise the ECJ and its monist and "supranational" vision of the Community.

The tortuous accommodation of supremacy by French, Italian, and—as we will see below—German legal systems contrasts sharply with how smoothly supremacy was received by judiciaries of the other three member legal systems included in our project. In each of these systems, judicial review is prohibited, and constitutional review by a specialised constitutional jurisdiction does not exist. Claes and DeWitt's Report on the Netherlands (Ch 7) documents the clearest case we have of reception proceeding according to the design of the European Court. In the Dutch constitutional order, the authors demonstrate, "monism reigns without dispute". Articles 65 and 66 (dating from 1953, today renumbered as articles 93 and 94) provide both for the direct applicability of international agreements and their primacy in any conflict with national legal norms, whether the latter norms were produced prior or subsequently to the former. The next article extends the rules governing direct applicability and primacy to decisions taken by international organisations. Even more extraordinary, the doctrinal community interprets the supremacy clause as bestowing upon international agreements supremacy even over the Constitution itself. Given the prohibition of constitutional review, write Claes and DeWitt (Ch 7), "treaties are more effectively enforceable than the Constitution".

---

[25] *Vabre*, Paris District Trial Court 1971, reported in [1976] CMLR 43.
[26] Reported in Ch 2, Report on France, p. 46.

Belgium provides a more rigorous test of the power of the ECJ's jurisprudence to reshape national legal orders. In Belgium, the Constitution tends toward a dualist relationship between international and municipal law; further, prior to the constitutionalisation of the treaties, the *lex posteriori* doctrine was securely in place. But, as the Report on Belgium (Ch 2), documents, Belgian courts easily swept aside these potential obstacles, on their own, without formal constitutional authorisation. The doctrine of *lex posteriori* was abandoned in the *Le Ski* judgment, rendered in 1971 by the Cour de cassation.[27] Cassation was supported in this endeavour by the Procureur général and the doctrinal community, both of which had been won over by the European Court's jurisprudence. The judgment proclaims its acceptance of supremacy and direct effect in monist terms: "The primacy of the Treaty results from the very nature of international law". Although one notices that this formulation differs from the European Court's insistence on the "autonomy" and "specificity" of the EC legal order as the basis for supremacy, the decision would probably not have been rendered in the absence of the ECJ's jurisprudence. In any event, according to Bribosia, there appear to be "no substantial legal consequences" to be drawn from this difference in language.

In terms of formal constitutional doctrine, supremacy and direct effect should arguably have met their chilliest reception in the courts of the United Kingdom. In the United Kingdom, the organising precept of constitutional law is the doctrine of Parliamentary sovereignty: the only legal limitation to legislative power is that a parliament of today cannot, with legislation, bind a parliament of tomorrow. The doctrine prohibits judicial review of legislation, and implies a rigid *lex posteriori* solution. Further, the United Kingdom constitutes the archetype of a dualist regime.[28] The formal acceptance of supremacy by the House of Lords, the United Kingdom's sole final judicial authority, came in 1991, in *Factortame II*.[29] Before this decision, when faced with statutory provisions that seemingly did not conform to Community norms, Paul Craig reports (Ch 8), UK courts either (1) applied the UK provisions, invoking *lex posteriori*, under the guise of "implied repeal" of the EC norm, a solution in open violation with the ECJ's jurisprudence of supremacy; or, (2) engaged in "strong principles of construction", in order to "read" the UK norm "so as to be compatible with Community law requirements". This latter practice, aided and abetted by an increasing use of article 177 references, appears to have prepared the way for full acceptance of supremacy, since it involved UK judges in techniques of interpretation associated more with continental than with native judging.

---

[27] Reported in Ch 1, Report on Belgium, p. 10. Bribosia asserts but does not explain exactly how this judgment could settle the question for the administrative courts, an autonomous judicial order.

[28] That is, any norm of international law that modifies the legal rights and obligations of UK citizens must be transposed to have effect within the United Kingdom. This law is then subject to implied repeal (*lex posteriori*).

[29] Reported in Ch 7, Report on the United Kingdom, p. 201 ff.

In *Factortame II*, the House of Lords implemented an ECJ ruling which all but required the construction of a theory of national sovereignty capable of receiving the supremacy doctrine. This the Lords did at the cost of abandoning, but only with respect to EC law, the implied repeal doctrine: the European Communities Act 1972, which states that the effect of all British statutes is subject to the terms of Community law, binds UK courts, at least unless Parliament *expressly* states that it wishes to derogate from Community law. Although Lord Bridge asserts that the nature of the 1972 Act "has always been clear", and that "there is nothing in anyway novel in according supremacy to rules of Community law", the fact remains that no court would have recognised either in 1972. The acceptance of supremacy is a surface manifestation of a much deeper process—a "Europeanisation" of British judging.[30] Europeanisation has enhanced the power of judges to control policy outcomes, to the detriment of traditional conceptions of Parliamentary sovereignty.[31]

Supremacy and the problem of fundamental rights

One hugely important, but wholly unintended, consequence of the ECJ's elaboration of the supremacy doctrine has been the progressive construction of a charter of rights for the Community. The EEC Treaty originally contained no such charter, although several provisions of the treaty—including the principles of non-discrimination based on nationality (article 7), and equal pay for equal work among men and women (article 119)—can be read as rights provisions. Their purpose was not so much to create rights claims for individuals, as to remove potential sources of distortion within an emerging common market. If, in 1959, the ECJ declared itself to be without power to review Community acts with reference to fundamental rights,[32] in 1969 the Court ruled that it had a positive duty to ensure that Community acts conform to fundamental rights;[33] and, in 1989, the Court secured the power to review the acts of the Member States for rights violations.[34] The Court has thus radically revised the Treaties, "wisely and courageously" in Weiler's terms.[35]

The move, however, was not voluntary.[36] An incipient rebellion against supremacy, led by national courts, drove the process. Just after the the

---

[30] Jonathan E. Levitsky, "The Europeanization of the British Style", *American Journal of Comparative Law* 42 (1994), 347–80.

[31] See also P. P. Craig, "Sovereignty of the UK Parliament After Factortame", *Yearbook of European Law* (1991), 221–56.

[32] *Stork*, ECJ 1/58

[33] *Stauder* v. *City of Ulm*, Case 26/69, [1970] CMLR 112.

[34] *Wachauf* v. *State*, Case 5/88, [1991] 1 CMLR 328.

[35] Joseph H. H. Weiler, "Eurocracy and Distrust", *Washington Law Review* 61 (1986), 1105–6.

[36] Mancini and Keeling are careful to state that the ECJ was not "bulldozed" but only "forced" by national courts into recognizing fundamental rights, G. Federico Mancini and David T. Keeling, "Democracy and the European Court of Justice", *The Modern Law Review* 57 (1994), 187.

doctrine of supremacy was announced, Italian and German judges noticed that supremacy would work to insulate EC law from national rights protection. They began challenging—in references to the ECJ and to their own constitutional courts—the legality of a range of EC legislative acts, on the theory that these acts violated national constitutional rights. The *International Handelsgesellschaft* case provides an important example. The case involved a financial penalty (the forfeiture of an export deposit) permitted by EC regulations adopted in 1967, and administered against a German exporter by the German Government. In its referral to the ECJ, the administrative court of Frankfurt complained that the regulations appeared to violate German constitutional rights. In its response, the ECJ declared that EC law could not be overridden by national rights provisions "without the legal basis of the Community itself", i.e., supremacy, "being called into question". But recognising the seriousness of the challenge, the Court declared that "respect for fundamental rights"—"inspired by the constitutional traditions of the member states"—"forms an integral part of the general principles of law protected by the Court of Justice". Although the German Government argued that the Court had no power to do so, the ECJ then reviewed the regulations for their conformity with these fundamental rights, but found no violation.[37] As Juliane Kokott reports, the case did not end there. Disappointed with the ECJ's ruling, the Frankfurt court asked the German Federal Constitutional Court (GFCC) to declare the EC rules unconstitutional. Although the GFCC refused to do so, it declared (by a 5–3 vote) that "*as long as* the integration process has not progressed so far that Community law also possesses a catalogue of rights . . . of settled validity, which is adequate in comparison with a catalogue of fundamental rights contained in the [German] constitution", the GFCC would permit German constitutional review of EC acts.[38] The decision is today known as the *Solange I* (the first "as long as") decision.

In response to cases like these, the ECJ became increasingly explicit about the fundamental rights it had promised to protect. In *Nold*,[39] the Court declared that it would annul "[Community] measures which are incompatible with fundamental rights recognised and protected by the constitutions of the member states". In the same case, the Court also announced that international human rights treaties signed by the Member States, including the European Convention on Human Rights, would "supply guidelines" to the Court. The Court has thereafter referred to the Convention as if it were a basic source of Community rights, and has invoked it in review of Member State acts (*Rutili*,[40] *Commission* v. *Germany*).[41] Although some uncertainty remains,

---

[37] *Internationale Handelsgesellschaft Gmbh* v. *Einfuhr-und-Vorratsstelle für Getreide und Futtermittel*, Case 11/70, [1972] CMLR 155.

[38] GFCC decisions mentioned here are reported in Ch 4, Report on Germany, p. 79 ff.

[39] *Nold* v. *Commission*, Case 4/73, [1975] ECR 985.

[40] *Rutili* v. *Ministry of the Interior*, Case 36/75,]1975] ECR 1219.

[41] Case 249/89, [1990] 3 CMLR 540.

national courts have generally been persuaded by these moves. In 1986, the GFCC set aside *Solange I*. In *Solange II*, it declared that "a measure of protection of fundamental rights has been established . . . which, in its conception, substance and manner of implementation, is essentially compatible with the standards established by the German constitution". The GFCC then prohibited preliminary references from German courts attacking the constitutionality of EC acts "*as long as* the EC, and in particular the ECJ, generally ensures an effective protection of fundamental rights".

The European Court's jurisprudence of supremacy and fundamental rights are tightly linked, to each other, and to a particular vision of the Community. Without supremacy, the ECJ had decided, the common market was doomed. And without a judicially enforceable charter of rights, national courts had decided, the supremacy doctrine was doomed. The ECJ could have maintained its original position which, in effect, held that fundamental rights were part of national—but not Community—law; the courts of the Member States could have begun to annul EC acts judged to be unconstitutional. In either event, legal integration might have been fatally undermined. As it happened, no EC act has ever been censored, by the ECJ or a national court, for violating Community or national rights provisions.

Supremacy and the constitutional limits to integration

Interactions between the European and national constitutional courts have led to stable accommodations on rights and to the obligation of ordinary courts to enforce EC law. But they did not resolve the fundamental problem posed by supremacy: who has the *ultimate* authority to determine the constitutionality of EC acts? The author's position is that the problem, however worrying to some, is in fact irresoluble. On the one hand, the logic of supremacy suggests that the ECJ alone should have such authority, as guardian of the constitutional order of the EC, and the Court—in *Foto-Frost*[42]—has declared as much. On the other hand, as all of our reports show, national constitutional courts, guardians of their own constitutional orders, view Community law as a species of international law which must either conform to national constitutional rules or be invalid as law. These courts, even at their most integration-friendly, have always been careful to reserve for themselves the final authority to determine the constitutionality of EC acts.

The German Constitutional Court's decision on the Maastricht Treaty on European Union (TEU) is the most unequivocal such ruling to date. Because of its far-reaching scope, the Maastricht Treaty required an accommodation between the European and national constitutions. The TEU (which also commits EC Member States to enhanced cooperation in foreign policy, security,

---

[42] *Foto-Frost* v. *Hauptzollamt Lübeck-Ost*, Case 314/85, *The Times*, 30 December 1987.

and social policy) established European citizenship for all EC nationals and a step-by-step process to European monetary union (EMU). These provisions forced most Member States to amend their Constitutions: the granting of a right to vote in local elections to all EC citizens, wherever they lived within the Community, conflicted with those constitutional provisions restricting voting rights to nationals; and the transfers of sovereignty involved in the EMU, the core of which is a single European currency managed by an independent European Central Bank, also required constitutional authorisation.

In December 1992, four articles of the German Constitution were amended to enable ratification, and the German Bundestag (by a 543–25 vote) and the Bundesrat (unanimously) then ratified the Treaty. In amending the Constitution, as Juliane Kokott reports (Ch 4), the Government and the legislature were careful to pay tribute to the GFCC's jurisprudence on legal integration. Article 23, which even before revision had constituted one of the most international law-friendly constitutional provisions to be found in the Community (allowing transfers of sovereignty by ordinary legislation), now states that Germany:

> "shall cooperate in the development of the European Union in order to realise a united Europe which is bound to observe democratic . . . principles . . . and which guarantees the protection of basic rights in a way which is substantially comparable to that provided by this constitution".

Further, rules (article 23) governing transfers of governmental authority from Germany to the EC were tightened: such transfers, which previously could be effected by a simple majority, now must be approved by two-thirds of the Bundestag and the Bundesrat.

The law ratifying the Treaty was suspended[43] when four members of the German Green Party and a former German EC Commissioner attacked its constitutionality in separate constitutional complaints. Although a dozen often contradictory arguments were invoked, complainants focused on the alleged "democratic deficit" afflicting the EC: that the expansion in the Community's policy-making powers had so far outpaced democratisation in the Community that in many areas Germans do not effectively participate in their own governance.

In a long and complex ruling rendered in October 1993, the GFCC dismissed the complaint as unfounded, clearing the way for German ratification of the Treaty. Given the care in which article 23 and other constitutional provisions had been revised, this outcome was hardly surprising. More extraordinary, the Court used the opportunity to introduce a new basis in which to challenge EC norms: the *ultra vires* nature of EC acts.[44] The ruling thus repudiates the ECJ's doctrine in *Foto-Frost*.

---

[43] The German President refused to sign the bill pending the GFCC's decision

[44] *Ultra vires* acts are governmental acts that are not legally valid to the extent that the governmental entity taking them has exceeded its legally prescribed authority.

The decision rests on two interpretive pillars, both revelatory of how the Court understands the nature of the EC polity and Germany's place within it. First, the Court subjugated article 23 to article 38, which establishes that the Bundestag is to be elected by "general, direct, free, equal, and secret" elections. The GFCC read article 38 to mean not only that Germans possessed a right to participate in such elections, but that "the weakening, within the scope of article 23, of the legitimation of state power gained through an election" was prohibited. Thus, a vote of the Bundestag, issuing from legislative elections, constitutes the sole means of conferring legitimacy to all acts of public authority within Germany, *including acts of the EC*. Secondly, the GFCC announced that it would view the EC integration as compatible with the German Constitution to the extent that Member State Governments "retain their sovereignty", and "thereby control integration". Willfully ignoring a good deal of reality, the GFCC declared the EC to be a strictly "intergovernmental Community", in which the Government of each Member State is a "master" of the treaties, possessing the power to veto Community acts and the right to withdraw from the EC.

The operative part of the judgment is derived from these two interpretive moves. Most important, the Court declared that integration must, in order to conform to constitutional dictates, proceed "predictably", that is, intergovernmentally. At the Community level, the German Government negotiates and authorises, by treaty law, whatever there is of EC governance; at the national level, the Bundestag legitimises and transposes these authorisations into national law. The Court then asserted its jurisdiction over EC acts:

> "If . . . European institutions or governmental entities were to implement or develop the Maastricht Treaty in a manner no longer covered by the Treaty in the form of it upon which the German [ratification act] is based, any legal instrument arising from such activity would not be binding within German territory. German state institutions would be preve nted, by reasons of constitutional law, from applying such legal instruments in Germany. Accordingly, the GFCC must examine the question of whether or not [these] legal instruments . . . may be considered to to remain within the bounds . . . accorded to them, or whether they may be considered to exceed these bounds".

Thus, the GFCC possesses the authority to void any EC act having the effect of depriving German legislative organs of their substantive control over integration. In terms of constitutional review processes, litigants now possess the right to plead the *ultra vires* nature of Community acts before all German judges, and could then initiate concrete review processes before the GFCC.

Not surprisingly, the GFCC's decision has been the target of sharp criticism, particularly by Community lawyers who see a repudiation of the underlying bases of European legal order. A glaring irony runs through the decision. Supra-national aspects of the TEU, such as the enhancement of certain powers of the European Parliament and the establishment of a general right to vote in local elections, sought to close, however slightly, the Community's democratic deficit. The revision of the German Constitution, necessary for ratification of the Treaty, also strengthened democratic controls over integration.[45] Nevertheless, in privileging a traditional international law and organisation approach to the EC, the Court legitimises the very source of the alleged deficit: the Community's inter-governmental elements. The irony can be drawn out further. The process by which the Treaties were constitutionalised, widely viewed as both strengthening the supra-national and the democratic character of the EC, escaped the control of national governments. Had the rules the GFCC laid down in its *Maastricht* decision been in place two decades earlier, the construction of an EC charter of rights, which the GFCC itself required in the name of democracy, would presumably have been unconstitutional.

Both the French[46] and Italian[47] constitutional courts have also, at different points of time and by different means, asserted their power to set national constitutional limits on European integration. In France, this has occurred in the guise of a convoluted jurisprudence on the constitutional limits to how much sovereignty national governments can "transfer" to EC institutions. In 1992, the French Council, in it's decisions on the constitutionality of the Maastricht Treaty, definitively abandoned an integration-hostile case law dating from the 1970s, a case law that had, in any case, undergone significant modification. The Council has signalled that it will use its power to review the constitutionality of international agreements only to instruct the Government and Parliament as to how the Constitution must be revised in order to permit the agreement to enter into force. It has further signalled that the constituent assembly's authority to revise the Constitution is virtually without limits. Nevertheless, as Jens Plötner's Report (Ch 3) implies, the Council seems to have reserved for itself the power to defend certain core values, first identified in a 1985 decision, namely "the respect for republican institutions, the continuity of the life of the nation, and the guarantee of civil rights and liberties".

The Italian court's jurisprudence locates *Kompetenz-Kompetenz* in Italy. In the words of a former ICC judge:

> "Italy applies Community law because the Constitutional Court interprets Italian constitutional principles as indicating that the Italian legal order chooses not to impede the application of Community law, not because Italian law is subordinate to Community law as maintained by the Court of Justice".[48]

---

[45] In addition to the revisions of article 23 discussed above, the powers of Bundestag and Bundesrat committees to be informed of and to scrutinise the Government's activities at the EC level were enhanced.

[46] See Alec Stone, "Ratifying *Maastricht*: France Debates European Union", *French Politics and Society* 11 (1993), 70–88.

[47] See Antonia La Pergola and Patrick Del Duca, "Community Law, International Law, and the Italian Constitution", *American Journal of International Law* 79 (1985), 598–621.

[48] La Pergola and Del Duca, n. 47 above, at 615.

After the ECJ's decision in *Simmenthal* and before the ICC's decision in *Granital*, at least parts of the Italian judiciary refused to be bound by the latter, one court even declared the *Simmenthal* judgment *ultra vires*.[49] But even at its most accommodating, the ICC has declared, in *Frontini* and *Granital* and contrary to the ECJ in *Simmenthal*, that preliminary references to the ICC continued to be required in three cases:

(1) when a national law conflicts with an EC norm in an area in which EC competence had not beforehand been exercised;

(2) when the national law expresses, explicitly, the legislator's will to derogate from the Community regime; and,

(3) when an EC rule may violate core, unspecified "values" of the constitution or the constitutional rights of Italian citizens.

More recently, in *Fragd* (1989), the ICC signalled that it is willing to begin "to test the consistency of individual rules of Community law with the fundamental principles for the protection of human rights that are contained in the Italian constitution".[50] (Unlike the German constitutional court, the ICC has not formally acknowledged the development of a rights jurisprudence by the ECJ.)

In the other three Member States, again, the problem of determining the constitutional limits to European integration, or the "who is competent to decide" problem has, notwithstanding an interesting new development in Belgium, been largely irrelevant. What drama exists in the Belgian case is of recent vintage, developing along with the consolidation of the institutional position of the Cour d'arbitrage, a constitutional jurisdiction that began functioning in the mid-1980s. The Cour d'arbitrage exercises those constitutional review powers necessary to defend the new Belgian federal order and to protect the fundamental rights of equality and education. Beginning in 1991, the Court asserted the power of indirect review of treaty law, indirect because review occurs after treaty law has been transposed into national law. Its subsequent jurisprudence has made it clear that treaty law that violates the constitution will be voided, a position criticised, according to Hervé Bribosia's Report (Ch 2), by the doctrinal community, the Procureur général, and the Belgian Prime Minister. Although Bribosia reports that the issue of *Kompetenz-Kompetenz* had been seemingly settled by *Le Ski* (it rested with Community organs), the Cour d'arbitrage has laid the foundations for a (German or Italian-style) constitutional jurisprudence on supremacy. The next stage will be the Belgian Court's decision on the Maastricht Treaty, now pending.

---

[49] Reported by Barav, n. 23 above, at 328.

[50] Giorgio Gaja, "New Developments in a Continuing Story: The Relationship Between EEC Law and Italian Law", *Common Market Law Review* 27 (1990), 94.

A preliminary assessment

Whether one considers Proposition 1a to be more or less valid depends heavily on one's relative tolerance for deviance. In support of the proposition, we see that the high courts of each of the national court systems have accepted judiciary supremacy and—with at least two exceptions[51]—are doctrinally positioned to enforce the direct effect of EC law. National solutions to the doctrinal problems attending the reception of supremacy differ, but the desired end—the uniform application and effectiveness of EC law across the Community—can surely be achieved by various means. This pragmatism may not satisfy everyone. Schermers, for example, has argued that, in order to resolve potential conflicts about rights between the ECJ and national constitutional courts, that the ECJ should be placed under the tutelage of the European Court of Human Rights, by way of a preliminary reference procedure.[52] We do not have to take legal coherence this far. After all, we ought to admit that intra-judicial conflict has driven the constitutionalisation process in important ways, and more often than not to the benefit of the European Court. Further, the new reticences of the German and Italian constitutional courts may turn out to be essentially rearguard actions—the erection of symbolic firebreaks to legal integration—in response to an ever-deepening constitutionalisation of EC law. On the other hand, constitutional courts may begin to actually exercise powers of review over Community acts.

It appears that Proposition 1b can not be sustained. Two findings are relevant here. First, the nature of constitutional provisions themselves appear to have no impact across cases. The Dutch case provides evidence for the proposition that the more monist the constitution, the smoother the reception of supremacy. The Belgian case tells us that a dualist tendencies can facilitate an equally smooth reception, while the French case provides an example of a legal system that, despite strongly monist constitutional provisions, partly operated in dualist terms (until 1989 in the case of the administrative courts). Generally, constitutional provisions tell us little in and of themselves. We have to know how they are interpreted by judges. The French, German, and Italian Constitutions expressly provide for transfers of sovereign powers to international organisations, for example, yet these provisions have not always been enough to legitimise the legal effect (i.e., supremacy) of such transfers within the municipal legal system. In the United Kingdom, judges, who had not done so before, swept aside a central precept of Parliamentary sovereignty in order to make supremacy juridically effective.

[51] The French Council of State and the Spanish Supreme Court refuse to give direct effect to directives under certain circumstances. See Ch 2, Report on France, and Diego J. Liñan Nogueras and Javier Roldán Barbero, "The Judicial Application of Community Law in Spain", *Common Market Law Review* 30 (1993), 1135–54. There may be other exceptions as well.

[52] Henry G. Schermers, "The Scales in Balance: National Constitutional Court v. Court of Justice", *Common Market Law Review* 27 (1990), 97–105.

This brings up my second point, one which can only be arrived at by examining the constitutional dialogues on supremacy comparatively. Member States possessed of specialised constitutional courts—France, Germany, and Italy—invariably develop problems associated with the *Kompetenz-Kompetenz* issue. Constitutional courts, far from facilitating the reception of supremacy, make that reception contingent. Most important, constitutional courts insist, whereas other high courts often do not insist, that it is the national constitution, and not the ECJ or the EC Treaties, that mediates the relationship between EC law and national law. Constitutional judges work to weaken integration-friendly provisions by interpreting them into a subordinate relationship to other constitutional provisions. That is, they engage in intra-constitutional interpretation in order to establish an intra-constitutional hierarchy of norms governing European integration. This exercise serves to establish formal, constitutional limits on European integration as well as to reserve for national constitutional courts the ultimate authority to control the legality of European integration. Member States that do not possess such courts are precisely those in which the *Kompetenz-Kompetenz* issue has been of little or no interest. Belgium provides dramatic validation of this point: its situation resembled the Dutch situation, until a new constitutional jurisdiction was established. That constitutional court has now begun to behave as have other constitutional courts.

A criticism

However excellent on their own terms, the national reports (and studies like them) collectively suffer from a fatal flaw: the privileged focus on formal doctrine. Far more important is what is ignored: how courts are actually resolving EC legal disputes. The distinction between doctrine and (for lack of a better phrase, case law) is endemic to traditional European legal scholarship. Whatever its virtues, it seriously undermines our capacity to evaluate the impact of constitutionalisation on the work of national judiciaries. Most important, although the national reports document a general move to embrace supremacy, this move appears to mask some extremely important differences in the day-to-day implementation of EC law. These differences, further, appear to be patterned across national and jurisdictional boundaries. If we are to progress in our understanding of legal integration processes, we need to begin mapping and accounting for these differences. This is the subject of the next section.

CONSTITUTIONAL DIALOGUES:
SUPREMACY, LITIGATION, AND POLICYMAKING

The constitutionalisation of the treaty system generated a structured and ongoing, intra-judicial dialogue, judges speaking to each other through the medium of legal discourse. Constitutionalisation also upgraded the capacity of European courts to intervene in policy processes and to shape policy outcomes. Approaches 2 and 3 direct our attention to another highly structured set of interactions, between legislators, litigators, and judges. Although our project was not designed to assess propositions 2 and 3, the national reports make it clear that the evolution of the EC legal system has been a messier, far less coherent process than the proponents of these imagined it to be. What follows is the urging of a research agenda capable of better explaining the dynamics of legal integration.

This agenda integrates the following four research priorities:

Study the case law of national courts

It is crucial that we abandon the widespread, but artificial, distinction between doctrine and case law, and study what judges actually are doing when they resolve legal disputes involving EC law. This is not an argument for lawyers to behave as political scientists. On the contrary, research into how courts construct a living jurisprudence from litigation and legal materials is essentially a lawyer's business. We should ask three interrelated research questions. Each forces us to consider the importance of EC law and supremacy doctrines in light of the day-to-day work of national judges.

(1) First, how many and what kinds of EC law disputes are national courts adjudicating? Astonishingly, neither the national reports nor existing published research is much concerned with what areas of EC law are being litigated and with what intensity.

(2) Secondly, what differences exist—within nation states and cross-nationally—in how national judges "implement" EC law and the ECJ's jurisprudence? We have to disaggregate EC law along sectoral lines— e.g., free movement, labour law, environmental protection, etc.—and plot how judges are deciding these cases. Is the French Cour de cassation more receptive to enforcing EC law in some areas than it is in others? Is Cassation more receptive to enforcing EC law than is the French Conseil d'état? Are Dutch courts more environmentally-friendly than Italian courts?—many such questions could be asked.

(3) Thirdly, under what circumstances—that is, how and with respect to what kinds of cases—do judges invoke supremacy and apply Community law against conflicting national law?; and under what circumstances do judges choose to ignore relevant Community law in order to maintain national policies? The logic of supremacy, of course, suggests that this choice does not exist; and the national reports generally assume that once supremacy is secured, judges behave as expected, according to the logic of supremacy. Yet we know (the next priority below) that judges may accept supremacy as a matter of doctrine, while ignoring it for the

purposes of deciding certain kinds of cases. These questions are of practical as well as scholarly importance for lawyers.

Without answers to questions like these, theorising about legal integration is putting the cart well before the horse. As will become clear, we can not move beyond speculation—of which we have had more than enough—until we have some minimal comparative understanding of how EC law is being adjudicated.

(Re)-specify judicial interests

When adjudicating EC law, judges are subject to conflicting pressures, pressures from which we can deduce individual and institutional interests. These deductions can imply either compliance with, or resistance to, the penetration of EC law within national systems. A first approach is to identify three clusters of interests which, taken together, appear to organise the most important non-legal, contextual factors suggested by the reports and by scholarship elsewhere.

The first is a judge's personal self-interest conceived as a career interest. Although the reports do not emphasise this factor, the self-interest of judges may conflict with the "judicial empowerment" hypothesis—the putative bureaucratic interest in seeing the courts gain in power at the expense of the political branches. As Shapiro has neatly put it, it is a "surprise" that some national courts have gone along with the ECJ, given that "such judges must attend to their career prospects within hierarchically organised national systems" of recruitment and promotion.[53] We would need to know more than we do about the bureaucratic pressures individual judges may be under to conform to national rather than supra-national norms of judging. It appears from the data collected by our project that disincentives to playing the "Eurolaw game" are surprisingly low or non-existent in many systems. But the national reports, again, do not take us beyond the formal reception of supremacy to what really counts: how supremacy is used or ignored by judges.

The second interest is in "judicial empowerment", by which is meant a court's institutional interest in enhancing its autonomy in and control over legal, and therefore policy, processes. The reports give us some clues as to how these interests actually play out. Constitutional courts are simply not empowered by the ECJ's jurisprudence of supremacy and its vision of a partnership with national judges. Constitutional courts instead develop their own vision of the relationship between the EC and national legal orders, which not surprisingly never quite fits with the ECJ's vision. Courts prohibited from

---

[53] Martin J. Shapiro, "The European Court of Justice", in A. Sbragia (ed.), *Euro-politics* (Washington, D.C.: Brookings Institution), 128.

reviewing the legal validity of national legislation have, *a priori*, a powerful institutional interest in obtaining such authority. Perhaps this explains why the civil courts, including the supreme courts of civil jurisdictions, have had the least difficulty accepting, without complex, the ECJ's authority and the specificity of the EC legal order as interpreted by the ECJ.

The third is a court's interest in using its decisions to make good policy. Garrett raises this point directly but in an unusably simplistic form: courts are machines whose work governments have set in motion and whose output they ultimately control. But the point can be refined, by assuming what Garrett denies: that courts have a meaningfully autonomous capacity to evaluate the policy impact of their decisions. In doing so, the legal integration process instantly becomes much more complex. In adopting a policy perspective, some important puzzles emerge, puzzles that we can only begin to explain by combining the first and second research priorities. Two examples:

Jens Plötner's Report (Ch 3) suggests that the ease in which the civil courts accepted supremacy simply "fit" with civil judges' own self-conception as guarantors of a kind of economic constitution. As national and Community economies merged, we might say, the distinction between national and EC law became untenable. Supremacy, civil courts may have (at least implicitly) understood, enables the judiciary to ensure that economic actors are regulated on an equivalent basis. Plötner further speculates that the French Conseil d'état's conversion to supremacy occurred in the context of an increasing number of cases of a commercial, rather than a traditionally administrative, nature. Thus, we might propose, informed by the approach proposed by Slaughter and Mattli, that the more a court is faced with commercial litigation, the more pressure a court comes under to function as a Community court. But, again, we would need to know more than we do about litigation patterns and how national courts are actually deciding commercial disputes to evaluate this proposition.

In contrast, courts may also have good reasons for maintaining existing lines of case law, case law that they have produced and which they control, rather than participating in that law's demise. In her Report (Ch 4), Juliane Kokott documents the fascinating behaviour of the high tax and labour courts of Germany who, in their references to the ECJ, are challenging the ECJ to be more sensitive to national solutions to legal problems of a mixed national and Community law nature. These courts have thus engaged the ECJ in a dialogue whose purpose is to inform the European Court of the difficulties German courts might have in implementing the ECJ's decisions, in the hope that the European Court will revise its own case law. These initiative have even succeeded at times. Similarly, the House of Lords combines the doctrine of supremacy with its discretionary power over article 177 referrals to enhance its own autonomy and what could be called a policy-making capacity. The Lords have not hesitated to use the powers afforded by supremacy not only to enforce EC law but to reshape the national law on sex discrimination in the workplace.[54] But, as Jonathon Golub has shown,[55] in the area of environmental policy, the Lords regularly enforce national legislation in clear violation of EC directives, without bothering first to refer the matter to the ECJ. Unfortunately, apart from the example provided by Kokott's Report, none of the other national reports examine such instances of discrete, case law-specific, judicial resistance to supremacy with reference to EC law or the case law-specific policies of the European Court. Yet such resistance may be widespread. A proposition: when judges are convinced of the superiority of national policies, they ignore the rules attending supremacy. Put differently, supremacy enables judges to pick and choose from a menu of policy choices; in so choosing, judges determine which rule will do the most good and the least harm to the society it helps to govern.

Correlate judicial outcomes with factors external to the law

Taking Proposition 2 seriously, the research on judicial outcomes ought to be correlated with certain social and economic data. Garrett has asserted, for example, that the ECJ's decision in *Cassis de dijon* ratified the policy goals of Germany and France, since both of these states benefit from an open market. In contrast, Hervé Bribosia, in his Report on Belgium (Ch 2), proposes that the courts of small states may be more open to enforcing EC law precisely because small states depend relatively more heavily on external markets for their prosperity. One could test propositions such as these (i.e., those derived from an alleged "national interest") by correlating economic data—the ratio of trade receipts to GDP, for example—with levels of litigation of selected areas of EC law. It may be, for example, that Bribosia is right, and the more dependent upon trade is a Member State, the more courts encourage litigation of EC law by enforcing that law. It may also be that in non-economic areas of EC law—social policy and the environment, for example—that we find a very different dynamic, similar to the one Golub and Kokott have identified, where courts are engaged in meaningful policy evaluation on an ongoing basis, vigilant about protecting their own national policies when deemed superior to EC policies.

---

[54] Sally J. Kenney (University of Minnesota), "Pregnancy Discrimination: Toward Substantive Equality", 10 *Wisconsin Women's Law Journal* (1996): 351–402, Sally J. Kenney, "Pregnancy and Disability: Comparing the United States and the European Community", *The Disability Law Reporter Service* 3 (1994), 8–17.

[55] Jonathon Golub (European University Institute) "Rethinking the Role of National Courts in European Integration: A Political Study of British Judicial Discretion", unpublished manuscript, 1995), 36 pp.

Study the behaviour of litigators

As Slaughter and Mattli have emphasised, the fuel for legal integration is the pursuit of private interests by legal means. Yet we know surprisingly little about the behaviour and organisation of litigators of EC law,[56] and nothing from a comparative perspective. Who litigates what and where? We desperately need comparative studies of whether, how, and why national and transnational litigation groups form; the impact of the case law of the European and national courts on litigation behaviour; and the extent to which this behaviour has risen or fallen over time. As with the study of case law, litigation activity must be studied cross-sectorally and cross-nationally.

CONCLUSION

The constitutionalisation of the EC Treaties begat the complex process of coordinating national and supra-national systems of law and policy-making. Cataloguing the jurisprudential techniques and mechanisms by which national jurisdictions have received the ECJ's doctrines of supremacy and direct effect is an indispensable first step towards a better understanding of the dynamics of European legal integration. The most important questions, however, have been left unanswered: does the constitutionalisation of the Treaties make a difference to legal and political outcomes, and if so how?; to what extent does the law and politics of litigating European law vary across jurisdictional and national boundaries?; are some jurisdictions more receptive than others to enforcing EU law? This chapter has been asking too many questions, but they are crucial. To answer them, we will need a much better understanding of the constitutional dialogues currently underway than we now possess. The general lines of inquiry, however, are clear. We need contextually-sensitive, policy-relevant studies of the interaction between legislators, litigators, the ECJ, and the national courts.

---

[56] What exists is recent and impressionistic. For a review of the literature, see Carol Harlow, "Towards a Theory of Access for the European Court of Justice", *Yearbook of European Law* 1992, 213–48.

12

Constitutional or International? The Foundations of the Community Legal Order and the Question of Judicial Kompetenz-Kompetenz[1]

J.H.H. WEILER AND ULRICH R. HALTERN

I. INTRODUCTION

Ever since the introduction of widespread majority voting in the wake of the Single European Act, the principal constitutional battleground in the Community shifted from issues of direct effect, supremacy and the like to that of material competences and jurisdictional lines. The most contentious issue in this battle concerns what has been called in this volume *Judicial Kompetenz-Komptenz*, the question as to which jurisdiction, Community or national, has the ultimate authority to declare the unconstitutionality of Community measures on the grounds of *ultra vires* and effectively to become the arbiter of the jurisdictional limits of the Community legal order. Inevitably the debate has moved from doctrine to theory, calling into question the very foundations of the Community legal order.

Theodor Schilling, in *The Autonomy of the Community Legal Order—An Analysis of Possible Foundations*,[2] challenges, to use his own language in the opening phrase of his piece, no less than "[t]he single most far-reaching, and probably most disputed, principle of the European Community . . . its claim to a legal order autonomous from Member State law".[3] In his attempt to explore the foundations of this claim to autonomy, he pricks one of the biggest hot-air balloons of European law[4]—its alleged "new" constitutional

---

[1] Adapted from J.H.H. Weiler & Ulrich R. Haltern, *The Autonomy of the Community Legal Order—Through the Looking Glass* 37 Harv. Int'l L. J.(1996)

[2] 37 Harv. Int'l L. J. 389 (1996).

[3] Id. at 389.

[4] While Dr. Schilling's article mostly refers to the law of the European Community, we will use the term "European Law" to describe either European Community Law or European Union law as the case may be. Only when distinctions matter, will we flag them. Our references include the Treaty Establishing the European Economic Community [EEC Treaty]; Treaty Establishing the European Coal and Steel Community [ECSC Treaty]; Treaty Establishing the European Atomic Energy Community [Euratom]; Single European Act [SEA]; and Treaty on the European Union [TEU].

garb—and exposes, if not its nakedness, at least its comfortable old togs of international law.

The bulk of the Schilling article is dedicated to the theoretical exercise of exploring the foundations of the autonomy claim: are these foundations constitutional or international? But fear not: this is not theory merely for the sake of theory. There is a distinct political context to the heavy theorizing. It comes in the very final passages of Schilling's piece, in what he himself describes as "The Decisive Question".[5] Schilling also makes no bones that his article is meant to be instrumental in the battles surrounding this "Decisive Question".[6]

What, then, is the "Decisive Question"? As stated, it is the most recent flash point (or "flash-in-the-pan") in the evolving relationship between Community law and Member State law.[7] The supremacy of Community law over, and the direct effect of Community law within, the Member States' legal orders, once all the rage, are now well-established if not *de jure* at least *de facto*. They are accepted by both the constitutional and the international law accounts of the system and confirmed, by and large, in practice. But, as all interpretative communities at least verbally affirm,[8] the Community is a system of "attributed", "enumerated", "limited" competences.[9] The writ of the Community is thus supreme only when enacted within its jurisdictional limits. An *ultra vires* Community measure should not be and would not be supreme. The "Decisive Question" is, therefore, as follows: when the legality of a Community mea-

---

[5] Schilling, *supra* note 1, at 404.

[6] *Id.* at 408-9.

[7] J.H.H. Weiler, Ulrich R. Haltern & Franz C. Mayer, *European Democracy and Its Critique*, W. Eur. Politics, July 1995, at 4.

[8] *See*, e.g., Bengt Beutler *et al.*, *Die Europäische Union: Rechtsordnung und Politik* 82 (4th ed. 1993); Thomas Oppermann, *Europarecht* 168–69 (1991); Philippe Manin, *Les Communautés Européennes—Droit institutionnel* 62 (1993); Antonio Tizzano, *Les compétences de la Communauté*, in *Trente ans de droit communautaire* 45 (Commission des Communautés européennes ed., 1981); Roland Bieber, *Artikel 4*, in *Kommentar zum EWG-Vertrag* para. 38 (Hans von der Groeben *et al.* eds., 4th ed. 1991). The virtual disappearance of the principle of enumerated powers, as a constraint on Community material jurisdiction, is analysed in detail by J.H.H. Weiler, *The Transformation of Europe*, 100 Yale L.J. 2403, 2431–53 (1991). The diminishing practical significance is also noted by T.C. Hartley, *The Foundations of European Community Law* 110–119 (3d ed. 1994).

[9] This has been confirmed by the Court of Justice early on. E.g., Case 26/62, *Van Gend & Loos* v. *Nederlandse Administratie der Belastingen*, [1963] ECR 1 (the Community constitutes "a new legal order of international law for the benefit of which the states have limited their sovereign rights, *albeit within limited fields*. . ." (emphasis added)). For even more striking language (albeit related to the Coal and Steel Community), see Joined Cases 7/56 & 3-7/57, *Dineke Algera et al.* v. *Common Assembly of the European Coal and Steel Community* [1957] ECR 39, Opinion of Mr. Advocate General Lagrange, 69, at 82 ("The Treaty is based upon delegation, with the consent of the Member States, of sovereignty to supranational institutions *for a strictly defined purpose*. . . . The legal principle underlying the Treaty is a principle of *limited authority*. The Community is a legal person governed by public law, and as such, it shall enjoy the legal capacity *it requires to perform its functions and attain its objectives*, but only that capacity. . . .") Much of this, today, is mere lip-service. Koen Lenaerts, for instance, concludes, "There simply is no nucleus of sovereignty that the Member States can invoke, as such, against the Community." Koen Lenaerts, *Constitutionalism and the Many Faces of Federalism*, 38 Am. J. Comp. L. 205, 220 (1990); Weiler, *supra* note 7, at 2431–6.

sure is challenged on the grounds of *ultra vires* who, in law, gets to make the final determination? Is it the European Court of Justice (ECJ) or the (highest) courts of the individual Member States? Since the jurisdictional limits laid out in the European Treaties are notoriously difficult to identify with precision,[10] the question of who gets to decide is of tremendous political importance for the relationship between the Community and the Member States.

The standard answer to the "Decisive Question", the "imperious answer" if you wish, put forward by most commentators as well as by the ECJ, is that the final determination of this issue, as with any other legal challenge to the legality of a Community measure, rests with the ECJ.[11] The ECJ has the competence, an exclusive competence, to invalidate a Community measure on any ground, including the ground that the measure was *ultra vires*. We may call this *Judicial* Kompetenz-Kompetenz: the competence to declare or to determine the limits of the competences of the Community.

This issue, dormant for years,[12] was suddenly thrown into the limelight by the famous (or infamous) 1993 *Maastricht* Decision of the German Federal Constitutional Court.[13] While conceding that the ECJ had a role to play, the German court held that from a German constitutional perspective, the ultimate authority to determine this issue rested with domestic law. Indeed, any German court or other emanation of the State had a duty not to apply Community measures which in its eyes were *ultra vires*.[14] In the case of a dispute, the German Federal Constitutional Court itself would have the final say.[15] The German court arrived at this conclusion based on a reasoning of German constitutional law. Though the reasoning has not met with uniform approval, to put it mildly, even among German constitutionalists,[16] we do not

---

[10] Weiler, *supra* note 7, at 2436–53.

[11] Case 314/85, *Foto-Frost* v. *Hauptzollamt Lübeck-Ost* [1987] ECR 4199. (This, it seems, has also been Schilling's first intuition.) *See* Schilling, *supra* note 1, at 405 ("According to the ordinary meaning of this provision, the ECJ is the ultimate umpire of the European system").

[12] Jean Paul Jacqué & J.H.H. Weiler, *On the Road to European Union—A New Judicial Architecture: An Agenda for the Intergovernmental Conference*, 27 CMLRev. 185 (1990); Jean Paul Jacqué & J.H.H. Weiler, *Sur la voie de l'Union européenne, une nouvelle architecture judiciaire*, 26 Revue Trimestrielle de Droit Européen 441 (1990).

[13] German Constitutional Court, Judgment of Oct. 12, 1993, 89 BVerfGE 155, *English translation in* 33 I.L.M. 388, 422-3 (1994).

[14] "If, for example, European institutions or governmental entities were to implement or to develop the Maastricht Treaty in a manner no longer covered by the Treaty in the form of it upon which the German Act of Acession is based, any legal instrument arising from such activity would not be binding within German territory. German State institutions would be prevented by reasons of constitutional law from applying such legal instruments in Germany." *Id.* at 188.

[15] This is the consequence of the German system of centralized judicial review, with the Bundesverfassungsgericht at its core.

[16] *See*, for instance, Christian Tomuschat, *Die Europäische Union unter Aufsicht des Bundesverfassungsgerichts*, 20 Europäische Grundrechtezeitschrift 489, 494 (1993); Jochen A. Frowein, *Das Maastricht-Urteil und die Grenzer der Verfassungsgerichtsbarkeit*, 54 Zeitschrift für ausländisches öffentliches Recht und Völkerrecht 1, 8–10 (1994); Meinhard Schröder, *Das Bundesverfassungsgericht als Hüter des Staates im Prozeß der europäischen Integration—Bemerkungen zum Maastricht-Urteil*, 1994 Deutsches Verwaltungsblatt 316, 323–24; Jürgen

plan to take issue with it in this essay.[17] After all, if the German court understands its authority as flowing from, and its loyalty flowing to, the German Constitution, it could hardly hold otherwise if it came to the conclusion that this is what the German Constitution mandated. Other courts, some with considerably longer traditions of constitutionalism and democracy than their German counterpart, have upheld positions that they thought were mandated by the genesis or function of their constitutions, even if this created or sanctioned a violation of the international obligations of their respective States.[18]

Some German courts, taking their cue from the German Federal Constitutional Court, have already set aside Community law that in their eyes was *ultra vires*.[19] If the German Constitutional Court itself were to do this, it would clearly be illegal under Community law. Schilling, however, does not reason ostensibly from a national constitutional law perspective, though he clearly supports the German result. Schilling tries to render this constitutional swine—if that is what it is—kosher by relying on public international law, his

Schwarze, *Europapolitik unter deutschem Verfassungsvorbehalt—Anmerkungen zum Maastricht-Urteil des BVerfG vom 12.10.1993*, 48 Neue Justiz 1, 3 (1994); Karl M. Meessen, *Maastricht nach Karlsruhe*, 9 Neue Juristische Wochenschrift 549, 552–3 (1994).

[17] For an extensive discussion, *see* J.H.H. Weiler, *The State 'über alles': Demos, Telos and the German Maastricht Decision, in* Festschrift für Ulrich Everling 1651 (Ole Due *et al.* eds., 1995).

[18] For example, English courts have held that English statutory law is binding upon them even if conflicting with international law. *See*, e.g., *R. v. Chief Immigration Officer, ex parte Salamat Bibi* [1976] 3 All ER 843; *R. v. Secretary of State for the Home Dept., ex parte Thakrar* [1974] 2 All ER 261; *Woodend (K. V. Ceylon) Rubber and Tea Co. v. Inland Revenue Commissioners* [1970] 2 All ER 801. Under US law, courts have occasionally subordinated treaties to subsequent statutes and held that the US has the perogative to violate its international commitments. *See*, above all, references *in* Louis Henkin, *The Constitution and United States Sovereignty: A Century of Chinese Exclusion and Its Progeny*, 100 Harv. L. Rev. 853 (1987), and the response by Peter Westen, *The Place of Foreign Treaties in the Courts of the United States: A Reply to Louis Henkin*, 101 Harv. L. Rev. 511 (1987). As to US statutes and international treaties see, *inter alia*, the *Head Money Cases*, 112 US 580 (1884); *Whitney v. Robertson*, 124 US 190 (1888); *Chinese Exclusion Case*, 130 US 581 (1889). As to US statutes and customary international law see, *inter alia*, the dictum in the *Paquete Habana Case*, 175 US 677, 700 (1900) ("International law is part of our law, and must be ascertained and administered by the courts of justice . . . For this purpose, *where there is* no treaty and *no controlling executive or legislative act* or judicial decision, resort must be had to the customs and usages of civilized nations . . ."). Under German law, international treaties do not have a higher status than federal laws, with the consequence that the principle *lex posterior derogat legi posteriori* is applicable and that the treaty must be consistent with the German Constitution, or Grundgesetz [GG]. For the obligation to choose the interpretation of an international treaty that is in accordance with the Constitution, *see*, *inter alia*, Judgment of May 4, 1955, BVerfG, 4 BVerfGE 157, 168 translated in 1 *Decisions of the Bundesverfassungsgericht—Federal Constitutional Court—Federal Republic of Germany: International Law and Law of the European Communities 1952–1989* (pt. 1) 70, 77 (1992). Article 25 of the Basic Law, which could be read as an affirmation of the supremacy of international law (although many disagree; *see*, e.g., Knut Ipsen, *Völkerrecht*, 1091–3 (3d ed. 1990)), does not apply to treaties but only to general customary rules of international law. Grundgesetz [GG] art. 25 (FRG). For further reference, also relating to other countries, see *Oppenheim's International Law*, Vol. I: Peace 54–81 (Sir Robert Jennings & Sir Arthur Watts eds., 9th ed. 1992). *See also* Eyal Benvenisti, *Judicial Misgivings Regarding the Application of International Law: An Analysis of Attitudes of National Courts*, 4 Eur. J. Int'l L. 159 (1993).

[19] *See* Norbert Reich, *Judge-made 'Europe a la carte': Some Remarks on Recent Conflicts between European and German Constitutional Law Provoked by the Banana Litigation*, 7 Eur. J. Int'l L. 103 (1996).

preferred foundation for the European Community legal order. His conclusion is uncompromising:

> The international law interpretation of the European Treaties thus leads to the conclusion that the ECJ is not the ultimate umpire of the system . . . Therefore, the Member States, *individually*, must have the final word on questions concerning the scope of the competences they have delegated to the Community.[20]

The stakes for Schilling are high: the "Rule of Law" itself is at issue. In Schilling's eyes, it is mere rhetoric when, on the "Decisive Question", the ECJ relies on the principle of the Rule of Law.[21] The "Truth" has been recognized by the German Constitutional Court, which according to Schilling, does not merely constitute, in law, the "final umpire of the system", but is also the clarion of the Rule of Law itself and has positioned itself, with the help of Schilling, "for eventually holding the ECJ in breach of that rule".[22]

We confess to finding these conclusions, and the reasoning on which they are based, puzzling. They evoke a reaction not unlike that of Alice when she peers into the LookingGlass House: "that's just the same . . . only the things go the other way."

Whatever the merits, or lack thereof, of a constitutional foundation for European law, the European Court, in adopting its position on judicial *Kompetenz-Kompetenz*, was not following any constitutional foundation but rather an orthodox international law rationale. In other words, even if we agreed with Schilling that international law provided the only basis on which to found the Community legal order, we would argue that this very foundation in international law mandates the opposite conclusions than the ones he reaches: the European Court does hold the position of "ultimate umpire of the system." Furthermore, international law certainly would not give the States, *individually*, the right to have the final word on questions concerning the competences of an international organization, just as it would not give such decisional finality to a State over any aspect of a Treaty to which it was party. Regardless of whether the position of the German Constitutional Court is justified under German constitutional law, it is not defensible under public international law. At most, all Member States of the Union, acting in unison, usually by following the Treaty-amendment procedure, may determine, amend, and modify the Treaties, including their jurisdictional reach.[23]

---

[20] Schilling, *supra* note 1, at 407 (emphasis added).

[21] *Id*. at 408.

[22] *Id*. at 409.

[23] This is, of course, not just a theoretical suggestion. The Member States have altered the Treaties several times, the latest examples being amendments to the framework of Maastricht. The most important example is the Protocol Concerning Article 119 of the Treaty Establishing the European Community, annexed to the EC Treaty which, according to EC Treaty art. 239, is an "integral part" of it. This protocol—the so-called "Barber" Protocol—was a reaction to the ECJ judgment in Case C-262/88, *Barber* v. *Royal Guardian Exch. Assurance Group*, 1990 ECR 1889. Being the prototype of a consensus reaction of the Member States to a binding decision of the ECJ, the Barber Protocol is considered by some to be a warning to the Court. See, e.g., Deirdre Curtin, *The Constitutional Structure of the Union: A Europe of Bits and Pieces*, 30

Ironically, as we argue later in this article, a constitutional law approach to the Community legal order would be more solicitous to an involvement of national jurisdictions in the determination of the jurisdictional limits of the Community legal order.

This, then, is how we plan to proceed. We shall say first a few words on Schilling's "constitutional-international" analysis—a few words only because, for the purposes of this essay, we are happy to remain agnostic on this issue. We agree with much of what Schilling says and our disagreements are mostly unrelated to the so-called "Decisive Question". We will thus be willing to accept, at least *arguendo*, his international law characterization of the Community legal order as the premise for analysing his "Decisive Question". On this basis we then proceed to analyse with some care the reasoning on which Schilling bases his conclusions. Lastly, we shall conclude by addressing, in a somewhat less doctrinal manner, the stand-off between the ECJ and the German Constitutional Court on the issue of judicial *Kompetenz-Kompetenz*.

II. THE COMMUNITY LEGAL ORDER: CONSTITUTIONAL OR INTERNATIONAL?

Schilling goes to great lengths to debunk the alleged constitutional foundations of the Community legal order. One could, of course—and, in our view, one should—call into question the very dichotomy between "the international" and "the constitutional" implicit in Schilling's argument. The blurring of this dichotomy is precisely one of the special features of the Community legal order and other transnational regimes.[24] But our critique of the Schilling piece does not go, as stated, to his whole argument. We are willing to share with him the constitutional-international distinction and even go further and share with him much of his critique of the constitutional-foundation thesis.

The European legal order was begotten from public international law in the normal way that these things happen: there was a communion among some States—the High Contracting Parties—which negotiated, signed, and subsequently ratified the constituent Treaties which brought into being, first the nascent European Coal and Steel Community and then, its twin siblings, the

CMLRev. 17, 51 (1993). Another example of the Member States altering the Treaties is the Protocol Annexed to the Treaty on European Union and to the Treaties Establishing the European Union (the so-called "Irish Abortion" Protocol). Curtin submits that "the whole purpose of including the Protocol in the first place was to close the door that seemed to be left ajar . . . by the [ECJ] ruling in *SPUC* v. *Grogan* [Case C-159/90, 1991 E.C.R. I-4685]." *Id.* at 49. Further examples—outside the "special case" protocols—include the new provisions on culture (*see* EC Treaty arts. 3 (p) and 128) and on public health (*see* art. 3 (o) and Title X of the EC Treaty).

[24] *See* José de Areilza, *Sovereignty or Management?: The Dual Character of the EC's Supranationalism—Revisited* (Harvard Jean Monnet Working Paper No. 2/95, 1995).

European Economic Community and Euratom. We know their progeny today as the three-pillared European Union. This manner of conception would, in the normal course of international life, determine the genetic—as well as legal—code of the new infant: an international organization with a separate legal personality but with no measure of independence or power to eradicate its subordination to its States parents and its subjection to the classical laws governing the States' treaty relations. The States, like the Olympian Gods, would forever remain ultimate masters of their creation. The Germans have a nice phrase for this: the Member States are called the "Herren der Verträge".[25]

This mastery of the States over their offspring does not prevent, as with other Almighties, acts of self-limitation: in the begetting of an international organization through an international treaty, the High Contracting Parties may decide to bestow on their offspring the power to make decisions which will bind them. They may even privilege a few States in the process.[26] But, at any point, as long as the Member States act in unison, they may change the status or the capacities of the organization. The basic principles of the law of treaties would apply to privilege the makers of the treaty at all critical junctures in the life of a treaty—treaty-making, amendment, interpretation and termination. As masters of the treaty, States are also masters of the organization. Thus, for example, not infrequently will States amend a treaty—including one setting up an international organization—in violation of its specific amendment procedures. As long as the amendment is in accord with the collective will of all parties, it would be considered valid.[27] Likewise, should

---

[25] *See,* e.g., German Constitutional Court, Judgment of Oct. 12, 1993, 89 BVerfGE 155, 190 (FRG). But see Markus Heintzen, *Die "Herrschaft" über die Europäischen Gemeinschaftsverträge—Bundesverfassungsgericht und Europäischer Gerichtshof auf Konfliktkurs?,* 119 Archiv des öffentlichen Rechts 564 (1994).

[26] The UN Charter empowers a small number of States in the Security Council to make decisions binding on the international community as a whole. UN Charter arts. 23–32. The Charter further privileges some States by giving them permanent membership in the Council and veto power. *Id.* Other organizations privilege States by according their votes more weight. Henry G. Schermers & Niels M. Blokker give some examples including the International Monetary Fund (IMF, art. 12, sec. 5(a)), the World Bank (World Bank, art. 5, sec. 3), the International Fund for Agricultural Development (IFAD, art. 6(3); Schedule II), the International Sugar Council (International Sugar Agreement, art. 25 and Annex), the Multilateral Investment Guarantee Agency (MIGA, art. 39), the Common Fund for Commodities (UNCTAD, Fundamental Elements of the Common Fund, para. 24), the International Energy Agency (IEA, art. 62), and the International Maritime Satellite Organization (INMARSAT, art. 14(3)). Henry G. Schermers & Niels M. Blokker, *International Institutional Law,* §§ 799–812 (3d ed. 1995).

[27] This so-called "freedom of form" rule seems to be confirmed by art. 39 of the Vienna Convention. UN Convention on the Law of Treaties, opened for signature May 23, 1969, art. 39, 1155 U.N.T.S. 331, 340 [Vienna Convention] ("A treaty may be amended by agreement between the parties. The rules laid down in Part II apply to such an agreement except in so far as the treaty may otherwise provide." Part II deals with the conclusion (and entry into force) of treaties.). Art. 11, which is part of Part II, provides that the consent of a State to be bound can be expressed in any form agreed between the parties. However, art. 39 subjects this freedom to the condition that the treaty does not provide otherwise. We find an interpretation contrary to the "freedom of form" rule unconvincing. There are two arguments clearly confirming the

there be a disagreement over the interpretation of a clause within a treaty, an agreement of all parties will normally be the final word as either an authentic interpretation[28] or a *de facto* amendment.[29]

There is a different manner in which disparate States may bring into being a new legal order, by "constitutional" fusion. Birth may take different forms, from constitutional convention[30] to treaty.[31] Arguably each new creature inherits a genetic and legal code altogether different from that of their parents. The constitutive act may explicitly or implicitly extinguish the separate existence of the constituent units,[32] but, in any event, it will subordinate the constituent units to the new creation. Thus, it is sometimes thought that whereas the subjects of a treaty (or a treaty-based international organization) are the States composing it, the subjects of, say, a federal constitutional order are not only its constituent States, but also its common citizenry. This difference is thought to create a different level of legitimacy for the constitutional

freedom of form. First, special revision clauses are intended to *facilitate*, not to complicate, the ordinary amendment process. The special amendment procedure, then, bars single States from insisting on amendment by consensus if the treaty provides for a more efficient procedure. There is, however, no reason why in cases in which all parties agree to consensus procedure they should not be able to do so. Second, *argumentum a maiore ad minus* ex Vienna Convention art. 54. If treaties can be terminated at any time by the consent of all the parties, then the parties must also be able to employ the less significant measure, the amendment or revision of the treaty by the consent of all the parites. Both arguments are put forward by Wolfram Karl, *Vertrag und spätere Praxis im Völkerrecht* 341–43 (1983); Bruno de Witte, *Rules of Change in International Law: How Special is the European Community?*, 25 Neth. Y.B. Int'l L. 299, 313 (1994).

[28] *See, e.g.*, 1 *Oppenheim's International Law*, *supra* note 17, § 630, at 1268–69; Alfred Verdross & Bruno Simma, *Universelles Völkerrecht: Theorie und Praxis* § 775, at 490–91 (3d ed. 1984); Knut Ipsen, *Völkerrecht* 120–21 (3d ed. 1990). *See also* Vienna Convention art. 31(3)(a), *supra* note 26, 1155 U.N.T.S. at 340.

[29] It may be difficult to draw a clear line between the two. Authentic interpretation, along the lines of art. 31(3)(a) of the Vienna Convention, can, substantially, be conceived of as a material amendment to the Treaty. Vienna Convention, *supra* note 26, 1155 U.N.T.S. at 340 [Vienna Convention]. This may have decisive implications, especially in municipal law. While amendments to international treaties generally have to be ratified by a competent body under national law, one could well argue that interpretive declarations do not have to be so ratified. This question arose, for example, under German law when the Bundesverfassungsgericht had to decide upon the constitutionality of the deployment of German armed forces "out of area". Judgment of July 12, 1994, 90 BVerfGE 286; *see* Wolff Heintschel von Heinegg & Ulrich R. Haltern, *The Decision of the German Federal Constitutional Court of 12 July 1994 in Re Deployment of German Armed Forces "Out of Area"*, 41 Neth. Int'l L. Rev. 285, 305–7 (1994).

[30] Consider, for example, the constitutional convention founding the United States. *See, e.g.*, Max Farrand, *The Framing of the Constitution of the United States* (1913); Gordon S. Wood, *The Creation of the American Republic 1776–1787* (1969).

[31] Consider the Einigungsvertrag of Aug. 31, 1990 [FRG—GDR: Treaty on the Establishment of German Unity] 1990 Bundesgesetzblatt Teil II [BGBl. II] 889, translated and reprinted in 30 I.L.M. 457 (1991)(leading to German unification). *See, e.g.*, Peter E. Quint, *Constitution-Making by Treaty in German Unification: A Comment on Arato, Elster, Preuss, and Richards*, 14 Cardozo L. Rev. 691 (1993). As far as German law is concerned, according to GG art. 23, unification was implemented by the accession of the German Democratic Republic to the Federal Republic of Germany.

[32] On October 3, 1990, the GDR ceased to exist. Its territory became part of the Federal Republic of Germany. The five states (*Länder*) that formed the GDR became states of the Federal Republic. *See*, generally Jochen Abr. Frowein, *The Reunification of Germany*, 86 Am. J. Int'l L. 152 (1992).

order, one where its legitimacy does not come only from the consent of sovereign States but from the broader and more direct consent of the citizens of those constituent units. Typically, the international organization is governed by international law and the constitutional order by its own municipal law.

There is no doubt that the European legal order started its life as an international organization in the traditional sense, even if it had some unique features from its inception.[33] This original internationalism was evident in, for example, the attitude of the institutions of the Communities themselves, including the vaunted ECJ,[34] as well as in the attitude of the Member States receiving expression in, for example, early instances of Treaty amendment.[35] We entirely share, then, Schilling's critique of those who hold that the Community legal order was born as a constitutional order.[36] It should be stated that few would ascribe original constitutionalism to the Community legal order.

Nevertheless, one of the great perceived truisms, or myths, of the European Union legal order is its alleged rupture with, or mutation from, public international law and its transformation into a constitutional legal order.[37] This mutation takes place, allegedly, from 1963 onwards and is reflected in landmark cases of the ECJ—in dialogue with national courts. The Court talks first of a "New Legal Order of International Law"[38] and then of a "New Legal Order" *simpliciter*. The "newness" of the legal order is characterized as "constitutional" and the process as "constitutionalization." The subjects of the new order are said to be not only States, but also individuals. Most commentators focus on the legal doctrines of supremacy of European law, the direct effect of European law, implied powers and pre-emption, and on the evolution of the protection of fundamental human rights as hallmarks of this "constitutionalization".[39]

---

[33] These unique features are so well known as to obviate extensive description. We content ourselves to point to EEC Treaty art. 189, the possibility of binding decision-making and majority voting under EEC, and the extraordinary powers of the High Authority under ECSC.

[34] *See*, e.g., *Dineke Algera v. Common Assembly of the European Coal and Steel Community, supra* note 8.

[35] In 1956 and 1957, the six original Member States of the European Coal and Steel Community twice modified the ECSC Treaty by informal agreement, disrespecting the formal procedure laid down in ECSC Treaty art. 36. *See* de Witte, *supra* note 26, at 316; Werner Meng, Artikel 236, in *Kommentar zum EWG-Vertrag, supra* note 7, para. 31, at 5844. *See also* J.H.H. Weiler & James Modrall, *Institutional Reform: Consensus or Majority?*, 10 Eur. L. Rev. 316 (1985); J.H.H. Weiler & James Modrall, *La création de l'Union européenne et sa relation avec les traités CEE*, in *Perspectives européennes—L'Europe de Demain* 173 (Commission des Communautés Européennes ed., 1985).

[36] Schilling, *supra* note 1, discussion part II.A. (at 390–5).

[37] Literature on this subject is endless. For a recent contribution *see The European Constitutional Area* (Roland Bieber & Pierre Widmer eds., 1995), and references therein.

[38] *Van Gend & Loos v. Nederlandse, supra* note 8.

[39] E.g., G. Federico Mancini, *The Making of a Constitution for Europe*, 26 CMLRev. 595 (1989); Eric Stein, *Lawyers, Judges, and the Making of a Transnational Constitution*, 75 Am. J. Int'l L. 1 (1981).

Whether or not, from the perspective of legal theory, these specific legal doctrines constitute real hallmarks of a constitutional order, as distinct from a classical international law order, can be—and has been—open to debate.[40] Assuming the distinction between an international and a constitutional order makes any sense at all—and this too can be doubted!—we would prefer to focus on the following features which distinguish the European legal order from public international law: the different hermeneutics of the European order, its system of compliance which renders European law in effect a transnational form of "higher law"[41] supported by enforceable judicial review, as well as the removal of traditional forms of State responsibility from the system.[42] We shall deal with these issues extensively in a separate article.[43]

However flawed the "constitutionalization" thesis may be from the perspective of legal theory, it has enjoyed huge success in the discourse of European law, and this from all actors concerned. The evidence is everywhere, both sublime and ridiculous—let the reader be the judge of which is which.

For its part, the ECJ did not hesitate to abandon the New Legal Order vocabulary in favor of an explicit constitutional rhetoric. [44] And whatever European law is called elsewhere, it has been treated frequently and consistently by national courts differently from most other treaty law and from the decisions of most other international organizations.[45] Not surprisingly, Community law is often practised, taught, and studied by different sets of professionals. In what many consider the pre-eminent English-language inter-

[40] *See* Derrick Wyatt, *New Legal Order, or Old?*, 7 Eur. L. Rev. 147 (1982); Bruno de Witte, *Retour à "Costa": La primauté du droit communautaire à la lumière du droit international*, 20 Revue Trimestrielle de Droit Européen 425 (1984).

[41] Mauro Cappelletti & David Golay, *The Judicial Branch in the Federal and Transnational Union: Its Impact on Integration, in* 1 *Integration Through Law—Europe and the American Federal Experience: Methods, Tools and Institutions* No. 2, Political Organs, Integration Techniques and Judicial Process 261 (Mauro Cappelletti et al. eds. 1986).

[42] Weiler, *supra* note 7, at 2422.

[43] We are aware that this issue is disputed. *See*, e.g., Christian Tomuschat, *Völkerrechtliche Schadensersatzansprüche vor dem EuGH*, in *Europarecht—Energierecht—Wirtschaftsrecht, Festschrift für Bodo Börner* 441 (Jürgen F. Baur et al. eds., 1992); Bruno Simma, *Self-Contained Regimes*, 16 Neth. Y.B. Int'l L. 111, 123–29 (1985).

[44] *Parti Ecologiste "Les Verts"* v. *European Parliament* [1986] ECR 1339.

[45] This situation becomes most obvious in Member States with a (mitigated) dualist system, above all Germany and Italy. In Germany, the Bundesverfassungsgericht in the German *Handelsgesellschaft* Case held that "[t]his Court—in this respect in agreement with the law developed by the European Court of Justice—adheres to its settled view that Community law is neither a component part of the national legal system *nor international law*, but forms an independent system of law flowing from an autonomous legal source." German Constitutional Court, judgment of May 29, 1974, BVerfGE 37, 271, translated in English in 1 Decisions of the Bundesverfassungsgericht—Federal Constitutional Court—Federal Republic of Germany: International Law and the Law of the European Communities 1952–1989 (pt. I) 270, 274 (1992) (emphasis added). The Italian Corte Costituzionale in the Italian *Frontini* Case held, "Fundamental requirements of equality and legal certainty demand that the Community norms, which *cannot be characterised as a source of international law*, nor of foreign law, nor of internal law of the individual States, ought to have full compulsory efficacy and direct application in all the Member States . . ." Judgment of Dec. 27, 1973 (Italian *Frontini* Case, No. 183) Corte Cost., *translated in* [1974] 2 CMLR 386, 387 (our emphasis). The different treatment of Community

national legal journal, *The American Journal of International Law*, you will hardly find articles dealing with European law, ever since Eric Stein published his celebrated article consecrating the European legal order in federal constitutional terms,[46] for the simple reason that the journal does not consider it international law! Even that cheeky upstart rival, *The European Journal of International Law*, treats the European Union as a polity in whose internal law it has little interest, for, again, it is not considered international law. By contrast, this last journal takes trouble to publish the European Union's "State Practice" in international fora for the benefit of its readers, in the way international law journals occasionally publish surveys of the state practice of the nation from which they publish. Furthermore, at most institutions of higher learning, knowledge of international law is not a requisite for the study of European law. It has, in our view, become increasingly artificial to describe the legal structures and processes of the Community with the vocabulary of international law.

Schilling himself is not impressed by the "constitutionalization" thesis. Even if the Community, like a precious metal, has some of the characteristics of a constitutional legal order, it lacks the most fundamental property: legitimation through a popular constituent power which in this case can only be the European people(s). From a purist, Kelsenian, perspective, Schilling argues, European constitutionalism is ersatz gold. Schilling thus reverts back to the origins of the Community and places his bet on international law.[47]

But what of the realist perspective? In light of the overwhelming practice of the last three or four decades, if the Community order is treated as constitutional who cares what it "really" is? Schilling does not shy away from the realist perspective, which he calls the Hartian perspective.[48] His critique is more refined. He claims

---

law and other international treaty law is confirmed in the *Granital* decision. Judgment of June 8, 1984 (*Granital* v. *Amministrazione delle Finanze dello Stato*, No. 170), Corte Cost., *translated in* 21 Common Mkt. L. Rev. 756 (1984). *See* Francesco P. R. Laderchi, *The European Court and National Courts, Doctrine and Jurisprudence: Legal Change in Its Social Context, Report on Italy* (EUI Working Paper RSC No. 95/30, 1995). See also Henry G. Schermers & Denis Waelbroeck, *Judicial Protection in the European Communities* 127–38 (5th ed. 1992). However, the issue of Kompetenz-Kompetenz has led the German Constitutional Court to seek distance from the rhetoric of an "autonomous legal order" and to retreat to "international law" rhetoric, as in the German *Maastricht* decision, *supra* note 16. *See* on this development Juliane Kokott, *The European Court and National Courts, Doctrine and Jurisprudence: Legal Change in Its Social Context, Report on Germany* (EUI Working Paper RSC No. 95/25, 1995) 9–13, 23–25.

[46] Stein, *supra* note 38.

[47] Schilling, *supra* note 1, at 397–8 ("There are, in fact, some indicators that point in the opposite direction, away from constitutionalization. Importantly, the European Treaties continue to be amended by treaties and provide for future amendments. The minor role that Maastricht Treaty art. N(1)(2) gives the European Parliament in preparing the draft of amending treaties cannot be an indication that the European people has adopted the treaties as a constitution. In addition, it cannot be claimed that there is, with the European people, a custom supported by a common *opinio juris* that regards the European Treaties as the constitution of an autonomous Europe. While some Europeans take this view, there are as many who do not share it. This is not enough to create a custom.").

[48] E.g., Schilling, *supra* note 1, at 398–400.

that if one takes the realist approach one buys a European constitutional construct by compromising the legitimacy of the European public sphere.[49]

We cannot accept the purist approach. We do not think that a reversion to public international law is any less artificial than the constitutional characterization. The Community lacks, in our view, some of the fundamental properties of internationalism. We are, however, very sympathetic to Schilling's assessment of the realist perspective. We too have characterized this system as a constitutional order without constitutionalism.[50] We think that the legitimacy gap is for real. The Community has adopted constitutional practices without any underlying legitimizing constitutionalism. Yet, attempts such as those by the German Constitutional Court[51] and by Schilling to try to push the toothpaste back in the tube by asserting that the Community is nothing more than an International Organization are self-serving (to the Court) and unhelpful in addressing the real problem of legitimacy. The legitimacy problem that Schilling points out will not go away if we change the theoretical foundation of the legal order from a constitutional one to an international one. Be this as it may, the implication of the internationalist premise on the "Decisive Question" is of greater interest.

III. Judicial Kompetenz-Kompetenz

How then does Schilling deal with the "Decisive Question" of the ultimate power to invalidate *ultra vires* Community law? And how does he reach the conclusion that an ". . . international law interpretation of the European Treaties thus leads to the conclusion that the ECJ is not the ultimate umpire of the system . . ." from which he believes that it follows that ". . . the Member States, *individually*, must have the final word on questions concerning the scope of the competences they have delegated to the Community"?[52] It is worth following his reasoning with some care.

His first argument, referring to Kelsen's 1952 treatise,[53] is to claim, somewhat surprisingly, that "[g]eneral international law does not provide any guidance on this question because it does not know of international institutions".[54] He then relies on a 1953 essay by Leo Gross[55] to support his thesis that "[t]he accepted method for the interpretation of international treaties, in the absence

---

[49] *Id.* at 399–401.

[50] J.H.H. Weiler, ". . . *We Will Do, And Hearken*" *(Ex. XXIV:7): Reflections on a Common Constitutional Law for the European Union*, in *The European Constitutional Area, supra* note 36, at 413.

[51] *See* Weiler, *supra* note 16, at 1669–70.

[52] Schilling, *supra* note 1, at 407 (emphasis added).

[53] Hans Kelsen, *Principles of International Law* (1952).

[54] Schilling, *supra* note 1, at 404.

[55] 1 Leo Gross, *States as Organs of International Law and the Problem of Autointerpretation*, in *Essays on International Law and Organization* 367, 382–96 (1993).

of treaty institutions, is autointerpretation".[56] We doubt whether either of these statements is an accurate reflection of their authors' intentions[57] or, in any event, of international law in the 1990s. When we offer our alternative construct, we shall return to these points.

First, we think that Schilling mischaracterizes the issue of autointerpretation. Even in treaties without centralized institutions, which is not the case of the European Treaties, autointerpretation, *by each state individually*, is mostly accepted as a practical inevitability with little, if any, normative value. The very article by Leo Gross on which Schilling seems to rely[58] is most eloquent on this issue. Gross explicitly avoids giving any normative spin to autointerpretation and clearly labels it as a *de facto* stand-off when he denies it any binding force. It is useful to quote Gross more extensively.

> This interpretation [of the individual states], however, is not a "decision" and is neither final nor binding upon the other parties . . . [We] may never know . . . which autointerpretation was correct. A controversy, in other words, may remain unsettled forever or for a long time.[59]
>
> It can be shown, I believe, that states have the right of autointerpretation but not the right to decide questions of international law, that is, to make binding decisions for others.[60]
>
> In a dispute regarding the interpretation of a bilateral treaty, the competent authority is the composite organ formed by the two contracting parties, or a tribunal instituted by the parties with the power to settle the dispute. To attribute to one party alone the capacity of an organ, that is, the right to decide the meaning of a treaty, would amount to conferring on it the right to create a norm binding on the

---

[56] Schilling, *supra* note 1, at 404.

[57] While Schilling's text conveys the impression that "general international law" is to be understood in contrast to "Community law", this is not what Kelsen had in mind. Kelsen was describing the difference between international and national law, characterizing the former as "a relatively decentralized" and the latter as a "relatively centralized" coercive order. Kelsen, *supra* note 52, at 402–3. For example, Kelsen talks about custom and treaties as "decentralized methods", and mentions that "there are under general international law no special organs for the application of the law and especially no central agencies for the execution of the sanctions", the implication being that national legal orders typically have a special organ to enforce the law. Even more revealing, however, is the fact that Kelsen, writing in 1952, observes that international law is moving towards international institutions. He calls the law of international organizations, which in 1952 was far from being fully-developed, "particular international law", as opposed to general international law: "But under particular international law, the creation as well as the application of the law may be—and actually is—centralized; and this process of centralization is steadily increasing by the establishment of international organizations instituting international tribunals and international executive agencies." Kelsen, *supra* note 52, at 403.

[58] It seems that Schilling draws on the following quotation from Gross: "It is generally recognized that the root of the unsatisfactory situation in international law and relations is the absence of an authority generally competent to declare what the law is at any given time, how it applies to a given situation or dispute, and what the appropriate sanction may be. In the absence of such an authority, and failing agreement between the states at variance on these points, each state has a right to interpret the law, the right of autointerpretation, as it might be called." Gross, *supra* note 54, at 386.

[59] *Id.*

[60] *Id.*

other state, that is, juridically speaking, subordinate the other state to the jurisdiction of the former. If no other principle of international law then certainly the principle of equality militates against such an attribution. Obviously, autointerpretation has no binding character. In autodecision, such a character is implied, but without any justification in general international law.[61]

The same consideration applies in multilateral treaties. Each contracting party has a right of autointerpretation, but not of autodecision. The right of authentic interpretation is vested in the composite organ formed by all the contracting parties. Unless the treaty provides for an alternative procedure, an authoritative interpretation can result from negotiations leading to an agreement, or from arbitration or adjudication.[62]

It is part of the principle of *pacta sunt servanda* that the right of authentic interpretation belongs to the composite organ which created the treaty and not to any of the states members of that organ.[63]

Arbitration and adjudication appear to be among the classic methods for seeking and obtaining an authoritative interpretation on questions arising from the autonomous application and interpretation of international law.[64]

Gross warns explicitly against Schilling's mistake:

Autointerpretation is easily presented, or rather misrepresented, as autodecision for want of a compulsory procedure leading to a heteronomous and binding decision. But appearances are misleading . . . [65]

Presupposing the absence of any mechanism of dispute resolution, we consider autointerpretation as a factual inevitability in a realm of little legal sophistication, and equally little shared goals and co-ordination.[66] It is not by accident that Gross discusses the issue of autointerpretation in reference to Kelsen's theory that States act as organs of the international community,[67] which is closely related to the problem of *bellum justum*.[68] Neither is it by accident that the most notable and recent case on the subject touched upon the unilateral re-interpretation of a cold war arms control treaty between the

---

[61] *Id.* at 390–1.

[62] *Id.* at 391.

[63] *Id.* at 392.

[64] *Id.* at 393.

[65] *Id.* at 394.

[66] Schilling himself acknowledges this: "The accepted method for the interpretation of international treaties, in the absence of treaty institutions, is autointerpretation by the contracting states." Schilling, *supra* note 1, at 404.

[67] Gross' article originally appeared in a volume devoted to Kelsen's theory of international law, *Law and Politics in the World Community: Essays on Hans Kelsens' Pure Theory and Related Problems in International Law* (George A. Lipsky ed., 1953).

[68] It would be interesting to analyse the theory of autointerpretation as conceived of by Leo Gross and also Hans Kelsen in relation to the claim that the right of self-defence is self-judging. Such an undertaking, however, goes beyond the limits of this article. *Cf.* Paul W. Kahn, *From Nuremberg to The Hague: The United States Position in Nicaragua v. United States and the Development of International Law*, 12 Yale J. Int'l L. 1 (1987) (concluding that the claim that, under international law, self-defence is a self-judging function that resists third-party review is incompatible with modern developments in international law).

US and the Soviet Union.[69] Yet even to say that autointerpretation under these conditions would be an "accepted method" proves too much.[70] Both jurisprudential[71] and functional[72] arguments are powerful enough to cast more than a shadow of doubt on a normative claim to autointerpretation.

These difficulties with autointerpretation, both jurisprudential and pragmatic, have increasingly induced States to create a variety of mechanisms to settle disputes—ranging from voluntary arbitration to the creation of international tribunals and a binding commitment to judicial dispute resolution. The extensive experience with international institutions in the last four decades, while it has become part of general international law, has also revealed the intricate problem of *quis judicabit*—who is competent to decide upon measures adopted by international organizations?[73] While we expect

[69] In 1985, the Reagan administration attempted to re-interpret the Anti-Ballistic Missile Treaty of 1972. *See* Robert Johnson, Recent Development, *Arms Control: Re-interpretation of the Anti-Ballistic Missile Treaty of 1972*, 27 Harv. Int'l L. J. 659 (1986).

[70] *Cf.* Ebere Osieke, *The Legal Validity of Ultra Vires Decisions of International Organizations*, 77 Am. J. Int'l L. 239, 254 (1983) (hereinafter *Legal Validity*) (noting that "[t]he right of member states to reject decisions they consider unconstitutional in the absence of a legal determination by a review body to that effect has not been generally accepted by international lawyers").

[71] A jurisprudential argument would rely on the principle of *pacta sunt servanda*. See, e.g., Abram Chayes & Antonia Handler Chayes, *Testing and Development of "Exotic" Systems under the ABM Treaty: The Great Reinterpretation Caper*, 99 Harv. L. Rev. 1956, 1970 (1986) (stating that treaty provisions cannot be altered unilaterally since they "represent a solemn engagement between nations, binding at international law").

[72] A functional argument would stress the fact that self-interpretation places the very objectives of a treaty in danger. *See*, e.g., Donald G. Gross, *Negotiated Treaty Amendment: The Solution to the SDI-ABM Treaty Conflict*, 28 Harv. Int'l L. J. 31, 51–2 (1987) ("In an atmosphere where each side felt free to reinterpret treaties to its own advantage, agreement on strategic matters would be exceedingly difficult to attain. Engaging in strained legal interpretation makes a mockery of the negotiating process . . . A strained unilateral interpretation dilutes the legal validity of the Treaty and undermines the mutual intention of controlling arms proliferation which lies at the base of the document . . . [T]he cost of unilateral reinterpretation would be high. If observed in practice, without the prior acquiescence of the Soviets, reinterpretation could trigger a complete breakdown of arms control. Both parties would be forced to reassess the value of treaties—fragile legal instruments—for controlling nuclear arms in a world where deft manipulations of language can alter previously understood meanings.").

[73] This problem should not be confused with the undisputed proposition that member states of an international organization have the right to challenge the acts and decisions of the organization. Only the competence to decide on these challenges is in question. Osieke, *Legal Validity*, *supra* note 69, at 240–1. This competence could lie either with the organization that has already acted, or with the challenging member state, or with a different organ, most likely judicial, either part of the organization or independent of it. We must first distinguish between two scenarios, one in which the parties to the treaty or the member states of the organization have not provided for a mechanism to settle disputes arising out of the treaty (Scenario 1), and one in which they have (Scenario 2). If no dispute-settlement mechanism was created, the problem of *nemo debet esse judex in propria causa* (no person should judge his or her own case) arises. Since there is no (judicial) institution to rule on challenges to the actions of the international organization, the competence to judge those actions must lie either with the organ itself or with the challenging member state. Both would be judging their own case. In addition, surveys of state practice have led to the result that it was always the organ whose act had been challenged that decided the claims of unconstitutionality. For example, in relation to the International Labor Organization Ebere Osieke concludes, "[s]ome very interesting principles seem to emerge from the foregoing examination of the practice of the International Labour Organization in the determination of claims of illegality or unconstitutionality concerning the acts of its organs . . . The fact which

that the Messiah will have to arrive before total consensus among international lawyers can be reached on any issue, state practice confirms the over-

emerges from the study is that all the claims of unconstitutionality were decided by the organs
whose acts were challenged." Ebere Osieke, *Ultra Vires Acts in International Organizations: The
Experience of the International Labour Organization*, 48 Brit. Y.B. Int'l L. 259, 273–4 (1977) [here-
inafter Osieke, *ILO*]. The organs whose acts were challenged decided their claims not only when
those claims arose in the Governing Body of the International Labor Office but also when they
arose at the International Labor Conference. Osieke, *ILO, id.* at 262–73. In a different study
on the ICAO, Osieke finds that even organizations that have established a review mechanism tend
to decide their own case, at least in the first instance. Under Art. 84 of the Chicago Convention,
contracting States may appeal to an arbitral tribunal or to the ICJ against a decision of the
Council on any disagreement between two or more contracting States relating to the interpretation or application of the Convention. Osieke finds that "[i]n all the cases examined in the present study, the objects were decided, in the first instance, by the organ whose competence or
jurisdiction was challenged." Ebere Osieke, *Unconstitutional Acts in International Organisations:
The Law and Practice of the ICAO*, 28 Int'l & Comp. L. Q. 1, 23–4 (1979) [hereinafter Osieke,
ICAO]. Again, this is true both for objections raised in the Council of the ICAO and for those
raised in the Assembly of the ICAO. "This [the result that all claims of unconstitutionality were
decided by the organs whose acts were challenged] appears to be the position in international
organisations generally . . ." Osieke, *ILO*, supra, at 274. Furthermore, "[t]his principle appears
to have been generally accepted in the law of international organizations . . ." Osieke, *ICAO*,
supra, at 24. This view is supported by the *Certain Expenses* case:
    In the legal systems of States, there is often some procedure for determining the validity of even
a legislative or governmental act, but no analogous procedure is to be found in the structure of
the United Nations. Proposals made during the drafting of the Charter to place the ultimate
authority to interpret the Charter in the International Court of Justice were not accepted; the
opinion which the Court is in course of rendering is an *advisory* opinion. As anticipated in 1945,
therefore, each organ must, in the first place at least, determine its own jurisdiction.
Certain Expenses of the United Nations, 1962 ICJ 151, 168 (July 20). The state practice privileges the organization rather than the individual member states for practical reasons. Denying
international organizations the competence to decide claims challenging its authority would "seriously impede the effective attainment of [the] objects and purposes [of those international orga-
nizations] because all that a member state would have to do to create an impasse or prevent the
adoption of a decision is to challenge the competence of the organ or the organization, or indeed
the legal validity of the decision." Osieke, *Legal Validity*, supra note 69, at 242. However, we do
not wish to take final sides on this question. Indeed, there also seems to be some state practice
to the contrary. *See*, e.g., Dan Ciobanu, *Preliminary Objections: Related to the Jurisdiction of the
United Nations Political Organs* 175–9 (1975) (stating that the member states of an international
organization have a "right of last resort", because they may claim that their interpretation of the
constituent documents is the correct one. He also states that they may refuse to comply with decisions if they think that those decisions are *ultra vires*). While Ciobanu argues in favour of such
a right of last resort for the member states, he also acknowledges that "what might be called the
right of autointerpretation of what international law prescribes has not found unanimous, and
perhaps [not] even general, support in the doctrine". Ciobanu, *id.* at 173 n.58. From the realist
point of view, this is not satisfactory. The solution, according to the overwhelming majority, is
the establishment of legal organs competent to make such decisions. See, e.g., *Legal Consequences
for States of the Continued Presence of South Africa in Namibia (South West Africa)
Nothwithstanding Security Council Resolution 276 (1970)*, 1971 ICJ 16, 2998 (June 21) (dissenting opinion of Judge Sir Gerald Fitzmaurice). This is scenario 2. Of course, once such an organ
is established, it holds, under general public international law, the competence to decide upon the
legality of the acts of the international organization. Even if we acknowledged, *arguendo*, the
right of an alleged member state to determine the validity of the act of the international organisation, this right would have been transferred to the judicial organ through the act of establishing it. See Schermers & Blokker, *supra* note 25, § 600, at 408, who, in this context, assert that
this transfer to a judicial organ would bring about "an important restriction on the states' right
of autointerpretation which many states do not wish to accept".

whelming view that when a treaty sets up a procedure for binding dispute resolution, particularly judicial organs, autointerpretation is legally squelched.[74] Tribunals do have jurisdiction to determine their own competence by interpreting their constitutive instruments.[75] Likewise, under general international law, the competence of a tribunal to determine the illegality of the actions of an international organization presumptively includes all grounds of illegality, including, we would submit, this international organization's lack of competence to act.

When the stakes are sufficiently high and States do not want to risk the outcome of a binding resolution, these States can use well-established and widely-practiced techniques to preserve their position. Instead of binding judicial resolution, States can, for instance, empower panels or committees to issue recommendations and help in conciliation.[76] But as a general proposition,

[74] *See* disscussion *supra* note 72. It should also be mentioned that in the rare cases where this right is claimed a central judicial organ had *not* been established. *Cf. Certain Expenses of the United Nations*, 1962 ICJ 151, 232 (Winiarski, B., dissenting); *Interpretation of the Agreement of 25 March 1951 between the WHO and Egypt*, 1980 ICJ 73, 104 (Dec. 20) (Gros, A., separate opinion); Ciobanu, *supra* note 72, at 162–79 (distinguishing between "judicial determination" and "political determination", with his examples of autointerpretation illustrating the latter category). Even where non-judicial organs of the international organization have interpreted the constituent document of that organization, their interpretations have been recognized as binding upon the State concerned. *See*, e.g., Ervin P. Hexner, *Interpretation by Public International Organizations of Their Basic Instruments*, 53 Am. J. Int'l L. 341, 352–6 (1959) (providing as early as 1959 telling examples relating to the IMF and the World Bank on the one hand and the Federal Communications Commission on the other). For examples referring to the U.N., see *supra* note 25.

[75] This principle has been long established in international arbitration. *See*, e.g., *Nottebohm Case (Liechtenstein v. Guatemala)*, 1953 ICJ 111, 119–20 (Nov. 18)(preliminary objection) ("Since the *Alabama* case, it has been generally recognized, following the earlier precedents, that, in the absence of any agreement to the contrary, an international tribunal has the right to decide as to its own jurisdiction and has the power to interpret for this purpose the instruments which govern that jurisdiction. This principle was expressly recognized in Articles 48 and 73 of the Hague Conventions of July 29th, 1899, and October 18th, 1907, for the Pacific Settlement of International Disputes . . . The Rapporteur of the Convention of 1899 had emphasized the necessity of this principle, presented by him as being 'of the very essence of the arbitral function and one of the inherent requirements for the exercise of this function.' This principle has been frequently applied and at times expressly stated. This principle, which is accepted by general international law in the matter of arbitration, assumes particular force when the international tribunal is no longer an arbitral tribunal constituted by virtue of a special agreement between the parties for the purpose of adjudicating on a particular dispute, but is an institution which has been pre-established by an international instrument defining its jurisdiction and regulating its operation . . ."). *See also* Ibrahim F.I. Shihata, *The Power of the International Court to Determine Its Own Jurisdiction—Compétence de la Compétence* (1965).

[76] Consider, for instance, the dispute settlement mechanism established by the United States— Israel Free Trade Area Agreement, April 22, 1985, 24 I.L.M. 653 (1985) (entered into force August 19, 1985) [hereinafter FTAA]. Article 19 establishes a hierarchy of intra-FTAA fora: informal consultations, referral to the Joint Committee, and referral by the Joint Committee to a conciliation panel. This panel will then try to get the parties to sign an agreement to resolve the dispute. A report containing the finding of facts will be drawn up and a resolution will be proposed. The report is non-binding. FTAA art. 19, *id.* at 664-65. It has been uniformly concluded that this dispute settlement mechanism "has the advantages of informality and administrative ease." Nicholas A. Aminoff, *The United States-Israel Free Trade Area Agreement of 1985: In Theory and Practice*, 25 J. World Trade 5, 23–24 (1991).

practically self-evident, it would empty binding judicial dispute resolution of its meaning if States subject to such procedures were then, in law, free to resort to "autointerpretation" and disregard the decision of the international tribunal.

We do not wish to minimize the "hard case" scenario. Arguably, a State is not obligated by an otherwise-binding resolution if this resolution was adopted *ultra vires*. But why limit this result to resolutions adopted *ultra vires*? Arguably, a State is not obligated by an otherwise-binding resolution if it was illegal for whatever reason, e.g. a procedural failure or a conflict with *jus cogens*. The nature of a mechanism providing for binding judicial resolution is that a State has to live with the risk of an adverse decision.

Under general international law, the State does have certain options. It can, for example, seek to convince all parties to the treaty to adopt its position. If successful, as masters of the treaty, the member States can jointly modify the treaty provision or the measure in question to remove the alleged illegality. A state can, if allowed, withdraw from the organization.

Of course, it can also decide to follow its own understanding of the law and disregard the tribunal, as States have sometimes done, but by doing so it would be violating international law and incurring State responsibility. While such a violation is a pragmatic option, in that States can, in fact, take this course of action, this option should not be cloaked with the mantle of legality.

Therefore, general international law does give us some guidance, and the guidance it gives us runs counter to Schilling's argument. Be that as it may, Schilling does not stake his claim on general international law, but on an international law interpretation of the EC Treaties. We must therefore turn to these. Do the European Treaties create some exception to the thrust of general international law?

Faithful to his internationalist approach, Schilling brushes aside the rather particularized hermeneutics, developed and applied for years within the European legal order,[77] and exhorts us to return to article 31(1) of the Vienna Convention on the Law of Treaties. Interpretation is to follow ". . . the ordinary meaning to be given to the terms of the treaty in their context and in the light of its object and purpose".[78]

The relevant provisions, according to Schilling, are EC article 164 and EC articles 169–183. In particular, he focuses on EC article 171, which states that "[i]f the Court of Justice finds that a Member State has failed to fulfill an obligation under this Treaty, [it] . . . shall be required to take the necessary

---

[77] We do not wish to deal, *in extenso*, with the highly complex debate about the different hermeneutics in European law, as opposed to general public international law. When we talk, hereinafter, about "international law interpretation", we mean a hermeneutics that pays great deference to the text and to the presumed intentions of the High Contracting Parties, and that is *not* informed by the teleology of European integration.

[78] Vienna Convention, art. 32(b), *supra* note 26, 1155 U.N.T.S. at 340.

measures to comply with the judgment of the Court of Justice." Schilling finds the ordinary meaning of this provision to indicate that the Court ". . . is the ultimate umpire of the European system."[79] We concur, reading the plain language of the article—which does not restrict the duty of obedience *ratione materiae*. If a Member State were to decide that it did not have to follow a measure it viewed as *ultra vires* but the ECJ thought otherwise, article 171 would require that the Member State obey the ECJ. But Schilling tries to overturn his own understanding of the ordinary meaning of the words by demonstrating that such a plain meaning would be inconsistent with the context of the provision and the object and purpose of the European Treaties.

Before we turn to his analysis of context, object and purpose, we must raise a more fundamental question: should Schilling have focused solely (or even principally) on EC Treaty article 171 in his international law interpretation of the European Treaties on the issue of judicial *Kompetenz-Kompetenz*? We think that articles 173 and 177 are also worthy of special mention.

Taking an internationalist, voluntarist, positivist approach, we recall that the High Contracting Parties to the European Treaties set up a court, the ECJ, to settle disputes arising under the Treaties. In their wisdom, they granted that Court wide jurisdiction, including jurisdiction to review the legality and validity of Community measures.[80] They even set out the criteria which the Court was to employ when engaging in such review.[81] They could have restricted the competence of the Court to review, for example, infringements of procedural requirements. They also could have given wide grounds of review in some fields while excluding others entirely. Schilling claims that a correct internationalist interpretation of the Treaties gives the individual supreme courts of the Member States, acting separately, the final say on the competences of the EC. The Member States could have spelled that out, but they did not. In fact, they appear to have spelled out the opposite. In article 173, the grounds for review are listed as ". . . *lack of competence*, infringement of an essential procedural requirement, infringement of this Treaty or of any rule of law relating to its application, or misuse of powers."[82]

The first ground for declaring the illegality of an act of a Community institution is lack of competence. This lack of competence might be internal, i.e., if the competence belongs to another institution,[83] or external, i.e., the Community, as such, lacks competence.[84]

But why read article 173 as making the European Court the "ultimate" umpire? This is what Schilling would have us believe is a correct international

---

[79] Schilling, *supra* note 1, at 405.

[80] *See* EC Treaty arts. 173-7.

[81] *See*, e.g., EC Treaty art. 173(1).

[82] EC Treaty art. 173 (emphasis added).

[83] Of course, that situation would also be illegal because it would be an infringement of the Rule of Law relating to the application of the Treaty.

[84] *See*, e.g., Schermers & Waelbroeck, *supra* note 44, at 194-95; Hans Krück, *Artikel 173*, in *Kommentar zum EWG-Vertrag*, *supra* note 7, at para. 73; and Hartley, *supra* note 7, at 428.

law interpretation of this provision: the High Contracting Parties set up the ECJ and gave it explicit jurisdiction to adjudicate challenges to Community measures by, among others, Member States on the grounds of lack of competence. That is, a Member State in dispute with a Community institution or with other Member States regarding the observance of Community law, if it believes that it may disregard a Community measure because it was taken *ultra vires*, is given a specific judicial remedy before the ECJ. But according to Schilling, the High Contracting Parties intended with this provision that the State challenging the legality of a community measure, if it lost in front of the ECJ, could nonetheless disregard the Community measure in question by using its right to "autointerpretation". "Heads I Win, Tails You Lose," is what we used to call that form of adjudication in kindergarten. This, we think, flies against the ordinary meaning and the entire judicial review context of the provision.

It also flies against the purposes of the treaties which include, according to article 2, harmonious and balanced development, social cohesion, and solidarity among Member States.[85] Consider, as just one example, the pragmatic nightmare that would ensue in a treaty as long, complex, and, by its own terms, open-textured as the EC Treaties if such an interpretation were adopted. State A, in the face of an unfavorable judicial decision, unilaterally abrogates Treaty provision *x* on the grounds that it is, in its eyes, *ultra vires*. The international law principle of reciprocity would mean that that particular obligation would cease to be operative between A and all the other Parties B–Z. So now there would be two co-existing regimes in relation to provision *x*; *x* is applied as among Parties B–Z, but inapplicable in the relationship of B–Z with A. Now imagine that State B abrogates, on the same grounds, Treaty provision *y*, and that State C does likewise with Treaty provision *z*. Some harmonious relations; Garry Kasparov would, we think, have difficulties in sorting out the permutations.

The Vienna Convention, in article 32(b) suggests that when the ordinary meaning leads to a result manifestly absurd or unreasonable, we may resort to subsidiary means of interpretation, including the *travaux préparatoires*.[86] The *travaux préparatoires* of the EC Treaties have not been published and are not pleaded before the Court.[87] Fortunately, we do not need them. In our view, this absurdity does not result from the ordinary meaning of the treaty, but rather from the extraordinary meaning that Schilling's construct would put on this provision.

Is it not more reasonable to imagine that, given the wide economic and social catch of the European Treaties and their unprecedented institutional scope, the delicate compromises which the various substantive obligations must have entailed, and the temptation by States to find excuses to escape the

---

[85] TEU art. 2.

[86] Vienna Convention, *supra* note 26, 1155 U.N.T.S. at 340.

[87] Which also throws doubt on the applicability of the Vienna Convention rules of interpretation to the European Treaties.

results of hard bargains, the High Contracting Parties established such elaborate provisions for centralized judicial review in order to, among other reasons, escape the pragmatic nightmare just mentioned, and not in order to place their multilateral bargains hostage in the hands of oft-partisan national courts?

In addition, the European Treaties, as Schilling himself points out, have been amended frequently and "re-ratified" on each instance of enlargement. For Schilling, this practice is a reminder of the international law character of the Community. So be it. But if the High Contracting Parties disagreed with the Court's understanding of its role and powers, wouldn't they have used these repeated occasions to "set the record straight" on what they had in mind?[88] After all, they used these occasions to set the record straight on other issues.[89] Instead, not only did the Member States fail to introduce any clarification in the sense argued by Schilling, they also amended the treaty in the opposite way. Rather than mentioning the right to disobey the ECJ through autointerpretation of measures taken *ultra vires*, the Member States modified article 171 to allow for imposing penalties against Member States who disobey the ECJ. And note that we are talking about the very practice which, to Schilling, confirms the international legal character of the Treaties.

Consider next the most celebrated legal provision in the Treaty, EC Treaty article 177.[90] The High Contracting Parties envisaged a role for national courts in the interpretation and application of Community law and in determining questions of its validity—not excluding, one may assume, a challenge to a Community measure alleged to be *ultra vires*. But as hardly needs reminding, when it comes to the highest national courts, against whose decisions there is no judicial remedy (which on any reading of article 177 would include the highest courts in the land, those courts to which Schilling would give the final say on the jurisdictional limits of the Community), Community law obligates them to make a preliminary reference to the ECJ.[91] That is the text.

---

[88] J.W.R. Reed, *Political Review of the European Court of Justice and its Jurisprudence* (Harvard Jean Monnet Working Paper No. 13/95, 1995).

[89] As they did in the so-called Barber Protocol, *supra* note 22.

[90] The Court of Justice shall have jurisdiction to give preliminary rulings concerning:
(a) the interpretation of the Treaty;
(b) the validity and interpretation of acts of the institutions of the Community and of the ECB;
(c) the interpretation of the statutes of bodies established by an act of the Council, where those statutes so provide.

    Where such a question is raised before any court or tribunal of a Member State, that court or tribunal may, if it considers that a decision on the question is necessary to enable it to give judgment, request the Court of Justice to give a ruling thereon.

    Where any such question is raised in a case pending before a court or tribunal of a Member State against whose decisions there is no judicial remedy under national law, that court or tribunal shall bring the matter before the Court of Justice.

EC Treaty art. 177.

[91] Case 283/81, *CILFIT* v. *Italian Ministry of Health* [1982] ECR 3415. Further important decisions on the obligation to ask for a preliminary ruling are Case 6/64, *Flaminio Costa* v. *ENEL* [1964] ECR 585; Joined Cases 28/62-30/62, *Da Costa en Schaake et al.* v. *Nederlandse Belastingadministratie* [1963] ECR 31.

Its ordinary meaning is quite clear. Moreover, the purpose of this provision is the same as the purpose of the comparable provisions in domestic constitutional systems such as Germany[92] and Italy,[93] namely to ensure uniform interpretation of treaty provisions throughout the jurisdiction.[94]

Schilling, who champions the rule of law, insists that article 177 has to be "scrupulously respected".[95] He would, however, have us believe, in accordance with his understanding of the ordinary meaning of this provision and other international legal rules of construction, that article 177 and the duty to refer are "scrupulously respected" when the highest national court makes a reference to the ECJ but, once this was done, presumably after saying a polite thank you, ". . . the Member States can use autointerpretation",[96] meaning the national court can go on to do what it wished to do anyway. Again, "Heads I Win" (if the Preliminary Ruling finds in my favor), "Tails You Lose" (if it does not, but then I get to invoke autointerpretation). This, following Schilling, is to be considered a scrupulous observance of article 177 according to international law? And this is also to be considered the basis from which the German Federal Constitutional Court is to give the ECJ lessons in observing the rule of law?

Schilling's interpretation hardly squares with the ordinary meaning of the words of EC Treaty article 177. It contradicts the object and purpose of article 177 without the need to invoke any of the rhetoric, presumptions, or hermeneutics of European constitutionalism. It is, perhaps, not surprising that Schilling decides to stake his claim on EC Treaty article 171 and to somehow leave articles 173 and 177 in the shadows.

We now come to one of the most puzzling passages in the entire Schilling argument, the one which uses the object and purpose of the European Treaties as a way to negate the ordinary meaning of EC Treaty article 171. It is worth citing *in extenso*.

> The purposes of the EC Treaty, as stated in article 2, relate to the activities of an economic community and, therefore, are arguably restricted to these activities. It follows that the European Treaties should not be interpreted as granting the Community unrestricted powers, in particular *Kompetenz-Kompetenz*. But such a conclusion is at odds with a *Kompetenz-Kompetenz* of the ECJ over questions of the respective competences of the Community and the Member States.[97]

---

[92] *Cf.* GG arts. 93–94, 99–100.

[93] *Cf.* Costituzione art. 134-7. For an exposition of the different conceptions of centralized and decentralized judicial revew, see Mauro Cappelletti, *The Judicial Process in Comparative Perspective* 117-49 (1989).

[94] See, e.g., Schermers & Waelbroeck, *supra* note 44, at 393–4; Hans Krück, *supra* note 83, paras. 10–14. The European Court of Justice, in the Second *Rheinmühlen* Case, held, "Article 177 is essential for the preservation of the Community character of the law established by the Treaty and has the object of ensuring that in all circumstances this law is the same in all States of the Community. . . . [I]t thus aims to avoid divergences in the interpretation of Community law which the national courts have to apply . . ." Case 166/73, *Rheinmühlen-Düsseldorf* v. *Einfuhr- und Vorratsstelle für Getreide und Futtermittel* [1974] ECR 33, 38.

[95] Schilling, *supra* note 1, at 408.

[96] *Id.*, at 408.

[97] *Id.*, at 406 (footnotes omitted).

In part, we believe the problem comes from the language, in particular from a possible conflation of the term *Kompetenz-Kompetenz*, which means two different things when applied to the Community and the Court. In part, the statement is simply misconceived.

Let us take the argument step by step.

First, it should be noted that the object and purpose of the European Treaties, even of the rather narrow Treaty of Paris establishing the European Coal and Steel Community, are by no means economic only. While preambles do not create positive legal obligations, they can help in understanding the purpose of a treaty, as expressly provided for in article 31 of the Vienna Convention on the Law of Treaties.[98] Entire chunks of the politically-charged and visionary Schuman Declaration are written into the Preamble of the Treaty of Paris.[99] And the Treaty of Rome commences with that highly economic objective of laying the foundations ". . . of an ever closer union among the peoples of Europe".[100] Do these texts have no hermeneutic significance in international law? We have always believed that the genius of the Treaties was to have political ends achieved by economic means.

[98] 1. A treaty shall be interpreted in good faith in accordance with the ordinary meaning to be given to the terms of the treaty in their context and in the light of its object and purpose.

2. The context for the purpose of the interpretation of a treaty shall comprise, in addition to the text, *including its preamble* and annexes: . . .

Vienna Convention, art. 31(1)-(2), *supra* note 26, 1155 U.N.T.S. at 340 (emphasis added). See also *Case Concerning the Rights of Nationals of the United States of America in Morocco*, 1952 ICJ 176, 196 (Aug. 27), where the ICJ had regarded the preamble of certain treaties as showing their object and purpose.

The principle that preambles can be used for the contextual and purposive interpretation of treaties is not only a principle of general international law but is also part of the hermeneutics of Community law. The European Court of Justice has referred to the Preamble of the EEC Treaty for the interpretation of that Treaty several times. E.g., *Van Gend en Loos*, *supra* note 8, at 12; Case 32/65, *Italy v. Council and Commission* [1966] ECR 389, 408. See also Stefan Schepers, *The Legal Force of the Preamble to the EEC Treaty*, 6 Eur. L. Rev. 356 (1981) (arguing that parts of the preamble to the EEC Treaty enjoy the same legal force as specific articles of the Treaty); Manfred Zuleeg, *Präambel, in* Kommentar zum EWG-Vertrag, *supra* note 7, para. 3 (arguing that the commitment to democracy and the fundamental rights and freedoms laid down in the Preamble to the Single European Act form part of the Community law as unwritten principles).

[99] The Heads of Government and State,

. . . Considering that world peace can be safeguarded only by creative efforts commensurate with the dangers that threaten it,

Convinced that the contribution which an organised and vital Europe can make to civilisation is indispensable to the maintenance of peaceful relations,

Recognising that Europe can be built only through practical achievements which will first of all create real solidarity, and through the establishment of common bases for economic development,

Anxious to help, by expanding their basic production, to raise the standard of living and further the works of peace,

Resolved to substitute for age-old rivalries the merging of their essential interests; to create, by establishing an economic community, the basis for a broader and deeper community among peoples long divided by bloody conflicts, and to lay the foundations for institutions which will give direction to a destiny henceforward shared,

Have decided to create a European Coal and Steel Community . . .

Preamble to the ECSC Treaty.

[100] Preamble to the EEC Treaty.

Even in article 2 EEC Treaty, which Schilling privileges in his view as to where one should look to determine the object and purpose of the EC Treaties, he glosses over the explicit task of creating closer relations among the States of the Community which takes place alongside the more economic tasks.[101] Maastricht rejects any claim that the Treaties are aiming, "basically" or otherwise, purely at economic goals. As one example undermining the claim of a "basic" economic community, it is sufficient to note that the Maastricht Treaty introduces a European citizenship.[102] The alleged "basic" economic nature of the EC Treaties is a tired old horse that should be let out to graze.

Nonetheless, let us assume, *quod non*, that the objects and purposes of the European Treaties were basically economic. Independently of that assumption, we can agree that the EC Treaty should not be interpreted in such a way as to give the Community organs unrestricted powers, in particular *Kompetenz-Kompetenz*. This would be true regardless of whether the purposes of the Treaties were broad or narrow. For let us be clear: n this context, *Kompetenz-Kompetenz* takes its meaning from its traditional usage in German Constitutional law. This is the power of the Community to determine (or enlarge) its own competences.[103] We agree that the competences of the Community, however broadly or narrowly defined, should remain attributed—i.e., limited by the explicit or implicit grants in the Treaty, as interpreted by the rules of international law.[104]

[101] Also, most people would consider the more explicit economic objectives part of a political-economic vocabulary. For example, EEC Treaty art. 2 reads as follows:

The Community shall have as its task, by establishing a common market and an economic and monetary union and by implementing the common policies or activities referred to in Articles 3 and 3a, to promote throughout the Community a harmonious and balanced development of economic activities, sustainable and non-inflationary growth respecting the environment, a high degree of convergence of economic performance, a high level of employment and of social protection, the raising of the standard of living and quality of life, and economic and social cohesion and solidarity among Member States.

EEC Treaty art. 2.

[102] 1. Citizenship of the Union is hereby established.

Every person holding the nationality of a Member State shall be a citizen of the Union.

2. Citizens of the Union shall enjoy the rights conferred by this Treaty and shall be subject to the duties imposed thereby.

TEU, art. 8.

[103] This is the meaning the German Constitutional Court gave to "*Kompetenz-Kompetenz*" in the *Maastricht* Decision in relation to TEU art. F(3). 89 BVerfGE 155, 194–9, *english translation in* 33 I.L.M. 395, 428–32 (1994). (we believe that the English translation of this part of the decision is misleading because the Court's notion of *Kompetenz-Kompetenz* has been transformed into "exclusive competence for jurisdictional conflicts" and this is exactly what it does not mean, as used by the Bundesverfassungsgericht). On the history of "Kompetenz-Kompetenz" *see* Peter Lerche, "*Kompetenz-Kompetenz*" *und das Maastricht-Urteil des Bundesverfassungsgerichts, in* Verfassungsrecht im Wandel 409 (Jörn Ipsen *et al.* eds. 1995).

[104] International law accepts that powers of an organization can be implied. In its Advisory Opinion of 11 April 1949, *Reparations for Injuries Suffered in the Service of the United Nations*, the ICJ held that "[u]nder international law, the Organization must be deemed to have those powers which, though not expressly provided in the Charter, are conferred upon it by necessary implication as being essential to the performance of its duties." 1949 ICJ 182. For writing on the implied powers doctrine in relation to international organizations, *see* references *in* Schermers & Blokker, *supra* note 25, at § 232–§ 236.

The crunch comes at this point in the Schilling text. Even if all the above is true, why does this imply that the ECJ, charged with adjudicating disputes arising from the Treaties and seeing that in the interpretation and application of the Treaty ". . . the law is observed",[105] cannot also decide disputes over the jurisdictional reach of the Community between the various actors? And why can it not be the ultimate umpire of such disputes? Why does it follow that if one of the purposes of the Treaties was to create an international organization with limited powers, the Community, and with no *legislative Kompetenz-Kompetenz* (i.e. without the power to extend its own jurisdiction), the Treaties cannot establish a court, the ECJ, with *judicial Kompetenz-Kompetenz* (i.e. the power to be the ultimate arbiter of disputes concerning the extent of those limited competences), giving one decisive answer, valid for everyone, which would ensure that the same measure of Community law is not considered legal in one jurisdiction and illegal in another?

The assumption that a Community without legislative *Kompetenz-Kompetenz* cannot contain a court with judicial *Kompetenz-Kompetenz* is at the core of Schilling's argument. It is not self-evident. In fact, we think it is false. Because Schilling assumes it without proof, Schilling's reasoning is, in our view, a classical *non-sequitur*, presuming that which he needs to prove and resting on assertion rather than reason.

Imagine a far-narrower treaty than the European Treaties, for instance, a treaty setting up among several States a transnational regime with law-making institutions empowered to regulate all matters affecting, say, migratory birds. Inevitably, by the very nature of language and law, there will be a "twilight zone" where the precise jurisdictional limit of which matters affect migratory birds will be disputed. Imagine further that the High Contracting Parties of this hypothetical organization set up a Court with judicial review provisions identical to those of the ECJ. Schilling himself admits that the ordinary meaning of the EC Treaty provisions clearly points to that Court being the ultimate umpire on the jurisdictional limit of the organization. Why does the fact that the purpose of this hypothetical organization is rather narrowly defined necessarily lead one to the conclusion that the ordinary meaning is to be overturned? Given that any jurisdictional limit is going to have a grey zone, why not, in the interest of avoiding otherwise insoluble disputes, empower a centralized Court to be the ultimate umpire? This question is even more legitimate in the light of the fact that the law-making institutions envisioned by the Treaty legislate by majority voting, and that the Treaty has notoriously open-textured provisions such as article 100 and its progeny, and article 235.

Once again, the spectre of Alice hovers. If at all, it is just the other way around: the narrower the purposes and jurisdiction, the more willing the parties will be to entrust adjudication to judicial organs because the stakes, even if the Court were to err, would not be so high. By contrast, if the organization

---

[105] EC Treaty art. 164.

was given broader powers, states may hesitate to entrust to a transnational court such power. Proof of this may be found in the EU Treaties. The Maastricht Treaty expanded the reach of the Union in a few notable areas.[106] The Member States were quick to seek to disenfranchise the ECJ when engaging in foreign policy, security, and their immigration policies.[107] Likewise, in drafting the UN Charter with its extremely broad objectives and jurisdiction, the Member States were careful not to enfranchise the International Court of Justice.[108]

Schilling raises one last argument to "buttress" the presumptive will of the Member States in entering into the European Treaties. He cites Advocate General Warner in the *ICRA* case:

---

[106] *See*, e.g., TEU arts. J-J. 11 (providing for a common foreign and security policy); TEU arts. K-K.9 (providing for co-operation "in the fields of justice and home affairs").

[107] According to TEU art. L, the common policy in foreign affairs and security matters is not subject to the jurisdiction of the ECJ. Although Neuwahl argues that the Court's jurisdiction is not as restricted as it may seem at first sight, it is fair to say that judicial review of Community acts in the field of the CFSP is limited. Nanette Neuwahl, *Foreign and Security Policy and the Implementation of the Requirement of "Consistency" under the Treaty on European Union*, in *Legal Issues of the Maastricht Treaty* 227 (David O'Keeffe & Patrick M. Twomey eds. 1994) (arguing that the Court's jurisdiction also covers, *inter alia*, questions as to the compatibility with Community law of the CFSP acts of the Council). Also, Article L TEU excludes jurisdiction of the Court of Justice over justice and home affairs (with the exception of conventions concluded under Article K.3(2)(c) TEU), leaving the Third Pillar structure essentially without judicial review. For reform proposals, see, e.g., David O'Keeffe, *Recasting the Third Pillar*, 32 CMLRev. 893, 909–11 (1995). See also J.H.H. Weiler, *Neither Unity Nor Three Pillars—The Trinity Structure of the Treaty on European Union*, in *The Maastricht Treaty on European Union: Legal Complexity and Political Dynamic* 49 (Jörg Monar *et al.* eds., 1993).

[108] During the UN Conference on International Organization in 1945, Belgium repeatedly suggested that the World Court should play a significant role in the peaceful settlement of disputes and proposed that the World Court be given the power of judicial review. The Conference rejected these proposals and, instead, adopted the report of the Legal Committee IV/2. With this report, it renounced the idea of setting up a specific mechanism for interpreting the Charter provisions, and recognized that each organ would inevitably interpret from day to day those provisions of the Charter which concerned its activities. It also invited the Organization and States to consider themselves legally bound by any "generally accepted" interpretation, pragmatically leaving the question of an authoritative interpretation of the Charter open for the time being. In addition, a "committee of experts" was entitled to make suggestions for the creation of a special organ for giving official interpretations of the Charter. Geoffrey R. Watson, *Constitutionalism, Judicial Review and the World Court*, 34 Harv. Int'l Law J. 1, 1-14 (1993).

The Lockerbie Decision, *Case Concerning Questions of Interpretation and Application of the 1971 Montreal Convention Arising From the Aerial Incident at Lockerbie*, 1992 ICJ 114, has stirred up the debate over whether or not the ICJ has the power of judicial review within the UN legal system. *See*, e.g., Michael Reisman, *The Constitutional Crisis in the United Nations*, 87 Am. J. Int'l L. 83 (1993); Thomas Franck, *The 'Powers of Appreciation': Who Is the Ultimate Guardian of UN Legality?*, 86 Am. J. Int'l L. 519 (1992); Christian Tomuschat, *The Lockerbie Case before the International Court of Justice*, 48 Int'l Commission of Jurists Rev. 38 (1992); José Alvarez, *Theoretical Perspectives on Judicial Review by the World Court*, in Proceedings of the 89th Annual Meeting 85 (Am. Soc'y Int'l L. ed., 1995); Vera Gowlland-Debbas, *The Relationship Between the International Court of Justice and the Security Council in Light of the Lockerbie Case*, 88 Am. J. Int'l L. 643 (1994). Even though the focal point of the discussion was the relationship between the Court and the Council, no one suggested that the member states had the power to make the final decision on the legality of a Council measure.

No Member State can . . . be held to have included, in [the partial] transfer [of sovereignty to the Community] power for the Community to legislate in infringement of rights protected by its own constitution.[109]

Warner was writing in the context of European Community protection of fundamental human rights. He also makes clear the consequences of his statement:

. . . a fundamental right recognized and protected by the Constitution of any Member State must be recognized and protected also in Community law.[110]

If not, it would indeed mean that a Member State would have transferred to the Community the power to violate its constitution.

A seductive proposition but, alas, not good law. With all respect to former A.G. Warner, his construct has been flatly rejected by the ECJ, and for good reasons. In *Hauer*, decided after *ICRA*, the ECJ forcefully states:

[T]he question of a possible infringement of fundamental rights by a measure of the Community institutions can only be judged *in the light of Community law itself*. The introduction of special criteria for assessment stemming from the legislation *or constitutional law of a particular Member State* would, by damaging the substantive unity and efficacy of Community law, lead inevitably to the destruction of the unity of the Common Market and the jeopardizing of the cohesion of the Community.[111]

Schilling may argue that he finds the Advocate General more persuasive than the Court. Advocate Generals often are! But not here. *Grogan*,[112] the celebrated abortion rights case, provides a classic illustration of why the approach of Warner was rejected and why it cannot, both as a matter of policy and logic, be accepted in most instances. What if the constitution in one Member State guaranteed the near absolute right of the fetus to life, yet in another Member State, the "opposing" right of a woman to autonomy over her body was constitutionally guaranteed, including the right to abort a foetus in certain circumstances? Which of the two rights would Warner have the ECJ choose to recognize as a Community right? In the case of abortion, how can the ECJ recognize the near absolute right of the unborn in the Irish

---

[109] Case 7/76, *Industria Romana Carni e Affini, S.p.A.* v. *Amministrazione delle Finanze dello Strato* [1976] ECR 1213, 1230 (Opinion of Advocate-General Warner of June 22, 1976 on the preliminary ruling requested by the Ufficio di Conciliazione). Schilling refers to a critique of that statement in Michael Akehurst, *The Application of General Principles of Law by the Court of Justice of the European Communities*, 52 Brit. Y.B. Int'l L. 29, 44 (1981). Schilling cites A.G. Warner. Schilling, *supra* note 1, at 407.

[110] *Industria Romana Carni e Affini*, *supra* note 108, at 1237 (opinion of Advocate-General Warner).

[111] Case 44/79, *Hauer* v. *Land Rheinland-Pfalz* [1979] ECR 3727, 3744 (emphasis added).

[112] Case C-159/90, *Society for the Protection of Unborn Children Ireland Ltd.* v. *Stephen Grogan et al*, [1991] FCR I-4685, reported in Dena T. Sacco & Alexia Brown, Recent Developments, *Regulation of Aborion in the European Community: Society for the Protection of Unborn Children Ireland Ltd. v. Grogan, Judgment of the European Court of Justice of 4 October 1991 in Case C-159/90 (1991)*, 33 Harv. Int'l L. J. 291 (1992).

constitution[113] and at the same time uphold a woman's right to self-determination?[114] Even for a Court guilty of constitutionalism run amok, this would be one twist too far.[115]

Two further things ought to be mentioned in this context. First, it seems that Schilling is moving beyond the limited proposition that the final say on issues of competences and *ultra vires* rests with the highest jurisdictions of the Member States, and is expanding the proposition to any rule or principle of national constitutional law. That conclusion would logically follow from his reasoning. If the proposition is that the Member States could not delegate to the Community matters reserved to them by their respective constitutions, surely this could not be limited to issues of jurisdiction but would extend to all material conflicts with a national constitution. The practical nightmare would be considerable.

But most surprising, and most telling, is that Schilling endorses the view of Warner from an international law point of view. The general rule of international law does not allow, except in the narrowest of circumstances which do not prevail here,[116] for a State to use its own domestic law, including its own domestic constitutional law, as an excuse for non-performance of a treaty. That is part of the "abc. . ." of international law and is reflected in the same Vienna Convention on which Schilling relies.[117] The authoritative treatise, *Oppenheim's International Law* is clear:

> It is firmly established that a state when charged with a breach of its international obligations cannot in international law validly plead as a defence that it was unable to fulfill them because its internal law . . . contained rules in conflict with international law; this applies equally to a state's assertion of its inability to secure the

---

[113] Irish Constitution art. 40, §3(3). See also Caroline Forder, *Abortion: A Constitutional Problem in European Perspective*, 1 Maastricht J. Eur. & Comp. L. 56 (1994) (discussing the restrictive interpretation of this article by the Irish Supreme Court and the other constitutional problems of Ireland).

[114] J.H.H. Weiler & Nicolas J.S. Lockhart, *"Taking Rights Seriously" Seriously: The European Court and its Fundamental Rights Jurisprudence*, 32 CMLRev. 51, pt. 2, 579, 598 (1995).

[115] For a full discussion, see J.H.H. Weiler, *Fundamental Rights and Fundamental Boundaries: On Standards and Values in the Protection of Human Rights*, in *The European Union and Human Rights* 51 (Nanette Neuwahl & Allan Rosas eds., 1995); Weiler & Lockhart, *supra* note 113.

[116] One cannot rely on Vienna Convention art. 46, *supra* note 26, 1155 U.N.T.S. at 343, for this proposition. First, a minor violation of the Constitutional law of each Member State concerning the jurisdictional reach of the Community could hardly be said to be manifest and objectively evident. The fracas following the *Maastricht* Decision of the German Constitutional Court within the public law community in Germany itself would testify to that. See also the analysis of Mendelson as to the non-applicability of the decision in the Community context, M.H. Mendelson, *The European Court of Justice and Human Rights*, 1 Y.B. Eur. L. 125, 155 (1981). But more importantly, Article 46 can be invoked when a State claims that its very consent to be bound was given in violation of its constitution. Schilling is arguing for a far more comfortable position: he affirms the consent to be bound, but allows the State to pick and choose what it consented to in relation to specfic EC provisions.

[117] Vienna Convention, art. 27, *supra* note 26, 1155 U.N.T.S. at 343. See also, e.g., Louis Henkin *et al.*, *International Law: Cases and Materials* 149-53 (3d ed. 1993).

necessary changes in its law by virtue of some legal or constitutional requirement . . . [118]

In the PCIJ *Decision on Treatment of Polish Nationals in Danzig*,[119] the World
Court held explicitly that a State cannot adduce its own constitution in order
to evade obligations incumbent upon it under international law.

International law, thus, turns out to be a broken reed for the propositions
advanced by Schilling. Indeed, after all his advocacy of an international law
approach, at the end of the day, it is national constitutional authority which
seems to animate him.

IV. REDEFINING THE DECISIVE QUESTION

This analysis is telling because, we think, it leads us to identify what we
believe is the real concern of Schilling and the German Federal Constitutional
Court to whose support he runs. The real concern is not with the integrity of
the Treaty under international law, nor even with the Rule of Law. On the
one hand, there seems to be an unhappiness with the erosion of State sovereignty in a classical sense in a materially and legally inter-dependent world.[120]
It is really State rights which concern Schilling, albeit cloaked in a would-be
mantle of international law.

But there probably is yet another concern for which we have greater sympathy. Imagine the unlikely scenario that Schilling were persuaded by our

[118] *Oppenheim's International Law, supra* note 17, at 84–5.

[119] *Treatment of Polish Nationals and Other Persons of Polish Origin or Speech in the Danzig
Territories*, 1932 PCIJ (ser. A/B) No. 44, at 24 (Feb. 4) (advisory opinion).

[120] Schilling also asserted classical State sovereignty in his 1990 article in the German public
law journal "Der Staat." Theodor Schilling, *Artikel 24 Absatz 1 des Grundgesetzes, Artikel 177 des
EWG-Vertrags und die Einheit der Rechtsordnung*, 29 Der Staat 161 (1990). In that article, he
used, as he does here, an interpretation reconciling two allegedly incompatible legal provisions
(German constitutional legal doctrine calls this concept *"praktische Konkordanz"*) in relation to
Article 177 EEC Treaty and the former Article 24 of the Geman Basic Law. The outcome was
exactly the same: the interpretation of EEC Treaty art. 177 along the lines of GG art. 24(1)
demanded that ECJ decisions had only persuasive power, *i.e.*, that of an advisory opinion, if (a)
the legal question touched upon the issue of competences, and (b) the ECJ's interlocutor was the
German Federal Constitutional Court. Schilling, in the article that we are responding to, "inter-
nationalizes" this conclusion by undertaking a similar interpretation of EEC Treaty art. 171 in
relation to EEC Treaty art. 2. Even more revealing is Schilling's recent article on the "Sovereignty
of the Members of the United Nations". Theodor Schilling, *Die 'neue Weltordnung' und die
Souveränität der Mitglieder der Vereinten Nationen*, 33 Archiv des Völkerrechts 67 (1995). There,
Schilling turns against another international institution that, in the name of international integration, fetters national sovereignty, namely the Security Council using its right to make decisions
that are legally binding upon the Member States of the UN. *Id.*, at 92–103. He argues that the
Member States are bound only by *legal* decisions of the Security Council. *Id.* Since the ICJ can
only review Council acts *incidenter*, he asserts that the State in question has the power to judge
for itself whether or not a measure of the Council is legal. Yet that state is, according to Schilling,
not necessarily the judge of its own cause because its decision can be reviewed by a "decentral
decision of the state community" (*"dezentrale Entscheidung der Staatengemeinschaft"*). *Id.*, at
101–103. Schilling dismantles the UN mechanism of dealing with breaches of peace and brushes
away "certain doubts" in the name of state sovereignty. *Id.*, at 101.

arguments. Would he really be happy to see the European Court remain in its pivotal position as ultimate umpire on questions of competences? We doubt it. His other concern, we think, is not with the *idea* of a centralized court that States may create to police their transnational legal undertakings (which from an international law perspective is legitimate and unexceptional), but with the *performance of this particular Court*, especially on the issue of competences.

The decisive question that truly underlies Schilling's engagement with international law is quite different from the one he poses. The question is not, do the European Treaties make the European Court the final umpire over Community competences?, but rather, can we trust and have confidence in the ECJ to perform the task of ultimate umpire of the jurisdictional limits? The issue, then, is not one of formal definition of task, but of trust in the performance.

The history of the Community jurisdictional powers explains Schilling's concerns. He is not alone in developing that sensitivity. During the debate accompanying the Maastricht Treaty, there erupted the dormant question of Community "competences and powers".[121] This question and the accompanying debate found their code in, for example, the deliciously vague concept of "subsidiarity". This question has been inevitably connected to the continued preoccupation with governance structures and processes, with the balance between Community and Member States, and with the questions of democracy and legitimacy of the Community to which the Maastricht debate gave a new and welcome charge.

What accounts for this eruption?[122]

First, a bit of history. The student of comparative federalism discovers a constant feature in practically all federal experiences: a tendency towards concentrations of legislative and executive powers in the center or general power at the expense of constituent units.[123] This concentration apparently occurs independently of the mechanism allocating jurisdiction / competences / powers between center and "periphery". Differences, where they occur, depend more on the ethos and political culture of polities than on legal and constitutional devices.[124] The Community has both shared and differed from this general experience.[125]

It has *shared* it in that the Community, especially in the 1970s, had seen a weakening of any workable and enforceable mechanism for allocation of jurisdiction/competences/powers between Community and its Member States.

---

[121] See generally Weiler, *supra* note 7, at 2431–53.

[122] In this part of the article, we are relying on Weiler, Haltern & Mayer, *supra* note 6.

[123] See generally *Europe After Maastricht: An Even Closer Union?* (Renaud Dehousse ed. 1994).

[124] *See* J.H.H. Weiler, *Limits To Growth? On the Law and Politics of the European Union's Jurisdictional Limits, in* State and Nation—Current Legal and Political Problems Before the 1996 Intergovernmental Conference, IUSEF No. 15, 1-32 (1995).

[125] We are relying here on Jacqué & Weiler, *supra* note 11.

How has this occurred? It has occurred by a combination of two factors.

(a) Profligate legislative practices especially in, for example, the usage of article 235.

(b) A bifurcated jurisprudence of the Court which on the one hand exten-sively interpreted the reach of the jurisdiction/competences/powers granted the Community and on the other hand had taken a self-limiting approach towards the expansion of Community jurisdiction/compe-tence/powers when exercised by the political organs.[126]

To make the above statement is not tantamount to criticizing the Community, its political organs and the ECJ. The question is one of values. It is possible to argue that this process was beneficial overall to the evolution and well-being of the Community as well as beneficial to the Member States, its citizens and residents. But this process was also a ticking constitutional time bomb which one day could threaten the evolution and stability of the Community. Sooner or later, "supreme" courts in the Member States would realize that the "socio-legal contract" announced by the ECJ in its major con-stitutionalizing decisions—namely, that "the Community constitutes a new legal order . . . for the benefit of which the States have limited their sovereign rights, *albeit within limited fields*"[127]—had been shattered. Although these "supreme" courts had accepted the principles of the new legal order, supremacy and direct effect, the fields seemed no longer limited. In the absence of Community legal checks, they would realize, it would fall upon them to draw the jurisdictional lines of the Community and its Member States.

Interestingly enough, the Community experience differs from the experience of other federal polities, in that despite the massive legislative expansion of Community jurisdiction / competences / powers, there had not been any polit-ical challenge of this issue from the Member States.

How so? The answer is simple and obvious, and it resides in the decision-making process as it stood before the Single European Act (SEA). Unlike the state governments of most federal States, the governments of the Member States, jointly and severally, could control the legislative expansion of Community jurisdiction/competences/powers. Nothing that was done could be done without the assent of all States. This diffused any sense of threat and crisis on the part of governments. Indeed, if we want to seek "offenders" who have disrespected the principle of limited competence, the governments of the Member States, in the form of the Council of Ministers, conniving with the Commission and Parliament, would be the main ones. How convenient to be able to do in Brussels what would often be politically more difficult back home, and then exquisitely blame the Community! The ECJ's role has been historically not one of activism, but one of, at most, active passivism. Nonetheless, it did not build up a repository of credibility as a body which

---

[126] *See* Weiler, *supra* note 7, at 2453-63.
[127] *Van Gend en Loos, supra* note 8, at 2 (emphasis added).

effectively patrols the jurisdictional boundaries between the Community and Member States.

This era passed with the shift to majority voting after the entry into force of the SEA and the seeds—indeed, the buds— of crisis became visible.[128] It became a matter of time before one of the national courts would defy the ECJ on this issue. Member States would become aware that in a process that gives them neither *de jure* nor *de facto* veto power, the question of jurisdictional lines has become crucial. The *Maastricht* Decision of the German Federal Constitutional Court fulfilled this prediction, albeit later than anticipated.

Of course, the German decision is an egregious violation of the Treaty— ironically, especially if understood in classical international legal terms. But this view is grounded in the classical, hierarchical, centrist view of the European legal order. How should one evaluate this development given the questions concerning the normative authority of European constitutionalism and a more horizontal, conversation-based view of that very same constitutionalism?

Somewhat inappropriately, given the conversation metaphor, we want to use some of the dynamics of the Cold War as a device for evaluating the judicial *Kompetenz-Kompetenz* aspect of the *Maastricht* Decision of the German Federal Constitutional Court.

According to this analogy, the German decision is not an official declaration of war, but the commencement of a cold war with its paradoxical guarantee of co-existence following the infamous MAD (Mutual Assured Destruction) logic. For the German Court actually to declare a Community norm unconstitutional, rather than simply threaten to do so, would be an extremely hazardous move so as to make its usage unlikely. The use of tactical nuclear weapons was always considered to carry the risk of creating a nuclear domino effect. If other Member State courts followed the German lead, or if other Member State legislatures or governments were to suspend implementation of the norm on some reciprocity rationale, a real constitutional crisis would arise in the Community—the legal equivalent of the Empty Chair political stand-off in the 1960s.[129] It would be hard for the German government to remedy the situation, especially if the German Court decision enjoyed general public popularity. Would the German Federal Constitutional Court be willing to face the responsibility of dealing such a blow to European integration, rather than just threatening to do so?

Maybe not, but the logic of the Cold War is that each side has to assume the worst and to arm as if the other side would actually deal the first blow. The ECJ would then have to watch over its shoulder the whole time, trying to anticipate any potential move by the German Federal Constitutional Court.

If we now abandon the belligerent metaphor, it could be argued that this situation is not *per se* unhealthy. The German move is an insistence on a more

---

[128] *See* Weiler, *supra* note 7, at 2453–63.
[129] Weiler, Haltern & Mayer, *supra* note 6.

polycentered view of constitutional adjudication and will eventually force a more even conversation between the European Court and its national constitutional counterparts. We would suggest that, in some ways, the German move of the 1990s in relation to competences resembles their prior move in relation to human rights.[130] It was only that move which forced the European Court to take human rights seriously.[131]

The current move could also force the Court to take competences seriously. This view is not without its functional problems.

(a) here is no "non proliferation treaty" in the Community structure. MAD works well, perhaps, in a situation of two superpowers. But there must be a real fear that other Member State Courts will follow the German lead in rejecting the exclusive *Kompetenz-Kompetenz* of the ECJ. The more courts adopt the weapon, the greater the chances that it will be used. Once that happens, it will become difficult to push the paste back into the tube.

(b) courts are not the principal Community players. But this square-off will have negative effects on the decision making process of the Community. The German Government and Governments whose courts will follow the German lead, will surely be tempted to play that card in negotiation. ("We really cannot compromise on this point, since our Court will strike it down . . .")

Here, too, we find an interesting paradox. The consistent position of the ECJ, as part of its constitutional architecture, has been that it alone has judicial *Kompetenz-Kompetenz* because the jurisdictional limits of the Community are a matter of interpretation of the Treaty. The German Federal Constitutional Court, as part of its reassertion of national sovereignty and insistence of legitimization of the European construct through States' instrumentalities and the logic of public international law, has defied the ECJ. As we argued throughout this article, the internationalist logic claimed by the German Court negates its own conclusions. Surely, the reach of an international treaty is a matter of international law and depends on the proper interpretation of that treaty. Therefore, from the internationalist perspective, the ECJ must be the final umpire of that system.

If, however, the European polity constitutes a constitutional order as claimed by the European Court of Justice, then this issue is far more nuanced. There has been no constitutional convention in Europe. European constitutionalism must depend on a common-law type rationale, one which draws on and integrates the national constitutional orders. The constitutional discourse in Europe must be conceived as a conversation of many actors in a constitutional interpretative community, rather than a hierarchical structure with the ECJ at the top. It is this constitutional perspective that, paradoxically, gives credibility to the claim of the German Court. A feature of neo-constitutionalism in this case would be

---

[130] *See* German Federal Constitutional Court, judgment of May 29, 1974, 37 BVerfGE 271 (*"Solange I"*); judgment of October 22, 1986, 73 BVerfGE 339 (*"Solange II"*).

[131] *Cf., in extenso*, Weiler & Lockhart, *supra* note 113.

that the jurisdictional line (or lines) should be a matter of constitutional conversation, not a constitutional *Diktat*.

And yet, the solution offered by the German Federal Constitutional Court and endorsed by Schilling is no conversation either. Although the German Court mentions that these decisions have to be taken in co-operation with the ECJ, it reserves the last word to itself. A European *Diktat* is simply replaced by a national one. And the national *Diktat* is far more destructive to the Community, if one contemplates the possibility of fifteen different interpretations.

How, then, can one square this circle?

One possible solution is institutional and we would like to outline only its essential structure. We have proposed the creation of a Constitutional Council for the Community, modeled in some ways after its French namesake. The Constitutional Council would have jurisdiction only over issues of competences (including subsidiarity) and would decide cases submitted to it after a law was adopted but before coming into force. It could be seized by any Community institution, by any Member State or by the European Parliament acting on a majority of its Members. Its president would be the President of the ECJ, and its members would be sitting members of the constitutional courts or their equivalents in the Member States. Within the Constitutional Council, no single Member State would have a veto power. The composition would also underscore that the question of competences is fundamentally also one of national constitutional norms, but still subject to a Union solution by a Union institution.

We will not elaborate in this article some of the technical aspects of the proposal.[132] The principal merit of this proposal is that it addresses the concern over fundamental jurisdictional boundaries without compromising the constitutional integrity of the Community, as did the *Maastricht* Decision of the German Federal Constitutional Court. Since, from a material point of view, the question of boundaries has a built-in indeterminacy, the critical issue is not what the boundaries are, but who gets to decide. On the one hand, the composition of the proposed Constitutional Council removes the issue from the purely political arena; on the other hand, it creates a body which would, we expect, enjoy a far greater measure of public confidence than the ECJ itself.

---

[132] For a more elaborate description of this proposal, see Weiler, Haltern & Mayer, *supra* note 6.

Epilogue

The European Courts of Justice:
Beyond 'Beyond Doctrine' or the Legitimacy
Crisis of European Constitutionalism[1]

J.H.H. WEILER

PROLOGUE—FROM SOCIAL SCIENCE TO NORMATIVE THEORY

The methodological approaches adopted in this volume in going 'beyond doctrine' mostly belong to the realm of the social sciences, principally political science. In going beyond doctrine the question requiring explanation was an emergent constitutionalism, constituted by, and reflected in, the relationship between the European Court and its national brethren. Political science attempts to explain the reasons for, and the implications of, that relationship. Why, for example, did national courts accept (when they did) direct effect and supremacy? Doctrine, if it bothers to explain that at all, will explain that this was because "the law" so required. Social science will look to factors such as empowerment, legal culture and many other factors, some of which we listed in the Preface to this volume and many of which feature in several of the national studies and the crosscutting essays which theorize about the relationship. When national courts are tardy in accepting some of the ECJ's constitutional doctrines, or accept then partially, or change their minds or end up rejecting what they had hitherto accepted—and this volume gives examples of all of the above—doctrine (if it does not simply stick its head in the sand or splutter about illegality) really has very little to offer by way of explanation and social science is all we have.

But there is one dimension of the constitutional conversation which goes even beyond "beyond doctrine" since it goes beyond social science too.

Direct effect and supremacy are at the core of the constitutional construct: If, as Alec Stone explains in this volume, constitutionalism is the process by which the EC Treaties evolved from a set of legal arrangements binding upon sovereign states, into a vertically integrated legal regime conferring judicially enforceable rights and obligations on all legal persons and entities, public and private, within the sphere of application of EC law—enforceable even against the Member States and national law, a different question may be asked: by

---

[1] For the last three years I have been grappling with what I think of as the legitimacy crisis of European Constitutionalism understood from the perspective of normative political theory. This essay tries to pull together a variety of strands into one synthetic concluding reflection. My principal intellectual debts and references to the work of all authors alluded to in the text will be acknowledged in the bibliographical note attached to this concluding essay.

what authority, then, if any—*understood in the vocabulary of normative polit-ical theory*—can the claim of European law to be both constitutionally supe-rior and with immediate effect in the polity be sustained? Who is the constituent power? Why should the subjects of European law in the Union, individuals, courts, governments etc. feel bound to observe the law of the Union as higher law, in the same way that their counterparts in, say, the USA are bound, to and by, American federal law? It is a dramatic question since constitutionalization is, effectively, with us, and to give a negative answer—as has been recently been given by actors and "observers"—would be tanta-lizingly subversive. The failure to address this question is partly why the critique of European Union constitutional democracy is often conflicted. One can, it seems, proclaim a profound democracy deficit and yet insist at the same time on the importance of accepting the supremacy of Union law. It is a dra-matic question too, since it goes to membership, to citizenship and national-ity and, thus, seems to bring European constitutionalism into direct conflict with the constitutionalism of its Member States. To whom is primary alle-giance owed? By whom is it owed? In this last respect this essay dovetails neatly with Bruno de Witte's provocative reflections in this volume.

This is no longer a theoretical issue. After all, as has been evident for some time now, and as is reflected in several of the national studies in this volume the constitutional honeymoon has ended; national Sleeping Beauty has woken up and discovered that she did not like the European Union Prince at all.

THE CHANGING CLIMATE OF EUROPEAN CONSTITUTIONALISM

The following is a non-exhaustive list of some of the signs of the new, more hostile, constitutional landscape.

(i) There are challenges from the collectivity of States. Consider first the Maastricht Treaty itself under the shadow of which we are still operating. In a praise-worthy and deservedly famous article reflecting on the consti-tutional dimensions of Maastricht—*The Constitutional Structure of the Union: A Europe of Bits and Pieces*—Deidre Curtin criticized the fragmen-tation and constitutional incoherence of the Union structure and had, too, harsh words for a certain assault on the Court in the Maastricht process. Amsterdam is generally more anaemic, but whilst expanding somewhat the role of the European Parliament in the decisional process, one cannot but notice a growing reticence towards the constitutional architecture on issues such as majority voting, Commission role and foreign policy.

(ii) There are challenges from individual Member States. In the Maastricht process it was the UK and Denmark. In the current IGC there was the Franco-German (!) initiative which introduced such variable geometry as to make the Community Pillar itself one of bits and pieces. The final ver-sion, under strenuous pressure from small Member States emasculated much of the original initiative. But its very proposal is of some significance. In the same breath one could mention the breathtaking proposal which surfaced during the IGC to amend Article 189a which requires unanimity to modify a Commission proposal. A better targeted attack on the constitutional powers of the Commission is more difficult to imagine. This proposal was blocked—a deal breaker for the Commission—but it is a sign of the attack on the *acquis.*

(iii) There are challenges from constitutional actors within Member States. Most interesting to the theme of Constitutionalism are the challenges coming from the national judiciary and in particular the highest courts. The German Constitutional Court and its Belgian counterpart have been most explicit on the issue of jurisdiction. The Italian Court, in declaring that it was under no duty to make references to the European Court ex Article 177 since it was not a "jurisdiction" in the sense of the Treaty has been more subtle and more insidious at the same time. There are signs from others as well, challenging precisely the hegemony of the European Court of Justice. There has been an understandable reaction trying to minimize and paper over the cracks. But it is there for anyone who wishes to look.

(iv) There are challenges from, yes, new constituencies within the Court of Justice. (We should not commit the error of imagining the Court as an homogeneous actor free of internal factions, disagreements and internal conflicted views on many issues, including the contours of Constitutionalism. The oft deep divisions on fundamental issues between Advocates General—full Members of the Court—and the Court itself surely mirror similar divisions within the College of Judges.) Consider the post-Maastricht jurisprudence of that Court itself—for example its famous (or, to some, infamous) *Keck* Decision which shifted the balance back to the Member States in the critical area of the internal market. Assailed by many champions of the Single Market as a heresy, Norbert Reich used that Decision among those justifying his analysis of a veritable Economic Constitutional *Revolution.* But there were others such as the controversial decisions which cut the role and power of the Community in the WTO or the one which denied the Union the competence to adhere to the European Convention on Human Rights.

(v) Most important, in my view, are the challenges from general public opinion in several Member States. Maastricht, refreshingly, gave the lie to years of a Eurobarometer ostrich syndrome. It is clear that Euroscepticism is not just another English vice. At a minimum, "Europe" is no longer part of consensus, non-partisan politics in many Member States, not least the new ones. Politicians can no longer count on automatic approval of their architectural changes to Community and Union. I have already suggested that though the discontent is in many instances non-specific, it goes often to what one would consider as the constitutional *acquis.*

It is hard to gauge the depth behind these challenges and it is even harder to explain the reasons for it. I would like to offer my own pet speculations on what may account for this change of mood.

(i) As regards Governments and States I believe that one explanation must rest with the hugely expanded role of majority voting which came into effect with the Single European Act. How and why the Governments accepted this sea-change is a story for another day. Clearly majority voting has been fundamental in the ability of the Community to move ahead with the creation of a Single Market (of sorts) and has generally transformed the climate of decision making. But it also removed one of the key political artifacts which had facilitated the acceptability of Constitutionalism. Constitutionalism with a veto and without a veto are two very different games and what we are seeing in the challenges of Member States—individual and collective—is an adjustment to that reality.

(ii) I do not wish to dwell here much on courts. The dialogue between the European Court and national courts has become more complex, nuanced and, at times, terse. In part courts are part of their national context and reflect the changing mood of public opinion—both elite and popular. In part certain strands of the European jurisprudence and certain failures of the European Court (as perceived by its interlocutors) in such areas as competences, have become more visible and less acceptable. In part the national challenges are a paradoxical sign of an acknowledgment by national courts of the constitutional nature of the European Court's posture: It is, strangely, easier to deal with the doctrinal elements of Constitutionalism (which after all constitutes the official vocabulary of the inter-court dialogues) when they can be pigeonholed as international law. A constitutional-constitutional dialogue has its inbuilt conflictual elements. Likewise, whilst reserving chapter and verse for another occasion, all of the "strange" decisions of the European Court should be seen as part of *its* response both to the general European context in which *it* finds itself and as part of its dialogue with a much more difficult national interlocutor.

(iii) The change in general public opinion is most interesting and, in my view, conditions much of the other responses.

There is, first, what one could term the paradox of success. In its foundational period, the European construct was perceived as part of a moral imperative in dealing with the heritage of World War II. Governments and States may have been happily pursuing their national interest but the European construct could be cloaked with a noble mantle of a new found idealism. Within Europe war may be possible but it is certainly unthinkable and with that huge success of its principal objective what Europe now is presented as delivering is bread and circus. Remove the moral imperative, remove the mantle of ideals, and its politics as usual with the frustrating twist that in Europe you cannot throw the scoundrels out at election time. So you try and throw the whole construct out.

Arguably, public attitudes go even deeper than that. We come here to a more sobering consideration in this regard, whereby European Union may be seen not simply as having suffered a loss of its earlier spiritual values, but as an actual source of social *Ressentiment*. Here are the highlights of what surely deserves much more than this superficial summary.

In his pre-choleric days, Ernst Nolte wrote a fascinating study on the origins of fascism in its various European modes. Consider, chillingly, the turn to fascism in Italy, France and Germany at the beginning of the century. In his profound comparative analysis of the cultural-political roots of the phenomenon the common source was identified as a reaction to some of the manifestations of modernity.

At a pragmatic level the principal manifestations of modernity were the increased bureaucratization of life, public and private; the depersonalization of the market (through mass consumerism, brand names and the like) and commodifaction of values; the "abstractism" of social life, especially through competitive structures of mobility; rapid urbanization and the centralization of power.

At an epistemological level modernity was premised on, and experienced in, an attempt to group the world into intelligible concepts which had to be understood through reason and science—abstract and universal categories. On this reading, fascism was a response to, and an exploitation of, the angst generated by these practical and cognitive challenges. Up to here this is a fairly well known story.

Eerily, at the end of the century, European Union can be seen as replicating, in reality or in the subjective perception of individuals and societies, some of these very same features: it has come to symbolize, unjustly perhaps, the epitome of bureaucratization and, likewise, the epitome of centralization. One of its most visible policies, the Common Agriculture Policy, has had historically the purpose of "rationalizing" farm holdings which, in effect, meant urbanization. The single market, with its emphasis on competitiveness and transnational movement of goods can be perceived as a latter day thrust at increased commodification of values (consider how the logic of the Community forces a topic such as abortion to be treated as a "service") and depersonalization of, this time round, the entire national market. Not only have local products come under pressure, even national products have lost their distinctiveness. The very transnationalism of the Community, which earlier on was celebrated as a reinvention of the Enlightenment idealism is just that: universal, rational, transcendent: wholly modernist.

To this sustained and, in my view, never resolved angst of modernity we have new, *fin de Siècle* added phenomena as illuminated brilliantly by Brian Fitzgerald.

To capture these phenomena we can resort to what Jose Ortega y Gasset called *creencias*—the certainties of life which needed no proof—both in the physical and social world: water falls downward, there is a difference between machines and humans, higher forms of life differentiate by gender etc. To the sustained challenge of modernity is added a profound shattering of the most fundamental *creencias*—deeper still, a shattering of the ability to believe in anything. It is worth tracing some of the manifestations of this process.

There is first, or was, for a sustained period in this century the assault of the reductive social sciences. Not only are things not what they seem to be, but their reality always has a cynical malevolence. Public life and its codes is a mask for exploitation and power; private life with its codes is a mask for domination. By an inevitable logic this assault turned on itself, whereby the illumination brought by these insights was not a vehicle for liberation but in itself for manipulation. The epistemic challenge of post modernism deepens the shattering. For, in the old, modernist perspectives, there was at least a truth to be explored, vindicated—even if that truth was one of power, exploitation and domination. One can find distasteful the post modernist self-centred, ironic, sneering posturing. But, without adjudicating the philosophical validity of its epistemic claim—there is no doubt that the notion that all observations are relative to the perception of the observer, that what we have are just competing narratives, has moved from being a philosophic position to a social reality. It is part of political discourse: multiculturalism is premised on it as are the breakdown of authority (political, scientific, social) and the ascendant culture of extreme individualism and subjectivity. Indeed, objectivity itself is considered a constraint on freedom—a strange freedom, empty of content. Finally, the shattering of so many *creencias* (of the notion of *creencia* itself) has found a powerful manifestation in the public forum: it is dominated by television which means by image, by non active discourse, by mediated information, by aloneness—a vertical one-on-one forum rather than a horizontal discourse.

To the angst of modernity is added the end of century fragmentation of information, disappearance of coherent world view, belief in belief and in the ability to know, let alone control.

There are many social responses to these phenomena. One of them has been a turn, by many, to any force which seems to offer "meaning". Almost paradoxically, but perhaps not, the continued pull of the Nation State, and the success in many societies of extreme forms of nationalism (measured not only in votes and members but in the ability of those extreme forms to shift the centre of the public debate) are, in part of course, due to the fact that the Nation and State are such powerful vehicles in responding to the existential craving for meaning and purpose which modernity and post-modernity seem to deny. The Nation and State, with their organizing myths of fate and destiny provide a captivating and reassuring answer to many.

Here too the failure of Europe is colossal. Just as I argued that Europe fuels the angst of modernity it also feeds the angst of post-modernity: giant and fragmented at the same time, built as much on image as on substance, it is incomprehensible and challenges increasingly the *creencias* of national daily life. I am not suggesting that Europe is about to see a return to fascism, nor most certainly should this analysis, if it has any merit, give joy to *fin-de-siècle* chauvinists, whose wares today are as odious as they were at the start of the century. But I am suggesting a profound change in its positioning in public life: Not, as in its founding period as a *response* to a crisis of confidence, but fifty years later as one of the causes of that crisis.

We come to understand here one of the profound paradoxes of European Integration. These very values, which find their legal and practical expression in, e.g., enhanced mobility, breakdown of local markets, and insertion of universal norms into domestic culture are also part of the deep modern and postmodern anxiety of European belongingness and part of the roots of European angst and alienation. A meaningful, legitimate and legitimating concept of Constitutionalism would have to face and mediate this paradox.

(iv) There is also a change in the academic discourse of Constitutionalism. Recall those two remarkable articles by Curtin and Reich. Their critique is as telling as the phenomena criticized. On my reading, the implicit view from which it is made is the classical European constitutional vision which privileges an image of a mono-centered, vertically integrated, polity; of a single "Single Market" as a constitutional value—part of the economic constitution of the Union—of an authoritative Court which enjoys and deserves deference both from national courts and all other political actors, of a respect for Member State diversity which, however, has to be subject to a Community discipline in the sphere of application of Community law.

Maastricht did represent a "rebellion" against that image of Constitutionalism. It is clear that the principal *raison d'être* of the Pillar structure, with the meticulous and explicit attempt to exclude the Court, was the wish of the Member States to operate outside a constitutional structure. And if one finds a certain emotional edge in the articles dealing with Decisions of the European Court in cases such as *Keck* and others like it, this is understandable. These decisions are painful since they seem like a betrayal from within the Vatican itself.

The *Weltanschauung* from which the critique is made is also totally understandable. It is entirely consistent with the repeated vocabulary of classical European Constitutionalism. Consider the legal underpinnings of Constitutionalism in, say, Article 177—with its explicit rationale of a uniform interpretation (and application) of Community law. This view has a compelling pragmatic rationale to it, as well as embodying a certain vision of equality before the law. But is it not too the *par-excellence* mono-centric view of the polity? Or of the potent idea of the Rule of Law which, in the rhetoric of the European Court, meant that any legal act is to be subject to judicial scrutiny. This is noble and in many ways persuasive. But it has, too, far reaching consequences to the primordial self-positioning of the Court. And to anyone who grew up on the original Court cases opening up the Common Market to free trade and smashing Member State protectionism affirming not only the substantive unity of the Market, but also the subjection of any fragmentation to Euro-scrutiny, the notion of exclusion from such scrutiny *à la Keck* is sacrilege.

We witnessed in recent years the emergence of a new academic discourse which attempts to rethink the very way in which classical Constitutionalism was conceptualized. For me, the most powerful and influential voice is that of MacCormick in his Trilogy *Beyond the Sovereign State; Sovereignty, Democracy and Subsidiarity* and *Liberalism, Nationalism and the Post-Sovereign State*. Here is a discourse which understands the impossibilities of the old constitutional discourse, in a polity and a society in which the key social and political concepts on which classical constitutionalism was premised have lost their meaning. I would mention in particular two of the hallmarks of this new reformed discussion: the first is a more explicitly normative and critical discussion of constitutionalism. The second is its challenges to the dualist prism of the traditional constitutional image. The dualist approach places the relationship between Community/Union and the Member States at the centre of the discourse and, likewise, places a huge premium on a Hierarchy of Norms—centrist and uniform—as a representation of, and resolution to, constitutional conflict. The new reformed discussion—in MacCormick, de Areilza, Dehousse, Slaughter, de Witte, Joerges—recognizes and at times suggests a different, "horizontal", "poly-centred" "infranational" image of the European polity and its constitutional framework.

Finally, we return to the issue with which I started this reflection: the need for a normatively convincing justification, rooted in political theory, of the claims of constitutionalism. The absence of such justification coupled with the signs of a changed constitutional climate suggest the potential for a true legitimacy crisis at a new more profound level than before.

LEGITIMACY AND ILLEGITIMACY IN THE CONSTITUTIONAL DISCOURSE OF THE EC

Legitimacy and illegitimacy are notoriously elusive concepts in political theory—suggestive rather than analytically rigorous—overreaching and under specified. One defining characteristic of legitimacy/illegitimacy discourse—in its multiple applications—is its appeal to foundations. Legitimacy and illegitimacy pertain to roots rather than foliage; to deep structure rather than surface. The following examples, turning on different situations in which appeals to "legitimacy" or "illegitimacy" are frequently made, are meant not simply to illustrate the foundational appeal of legitimacy discourse, but to create a (non-exhaustive) categorization and taxonomy which will make the elusive concept more usable.

Legitimacy/illegitimacy as a category of formal legal validity

I can, for example, be wholeheartedly and fundamentally opposed to the pro-gramme of, or the laws enacted by, a government, but not deny their legal validity and hence legitimacy. The recent Conservative Government in Great Britain was thought to be very unpopular. It was defeated in the last election but its legality and the legitimacy of its enactments were not challenged in a foundational sense. In this example, legitimacy appeals to some deeper vali-dating legal rules of recognition (rules about rules) and not to programmatic content or specific enactment.

Legitimacy/illegitimacy by reference to deontological (non-legal) discourse

Notions of legitimacy and illegitimacy can extend beyond issues of legal valid-ity. Thus, to give another example, I can acknowledge the perfect legality and formal validity of a programme or a law enacted by the government in terms of its self-referential positive rules but deny the very legitimacy of those rules. Even though legal I could still claim: "They are illegitimate." In this case I will be appealing to a deeper normative invalidating "rule". This invalidating rule may pertain to some normative political theory which sets out conditions for "legitimate" *government*—democracy, for example. It may also pertain to ethics and morality as providing a deeper order of legitimacy against which even formally valid acts of *governance* must be checked.

Legitimacy/illegitimacy by reference to foundational myths

There is one additional aspect of legitimacy/illegitimacy in relation to gover-nance which goes beyond formal validity and/or deontological discourse. Let us assume that we would posit today that democratic government and gover-nance would be necessary conditions for an objective determination of the legitimacy of a polity. There would, however, be a condition precedent to such legitimacy—namely, the existence of a *demos* for which and by whom the democratic structure and process is to take place. In defining the *demos* one has to abandon the categories of formal validity or normative rationality.

The existence of the *demos* depends mostly on the subjective feelings of its members. Even to the extent that formal categories can exist, it has been cogently argued, by Böckenförder for example, that different nationalisms define differently the condition for their membership, which in turn become the ultimate referent for subjective, social legitimacy since the very under-standing of the self, individual and collective, depends on it. The definition of *demos* is intricately connected to the definition of the *telos* of the polity, a *telos* the furtherance of which is the ultimate legitimating referent of the polity. It is to this stratum of legitimation then, rooted in the constitutive myths of the polity itself, that an appeal is made, and the explanation is given, for legitimacy of governance which transcends the normativity of the system of governance. This analysis explains not only social legitimation but also social illegitimation, i.e. the possibility of observing a polity which, on the surface is deontologically legitimate but to claim that beneath the surface there is a legitimacy problem gnawing at its roots. The Weimar Republic, for example, was legal and democratic. But it had, and was, felt to be betraying the "destiny", the "honor" etc. of the German nation and hence thought by many to be illegitimate.

Legitimacy/illegitimacy as a social and political category

This last category leads us to a final distinction in legitimacy/illegitimacy discourse. Formal validity and the deontological criteria, subject, of course, to the usual problems of epistemological uncertainty and moral relativity, are supposedly objective categories providing yardsticks for the legitimacy of a regime independently of its acceptance or otherwise by the governed. The fact, for example, that National Socialism was a hugely popular regime almost until its defeat, would be irrelevant to a determination of its legitimacy by reference to deontological criteria.

But the existence of myths going to the very foundation of the *demos* is clearly a matter which in large part goes to an empirically observable social reality. Social acceptance is a different face of Legitimacy/Illegitimacy discourse. The foundational nature of legitimacy/illegitimacy remains intact also in relation to this social-empirical dimension of the concept. When the claim is made that a regime is illegitimate in the empirical-social sense, more than mere unpopularity is implied. The extreme religious right in Israel, in its rejection of the Rabin/Peres peace plan, do not deny its formal validity of the government or its democratic nature. The policies, and the government which promotes them, are illegitimate since through their eyes they strike at some foundational understandings of the Jewish/Israeli Nation State. The Separatists in Quebec, say, are not opposed to the federal government simply or primarily because of specific policies but because its very authority over Quebec is an affront to their self-understanding as an autonomous people.

There is no necessary connection between the objective strands of legitimacy/illegitimacy and its social manifestations. National Socialism had scarce legal validity and would require considerable contortions to justify its programme and acts under conventional normative theories—though of course apologists who used their intelligence to provide the contortions were not in short supply. Its considerable popular appeal and deep legitimacy in German society did not result from the consistency or otherwise of National Socialism with normative rationality. Legitimacy was acquired by an appeal to deeper strata in the human psyche where profound existential needs for meaning and belonging were met with captivating national myths.

The relations between the categories of legitimacy/illegitimacy

In one sense there is a clear division between formal and normative-deontological concept of legitimacy/illegitimacy and its social manifestations. The pretense of the first two categories is to be able to pronounce on the legitimacy/illegitimacy of governance without reference to its social reality. In that it is like most normative judgments which are supposedly meant to be detached from their objects.

But the categories of legitimacy/illegitimacy are by no means watertight. How could it be otherwise. Surely the structure and process of government and the legality of its acts of governance will contribute to its legitimacy empirically defined. Supposedly in the liberal West there is meant to be a high degree of consonance between normative-deontological legitimacy/ illegitimacy and its empirical manifestations. Supposedly a non-democratic regime would enjoy low empirical legitimacy, or none at all—i.e. that normative legitimacy would be at least a necessary condition for social legitimacy and vice versa. Supposedly a similar measure of consonance exists between formal legitimacy and its other manifestations.

Reality is, as usual, more complex than any modeling. The European Union itself, in certain periods, will provide an example of a cleavage between low normative legitimacy and high social legitimacy.

One interesting feature of legitimacy/illegitimacy discourse, despite its vagueness and under specificity, is its relative prominence in academia as well as everyday politics. The foundational nature of the discourse and interplay between the normative and the empirical may account for this popularity. First, we note that legitimacy or illegitimacy are applied not only to outcomes (laws and programmes) but also to institutions, processes and, at times, the whole polity. For the academic to make a claim about illegitimacy, because of the foundational quality, is in the first place to be consequential. If there is a problem of legitimacy, there is a legitimacy crisis. Crisis is important. Second, to make a claim about illegitimacy is also to be deep, because definitionally it is a statement about something that goes beyond the surface, that pertains to the foundations. It enables us to search for, and talk about, legitimating myths and narratives. It is also appealing because legitimacy legitimates the introduction, in broad daylight, of normative and moral discourse into "scientific" observation and analysis. Finally, it is appealing since the inbuilt softness of the components of the concept creates a wonderfully broad area in which it is hard, perhaps impossible, to "prove" either in normative or empirical terms the legitimacy or illegitimacy of outcomes, institutions,

processes or polities. The discourse of legitimacy has the attraction of speculation.

The discourse of legitimacy/illegitimacy in the evolution of European constitutionalism

European constitutionalism provides a useful prism through which to understand the legitimacy/illegitimacy discourse of the Community since through it
intersect both the legal structure and the political process of European integration. The evolution of European constitutionalism has, in my view,
brought into play, in different ways the different faces of Legitimacy/
Illegitimacy.

The discourse of legitimacy/illegitimacy in the evolution of European constitutionalism—legal doubts and political legitimacy

The first legitimacy/illegitimacy issue was associated with what could be considered the most orthodox version of European constitutionalism which finds
expression in the well known key legal doctrines, developed in the 60s and
early 70s, which determined the relationship between the Community and
Member States and discussed amply elsewhere.

Constitutionalism thus understood is very much a creature of legal discourse. It was, however, in many ways a far-reaching discourse, surprising in
its reach and, arguably at least, pushing to the boundaries of the accepted
canons of legal construction. The legitimacy/illegitimacy issues turn thus on
the validity of the juridical constructs adopted in the legal community especially by the European Court of Justice. Rassmussen, most famously, in his
1986 book *On Law and Policy in the European Court of Justice* challenges the
legitimacy of the EC constitutionalism in terms of their legal validity as measured by hermeneutical norms. It is not the place here to rehearse this debate
but simply to note that in objective terms the challenge was far from specious.

The relationship in this discussion between normative and social legitimacy
is fascinating. Despite the legally problematic nature of the emerging constitutional structure of the Community, the most striking feature of the first
phase of European Constitutionalism was its acceptance by a series of
Member State interlocutors—an acceptance which, at first blush, may have
seemed counter intuitive since, *prima facie*, European constitutionalism places
shackles of Member State legal and political freedoms under less constitu-
tionalized transnational regimes. To explain how a radical constitutional construct, with, at best, fragile legal validity could generate such a high measure

of empirical legitimacy by national political institutions is an integral part of that legitimacy/illegitimacy debate.[2]

The discourse of legitimacy/illegitimacy in the evolution of European constitutionalism—the democratic deficiencies and social legitimacy.

The second issue of legitimacy/illegitimacy relating to European Constitutionalism may seem even more intriguing. It is hardly contested in both the political and academic worlds that the Community, especially in the period leading up to Maastricht, has suffered from serious democratic deficiencies in its mode of government—often referred to as the Community democratic deficit. Later in this essay I shall attempt to capture the essential strands of that critique. Here too, the transparent democratic deficiencies did not prevent not simply an acquiescence by national political institutions in the new constitutional architecture but also a generally supportive public opinion which reaches a certain crescendo, almost a transnational psychosis, in the celebration of the 1992 plan and the Single European Act. This cleavage between normative-deontological legitimacy and its social counterpart is probably even more poignant than the cleavage between formal legal legitimacy and political acceptance.[3]

The discourse of legitimacy/illegitimacy in the evolution of European constitutionalism—challenging the foundational myths of the Union

I think that since Maastricht, the legitimacy/illegitimacy debate has changed considerably. First, it is evident that general public opinion has taken a much more sceptical and critical approach towards the European construct. Measurement of empirical illegitimacy is difficult. Whether the serious erosion in public support for the European construct could be construed as a veritable legitimacy crisis is moot. This is certainly the spirit which imbued the 1996 IGC Reflection Group's Report, the proceedings of the IGC and, to some respect the final Amsterdam Treaty.

Why there has been this erosion has been the subject of considerable speculation to which I do not wish to add. Of greater interest to me is the emergence of a new discussion which goes to the fundamental myths of the Community or Union calling into question the very foundations of European constitutionalism. I propose to explain the contours of this new legitimacy/illegitimacy challenge. I am not indifferent to this challenge and thus I propose also to offer some ways of thinking and even responding to it.

[2] I have tried to answer this question in *Journey to an Unknown Destination: a Retrospective and Prospective of the European Court of Justice in the Arena of Political Integration*. 31 Journal of Common Market Studies 418 (1993)

[3] I attempted to explore the aspect of legitimacy/illegitimacy in *Parlement Europeen, Integration Europeenne, Democratie et Legitimite*. In Louis and Waelbroeck (eds) *Le Parlement Européen* (Etudes Européennes, 1988).

THE EVOLVING DEBATE ON EU CONSTITUTIONAL LEGITIMACY

	Normative—Deontological Issue	Empirical—Social Responses
First Debate	Formal Validity: The Legitimacy of ECJ Constitutionalising Legal Discourse	Acceptance by National Political Interlocutors
Second Debate	Deontological Concerns: The Democracy Deficit	Social Acceptance
Current Debate	Foundational Myths: Issues of European Identity and Demos	Social Skepticism

RECONSTITUTING THE EUROPEAN POLITY

So where can one search for a construct which can offer normative legitimation to constitutionailsm?

One place to look for the answer to the issue of normative authority would be international law. The High Contracting Powers—the Member States of the European Union—entered into an international Treaty based on international law which created an organization with these wide capacities and established its institutions empowered to exercise the various powers. What, then, of authority? On this view the transnational authority of the Union writ, so long as *jus cogens* was not violated (and it clearly was not), derives from international law: *pacta sunt servanda*. The internal authority of the Union writ, so long as internal constitutional norms were not violated (and apparently they were not) derives from the constitutional authority which governments enjoy to engage their respective States, including the authority to undertake international obligations with internal ramifications in national law. The nature of the European polity on this reading is an international organization belonging to the States which created it.

For a long time the international view has been out of vogue. Despite its terse elegance the international view runs against one of the great orthodoxies of the system: if we look to the rhetoric of the European Court in the celebrated *Van Gend en Loos* case—the embodiment of constitutional orthodoxy—the Community is not an "old" order of international law; it is more than

> an agreement which merely creates mutual obligations between the contracting states . . . the Community constitutes a new legal order of international law for the benefit of which the states have limited their sovereign rights. . . .

In subsequent cases the Court dropped the reference to international law altogether and in the 80s, in cases such as *Les Verts*, it referred to the Treaties as the Constitutional Charter of the Union.

The internationalist view does not simply contradict this rhetoric. Given the massive transfer of competences to the Union, the unprecedented empowerment of Community institutions (and through them, indirectly, of the executive branch of the Member States at the expense of, say, national parliaments) and the consequent creation of considerable democratic deficiencies in central aspects of European public life, the internationalists' construct provides a poor legitimation to this new architecture of power.

But if we reject the internationalist view as grounding direct effect and supremacy what comes in its place? Answering this question is exactly where, at least in the first place, political theory has to replace social science.

As already noted, in Western, liberal democracies, under one guise or another, public authority requires legitimation through one principal source: the citizens constituting the political subjects of the polity. The principal hallmark of citizenship is not simply the enjoyment of human rights characterized by their extension to all in their quality as humans rather than citizens. The deepest, most clearly engraved hallmark of citizenship in our democracies is that in citizens vests the power, by majority, to create binding norms, to shape the political, social and economic direction of the polity. More realistically, in citizens vests the power to enable and habilitate representative institutions which will exercise governance on behalf of, and for, citizens. Note too, that this huge privilege and power of citizenship has, traditionally, come with duties—not simply a duty to obey the norms (that falls on non-citizens too) but a duty of loyalty to the polity with well known classical manifestations. Citizenship is so basic that, for the most part, it is simply assumed in democratic political theory which engage mostly in the conditions and practice of its exercise.

One might think that this issue has been addressed in the Community constitutional architecture. In the same *Van Gend en Loos* we read:

> Independently of the legislation of Member States, Community law . . . not only imposes obligations on individuals but is also intended to confer upon them rights which become part of their legal heritage.

This phrase wonderfully sharpens the issue: for here are obligations imposed on individuals *independently of the legislation of Member States*. Member State legislation derives its authority and legitimacy to impose obligations on individuals because it is made by, or in the name of, its subjects— the citizens of the Member States. If Community law imposes obligations independently of the legislation of Member States, who are its subjects?

Surely this is where the legal doctrine of Direct Effect is so significant. For Direct Effect purports not simply to address the issue of the status of norms (so essential to individual *qua* litigants—and thus to their lawyers) but also the political status and identity of the subjects of those norms.

Lawyers recite dutifully that the

> Community constitutes a new legal order . . . for the benefit of which the states have
> limited their sovereign rights, albeit within limited fields, and the subjects of which
> comprise not only Member States but also their nationals.

Individuals, not only States, are thus subjects. Semantically, in English, "subjects" is often synonymous with citizenship. The Queen's subjects of old are the present citizens of the Realm. It could seem, thus, that in the very articulation of one of the principal "constitutionalizing" doctrines—direct effect—the condition for its authority was provided by elevating individuals to the status of full subjects along side Member States.

But this would be a highly problematic construction.

Direct Effect means that obligations among States created by a Treaty confer rights on individuals which courts must protect, even against their own statal public authorities. It is in this sense that calling individuals subjects of the Treaty alongside Member States may be justified. But note, individuals are "subjects" only in the (direct) *effect* of the law. In this sense alone is Europe a new legal order. Consider the following *reductio ad absurdum*: imagine three States which still allow slavery. There is trade among these States, including trade in slaves. Imagine further that the three get together and conclude a treaty which creates mutual obligations among them such as prohibiting a workday for slaves of more than twenty hours. They also create institutions which are henceforth empowered to regulate all matters concerning slavery. Imagine now that they do not wait for a judicial decision but include explicitly in their treaty what the ECJ "found" in *Van Gend en Loos*: that these obligations, are, independently of national legislation, intended to create rights for the slaves themselves, and that national courts would have to protect those rights. Another new legal order will have come into being. Does the fact that the obligations *created by the States, the High Contracting Parties* which bestow rights on our poor slaves make them subjects of the Treaty? Yes in the limited sense of deriving rights created by others. No, in the sense that they have no say in the making of those rights. Enjoying rights created by others does not make you a full subject of the law. Thus, in *Van Gend en Loos*, to the extent that the High Contracting Parties retained the prerogatives to make the obligations, bestowing rights on individuals, there was, in this sense, little new in the legal order, except that it *accentuated* the problem of legitimacy. For if the Community and Union have the capacity to exercise law making power over individuals *independently of national legislation*, by whose authority does it enjoy that power?

One could object to my absurd example and claim that in the Union context the Member States are composed of citizens, not slaves; citizens who enabled their States to create institutions which create obligations. That the act of authorization of the Treaties, which bestow these powers on the Community, by national parliament provides the authority. That is true, but

note, first, how that argument re-introduces legitimation through the media-
tion of the State and authority through public international law, thus waving
good-bye to the "new legal order" and constitutionalism. Note, too, that in a
strange, paradoxical balance of what is gained and lost, there is one respect
where the citizens' relative position has worsened compared to the slaves'.
Whereas before all obligations were created in a national forum over which
they exercised citizen control, the European situation as described/created by
Van Gend en Loos is that now they will be subject to obligations "independently of the legislation of Member States" i.e. without that direct legitimation.

To use our current vocabulary, though, the Community seen through the
eyes of *Van Gend* recognized nationals as subjects in one sense (effect of law),
it stripped them of citizenship in another. One paradox, then, has been that
the very doctrine which is foundational to European constitutionalism is, at
the same time, its denial.

Citizens constitute the *demos* of the polity. This is the other, collective side,
of the citizenship coin. *Demos* provides another way of expressing the link
between citizenship and democracy. Democracy does not exist in a vacuum.
It is premised on the existence of a polity with members—the *demos*—by
whom and for whom democratic discourse with its many variants takes place.
The authority and legitimacy of a majority to compel a minority exists only
within political boundaries defined by a *demos*. Simply put, if there is no
demos, there can be no operating democracy.

Is there, can there be a European *demos* which would legitimate the authority of European constitutionalism?

As part of this debate there has emerged an articulate and powerful No
Demos Thesis. One implication of this thesis, espoused, among others, by the
German Constitutional Court, is to deny any meaningful democratization of
the Union at the European level, to reassert the implicit underpinning of the
Community legal order in international law, and if one is to be intellectually
consistent, to negate likewise any meaningful content to European
citizenship. Time does not permit full elaboration but a few hints will suffice.

Under this view, the nation or the people, which is the modern expression
of *demos*, constitutes the basis for the modern democratic State: the nation
and its members—which may be defined in many different ways—constitutes
the polity for the purposes of accepting the discipline of democratic, majoritarian governance. Both descriptively and prescriptively (how it is and how it
ought to be) a minority will/should accept the legitimacy of a majority decision because both majority and minority are part of the same *demos*, the same
people. That is an integral part of what rule-by-the-people, democracy, means
on this reading. Typically (though not necessarily) the State constitutes the
arena, and defines the political boundaries within which the nation/people
exercise their democratic power. The significance of the political boundary is

not only to the older notion of political independence and territorial integrity, but also to the very democratic nature of the polity. A parliament is, on this view, an institution of democracy not only because it provides a mechanism for representation and majority voting, but because it represents the *demos*, often the nation, from which derive the authority and legitimacy of its decisions. To drive this point home, imagine an *Anschluß* between Germany and Denmark. Try and tell the Danes that they should not worry since they will have full representation in the Bundestag. Their screams of grief will be shrill not simply because they will be condemned, as Danes, to permanent minorityship (that may be true for the German Greens too), but because the way nationality, in this way of thinking, enmeshes with democracy is that even majority rule is only legitimate within a *demos*, when Danes rule Danes.

Turning to Europe, it is argued as a matter of empirical observation that there is no European *demos*—not a people not a nation. Neither the subjective element (the sense of shared collective identity and loyalty) nor the objective conditions which could produce these (the kind of homogeneity of the organic national-cultural conditions on which peoplehood in the European tradition depend such as shared culture, a shared sense of history, a shared means of communication) exist. Long term peaceful relations with thickening economic and social intercourse should not be confused with the bonds of peoplehood and nationality forged by language, history, ethnicity and all the rest.

The consequences of the No *Demos* Thesis for the European construct are interesting. The rigorous implication of this view would be that absent a *demos*, there cannot, by definition, be a democracy or democratization at the European level. This is not a semantic proposition. On this reading, European democracy (meaning a minimum binding majoritarian decision-making at the European level) without a *demos* is no different from the previously mentioned German-Danish *Anschluß* except on a larger scale. Giving the Danes a vote in the Bundestag is, as argued, ice cold comfort. Giving them a vote in the European Parliament or Council is, conceptually, no different. This would be true for each and every Nation-State. European integration, on this view, may have involved a certain transfer of State functions to the Union but this has not been accompanied by a redrawing of political boundaries which can occur only if, and can be ascertained only when, a European people can be said to exist. Since this, it is claimed, has not occurred, the Union and its institutions can have neither the authority nor the legitimacy of a *demos*-cratic State. Empowering the European Parliament is no solution and could—to the extent that it weakens the Council (the voice of the Member States)—actually exacerbate the legitimacy problem of the Community. On this view, a parliament without a *demos* is conceptually impossible, practically despotic. If the European Parliament is not the representative of *a* people, if the territorial boundaries of the EU do not correspond to its political boundaries, then the writ of such a parliament has only slightly more legitimacy than the writ of an emperor.

But the problem goes even deeper. The No-*Demos* Thesis in its strongest version is not descriptive. It is not simply an empirical observation that *as yet* the conditions for European peoplehood do not exist. At its most serious the thesis is normative. The *telos* of European integration is ". . . an ever closer union among the *peoples* of Europe". Europe is not meant to be about nation building, or a melting pot—quite the contrary. There is no European *demos* and there should not be one.

Here, then, is the second paradox. The constitutional architecture is a feature of the Union which defines its uniqueness and, functionally, emerged as necessary for attaining the objective of an ever closer union among the peoples of Europe. The normative legitimation of this constitutionalism requires a *demos*, the emergence of which would however negate that very basic *telos*. Put differently: to realize the objectives of the Union in a democratic way, the only way which enjoys political legitimacy, a European *Demos* would seem necessary. But a European *demos* would seem to negate those very objectives.

European citizenship and peoplehood are problematic in another sense. The "Union among Peoples" *telos* does not represent a second best option chosen out of political pragmatism. It is not simply the most that would be acceptable politically in Europe, but something falling short of the ideal-type—a European people. The "Union among Peoples" *telos* is, instead, a reflection of a deep moral ethos. The alternative *telos*, creating one people out of the many would contradict one of the most basic European ideals: inventing new ways and contexts which would enable distinct nations and States to thrive, interact and resolve their conflicts without the disastrous apocalyptic results witnessed in Europe this century. The Union among Peoples is, in part, about creating a political culture which learns new ways to deal with the Other. A European citizenship could be seen, on this view, as part of a statal *telos* and an exclusionary ethos—according to which Europe is about redefining a polity in which the Us may no longer be Germans or French or Italians and the Them no longer British, or Dutch or Irish. The Us would become European and the Them non-European. Of course the question could then be asked: if Europe, part of whose roots were an attempt to tame the excesses nationalism and the classic Nation-State embrace, even if "only" at the symbolic level European citizenship, by simply defining a new Other—on what moral ground can one turn against French National Fronts, German Republicans and their brethren elsewhere who embrace Member State nationalism. On the ground that they chose the wrong nationalism which to embrace?

Is one faced, then, with a "tragic choice" in which absent citizenship the normative authority of European constitutionalism would become untenable but in which the introduction of citizenship would not only mean a redefinition of the "peoples" *telos*, but introduce an exclusionary ethos of dubious moral credentials?

CITIZENSHIP AND DEMOS: A REFORMED DEBATE

The choice would, indeed, be tragic if the understanding of European citizenship and European *demos* were to embrace that strand in European political thought and praxis which a: understands nationality in the organic terms of culture and/or language and/or religion and/or ethnicity; and b. conflates nationality and citizenship so that nationality is a condition for citizenship and citizenship means nationality.

Is it mandated, we should ask, that *demos* in general and the European *demos* in particular be understood exclusively in organic cultural homogeneous terms? Can we not break away from that tradition and define membership of a polity in civic, non-organic-cultural terms? Can we not imagine a *demos* understood in non-organic terms, a coming together on the basis not of shared ethnos and/or organic culture, but a coming together on the basis of shared values, a shared understanding of rights and societal duties and shared rational, intellectual culture which transcend organic-national differences. The Treaty (in its English language version) gives us here unexpected aid:

> Citizenship of the Union is hereby established. Every person holding the nationality of a Member State shall be a citizen of the Union [Maastricht] Citizenship of the Union shall complement and not replace national citizenship.[Amsterdam]

The introduction of citizenship to the conceptual world of the Union could be seen as just another step in the drive towards a Statal vision of Europe, especially if citizenship is understood as being premised on statehood. But there is another more tantalizing and radical way of understanding the provision, namely as the very conceptual decoupling of nationality from citizenship and as the conception of a polity the *demos* of which, its membership, is understood in the first place in civic and political rather than ethno-cultural terms. On this view, the Union belongs to, is composed of, citizens who *by definition* do not share the same nationality. The substance of membership (and thus of the *demos*) is in a commitment to the shared values of the Union as expressed in its constituent documents, a commitment, *inter alia*, to the duties and rights of a civic society covering discrete areas of public life, a commitment to membership in a polity which privileges exactly the opposites of nationalism—those human features which transcend the differences of organic ethno-culturalism. On this reading, the conceptualization of a European *demos* should not be based on real or imaginary trans-European cultural affinities or shared histories nor on the construction of a European "national" myth of the type which constitutes the identity of the organic nation. The decoupling of nationality and citizenship opens the possibility, instead, of thinking of co-existing multiple *Demoi*.

MULTIPLE DEMOI AND THE FRACTURED SELF

One view of multiple *demoi* may consist in what may be called the "concentric circles" approach. On this approach one feels simultaneously as belonging to, and being part of, say, Germany and Europe; or, even, Scotland, Britain and Europe. What characterizes this view is that the sense of identity and identification derives from the same sources of human attachment albeit at different levels of intensity. Presumably the most intense (which the nation, and State, always claims to be) would and should trump in normative conflict.

The problem with this view is that it invites us to regard European citizenship in the same way that we understand our national citizenship. This was precisely the fallacy of the German Constitutional Court in its *Maastricht* decision: conceptualizing the European *demos* in the way that the German *demos* is conceptualized.

One alternative view of multiple *demoi* invites individuals to see themselves as belonging simultaneously to two *demoi*, based, critically, on different subjective factors of identification, in the way someone may regard himself or herself as being German and Catholic. I may be a German national in the in-reaching strong sense of organic-cultural identification and sense of belongingness. I am simultaneously a European citizen in terms of my European transnational affinities to shared values which transcend the ethno-national diversity.

On this view, the Union *demos* turns away from its antecedents and understanding in the European Nation-State. But equally, it should be noted that I am suggesting here something that is different from simple American Republicanism transferred to Europe. The values one is discussing may be seen to have a special European specificity, a specificity I have explored elsewhere but one dimension of which, by way of simple example, could most certainly be that strand of mutual social responsibility embodied in the ethos of the Welfare State adopted by all European societies and by all political forces. Human rights as embodied in the European Convention on Human Rights would constitute another strand in this matrix of values as would, say, the ban on discrimination on grounds of nationality and all the rest.

But this view, too, has its problems. In the first place it is not clear how this matrix of values would be qualitatively different from the normal artefacts of constitutional democracy practised in most European Nation States. After all, all of them are signatories to the European Convention on Human Rights, all of them, to varying degrees share in those "European values". Secondly, a community of value expressed in these terms provides a rather thin, even if laudable, content to the notion of citizenship. And as A.N. Smith convincingly argues, without resonant fiction of relatedness through memory, and myth and history and/or real kinship, a real sense of membership is hard to come by. It is noticeable that even national polities who supposedly understand themselves as communities of values, such as France or the United States, cannot avoid in their evolution, self-understanding and even self-definition many of the features of communities of fate.

I want to offer a third version of the multiple *demoi*, one of true variable geometry. It is like the second version in one crucial respect: it too invites individuals to see themselves as belonging simultaneously to two demoi, based, critically, on different subjective factors of identification. And in this version too the invitation is to embrace the national in the in-reaching strong sense of organic-cultural identification and belongingness and to embrace the European in terms of European transnational affinities to shared values which transcend the ethno-national diversity.

But there are too critical differences. One can be German without being Catholic. One can be Catholic without being German. In this model of European citizenship, the concepts of Member State nationality and European citizenship are totally interdependent. One cannot, conceptually and psychologically (let alone legally) be a European citizen without being a Member State national. It is in this respect the mirror of my analysis of supranationalism itself, which, as I was at pains to argue, had no ontological independence but was part and parcel of the national project, in some way its gate keeper.

There is a second critical difference to this model of multiple *demoi*: its matrix of values is not simply the material commitment to social solidarity, to human rights and other such values which, as I argued, would hardly differentiate it from the modern constitutional, West European liberal state. It has a second important civilizatory dimension. It is the acceptance by its members that in a range of areas of public life, one will accept the legitimacy and authority of decisions adopted by fellow European citizens in the realization that in these areas preference is given to choices made by the outreaching, non organic, *demos*, rather than by the in-reaching one. The Treaties on this reading would have to be seen not only as an agreement among States (a Union of States) but as a "social contract" among the nationals of those States—ratified in accordance with the constitutional requirements in all Member States—that they will in the areas covered by the Treaty regard themselves as associating as citizens in a broader society. But crucially, this view preserves the boundaries, preserves the Self and preserves the Other. But it attempts to educate the I to reach to that Other. We can go even further. In this polity, and to this *demos*, one cardinal value is precisely that there will not be a drive towards, or an acceptance of, an over-arching organic-cultural national identity displacing those of the Member States. Nationals of the Member States are European citizens, not the other way around. Europe is "not yet" a *demos* in the organic national-cultural sense and should never become one. The value matrix has, thus, two civilizing strands: material and processual. One that subordinates the individual and the national society to certain values and certain decisional procedures representing a broader range of interests and sensibilities. Of course the two are connected. We are willing to submit aspects of our social ordering to a polity composed of "others" precisely because we are convinced that in some material sense they share our basic values. It is a construct which is designed to encourage certain virtues of tolerance and humanity.

The discourse of European democracy, too, takes an additional significance in this context. The primary imperative of democracy in Europe is in bestowing legitimacy on a "formation"—the Union—which, want it or not, exercises manifold state functions. It was this imperative from which the search for *demos* and European citizenship emerged. But now we have seen that our construct of European citizenship was also seen as having a particular supranational educational, civilizing function, by submitting certain aspects of our national autonomy to a community which in significant aspects is a community of "others". But the civilizing impulse would, surely, be lost if in the Community decisional process, the individual became totally lost, and instead of a deliberative engagement across differences we had bureaucratic subordination.

One should not get carried away with this construct. Note first that the Maastricht formula does not imply a full decoupling: Member States are free to define their own conditions of membership and these may continue to be defined in national terms. But one should not read this construct as embracing an unreconstructed notion of nationalism within each Member State. I have already argued: a nationalism which seeks to overwhelm the self has been a major source of bigotry and prejudice. A nationalism which acknowledges the multicultural self, can be a positive unifying concept. On this reading European citizenship as a reflection of supranationalism can be regarded as part of the Liberal Nation project. That, in my view, is the greatest promise of introducing supranational citizenship into a construct the major components of which continue to be States and nations. The national and the supranational encapsulate on this reading two of the most elemental, alluring and frightening social and psychological poles of our cultural heritage. The national is Eros: reaching back to the pre-modern, appealing to the heart with a grasp on our emotions, and evocative of the romantic vision of creative social organization as well as responding to our existential yearning for a meaning located in time and space. The nation, through its myths, provides a past and a future. And it is always a history and a destiny in a place, in a territory, a narrative that is fluid and fixed at the same time. The dangers are self-evident. The supranational is civilization: confidently modernist, appealing to the rational within us and to enlightenment neo-classical humanism, taming that Eros. Importantly, the relationship is circular—for its very modernism and rationalism are what, as I sought to show earlier, is alienating, and would have but an ambivalent appeal if they were to represent alone the content of European identity.

Martin Heidegger is an unwitting ironic metaphor for the difficulty of negotiating between these poles earlier in this century. His rational, impersonal critique of totalistic rationality and of modernity remain a powerful lesson to
this day; but equally powerful is the lesson from his fall: an irrational, personal embracing of an irrational, romantic pre-modern nationalism run amok.

For some European citizenship is an icon signifying the hope of transcending
State and national society altogether. For others it is no more than a symbol for
the demise of the classical European Nation-State in the bureaucratic, globalized
market. For others still it is the icon of a shrewd, Machiavelli-like scheme of
self-preservation of the same statal structure which has dominated Europe for a
century and more. Finally it could be regarded as emblematic of that new liberal effort which seeks to retain the Eros of the national, its demonic aspects,
under civilizatory constraints and thereby to provide that elusive legitimating
dimension of European constitutionalism. The persuasiveness of this construct
is for the reader to judge. But European constitutionalism cannot proceed without a working out of its necessary legitimating foundations.

ESSENTIAL BIBLIOGRAPHICAL NOTE AND FURTHER READING

On European Constitutionalism and Democratic Governance—Classical Approaches

Curtin D., "The Constitutional Structure of the European Union: A Europe of Bits and
    Pieces", 30 CML Rev. 65 (1993)
Green A. W., *Political Integration by Jurisprudence* (Sijthoff, Leyden, 1969)
Laenarts K., "Constitutionalism and the Many Faces of Federalism", 38 A.J. Com.
    Law 205 (1990)
Lodge J., "Transparency and Democratic Legitimacy", 32 JCMS 343 (1994)
Mancini F., "The Making of a Constitution for Europe", 26 CML Rev. 595 (1989)
Neunreither, "The Democracy Deficit of the European Union", 29 Government and
    Opposition 299 (1994)
Reich N., "The 'November Revolution' of the European Court of Justice: Keck, Meng
    and Audi Revisited" 31 CML Rev. 459 (1994)
Schermers H.G. & D. Waelbroeck, *Judicial Protection in the European Communities*
    (5th ed, Kluwer, Deventer & Boston, 1992)
Stein E., "Lawyers, Judges and the Making of a Transnational Constitution", 75 A.J.
    I.L 1, 1 (1981)

Political and Social Science Discovers European Constitutionalism and Constitutionalism Discovers Political and Social Sciences

General

Haas E., *The Uniting of Europe* (London: Stanford Univ. Press, 1958)
Haas E & Scmitter Ph., "Economics and Differential Patterns of Political Integration",
    18 International Organization 7070 (1964).

Sbragia A. (ed) *EuroPolitics: Institutions and Policymaking in the "New" European Community* (Washington DC, Brookings 1992)

Pelkmans J. and Robson P., "The Aspirations of the White Paper" 25 JCMS 181 (1987)

Snyder F., *New Direction in European Community Law* (London: Wiedenfeld & Nicholson, 1990)

Fligstein N. & MaraDrita I, "How to Make a Market: Reflections on the Attempt to Create a Single Market in the European Union", 102 American Journal of Sociology 1 (1996)

Jacquemin A., "Imperfect Market Structure and International Trade", 35 Kyklos 1 (1982)

Lindberg L.N. and Scheingold S.A., *Europe's Would Be Polity* (Englewood Cliffs, NJ: Prentice Hall, 1970)

Adams W. J., "Economic Analysis of European Integration", AEL Vol. IV. Book 1 (1995)

Scharpf F.W., "The Joint Decision Trap: Lessons From German Federalism and European Integration", Public Administration 66 (1988), 239

R. O. Keohane & S. Hoffmann, "Institutional Chance in Europe in the 1980s" in R.O. Keohane & S. Hoffmann, *The New European Community: Decisionmaking and Institutional Change* (Westview Press, Boulder, San Francisco, Oxford 1991)

Intergovernmentalism

Moravcsik A., "Preference and Power in the European Community: A Liberal Intergovernmentalist Approach, in Economic and Political Integration" in *Europe: Internal Dynamics and Global Context* (S. Bulmer & A. Scott eds, Oxford/ Cambridge (Mass.) 1994)

Moravcsik A., *Why the European Community Strengthens the State: Domestic Politics and International Cooperation*, Harvard University CES Working Paper Series #52 (1994)

On New Institutional Thinking of the Union

Bulmer S.J., "The Governance of the European Union: A New Institutionalist Approach", Journal of Public Policy 13 (1994), 351

Bulmer S.J., "Institutions and Policy Change in the European Communities: The Case of Merger Control", Public Administration 72 (1994), 423

The Court

Alter, K., *Explaining National Court Acceptance of the European Court Jurisprudence*: A Critical Evaluation of Theories of Legal Integration, EUI Working Paper RSC 1995

Burley A.M. & Mattli W., "Europe Before the Court: A Political theory of Legal Integration", 47 International Organization 41 (1993).

Rasmussen H., *On Law and Policy in the European Court of Justice* (Martinus Nijhoff, Dordrecht, Lancaster, Boston, 1986)

Stone Sweet A., Constitutional Dialogue in the European Community, EUI Working Paper RSC 1995.

Stone Sweet A., *From Free Trade to Supranational Polity: The European Court and Integration*, Working Paper 2.45, Center for German and European Studies, University of California, Berkeley

Wincott D., "Political Theory, Law, and European Union" in Shaw J. & More G., *New Legal Dynamics of European Union* (Clarendon Press, Oxford, 1995)

The New Constitutionalism: Horizontal, Fragmented, Infranational Approaches to European Constitutionalism and Governance

Dehousse R, *Intégration ou Disintégration: Cinq Thèses sur l'incidence de l'intégration européenne sur les structures étatiques*, EUI Working Paper RSC 96/4 1996.

De Witte B., "Droit Communautaire et Valeurs Constitutionelles Nationales", 14 Droit 87 (1991)

MacCormick N., "Sovereignty, Democracy & Subsidiarity in Bellamy R., Bufacchi V., Castiglione D. (eds), *Democracy and Constitutional Culture in the Union of Europe* (Lothian Foundation, London, 1995)

MacCormick, N., "Beyond the Sovereign State", 56 Modern Law Review 1 (1990)

Majone G., "Regulating Europe: Problems and Prospects", in *Jahrbuch zur Staats und Verwaltungswissenschaft 1989* (T. Ellwein *et al.* eds.), 159

Shaw J. & More G. (eds.), *New Legal Dynamics of European Union* (Clarendon Press, Oxford 1995)

Joerges Ch. & Neyer, *MultiLevel Governance, Deliberative Politics and the Role of Law*, European University Institute, RSC Working Paper 1997.

Slaughter A-M., "International Law in a World of Liberal States", 6 EJIL 503 (1995)

The New Constitutionalism: The Debate about Identity, Demos and Democracy

Boeckenfoerde E.W., "Die Nation: Identitaet in Differenz", Politische Wissenschaft 1995, 974

Bogdandy A. von (ed.), *Die Europäische Option* (BadenBaden 1993)

Habermas J., "Staatsbhrgerschaft und nationale Identitat" (1990), in *Faktizitat und Geltung. Beitrage zur Diskurstheorie des Rechts und des demokratischen Rechtsstaats* (Frankfurt/Main 1992)

Meehan E, *Citizenship and the European Community* (London, 1993)

Oldfield, A., *Citizenship and Community* (London: Routledge 1990)

Preuss U.K., "Constitutional Powermaking for the New Polity: Some Deliberations on the Relation Between Constituent Power and the Constitution", 14 Cardozo Law Review 639 (1993).

Preuss U.K, "Citizenship and Identity: Aspects of a Political theory of Citizenship" in Bellamy R., Bufacchi V., Castiglione D. (eds), *Democracy and Constitutional Culture in the Union of Europe* (Lothian Foundation, London, 1995)

Soledad G. (ed.), *European Identity and the Search for Legitimacy* (London 1993)

Telo M. (ed.), *Democratie et construction européenne* (Bruxelles 1995)

Other Authors Mentioned

Fitzgerald B., "The Future of Belief", 63 First Things 23 (1996)
E. Nolte, *The Three Faces of Facism* (Wiedenfeld and Nicolson, London, 1965)

Index